INTERNATIONAL
SOCIAL
WORK

INTERNATIONAL SOCIAL WORK

Issues, Strategies, and Programs

DAVID COX
La Trobe University

MANOHAR PAWAR
Charles Sturt University

SAGE Publications
Thousand Oaks ▪ London ▪ New Delhi

For information:

Sage Publications, Inc.
2455 Teller Road
Thousand Oaks, California 91320
E-mail: order@sagepub.com

Sage Publications Ltd.
1 Oliver's Yard
55 City Road
London, EC1Y 1SP
United Kingdom

Sage Publications India Pvt. Ltd.
B-42, Panchsheel Enclave
Post Box 4109
New Delhi 110 017 India

Printed in the United States of America

Library of Congress Cataloging-in-Publication Data

Cox, David R. (David Ray)
International social work : issues, strategies, and programs/David Cox, Manohar Pawar.
   p. cm.
Includes bibliographical references and index.
ISBN 1-4129-1407-8 (cloth)—ISBN 1-4129-1408-6 (pbk.)
  1. Social service—Cross-cultural studies. 2. Social problems—Cross-cultural studies.
3. Human services—Cross-cultural studies. 4. Globalization. 5. Social change.
6. Social work education. I. Pawar, Manohar S. II. Title.
HV40.35.C68 2006
361—dc22   2005012706

This book is printed on acid-free paper.

05   06   07   08   09   10   9   8   7   6   5   4   3   2   1

Acquiring Editor:	Arthur T. Pomponio
Editorial Assistant:	Veronica Novak
Project Editor:	Beth A. Bernstein
Copy Editor:	Cate Huisman
Typesetter:	C&M Digitals (P) Ltd.
Indexer:	Naomi Linzer
Cover Designer:	Edgar Abarca

Contents

Introduction

Goals

We take pleasure in introducing you, the reader, to the interesting and challenging field of international social work. The main goal of this text is to share our understanding of international social work with social workers, development workers, and members of the helping professions generally. Our focus is particularly on the programs and strategies that are being applied to a range of situations involving needy individuals in developing countries. Our second goal is to encourage social workers around the world to consider how traditional social work might be applied more effectively to global concerns. Third, we aim to encourage social workers and others to consider devoting some part of their working lives to responding to the needs faced by developing countries, and especially the poorer ones where the helping professions are not well established. Fourth, we would like to see social workers and others contributing to the process of devising social policies and programs appropriate to this era of rapid globalization. Finally, we are convinced that an understanding of international social work will contribute to the effectiveness of social work and development practice wherever it is undertaken.

Readership

This book is written for those who take an active interest in, or intend working in, the field of international social work and social development. It is designed to inform undergraduate and postgraduate students in social work, and to contribute to the understanding of relevant human services professionals engaged in international work, especially in the poorer developing countries. Higher-degree research students and social researchers may also find the book a useful reference source.

Organization

The book is organized in fourteen chapters. The first chapter introduces the concepts of social work and international social work. It is important for social work readers to possess a general overview of social work globally. The second chapter continues in outlining our conceptual model of international social work by introducing the importance of utilizing an integrated-perspectives approach, which for us outlines the values, principles, and goals that international social work espouses. The third and final introductory chapter presents the global context of international social work. That context is complex, consisting of a range of global problems, a myriad of agencies established to respond to these problems, and various sets of conventions and policies, all of which reflect historical realities and the changing ideologies that surround these.

Chapters 4 to 13 constitute the core of the text, focusing on specific fields in which international social work is involved, and introducing the major programs and strategies that characterize these fields. Chapter 4 introduces some key programs and strategies that tend to characterize intervention in all fields. Chapters 5 to 12 consider four significant fields, with one chapter introducing the field and a second outlining the main programs and strategies currently used. The four fields are development, poverty, conflict and post-conflict reconstruction, and displacement and forced migration. Readers who are already relatively familiar with a field may omit the first chapter on that field and focus on the programs and strategies outlined in the second chapter. In general terms, however, we consider that readers should possess some understanding of the field as a whole, and the issues that run through it, before turning their attention to intervention approaches. Chapter 13 does not cover a major field but introduces the international response to specific needy populations. As examples of intervention focused on selected populations, we outline the situation of, and responses to, four groups: street children, child laborers, migrant workers, and AIDS orphans.

The final chapter poses some challenges for international social work's further development, and suggests some steps for addressing those challenges.

Special Features

This book has several features that should be found useful by various groups of readers. Each chapter commences with a set of learning objectives. In the chapters relating to intervention, we have provided a number of short case examples and a few longer case studies. We hope that these will assist in grounding the discussion. Although the intention was to draw case examples from as wide a range of countries as possible, we are conscious that they do not represent all parts of the world. At the conclusion of each chapter, we have included a chapter summary, a list of questions for discussion, a list of possible research topics, and some references for further reading. The last three are, of course, only suggestive, especially the research topics. The suggested readings contain both recent and older publications, our criterion being those references known to us that were readily available and which we considered the most useful. The IFSW/IASSW's "Ethics in Social Work, Statement of Principles" is provided as an appendix because it represents in effect the only formal internationally devised and approved charter for social work as a global profession. Finally, a list of acronyms used in the book is included at the end of the text.

Feedback

The goal of this text is to meet the needs of students studying International Social Work. To better meet your needs with any future editions we would appreciate your feedback on the effectiveness of this edition. You can quickly and easily complete a questionnaire by going to: www.sagepub.com/coxsurvey. To show our appreciation, we would like to offer you a free SAGE book (your choice, up to a $50 value). Many thanks!

Acknowledgments

We would like to acknowledge here the love and support of our families over the years—our wives, parents, and children. It is they, above all others, who have made possible our involvement in international social work and our commitment to the preparation of this text. We would also like to thank the peer reviewers for their helpful comments and suggestions, and the team at Sage for their efficient, patient, and friendly steering of the manuscript through to printing.

1

International Social Work

In this chapter we introduce the concept of social work, especially from the global perspective. A general understanding of how social work has evolved, and continues to evolve, and has spread globally is central to assessing the current and future roles of social work as a global profession. We then introduce our definition and understanding of international social work, for it is that aspect of social work, and the international field within which it operates, that is the topic of this text.

Social Work

The topic of social work will require no introduction to the majority of readers, but before moving to consider social work as a global profession and our definition of international social work, it may be useful to say a few things about social work generally in this context. We are concerned when colleagues in a developing country seriously contemplate dispensing with the term *social work* because locally it is widely misunderstood. Sometimes it is said that social work is viewed in a specific context as virtually synonymous with, to give a few examples, charitable work, one-to-one intervention by highly qualified professionals

utilizing a therapeutic approach, the welfare state, and emerging urban concerns. Clearly these views are erroneous, given the nature and scope of social work throughout its history; however, the apparent prevalence in some contexts of such views as those listed suggests that the social work profession has not been as successful as it might have been in projecting an acceptable image across the developing world. A perceived tendency to distinguish social work from, for example, policy concerns, community and social development, and community-based responses to welfare needs, suggests that a very narrow understanding of social work is more prevalent than we would like to see. Furthermore, we should perhaps acknowledge that, while many of us would regard the breadth of social work as one of its strengths, it is very likely that that same breadth makes it difficult for many outside observers to, as Hartman (1994, p. 14) puts it, distinguish a common thread that typifies the core of social work. Hartman writes (p. 13),

> Social work includes a broad and varied array of activities and is practiced with different size systems and in a variety of arenas. There is scant agreement in the field on the worldview, epistemology, or even on the principles

Learning Objectives

The main objective of this chapter is to provide a broad introduction to social work and to discuss the concept of international social work. After studying this chapter, readers should be able to reflect on

- Widely agreed definitions of social work, unique features of social work in some countries, origin of professional social work in the west and its expansion through colonization, and indigenous social work in developing countries.
- Some recent trends and critical issues in social work that are of relevance to international social work.
- Global social work organizations.
- The definition and scope of international social work.

or shape of practice. Volumes have been published on the different models (Turner 1986; Dorfman, 1988) and some have concluded that the only common thread that runs through all of social work is a shared value stance (NASW, 1981).

The 1990s saw the publication of several texts that provided an overview of social work around the world by presenting chapters on social work in various specific countries. (See, for example, Hokenstad, Khinduka, and Midgley, 1992, and Mayadas, Watts, and Elliott, 1997.) These texts make very interesting reading, highlighting major differences in, to use Elliott's analysis (1997, p. 441), the ways in which social work is "socially constructed" in various parts of the world. As one reflects on the reported differences in the predominant forms that social work has adopted in various regions and countries, one may well wonder whether this diversity can meaningfully be seen as different expressions of one and the same profession. It is said, for example, that "the individual paradigm is strongly represented in American social work" (Elliott, p. 441); that in China the focus is on the mobilization of the masses to address social problems (Chow, 1997); that in Latin America social work presents a strong emphasis on social justice and

social action (Kendall, 2000, pp. 107–108); and that in Africa there is an increasing emphasis on social development as defined by, for example, the UNDP (United Nations Development Programme) (Healy, 2001, p. 102); while the rebirth of social work in Eastern Europe since 1990 has seen a strong emphasis on social reconstruction or the building of civil society (Constable and Mehta, 1994).

While it has been common in the literature to highlight some dominant forms adopted by social work in specific countries, a closer analysis reveals that, in virtually all countries, there exists a range of sometimes competing and sometimes complementary forms of social work—a range that is commonly expanding as social work agencies and practitioners venture into new fields of practice as an ever widening range of social problems is recognized. All such developments, however, add to the difficulty, even for social workers, of defining social work, and of non–social workers perceiving a common thread running through the diverse approaches that constitute contemporary social work globally.

At the international level, social work has striven, since at least the 1970s, to define itself as a global profession and to agree internationally on a common code of ethics. The foreword to the international code developed by the IFSW

(International Federation of Social Workers) and adopted at its general meeting in Puerto Rico in 1976 states,

> Social work originates variously from humanitarian, religious, and democratic ideals and philosophies and has universal application to meet human needs arising from personal-societal interactions and to develop human potential. Professional social workers are dedicated to service for the welfare and self-fulfillment of human beings; to the development and disciplined use of scientific knowledge regarding human and societal behavior; to the development of resources to meet individual, group, national and international needs and aspirations; and to the achievement of social justice. (quoted in Alexander, 1982, p. 47)

At its general meeting in 2004, the IFSW and IASSW (International Association of Schools of Social Work) approved the following definition of social work:

> The social work profession promotes social change, problem solving in human relationships and the empowerment and liberation of people to enhance well-being. Utilizing theories of human behaviour and social systems, social work intervenes at the points where people interact with their environments. Principles of human rights and social justice are fundamental to social work. (IFSW and IASSW, 2004)

Given that professional social work has been guided by developments in the United States more than anywhere else, it is appropriate to consider here a recent definition of social work in the United States:

> Social work is the applied science of helping people achieve an effective level of psychosocial functioning and effecting societal changes to enhance the well-being of all people. (Barker, 1999, p. 433)

It is important that the profession is able to present to the outside world an understanding of its core nature, and of the relevance of that core nature to the fields of work on which the international community is focused and with which the developing countries are concerned. At the same time, it is important that the profession remains flexible, and is able to adapt itself to changing conditions and needs either as the world changes or as the profession moves into new environments. It would indeed be amazing, and reflect poorly on the profession, if social work did not present many different faces globally, given the wide range of national and local conditions to which it is called upon to respond. Nor does the presenting diversity represent a source of division within the profession. The only concern is that the diverse nature of social work sometimes results in non–social workers failing to appreciate the full nature of social work, and perceiving social work, whether positively or negatively, in terms of only one of its many faces.

The Global Spread and Organization of Social Work

The history of social work reveals its links with social welfare and social development, with other professions such as medicine, and with the charitable movement that emerged in the nineteenth century. This history has been explored by a range of writers (e.g., Kendall, 2000) and requires in this context little more than a summary of the major points.

Professional Social Work's Western Origins

It is generally agreed that social work grew out of the urban destitution that characterized post–Industrial Revolution England and the government's response to this situation through relief for the poor. As Midgley (1981, p. 17) puts it,

As the rural poor were drawn into and concentrated in the industrialising cities during the nineteenth century, the problem of urban destitution became more acute and conventional public poor relief provisions were strained; social work attempted to provide an alternative which would lessen the burden of public assistance borne by taxpayers, be more humane and seek to rehabilitate the destitute.

A large number of charitable organizations emerged in the United Kingdom and continental Europe, and subsequently in the United States and elsewhere (e.g., Australia), and these had an enormous influence on the profession's development. Their emergence led in particular to the profession's focus on social casework.

The conditions in the newly emerging cities gave rise also to the settlement movement, designed to bring the middle classes into contact with those in poor urban areas and, through the cross-class contacts that occurred and the recreational and educational activities that were arranged, to "inculcate moral values and reform the habits of slum dwellers," as Midgley (1981, p. 22) describes the goals. This settlement work can be seen as one important set of roots for the profession's embrace of community work, for it advocated community-based responses to social problems and social reforms. Leighninger and Midgley (1997, p. 10) describe this settlement movement as it emerged in the United States, showing how it led the emerging profession to focus on the causes of social problems and explore responses to them at both a government policy and a community level.

Leighninger and Midgley (1997, p. 11) provide a succinct summary of the impact of this early history on the social work profession:

Individualist approaches, social reform movements, and the growth of public social services have all played a role in social work's development. The profession's leaders were able to amalgamate individually focused treatment, organized group pursuits, community activism, social reform, and other activities into a loosely defined practice methodology which formed the basis of social work's professional identity.

This shows why casework, community work, and group work were all important to this early development.

In the following decades, the fledgling profession was to broaden considerably in response to other developments in its environment, especially in the United Kingdom and United States. For example, developments in the field of law and order resulted in a focus on young offenders and the establishment of a probation service in which social work would play a leading role. Similarly, developments in the health field led to the emergence of hospital social work and later a strong emphasis on psychiatric social work. Indeed, the medical model had a significant impact on social work in the late nineteenth and early twentieth centuries, and psychiatric social work, according to Midgley (1981, p. 29), was boosted by the frequent use of social workers in work with shell-shocked patients during World War I.

The development of social work education closely reflected the above historical roots. It began usually with in-service training for various areas of work, established initially by either private societies or government departments, depending on where the majority of workers were employed. Then over the years these training courses were moved into the educational institutions, and particularly universities. The curricula taught initially reflected the prevailing practice contexts; however, eventually they came to incorporate the breadth of social work activities that emerged, including new bodies of knowledge and new practice methodologies.

We have referred so far mainly to developments in the United Kingdom and United States, and these two countries certainly led in the emergence of professional social work. The situation on the European continent, as Rowlings (1997) points out, was and is highly varied and often in marked contrast to that of the United Kingdom and United States. Rowlings comments,

> Europe incorporates multiple and varied structures through which social work and social welfare services are delivered. These reflect very different views on the role of the state in the direct or indirect provision of welfare and on the responsibility of the family, and more particularly of women, for the survival and well-being of dependent family members. (p. 114)

The writer goes on to contrast north and south Europe, there being a long-established tradition of state delivery of welfare services in the north, mostly through local government structures, while in much of southern Europe there was no tradition of active state involvement in welfare. However, whatever the local tradition historically, a mixed welfare system has now emerged or is emerging in most of Europe, influenced most recently by the social policies of the European Union.

These differing welfare structures across Europe have resulted in significant differences in social work, including in its definition. Rowlings explains that in France, for example, "social work" is a collective term covering eight or nine occupational groups usually regarded elsewhere as paraprofessional groupings. By contrast, in Germany the term "has the narrower meaning of individualized casework by workers operating from local community-based offices, hospitals, clinics, or voluntary organizations" (p. 116).

This author thus points out that the parameters of social work vary across Europe. For example, in Sweden it does not include work with older people but in many other countries it does. Similarly, she notes that in the United Kingdom "income support (or social assistance) is provided by civil servants employed in a national social security system," whereas in continental western Europe "qualified social workers assess and administer the benefits system" (p. 117).

Social work in Europe, while varied, does contain indigenous roots that reflect the peculiar culture and social structure of each state. By contrast, the new industrialized countries, founded by European states as colonies, tended to inherit their social work structures along with the colonial social welfare system. For example, the United Kingdom exported its welfare system and its charitable organizations to Australia, and training courses were established to provide in-service training for the staff of these departments and organizations. The social work profession, as Ife (1997, p. 383) notes, also received significant impetus from the medical field with "a perceived need for trained hospital almoners." In addition, the ongoing development of social work was much influenced by developments in the United Kingdom but particularly the United States, as many social work leaders went to these countries for advanced education in social work. Indeed, these ties of Australian social work to the United Kingdom and United States have been lamented by some observers, as having held back the emergence of an indigenous profession within this and other former colonies. While most industrialized western countries eventually broke free of their colonial heritage to a large degree, and began to forge their own indigenous approach to social work, they could also not avoid altogether the influence of their roots and the basic systems inherited from particularly the United Kingdom and United States, nor of the ongoing developments in these countries.

The Expansion of Social Work Through Colonization

Social work accompanied colonialism essentially to meet the needs and aspirations of the colonial powers, rather than to allow social work to make a contribution to these countries' development. The colonial powers believed that they were bringing these territories into the modern civilized world, and such social welfare services as were established reflected this objective. This objective, together with the fact that those who administered these services were social workers and others recruited from the home country, resulted in the imposition on these lands of a usually rudimentary western welfare system staffed, or at least administered, largely by westerners. For the most part, the emphasis was on health, education, and law and order, especially in urban areas, but often confined to the support and protection of those classes whose roles were important to the colonial system, with the needs of many others ignored except where Christian or humanitarian motivated services reached out, more often than not to civilize and Christianize rather than meet welfare, let alone development, needs (see Hoogvelt, 2001, p. 20).

In a number of colonies, social welfare and community development training courses were introduced as more and more local people were recruited to staff the developing social services. To some extent these early training courses formed a basis for the establishment of modern social work, although it is also true that when modern social work per se was introduced, usually after independence had been obtained, it represented to some degree a new import from the West with American schools and training models often used as the models for these developments (Midgley, 1981, pp. 56ff.). As Midgley points out, the UN also took a strong interest in the establishment of professional social work in developing countries in the 1950s and 1960s, as too did a number of social work professionals from the Western world who initiated many new developments. Inevitably the schools of social work established in this period had to draw heavily on expatriates as teachers, who invariably taught according to the models and curricula with which they were familiar. Midgley (1981, p. 60) comments,

To promote "modern" social work, western social work experts used as models the approaches to social work education which had developed in their own countries. Motivated by the demands of modernization, they designed curricula which replicated the content of western social work training, urged that social work courses be established in universities and recommended the adoption of western professional standards.

Although Midgley argues that even those countries that were not colonized were affected by colonialism, the reality is that a number of developing countries, including many that were later designated by the UN as the Least Developed Countries (LDCs), did not establish either state-run social services or modern social work, despite the presence in most of these countries of some international agencies providing a range of services through largely expatriate staff. The absence of the colonial powers from these countries, as well as their extremely slow development process, are presumably reasons why most of these countries still lack professional social work, in terms of modern social work education and associations of social workers. While colonialism involved imposing a western stamp on early social work developments in the developing world, it at least laid some foundations for modern social welfare and social work developments. It is a matter of judgment whether this western stamp was overall negative or positive. On the one hand, it resulted in what were often perceived to be inappropriate forms of social work education and practice; on the other hand, in many of those countries without any direct colonial influence, social work had not developed roots at all, despite the existence of environments that required initiatives along social work lines. The one situation cried out for reform; while the other situation awaited the introduction of appropriate social work systems.

The above discussion suggests that the origins of modern social work were everywhere very similar. This in fact is not the full story. Whether in response to local circumstances or, more likely, reflecting the priorities of influential parties, social work emerged in the various countries with somewhat distinctive priorities. In India, for example, industrial social work has thrived from an early stage (Bose, 1992, p. 75).

Regarding such developments, Pawar (1999) has noted that social work programs possessing a labor market specialization tend to produce two cadres of personnel with opposing interests. On the one hand there are the labor welfare and personnel management graduates who identify with management; on the other hand, there are the social workers who focus on the labor force.

Regarding Egypt, Abo-El-Nasr (1997, p. 206) notes that "the keynote of the early practice of social work in Egypt was in two fields: community development projects in rural areas and schools in urban areas." This author sees social work "as an adjunct or auxiliary to the achievement of the primary organizational goals of education, medicine, and production." Egypt is thus also another of the few countries where industrial social work has flourished.

In a case study of social work in the Philippines, Midgley (1981, p. 58) points out that there the Department of Social Welfare was the major employer of social workers, and that it "was concerned chiefly . . . 'with the welfare of the handicapped, the unwanted and the unloved, like the orphans and waifs who either ran away from home or were turned out by their parents.'" Hence "child care was among the first responsibilities assumed by public welfare services in the Philippines." Midgley goes on to explain that social work in the Philippines adopted casework methods as its major thrust, was very urban-oriented, and thus in these early stages lacked relevance to the (developmental and rural) needs of the Philippines.

Thus a closer study of the emergence of social work in the developing world indicates that, while the influences of colonialism and of the Western world generally were commonly of great importance, the precise nature of the fledgling profession in the various countries or regions was not identical, in part because their sociocultural and political economy contexts were different. It further indicates that these early priorities in the functions and practice of social work have usually had an ongoing influence on the profession's image and subsequent development in the various countries. (For examples of this diversity, see Hokenstad et al., 1992, and Mayadas et al., 1997.)

The Focus on Indigenous Social Work in Developing Countries

Reading reports on social work around the world today reveals a consensus between writers on a number of points. First, it is clear that organized professional social work exists to varying degrees in the majority of countries (many LDCs being the exception), and that the various national social work structures recognize each other as sharing much in common and as being part of a global profession. Second, social work everywhere shares the same ethical underpinnings, as revealed not only in joint ethical statements but also in shared concerns. Third, there is a strong sense that "social workers are coping with similar social problems in many if not most countries" (Healy, 2001, p. 100), and the programs and discussions at international social work conferences drive home this point. Fourth, social work almost everywhere in the developing world shares a sense of possessing a low status among the professions, seemingly due to common images of what social work is and does—images that often, unfortunately, contain a degree of accuracy regarding social work in that country, although not globally. Finally, there is a widely held fear in many developed countries that social work is in several specific types of danger, especially those of merging with the bureaucracy, moving extensively into private practice, becoming the servant of government through its role in the trend to contract services out, and of weakening along with the so-called demise of the welfare state and formal welfare structures as part of the application of neoliberal ideology (see Pierson, 1998; Hutton, 2003).

While there is agreement that social work around the world shares much in common, some writers also recognize the existence of significant differences. At one level these differences are those that could be anticipated within any global profession—differences from country to country in emphases, in the strength of the profession, and in the details of professional education and practice, reflecting in large part the sociocultural-economic differences in prevailing environments but also historical factors. At another and far more significant level are the differences that reflect the profession's specific regional, national, and local responses to changing need profiles, changing resource issues necessitating changes in prevailing methodologies, and so on. These changes, as they occur in particular places, can begin to change the face of the profession quite markedly; however, such changes tend to occur slowly and initially only within small sections of, or even on the margins of, the overall profession.

It is clear that in Latin America, for example, social work has been influenced in places, and to some degree overall, by liberation theology adopted by sections of the Catholic Church and the *conscientization* (consciousness-raising) focus of Paulo Freire (1972), resulting in a strong social justice and social action focus and a commitment to revolutionary change (Kendall, 2000, pp. 107–108). In many parts of Africa, as a second example, social work has been strongly influenced by recent social development thinking, and social workers have been actively promoting a social development perspective within the profession (see Healy, 2001, p. 102; *Journal of Social Development in Africa*). As a third example, in parts of India, there has in recent times been a strong focus on rural social work, involving the recruitment of rural students to study in new rural-oriented schools of social work and to go on to practice rural social work. Another example is the People's Republic of China, where the introduction of professional social work from the West has been resisted because it does not dovetail with Chinese cultural values and practices. Indeed, in most regions the need for culturally sensitive social work education and practice is increasingly recognized by those who are involved at grassroots levels.

Finally, the birth or rebirth of social work in Eastern Europe in the aftermath of the end of the Cold War (1989), and the collapse of communist and socialist regimes that followed, has seen a strong emphasis on social reconstruction or, as some express it, the building of civil society (the network of organizations that mediate between the people and state political and economic structures). This has often been seen as an essential first step to many other necessary developments (see Constable and Mehta, 1994). However, in all of the above examples, except for the last one perhaps, these distinctive characteristics exist alongside a set of mainstream social work characteristics that have not changed greatly over recent decades. While they are significant and interesting developments, they remain in a sense marginal.

In such examples, social work is changing, albeit often slowly, as a result of a critical examination of its roles in the light of recent developments. While change has, to some extent, been endemic to social work since the outset, these recent changes are quite radical and could result in major changes to the overall profession in the long term. Whether these changes will result in a broadening of the profession under common professional auspices, or a splitting of the profession into various schools such as the clinical and social development approaches, only time will tell. We believe, however, that these new emphases are timely if social work is to retain its integrity, be true to its value base, and play a worthwhile role in the major challenges confronting the contemporary world. To a very large degree those people driving such changes are doing what Midgley (1981, p. 157) said was required to modify the welfare approach, which included wrong priorities and inappropriate structures introduced from the West: "Solutions to these problems can be found only if social workers attempt to identify and rectify inappropriate forms of social work education and practice in their own countries." Gradually solutions are being found, usually by expanding the breadth of social work, although it is probably true to say that the process is still in its infancy.

An article that exemplifies many of the above points in the African context is that of Osei-Hwedie (1993). This writer is concerned about the gap between western theory, especially social science theory, and social work practice in Africa. He suggests that the indigenization of social work in Africa "must start from within, determine what our problems and requirements are, what resources and skills are available to us and what processes and procedures we can borrow from others" (p. 22). He argues that it may be necessary to redefine social work "in the context of social development and social development concerns" (p. 23). He continues, using a line of argument that can be applied in much of the developing world:

Increasing social work effectiveness in Africa means perfecting the professional expertise, and establishing greater legitimacy and societal acceptability. The struggle to define social work and charter its course also involves the issue of control. It is a struggle about who defines and controls the profession and therefore assigns its socioeconomic status. By necessity whoever defines the field must also set the agenda. A major problem is that the social work agenda is set by other people, especially politicians, and that to a large extent, social work training is dictated by the nature of employment, in almost all cases, as offered by government and nongovernment organizations. Once again, indigenization of the field must resolve the question of who sets the agenda, and remove the content of practice from the political to the professional arena.

Finally, Osei-Hwedie (1993, p. 27) charts the difficult road ahead for social work:

The profession must . . . locate the basis of the profession and its rationale; develop a

process which enables refined knowledge and skills to emerge out of practice; define social work and its mission to capture the African world view; clarify the domain and expertise of social work; and identify the knowledge, philosophy and value bases of the profession.

The processes either of adapting inherited western social work knowledge and skills to local situations, or of devising an indigenous form of social work from scratch drawing on external and local expertise, are by no means easy for anyone, and especially for social work leaders in the poorer developing countries. This is an area with which the global profession should be prepared to assist. In relation to the first situation, Pawar (1999) has suggested ten steps for developing indigenous social work education:

1. acceptance by social work educators of the fact that they are teaching a western social work model, resulting in

2. a questioning of the model and the local relevance of the various subjects and specializations;

3. identifying what is and is not relevant and why;

4. identifying the various factors, conditions, and circumstances that result in aspects of the model being irrelevant;

5. discovering solutions, perceptions, and coping strategies that exist within local culture, traditions, and practices;

6. documenting these and incorporating them into classroom teaching and field education;

7. undertaking a micro level series of exercises that will facilitate the development of indigenous curricula;

8. documenting and disseminating effective social work practices;

9. revising subject curricula to incorporate the above; and

10. organizing curriculum development workshops at the school level, involving educators, practitioners, and students; and later at interschool levels.

Given the focus of this text on the developing world, we have referred only to the indigenization of social work in developing countries, seemingly implying that this trend has no relevance for western industrialized countries. Such, however, is not the case. Although it is not appropriate to detail these developments here, it should be noted that social work in several western countries has identified the importance of developing forms of indigenous social work in relation to various local situations. One example is in the field of social work among indigenous minorities, where work has been proceeding in at least Australia, Canada, New Zealand, and the United States.

Recent Trends in Social Work of Relevance to International Social Work

It can be said that, over its long history, social work has evolved to serve three major areas of practice.

The first area sees social work as an arm of the welfare state. Within this area, the state effectively dictates the specific fields of practice on which the profession focuses, and the majority of social workers are either employed directly by the state or by agencies that are funded, and therefore effectively controlled, by the state. This area of practice includes the following specific fields of work: work with juvenile delinquents and adult criminals through, for example, probation and parole work and working within correctional institutions; family welfare services; work in the child protection and child adoption fields; and work in the fields of social security, family assistance, and similar welfare and assistance schemes. There are strong elements of social control and protection in this general area.

The second area sees social work as committed to enhancing the social functioning or well-being of individuals and families by working directly with clients experiencing problems. This area of practice has had several offshoots, including clinical social work, family therapy and marriage guidance, medical and psychiatric social work, and work within the so-called psychotherapies. In this area of social work, workers are very much serving individual people who become their clients, epitomized in its extreme form by private practice. However, it also covers practice in state and private institutional settings, such as, for example, hospitals.

The third area of social work sees the profession as seeking to contribute to the building of healthy, cohesive, and enabling communities and societies, and by this process promoting the well-being of people. The fields of practice in this area range from community development to macro social policy formulation, and can today be summarized perhaps as social development: the basic goals are always related to improving the environments or societies within which people develop and live. Here social work is to some degree the servant of the people within selected contexts, including communities and population groupings such as ethnic groups, regions, and nations, but it also reflects the profession's mission to contribute to the building of a better world at various levels. The majority of social workers employed in this area work for the agencies of civil society, although some will work for the state, especially in the fields of social administration, social policy, and state-devised community development or social development programs, but with goals similar to the goals of those working within civil society.

Throughout the history of social work, questions have periodically arisen about the validity of these three areas and the nature of the balance between them. Let us consider how such questions have been answered in recent times. We shall see that the criticisms leveled at the profession, most frequently from within its own ranks, are of three types. There are those who criticize the balance within the profession between the three areas specified above, however these areas are delineated. Second, there are those who criticize the profession for effectively neglecting certain fields of practice altogether, and the fields referred to lie mainly within the third area outlined—the area which can be referred to as social development. Finally, there are those who criticize the profession for ignoring selected population sectors altogether, which means that all three areas of practice delineated above are not applied to any significant degree to designated population groupings. Let us consider these three types of criticisms in more detail.

The Question of Balance Between the Three Areas of Practice

The criticism that the profession is unbalanced in the selection of the areas of education and practice on which it focuses takes different forms in different countries, reflecting the fact that the actual balance between the three areas varies significantly from country to country. The United States is a nation where some believe that social work has focused excessively on the area of micro practice with individuals and families, utilizing a largely clinical model in its practice across this area. In 1990, Specht (1990, p. 345) warned, "As things currently stand, there is good reason to expect that the profession will be entirely engulfed by psychotherapy within the next 20 years, and social work's function in the public social services will become negligible." In conclusion, Specht (1990, p. 354) writes, "The central point of this article is that the psychotherapies have diverted social work from its original vision, a vision of the perfectibility of society, the building of the 'city beautiful,' the 'new society,' and the 'new frontier.'"

Writing about social work in the United Kingdom, Harris (1990, pp. 204–205) criticizes what he regards as an unacceptable imbalance, albeit a different imbalance to that perceived by Specht as applying to social work in the United States. Harris writes in a critical tone,

> In the United Kingdom the debate about "what is social work?" has for many years been a central existential concern. It is variously answered. My own view is that it is in essence a state-funded activity concerned to deal individually with a range of "hard cases" in relation to which the routine application of the rules and law and policy are wanting: social work enforces rights which have not been elsewhere enforced and duties which the social worker's clientele have abrogated: social work is, therefore, a state-centred, not a client-centred enterprise. . . .

Finally, writing out of the African context, Kaseke (1990, p. 19) reflects a common African view that social work has been too preoccupied on that continent with state welfare and remedial approaches and too little with the social development field. He writes,

> Social development has evolved out of the frustration of social workers operating within the framework of the remedial approach. Their impressive intervention skills at the micro level have not helped to provide a permanent solution to problems which continue to resurface in dimensions much beyond the capacity of social workers with their current operational parameters.

Mupedziswa (1992) shares this view. He writes,

> The problems raised in this paper [unemployment, refugees, AIDS, ecology and structural adjustment programs] are major challenges for the social work profession. There is need for the social work profession to adopt what Ankrah (1987) has termed a "futuristic orientation", that is to anticipate what human needs are likely to be and what conditions will ensure that these are met, if social work hopes

to get on top of the situation. The profession just must become more aggressive, and more adventurous, if it is to be taken seriously and indeed if it is to become more relevant. (p. 29)

Most writers on social work across Africa discuss the variety of influences on and emerging forms of the profession, alongside many attempts at indigenization (see Asamoah, 1997), and go on to conclude that the indigenization process must be taken further and that social work must become more responsive to the major problems confronting the continent by adopting a largely developmental approach. (See, for example, Osei-Hwedie, 1993.)

The Neglect of Certain Fields of Practice and Certain Population Groupings

The second criticism of contemporary social work that is frequently encountered is that it tends to ignore or neglect certain vital issues or areas of need. Lobo and Mayadas (1997) describe the emerging model of social work within the field of work with refugees and displaced persons as a major challenge for international social work, while implying that this field is not significantly addressed by the profession. Back in 1982, and these views are probably still accurate, Sanders wrote that "the refugee problem and the unprecedented involuntary movement of people across national borders is a challenge to the conscience of the international community and the social work profession." Another issue that Sanders (1985, 1988) and others often wrote and spoke about was peace, emphasizing that peace and social development issues were closely related and should constitute social work concerns.

Other writers have lamented social work's effective neglect of extreme poverty in developing countries. Gore (1988, p. 3) writes of the situation in India, "It is often said in criticism of social work in India that the professional social workers address themselves to the consequences of poverty—such as destitution, lack of shelter, broken family, delinquency—rather than to poverty itself."

This is a fairly common view across the developing world. In developing countries, writers tend to refer to all major development-related needs, including poverty, as in practice effectively lying outside the usual scope of social work practice. They lament, for example, the neglect of rural areas, child labor, street children, migrant workers, illiteracy among and discrimination against women, and other fields. Usually the reasons stated or implied include that the state welfare system has not ventured into these areas and that aid agencies will not readily fund projects in such areas. Other reasons, however, relate to the urban and middle-class nature of the social work profession and the tendency of its graduates to choose other more acceptable and easier or more comfortable fields of practice over these neglected ones. Finally, social work n some developing countries is criticized as neglecting the field of social policy.

Allied to the criticized tendency of social work to avoid selected issues or fields is the criticism that it effectively turns its back on certain populations—usually populations that constitute unpopular minority groups within a state. The criticism is made of social work's role among indigenous minorities in most countries, among the Gypsy or Roma population of Europe, among asylum seekers and illegal migrants in some countries, and among certain castes in India. Frequently the view is put that the only way to rectify this situation is for schools of social work to adopt a policy of positive discrimination, selecting students from such backgrounds, and incorporating relevant material in the curriculum. While admirable in some senses, there are also dangers in such a policy, especially that of relegating a massive set of problems to a handful of graduates from a specific background. Of course one can explain an absence of social work services in certain contexts as simply reflecting a lack of employment opportunities and funding, but we believe the reasons to be more complex than this and have much to do with perceptions of mainstream social work in some countries, within and outside the profession.

Factors That Influence the Choice of the Three Areas of Practice and the Balance Between Them

Complexity of Factors

We have discussed this topic largely as if it were a matter of worker preference as to where social workers practice, and that their choices tend to reflect attitudes within the profession as much as personal preferences. The question of what determines social work deployment patterns is in reality quite complex. It involves the backgrounds and motivations of those who apply for and are accepted into schools of social work, and that population today in developing countries is usually a biased one favoring well-educated, urban middle-class persons. It involves the values, curriculum, staff profile, and other factors pertaining to the social work schools, for specific types of schools and curricula attract specific types of students, and in turn influence the employment preferences of graduates. It involves the employment market, for most persons will not choose to study particular emphases of a profession if the employment opportunities do not exist. It involves community attitudes prevailing among government personnel who make decisions about education, and among education administrators, education funding bodies, and parents of potential students, as well as in the range of government and nongovernment welfare services. If community values and attitudes are strongly against certain fields of practice or certain potential target populations, it is unlikely that courses, staff, or students will embrace those fields of practice to any significant degree. In such situations, it is often left to a handful of individuals or agencies to pioneer social work practice in unpopular areas, with the hope that they might eventually demonstrate the efficacy and necessity of such work.

Local Issues, Needs, and Contexts

A major difficulty may seem to be that most of those commentators who criticize the balance within or coverage of social work are not recommending that any areas or fields be dropped. They are usually not against what most social workers do but would like to see the scope of their reach expanded. Indeed, those who analyze the situation closely are disinclined to focus excessively on the differences between the areas of practice because they are aware of the large and necessary degree of overlap. For example, those who support a strong social development focus commonly do not exclude casework from such a focus, and certainly embrace both state-based and civil society–based intervention programs. The problem that then emerges is that of constantly expanding the areas or fields of practice, within an already overloaded curriculum and possibly an overstretched profession.

However, while few may wish to move social work out of any fields of activity, it is important in every profession to allow an assessment of the prevailing situation to determine issues like the balance between various areas of practice. It is clearly unacceptable that social work in Africa, to take but one example, should focus excessively on either the area of casework or that of social control measures initiated by governments. While both areas of practice have their place and generate skills that have wider applicability, social work in Africa should focus predominantly on addressing those needs that afflict the great majority of the population and cause widespread suffering, such as poverty, HIV/AIDS, and low levels of social development. Hence the call for a social development focus in many African countries and elsewhere would seem a completely logical decision for social work to make in that context.

The Need for a Comprehensive and Integrated Response

An alternative to expanding the scope of social work may be seen to be the development of new professions, such as social development workers, conflict and trauma counselors, and peace workers engaged in community reconciliation. We would, however, argue strongly against such a response. The reality is that need is holistic, and that persons, families, communities, regions, and even states must to a large degree be perceived as integrated wholes. The range of needs will vary, and specialist intervention will often be necessary, but it will always be important that there are those professionals who are able to see, understand, and assess the wider picture, and then work to ensure that the overall response to the overall situation is both comprehensive and integrated. This is indeed one of the major lessons to emerge from social work generally and social development work to date.

Let us take an example. If one works in a country that has been through a period of conflict, it is very obvious that workers are confronted with a range of interacting needs including, for example, needs to achieve reconciliation between parties to the conflict, to reintegrate returning displaced persons, to assist those who have been traumatized by events, to help communities to reestablish and work together, to build income-generation opportunities while distributing aid as necessary, to reconstruct society from the state institutions down to the local level, and to assist individuals with personal needs ranging from medical to marital problems. While inevitably some agencies and workers will be focusing on but one of these areas, there is the need for workers who can appreciate the larger picture; develop and implement a comprehensive set of policies and programs; deploy, support, and coordinate specialist workers; and generally ensure that developments in any one area will complement those in other areas so that people's well-being as a whole and the future development of the country are ensured.

Levels of Deployment of Social Workers

This perception of the need for a comprehensive and integrated approach to situations of poverty and displacement, postconflict situations, and social development generally, immediately suggests the importance of workers operating at different levels. A critical problem for social work in many contexts internationally, we believe, is its focus largely on the one level—that of the university graduate professional social worker. In some countries, we see the employment of welfare workers at a level below graduate social workers, and social administrators and supervisors at a level above, but usually with clear demarcations between roles and levels. The difficulties encountered with the one graduate level model are several: the education is expensive for all parties; in developing countries it results in relatively small graduate numbers; graduates expect to be paid well and to enjoy relatively good working conditions; and graduate profiles reflect the education level, being commonly predominantly urban middle-class.

The work situation, by contrast with the prevailing model, suggests the need for at least three levels of worker, and hence of training. Any efforts to alleviate poverty, tackle local-level development, engage with large populations of displaced persons, or embark on postconflict reconstruction will require very large numbers of workers able and willing to work in frontline operations with often difficult work environments. The training of these personnel can be, however, relatively short and limited to selected work roles, provided that adequate supervision is made available. A second level required is that of workers who can devise and implement local programs; train, supervise and support frontline workers; and interact with broader levels of society as necessary. Numbers at this level will need to be considerable, although much less than the numbers of frontline workers, while the complexity of the work calls for a basic university education. Finally, there is a need for workers with advanced training able to work effectively at the macro policy and planning levels, relate local programs to the broader societal situation, participate in the education of the second level of workers, prepare materials for use in the field, and otherwise facilitate a comprehensive and integrated approach to presenting situations.

We can refer to the three levels outlined in various ways. They can be seen as the local, intermediate, and central levels of operation; or the three levels of graduates can be described as social work assistants, social workers, and senior social workers; or alternatively, they can be regarded as paraprofessionals, professionals, and senior professionals. The terminology is not as important as is the acceptance of the three basic levels to implementing a comprehensive strategy in responding to presenting national and international needs. We would also argue that it is important that the three levels are all levels within the profession of social work with articulation from one level to the next well provided for, and that the training and numbers trained at each level reflect prevailing requirements at the three levels. It should be noted that we are not alone in reaching this conclusion. For example, Constable and Mehta (1994, p. 117), in concluding a study of social work education in Eastern Europe, argue the overall need for four levels, namely, in their terms: paraprofessional auxiliary level, first diploma level, second diploma level, and doctoral level. It has been pointed out to us by social workers in Hong Kong that they have long utilized a clearly delineated three tier system, while a de facto three tier system can be seen as operating in many western countries, whether or not workers at all levels and the profession consciously endorse this situation. (This topic is developed further in Chapter 14.)

In conclusion, it seems to us that social work has the responsibility and the potential to respond to the various situations of need that have dominated the international scene in recent times. Furthermore, we would strongly support the focus of social work simultaneously on the three areas that can be described as supporting the welfare state, providing casework services to community members in need of such, and engaging in social development as we have defined it (see Chapter 2). However, the balance between these three areas should vary from country to country, reflecting the balance between presenting needs and commonly agreed-upon responses to meeting those needs. Clearly, therefore, schools of social work internationally should be encouraged to reflect all three areas in the curriculum offered to students (although individual schools may reflect the three areas in different ways, perhaps complementing each other).

Furthermore, the need for social workers to contribute at the three levels, which we might refer to as local, intermediate, and central, necessitates the basic division of the profession into the three levels of assistant social workers, social workers, and senior social workers, with levels of entry to the profession and education and training offered reflecting these three levels of work in the field. In addition, the numerical balance between the three levels of recruitment and education will reflect the socioeconomic and development realities and need profiles prevailing in any country or region. We reach these conclusions from our examination of international social work. We cannot see how social work can make a significant response to the several aspects of international social work canvassed in this text unless these changes to the prevailing situation in the profession are made. Moreover, we believe that the profession is capable of undergoing change and agree with Kendall (2000, p. 107) when she writes, "It appears to be true that social work, perhaps more than any of the professions, is necessarily responsive to the social, political, economic and cultural conditions of the countries in which it is practiced."

The "Professionalization" of Social Work

A core problem concerning the "professionalization" of social work in the developing country context was set out by Midgley as early as 1981. He wrote,

> Because schools of social work in the United States and Britain were established at universities, it was recommended that social work training in the Third World should be introduced at the same level. In some countries, where there is a surplus of graduates, university trained social workers are employed as field workers but in many others, where a university education holds the prospect of rapid promotion, graduates are not eager to begin their careers at field level positions and are especially anxious to avoid a posting in the rural areas. Frequently, graduates are given responsibility for administration for which they have not been trained properly and, at the same time, inadequate training facilities for field level workers are provided. (1981, p. 153)

It is clear that social work in the West has deliberately taken on the mantle of a profession, especially in terms of the level of education required for practice, and Midgley is emphasizing the inappropriateness of these education levels for at least some developing countries. It is important, however, to consider the degree of professionalism in the light of the roles of social work. Here there are two major considerations. One is that social workers exercise a significant degree of control or influence over people's lives and well-being, and the principle of accountability or responsible behavior would necessitate that all social workers are trained to the highest level possible. And as professional education in the Western world has become a province of the universities, it is appropriate that social work education is located there

and its levels monitored closely. The second consideration is related to the key role of social work in integrating a variety of welfare or development inputs. If social workers are to be expected to give full consideration to social, economic, political, technological, ecological, cultural, legal, and other factors, while often coordinating a range of inputs in any situation, the level of education needs to be at least at the level of these other disciplines, and possibly for a slightly longer period of education than some disciplines. Once again, therefore, the logic implies a tertiary level of preparation.

We would certainly want to argue that social work has a responsibility to be as professional as possible, given that doing so does conform with the important principle of accountability and ensure that all practice has the potential to raise levels of well-being to the highest possible in a given environment. However, professionalism in social work does not necessitate a certain level of training for all workers, or certain levels of salary and work conditions for that matter. The objective, and indeed obligation, is to provide a service at the highest level possible in a given context. While that level will inevitably vary to some degree, the existence of global guidelines established by the IFSW (IASSW and IFSW, 2004) is very important. The nine standards being developed cover the social work school's core purpose or mission, program objectives and outcomes, program curricula including field work, core curricula, professional staff, student body, structure, administration, governance and resources, cultural and ethnic diversity and gender inclusiveness, and social values and ethical codes of conduct. However, we might argue that, above all other considerations, countries' resource levels should never preclude social work altogether or specific levels of social work practice, as appears currently to occur. Rather social work should be geared to the resources available, with external supports in the case of many LDCs. We shall return to the question in Chapter 14.

The Global Organization of Social Work

As the global organization of social work will enter into our discussions at several points, it will be helpful to present a brief overview of this. The three main international social work organizations were all in effect founded in the late 1920s, all emerging out of an international conference on social work in Paris in 1928. The International Conference on Social Work, the predecessor of the International Council on Social Welfare (ICSW), and the International Permanent Secretariat of Social Workers, the predecessor of the International Federation of Social Workers (IFSW), were both founded in 1928, and the International Association of Schools of Social Work (IASSW) in 1929. These three international organizations continue to be the key global organizations uniting social work internationally, although each has over the years evolved distinctive roles. Other international organizations have been field-specific in nature (for example, in the fields of aging and child welfare), but we do no more than note their existence in this context, important though they are. We should also note that our three global organizations developed regional associations which have often played key roles within the regions, while individual schools, social workers, and NGOs are usually united at state level within national associations.

A brief history of the three global organizations—IASSW, IFSW, and ICSW—can be found in Healy (1995b, pp. 1505–1506, and 2001, pp. 48–62). We shall provide only an introduction to each of the three organizations.

International Association of Schools of Social Work—IASSW

The IASSW began with 46 founding members from 10 countries in 1929, growing by 1939 to 75 member schools from 18 countries. After a temporary setback resulting from World War II,

the association continued to expand, to organize international conferences and seminars to facilitate interchange, and to develop general standards for social work education. It established an independent secretariat in 1971, led initially by the highly respected Katherine Kendall as the first secretary-general. This office was maintained until the late 1990s when the financial situation necessitated a change to a voluntary secretariat. The IASSW newsletters, publications, and conferences represent major links between schools of social work in developed and developing countries, assisting the former to reflect global realities in their curricula, and the latter to grow stronger and promote social work in their respective countries.

International Federation of Social Workers—IFSW

The predecessor of the IFSW, the International Permanent Secretariat of Social Workers, was founded in Paris in 1928 by social workers from several European countries and the United States. Dissolved during World War II, the organization was reformed in the 1950s, emerging eventually as the IFSW in 1956. The primary aim of the IFSW was to promote social work as a profession with professional standards and ethics. The International Code of Ethics was initially adopted in 1976, to be later revised. Another important goal was interchange between social workers around the globe, and the IFSW's regular conferences were organized largely to this end. The association has also represented social work's views on major world issues through position papers and its consultative status to the UN.

International Council on Social Welfare—ICSW

The ICSW began its life in 1928 as the International Conference on Social Work, becoming the ICSW in 1966. It is essentially an international council composed of national social welfare councils together with some international associations. Healy (2001, p. 59) reports that "there are currently 51 national committees and 31 other national associations," with 14 international organizations also being members. The ICSW embraces "practitioners from various disciplines and lay people interested in social welfare" (Healy). In 1982 the organization expanded its full name to International Council on Social Welfare: A World Organization Promoting Social Development, thus beginning to identify more closely with the development movement.

All three organizations are active at the UN level, promote and engage in global social welfare and social development agendas, interact with each other and with a range of other global associations, and generally facilitate their membership's active and professional contribution to international affairs. At the same time, each seeks to assist its membership and to promote social work and social welfare at regional, national, and local levels. Together they publish the journal *International Social Work*.

In addition, there are two more international organizations that are relevant to the profession and of interest to students of international social work. These are the Interuniversity Consortium for International Consortium of Social Development (ICSD) and the Commonwealth Organization for Social Work (COSW).

The ICSD was started in the 1970s by a group of social work educators to respond to pressing human concerns from an international, multidisciplinary perspective. It has members in dozens of countries and branches in Europe and the Asia-Pacific region. The organization seeks to develop conceptual frameworks and effective intervention strategies geared to influencing local, national, and international systems. It organizes an international symposium every two years and publishes the journal *Social Development Issues*. ICSD serves as a clearinghouse for information on international social development and fosters collaboration with a variety of international bodies. Further information may be

obtained from its Web site (www.iucisd.org) (see Healy, 1995b, p. 1506).

The Commonwealth Organization for Social Work had its beginnings in the early 1990s at the IFSW conference in Sri Lanka. It is an emerging organization open to citizens, including of course social workers, from Commonwealth countries (the Commonwealth is an association of 53 independent sovereign countries committed to the Declaration of Commonwealth Principles agreed to in Singapore in 1971 and reaffirmed in the Harare Declaration of 1991) who are interested in supporting social work and social development. It is based in London with an honorary secretary-general. COSW's main objectives are to promote and support communication and collaboration between social workers and social work associations in commonwealth countries, and to uphold and promote the code of ethics of the IFSW. The organization has the potential to contribute significantly to international social work's development.

However, it must be acknowledged that all five organizations seek to carry out their diverse and important roles with very limited resources, both financial and in terms of full-time personnel. International work is rendered expensive by the costs of travel and of maintaining effective communication links globally. Moreover, the difficulties inherent in consolidating a diversity of international views into a cohesive and meaningful statement or position paper for presentation in a variety of contexts should not be underestimated. Despite these inherent limitations, the work of these five global organizations has been and continues to be highly commendable, often in large part due to the dedicated contributions of a relatively small number of committed individuals. However, we might also note that the three main global social work organizations represent probably fewer than half of the world's nations, reflecting the still limited spread of social work globally.

From the perspective of international social work, the IASSW and IFSW in particular must be seen as carrying significant responsibility for the ongoing development of this field of practice. In particular, they should be able to assist developed and developing countries in their struggle to promote social work education and practice, to speak with governments, to assist in developing curricula, to facilitate visits to these countries by experienced practitioners and educators, to assist with the securing of appropriate social work literature, and to ensure that personnel within these countries are linked into global social work networks. Much activity along these lines has occurred in the past, but much more remains to be done, and it is to be hoped that the IASSW and IFSW will prove increasingly able to rise to the challenge.

International Social Work

Accepting that social work is an international unified profession with a common core, let us turn to a consideration of international social work. In the above discussion of social work we have implied that social work possesses all of the elements of a global profession, despite its inherent diversity. This is argued by Midgley (1995b, p. 1494), by Elliott (1997) after considering social work practice in 17 countries, by Healy (2001) after considering social work education around the world, and by Kendall (2000) after considering the organization of social work as an international profession. (See also Midgley, 2001.) In this text, the focus in defining international social work is not on social work as a global profession but rather on the roles of the profession in the international field.

The Definition of International Social Work

In her text on international social work, Healy (2001, p. 7) defined international social work as follows:

International social work is defined as international professional practice and the capacity for international action by the social work profession and its members. International

action has four dimensions: internationally related domestic practice and advocacy, professional exchange, international practice, and international policy development and advocacy.

Let us consider this definition. Healy commences by stating that international social work is social work practiced internationally, as distinct from locally and nationally. The assumption is that there are situations that are global in nature, thus requiring a global approach. In our understanding of international social work, however, we shall include practice pertaining to global concerns but taking place at national and local levels within countries. In the light of these global needs, Healy asserts that social work has the capacity to take international action—an assertion that we also set out to affirm in this text. Healy then lists four dimensions of international action, each of which is important.

The first dimension reflects an appreciation that, in an era of globalization, much if not all domestic practice requires an international perspective. We accept the importance of this dimension. Healy's second dimension, professional exchange, suggests that an international profession requires an international structure that encourages its members around the world to engage in mutual exchange at various levels and facilitates this process. Without this, a profession internationally is no more than a collection of national structures and outlooks. In our view of this professional exchange aspect of international social work, part of its importance is the extent to which social work in the developed industrial world can learn from innovations in the developing world. The third dimension, international practice, is the key focus of this text. It implies a need and a capacity for social work to engage in a range of actions at the international level, reflecting the same values, goals, and practice methods that apply at other levels. Finally, Healy includes the policy dimension, or the need for social work to advocate for the development and effective implementation of policies protecting the rights and enhancing the well-being of all peoples of the world. Some writers have focused exclusively on this policy dimension (e.g., Deacon, 1997).

One aspect of international social work that we find missing from Healy's definition is the goal of the profession to see itself established around the world. The current reality is that social work is virtually nonexistent in all of the poorest countries of the world (the UN's Least Developed Countries or LDCs of which there are some 48) and is in an embryonic stage in many other developing countries. It is not professional ambition that leads to our desire to see a strong social work profession in all countries. Rather it is our vision of the roles that social work can play, and should be playing, in the least or lesser developed countries; and our concern as we discuss international social work is that it does not represent a form of neoimperialism, with the western branches of the profession spearheading its emergence as a truly international profession.

While we appreciate Healy's definition of international social work, we shall define it a little differently to be in keeping with the purpose of this text:

> International social work is the promotion of social work education and practice globally and locally, with the purpose of building a truly integrated international profession that reflects social work's capacity to respond appropriately and effectively, in education and practice terms, to the various global challenges that are having a significant impact on the well-being of large sections of the world's population. This global and local promotion of social work education and practice is based on an integrated-perspectives approach that synthesizes global, human rights, ecological, and social development perspectives of international situations and responses to them.

There are several important aspects of this definition. The definition commences with the importance of action: international social work consists essentially of active promotion by the profession at various levels of the profession's involvement in global challenges. The link between education and practice is important in all professions, and international social work requires a much stronger focus within social work education curricula than it has received to date (Healy, 2001, chap. 11) if its scope is to expand. The emphasis on an integrated profession reflects the ever-present danger of the West imposing on other countries its basic understanding of the nature and roles of social work. We have already seen significant departures from western social work traditions in Latin America (Queiro-Tajalli, 1997) and in Africa and Asia (Mayadas et al., 1997; Kendall, 2000), as well as concerns about professional development trends in the United States (Specht, 1990), United Kingdom (Harris, 1990), and elsewhere. It is important to accept the necessary diversity across the profession within an integrated overall acceptance of the essential nature of social work. The key emphasis of the definition is that social work should engage in responses to the significant global challenges that are consistent with the essential nature of social work and in responses that are effective within the context of these global challenges. These responses are informed by the integrated-perspectives approach outlined in Chapter 2. Finally, the social work focus in participating in the international response to global challenges is driven by a concern for individual and collective well-being, reflecting the core values and goals of the profession as well as our integrated-perspectives approach.

Some important features of the definition are these:

- Action to address social work education and practice at global and local levels.
- Links between education and international practice.
- Integration of diverse practices rather than domination by one country or culture.
- An integrated-perspectives approach to practice—i.e., a synthesis of global, human rights, ecological, and social development perspectives.
- Individual and collective well-being.

In using the term *international social work*, there is always a danger that some will interpret it as applying only to one specific level of intervention, namely the international. However, as is commonly stressed, the focus in any context needs to be on all levels, from the local or domestic to the global or international. Whether the concern is with conflict, poverty, displacement, ecological degradation, or development in any of its dimensions (economic, political, social, cultural, or legal), the local, regional, national, and international levels will be significant, and our exploration of international social work practice will reflect this same range of levels.

The focus of this text is on international social work responding to global challenges and the social realities within the developing world, while appreciating that international social work has also many applications within the so-called developed world. Indeed, the utilization of the terms *developed country* and *developing country,* while widespread in the literature, is in fact ambiguous. It is far better to think in terms of degrees of development along a pathway that possesses no preordained destination, or perhaps, more precisely, we should think in terms of a greater range of categories of countries defined in terms of their level and type of development (see World Bank, 1997, p. 265).

The Scope of International Social Work in Terms of Its Response to Global Concerns

In this text there is frequent reference to different fields of international concern and activity, reflecting an international tendency to use this language. For example, we have the fields of poverty and its alleviation, development, natural disasters and responding to them, health concerns, and so on. Much of the organization within the international community and the literature is along these lines. However, social work and the various helping professions, in addition to focusing on fields as defined, frequently also focus on specific populations, either within fields, cutting across fields, or seeing the fields as factors affecting the specific population. Examples include

women in poverty, street children, indigenous minorities, sufferers of HIV/AIDS, and so on. Whatever the specific focus of any agency or body of literature, it is important to appreciate that the various fields are highly interactive and need to be appreciated as such. For example, the fields of poverty, conflict, and ecological degradation are often closely related in cause-and-effect terms— that is, both poverty and conflict can contribute to ecological degradation, while poverty and ecological degradation can contribute to conflict, and so on. Hence, appreciating the context in which any specific population lives requires understanding the ways in which several fields interact as they impinge on the specific population in question. Finally, in responding to specific fields or populations, there is the question of the level of the response. Responses can usually be found at at least three levels: international, national, and local; however, the fourth level of *regions* could also be included. For example, in relation to some particular aspect of development, or some particular situation of conflict, responses may come from the UN (international), the European Union (regional), various governments (national), and local organizations and movements (local).

Our understanding of international social work is that its potential relevance covers virtually all of the fields of activity that concern the international community, a wide range of specific populations within each field (or cutting across fields), and all levels at which intervention is necessary and possible. In this text, we have selected a few fields and a few specific populations on which to focus, not only because of their importance but as examples, and have confined our discussion largely to the local level, without negating the importance of the other levels both per se and as areas of activity for social workers. We focus on the local level partly because of its neglect by social work in many developing country contexts, and partly because it represents in most cases the field work on which social work at the other levels, and on which policy and advocacy work and so on, should be based. Local work represents both our right to speak out and engage in policy and planning activities, and the source of the knowledge and experience on which, to a large degree, we base our work at the other levels.

Conclusion

Social work has emerged as a very broad profession, both within individual countries and in a global comparative sense. While its western and colonial origins have left their imprint on the profession, we can still see social work evolving in a range of very different contexts with highly varied emphases. In this chapter, however, our focus is limited to the international scene, and in two particular ways. First, there is the question of social work's potential to contribute to the alleviation of the major social problems and areas of need that preoccupy large sections of the international community. Second, and closely related to the first, is the potential of social work to contribute to confronting these global needs as they are experienced in the least developed countries and areas of the world. We agree with many other commentators that social work does have the potential to contribute much in these interrelated areas, and we shall go on in this text to suggest how that goal might be achieved, both generally and in relation to specific fields of work.

Summary

- The understanding of social work, and its application of knowledge and skills, varies greatly across the globe. Despite such variation, the IFSW social work definition is accepted by many countries and can be adopted by many other countries. However, what is commonly accepted by all is its value base and commitment to social change.

- Formal social work education originated, and developed, as a full-fledged profession in the West. Later it spread to many countries, including former colonies. By and large this western social work education pattern prevails in most parts of the world, though each country has added its own unique features to its education and practice model. There is a need to indigenize social work education in accordance with the varied country contexts.

- Social work education, practice, and professional organizations vary significantly in terms of the balance between the three areas of practice, namely supporting the welfare state, providing casework services, and engaging in social development. Several complex factors influence the balance between these practice areas, which is often a source of criticism of the profession that raises several critical issues. A comprehensive and integrated response is needed at both local and global levels.

- International social work organizations have a significant responsibility and can play crucial roles in further developing social work as a global profession.

- International social work needs to be understood in terms of education and practice and of interdependence between the two, resulting in diversity that is nonetheless held together by the four integrated perspectives geared essentially to the promotion of individual and collective well-being.

Questions and Topics for Discussion

- Compare and contrast the IFSW's and Barker's (1999) social work definitions.
- Summarize the main points you have noted while studying the origins of social work in the West, expansion of the profession into former colonies, and indigenization of social work.
- Does the suggested division of social work into three main areas make sense according to your experience?
- Why do you think there is an imbalance in the practice of the three areas in different national contexts, and what kind of issues does it raise for the profession?
- As an exercise, visit the Web sites of international social work organizations; study their aims, objectives, and current activities; and discuss these with peers.
- Compare and contrast the two definitions of international social work (one by Healy, 2001; and another by the authors of this text).
- Discuss recent trends and key issues in international social work practice.

Possible Areas for Research Projects

- Carry out an analysis of varied conceptions of international social work and of how professional social workers and other relevant professionals perceive international social work.
- Examine the impact of western social work models and the extent of indigenization of social work in selected developing countries.
- Study the factors that enhance and hamper indigenization of social work education and practice within a particular place.
- Examine the factors that have influenced the choice of areas of practice locally and explore strategies for developing a good balance in practice.
- Develop case studies on selected professional social work organizations.

Further Reading

Healy, L. (2001). *International social work: Professional action in an interdependent world.* New York: Oxford University Press.

Mayadas, N. S., Watts, T. D., & Elliott, D. (Eds.). (1997). *International handbook on social work theory and practice.* Westport, CT: Greenwood.

Ramanathan, C. S., & Link, R. J. (Eds.). (1999). *All our futures: Principles and resources for social work practice in a global era.* Boston: Brooks/Cole.

2

The Integrated-perspectives Approach to International Social Work

The definition of international social work given in Chapter 1 contains reference to an integrated-perspectives approach as a framework for international social work practice, and it is to this approach that we now turn. The model in Figure 2.1 shows the integration of four perspectives to constitute the integrated-perspectives approach. We shall consider each of the four perspectives in its own right before considering the integration of the four as the overall approach to international social work practice suggested here. However, a summary of the part played by the four perspectives may be helpful at this point.

The global perspective establishes the boundaries of the approach and highlights the essential unity of the earth. The global perspective omits no person or population or place. It is all-inclusive, with the implied importance of

Learning Objectives

The main objective of this chapter is to discuss the integrated-perspectives approach to international social work practice. After studying this chapter, readers should be able to understand

- Several dimensions of each of four perspectives—global, human rights, ecological, and social development—of the integrated approach.
- The connections among the various dimensions of each perspective and between the four perspectives in an integrated manner.
- The significance of such an approach for international social work practice.
- The potential of the integrated-perspectives approach to be employed as a tool to analyze issues and needs, and to develop appropriate responses to address the same.

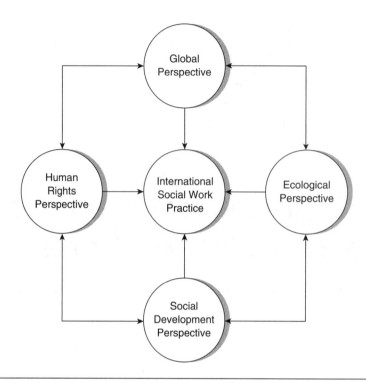

Figure 2.1   An integrated-perspectives approach for international social work practice

each person, population, and place being reinforced by the human rights and ecological perspectives respectively. It is also a unifying perspective, suggesting the basic global village concept, and this unifying element is reinforced by all three of the other perspectives.

The human rights perspective represents the key value base of international social work. All aspects of international social work should be guided by those fundamental rights and freedoms that have been globally endorsed within a series of international conventions and declarations. Its core emphases are consistent with the value base adopted by social work from the beginning. This human rights perspective underpins the global perspective and is elaborated through the ecological and social development perspectives. It establishes in general terms the vision and goals that drive international social work.

The ecological perspective reflects the importance of the natural world within which human beings must live and of which they are a part. It

is a critical aspect of the environment within which all international development and all social work practice takes place. Although the ecological perspective is one important aspect of the global perspective, it is treated separately because of its inherent distinctive importance and the danger of it being overlooked. The ecological dimension is also one dimension of multidimensional social development, so that the social development perspective reinforces its importance.

The social development perspective encompasses a major component of international social work in that much international social work is engaged in the various aspects of social development, while its goals and value base underpin international social work. Whatever the context, and whatever the need for remedial and preventative action, the focus is ultimately on enhancing the social development of the people involved, while protecting or seeking to improve the environments within which they function. Social development is essentially a

value-b
approa
the ult
being
nation
on spe
often
of soc
is also
guide
social
conte
reinf
persp
T
inter
with
pers
whi
of t
alo
into

presented here
The first dim
principles
second
the t
th

Nations Research Institute for Social Development (UNRISD, 1995b, p. 12) writes,

Citizenship has three central propositions: equality in individual and human rights; free and universal political participation; and state responsibility to ensure adequate standards of human welfare. The time has come to extend these principles internationally: to foc attention explicitly on global citizenship

For many writers (e.g., Muet Smith, 2002; Kaldor, 2003), the c or global citizenship is linke perceived emergence of Participating through gl of the world are s the democratiza process—or g while camp and enh their ab

base,

- the ecological perspective the essential link between humanity and nature, and
- the social development perspective the overall guide to action or sense of direction underpinning action.

The following sections will elaborate on each of the four perspectives.

The Global Perspective

The first component of our integrated-perspectives approach is the global perspective, an obvious component perhaps given our emphasis on international concerns. The concept of *global* and the recent preoccupation with globalization trends are, however, far from constituting a unitary concept. This perspective is in reality and in

diversity presenting as dimensions of global, a third and a reconciling dimension to at least some degree is interdependence. Our second set of binary opposites, globalization and localization, are here reconciled by our final dimension of world citizenship. Thus our six dimensions of the global perspective are unity, diversity, interdependence, globalization, localization, and world citizenship. Let us outline briefly our understanding of each dimension.

Unity

The hub of global unity is obviously the fact that all human beings derive from the same origins, inhabit the same planet, and exhibit the same basic needs. And while there exists diversity across the human race, in the specific environments it inhabits and in its cultural in terms of four dimensions. The first dimension consists of the values and principles on which human rights are based; the second dimension is the set of rights themselves; the third dimension is the universality of both the values and the rights derived from them; and the fourth dimension is the role of human rights as a guide to living and behavior in all contexts, and hence to professional practice.

Values and Principles

While human rights themselves are often traced back to the eighteenth century, where they culminated in the American Declaration of Independence and the French Declaration of the Rights of Man, many of the core elements of human rights were present and enforced in western and nonwestern cultures and societies from ancient times (UNCHR, 1992, p. 12). The essential value foundation of human rights lies in what it means to be human. Donnelly (1993, p. 19) expresses it very well:

> The very term human rights indicates both their nature and their source: they are the rights that one has simply because one is human. They are held by all human beings, irrespective of any rights or duties one may (or may not) have as citizens, members of families, workers, or parts of any public or private organization or association. In the language of the 1948 declaration, they are universal rights.
>
> If all human beings have them simply because they are human, human rights are held equally by all. And because being human cannot be renounced, lost or forfeited, human rights are inalienable. Even the cruelest torturer and the most debased victim are still human beings. In practice, not all people enjoy all their human rights, let alone enjoy them equally. Nonetheless, all human beings have the same human rights and hold them equally and inalienably.

...elfeldt and ...ncept of world ...d closely with the ...global civil society. ...bal civil society, peoples ...en to be contributing to ...ion of the world's political ...ing globalization a human face, ...aigning actively to protect the rights ...nce the well-being of all peoples within ...local context. Global citizenship is invari-...ly expressed at both the global and local level, with action at the global level being frequently geared to outcomes at the local level. From a world citizenship perspective, the global and the local are closely linked, indeed inseparable. Citizenship can never be limited to nationality and territory. We are all first and foremost citizens of the world, entitled to the protection of the international community, while ideally also citizens of a state and belonging to a specific homeland. If we cannot assert this in principle, and strive for it in practice, then the global perspective is meaningless. (See work of Falk, 1993; and Kaldor, 2003.)

The Human Rights Perspective

The human rights perspective is an essential component of the integrated-perspectives approach, basically providing the values and rights basis of international social work practice. The human rights perspective is understood and

In Donnelly's eyes, human rights are "paramount moral rights" (1993, p. 20) that rest on "a moral account of human possibility."

> Human rights rest on an account of a life of dignity to which human beings are "by nature" suited and the kind of person worthy of and entitled to such a life. And if the rights specified by the underlying theory of human nature are implemented and enforced, they should help to bring into being the envisioned type of person. The effective implementation of human rights should thus result in a self-fulfilling moral prophecy.

In what they describe as an "illustrative rather than exhaustive" list of the values and principles on which human rights are based, the United Nations Centre for Human Rights (UNCHR, 1992, pp. 13–19) discusses eight "philosophical values." These are

1. Life—"The worth of life, human and non-human existence is the fountainhead of all the other ideals and values."

2. Freedom and liberty—The UN Universal Declaration of Human Rights asserts that "all human beings are born free," and it proceeds to list a set of fundamental freedoms, including the right to liberty and the right to freedom from slavery and servitude, torture, arbitrary arrest, and arbitrary interference with privacy, family, and home.

3. Equality and nondiscrimination—The same UN declaration sets out the fundamental principle of equality of all human beings.

4. Justice—"Various aspects of justice have to be taken into consideration: the legal, judicial, social, economic and other aspects which constitute the basis of a society upholding the dignity of its members, and ensuring security and integrity of persons."

5. Solidarity—"Solidarity is another fundamental value which implies not only understanding and empathy towards humankind's pain and suffering, but identifying and taking a stand with the sufferers and their cause."

6. Social responsibility—"Social responsibility is action undertaken on behalf of sufferers and victims: standing for them, championing their cause and helping them. It could thus be said that social responsibility is the implementation corollary of solidarity."

7. Evolution, peace, and nonviolence—Peace is presented here as "a distinct value and not simply the absence of organized conflict." The ultimate goal of peace is "achieving harmony within the self, with others and with the environment."

8. Relationships between humankind and nature—The final value or principle is that of harmony with nature as the necessary basis for preventing environmental degradation.

While this list is not exhaustive it does indicate the nature of the value foundations on which human rights are based.

Human Rights

There has been an evolution in the understanding of human rights, as a UN publication (UNCHR, 1992, p. 12) makes clear:

> The development of human rights has been one of evolution. A concern for civil and political rights, which was the initial spur to the conceptualization of human rights in the eighteenth century, was gradually matched by a demand for economic, social and cultural rights. Now a third generation of rights is increasingly recognized as a legitimate universal aspiration for humankind—rights to peace, development and a clean environment protected from destruction.

Ife (2001, pp. 24ff.) discusses these three generations of human rights at more length. First generation rights, sometimes referred to as negative rights, emphasize protection. They "involve the prevention of human rights abuses and the safeguarding or protection of rights rather than the more positive assertion, provision and realization of human rights" (p. 25). Ife continues: "The second generation of human rights is the constellation of rights known as economic, social and cultural rights." These are concerned with social provision, thus requiring "a stronger and more resource-intensive role for the state" (p. 26). Then,

> The third generation of human rights involves rights which only make sense if defined at a collective level; they are rights that belong to a community, population, society or nation rather than being readily applicable to an individual, though individuals can clearly benefit from their realization. (p. 27)

These third generation rights include the right to economic development, to clean water, and so on. The various rights recognized by the international community are contained within a set of declarations and conventions listed in Appendix A and presented in Part III of the UN's 1992 text. (See also Laqueur and Rubin, 1990.)

Universality

The dimension of universality is included here because of its importance but also controversial nature. As Donnelly (1993, pp. 34ff.) discusses, the debate is between the relativists (e.g., Huntington, 2002, p. 196), who argue that the moral values on which rights are based are "historically or culturally specific" (p. 35), and the universalists who argue that all values and human rights "are entirely universal" (p. 36). Donnelly himself supports a position that he describes as "weak cultural relativism" (p. 36). He writes that "internationally recognized human

rights represent a good first approximation of the guarantees necessary for a life of dignity"; however, "universality is only an initial presumption. Some deviations from international human rights norms may be justified—or even demanded." His final conclusion is this: "The possibility of justifiable modifications, however, must not obscure the fundamental universality of international human rights norms. Deviations should be rare and their cumulative impact relatively minor" (p. 37).

This position is perhaps not all that different from Ife's (2001, p. 7) position, with which we are in agreement:

> The universality of human rights must not be confused with a static unchangeable notion of human rights. Because human rights must be seen as constructed rather than objectively existing, the important thing is the process of dialogue, discussion and exchange that seeks to articulate such universal values.

A Guide to Living and Behavior

The final dimension of our human rights perspective relates to the ultimate objective of the perspective, namely that these human rights (however defined in any specific context), and the principles and values on which they are based, should determine how humanity lives, and is permitted to live, at all levels. Human rights are not just protection from certain forms of abuse, or the right to receive certain forms of social provision. They are also guides for behavior from the individual (e.g., how an individual soldier treats an enemy prisoner) through to the international level (e.g., how the UN Security Council reaches decisions). In a sense, human rights constitute the overall universal norms within which all societies should be set and against which they can be judged. In this context, it is significant to note that the values on which human rights are based conform to the basic teachings of all of the world's major religions. In very basic terms, they set out how people should both treat each other (as individuals, groups, or collectives) and relate to nature. (For important discussions on human rights as a guide to development generally, see UNDP, 2000; and Uvin, 2004.)

Long term locally and world perspective in terms of the environment

The Ecological Perspective

The ecological perspective leads us to focus on the natural environment within which human life is and must be lived—the natural environment on which all life ultimately depends. Ife (2002, chap. 2) refers to the environmental crisis that is widely seen to be of great importance today and compares two types of responses to this crisis. One is the environmental response Ife describes as seeking "to solve specific problems by finding discrete solutions." He comments:

> Such an approach is characteristic linear thinking, which has played a dominant role in the Western world view within which industrial and technological "progress" has developed. (p. 22)

In relation to the second type of response, Ife (2002, p. 23) writes,

> By contrast, the Green response to environmental problems takes a more fundamental or radical approach. It sees environmental problems as being merely the symptoms of a more significant and underlying problem. They are the consequence of a social, economic and political order which is blatantly unsustainable, and thus it is the social, economic and political order that needs to be changed.

Ife's own ecological perspective adopts the Green view of ecological problems. As he states,

> If the ecological crisis is to be effectively resolved, it will be through social, economic and political change, rather than through scientific and technological progress.

There is in the literature a third type of response to the ecological crisis that we might call the spiritual response. Nasr (1990, p. 3) presents this approach as follows: "The blight wrought upon the environment is in reality an externalization of the inner state of the soul of that humanity whose actions are responsible for the ecological crisis." In this view, the ecological crisis stems fundamentally from "the attitude of simple domination and plunder of nature that developed later in the history of the West" (p. 5). Within this attitude, "Man is made absolute, his 'rights' dominating over both God's rights and the rights of His creation" (p. 6). Drawing on various spiritual traditions, especially those of indigenous peoples such as Australia's aboriginal population, other writers refer to "ecospirituality." For example, Tacey (2000, p. 162) writes that "the environmental crisis . . . is a spiritual problem about how we experience ourselves in the world." He continues,

> Today's society shows scant regard for the environment and little commitment to nature. Secular materialism and egotistical desires govern our relations with the land, we have no cosmology to link us spiritually with the world, and our official religious tradition is concerned more with heaven than with earth. It is hardly surprising, in view of this, that we face the prospect of ecological disaster. (p. 163)

By contrast, "there is a profound sense of spiritual kinship with the environment" in aboriginal Australia (p. 164), as is also the case with many other indigenous peoples.

In our ecological perspective we shall acknowledge the importance of all three responses to the ecological crisis. It is important to identify specific problems and appropriate responses, even if these tend to be short-term remedial measures. However, we agree with Ife that the more long-term and sustainable response will involve significant social, economic, and political change. Yet in the final analysis it does seem essential that humanity rediscovers the spiritual link between humankind and nature. As Tacey (2000, p. 177) puts it,

> The ecological benefits of an ecospirituality are virtually incalculable, and purely on practical and survival grounds, there are many arguments to be put for why we alienated moderns must strive towards a recovery of mythic imagination, expanded subjectivity and a cosmic identity.

We have identified four dimensions to the ecological perspective, and in this we are in complete agreement with, and much indebted to, Ife (2002).

Holism and Unity

The essence of this dimension, as Ife describes it, is that the world and all phenomena are "part of a seamless web of complex interconnecting relationships," characterized by "integration and synthesis" (p. 41). As Ife explains, this approach leads to an ecocentric view of the world rather than an anthropocentric one, resulting in a "respect for all life, the intrinsic value of the natural world and, hence, a strong conservationist ethic" (p. 41). It is important to emphasize that this holistic approach emphasizes the unity or oneness between humankind and nature, from both a spiritual and a practical perspective.

Diversity

As with our global perspective, within the ecological perspective unity or holism is balanced by diversity. Just as humanity benefits from its immense diversity on many levels, so nature benefits from, indeed requires, diversity—diversity of species and conditions within the web of life. The alternative to diversity is uniformity, and, as Ife puts it, "uniformity is a recipe for ecological disaster" (p. 43).

Equilibrium

A further dimension to the existence of diversity within an overall unity is that of equilibrium. Nature demonstrates clearly the importance of balance between the various species and between differing conditions, such as wet and dry or hot and cold conditions. Similarly, the impact of people on an environment and the inherent needs of that environment must be kept in balance, as indeed happens with many other species—for example, we see the reproductive rates of many species varying so as to maintain a balance between a species' needs and those of the environment during, for example, extreme climatic conditions. Thus equilibrium is maintained. Humanity, however, appears to have lost all consciousness of such a need, and still acts largely on the assumption that any depletion of the environment caused by a lack of equilibrium can be offset by mankind's scientific abilities.

Sustainability

The principle of sustainability has become of central importance in ecological and development thinking, with the term "sustainable development" being now commonplace (see World Bank, 2003). Humanity needs to draw on nature for its very survival, but it must do so in ways and at rates that are sustainable across generations. The danger of exhausting land, water, fish, mineral, and other stocks is very real in many parts of the globe, and only an active concern with the principle of sustainability will result in careful management of all natural resources. The basic concern is well-known and frequently enunciated. Back in 1992, the World Bank expressed it as follows:

> Sustainable development is development that lasts. A specific concern is that those who enjoy the fruits of economic development today may be making future generations worse off by

excessively degrading the earth's resources and polluting the earth's environment. The general principle of sustainable development adopted by the World Commission on Environment and Development (WCED, 1987)—that current generations should "meet their needs without compromising the ability of future generations to meet their own needs"—has become widely accepted. (p. 34)

Elliott (1994, p. 3) defines sustainable development as "development that is likely to achieve lasting satisfaction of human needs and improvement of the quality of human life." (For further material on the ecological perspective, see Brown et al., 1991; George, 1990; and Suter, 1995.)

Covers all the other Perspectives

The Social Development Perspective

The term *social development* has commonly been used in two distinct ways. One way is to use *social* as contrasting with economic, political, cultural, legal, and ecological. The focus on social development is then often to counteract what is seen as an excessive emphasis on economic development, and specifically on economic growth. In our view, it is better to adopt the UNDP convention of using *human development* for this purpose (UNDP Human Development Reports since 1990; Ul Haq, 1995; Sen, 2001). The second way, which really flows from the logic of a people-centered approach to development, is to see social development as signifying the development of society as a whole, in all its complexity and with all its dimensions. In this text we are using *social* in the second sense of societal development, or development pertaining to a society.

Two views of social development that are consistent with this understanding are the following:

Social development is a process of planned social change designed to promote the well-being of the population as a whole in conjunction with the dynamic process of economic development. (Midgley, 1995a, p. 8) (See also Midgley, 1996a)

Todaro and Smith (2003, p. 23) present their very comprehensive understanding of development in terms of three key objectives:

1. to increase the availability and widen the distribution of basic life-sustaining goods,

2. to raise levels of living—economic and social, and in terms of cultural and human values, and

3. to expand the range of economic and social choices.

In our view, the concept of social development as it has evolved since the early 1990s has had five key elements:

1. a foundation of principles or values;

2. a focus on people and human resources through such measures as capacity building;

3. the establishment of an adequate and appropriate network of national institutions and structures;

4. a satisfactory system of micro-macro relations, achieved through, for example, the freedom of people to participate; and

5. the creation by the state of an enabling environment, in economic, political, social, legal, and cultural terms.

In elaborating on the social development perspective we shall focus on four dimensions: this perspective is value-based, involves proactive intervention, is multidimensional, and is multilevel.

Value-based

The value-based dimension of social development stems essentially from the acceptance of development of societies at any level as being essentially for the benefit of the people who form, or will in the future form, those societies. Development is focused on and geared to the enhancement of the well-being of people, because people are valued over systems and structures. The first of the UNDP's Human Development reports in 1990 established that the basic objective of human development was to enlarge the range of people's choices. The 1991 report expanded on this theme:

> The basic objective of human development is to enlarge people's choices to make development more democratic and participatory. These choices should include access to income and employment opportunities, education and health, and a clean and safe physical environment. Each individual should also have the opportunity to participate fully in community decisions and to enjoy human, economic and political freedoms. (p. 1)

In a later report, the UNDP would maintain that development should be "of the people, by the people and for the people" (UNDP, 1993, p. 3). In a similar vein, in its *World Development Report* in 1991, the World Bank stated that "the challenge of development in its broadest sense is to improve the quality of life" (1991b, p. 4). The value base of social development stems from this people-centered goal embodied in the term *human development* and at the heart of social development.

The specific values that are listed as fundamental to development or social development will vary. Todaro and Smith (2003, pp. 21–22) suggest three core values: "1. sustenance—the ability to meet basic needs; 2. self-esteem—to be a person; and 3. freedom from servitude—to be able to choose." An unpublished ESCAP (United Nations Economic and Social Commission for Asia and the Pacific) paper (D. Cox, training notes, 2000) suggested the following:

Participation, incorporating the principle of equity and equality of opportunity, so that development is participatory and equitable (see Stiefel and Wolfe, 1994);

Sustainability, or sustainable development (see World Bank, 2003);

Social integration, or social development that promotes social integration; and

Human rights and fundamental freedoms, or social development that reflects these fundamental rights and freedoms.

Other values commonly emphasized are self-reliance and empowerment, but an exhaustive list is not possible or necessary in this context.

Proactive Intervention

Social development differs from all forms of remedial intervention that function essentially as responses to identified problems. It even goes beyond preventative responses that foresee future problems and seek to avert them. Social development adopts what is basically a developmental approach, which means that it sets out to create (not in any final and certainly not in a social engineering sense, but in a dynamic process sense) the kind of society that reflects the values on which social development is based. It represents in this sense proactive intervention—intervention that always seeks to improve the status quo in the interests of enhancing the well-being of some or all sections of the population.

Multidimensional

Social development is multidimensional in two meanings of the term. First, it recognizes the inherent importance of the economic, social, political, cultural, legal, and ecological dimensions of a society's life, and seeks to develop each and all of these dimensions in an integrated and holistic sense. In a second meaning, the dimensions of a society can be envisaged in terms of social structures, social relations, social processes, and social values, and all four of these dimensions need to be considered whenever social development is considered. This implies that workers in social development need to think in broad multidimensional and societal terms, regardless of where their specific actions are being directed at any point in time.

Multilevel

Our final dimension of the social development perspective is that social development needs to be implemented at all of the levels at which a society functions. Sometimes these levels are expressed in terms of the local, regional, national or state, and global levels, signifying the perceived area and population covered by a development initiative. At other times, the focus is more on the sectors of society, essentially the individual/family/community sector, the civil society sector, the for-profit or corporate sector, and the state or national institutional sector. Social development may focus on any of these levels or within any of these sectors, but it is clear that it should never do so without keeping the other levels or sectors in mind, as all interact within the overall functioning of a society and are critical to the development of that society. Finally, social development incorporates the international level, thus stressing the significance of the interaction of all societies for the development of any one society or part thereof.

The Integrated-perspectives Approach as a Whole

The integrated-perspectives approach, as depicted in Figure 2.2, indicates the four perspectives that constitute the model and the key dimensions of each of the perspectives as we perceive them.

The Model

The model suggests that, in regard to any aspect of international social work practice, it is necessary to consider the presenting problem and response options from the point of view of each of the four perspectives.

For example, if a social worker is confronted with a situation involving asylum seekers in a particular country, the reaction could be to examine the needs presented by this asylum-seeker population and consider how those needs might be responded to as short-term immediate needs within the immediate context. While such a remedial response is at times necessary as an immediate short-term response, the preferred or ultimate response would be to also consider the situation as an aspect of international social work, and analyze it in terms of the four perspectives. It would then become clear, for example, that the local asylum-seeker problem is part of a global problem and has global aspects that should be considered in relation to any local response; it will also be clear that it is a human rights problem that should be examined and intervention options considered on the basis of those rights; furthermore, ecological concerns may well relate to the country and place of origin, contributing to displacement, and it will be apparent that any intervention strategy should take those ecological issues into account; and, finally, it will be apparent that the key concern is for the ongoing well-being of these asylum seekers, and for the social development issues concerning them and whatever country or place is considered as offering these people a future place of residence. The integrated-perspectives approach is thus

- a tool for analysis of every aspect of any situation coming under international social work practice,
- an approach to determining causation and consequences of past events,
- a model for identifying possible responses and their consequences, and
- an overview of the actual intervention process.

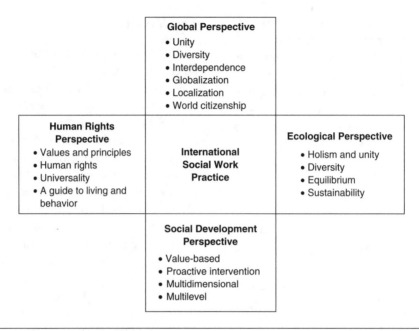

Figure 2.2   An integrated-perspectives approach for international social work practice

Justification of the Approach

While the need for an analytical model to guide international social work practice should be self-evident, the choice of perspectives included within the integrated-perspectives approach may not be and may require some justification. The inclusion of the global perspective should be self-evident when the focus is on the international and we are in an era of rapid globalization. The global perspective is basically a way of helping us to make sense of the term international, and the various dimensions identified assist in that process. Nor is the need to include a value perspective likely to be controversial. Why would one reach out to all peoples in all places and all conditions unless doing so is based on a set of values that drives such behavior? And what better set of values than the set of internationally endorsed human rights of universal applicability?

The inclusion of the ecological perspective is based on the logical importance of the ecological

context within which all human activity occurs, and on the perceived crisis threatening many aspects of that context. All action from here on must consider that crisis, address it where possible, find ways of operation that are ecologically sustainable, and ideally learn to respect the environment and live in harmony with it. Finally, the social development perspective reflects the need to place all social work action within the context of a vision, a set of goals, or a modus operandi, and what better modus operandi than the well-thought-out social development process, with its people-centered, all-inclusive, and integrated approach to maximizing well-being.

If the inclusion of these four perspectives is readily justified, we need to consider whether the exclusion of other possible perspectives is acceptable. While we consider it necessary to limit the number of perspectives for practical purposes, we would also argue that the four selected for inclusion are indeed very broad. Let us consider briefly alternative or additional perspectives. Within social work, the feminist or gender perspective might be one that immediately comes to mind. Given the centrality of gender concerns in many contexts, this is not surprising. However, our approach incorporates the gender perspective to a large degree through its place in all four of the perspectives, but especially within human rights and social development. Other readers might be inclined to stress a particular political-economic perspective, whether Marxist, socialist, capitalist, or some other, or an ideological perspective such as neoliberalism, neoconservatism, colonialism, neocolonialism, or neoimperialism, if only to ensure that such perspectives are avoided. We are not in favor of international social work practice being driven by or preoccupied with any particular ideology, while recognizing the centrality of ideologies and power struggles in international relations and in many of the specific situations concerning international social work practice. It is always crucial to contextualize international social work practice, and our integrated-perspectives approach already enables us to do this.

The Integrated-perspectives Approach and Existing Social Work Theories

The integrated-perspectives approach does not appear to be in conflict with existing social work theories, and indeed in many ways it represents an extrapolation or extension of existing theories. Payne (1997) has divided social work theories and models into three categories: reflexive-therapeutic, socialist-collectivist, and individual-reformist. While this categorization is helpful, we are of the view that twenty-first-century international social work practice needs to be informed by an integrated approach, and our four perspectives provide us with such an approach.

Many of the links between the four perspectives and existing social work theory will be obvious to many of our readers. The human rights perspective closely reflects the ethics,

values, and rights approach that social work endorsed from the beginning. Similarly, the ecological perspective is not new to social work practice. Various social work assessment and intervention models emanate from the ecological perspective: for example, systems theory (e.g., Compton and Galaway, 1999; Pincus and Minahan, 1973), ecological systems (e.g., Bronfenbrenner, 1979), and life model theories (e.g., Germain and Gitterman, 1980, 1996) have been extensively applied in social work practice, though not always addressing structural issues. Thus the ecological perspective connects well to current social work theories and provides a renewed direction to its practice.

The relevance of social development to social work has been an issue of some controversy in recent years. While some social workers have considered the essence of social development to be distinct from social work (e.g., Midgley, 1995a), others have argued for the incorporation of the social development approach within social work (e.g., Billups, 1994; Osei-Hwedie, 1990; Elliott, 1993; Gray, 1997a, 1997b; Meinert and Kohn, 1987; Elliott and Mayadas, 1996). In our opinion, social work can only benefit from drawing upon the insights of social development, while not losing its separate identity. In relation to the various social work methods, Ife (2002) presents a model of community development that resonates closely with social development; Elliott and Mayadas (1996, p. 61) see no conflict between social development and social work's clinical model of practice; while social policy has moved from an international comparative approach to the direct incorporation of global social policy.

Finally, the global perspective, we would argue, has been inherent in social work right through, even if not explicit until more recent times. Moreover, the global perspective is consistent with the renewed focus on structural issues (e.g., Mullaly, 1993; Fook, 1993), for the global perspective focuses closely on global economic and political structures.

Overreliance on one particular social work theory, approach, or methodology does not facilitate practice in the international arena. The effectiveness of social work intervention, especially in global contexts, requires a willingness to use a range of methods, and we see the integrated-perspectives approach as facilitating this.

The Application of the Integrated-perspectives Approach to International Social Work

We shall explore the integrated-perspectives approach in terms of workers' orientation, the process of analyzing situations, the planning of intervention strategies, and the implementation of intervention plans. Throughout we shall refer to the integrated-perspectives approach as "the approach."

Workers' Orientation

The approach represents an appropriate orientation to all professional social work that all social workers would benefit from adopting. With this orientation, workers would be in every context conscious of the global, human rights, ecological, and social development perspectives on their work. These perspectives would pervade all aspects of their practice, whether they were engaged in analysis of what is, or considering what might and should be. It would become second nature to think globally, be conscious of rights issues, consider ecological ramifications, and operate on the basis of a social development vision of a society that maximizes the well-being of all residents.

The importance of this orientation becomes clearer perhaps when we consider the exact opposites. An approach to social work that failed to see beyond the presenting client or client group, that saw presenting problems as requiring an exclusively remedial focus, that possessed no

sense of the possible importance of the natural environment, and that had no active vision for a better society for these and other clients could be potentially highly limiting when compared with the proposed approach.

People's well-being is certainly enhanced by the remedying of specific presenting problems: however, it is enhanced in more lasting ways by providing people with a better natural and societal context, and by ensuring the protection of people's rights.

Situation Analyses

The approach is a key to, or a tool for, situation analyses because it enables us to consider any situation at all levels, in all its dimensions and from several essential perspectives, thus enabling us to arrive at both an appropriately detailed but also a holistic understanding of situations. Let us consider this in terms of our four perspectives.

Global

The model leads us to consider whether there are any relevant global factors, either contributing to the existing state of affairs or presenting as potential solutions.

The significance of global factors can be found at a macro level. For example, is the plight of a small island state due to its marginalization within existing globalization processes—that is, this state has little to offer outsiders and simply lies hidden over the horizon when significant global affairs are being considered? Or is it apparent that the international mining of a developing country's natural resources is resulting in damage to that country's environment, is effectively exploiting that country's resources, and is undermining that country's culture while contributing little financial gain of long-term benefit? Or are a particular people being effectively dominated by some other group, with serious consequences for well-being, for example, through violence, human rights abuses, exploitation, and general subjugation to the interests of outsiders? Or is a particular local occurrence—perhaps an influx of people or a dumping of cheap products—due to occurrences in other parts of the globe, thus requiring tackling at its source if possible? Or is some local natural phenomenon, such as an increase in the severity of storms or a rising of sea levels, due in part to the impact of the behavior of other countries?

However, examples are also numerous at the micro level. For example, is a previous immigrant's inability to settle due to ongoing anxieties about situations in the home country? Are the solutions to an asylum seeker's predicament dependent on appropriate global policies? Is the well-being of an overseas-born child adopted locally dependent on the way in which inter-country adoptions are handled? Is the treatment of people with a serious illness dependent on international pharmaceutical companies' willingness to make the necessary drugs available locally and at an affordable price? Is a local problem being exacerbated by a lack of appropriate technology which is known to be available in other countries? Does the resolution of a marital problem require simultaneous work in two countries because the parties involved live in different countries? Is the local unemployment problem largely an outcome of the moving of jobs to other countries because labor there is cheaper? Is the prevailing level of wages in a developing country's free trade zone an example of multinational corporations exploiting the weakness of a government and the vulnerability of people?

Clearly, understanding many local situations and developing a constructive analysis of causal and other factors often requires a global perspective. Moreover, given the impact of globalization, it will always be beneficial to at least raise the possibility that global factors are relevant to a situation being analyzed. In addition, adopting an international comparative approach will often be a significant aspect of the global perspective for both analysis and intervention. For example, a worker confronting a particular situation might be helped by exploring how such a situation has been understood elsewhere, in terms, for example, of causal factors, and what successful intervention strategies have been utilized in other countries. This may apply, for example, to the situations of indigenous minorities, rural poverty, the HIV/AIDS pandemic, the isolated elderly, various forms of drug addiction, and so on.

Human Rights

The approach maintains that situations should always be considered from a human rights perspective. This involves always asking such questions as these: Are there human rights abuses in this situation? Has the situation been caused in part by such abuses, even if they lie in the distant past? Do human rights abuses continue to affect this situation? Is a people's seeming inability to act constructively in part a consequence of the legacy of human rights abuses in the past, evident in part in low levels of self-esteem?

Unfortunately, the prevalence of human rights abuse historically has been extremely high, and with often devastating consequences. One thinks, for example, of the prevalence and consequences of the slave trade, of the treatment of women as inferior and the possessions of men, of the abuse of children's rights because their births were unwanted (e.g., female infanticide), of the mass slaughter of indigenous minorities regarded as uncivilized savages, of the caste and class systems that relegated certain groups by birth to inferior status, of the subjugation of entire countries under the colonial system, and of systematic violence against ethnic groups simply because they were seen to be different. While historically we might say that such things occurred in the process of the world becoming a civilized place, and that people in the past acted on the basis of different values and understandings, the reality is that all of these examples of abuse are to be found in the modern world, even if the circumstances, extent, and details have obviously changed.

Again, the above examples focus on the macro level. Equally relevant to the social worker's role in any local context is to discern situations of abuse. Domestic abuse of women, children, and the elderly; abuse in the form of discrimination against members of perceived minorities; abuse of newcomers to an area; abuse of those thought to be, or found guilty of, offences against society; abuse in schools and the workplace in the form of bullying; and so on—such areas of abuse continue to be part of the reality of most countries and localities, although clearly much worse in some places than others.

Why is it important to identify abuse? The major reason is surely that abuse is inherently wrong, contrary to the principles by which all people should live, and therefore needing to be recognized for what it is and tackled in whatever ways possible. Second, if the abuse situation is not recognized and rectified, remedial intervention will be of limited long-term assistance. Providing welfare to people deprived of their human rights leaves such people in an invidious and unjust situation. A third reason is that, if past abuse is not identified, the worker is less likely to perceive and understand the long-term effects on individuals of abuse they have sustained. Too often victims of abuse have been attributed with cultural and personal characteristics that may even be seen as the reasons why they were abused rather than the consequences of abuse. For example, people found to be overly pliant, fatalistic, lacking in entrepreneurial zeal or a work ethic, and so on might be considered to possess a culture that was inappropriate for the modern world, rather than representing characteristics developed over the years as a defense against or consequence of abuse.

Abuse in many of the examples given is obvious and often blatant. As such it is readily perceived, although it may also be so widely accepted in the context that it is difficult to oppose. In other situations, abuse is either well hidden or devious in its perpetration, rendering it difficult to perceive (e.g., the abuse of migrant worker domestics or child prostitutes). This latter possibility is one reason why it is always important that we as social workers apply a human rights perspective, asking whether abuse is a factor in any situation, and not just acknowledging blatant examples of it.

Finally, and significantly, is the importance of approaching all people and situations instinctively on a human rights basis. A human rights orientation results in our immediate acceptance of the right of all individuals and groups to be different and to behave within their own set of assumptions, providing such behavior does not impinge on the rights of others. This orientation leads to a spontaneous acknowledgment of human equality—that all people are born equal and have equal rights. A human rights orientation is thus as much a positive element in our approach to social work as it is a tool for identifying underlying problems within a situation. Both aspects of this perspective are very important.

Ecological

Very important to our approach is the ecological perspective. As social workers consider any situation from an analytical perspective, the question of the possible relevance of ecological factors should always be present. Have the presenting problems been contributed to by ecological factors? For example, is poverty in a particular context due in part to ecological degradation? Do people appear to be negatively influenced by the natural surrounds, or lack thereof? Has the presenting displacement of people from their usual place of abode been due in part to ecological degradation? Is observed conflict in part a consequence of competition for scarce natural resources? Is the well-being of a group of refugees negatively influenced by their natural environment, or their rejection by locals due to their fear of the impact of the refugees on scarce natural resources?

Alternatively, is an existing state of affairs unsustainable because of its likely impact on the natural environment, on people's well-being, or both? For example: Are people's farming methods ecologically unsustainable? Are a company's mining activities likely to destroy the environment on which a people depends? Is a government's population relocation policy likely to prove unsustainable? Is logging in a tropical forest undermining a people's livelihood and likely to result in devastation of the natural environment? Is a dependence on certain forms of technology counterproductive long-term, and are alternatives available? Is poverty forcing people to destroy the environment on which they ultimately must depend, for example by using all growth for firewood, moving into ecologically fragile areas, or overfishing local waters? Are people placing themselves in great danger by building their homes on slopes prone to mudslides or beside rivers prone to flooding? Are people's livelihoods simply too risky, such as rummaging through garbage dumps? When situations of actual or potential ecological damage are detected, workers should proceed to explore the foundations of these situations. How much are the attitudes of the people, of governments, or of corporations responsible? How much are prevailing circumstances driven by necessity, even when the people involved recognize the danger? How much is ecological degradation an outcome of policies that have not been thought through and to which there are suitable alternatives? If workers are to engage in seeking to reverse unacceptable situations, a careful analysis of such contributing factors will be essential, and will of course help to lay the foundations for a suitable intervention strategy.

Finally, it is incumbent on social workers, as on others, to point the way in this regard. If workers are oriented toward sound environmental approaches in general terms, they will be endorsing the importance of such an orientation in all that they say and do. As such they are an important example to others, an educational tool, and a source of information regarding ecology. Alternatively, neglect of the ecological dimension by professionals sends a clear message in many contexts that this is not in fact an important perspective when people and groups are engaged in any aspect of social development at any level.

Social Development

Our final perspective of relevance to the process of analysis is the social development one. It will often be that a situation confronting a worker is one aspect of inadequate overall social development. For example, national social development may have focused on urban areas, emphasized industry over other productive pursuits, favored a particular class of people, possessed an ethnic or gender bias, or been marred by corruption and inefficiency. Understanding a local situation within its broader national social development context is most important. Alternatively, the social development process adopted locally might have been inappropriate or ineffectual in ways that can be identified. For example, the development might have been designed and pursued by some local elite group, with little regard for the wishes or culture of the populace; the development process might have focused on, for example, the economic dimension but ignored the political and legal developments that the economic goals depended on; or the local development process might have sought to rely on the inputs of a population without ensuring that people possessed the required capacities for playing those roles.

Other possibilities within this perspective are that the goals and values underpinning social development, at either the national or local level, might be related to elite group interests far more than the general public interest. In other words, the development process might have been effectively controlled by certain individuals, organizations, or groups operating almost exclusively on the basis of self-interest or selected group values, to the detriment of the majority.

The characteristics of social development emphasized earlier in this chapter are all relevant at the analytical level. Has the development process covered all dimensions of society and in ways that accommodated the necessary interaction between these dimensions? Has the process seen appropriate action at all levels within the nation, and where relevant at the international level? Has the process been based on the set of values that social development experience and analysis have revealed to be of central importance? And has proactive intervention been undertaken as required, without waiting for problems to emerge and require responses?

Ideally, local workers should possess not only an understanding of the social development process in theory but also a vision, based on the best and broadest possible analysis, of what should be the social development goals of a country or area within the foreseeable future. Both types of understanding are critical to knowing how to proceed in ways that are sound from the social development perspective.

Planning Intervention

The integrated-perspectives approach is as much a key to planning intervention as it is to analyzing a situation, as the previous discussion will have made apparent. Let us consider its role in the intervention context by envisaging a specific situation clearly warranting action.

Our hypothetical, but very common, situation is that of a marginalized, poverty-stricken population—a situation where a population has been relegated to the margins of society in every sense, suffers high levels of poverty, is extremely vulnerable to all sorts of events beyond its control, is faced with high levels of unemployment and underemployment, and has come to accept its situation with high levels of resignation and apathy. In such a context, how might our approach

be used to plan a comprehensive intervention strategy? The approach would ensure that several elements were central to the overall strategy adopted.

First, the overall strategy would be necessarily people-centered. This approach would flow from the human rights perspective and the social development principles.

Second, the overall strategy would contain a remedial component, necessitated not only by humanitarian and human rights concerns but by the need to ensure that as many people as possible were able to participate in the social development process by having any disabilities they possessed rectified as far as possible.

Third, the overall strategy would be planned with the natural environment in mind. If environmental degradation is contributing to the problems, can that be reversed or is relocation called for? Can the natural environment play a significant role in addressing the overall situation; for example, by being a potential source of future livelihood, by using its development for developing or enhancing skills, by the achievement of its renewal acting as a source of pride, or by a locally created pleasant environment contributing to a people's sense of well-being?

Fourth, the overall strategy would be planned with human rights very much in mind. We would need to draw on our understanding of any past human rights abuse, and of the impact of that on individual and group behavior. Based on this understanding, we might encourage people to campaign for their rights, or seek to inculcate a consciousness of their rights. It may be that the rights at issue are those of a subsection of the population, a conscious awareness of which does not permeate the wider population. Our intervention strategy would be designed to overcome existing rights problems, protect rights into the future, and build a community or society based on an acceptance of the rights of all members.

Fifth, the overall strategy would carefully consider the overall situation from a global

The Integrated-perspectives Approach to International Social Work

perspective, and seek to include a global intervention dimension consistent with conclusions from the analytical stage of the significance of the global dimension. Were global developments impacting negatively on these people and requiring action? Could global assistance of some kind contribute to a better future, and how could this be achieved? Would these people benefit from achieving access to various branches of the UN system, intergovernmental bodies, or their national government, and how could this be achieved? Do these people possess the potential to manufacture and sell certain products, for example their local crafts, in global markets?

Sixth and finally, addressing this situation would call for a social development approach to enhancing this people's overall development within the context of their regional and national development contexts. The intervention strategy would consider which dimensions of social development should ideally be addressed and how, and what levels of developmental activity should ideally be stimulated and how. This process should be undertaken using a people-centered approach so that it is the people who explore, albeit with assistance, their needs, goals, and options. There would be required a strong educational focus, wherever possible utilizing a social learning approach to this. A facilitation process would be best to assist people to feel supported but not guided or directed by outsiders.

Implementation of the Plan

Under the social development perspective of our approach, implementation is a process that in effect proceeds through the analysis, intervention planning, plan implementation, and evaluation phases, all interwoven within an overall process and underpinned throughout by the principles on which social development is based. Implementation is not in any sense the key phase or end goal, as outcome-oriented outsiders

might be inclined to think. It may be that what people learn through analyzing their own situation, or the confidence that they gain by making slight progress on narrow fronts, or the skills that they develop at any or every stage of the process, or even the impact of outsiders acknowledging their reality and demonstrating a degree of empathy, may loom larger in importance, at least in the short term, than the outcomes of carefully planned intervention.

Conclusion

As social workers, we tend to approach situations on the basis of certain values, beliefs, assumptions, and so on, some of which we are conscious of and others perhaps not. It is our belief that all our professional activities should be consciously guided by an appropriate set of values, beliefs, and understandings. Bearing in mind the range of fields in which international social work is active, we have sought to draw together an appropriate set of what we call *guiding perspectives*—perspectives that can serve as a guide to action at every stage in the social work intervention process and in any international context. While some readers may seek to modify the set of perspectives suggested, we would argue strongly that all four of the perspectives that make up our integrated-perspectives approach are extremely important, and that all four need to be applied within an integrated approach. In some circumstances, workers may well feel that, in a specific context, this approach requires modifications, perhaps by making some aspects more explicit, and thus emphasizing certain dimensions, and we would support using the integrated-perspectives approach in that way. On the other hand, we can envision no situation where any of the four perspectives that are now included should be ignored or even downplayed, because we regard each as fundamentally vital in all contexts of international social work in particular.

Summary

- It is suggested that international social work can be guided by the integrated-perspectives approach that synthesizes global, human rights, ecological, and social development perspectives.

- The global perspective is based on unity, diversity, interdependence, globalization, localization, and world citizenship dimensions. The human rights perspective draws on basic values and principles, human rights, and their universal application as a guide to behavior. Holism and unity, diversity, equilibrium, and sustainability dimensions constitute the ecological perspective. Drawing from and contributing to the other perspectives, the social development perspective emphasizes participatory, people-centered, and empowering values, proactive intervention, and multidimensional and multilevel approaches.

- For international social work practice, the global perspective represents the overall context, the human rights perspective provides the value base, the ecological perspective demonstrates the link between humanity and nature, and the social development perspective guides action and provides a sense of direction.

- Social workers and development practitioners can employ the approach to analyze and address needs and issues at local and global levels.

Questions and Topics for Discussion

- What do you think of the integrated-perspectives approach?

- Critically review all dimensions of each perspective.

- Summarize your understanding of the integrated-perspectives approach presented in this chapter.

- Discuss why you agree or disagree with the overall integrated-perspectives approach.

- Do you think the integrated-perspectives approach offers a useful framework for international social work practice?

- Compare the integrated-perspectives approach with social work theories you are familiar with, and discuss how the approach complements those theories and provides an improved approach for practice.

- What are the most important points that you take from this chapter?

Possible Areas for Research Projects

- Systematically analyze any issue or social problem of interest to you by employing the integrated-perspectives approach.

- Evaluate a social worker's and social work agency's practice with a view to determining to what extent the integrated perspective is in effect used, and suggest how the practice may be improved by deliberately employing the approach.

- Utilizing the integrated-perspectives approach, prepare a case study of a field of practice in a specific context with which you are familiar (e.g., poverty, education, health crisis, ecological degradation, refugees and displacement of people, postwar reconstruction, etc.), covering global, national, and local levels.

Further Reading

Elisabeth, R. (2003). *Social work and human rights: A foundation for policy and practice.* New York: Columbia University Press.

Midgley, J. (1995). *Social development: The developmental perspective in social welfare.* London: Sage.

Midgley, J. (1996). Involving social work in economic development. *International social work, (59)2,* 13–25.

Midgley, J. (2000). Promoting value-based social development: B. trainers' manual, UN/ESCAP. Unpublished manuscript.

UNDP. (1999). *Human development report: Globalization with a human face.* New York: Oxford University Press.

UNDP. (2000). *Human rights and human development—for freedom and solidarity.* New York: Oxford University Press.

Uvin, P. (2004). *Human rights and development.* Bloomfield, CT: Kumarian.

World Bank. (2003). *World development report: Sustainable development in a dynamic world.* New York: Oxford University Press.

These UN documents may be viewed on their respective Web sites:

Universal Declaration of Human Rights
http://www.unhchr.ch/udhr/index.htm

The International Covenant on Civil and Political Rights
http://www.hrweb.org/legal/undocs.html#CPR

3

The Global Context of International Social Work

Introduction

Whether working locally or internationally, social workers who desire to be tuned into international social work require a clear sense of the global context within which all such practice occurs. This is especially true when working in, or with regard to, developing countries. This global context will play various roles in relation to practice and the practitioner. At times it will represent the operational context within which the worker is employed, containing both the employing agency and the organizational network of which that agency is a part. At another level, the global context, or some aspects of it, will be a contributing factor in the presenting problems with which the worker is grappling, and appreciating its significance as a causal factor may be very important. Perhaps less frequently, the global context's potential role in achieving change will be an element in the worker's overall intervention strategy. Finally, whatever the specific roles that the global context is playing within specific situations, what is important is that the worker is always able to visualize the prevailing general global context,

analyze a presenting situation with that context as an element in the analysis, and develop an intervention strategy that holds together and integrates the local, national, and international levels of context.

We have separated out for discussion in this chapter four dimensions of the global context, namely the social problem, organizational, ideological, and policy dimensions. While all four dimensions are important in themselves, the four interact to constitute the global context as it impinges on international social work. The social problem context is often our starting point as social workers, in that it is our awareness of some global problems such as poverty, refugees, or the HIV/AIDS epidemic that leads us to take an interest in international social work. Pursuing that interest, whether at an academic or practical level, will inevitably lead us to consider what is being done, by what agencies, and perhaps with what employment opportunities for social workers. The organizational context thus becomes of key importance. Further consideration or involvement, however, will lead to an awareness that the motives behind the roles played by various agencies represent a very

Learning Objectives

The main learning objectives of this chapter are to alert readers to

- Major global social problems, such as poverty, conflicts and wars, forced migration, the AIDS epidemic, and so forth, and the need for international social workers to be aware of these problems.
- The range of organizations established by national governments, the UN, regional associations, and NGOs for addressing global social problems, and the importance of this organizational context for international social work practice.
- The ideological context in terms of dominant and competing ideologies, and their impact on international developments.
- Global economic, social, and related policies and their significance for international social work practice.
- The roles that these organizations, ideologies, and policies together play in responding to global problems.

important factor. Prevailing motivations reflect a variety of ideological stances and result in a range of policies at all levels of involvement. We shall, therefore, reflect briefly on the ideological and policy dimensions of the global context.

We shall commence with a brief overview of global social problems, using the term "social" because our focus is on the general relevance of global problems to the well-being of people and their communities and societies.

The Global Social Problems Context

This is not the place for a detailed analysis of global social problems, yet it is important that those working in, or proposing to work in, international social work possess a general understanding of at least the major global social problems. We need to be aware of several aspects of this dimension of the global context:

1. What are the main global social problems?

2. What numbers of people are affected by these problems and where in the world are they concentrated?

3. In general terms, what are the main causes of these problems, and to what degree are they interrelated?

4. In general terms, how has the international community been responding to these problems?

5. In general terms, have these problems been reducing significantly in scope and severity in recent decades, and if not, what additional types of intervention seem to be required?

We are distinguishing between, first, the need to understand the world as a whole in terms of the prevailing major global social problems; second, the need for the worker who specializes in a particular field of international social work to understand that field in some considerable detail for purposes of, for example, guiding overall policy and program developments; and third, the local workers specializing in one or more fields needing to appreciate not only the relevant global context but also all aspects of the field in which they are involved within a relatively circumscribed geographical area. At this point our focus is on the first level, namely a global understanding. For the fields that we have selected for more detailed attention later in this text, our focus will be on the second level, namely programs and strategies for responding to global social problems.

Poverty and Interacting Fields

Poverty, with its associated problems such as infant mortality, malnutrition, and vulnerability, is commonly regarded as the world's most serious problem. Depending on how poverty is defined and measured, no one would dispute the claim that, at the very least, approximately one in every three of the world's people lives in poverty. This is partly because many people around the globe exist so close to the poverty line that any one of a number of common occurrences, even at a minor level, will push them into poverty. Such occurrences include economic changes, such as increases in inflation rates, deteriorating trade arrangements, or reductions in a government's subsidies of basic necessities; ecological changes, such as deterioration of the environment or depletion of essential food sources; social conflict within a nation or war between nations; demographic changes through migration or natural increase; and natural disasters that destroy people's homes and livelihoods.

The international community has, in the post–World War II decades, made many commitments to reducing poverty rates, the most recent being to halve the global poverty rate by 2015. Moreover, much aid and development work has had this goal in mind, with funding agencies such as the World Bank increasingly requiring that every project submitted by states for funding contain a poverty reduction component. However, despite the best of intentions and endeavors, and while poverty rates have dropped significantly in a few countries, they have fluctuated significantly in many developing countries since the 1980s, and they have not been significantly reduced as a whole. This is partly because poverty is an outcome of many causal factors that are very difficult to control, partly because poverty rates are often maintained by high population growth rates in the poorest parts of the world, and partly due to a lack of commitment to reducing poverty on the part of many governments.

The Plight of Children

A recent report from the United Nations Children's Fund (UNICEF) presents the alarming situation that 50 percent of the world's children are significantly affected by poverty, conflict, or the AIDS epidemic. This alarming situation is reflected in high rates of malnutrition and high infant and child mortality rates in many parts of the world; large numbers of children being forced into deleterious child labor conditions; many children being vulnerable to child slavery, often associated with child prostitution and other abuses; and large numbers of orphans and other children being abandoned, or placed in poor quality orphanages, or otherwise subject to neglect and abuse.

The plight of children is clearly a multicausal situation. It is, moreover, a deteriorating situation, despite the work of organizations like UNICEF, Save The Children, and many others.

The Plight of Women

It might surprise some western readers that, after long and hard-fought campaigns for gender equality, we should still be highlighting the plight of women. In many contexts, women bear a disproportionate burden in relation to family life generally and such phenomena as displacement. Women are also more vulnerable than men in many contexts, especially during wars and civil conflict. In situations of poverty, women carry a disproportionate share of the risks and consequences, so that it is common to speak of the "feminization of poverty." Finally, in many nations, culture places women at a significant disadvantage. Among the customs that are the object of ongoing and active concern are arranged marriages; female genital mutilation; an inability of women to own property, access credit, or inherit; the acceptance of wife beatings, rape within marriage, and other forms of domestic abuse; and the virtual slavery conditions of many women within pre- and post-marriage contexts.

Once again, many organizations and movements are devoted to enhancing the rights of women, achieving gender equality, offering protection to vulnerable women, and responding directly to the needs presented by women. Unfortunately, progress in this area seems often to be painfully slow.

The Extent of Conflict

A reading of any global history reveals the extremely common inability of social groupings, nations, and empires to live at peace with their neighbors. In pursuit of territory, booty of all kinds, slaves, power, and status, conflict at all levels has been a significant aspect of the human story. The last century witnessed two of the worst wars known to history, and since the end of the Cold War in 1989 the scourge of civil war has intensified alarmingly. In recent times, the world has been experiencing upwards of 30 civil wars at any one time, with very high casualty figures, especially among civilians.

A major goal of the UN is world peace, yet its work and that of national governments and regional associations, along with that of many organizations of civil society, have together failed to do more than perhaps contain many situations. Only when we add together the widespread consequences of conflict on people's personal lives and social contexts, economic conditions, physical infrastructure, and the environment, do we begin to appreciate the enormity of this global problem. Yet because conflict once again has many causes, it seems difficult for the international community to significantly reduce the impact of conflict in the foreseeable future. Finally, it has become clear in recent times that rebuilding a society after conflict is a complex, hugely expensive, and extremely difficult undertaking.

Natural Disasters and Ecological Degradation

Recent reports reveal the extent to which natural disasters have increased in frequency and severity, whatever the reasons for this. The costs of responding quickly and effectively to natural disasters are truly great, yet they pale into insignificance when compared with the cost of repairing the damage caused by disasters, to say nothing of supporting the people until a modicum of economic and social functioning is restored.

Natural disasters are acute dramatic events that gain immediate attention. Ecological degradation is a more insidious problem that usually creeps up on people slowly, with its inevitable consequences gradually eating away at people's standards of well-being. Moreover, given frequent controversy over the precise causes of the degradation and the appropriateness of various possible responses, action tends to be piecemeal and insufficient until it becomes almost too late to act.

Both natural disasters and ecological degradation tend to have a greater impact on poorer people, partly because it is the poor who are obliged to live in areas more susceptible to both occurrences, and partly because the quality of their homes and the nature of their daily existence render them more vulnerable.

The Uneven Development of Nations

Allied closely to all of the above problems is the need for each country of the world to achieve a level and form of development that is consistent with that country's economic, social, political, cultural, and ecological needs. This goal was recognized and accepted internationally in the aftermath of World War II, with very high volumes of resources being devoted to global development since then. Yet despite all the efforts and expenditure, progress on the development front generally has been uneven and somewhat erratic. Some one-quarter of the world's approximately 200 nation-states remain classified as "least developed," while others are classified as "developing" but with unacceptable low achievement levels in some aspects of that development. There is also widespread concern at the plight of "failed states"—states where governance is not adequate to provide a basis for development. There is also an acknowledgment of the uneven development of many states—states where some sections of the country and populace have done quite well while others languish in poverty or with inadequate levels of development.

It would seem to be the case that, if development aid of all kinds were made available by states on the recommended basis of 0.7 percent of GDP, and if that aid were then devoted to global development on the basis of needs (not self-interest), the current development situation could be fairly speedily rectified. It seems, however, that this is unlikely to happen in the foreseeable future, and that the world will continue to be a very uneven place in terms of prevailing levels of development.

The Uneven Impact of Most Global Problems

Many readers will be familiar with the biblical saying that to those who have more will be given, and the relevance of this to the modern world is difficult to ignore. Many countries are vulnerable, in the first place, because their geographical conditions or location—for example, small, remote, landlocked, and island states—have held back their development. Some of these are also in regions of the world more prone to natural disasters. If these countries experience high rates of population growth, and especially if the land is ecologically fragile, poverty is likely to spread widely and development be further impaired. These outcomes may then result in low levels of social cohesion and poor governance, resulting in high levels of social tension, corruption, and inefficiency.

It is not a coincidence that some 90 percent of global population growth is in the poorer parts of the world, that most civil wars take place in developing countries, that poorer countries are more prone to the ravages of natural disasters, and that trade and investment flows tend to favor the better-off or more developed states. Hence many countries are very seriously affected by virtually all of the main global social problems, the cumulative impact of which can be horrendous.

Given this situation, one might think that the bulk of the efforts of the international community would be devoted to rectifying global inequality. Unfortunately, this is not the case. When countries or regions are given such labels as "basket cases" or "bottomless pits" in terms of absorbing aid, or when governments are corrupt or inefficient or have failed, there is a reluctance to devote too many resources to them because to do so seems to be an inefficient use of resources and is politically unpopular. Hence poor situations may deteriorate further.

The Displacement and Forced Migration of People

One inevitable consequence of extreme poverty, widespread social conflict, serious natural disasters, ecological degradation, and low levels of development is that many people are forced to leave their usual place of abode and seek refuge, assistance, or a better future elsewhere. In reality, only a small proportion of people affected by such events are able to leave. Many will stay and die, and many linger on in poverty and fear, for flight is simply not a viable or acceptable option for them.

Official figures place the numbers of displaced persons at around 50 million, although in many situations only rough estimates are possible. Even if this number is reasonably accurate, the impact of the displacement of 50 million people on the people themselves, often on the areas from which they originate, and certainly on the areas to which they flee, is substantial. The tasks of protecting, providing sustenance for on an ongoing basis, and finding a satisfactory solution to the plight of 50 million people are huge: when, however, those displaced are unwelcome guests in foreign lands, or are destabilizing local economic and social stability levels yet have nowhere else to go, the challenge becomes massive.

The UN and various organizations of global and local civil society have made the care of the world's displaced a major concern. However, these organizations can seldom influence the forces that cause displacement, and those forces frequently result in a sudden and massive exodus of people requiring a large-scale emergency response. Moreover, the huge cost of responding to displacement is seldom met by the international community, so that in recent times many displaced persons have not survived their ordeal. Nor is the situation helped by the fear of western and other countries that displaced persons might seek to breech their borders and impose themselves on a nation as uninvited guests.

The HIV/AIDS Epidemic and Other Global Health Concerns

HIV/AIDS became a significant health concern in the 1980s, and in the 1990s was seen as "the greatest shock to development" (UNDP, 2003, p. 41). This report estimates the numbers of people infected at around 42 million, with some 22 million already killed and 13 million left orphans. In addition to its destruction of human life, HIV/AIDS is throwing development off course in much of Africa by devastating workforces generally and key groups such as teachers particularly (e.g., Zambia lost 1,300 teachers in one year). Beyond Africa, China, India, and the Russian Federation are among

those countries experiencing soaring rates of infection, while few countries are escaping the epidemic.

While HIV/AIDS is the major current health concern, it is certainly not the only one. Maternal mortality, at its most urgent in sub-Saharan Africa; child mortality, especially in sub-Saharan Africa and South Asia; tuberculosis (killing up to two million people a year); and malaria (killing some one million people a year) are among other major health concerns.

Global Social Problems and International Social Work

There are several reasons why social workers contributing to international social work need to possess a general awareness of global social problems, in addition, of course, to a precise awareness of those social problems dominating the areas (field and geographical) where they are working.

First is the fact that it is these major social problems that largely determine the very nature and existence of the international community. The evolution of international structures, the work on global policy, and the deployment of resources are all largely determined by the focus on poverty, conflict and armaments issues, international terrorism, global crime, refugee movements, the abuse and exploitation of children and women, ecological concerns, and so on, and social workers need to be aware of how and why these concerns drive global agendas. (See the discussion of the international community's millennium development goals in UNDP, 2003.)

Second, there is virtually no work situation, especially in developing countries, in which international social workers are to be found that will not be affected at a significant level by probably several of these global concerns. No population or situation is immune, especially in developing countries, and social workers need to be able to relate local situations to global trends.

Third, it follows that wherever and at whatever level social workers are working, they should have in mind their obligation to contribute, where possible, to the evolution of global policies and programs relating to these global concerns. The knowledge and experience that international social workers derive from their fieldwork are of great importance when the international community at the macro level seeks to formulate a response to a global problem or some dimension thereof. For example, when the Hague Conference on Private International Law sought to establish a set of principles pertaining to international child abductions, they approached International Social Service and its workers worldwide to furnish them with relevant case data. In more recent years, it has been NGOs working in the HIV/AIDS field that have campaigned for international action, and contributed vital information and suggestions as to the directions that such action should take.

Fourth, an understanding of the global realities pertaining to any problem situation makes possible a better analysis of a local situation— for example, by incorporating the global dimension—and facilitates a better intervention strategy by encouraging the worker to draw on international experience as a guide. The international comparative approach has much to commend it.

Fifth, the fact that a network of agencies and conventions and so on have been brought to bear on any global social problem at the international level means that there is potentially available to workers in the field a wide range of resources—provided that workers are aware of what has been happening globally. Various UN agencies provide technical assistance to governments but also at times to NGOs; a range of international reports are potentially helpful to workers; workers may explore the relevant networks in search of advice; the relevant active international community agencies may be sources of funding or other resources to assist local initiatives; and so on. The possibility for local workers in the international field to tap the international community is always there and is usually highly beneficial.

The Organizational Context

The second dimension of the global context that international social workers need to understand is the organizational context. The global context can be conceived of as a range of international organizations, often referred to rather loosely as the *international community*. The range is extremely wide, consisting of several key categories of agencies, each of which is in itself highly varied and complex. The main categories of organizations are

- national governments and the agencies they establish for international work;
- intergovernmental agencies established by groups of nations, including regional associations such as the European Union and African Union;
- the UN system established and supported by the great majority of states;
- corporations, especially the transnational or multinational ones (TNCs or MNCs);
- nongovernment organizations operating internationally (INGOs); and
- the other organs of global civil society, such as social movements, labor movements, religious movements, and cultural associations.

Each of these categories has important roles to play internationally, and their actions determine much of the global context and its ongoing development. Furthermore, the interaction between these categories of organizations, and between the plethora of individual organizations of which each category is composed, is a further important dimension of global developments. While each category warrants a textbook, or at least a full chapter—given their size, complexity, and importance—we shall briefly comment on each category and leave it for the reader to explore further. Before doing so, however, let us reflect on what preceded the emergence of the international community.

The Beginnings of an International Community

For many centuries, world affairs were dominated economically by traders and trading routes and politically by the concept of "balance of power." As Eban (1983, pp. 243–244) explains, "balance of power" was an ambiguous concept. On the one hand, it implied a quest for equilibrium that, if achieved, would result in peace between nations with each apprehensive about taking up arms against another. Others, however, saw it more as a quest for superiority by states, so that balance really meant imbalance and the pursuit of national interests, including developing the ability to defeat aggressors. Within this system, war was the ultimate sanction: "The logic of the balance system requires that those who uphold it must threaten to fight against those who challenge it," and such a threat will supposedly deter would-be aggressors. However, as Eban points out, "both of the world wars . . . reveal the fragility of deterrent systems based on the assumption of total rationality" (p. 244). Hence not surprisingly, after the horrors of the First World War initially and then those of the Second World War, there was a drive to initiate what Eban calls "a new diplomacy"—"a movement for international organizations." This movement aspires to organize nation-states into a universal community, all of whose members are committed to mutual assistance in accordance with an objectively binding code. Its aim is nothing less than world peace under law. In this conception what each member of the community owes to the other does not depend on individual discretion according to each member's predilections, solidarities, and interests:

The UN system aspires to reconcile national sovereignty with world order. The guiding principle of the UN idea was collective security. This requires the creation of such a preponderance of power that no single state or group of states can hope to withstand it. (Eban, 1983, p. 239)

With hindsight, the Cold War that ran from the end of World War II to 1989, the division between western and third world or developing country interests (as reflected in, for example, the Bandung Conference in 1955 of nonaligned states and in voting patterns in the UN General Assembly), and the post–Cold War dominance by the United States as the only global power were among the many factors that worked against the short-term achievement of the vision that lay behind the establishment of the international community. Other ongoing concerns included the difficulty that states and international organizations often experienced in reconciling national interests or sovereignty and a new world order, the difficulty that the emerging INGO sector often had in collaborating with the global economic institutions such as the World Bank and the International Monetary Fund (IMF), and the difficulty in fitting the TNCs—with their apparently distinctive and self- or profit-centered goals—into the overall international community. Nonetheless, there was no doubt that an international community was and is emerging, and there continues into the twenty-first century to be great hopes for a future under its leadership.

National Governments and the Agencies They Establish for International Work

No matter how much some people might desire the focus to be on international organizations, there can be no doubt that the most significant players on the international stage remain the nation-states. Despite frequent claims that globalization has overtaken the state, and . . . are, the reality is that states remain very much alive and well. All major global economic and political associations are made up of member states, and although such associations may act against a state member or seek to influence its internal affairs (e.g., the World Bank or European Union), the status of the state retains its integrity and much of its importance. Moreover, individual states have shown themselves able to act unilaterally in either the pursuit of international goals (e.g., the United States) or in pursuit of national goals that contravene global agreements (e.g., Burma/Myanmar, North Korea, and many others).

At another level, many individual states pursue their national interests through the operation of internationally oriented agencies—the international or foreign aid departments that in the West are sometimes located within ministries of foreign affairs. These agencies frequently operate very large aid programs, working through both the NGO sector and through bilateral developments undertaken with other governments. States are interested in trade arrangements and frequently enter into bilateral arrangements in this area; they retain the need to be ready to defend themselves against possible aggressors, through intelligence gathering operations or military establishments; they relate to world population mobility through the establishment of various migration and asylum seeker programs and tourism arrangements; and they engage in aid and development work, partly at times for altruistic reasons but sometimes as an extension of the pursuit of national interests. Moreover, the network of diplomatic activity undertaken by states seeks to maintain a national awareness of developments around the globe, especially of those likely to constitute a potential threat to national interests, such as terrorism and human trafficking.

On another level again, writers on global development are very aware of the potential threat to global economic and political stability of what is commonly referred to as "poor governance." Such is the nature of global interconnectedness that poor governance not only undermines the well-being of the people of the state in question, but has potential consequences for many others (e.g., through encouraging asylum seekers or illegal migrants, causing internal conflict with widespread external ramifications, and undermining external economic relations).

A further important issue for the international community that will increasingly affect the roles of national governments is determining in what circumstances it should take action to change a course of events within a sovereign state, usually through the UN but also through regional state bodies such as the European Union and African Union. The international community, or various organs within it, have sometimes taken action and sometimes refrained from taking action, and have been criticized for both types of decisions. How important and how justifiable today is the maintenance of the integrity of the sovereign state? Does the sovereign state take precedence over the international protection of people's human rights, or international prevention of ecological vandalism, or international rejection of the perpetuation of extreme poverty, or an international right to bring to justice those accused of crimes against humanity?

Finally, the question of the long-term viability of states has to be considered seriously, especially as, on the one hand, some states are clearly failing, and, on the other hand, pressure is exerted to divide a number of states into their constituent ethnic or religious components, thus creating a larger number of smaller states. (See recent developments in the former USSR, Czechoslovakia, and Yugoslavia.) There is also a major concern for the world's poorest states—many of which are landlocked, small island states—and states that have never really achieved a significant measure of state identity or national governance. It may well be that the only answer for such states is to become members of wider regional associations that will underwrite their development and support their ongoing functioning, while recognizing their national identity and autonomy to a least some degree, as we have seen happen in the European Union and to some degree in the Pacific.

While states continue to be the major players on the world stage in many ways, a range of questions surrounds their very existence in some cases, and in all cases their specific roles within the world community. To what extent states will continue as we know them today remains one of the many ongoing questions in considering the global context. What is certain, however, is that many social workers engaged in international work will be employed by states, work under state auspices to some degree, interact regularly with state agencies, and be involved in addressing situations which are at least in part an outcome of state actions. (For detailed discussions of the future of modern states and their roles see, for example, World Bank, 1997; Holton, 1998; Randall and Theobald, 1998; and Duffield, 2001, pp. 163ff.)

Intergovernmental Agencies Established by Groups of Nations, Including Regional Associations Such as the European Union and African Union

The obvious distance between many states and international structures, such as the UN, can leave such states feeling insignificant and rather lost on this international stage. It is not surprising, therefore, that many political leaders and states have regarded associations of states within circumscribed areas, within which they share common interests and concerns, as essential to the state and as a necessary first step to effective global associations such as the UN. There are indeed many regional associations, of which some of the best known are the European Union (EU), Organization of American States, African Union (formerly the Organization of African

Unity), Asia Pacific Economic Cooperation (APEC), and Arab League. In addition, areas of Africa, Asia, and Latin America have formed many subregional associations, such as the Association of Southeast Asian Countries (ASEAN) and the Economic Community of West African States (ECOWAS). To a significant degree these regional and subregional associations remain in their infancy. Issues of a regional parliament, common policies and institutions, and a common currency have taken center stage in the evolution of the European Union; however, the question as to whether this union is a blueprint for other such developments, or whether Europe has unique characteristics that might render its export of the concept of a regional federation as dubious as its export of the concept of the nation-state in an earlier century, remains one that is difficult to answer. On the face of it, however, regional associations make much sense and could be an important stepping-stone to global security and well-being.

The United Nations System

The UN system is the first truly global system in history, with almost all states being members of it and supporting its key roles to at least a significant degree. That it remains an evolving system is obvious, with much of its structure reflecting the realities prevailing at the end of World War II when it was established, and so inevitably requiring reform 60 years later. Understandably, a key role of the newly established system was to seek to ensure that a war such as that recently endured during 1939–1945 would never be repeated. As Eban (1983, p. 239) writes of the UN: "While its responsibilities were to cover many fields of action and struggle, its major task had always been deemed to lie in the prevention, cessation and termination of armed conflict."

This task lay essentially with the Security Council, the composition of which has become increasingly outdated and ineffective in fulfilling its key role. In 2004, a UN panel called for the Security Council to be expanded from 15 to 24 members, giving broader representation to developing countries. It recommended that six new permanent members be added to the existing five—two from Asia, two from Africa, one from the Americas, and one from Europe.

The UN system was also to have a major role in global economic and social development. Key economic roles were given to the International Bank for Reconstruction and Development (later renamed the World Bank), the International Monetary Fund, and the General Agreement on Trade and Tariffs (later renamed the World Trade Organization, or WTO), and although these bodies were essentially independent of the UN itself they were clearly established as important components of the UN system. The World Bank is owned by its 181 member countries, controlled by its own board and based in Washington, D.C. It provides development funds, mainly in the form of interest-bearing loans, to needy developing states together with technical assistance. It has been agreed that the United States nominates the head of the World Bank. The IMF was set up to monitor and regulate the international monetary system. It is financially independent of the UN although it reports to it. Its short-term loans are designed to bring stability to international exchange rates and alleviate serious balance of payments problems. The perceived problem, however, is that the loans tend to be conditional on the recipient states adopting a range of policies—policies largely reflecting western neoliberal thinking. The WTO, with currently 142 members, has had as its core aim the reduction of tariffs on internationally traded goods and services based on a free trade philosophy. More recently, it has moved also into the protection of intellectual property rights. Considerable controversy surrounds almost all aspects of its work. (See Todaro, 1997, part 3; and Todaro and Smith, 2003, pp. 584–587 and 626–630 for a detailed discussion of these agencies.)

The roles of the mainstream UN system in economic and social development are more closely related to direct development aid, involving the provision of funding, technical assistance, and opportunities for states and agencies to share experiences and plan strategies. To carry out these purposes, there is a range of agencies reporting to either ECOSOC (the Economic and Social Council) or directly to the General Assembly. Gordon (1994, p. 72) sets out the goals underpinning this work:

> Chapter IX of the [UN] charter deals with the general subject of international economic and social cooperation, and chapter X deals specifically with the organisation and functions of ECOSOC. Article 55 of chapter IX reads:
>
> With a view to the creation of conditions of stability and well-being which are necessary for peaceful and friendly relations among nations based on respect for the principle of equal rights and self-determination of peoples, the United Nations shall promote:
>
> a. higher standards of living, full employment and conditions of economic and social progress and development;
> b. solutions of international economic, social, health, and related problems, and international cultural and educational cooperation; and
> c. universal respect for, and observance of human rights and fundamental freedoms for all without distinction as to race, sex, language, or religion.

Among the many agencies entrusted with these goals are the United Nations Development Programme (UNDP), World Food Programme (WFP), World Health Organisation (WHO), UN Environmental Programme (UNEP), UN Education, Scientific and Cultural Organisation (UNESCO), UN High Commissioner for Refugees (UNHCR), Human Rights Commission, Commission for Social Development, Food and

Agricultural Organisation (FAO), UN Children's Fund (UNICEF), and the UN Centre for Human Settlements (HABITAT).

In addition to the central UN agencies, with their global mandates, ECOSOC has its regional equivalents, such as the Economic and Social Commission for Asia Pacific (ESCAP), with their own divisions and programs.

A further important role of the UN system is its adoption of declarations and conventions on various topics. These have been of particular importance in the field of human rights, beginning with the Universal Declaration of Human Rights adopted in 1948 (see UNDP, 2000). The difficulty in this field has been in the area of compliance. As Donnelly (1993, p. 11) puts it, states "did not agree to let the UN investigate their compliance with these standards." The same situation has applied in the area of international law more generally. States were expected to sign the various UN treaties and incorporate their provisions within state legal systems. The outcome, as Donnelly says, is a body of international law—"Customary rules of international law are well-established state practices to which a sense of obligation has come to be attached." The difficulties here have been twofold. First, a number of states have either not ratified a treaty or have failed to incorporate it in state law. Second, the enforcement of international law remains highly problematic, despite the existence of the International Court of Justice, the International Criminal Court, and various specific tribunals to investigate crimes against humanity (see Robertson, 2000).

There are various texts describing the UN system and discussing its strengths and weaknesses (e.g., see Gordon, 1994). What is important is that the international social worker possesses a realistic appreciation of its effectiveness. From experience, it is all too easy to have far higher expectations of the UN than it is capable of fulfilling (e.g., because of its dependence on the support of states), and, alternatively, to become so skeptical of the body that

one overlooks both its past achievements and its future potential. It is a system with strengths and weaknesses; moreover, as is often said, in terms of a global system it is all that we have, and it is therefore incumbent on us all to do what we can to make it work, hopefully even better in the future than it has in the past.

Corporations, Especially the Transnational Ones

There is a tendency for international social workers to dismiss the private for-profit sector at the international level (the TNCs or MNCs) as either irrelevant to their work or as highly deleterious in their impact on states and on people's lives. Whatever one's view on the potential of TNCs to bring harm or good to the world, their existence and importance on many levels cannot be ignored. Todaro (1997, pp. 534–543) begins his discussion of MNCs as follows:

Few developments have played as critical a role in the extraordinary growth of international trade and capital flows during the past few decades as the rise of the multinational corporation (MNC).

Todaro proceeds to discuss the size of these bodies, pointing out that they are far larger than many states, that they control 70 percent of world trade, that they generally dominate the areas of production, distribution, and sale of many goods from developing countries, that they exercise power in a variety of ways, and that they are concentrated in a few western countries (44 of the 100 largest are headquartered in the United States alone). In terms of the controversy over the roles of TNCs, Todaro suggests that it is really a controversy over the development process. He writes,

The controversy over the role and impact of private foreign investment often has as its basis a fundamental disagreement about the nature, style, and character of a desirable development process. (pp. 537–538)

In his own assessment of the pros and cons of MNC activities, Todaro stresses the complexity of the question and concludes,

Perhaps the only valid general conclusion is that private foreign investment can be an important stimulus to economic and social development as long as the interests of MNCs and host country governments coincide (assuming of course that they don't coincide along the lines of dualistic development and widening inequalities). (p. 543)

Todaro accepts that MNCs will continue to "gravitate toward the most profitable investment opportunities, engage in transfer pricing, and repatriate profits" (p. 543), but he is uncertain as to whether the net outcome of their involvement will be positive or negative.

Other writers have a far more negative impression of the impact of MNCs or TNCs on economic development generally and developing countries in particular. One outspoken critic of TNCs is Korten (1995), who writes of the TNC agenda,

It is a conscious and intentional transformation in search of a new world economic order in which business has no nationality and knows no borders. It is driven by global dreams of vast corporate empires, compliant governments, a globalized consumer monoculture, and a universal ideological commitment to corporate libertarianism.

While much of what Korten and others say in criticism of the TNCs sounds convincing, the reality is that TNCs do exist and will continue to play major roles on the world stage. The goal should therefore be that the UN system and global civil society will increasingly be able to expand the potential for good that the TNCs certainly possess, influence their agendas by increasing their awareness of certain realities, and generally learn to cooperate with this critical sector.

Nongovernment Agencies Operating Internationally (INGOs)

International nongovernment organizations (INGOs) have a long history (see Kaldor, 2003, chap. 4). The oldest of the well-known INGOs is the Red Cross, founded in 1863, but many Christian humanitarian organizations, Jewish welfare agencies, and the American Medical Association were founded even earlier (Beigbeder, 1991, pp. 8–9). Many other NGOs were established in the period of the 1920s to the 1960s, but the great expansion of NGOs generally and of INGOs in particular began in the 1970s. The range of INGOs is enormous (see Korten, 1990, p. 2; Kaldor, 2003, chap. 4). Some have budgets larger than those of many nations, operate globally, and are widely known. Others have small budgets and a limited range of activities and are known only in the circles within which they operate. The internal structure of INGOs also varies greatly. Some are highly structured organizationally with an employer-employee structure, and others are extremely loose, operating largely as umbrellas for personal initiatives. Funding arrangements are a further important variable. Some INGOs are almost completely dependent on receiving contracts from other agencies or on donor agency funding for programs they develop, while others—especially the religious agencies—have a constituency on which they depend for donations. This funding variable is extremely important in determining the extent of the independence of agencies and hence their ability to display initiative.

As with all sections of global organizations, the INGO sector has its strengths and weaknesses. While it used to be widely assumed that all NGOs generally had more ability than other sectors to respond to newly emerging needs, in innovative ways, and on the basis of principles such as people's participation, this is certainly not a valid assumption today. As governments and the UN increasingly pursue their goals through the NGO sector, as NGOs and INGOs become more and more dependent on external formal funding sources, and as more and more INGOs for whatever reason adopt bureaucratic structures and administrative procedures, the nature of INGOs is inevitably changed. It used also to be assumed, perhaps wrongly, that the NGO sector shared common values and would instinctively work together for the common good. Whatever the past reality, a common complaint about INGOs is that they compete with each other—for funds, for a prominent share of a specific task, for media coverage, for personnel, and for kudos. There is a noted inability or unwillingness to cooperate or collaborate in many contexts, and a tendency for the sheer numbers of INGOs involved in many situations to constitute a major problem in efficiently and effectively responding to a designated area of need. (Examples include the refugee and post-conflict reconstruction field but also many aspects of local-level development. See, for example, Duffield, 2001, pp. 53ff.)

Understandably perhaps, the quality of the work carried out by INGOs varies greatly. This may be due in part to inadequate funding, inappropriate staff recruitment, poor program design or management, or inexperience in the field. The large number of NGOs and INGOs competing for funding even allows a few bogus NGOs to attempt to obtain a share of available funds fraudulently. Moreover, the tendency of INGOs to pursue funding sources, and therefore programs popular with donors, will adversely affect their ability to respond effectively to an overall presenting situation, thus detracting from the sector's ability to complement the contribution of the government and for-profit sectors. (On NGOs and INGOs in development, see Edwards and Hulme, 1992; Poulton and Harris, 1988; Korten, 1990; and UNDP, 1993, chap. 5.)

In addition to the variables affecting the nature and performance of the NGO sector

generally, there is a considerable literature on NGO-government relations in developing countries (e.g., Holloway, 1989; Fowler, 1991; UN/ESCAP, 1991; Clark, 1993; Heyzer, Riker, and Quizon, 1995). An ESCAP seminar on government-NGO cooperation in social development in 1991 revealed a tremendous diversity among states in the Asia-Pacific region in this regard, ranging from the practical outlawing of the NGO sector, to significant levels of mutual suspicion, to close cooperation, making it difficult and dangerous to generalize. What it did reveal was an issue requiring considerable work, and the report of the seminar makes a number of recommendations. This focus on barriers to state-NGO relations and development of recommendations for overcoming these is common to most writers in the field. The prevailing conclusions are that there remains a long way to go in building strong and cooperative state-NGO relations in many developing countries, that the goal is extremely important, and that there are a number of readily identifiable strategies for achieving this goal. Some of the literature focuses extensively on state legislation pertaining to the NGO sector, which currently varies greatly across states, as the starting point for achieving better relations.

We should also be aware of relationships between the INGOs and the UN system (see Otto, 1996; Willetts, 1996; Weiss and Gordenker, 1996). In his foreword to the Weiss and Gordenker publication, Boutros Boutros-Gali, then the secretary-general of the UN, stresses the importance of the NGO sector within the UN system in "the maintenance and establishment of peace" and "the areas of assistance, mobilization, and democratization activities." The only mention of NGOs in the UN charter is in article 71, which empowers ECOSOC to "make suitable arrangements for consultation with non-governmental organizations which are concerned with matters within its competence." Since 1968, NGOs having a representative and international character have been entitled to admission to consultative status in the UN, supervised by the Committee on NGOs. NGOs and INGOs also operate within the system as lobbyists (see Kaldor, 2003, pp. 90–91), and by attending the NGO forums that parallel most UN Global Forums composed of government representatives. How much influence the NGO sector has within the UN system is, however, very difficult to determine. Certainly the deliberations and recommendations of the transnational federations of NGOs and INGOs are much more likely to influence outcomes than are most individual NGOs and INGOs, and some agencies within the UN system (e.g., the UNHCR) have been instrumental in establishing or encouraging NGO federations able to provide an input within specific fields of work.

Finally, reference should be made to the important role of the INGOs within the emerging global civil society, but we shall defer discussion of this to the final section in this review of the organizational dimension of the global context.

Global Civil Society

Shaw (1994, p. 647) has defined civil society as follows: It consists of "the network of institutions through which groups in society represent themselves—both to each other and to the state." In effect, civil society stands alongside the other three components of modern society, namely the state or governance system, the market or economic systems, and people-in-community, which components Galtung (1995, p. 204) regards as the different types of power in society. Civil society is usually seen as constituting the linkages between people-in-community and the economic and political systems of the state. As such, it enables people to participate in society in strength, by working together within a range of voluntary associations, and so to keep political and economic systems accountable. Exactly the same argument applies to civil society at the

global level. However, despite these definitions, we need also to be aware that global civil society is, in the literature, seen in a variety of ways and given varying degrees of significance, as the following review demonstrates.

The UNDP's 1997 *Human Development Report* warned that, while globalization offers great opportunities, it represents also a major threat to global equity. Pieterse (1997, p. 374) goes further, commenting that globalization has led to "the overriding imperative of competitiveness, resulting in distortions and the sacrifice of the interests of the most vulnerable in society." Hence the key role of global civil society is, as it is at the state level, to seek to ensure that the political and economic forces and systems that operate are held accountable to the people. If national civil society aims "to limit arbitrary or abusive state power" (Polidano and Hulme, 1997, p. 7), so global civil society represents essentially "transnational political activity" (Pasha, 1996, p. 643) carried out on behalf of people to ensure that global developments are in the people's best interests.

Aziz (1995, p. 12) sees global civil society as spearheaded by grassroots movements, thus representing "globalization from below." These movements reflect concerns such as "the environment, human rights, women's issues, sustainable development, peace and justice, universal literacy, and liberation from oppression" (Aziz). Rosenau (1995, p. 387) emphasizes more the collaboration between INGOs, or what he calls *transnational NGOs* (TNGOs). Rosenau refers to the growth in TNGOs as "stunning," with numbers increasing nineteen times since 1956 to more than 18,000 in 1992. Clearly both INGOs (or TNGOs) and global movements come together to represent what Stern-Petersson (1993, p. 136) refers to as "the emerging third force in world affairs"—a third force that "shares authority and responsibility for global policy with actors representing the state and market." The Commission on Global Governance (1995, p. 254) comments that "global civil society is best expressed in the global nongovernment movement," but elsewhere its report points out that this movement covers a multitude of institutions, voluntary associations, and networks—women's groups, trade unions, chambers of commerce, farming or housing cooperatives, neighborhood watch associations, religion-based organizations, and so on (p. 32). This Commission recommended that there be established, within the UN system, an annual Forum of Civil Society.

Kaldor (2003, chap. 1) sets out five different versions of global civil society, all both normative and descriptive. The first is concerned with the rule of law or civility, with global civil society signifying cosmopolitan order; the second version is concerned broadly with all aspects of economic, social, and cultural globalization; the third version is the activist one concerned with political emancipation, where social movements and civic activists seek to influence the global sphere; the fourth version is that of the neoliberals promoting the benefits of western society through global privatization of democracy and humanitarianism; and, fifth, the postmodern version seeks "to break with modernity of which a key component was the nation-state," and sees global civil society as the "plurality of global networks of contestation." Kaldor's own approach incorporates various aspects of these five dimensions.

While many writers hold high aspirations for global civil society, and perhaps realistically so given developments to date, we would have to agree with Shaw (1994, p. 655) that "these developments have so far been limited, and that global civil society is still more potential than actual," in terms not so much of size as of fulfilling the global roles possible. What is important is that this "globalization-from-below" movement continues to strengthen, engage in social action, put forward alternative social and economic policies and development models, and advocate for the world's disadvantaged people. Six key roles for civil society, nationally and globally, emerge from the literature:

- mediating between people and national or global political structures;
- reinforcing social ties between differing, and potentially competing, groups in society and globally;
- the promotion of democracy or people's participation;
- the reflecting and managing of pluralism;
- the advocacy of the rights of the disadvantaged and marginalized or excluded; and
- the presenting of needs and of alternative development models or strategies.

Global civil society must be strong enough to interact effectively with global economic and political structures, strong enough to represent the needs of all peoples of the world, and strong enough to play a key role in the formulation of global policies and programs that will reflect the basic principles and rights that constitute the essence of humanity. (A further useful reference on the contribution of global civil society, especially at the values level, is Bruyn, 2005.)

The Global Organizational Context and International Social Work

Social workers who enter international social work will inevitably find themselves working within a section of the broad global organizational context. The choice of employment path is indeed one of the first decisions confronting the graduate who decides to enter international social work. Should they participate in their own nation's global outreach or move on to the international level? Should they aim to work for the UN or one of the INGOs? This decision is inevitably linked to the decision as to the field in which our graduate will specialize (refugee work, natural disasters, conflict resolution, postconflict reconstruction, etc.), and to a determination of the focus of the graduate's involvement—for example, policy formulation, program development and administration, research, or frontline operations. Some organizations are much stronger at one or more of these levels than others, while most international organizations specialize in a particular field of activity. Thus a knowledge of the organizational context of international social work is important for enabling a social worker to plan his or her career path.

Related to or even independent of their career paths, international social workers may choose to use their knowledge of the organizational context to contribute to the strengthening of one or more areas. They may, for example, admire the roles and work of the UN and seek to play a part in its strengthening in general or specific terms. Alternatively, workers may link up with particular INGOs, such as the Red Cross or Amnesty International, and similarly contribute to strengthening their international role. Similarly, many social workers have worked hard to strengthen global civil society, either at a general level by, for example, lobbying at the UN, or more specifically by helping to strengthen some component of global civil society, such as the green movement. Often of course, the social worker's contribution along such lines might be carried out through the profession's own global organizations, such as the IFSW.

Frequently an understanding of the global organizational context will become more critical as international social workers become involved in a specific local situation. They will want and need to know what elements within that organizational context are potentially relevant to what their local situation requires. Can they involve particular international agencies, or seek funding from them, or involve them in local training schemes, or have the agencies' experts placed with them for brief periods, and so on. This global organizational context is potentially the most important resource available to workers at the local level in most contexts.

Sometimes an understanding of the global organizational context is vital in helping workers to control their anger and frustration. From the perspective of their local level, workers may be asking: Why does not the UN intervene? Why cannot the various NGOs cooperate? Why are these national agencies blocking our endeavors?

Only by understanding the general nature and current realities of the global organizational context can workers begin to appreciate the possible roles, the weaknesses or imposed limitations, the organizational decision-making processes, and so on to the point where they can be realistic in their expectations and controlled in their reactions.

It is vital for many reasons, a few of which we have highlighted, that international social workers understand the nature of the global organizational context within which they operate and on which they will often be dependent.

The Ideological Context

The term "ideology" has been defined as "systems of thought and belief by which individuals and groups explain how their social system operates and what principles it exemplifies" (Gilpin, 1987, p. 25). Ideologies are essentially "intellectual commitments or acts of faith" (Gilpin, p. 4). The importance of ideologies is reflected in the existence throughout world history of religious and cultural systems, political and related social systems, economic systems, and so on, all based on ideology. One critical issue that arises is how these differing systems, coexist on the world stage. Do they tend to exist side by side in peace, compete with each other, or seek to dominate others? History would seem to demonstrate that, at any point in time, a range of ideologies or worldviews coexist and compete with each other with varying degrees of aggression involved. Because of this, there are those who present the global ideological context as a pervasive clash between competing ideologies or civilizations. Two examples of such writers are Huntington (2002) and Gilpin (1987). (See also Sachs, 2002.) Huntington's theme is that "human history is the history of civilizations" (p. 10) that are inevitably clashing with each other. Not surprisingly, the title of his well-known but highly controversial book is *The Clash of Civilizations.* Gilpin, by contrast,

Table 3.1   Summary of the three ideologies

Ideology	Thoughts and Beliefs	Actions	Impact

Liberalism	Liberty
	Freedom
	Rationality
	Individualism
	Free market
	Private property
		Democracy
		Minimum, but active
		  state intervention
		Competition
		Independence
		Choice
		Capital formation
		Colonization
			Social, economic, and political
			  conditions seem to improve
			Increasing inequality
			Weak distribution of resources
			  which concentrates them in
			  hands of a few

Nationalism	State-building Independence Defense Sovereignty Geographic location	Political autonomy Industrialization Military power Economic self-sufficiency Protection	Security and belongingness Strong and weak nations Colonization and exploitation Sanctions, conflict, and war

Marxism
Communism
	Class struggle
	Classless society
	Common ownership of
	  means of production
	Liberation for all
	  people
		Change through struggle
		Socialist/communist forms
		  of government
		Analyze and critique
		  capitalist structures and
		  actions
			Progress toward equality
			Better distribution of resources
			A strong center
			High initial growth
			  accompanied by stagnation
			Declining impact on states

presents a model based on conflict between ideologies. He argues that three competing ideologies of political economy have divided humanity since the 1800s. The three ideologies are liberalism, nationalism, and Marxism (see Table 3.1), of which he writes,

> These three ideologies are fundamentally different in their conceptions of the relationships among society, state and market, and it may not be an exaggeration to say that every controversy in the field of international political economy is ultimately reducible to differing conceptions of these relationships. The intellectual clash is not merely of historic interest. Economic liberalism, Marxism, and economic nationalism are all very much alive at the end of the twentieth century. (Gilpin, 1987, p. 25)

Other commentators on recent world history, who follow this basic type of approach to ideology, are those who focus on the rift between the ideology of "triumphant economic—and political—capitalist liberalism," as it had developed in the Western world, and the "New World" that the West set out to dominate (Hobsbaum, 1995, p. 201). This is a view shared by Worsley (1984) and Hoogvelt (2001, pp. 18–21). The tendency to divide the world into largely irreconcilable camps has long been evident and is still with us, exemplified in, for example, ongoing perceptions of the differences between East and West or Islam and the Judeo-Christian tradition.

All of the above schools of thought are examples of schools that see differing ideologies as coexisting but inherently in conflict to some degree. This is usually because of some element within each ideology that encourages its followers to proselytize or seek to subjugate competing ideologies.

A second type of school focuses on particular ideological trends which are in themselves, in the view of these schools, a danger to the global community. Adherents of these schools then seek to counteract these trends by promoting alternative ideologies. For example, many writers and activists have focused on the strong antifemale trend often found in religious, political, economic, cultural, and social systems, and have sought to counter this through the promotion of feminism. Others have identified the tendency in many ideologies and systems to have scant regard for the natural environment, and have sought to counter this trend through the promotion of green ideologies. Both feminist and green ideologies are widely espoused, in general terms, by a wide range of workers in the international field. This is because each of these ideologies is seen as having vital implications for human well-being.

A third aspect of the current ideological context that calls for attention is characterized by either opposition to, or major doubts concerning, various existing dominant ideologies. For the most part, however, this type of opposition or concern has not resulted in opposing ideologies in any full sense, but rather in protests against, and widely expressed opposition to, these ideologies. Well-known ideological movements of this kind include anticapitalism, antiglobalization, anti–free trade, and anti–transnational corporations. Supporters of these views, a very varied camp, have sought to disrupt many international gatherings in recent years and received considerable media coverage. Many books have also been published reflecting such concerns, as can be seen from titles such as Chua's *World on Fire: How Exporting Free Market Democracy Breeds Ethnic Hatred and Global Instability* (2003).

A fourth and very important type of global ideological thinking focuses not so much on criticizing existing ideologies as on highlighting what might be, and so promoting a particular ideology. Examples of such ideologies are humanitarianism, a focus on human rights, and various religious ideologies. The promotion of such ideologies usually emanates from a combination of a concern for some existing state of affairs and a belief in the efficacy of bringing a particular ideologically based approach to bear when addressing that state of affairs. The expression of these ideologies is, therefore, found not so much in protest movements as in the active engagement in the field at all levels of ideologically based agencies, religious and secular in nature.

From the above discussion, it can be seen that ideology can and does play significant roles in understanding the overall legacy of history, in analyzing existing socioeconomic-political situations and trends, and in developing intervention strategies.

The Significance of a Historical Perspective of Ideology

While the study of many areas of history has the potential to assist our understanding of the contemporary global context, we shall confine our comments here to the widely acknowledged significance of the history of capitalist expansion emanating from Europe as early as the fifteenth and sixteenth centuries. This history, as Hoogvelt perceives it, encompasses

the period of mercantilism of 1500–1800—that is, "the striving after political power through economic means" (p. 3);

the period of colonialism, 1800–1950, important in Hoogvelt's eyes because of its "legacy of the international division of labour, of resource bondage and the westernisation of the peripheral elites" (p. 26);

the period of neocolonial imperialism, 1950–1970—a period of "unequal exchange between the rich and poor worlds . . . mediated by neocolonial class alliances between international capital and third world bourgeoisies" (p. 47); and

the postimperial era from 1970 on, which saw a "transfer of economic surplus through debt peonage" (p. 17). (See also Potter, 1992.)

Whatever the details, this general pattern of western dominance is generally accepted, and is widely regarded as highly relevant to recent developments.

It is not, therefore, in this context, the details of the history of capitalist expansion that are important. They can readily be found in Hoogvelt (2001) and elsewhere. Rather it is the widely accepted conclusion that the ideologies of mercantilism, colonialism, imperialism, and modernization have left their mark on all of the countries directly involved, and most others, and have resulted in modern systems that reflect these historical events and contemporary realities that still bear the mark of this historical legacy. For example, in his well-known text on development, Black (1991) assumes throughout that the former colonial powers, now neocolonial powers, are as able today to control trade arrangements and to exploit tribal and ethnic animosities as they were during the colonial period.

Furthermore, the reality that the liberalizing elites in most former colonies—who achieved independence and guided postindependence development—were themselves strongly western in orientation contributed to this outcome (see, e.g., Hobsbaum, 1995). A further important factor contributing to the recent situation has been western control of the establishment and policies of the global economic institutions set out after World War II. Indeed, the history of capitalist expansion, and especially colonialism, has left its mark on the world in a whole range of ways, including through the imposition of arbitrary state boundaries, especially in Africa, by colonial powers; through western-engineered

state demographic profiles, as in Malaysia and Fiji; through western-influenced state political systems, introduced before conditions were conducive (e.g., in Papua New Guinea); and through the formation of western-style state welfare systems (see Chapter 1). These are but some of the important aspects of the colonial legacy. It is a legacy of which many of the general public in developing countries are strongly aware.

Economic Neoliberalism and its Neoconservative Wing—the New Right

Of the ideologies that have made up the global ideological context in recent times, none is more important than the ideological trend known by various names but which we shall refer to as *economic neoliberalism*. It is a highly controversial ideology, having a wide range of supporters, including many highly influential leaders and scholars, but also many critics, some of whom regard it as the most significant factor adversely influencing the well-being of a high proportion of the world's population. Some see this ideological development as a return to historical liberal capitalism, and some present it as the heritage of the "New Right" political forces, "a mixture of economic liberalism and renascent conservatism" (Pierson, 1998, p. 39) espoused by Margaret Thatcher (prime minister of the United Kingdom, 1979–1990) and Ronald Reagan (president of the United States, 1981–1988). Even more significantly, however, many see economic neoliberalism as the ideology underpinning, in particular, the work of the World Bank and IMF in terms of, for example, their structural adjustment packages (e.g., Randall and Theobald, 1998, pp. 160–161); the focus of the WTO and of many western states on free trade (e.g., Nader et al., 1993); the international movement of capital generally (Korten, 1995, pp. 79ff.); and the pursuit of policies designed to enhance economic growth at the expense of virtually all other economic and social concerns (e.g., Hutton, 2003; Hamilton, 2003).

Indeed, some commentators speak as if economic neoliberalism is at the heart of most of our global problems, although as Hoogvelt (2001, p. 187) and others point out, the precise nature of any causal link is difficult to detect. The fundamental issue, perhaps, concerns the question of the distribution of decision-making power, nationally and globally. Korten (1995, p. 86) comments that, at its core, this ideology is "not about the public interest" but "about defending and institutionalizing the right of the economically powerful to do whatever best serves their immediate interests without public accountability for the consequences." This seems to be a fairly widely held view in many quarters of the international field.

What are the key elements of this ideology of economic neoliberalism? Among the elements most commonly referred to are

- freeing up of the economy by essentially minimizing government interference—deregulation;
- maximizing trade potential by instituting a free trade regime—free of government subsidies and import-export controls;
- limiting or rolling back state power, in part by devolving more responsibility to communities, families, and individuals;
- placing a strong emphasis on individualism—often linked to private property, consumption, and the pursuit of entrepreneurialism; and
- a negative view of the welfare state as uneconomic, unproductive, inefficient, and a denial of freedom.

However, we need to be aware that discrepancies between what an ideology suggests and what a viable political economy permits are common, and that this ideology is seldom imposed as rigidly as it is sometimes presented or in a uniform manner.

International Social Work and the Ideological Context

It should be clear to readers that an understanding of the global ideological context, from both a historical and a contemporary perspective, is an important aspect of international social work. It is difficult to see how most situations could be analyzed, and therefore understood and responded to, without addressing this aspect of the global context. Let us develop this general conclusion a little further by focusing on three ways in which the global ideological context might be relevant to international social work.

The Worker's Own Ideological Position

No worker will enter the international field without some ideological baggage, whether related to general cultural background and upbringing or to specific experiences in the field. Indeed, many social workers entering international social work do so, from our experience, as a result of strong ideological motivation. Sometimes this motivation emanates from the worker's background, as with religious motivation; sometimes it comes from international experiences resulting in a desire to work toward achieving human rights and social justice or humanitarian goals; and sometimes it is a result of participation in a particular social movement possessing strong ideology, such as green or feminist movements.

Often strong ideological motivation drives the workers' degree of commitment, protects them against frustrations and disappointments, and provides them with strong support networks. If there is a negative aspect to this situation, however, it is the danger that workers who are strongly driven ideologically will find it difficult to be objective in their approach, or open and insightful in coming to an understanding of situations seemingly at variance with their ideological stance. There is a general cross-cultural issue involved here, and a considerable literature addresses this issue. In addition, we need to be aware of workers' often strong reactions to situations that for them are ideologically unacceptable, but to which, in reality terms, they have to demonstrate an objective approach and bring about, if possible, an outcome acceptable to all relevant parties. The question is whether most workers find it easy to make the necessary compromises.

Local People's Perceptions of Western Ideology

While they may not express it in ideological terms, many people in developing countries will have strong emotional reactions to the West, its agencies, and its personnel. The prevailing emotion may be anger, suspicion, or hatred, reflecting frustration that is related to perceptions of Western behavior in the distant past or in recent times. Emotions may be so strong that certain lines of action may be effectively closed to workers, or they may spill over into an inability to even accept workers with western connections, or they may be so strong that any forward movement at all might be deemed impossible. In any event, an awareness of the possibility of ideological reactions and an ability to analyze their nature and causes are crucial to intervention. Chua's 2003 text is a good example of this phenomenon, although at the macro level.

Workers' Reactions to Relevant Institutional Ideologies

It is not at all uncommon for workers in international social work to find themselves working in or for, or having to collaborate with, agencies or institutions possessing dominant ideologies to which they personally are inherently opposed. Seldom do all personnel in any agency reflect even similar ideologies among themselves, let alone the same ideology as the agency has endorsed at some formal level. Faced

with potentially conflicting ideological views, what are appropriate reactions? Should the worker withdraw, seek to change the organization's ideology from within, or accept the realities of ideological pluralism and develop an ability to work within such a situation? The decision will be an individual one, reflecting a range of considerations, and any of the above decisions may be thought appropriate. What is inappropriate is that workers fail to acknowledge the potential for tension or conflict, and carry on working regardless; for when this occurs, events may overtake decision making and leave the worker with few satisfactory options for resolving complex and difficult situations.

The Emerging Policy Context: The Emergence of Global Social and Economic Policy and of International Law, and the Significance of These for International Social Work Practice

While certainly the world is still a long way from functioning under a set of universal or global policies, ideologies, principles, and laws, there are many signs of the world moving in this general direction, no matter how slow, uneven, uncertain, and precarious the steps being taken. The subject is complex, but let us share our understanding of the current state of developments and encourage the reader to reflect on the potential significance for international social work of what seems to be occurring.

International Law

Let us commence with international law. There seems to be no doubt that, as Robertson (2000, p. 90) puts it, "for the present, international law comes courtesy of nation states if it comes at all." International law is not legislated by a parliament of nations with authority to do so but by a "hopelessly unrepresentative" General Assembly (GA) of the UN; while the International Court of Justice in The Hague "is not permitted to become a Supreme Court for Humankind" (Robertson, p. 90). Yet nonbinding resolutions of the GA do sometimes influence nations, while "customary international law" does at times "filter through into national law" (pp. 91–92). As Robertson points out,

> Some common law systems, including the British and American, accept customary international law as part of that common law, although treaties must be incorporated by specific legislation before they can have any direct legal effects. [However,] at the beginning of the twenty-first century, international law remains subordinate and subservient to state power, which tends to favour economic, political or military interests whenever they conflict with those of justice. [Yet] abusive exercising of state power is becoming harder to hide and easier to condemn and the legal theory that human rights can be subjugated to "state rights" is becoming recognized as a dangerous fiction. (pp. 91–92)

Social workers need to be aware of the gradual development of a body of international law, of the need for states to endorse it and incorporate it into state law, and of their role as social workers to seek to influence this last process.

Global Economic Policy

Global economic policy presents a different situation. The existence of a global economy is not disputed; nor is it disputed that, as a consequence of the operations of the global economy, "it is less and less possible for individual states to regulate the economic activity that goes on within and across their borders" (Pierson, 1998, p. 64; see also Randall and Theobald, 1998,

p. 253). The key issue, however, is the degree to which global economic policy is a reality, determined by global organizations and institutions relatively independent of states. Randall and Theobald (1998, p. 253) write,

> Capital flows and investment decisions, fiscal and even monetary policy are increasingly determined by the actions of international banks, commodity brokers, currency speculators, market makers and the like. Debtor nations must submit themselves to policies and programmes imposed by the IFIs [International Financial Institutions].

The prevailing reality would appear to be a degree of tension between state and global economic policies, with a variety of scenarios. Some states appear to be supporting, or even driving, global economic policy, while not always adhering to those economic policies in their own behavior. Other states appear to be subjugated to global economic policy, and, on the basis of some criteria, to be suffering accordingly. Other states again, however, remain reasonably successful in ignoring global economic policy and pursuing a largely state-determined economic path. In essence, then, the relationship between global and state economic policy differs from that pertaining to international law only in that the powers behind global economic policy are far more powerful than those behind international law—and certainly even less accountable to the people or to many states.

Global Social Policy

Over the last few decades, the focus in international social work has been mainly on comparative social policy and the emergence of social policy in developing countries. (See, for example, MacPherson and Midgley, 1987.) While that remains important, here we are more concerned with global social policy. In the first chapter of his text on global social policy, Deacon (1997) includes within the term the "globalization of social policy instruments, policy and provision" (p. 2), all viewed as in their early stages of development, and "the socialization of global politics"—"In other words the major agenda issues at intergovernmental meetings are now in essence social (and environmental) questions" (p. 3). Regarding the extent of the development of global social policy, Deacon writes,

> Social policy as an academic discipline or field of study has, we suggest, been rather slower to wake up to the impact of the new world (dis)order on its subject matter than some economists, political scientists, international relations students and sociologists. On the other hand, because of its commitment to welfare and the concern of its practitioners to not only analyse existing policy but prescribe better ways in which human needs might be articulated and met, its potential contribution to the new global politics is immense. (p. 8)

Deacon agrees with Townsend and Donkor (1995, p. 20) that

> the problems in the late twentieth century of the international market and the replacement of sovereignty and empire by international hierarchical power will demand the establishment of forms of an international welfare state.

However, while setting out the pressures for the globalization of social policy, Deacon warns,

> National and regional self-interest and protectionism are alternative strategies available to governments. Supranationalization can be resisted. (p. 14)

Emerging Global Policy and International Social Work

While it is clear that developments in all three areas of policy covered are to some degree or in some regards in their infancy, it is also clear that those developments that have occurred are already having an impact on world affairs and development. Robertson is convinced that customary international law is working to protect human rights, although much more needs to be done; while Deacon is convinced that global social policy, as manifested by developments within regional bodies such as the European Union and by the field of international economic and social development, is already opening up possibilities such as global policies, global taxation and redistribution of monies, and global provision for the welfare needs of populations such as refugees. Furthermore, the global agreement relating to welfare goals and agendas in a range of areas augurs well for the future. How far developments in global economic policy have proved beneficial to the world's people is a more contentious issue, but undoubtedly much good has been achieved and there is still much more potential for good. The key element lacking here would appear to be the incorporation of the least developed countries within a more equitable global economic order.

The significance of these developments for international social work practice is readily perceived. In the first place, they together constitute a policy context of which workers need to be aware as they seek to understand and respond to situations of any kind. In the second place, the policy context contains much potential for good, and international social workers need to be aware of the responsibility they carry to contribute to its appropriate and effective ongoing development. However, the significance of global policy does not detract from the continuing significance of national policy regimes, and international social workers will frequently find themselves seeking to balance and handle these two competing demands. When operating internationally, the importance of and inherent difficulty in grasping the intricacies of perhaps several sets of national policy, the interaction between these, and their relationship to emerging global policy will frequently confront workers, calling for a firm grasp of the policy field generally and of a large body of detailed knowledge, relating to the national and international levels, in specific fields of practice.

With the social work profession having increasingly found its place in the policy arena in recent years at the national level, it follows that the profession will be seeking to participate in policy concerns at the global level. Indeed, social work practitioners in some obvious contexts have long been aware of global policy needs and realities: for example, social workers in intercountry casework, intercountry adoption, other areas of child welfare such as custody disputes across borders, and the corrections field have long possessed some kind of focus on global social policy. At another level, social workers engaged in such fields as poverty alleviation, unemployment, and local-level development have often been very aware of how global economic policy was affecting the local situation. Finally, social workers who have specialized in human rights work, work with indigenous minorities, ecological concerns, and a range of other areas have either utilized international law and conventions as a vehicle for pursuing national or local change, or have contributed to the expansion of policy at the international level.

If the importance of global social and economic policy to social work has already been well established, there is little doubt that it will grow in importance in future years. High levels of international population mobility, various types of collaborative arrangements between states, global collaboration in responding to needs, and the ongoing process of globalization generally will all continue to possess a policy dimension, and probably on an increasing level. International social workers need to be aware of these processes and ready to play their part in ensuring that the policies that do emerge are in the best interests of human well-being, and not just of states and corporations, and especially of the more vulnerable of the world's people whose voice is often not heard at decision-making levels.

However, it is also important that, as global policies do evolve, international social workers especially, but increasingly all social workers, are familiar with them and aware of their relevance to their practice. Often it is social workers who will carry the responsibility of making individuals and groups aware of the global policies that might affect their situations, and who will facilitate their ability to interact with those policies and the agencies that administer them. This is, of course, already the situation in some areas of practice, as noted above, but the range of areas of practice to which global policies will apply is likely to expand.

In other words, just as social workers have always needed to possess a knowledge and understanding of national legal and policy regimes, so in an era of rapid globalization do they also need to be aware of global regimes.

Conclusion

The context of international social work is vast and complex, yet highly fascinating. More and more professionals, from a wide range of disciplines and countries, have moved into international work. They find a niche within that complex of international organizations, having frequently to interact with some or all of the sectors involved, and therefore needing to develop some basic understanding of the network of global organizations and how they function. Their work will see them focusing in often a relatively limited field, but almost invariably they are conscious of the impact on their field of a range of other fields, issues, and social problems. Many find themselves obliged to improve their cross-disciplinary abilities, as they wrestle with highly complex situations that are often underresourced in personnel and other terms. Increasingly too, workers encounter an ever growing array of international laws, conventions, and policies, some of which relate directly to what they are seeking to achieve. To understand this legal and policy context is not easy for most workers, but not to understand it, or have access to those who do, can often result in unfortunate outcomes. Finally, one is aware also of the existence of dominating or competing ideologies, and of the need at the very minimum to appreciate these as one aspect of one's operating reality.

While the above is true for all who enter the international field, for social workers and other members of the helping professions the focus required will be on specific elements of each of these four aspects of the international context. This should become clearer to readers as we consider various aspects of the field of international social work in subsequent chapters. At this point, however, we would hope that readers will have a basic understanding of these four aspects of the international context that have been discussed.

Summary

- It is important to have a clear understanding of the global context of international social work, and this context has been presented in terms of four dimensions: global social problems, global organizations, ideologies of global relevance, and global policy frameworks.

- A clear understanding of global social problems is necessary as these problems influence actions and resource allocations of national and international agencies. Such an understanding also helps social workers to analyze and relate to local situations and contribute to local and global policies.

- The organizational context for international social work is very vast and complex. The roots of the beginning of international organizations may be traced to the consequences of the two world wars. One way of understanding the overall organizational context is by looking at the national governments' agencies which serve international purposes, at intergovernmental agencies such as the European Union and African Union, at the UN system, and at some transnational corporations, INGOs, and global civil society. This understanding significantly helps social workers to contribute to international social work.

- Many countries have been strongly influenced by, if not the victims of, prevailing ideologies. Liberalism, colonialism, nationalism, Marxism, imperialism, and neocolonialism have all had an influence on the development of various nation-states and international developments. However, liberalism, in its many forms including neoliberalism, appears to have been the dominant ideology, although there have emerged strong ideologies opposing it. An understanding of these ideologies is an important part of the preparation for international social work.

- The global policy context is composed of international law, economic policy, and social policy, although social policy developments particularly are in their early stages. However, understanding such emerging policies is necessary for international social work practice.

Questions and Topics for Discussion

- After reading this chapter, what do you consider to be the main aspects of the global context of international social work?
- According to you, what are the main global social problems? Of these, choose a social problem of your interest, and discuss it in light of the four questions (nos. 2–5) posed in the global social problems context section.
- Why do you think social workers need to be aware of global social problems?
- Discuss the broad organizational context for international social work.
- Study any of the following organizations that interest you and identify roles for social workers:

  - A national government's agency established for international work.
  - An intergovernmental agency or regional association.
  - A UN agency, e.g., UNICEF, UNDP, etc.
  - An INGO.

- With the class divided into small groups, let each group consider the nature, strengths, weaknesses, and potential of one of the six categories of international organizations discussed and present their conclusions to the class.
- How can better coordination and cooperation be developed among international organizations?
- According to you, what are the most dominant ideologies in the contemporary world? Consider the merits of opposing ideologies to these dominant ideologies.
- Why is it important to understand these ideologies for international social work practice?
- Assume that, as an international social work practitioner, you are going to work in a specific field in a particular country. Discuss global and state policies possibly relevant to the chosen field and country.
- As an international social work practitioner, what aspects of the global context should be kept in mind for your practice?

Possible Areas for Research Projects

- Undertake a systematic analysis of any global social problem according to the four questions (nos. 2–5) posed under the global social problems context section.
- Undertake an analysis of a particular issue according to the four dimensions of the global context presented in this chapter.
- Examine the current level of coordination and cooperation (or lack of it) among the six categories of organizations in a country as a case study.
- Study the issues in implementing international law and global policies at the national level.
- Study what constitutes the global context of international social work in a selected situation.
- Undertake a study of how the organizational context matters in international social work by surveying social workers working in international organizations.

Further Reading

Deacon, B. (1997). *Global social policy: International organizations and the future of welfare.* London: Sage.

Gordon, W. (1994). *The United Nations at the crossroads of reform.* New York: M. E. Sharpe.

Hoogvelt, A. (2001). *Globalisation and the post-colonial world: The new political economy of development.* Basingstoke, England: Palgrave Macmillan.

Kaldor, M. (2003). *Global civil society: An answer to war.* Cambridge, England: Polity Press.

4

Basic Programs and Strategies for International Social Work

Introduction

One of the significant insights that emerges from studying international social work is that a great variety of workers, engaged in highly divergent fields, have adopted a number of common strategies. Some of these workers may have done so as a result of study, general reading, or training courses, but many others have done so because these strategies appeared to represent a commonsense or logical approach. Field-workers seem to appreciate instinctively that people's empowerment and capacity building are indispensable to progress. Similarly, they quickly realize that self-help and community-based approaches to change are both necessitated by resource shortages and right in principle. Along similar lines, workers perceive the necessity for communities and societies to pull together as far as possible, which is an outcome of social cohesion. Finally, it is common sense that alleviating poverty, accessing basic services, and acquiring a measure of freedom requires some income, so that income-generation strategies come to assume high priority.

Because these programs and strategies are clearly central to every international field of practice, we are outlining them in this chapter rather than in the chapters pertaining to specific fields. Clearly there is no clear dividing line or inherent difference between the programs and strategies discussed here and those discussed in the field chapters; however, those left to the field chapters tend to have specific relevance for a specific field, even if relevant elsewhere, whereas those discussed in this chapter possess general relevance across virtually all fields.

It should also be pointed out that some of the programs and strategies discussed in this chapter are obviously central to traditional social work, such as empowerment and community development; while others, or at least the terminology used to describe them, might appear to be more marginal, at least in the context of developed countries. Many social workers do not seem to engage in capacity building and income generation, at least by name, or to promote social cohesion. On further analysis, however, clearly much of social work is in effect geared to all three of these goals, albeit at varying

Learning Objectives

The main learning objectives of this chapter are as follows:

- To develop a critical understanding of the concept of empowerment and to employ it as a key principle and strategy in international social work practice.

- To understand the importance and the range of activities and targets covered under capacity building.

- To understand the importance of self-help groups, self-reliance, and the mobilization of local resources and means of achieving self-reliance.

- To understand the need and strategies for social cohesion in heterogeneous societies experiencing social tension, conflict, and civil war.

- To understand the importance of income-generation strategies and programs in the context of poverty alleviation, postconflict reconstruction, and recovery from disasters and displacement, bearing in mind given socioeconomic and political situations.

- To understand community development as a broad umbrella strategy encompassing several other strategies that emphasize the process of achieving community development.

levels and in different ways. For example, social workers in western countries will be more likely to facilitate unemployed people finding existing jobs than to initiate new income-generation programs; while capacity building is commonly an important element in social work with individuals, groups, and communities, without capacity building programs being as specific or as up-front as they are in most international social work.

Empowerment

As with a number of terms in social development and social work, empowerment and the process of empowering people has become something of a rhetorical refrain employed in virtually all contexts. Sometimes the impression gained is that the empowerment of some target population is simultaneously a key objective in itself and the answer to many presenting problems. If it is to be a useful term and an important strategy for workers in the field, then it is important that we clarify its meaning.

The Oxford English Dictionary defines power inter alia in these ways:

ability to do or effect something;

authority given or committed;

legal ability, capacity, or authority to act; and

possession of command or control over others.

To empower is to invest legally or formally with power, to impart or bestow power to an end or a purpose, or to assume or gain power over. Hence empowerment is the action of empowering or the state of being empowered. As Weissberg (1999, p. 16) says in his text on empowerment: "Plainly put, possessing 'power' means a capacity to impose one's will or achieve a position of superiority."

If we consider such definitions as these, then does empowering children, women, the poor, minority groups, and so on mean reversing existing power relations and giving them power over, respectively, adults, men, the rich, or dominant groups? From a wide-ranging examination of the literature on empowerment, Weissberg (1999, p. 17) concludes that the common element present in much writing, at least in the United States, is that "those empowered can orchestrate their lives and control the world around them." Clearly there is a difficulty in using the term in this extreme sense; however, this is not the meaning of empowerment found in most of the social work and social development literature. Let us consider a few of these writers to see what they mean by the term.

Turning first to the social work literature, we find that the focus is almost invariably on practice that enables members of stigmatized groups or minorities in a society to overcome the blockages imposed by stigma and realize their potential. In her book on the empowerment approach to social work practice, Lee (2001, pp. 83–84) quotes and adopts the definition of empowerment put forward by Solomon (1976, p. 19). Empowerment is

a process whereby the social worker engages in a set of activities with the client . . . that aim to reduce the powerlessness that has been created by negative valuations based on membership in a stigmatized group. It involves identification of the power blocks that contribute to the problem as well as the development and implementation of specific strategies aimed at either the reduction of the effects from indirect power blocks or the reduction of the operations of direct power blocks.

In her own understanding of empowerment in social work practice, Lee regards the empowerment approach as integrating social work's casework-, clinical-, and community-oriented approaches. She writes (2001, pp. 30–31),

The empowerment approach is an integrated method of social work practice driven by the unified personal political construct and a commitment to the unleashing of human potentialities toward the end of building the beloved community, where justice is the rule. It is therefore a clinical and a community-oriented approach encompassing holistic work with individuals, families, small groups, communities, and political systems.

In his text *Social Work and Empowerment*, Adams (2003, p. 8) quotes the *Dictionary of Social Work* definition of empowerment:

[Empowerment is] theory concerned with how people may gain collective control over their lives, so as to achieve their interests as a group, and a method by which social workers seek to enhance the power of people who lack it. (Thomas and Pierson, 1995, p. 134)

In their social work text on organizing for power and empowerment, Mondros and Wilson (1994, p. 6) define empowerment as referring to "a psychological state—a sense of competence, control, and entitlement—that allows one to pursue concrete activities aimed at becoming powerful." They argue that basically people need to feel empowered if they are going to take their place in society, and while some groupings in a society do feel empowered, others do not. The main strategy in such situations for achieving empowerment, according to these authors, is community organizing. However, the empowerment goal here is similar to Lee's (2001, p. 6).

While empowerment is a common and important concept in social work, it is also very widely used in the social development literature in a similar but somewhat broader sense. To go back to an early campaigner, Pandey (1996) sets out what Gandhi meant by his use of the term. He concludes that Gandhi saw empowerment as having three meanings. These were personal transformation, which embraced consciousness-raising and self-reliance in a search for self-realization and self-fulfillment; constructive work, which was directed toward building alternative social institutions with the fourfold roles of serving the oppressed, cultivating a non-violent lifestyle, building the image of a future society, and providing training to nonviolent workers; and nonviolent action as required to address a variety of concerns.

Although Freire (1972) uses different terminology from Gandhi's, it is a similar view of empowerment and one that has had widespread influence on social work and social development in Latin America and elsewhere. Freire saw empowerment as a product of critical consciousness, critical awareness, or conscientization. As he writes, "To surmount the situation of oppression, men must first critically recognize its causes" (pp. 24), and this recognition arises from "educational projects, which should be carried out with the oppressed in the process of organizing them" (p. 31). The critical consciousness that is achieved is akin to religious conversion (pp. 36–37) and removes that "fatalism in the guise of docility" that has rendered the oppressed unable to act in the past. Freire writes that the oppressed, ambiguous regarding the reasons for their oppressed state, "are reluctant to resist, and totally lack confidence in themselves. They have a diffuse, magical belief in the invulnerability and power of the oppressor" (p. 39). Through the process of learning, a transformation takes place:

> And as those who have been completely marginalized are so radically transformed, they are no longer willing to be mere objects, responding to changes occurring around them; they are more likely to decide to take upon themselves the struggle to change the structures of society which until now have served to oppress them. (p. 13)

Writing of the influence that Freire had on social work in Latin America, Kendall (2000, p. 107) writes,

> Borrowing a concept from the work of Paulo Freire on adult literacy and cultural action, social workers found in "conscientization" a new approach geared to changing social structures and complete identification with the powerless and the oppressed.

Freire's "new awareness of self in relation to all society" (Lee, 2001, p. 35) was a significant contribution to social work's understanding of the empowerment approach.

Anderson, Wilson, Mwansa, and Osei-Hwedie (1994, pp. 71–72), writing of the African context, present five dimensions of empowerment. These are

> personal empowerment (competency required for taking self-direction); social empowerment (comprising society's capacity for self-direction and control of community processes and resources); educational empowerment (the development of an educational system that prepares people for both their social and work life); economic empowerment (the development of the means to earn a sufficient income to live a life of dignity and to provide for the adequate fulfillment of the requisite needs of shelter, food and clothing); and political empowerment (involvement in democratic decision-making).

These five dimensions can, in the writers' words, be regarded as a combination of social development in terms of individual development (the micro level), and institutional development that avoids the domination of one social group or institution over another (the macro level) (p. 79). This reflects Lee's approach outlined above.

The World Bank in its 2000/2001 *World Development Report* contains a section on empowerment (Part III). By empowerment this report seems to mean making state institutions more responsive to public needs through such strategies as local organizational development and participatory political systems. This refers, then, to the state's obligation to empower people by facilitating their organizational development and political participation. While most writers see the empowerment approach as people-centered, this report is right in emphasizing the important roles that states can play in the process, as well as the importance of organizations that are empowering in their structures and operations.

Examining the definitions of empowerment used or implied by these and other writers in the social work and social development fields, we would have to conclude that they are not conforming to the common dictionary definition as given above and interpreted by Weissberg. They are not arguing for a reversal of the structures of power in society or for any target group to achieve power over others: rather, they are addressing the need to engage people more actively in addressing their personal needs and improving their wider environment. To use Weissberg's (1999, p. ix) words, there are those writers who focus mainly on personal empowerment, that is, to "seek power over their lives by gaining new skills, conquering bad habits or imposing self-discipline." Alternative terms here might include promoting self-realization or self-fulfillment, self-reliance, self-confidence, personal capacity building, and so on. At this level, empowerment might be either psychological (feeling empowered) or pragmatic (developing selected capacities and skills).

The second aspect that Weissberg (p. x) identifies is the need to play a more active community role. This need may be expressed by joining in local organizations with a range of objectives; by demanding a greater role in broader political and decision-making processes; and by lobbying for an improvement in the functioning of state institutions as such or in their roles in the distribution of the state's available resources. In other words, for the most part the use of the term *empowerment* can mean assisting individuals to exercise greater control over their own lives, and to exercise a stronger influence over the decision-making and structural developments in society that impact directly or indirectly on their lives and well-being. Both dimensions are not basically designed to give people power over others, but to improve people's lot in life by removing impediments to the development of their potential at as many levels as possible. As Lee (2001, p. 4) puts it in the social work context, "Assisting clients to challenge obstacles and actualize potentialities, to affirm life, build community,

and work to change structural arrangements and toxic environments is the aim of the empowerment approach."

Weissberg, in rejecting the strong emphasis placed on empowerment today, argues that exercising power over others does not necessarily bring greater happiness or improved well-being. Nor does it necessarily secure greater equity or a greater measure of participatory democracy in a society. He points out that power can corrupt, and in this and other ways a reversal of power can prove deleterious for all concerned. He goes on to say that, rather than focusing on how much power certain people have, the important questions to ask are these: What are the existing needs? What are the objectives in addressing these needs? And what will help to achieve these objectives? Empowerment, in the more limited sense that commonly applies in social work and social development, will often be a significant part of the answer to such questions, but seldom the complete answer. On the other hand, it is easy to agree with Weissberg that securing power for an oppressed or poverty-stricken or excluded population, in the sense of acquiring control over others, may in itself achieve little that is positive and potentially much that is negative.

Therefore, concludes Weissberg (1999, chap. 2), let us identify clearly what a specific situation requires and strive to achieve that change, but without using the term *empowerment* to define our strategy, and so implying that, if power is obtained by the target population, all else that is deleterious in the situation will automatically be rectified. If the goal is personal capacity building, or job creation, or political participation, or a stronger civil society, or community building, let us identify them as such and treat the distribution of power as one of the important variables likely to be involved in rectifying the situation. This is a view with which most social workers would be in agreement.

Is there then any benefit derived from using empowerment as a specific goal or strategy? There would certainly seem to be in relation, first, to making people feel empowered. We may refer to this as enhancing self-confidence or the motivation to engage in self and group development, and many professionals and others are in effect constantly engaged in helping individuals to feel empowered. Parents, teachers, psychologists, counselors, social workers, and others assist people to establish objectives, devise strategies, gain strength from small successes, understand better the nature of their environment and how they might engage with it, and in general learn to exercise some degree of control over their own lives or some sense of feeling empowered. This is one of the most common processes in which many of us engage at many levels.

Second, it is important that people feel that they can also directly exercise some control over their wider environment. Frequently individuals sense that personal control of broader societal developments is impossible. By coming together, however, in communities and organizations, people can find strength in numbers, while bringing together a diversity of insights, experiences, and capacities to be applied to the pursuit of common goals. Hence, social workers and others are frequently engaged in community organizing, community development, and strengthening the nongovernment sector or civil society. To refer to this process as empowering people is not inappropriate, for it is clearly part of the empowerment approach. It is a process aimed at people gaining some power within the decision-making and other structures of which their society is composed. It is not, however, aimed at gaining power over others, but rather at creating situations of shared power or, to use a common alternative term, at creating participatory approaches to the development and functioning of society.

As pointed out earlier, Weissberg summarized the literature on empowerment in the United States as suggesting that "those empowered can orchestrate their lives and control the world around them." He is probably correct in arguing that power and control are not ideal goals, and he might well have added that for the most part they

are also not usually achievable in this literal sense. What we understand the literature and workers to be saying, particularly in the social work–social development contexts, is that those who are empowered can increase the extent of control they exercise over their own lives, and can then participate with others in the development of the society around them in ways that will maximize equity, justice, and the well-being of all concerned. In other words, power and control are not the objectives of the process but rather means of achieving selected goals. Individuals and groups require a degree of power and control, exercised in conjunction with others within the contexts of family, group, community, and society, that enable them to play a meaningful and satisfying role within social development at all levels. Given that many people still cannot play such a role in many societies, empowerment is, therefore, a strategy of central importance.

The literature on how to achieve the key goals of empowerment is indeed vast, and even the key strategies are difficult to summarize here without devoting significant space to the task. (For example, Lee, 2001, devotes Chapter 3 to the how-to of applying the empowerment approach to practice, covering a range of skills in working with individuals, groups, and communities; while the book by Mondros and Wilson, 1994, is entirely related to community organizing strategies for empowerment.) There are many ways to empower individuals to take more control over their own lives, with the choice of strategies depending in large part on the nature of the barriers existing to their doing so:

- Are the barriers within the individual, within the family, within community relations, or within society's structures?
- Should the worker focus on counseling and therapy or on social change, or a mixture of the two?

As always a careful assessment of the situation is essential, followed by the selection of strategies that are appropriate and feasible in the context. Here the social worker may draw on virtually any of the strategies that compose the tools of social work. The worker's specific objective may be to strengthen the person or the group by engaging in awareness raising, capacity building, local organization development, promoting self-help group formation, identifying and facilitating income-generation schemes, or any other aspect of local-level development. All such strategies will be empowering if successfully implemented. In one sense empowering does not have its own unique strategies. Rather it injects into a situation an appreciation that a key part of the presenting situation is that individuals or groups lack sufficient power or control over the prevailing circumstances to feel able to engage in seeking to change them. It is a variable that must be addressed by ensuring that an empowering process is part of what transpires. In other words, what is important is for the worker to distinguish between those strategies and processes that have the effect of being disempowering, and those that are empowering, and then to ensure that only the latter are utilized.

Let us conclude with Lee's (2001, pp. 402–403) words regarding empowerment and international social work:

> The empowerment approach is a paradigm for international social work practice. . . . The approach relates to individuals as well as sociopolitical and economic developments and liberation in the face of human oppression. Additional to the range of social work skills, consciousness-raising, empowering group process, and the process of praxis—action-reflection-action—are the core processes of the empowerment approach and of conscientization and social development practice.

Capacity Building

The common focus on capacity building fits with the prevailing focus in development today on people-centered, participatory, and sustainable development. If people are to play an active role in the development of any aspect of their society or community, it is obvious that certain capacities will facilitate this role. If, therefore, certain obviously required capacities are not present, then a first step will be to rectify this situation. It is not surprising, therefore, that the strategy of capacity building has been around now for a long time, although becoming more common in recent years. Let us commence by reviewing a few of the recent texts.

Sometimes the literature restricts discussion to a specific context or level of capacity building. An Oxfam report (Eade, 1997), for example, focuses largely on the capacity building of local NGOs, while some internal UNHCR papers discuss capacity building as it relates to a refugee operation (UNHCR, 1997). At the other extreme, World Bank and Asian Development Bank literature tends to focus on capacity building at either the state level or the local government level, in terms of political activities, bureaucratic structures, and institutional building. (See, for example, the World Bank's [1991b; *Africa Capacity Building Initiative*.) In effect, capacity building can relate to individuals, families, communities, local organizations, local government, civil society organizations, state institutions, and even the private sector. The logic for enhancing capacity building will be similar in all these contexts, namely to enhance capacity to carry out roles necessary for the development or well-being of society at all levels, but clearly the actual strategies adopted will vary with context. The essential point here, however, is that capacity building applies at all levels of a society.

A second important point from the literature is that capacity building is closely linked to many important principles. It is linked to self-reliance, sustainability, participation, equity, human rights, and no doubt others. In all cases, it is difficult to see how these principles can be upheld, and the goals they imply achieved, if the people or institutions or even states concerned do not come to possess the capacities essential to implementing these principles and goals.

A third point implied by the above is that the actual capacities in question will be many and varied. In relation to people's capacities, they may be of a very general nature, such as an adequate level of self-esteem or of personal or group empowerment, or very specific in nature, such as literacy skills, the ability to manage certain disabilities or illnesses, or the knowledge and skills to carry out specific tasks. At the community level, the capacity may vary, for example, from those necessary to participate in the wider society, to those related to achieving sufficient income-generation opportunities, to those necessary for intergroup reconciliation and securing social cohesion, to those pertaining to establishing market structures or effective local governance. And there will be similar diversity at all other levels.

A fourth general point is that the modalities that can be used to build capacities will also vary greatly. They will include specific education, training, and instruction, of both an informal and formal nature; the provision of material goods without which the capacity to achieve some specific goal is minimal, such as seeds, machinery, raw materials such as cement, and access to technology such as telephone services; the opening of doors to selected opportunities, services, and decision-making bodies, involving issues of access; and the enhancing generally of education and health levels across a population. Indeed, if the starting point in any context is the identification of some deficiency in the available range of capacities, the list of modalities for rectifying this will be as long as workers' initiative and imagination make it.

While we can clearly discuss capacity building in terms of different levels and capacities, a crucial aspect of the recent focus on capacity building is that the term fundamentally implies a process that possesses certain characteristics. Among these characteristics are

- that all external intervention begins with identifying local capacities and building upon them, rather than introducing new structures, personnel, or approaches, without considering what local capacities already exist;
- that arguably the central purpose of all outside intervention in all situations is the building (or rebuilding in the case of postconflict situations) of capacities, even if some initial emergency care or aid is required, in that only by building capacities is the future assured as far as it is humanly possible to do so; and
- that people's improved capacities in all areas are valued in their own right as the most significant outcome of all intervention, and that people should then have the freedom to determine what they will do with their heightened capacities.

O'Shaughnessy (1999, pp. 10–11), in a paper on capacity building for World Vision, a prominent international development agency, highlights in a table the differences between piecemeal social engineering and people-centered capacity building, which picks up these and other essential characteristics of capacity building. In this sense, capacity building typifies a new way of describing the people-centered, bottom-up, and participatory style in the development field. As O'Shaughnessy writes,

> Capacity building . . . is a key concept in many of the new approaches to overseas aid proposed by donors and NGOs. Among other things, the new models call for more democratic and holistic approaches to assist communities to develop their own capacities and resourcefulness. (p. 16)

The rest of this World Vision document presents capacity building as a key organizing principle that both helps to determine the overall approach to development or aid work, and is relevant at each and every stage in an operation. The document makes it clear that the success of every project or program, especially in terms of sustainability, is that the people concerned possess, or come to possess, the capacities for handling the situation or aspect of development. For example, programs to provide credit to low-income people should see credit as the key capacity-building tool, and accept that the recipients of the credit may require basic business skills if they are to use the credit effectively and in a sustainable manner (O'Shaughnessy, 1999, p. 38). In addition, however, capacity-building principles will apply to the manner in which the scheme is proposed to the people, in the style of implementation, and in evaluation processes. In other words, capacity building permeates outsiders' intervention in virtually all situations at virtually all levels of intervention. Does it therefore possess any techniques or skills that practitioners can master, or is it relevant only, but importantly, at the principle or overall approach level?

A starting point to answering this question may be to identify what the term *capacity* might cover; and we can do this by using a checklist, such as that shown in Table 4.1, to identify deficiencies in the range of capacities required for achieving selected goals. Once the problem areas in terms of capacity levels have been identified from a checklist, some of the required strategies will be obvious or can be readily identified. It is not surprising that the literature makes constant reference to terms like awareness raising, enhancing self-esteem, raising literacy levels, confidence building, access to basic education and health services, empowerment, and so on. Even when the term *capacity building* is not used, the implication is usually that only minimal progress will be possible unless attention is given to a specific type of capacity. It follows, therefore, that the techniques and skills required for capacity building relate not so much to capacity building per se as to the specific type of capacity required within a specific situation to achieve selected goals.

Table 4.1   Capacity checklist

Personal Level

Emotional dimension

Confidence levels
Self-esteem levels
Consciousness or awareness levels
Empowerment level

Physical dimension

Capacity to work with any existing disabilities
Availability of basic health services

Cognitive dimension

Literacy skills
Basic education levels
Specific knowledge in relevant areas

Skills dimension

Skills specific to identified tasks

Group and Community Level

Strength of group or community identity

Degree of cohesion of group or community

Awareness of needs and well-being levels within group or community

Existence of common objectives and goals

Availability of appropriate leadership and governance

Systems and Organizations Level

Understanding of organizational objectives and goals

Identification and recruitment of personnel

Efficiency of operating systems

Availability of prerequisites for successful functioning

Awareness of potential barriers to processes and outcomes

Awareness of potential significance of context

In conclusion, what is important here is the recognition by practitioners of the overall importance of capacity building in all endeavors to enhance well-being, and the ability then to identify the particular areas or forms of capacity that require attention, with of course the cognizance and participation of those persons and organizations concerned. The ability of practitioners to then engage in capacity building will depend upon the understanding and skills they possess relating to the capacities in question or their ability to access such understanding and skills. (On capacity building, see also James, 1998, 2001.)

Self-help and Self-reliance

In this section we shall discuss self-help group formation as an important strategy in its own right, and as a strategy for achieving self-reliance, which is in itself a very important goal of social development. We should emphasize from the beginning, however, that there are two ways in which self-reliance is used in development circles that are not our concern here. One is a focus on self-reliance as a goal of state development. India, for example, has placed a strong emphasis on self-reliance, or self-reliant development, in its various five-year plans. Another country that has done this is Thailand, where the concept of self-reliance permeates most public statements regarding social and community development. A second important use of the term is in relationship to ecological sustainability. Ife (1995, p. 110) indeed claims that "the idea of community self-reliance derives directly from the ecological principle of sustainability." Sustainable self-sufficient living has been the central objective of many development projects (see Hoff, 1998), and the term usually incorporates the term *self-reliance*. Here, however, our focus is on community self-reliance, although we shall commence with a brief look at the concept of self-help groups.

Here we might digress to point out that the meaning of *self* in both self-help and self-reliance often carries a group significance more than an individual one. While it might be argued

that individuals become involved in all such initiatives essentially out of self-interest, the strategy is essentially a group strategy, and therefore perhaps more closely allied to family-based and community-based initiatives of the past, and now emphasized in many developing countries, than to the individualism of the modern world. Self-reliance even more particularly is self-reliance of the family group or community far more than it is of any individual involved. In most cases, however, the individuals involved compose a largely egalitarian group coming together on an equitable basis, so the strategy is suited best to communities or groups with these characteristics.

Self-help Groups

Most readers will be aware of the importance of self-help groups in at least the western world in recent decades, although it could validly be suggested that the developing world has reflected informal models of such for a long period. Taking Verhagen's (1987, p. 22) definition,

> Self-help is any voluntary action undertaken by an individual or group of persons which aims at the satisfaction of individual or collective needs or aspirations. The distinctive feature of a self-help initiative or activity is the substantial contribution made from the individual's or group's own resources in terms of labour, capital, land and/or entrepreneurial skills. Self-help can be concerned with political, economic, social or cultural activities.

In a study of all types of support groups in the United States, Wuthnow (1994, p. 76) estimated that there were some 500,000 self-help groups in the United States involving some 8 to 10 million members. These groups covered a wide variety of interests, needs, and aspirations. Social workers are perhaps most familiar with self-help groups organized to assist alcoholics, gamblers, persons suffering from certain psychiatric disorders and physical health conditions, and persons in particular social situations such as recently bereaved or widowed. However, as Adams (2003, pp. 18–19) points out, self-help had its roots "in the mutual aid and friendly society movements" that, in the United Kingdom, date from the eighteenth century. Adams also makes the very important link between self-help and empowerment: "Self-help is the most significant traditional activity in Britain on which empowerment practice draws."

In the developing countries, many, if not most, so-called Peoples' Organizations or Local Organizations are in reality what Verhagen (1987, p. 22) terms self-help organizations. He writes,

A self-help organization denotes the institutional framework for individuals or households who have agreed to cooperate on a continuing basis to pursue one or more objectives.

A self-help organization is a membership organization which implies that its risks, costs and benefits are shared among its members on an equitable basis and that its leadership and/or manager are liable to be called to account by membership for their deeds.

Self-help organizations are essentially the outcome of a group of people or a community engaging in a self-help strategy. And, as many people have observed, such organizational development forms the basis of local level development and of an active civil society at a wider level.

Self-reliance

According to Verhagen (1987, p. 23),

self-help is a means to achieve self-reliance. Self-reliance is a state or condition whereby an individual or group of persons having achieved such a condition no longer depends on the benevolence or assistance of third

parties to secure individual or group interests. By implication, a self-reliant group has developed sufficient analytical, productive and organizational capacity to design and implement a strategy which effectively contributes to the betterment of the conditions of life of its membership and the maintenance of its independent status.

Why should we attach importance to self-reliance? There are several reasons. One central reason is that there are dangers in being overly dependent on external resources, although no community or group today can be fully self-sufficient. In relation to communities and their development, Ife (1995, p. 111) expresses this reason in these terms:

Reliance on external resources comes at a price, namely the price of loss of autonomy and independence; genuinely autonomous communities can only flourish in the absence of such external dependency, as the experience of those who have to rely on government grants can clearly testify.

In many developing countries' contexts, there are even more compelling reasons for communities and groups to minimize their reliance on either the state or development projects. A second reason is the positive one that with self-reliance comes increased self-esteem, community pride, and enhanced community development initiatives; while a third reason is that all people, groups, and communities possess strengths, resources, and capacities that are frequently overlooked when external aid is readily available. Sometimes communities become convinced, often influenced by external attitudes, that by themselves they are weak and insignificant. One consequence of this is to impair self-esteem and self-confidence, while another is to deprive the community and state of the value of the local resources that are rejected or overlooked, and this can be disastrous when the total pool of resources is significantly limited.

Basically it makes sense to apply what the Europeans commonly term the principle of *subsidiarity,* namely that all activity and intervention should occur at the lowest level possible. It follows that individuals should learn to stand on their own feet and do what they can for themselves; that communities should become as self-reliant as possible, utilizing local human and other resources in a manner that is sustainable and enhancing of community life; that regions should tackle their own affairs, adopting policies and programs that are appropriate to the region's characteristics; and that the state then undertakes those responsibilities which cannot, and perhaps should not, be undertaken at any lower level, such as certain infrastructure developments and aspects of governance. Today some writers would add that nations should never become too reliant on the global market and other aspects of globalization.

Back in the 1970s and 1980s, many agencies within the UN were arguing that the world had sufficient resources to meet the basic needs of everyone, but only if development strategies adhered to certain principles. As one UN (UN/ Department of International Economic and Social Affairs, 1982, p. 10) document expressed these principles,

> The principles of "another development" are that it is: (a) geared to the satisfaction of needs, beginning with the eradication of poverty; (b) endogenous and self-reliant, that is, relying on the strengths of the societies undertaking it; and (c) in harmony with the environment.
>
> It is felt that such an approach would stimulate creativity, assure better utilization of factors of production, reduce vulnerability and dependence, enhance self-reliance and self-confidence, and foster dignity.

There is clearly ample support in the literature for self-reliance, and the concept seems logical in every sense. However, much that occurs throughout social development is not designed to promote self-reliance. There are two tendencies that should be borne in mind. One is the tendency to distrust self-reliance; with some governments and agencies distrusting the principle, fearing the implications of giving people excessive control over themselves and their communities. There is quite often a prevailing sense that governments, agencies, professionals, experts, and so on know best what people need, and that, in selecting resources for a project, the focus should be on selecting the best resources available—usually external resources. What is not emphasized is that the use of such resources will maximize profits, employment opportunities, and national pride in its status and achievements: in other words, that there are ulterior motives and vested interests involved in proceeding along these lines. The second tendency is that, in an attempt to promote self-reliance, an organization such as a government may utilize approaches that in practice exclude sections of a population, while assuming that the self-reliance policy is meeting all needs. For example, in the 1990s the Thai government initiated a "credit and loan scheme" designed to achieve self-reliance among the poor. Some research (Senanuch, 2005) suggests, however, that the scheme was not accessible to some of the poorest families, who were consequently left without support. In this case, the policy of community self-reliance imposed an unrealistic measure of individual self-reliance, with often significantly adverse outcomes in poverty terms.

Key Strategies for Achieving Self-reliance

We are unaware of any discussion on strategies, as distinct from policies, for achieving self-reliance, although many of these flow logically from the very nature of the principle. Let us list some of the key ones that appear logical in many circumstances.

Encourage Self-help Groups

Workers can encourage people who express certain needs or aspirations to consider forming a self-help group. Using examples from elsewhere, it is not difficult for people to understand and consider applying the basic idea, but they may require considerable encouragement and support initially until the group begins to function effectively.

Encourage Local Organizational Development

Local organizations are the building blocks of local development and ultimately of an effective civil society. However, they are also essentially self-help groups whose activities promote self-reliance. Strategies for facilitating local organizational development are discussed elsewhere (see Chapter 6); however, it is important to note Chambers's (1993, p. 11) conclusion "that most rural people are more capable of self-reliant organization than most outsiders are conditioned to believe is supported by much evidence."

Community Development

Ife (1995, p. 111) argues in his book on community development that "the aim of community development must ultimately be self-reliance," and this would seem to be right. All aspects of community development are based on the self-reliance principle, whether encouraging local leadership, local organizational development, local productivity and income-generation activities, social cohesion, or improved interaction with the wider society.

Encourage in People a Belief in Themselves and Their Capacities

Whatever their other activities, all local workers can and should be encouraging in people a belief in themselves—in their own capacities to take responsibility for their own situations, whether individually or in groups. Inherent in this is encouraging them to identify local resources and devise ways of utilizing them in improving their own and their community's well-being.

Encourage Appropriate External Agency Approaches

Workers can encourage government and nongovernment agencies and their personnel to be conscious of the dangers associated with excessive dependency, and the advantages of maximizing the utilization of local resources and thus promoting self-reliance. For the most part this will probably be done informally, but at times research and policy proposals may be called for.

Key Strategies for Achieving Self-reliance

- Encourage self-help groups
- Encourage local organizational development
- Community development
- Encourage in people a belief in themselves and their capacities
- Encourage appropriate external agency approaches

Enhancing Social Integration or Social Cohesion

Social cohesion is relevant to the majority of contemporary societies and localities because of the ease and frequency with which populations experience divisions. In the developed world, social cohesion is perhaps most frequently used in relation to divisions based on race, ethnicity, and migration status. In the developing world, the complexity of sources of division is usually much greater. In addition to the above, gender, class, caste, being the occupants of slums or squatter settlements, being rural dwellers, and so on can all result in strong divisions within communities, localities, and nations. These divisions can in turn affect access to various facilities, assets, and opportunities, can result in negative or hostile attitudes within the mainstream toward "undesirable" categories, and can be a source of conflict. Social cohesion is a key to all community and social development.

Enhancing social integration (or social cohesion or social harmony) within particularly racially or ethnically divided societies has become an extremely important focus in recent times, for two main reasons. The first reason is that the great majority of modern societies are heterogeneous, as a result of colonialism, occupation, migration of various kinds, and tourism. Second, most societies have in practice found it difficult to avoid a degree of tension and conflict arising out of their pluralistic nature, and are constantly seeking for the strategies that will bring about a reasonable level of harmony and cohesion.

A heterogeneous society may be such as a result of the coexistence of distinctive racial groupings. South Africa and the United States are good examples, but many societies today are multiracial to some degree, including virtually every western country. In other cases, heterogeneity is a product of the mixing of ethnic groups. This occurred widely on the African continent, as the colonial powers drew lines on a map to signify colonial possessions that paid no heed to ethnic group boundaries. Eventually these colonial territories won independence and became multiethnic states. Elsewhere, ethnic pluralism was a result of either migration or colonial action where colonial powers brought in members of a different ethnic group to fulfill a colonial need (e.g., Malaysia and Fiji). Religious pluralism is another important source of state diversity, and tension has arisen between religious groups in many countries, including Northern Ireland, Lebanon, Israel, Indonesia, India, and Turkey. In practice, it can be difficult to separate ethnic from religious factors, while such factors may also become confused with class, geographical, political, and other factors.

Symbolic of the significance of tension and conflict in heterogeneous countries is the extent of civil war since 1989, with the reality that diversity has been a major factor in the great majority of cases. This is not to say that diversity results inevitably in tension and conflict; the reality is rather that these divisions become significant when either political or socioeconomic realities render them such. Was the Yugoslav war in the early 1990s a war between Bosnians, Croats, and Serbs, or was an ethnic conflict provoked by leaders like Milosevic for political purposes? This confusion between the significance of underlying differences and political, economic, social, and other developments is a common one in recent civil wars. Nevertheless, since 1989 the world has witnessed annually in excess of 30 major civil wars and a much larger number of lower-intensity conflicts. Some of these conflicts have continued for periods well in excess of a decade, while others simmer over a long period with periodic flare-ups (see UNHCR, 1997/1998). The suffering resulting from these conflicts has been truly horrendous, affecting millions of people directly and even more indirectly (see Chapter 9).

However, the overall situation involving social integration, cohesion, and harmony is far more complex than the occurrence of civil wars would suggest. A consideration of the terminology in use will assist our understanding of the scope and diverse nature of the overall problem. *Social harmony* signifies the need for diverse groupings within a common society to live together in peace. The catastrophe to be avoided at all costs is *social conflict,* but even *social tensions* will bring a toll. *Social integration* is commonly applied to the need for newly arrived immigrant groups to find a place for themselves within their new society—a place of acceptance by, and as far as possible of equal opportunities to, the host society. Given the scope of modern migration, this goal is extremely important for both the immigrants involved and ultimately also for the cohesion of the societies of which they are now a part. Finally, *social cohesion* signifies a situation in society where all residents feel themselves to be stakeholders in that society's development, and not marginalized or excluded. This may apply to indigenous minorities, populations such as the Roma peoples of Europe, former immigrants and especially migrant workers and asylum seekers, selected ethnic groups, or people living in certain geographical regions.

In the European green paper on social policy in 1993, it was argued that "social policies now have to take on the more ambitious objective of helping people to find a place in society"—of ensuring that no one is socially or economically excluded (Commission of the European Communities, 1993, pp. 20–21). In reality, social integration, cohesion, and harmony, as commonly used, simply place slightly different slants on the same basic need, namely that of ensuring that all members of all social groupings find a place within a society in ways that are equitable, and ensure a society that is working together to secure the well-being of all. We shall use the term *social cohesion* from here on to signify all of the above objectives, and shall focus on strategies for achieving social cohesion.

Key Strategies for Achieving Social Cohesion

Social cohesion is one of those many objectives requiring action at both the macro and

micro levels; and, as is so often the case, social workers and other practitioners will find themselves working strenuously toward changes at the macro level while at the same time embarking on actions at the local level designed to achieve the same basic goals. Many types of strategies are commonly discussed; let us canvas these briefly.

A Buoyant Economy

This may seem like an unusual one to start with, but it is commonly accepted that a buoyant economy is a major protection against social conflict. In reality, however, the emphasis should be on economic growth with equity. In other words, where the economy is growing and the majority of people feel that they can participate and share in that growth, ethnic and other differences are less likely to surface in a negative sense. By contrast, in times of economic downturn or in the face of blatant economic discrimination against certain groups, ethnic and other tensions are likely to emerge. The editors' introduction, and papers from Siddique and others in Colletta, Lim, and Kelles-Vitanen (2001), constantly make this point in reference to the experience of southeast Asia during the financial and economic crisis of 1997. However, while governments like to place the focus for peace and harmony on economic growth per se, as Colletta et al. (2001, p. 4) point out in their introduction,

> The financial and economic crisis did not so much cause these weaknesses of fragile social cohesion and poor governance. Recent sectarian outbursts of violence in Indonesia and elsewhere in the region raise the question of the very nature of the development process. In the past, successful "market building" has taken precedence over "nation building." Social cohesion should be put back on the agenda as an independent policy goal.

So while economic growth may in practice preserve social harmony, it may in reality be only papering over the cracks of a divided society. When this is the case, an increase in inequality or unemployment, or an increase in interest or inflation rates, or some other economic development may give rise to an upsurge of violence along the fault lines of a pluralistic society.

The essential strategy here is, therefore, to create income-generation and other socioeconomic opportunities for all members of a pluralistic society, while remembering that it will still be necessary to tackle directly the problems potentially associated with diversity.

National Identity and Citizenship Campaigns

It is important that people are more than economic stakeholders. They need also to feel a sense of belonging to the country in which they reside, even though this will often be only one of several types of identity. While a permanent residence visa is a very important step for all newcomers to a country, bestowing citizenship rights is usually even more important, signifying acceptance by other citizens and the state as an entity, and opening the doors to involvement in the life of the state at all levels. The same need exists among members of indigenous minorities and other groups, who in some countries are denied full citizenship rights. The opposite reality to the sense of belonging that comes with citizenship is for people to feel second-class or unwanted in the very country where they are living and on which they depend.

Antidiscrimination Legislation and Policy Arrangements

A key cause of social disharmony is the experience of discrimination and the realities of inequality across many aspects of life. Even though systems seldom function perfectly, it is important for various types of minority group members to know that there is legislation against discrimination, racial vilification, and so on, and that they can appeal to the authorities to correct certain situations. It is also important that governments are doing all they can at the policy level to ensure the maximum possible degree of equality in society. Some governments have introduced affirmative action or positive discrimination policies; others have implemented access and equity procedures across the public and private sectors; and thus governments have sought to ensure that all members of a society have the same access to capacity-building opportunities and to situations where they can use these capacities. There is no doubt that these arrangements can be highly effective; yet it is also clear that, where the same measures do not reflect either government or public commitment, their existence on paper makes virtually no difference. In the end, the vital factor is the extent of the commitment to equality at all levels in a society.

Promotion of Multicultural Society

While the above specific strategies are important, even more important is the basic commitment to building a multiracial, multiethnic, or multicultural society. This involves exploring what multiculturalism means across all levels and areas of society. What are multicultural education, political life, social service delivery, community development, economic development, and legal development? Societies that have embraced multiculturalism have had to study carefully all dimensions of a society's life and development, seeking to apply a set of basic multicultural principles in all that they undertake. There is no blueprint for building a multicultural society. Each society's history, cultural makeup, and prevailing circumstances will largely dictate the way in which it should proceed along this path.

Participatory Democracy

While participatory democracy is a central element of a multicultural society, it is nonetheless important to emphasize it separately. Unless

---

Key Strategies for Achieving Social Cohesion

- A buoyant economy
- National identity and citizenship campaigns
- Antidiscrimination legislation and policy arrangements
- Promotion of multicultural society
- Participatory democracy
- Local-level applications of the above strategies
- Mediation and reconciliation strategies

---

and until a specific marginal population grouping is accepted into the political process, any negative experiences are likely to be blamed on those who wield power—whether an ethnic group, religious group, caste, class, or racial grouping. It is perhaps only when political participation coincides with the cessation of the conditions resulting in negative experience that those concerned will begin to appreciate the full realities of social development. Until participatory democracy is achieved, those who feel marginalized have a ready-made reason for blaming others for their condition, and therefore neglecting to take whatever action is in reality open to them. Participatory democracy is not a panacea for social cohesion, but it may be a necessary precondition.

Local-level Applications of the Above Strategies

While the above strategies are couched in macro-level terms, and so are largely applicable at the state level, it needs to be emphasized that they all have their equivalent at the micro or local level. The strategies are not always as clear-cut at the local level, but local-level income-generation, participatory politics, multicultural development, prosocial cohesion policies, and action against discrimination are all feasible and important. The means of pursuing and implementing them will depend entirely on a careful assessment of local conditions, and so the means

are likely to vary greatly, but as goals these are of central importance to building social cohesion at the local level.

Mediation and Reconciliation Strategies

In postconflict situations in particular, but sometimes also in others such as in the relationships between an indigenous minority and the dominant social grouping, it is important for workers to consider the need to develop strategies that will address past causes of enmity and division, and seek to bring sectional groupings into an acceptance of each other's presence and of the need to work together in harmony in building a community for all. How precisely such strategies are implemented may well be a challenge to the local worker. While some writers draw on the mediation and industrial relations literature, others suggest that this type of reconciliation represents largely uncharted waters for the helping professions (see Chapter 10).

Income-generation

There are many situations in the developing world where income-generation is the core basis of well-being. Many people in developing countries have had to, and still have to, survive on minimal resources, leaving them highly vulnerable to even minor changes in their environment; or they exist in poverty with all of the consequences of a hard life and low life expectancy; or they have faced or face situations of absolute destruction, such as conflict or a natural disaster can create, and are left completely dependent on outsiders. In such situations, aid is frequently essential as a short-term measure, but neither the practicalities of aid delivery nor the common impact of prolonged aid on people and communities will allow this to be a long-term solution. The alternative to aid in all such situations, or at least the step that must follow it, is providing people with the opportunities to earn an income sufficient for at least basic well-being—and such is the key goal of income-generation strategies.

It follows that income-generation measures constitute a key component of local-level development in poorer areas, poverty alleviation programs, postconflict reconstruction, and recovery from natural disasters. Even the plight of displaced persons may be able to be ameliorated by the creation of income-generation opportunities, during the period of displacement, on return home, and if resettled in third countries. In some situations, the objective of programs will be to improve the income-generation opportunities already available to people, in others to enable people to return to income-generation measures utilized in the past, and, probably in a majority of situations, to identify and make possible completely new income-generation measures. Without differentiating between the range of situations requiring income-generation initiatives, although in the field such differentiation is very important, let us consider the types of income-generation programs commonly employed.

In presenting the following income-generation strategies, we accept to a degree the common belief that an expanding economy should ultimately provide income-generation opportunities for all, but we stress the "should." As many commentators point out, and perhaps most vividly the UNDP (1996b), while economic growth is a necessary condition for significant employment generation and adequate income

levels, it is not a sufficient condition. Much depends on the nature and distribution of the economic growth. In this context and with the situations that we have in mind, we are assuming that either economic growth is minimal or it is not available to a particular population or in a given area. Workers in such situations in the field are, therefore, seeking to enhance income generation at the local level, utilizing usually minimal local resources and external inputs.

In addition to economic policy, there are other areas of government policy of indirect relevance to income-generation programs at the local level. Some key examples of these are land redistribution and utilization policies, and the development of national marketing infrastructure. The reality, however, is that even where such policies are initiated by central governments, their application at the local level in at least the poorer areas depends often on the initiatives taken by local workers.

Key Types of Income-generation Strategies

There are many situations in the field where poorer people are eking out a living by harvesting a local resource, either exclusively for consumption or also for income purposes. They will often be engaged in agriculture or fishing, but may also be engaged in some home-based production for the local market. Workers will be concerned by those situations where either the food harvested or the income achieved is insufficient for an adequate level of well-being, or is too precarious a source for people to depend on. They may also be aware that the input of some knowledge and training may make a significant difference to either the amount of food or income generated (or both) and to the dependability of the source. Let us consider a few examples.

Contributing Knowledge and Training to Existing Income-generation Enterprises

Agricultural extension workers and others have made a significant contribution to the well-being of people dependent on agriculture by sharing with them some knowledge relevant to the type of agricultural production being undertaken. They may suggest a new variety of seed, a simple irrigation system, a cash crop that can be produced in addition to basic food production, or improved basic tools. Sharing such knowledge and providing related training may result in higher yields (perhaps allowing a surplus for sale), more harvests per year, or additional income for minimal outlays. Sometimes the necessary resources may be already available through a government department without this fact being known to local people. In the area of fishing, a good example is the introduction of artificial reefs for breeding fish and some training in sustainable harvesting of fish stocks. Inland the focus may be on better utilization of fish ponds to produce, with minimal land, a regular and valuable source of protein or a highly marketable commodity.

Such initiatives are not the sole prerogative of agricultural personnel, who are, however, likely to be responsible for researching and making known such initiatives. In most situations, the actual dissemination of knowledge and training will be undertaken by local grassroots workers, whose numbers should include social workers.

Introducing Microcredit Schemes and People's Banks

To become a productive member of a community, and in so doing provide for oneself and one's dependents, requires access to a range of assets. For the landless poor in rural areas and those in urban areas with no assets other than their own labor, access to capital becomes vital. The sum required may be extremely small, but the reality is that it will not be provided to such clients by traditional banking systems, while the alternative of moneylenders leaves the poor vulnerable to exploitation of often extreme kinds. What has been seen to be clearly required is a system of loans provided without any surety and on terms that suit the purposes to which the money is being put.

With a little capital, poor persons may purchase some goods at the market or from fishermen on the beach and sell those goods elsewhere for a slight profit; or they might purchase an animal for income purposes (e.g., selling milk), or from which to breed and sell the offspring; or they may purchase some basic supplies and make something in their homes which they can then sell; or they may set up a stall on the street to sell their own cooked food to passers-by. There are in practice many opportunities for the poor to make a little money—assuming they have basic health and reasonable stability in their lives—provided that they have access to credit.

Hence a major initiative in development and poverty alleviation programs has been the establishment of credit schemes designed to meet the needs of low-income people. Some of these schemes have been set up as alternative institutional banking structures (e.g., the Grameen Bank of Bangladesh), and, while such have their place, the focus here is on schemes that are run by the people themselves. Community-based credit schemes can acquire their basic funds in one of two ways. Either the community acquires a small grant for this purpose from an aid agency, or the members of the scheme institute a savings scheme whereby they together create a pool of money from which individual members can borrow.

In the first approach, a community group receives a grant from which its members can borrow. A committee is formed to organize the scheme, but it is the members who make the decisions regarding loans, interest to be paid, and so on. In the second approach, a major emphasis is placed on savings methods, for the basic idea of poor people saving is on the face of it ludicrous. However, such schemes encourage members to devise, and share with other members, strategies for saving a few cents every week. These savings soon mount to a sufficient amount for individual members to put forward ideas for small income-generation projects requiring a loan. The group approves the application. In both approaches, a key program element is that the members take a vital interest in the progress of each enterprise funded. This interest is in reality a form of social or peer pressure on the borrower to be successful and eventually repay the loan, so that it is not surprising that repayment rates are invariably in excess of 90 percent. However, the interest in each borrower's enterprise is also an important source of social learning and support. Members learn from each other what can be done, how to handle certain occurrences, and the advantages of mutual support. Finally, the nature of fellow members' interest in each enterprise gives individuals confidence and a sense that they are not engaging in something alone. If things go wrong there are people around to make suggestions, the experience of others on which to draw, and a sense that one is not facing the problem alone or with an unsympathetic moneylender breathing down one's neck.

The importance and success of many such schemes cannot be overemphasized. Moreover, they are not resource-intensive. In some places, local poor people have picked up the idea and implemented it relatively unaided. More frequently, there has been a worker present to advise and encourage people to form such a scheme. The savings often used represent a resource possessed by the poor of which all had been unaware, and the grants sometimes used are minute in each case, especially compared with the expenditure on many aid projects carried out by well-paid experts. Finally, the ongoing organization of the scheme is provided by the people themselves, being therefore not only cheap but an excellent source of capability building and empowerment. (Discussions on credit schemes are numerous, but they include Hulme and Montgomery, 1995; IFAD, 1985; Chambers, 1993; and several articles in *Social Development Issues,* volume 25, numbers 1 and 2 [2003], devoted to this subject. For a discussion of microcredit or asset building in the United States, see Sherraden, 1991. For examples of credit schemes and people's banks, see Chapter 6.)

The Facilitation of Microenterprise Schemes

While the poor are themselves initiating very small microenterprises with the assistance of credit schemes, knowledge-building, and their newfound confidence, the poverty alleviation strategy itself may rely on the initiation of a microenterprise in which a large number of the poor may participate. In close consultation with the people, workers look for a microenterprise where there is a market for the product and where the skills and other inputs involved are within the current or future capabilities of the poor. These microenterprises require a certain amount of central planning and organization, and of course funding, but are essentially composed of a large number of very small units that individual households can operate, except for the need to draw on the centralized structures. Such enterprises are perhaps best run by an NGO adopting a highly consultative approach, while possessing the strengths and resources to make a success of the implementation of the plan.

Some well-known microenterprise schemes in the Asian region have revolved around, for example, the poultry industry and rabbit production. In regard to the former, one scheme in Bangladesh (UN/ESCAP, 1996a, pp. 1–9) trained individual women to play specific roles in the industry as relatively autonomous units, in close collaboration with other women playing other roles, but with the roles clearly demarcated, training arranged, prices of goods and services established centrally, the women well supported, and the fundamentals of the program protected by the NGO involved. Many thousands of women had their poverty alleviated through this scheme. An example of the rabbit production scheme is one in the People's Republic of China that involved poor households breeding rabbits for sale to a central factory at a set price where the rabbits were processed for the market. The households were set up and supported in a range of ways but operated largely independently.

A second form of microenterprise is that of the worker-owned enterprise. One example of this in the Philippines involved a significant number of poor families being taught to manufacture the separate components for an inexpensive form of housing developed by a western NGO. Once the families had agreed to become involved in this microenterprise, they were taught the skills involved and given credit to establish the business. They proceeded to establish a very successful collective enterprise, repay their loan, and raise their families out of poverty. At the same time, they were providing many other families with a form of housing that was both inexpensive and well suited to the environment of the country.

Microenterprises thus involve initially someone or some NGO formulating a plan for such. The plan is then discussed with families who might be interested and goes ahead only if sufficient members decide to be involved. The roles of the NGO from then on are facilitative and supportive, in terms of arranging training and providing credit as necessary and support until the program is well under way. Essentially it is the poor themselves who eventually run the program, at least to a significant degree, and through the income-generation potential of the program are able to enhance the well-being of their families. It is extremely important that the program is a sustainable one, possessing a long-term potential to provide income, and demanding inputs from the families concerned that are not beyond their potential.

Microenterprises will tend to be part of the informal economy, and it may be difficult early in the development process to impose standards common in the formal economy. It may also be important to watch that the microenterprise does not compete with the formal economy in ways that will bring resentment and a backlash. They should be essentially complementary to the formal economy, which will in any case often

be in only embryonic form in the places where such microenterprises can flourish. Given, however, that it has proved impossible to find income-generation opportunities within the formal economy for the majority of people in most countries, this focus on an alternative economy would seem essential and far better than the welfare alternative, which is, in any case, usually not feasible. (For a detailed discussion of social work and microenterprises, see Livermore, 1996.)

The Encouragement of Collective Action

In many communities facing underdevelopment and poverty, needs exist that can only or best be met by people working together to do so. A community may be faced with an environmental disaster emanating from a practice that community members have engaged in for a long time, and the solution may need to come from the community itself. A population of farmers may be finding it impossible to handle certain aspects of the work as individual farmers, and the answer may well lie in the farmers uniting to assist each other in turn. A community may be confronted with a social or health problem, such as drug addiction, HIV/AIDS, or water-related diseases, rendering the best response one undertaken by the community working as far as possible as a whole (usually referred to as *community-based service delivery*). A group of producers may face a long walk to the market to sell their produce, and may find it preferable that they take it in turns to convey everyone's produce to market in a vehicle obtained collectively for the purpose, and perhaps using a track that the producers together construct.

There are many examples of the best response to a situation being a community one. The question then is, will the people involved spontaneously come to this decision, or does the initial concept need to be put forward by a development or community worker who, as an outsider, can see the need for and potential of a

---

Key Income Generation Strategies

- Contributing knowledge and training to existing income generation enterprises.

- Introduce microcredit schemes and people's banks.

- Facilitate microenterprise schemes.

- Encourage collective action.

---

community-based response? The challenge for the worker is then to find ways of putting forward the idea that will give the people involved full rein to reach their own decision on the matter. It may be preferable to let members of the community see what other communities have achieved around a similar problem; it may be best to bring those involved together to discuss the problems and leave it for them to suggest solutions; or the worker may be convinced that it is preferable to be proactive and put forward a proposal. The process will depend on the worker's perception of cultural and other factors involved in the situation.

Community-based responses reflect the self-reliance principle while recognizing that the resources do not exist for sending appropriate professional workers and other essential resources into each and every poor community. If communities can themselves come to appreciate and take control of communitywide problems, the chances are that the experience of doing so will lead that community to initiate many other areas of activity.

Community Development

We address the strategy of community development (and community-based development) last in this chapter because it is a much broader strategy than the previous ones covered, and indeed potentially incorporates all of them within an integrated response to a wide range of situations. Campfens (1997), in the only recent international review of community development

known to us, provides some important insights in this regard. Regarding the first point, community development is commonly regarded as empowering (e.g., Campfens, 1997, p. 461), involving capacity building, focusing on self-help and self-reliance (Campfens, p. 462), concerned with questions of social cohesion (Campfens, p. 448), and either facilitating or utilizing income-generation strategies. In regard to the second point, community development is clearly a critical dimension of development and a basic tool for achieving social development (Stoesz, Guzzetta, and Lusk, 1999, chap. 7); is commonly included in postconflict reconstruction as community rebuilding; is utilized in a displacement context; and is certainly a key strategy in poverty alleviation. Indeed, it is difficult to envisage an aspect of international social work in which community development does not potentially play a vital role.

Before addressing community development as a strategy in international social work, we need to dwell a little on the meaning and significance of the concept. First, there is the question of terminology, with the diverse terminology reflecting the changes that have occurred in the conceptualization of community development. Ife (1995, p. 1) begins his discussion of community development by stating: "There is no clear agreement on the nature of the activity which is described as community work." Confusion in the terminology used is, he points out, reflected in the following list of common terms: "community work, community development, community organization, community action, community participation and community change." Outside social work, there is some confusion between *community development, social development, locality development, local-level development,* and *community-based development.* How do these terms relate to each other?

Let us commence by considering some definitions of community development advanced by recent writers who include in their discussion a consideration of social development. Stoesz et al. (1999, p. 129) write of community development: "'Community development' embodies the concept that collectivities of people who share common concerns have the potential capacity to deal jointly with those concerns in ways that advance the common interest."

In regard to the relationship between community development and social development, these authors suggest that "it is generally agreed that community development included social development, but they are not the same" (p. 129). While agreeing with other writers that community development can be described as "a method, a program, a movement, a process of change, and the preparation for change," they also agree that "the fundamental element in community development is change and that the intended change is always in a consciously chosen direction" (p. 130). They go on to make the important point that this focus on change renders community development essentially a political activity.

Campfens (1997, p. 20) agrees that community development constitutes essentially "the process of planned change," but that over time the nature of community development has changed from a process dominated by central authorities to "a more pluralistic and participatory approach to planning in which state agencies function more in partnership with NGOs and Community Organizations" (p. 21). Campfens's outline of what is community development reflects the complexity he sees in the use and practice related to the term worldwide:

Simply put, community development is a demonstration of the ideas, values and ideals of the society in which it is carried out. From a humanitarian perspective, it may be seen as a search for community, mutual aid, social

support, and human liberation in an alienating, oppressive, competitive, and individualistic society. In its more pragmatic institutional sense, it may be viewed as a means for mobilizing communities to join state or institutional initiatives that are aimed at alleviating poverty, solving social problems, strengthening families, fostering democracy, and achieving modernization and socio-economic development. (p. 25)

Regarding social development, Campfens's response is in effect that a wide range of understandings of, or at least types of approaches to, community development coexist, one of which is virtually synonymous with social development.

As a final example of a recent definition of community development, Ife (1995, p. 2) describes his approach:

This book . . . seeks to locate community work and community-based services within a broader context of an approach to community development. This latter term is seen as the process of establishing, or re-establishing, structures of human community within which new ways of relating, organizing social life and meeting human need become possible. In this context, community work is seen as the activity, or practice, of a person who seeks to facilitate that process of community development, whether or not that person is actually paid for filling that role. Community-based services are seen as structures and processes for meeting human need, drawing on the resources, expertise and wisdom of the community itself.

He also considers the question of the relationship between community development and social development, concluding,

Much of what is traditionally regarded as community development, in occupations such as social work, youth work, education and the health professions, can be understood as social development. (p. 133)

Before considering what are being presented as the key elements of community development today, we should note the consensus of these and other authors that community development has changed quite radically over recent decades. In their consideration of the historical background of community development, Stoesz et al. (1999, pp. 131ff.) begin by noting that community development really dates back to "mutual protection and economic enhancement" institutions found in most peasant societies, and to the activities of early religious communities. Post–World War II community development was basically a strategy for helping less developed countries to achieve self-sufficiency and political stability, although the authors point out that a range of quite different community development models in this period are presented in the literature. In relation to developing countries, these authors state,

> Historically, community development in developing countries has tended to be primarily (but not exclusively) local, relatively small-scale activity involving village-level workers, sometimes with outside assistance, although with the potential, through net-working, to expand into large-scale movements. By the middle of the 1960s, it was beginning to be replaced by "national planning" schemes but rebounded in the 1970s as "participatory development." (Stoesz et al., 1999, p. 145)

They go on to contrast this approach to the situation that applied in developed countries, especially the United States.

Campfens (1997, p. 17) highlights that historically, in the 1960s,

> CD [community development] programs were established to mobilize people in their local communities as an integral part of the five-year plans masterminded by national planners and operating under a centralized system of management and resource allocation. This model, adopted in much of South America and other Third World regions, was an unequivocal failure. . . .

Yet despite their failures, state-initiated and -administered CD programs continued to hold an appeal, especially among governments that, faced with heavy debt loads and limited capital resources, were looking for low-cost alternatives for meeting basic human and community needs.

Later in the text, Campfens suggests that early rural community development programs "favoured the rural elite and failed to reach landless, poor women, unemployed young people, and small farmers" (p. 453). These community development programs tended to be state-initiated. Other writers agree that most early large-scale and government-initiated community development programs in the developing world were a failure (e.g., Dore and Mars, 1981). It was presumably an appreciation of this history of failure that led to the temporary sidelining of community development; and, when it was revived, to changing the focus to a locality development model of community development, and one very different from what had earlier prevailed (Campfens, 1997, p. 449). The new focus was on a "bottom-up approach to effecting change at the neighborhood and regional level," based on partnerships between states, NGOs, and local organizations. Campfens (1997, p. 450) writes,

> These policies were aimed at revitalizing local communities, at fostering citizen participation, and at encouraging the economically and socially excluded (as organized groups) to get involved in improving their living conditions. This has led to a strong resurgence of interest in CD and in the training of community workers.

Campfens points out that, while traditionally it was the state that initiated community development and "sought local and community participation," in recent times "autonomous grassroots groups are now 'spontaneously' emerging to engage in community action" (p. 452). Furthermore, Campfens also found "that community development practice is moving away from a singular preoccupation with the local community, and toward a strategy that incorporates multiple targets" (p. 454). Finally, in this new model of community development, NGOs possessed a vital enabling role through which they "merged their own efforts with those of others" as "mediating institutions," utilizing a highly people-centered and participatory approach (p. 463).

Let us draw this discussion together by presenting our understanding of community development. The key for us can be seen in comments from two of our sources. Campfens (1997, p. 460) comments that "participation is the sine qua non of CD"; and Ife (1995, p. 131) writes that "the purpose of community development is to re-establish the community as the location of significant human experience and the meeting of human need." Community development must be participatory, and to be such it needs to operate at the community or locality level. We prefer to retain the term *social development* for Campfens's (p. 455) first type of approach to CD, viewing social development as a comprehensive and integrated approach to the development of society as a whole. Similarly, we prefer to use *social integration* and *social cohesion* as covering the programs and strategies that focus on intergroup relations (Campfens's eighth type of approach to CD). Locality development, Campfens's third type, we regard as synonymous with community development, its advantage being that it gets past the common debate on what is community in the modern world. The categorical concept—focusing on a category of people, Campfens's fifth type of approach to CD—we regard as an essential aspect of community development in many contexts. It highlights the existence within many communities or localities of categories of significantly disadvantaged, alienated, or excluded people, whose development may need to be initially tackled at the group or category level. Similarly, we would incorporate another two of Campfens's types within our concept of community development; namely, the

self-management concept "in which CD takes a bottom-up empowering approach to the development of communities or groups," and the social learning or educational concept of CD "which brings together professional experts, with their 'universal knowledge,' and the local residents with their popular knowledge and lived experience."

Key Strategies to Involve People in Community Development

This brings us to the question of programs and strategies for furthering community development. In the following discussion, we are very aware that, in terms of Stoesz et al.'s (1999, p. 129) depiction of community development as "process, method, program and movement," our focus is essentially on process. A wide range of methods and programs will potentially be utilized, but the critical issues are of a process nature.

Cultivate Desire and Commitment to Change

First, it is clear that community development is driven by a desire to change a situation along certain lines. Commonly, the intentions will include promoting human rights and social justice, helping a community to become more inclusive (i.e., promoting social cohesion), and finding ways that will enhance collective and individual well-being. This can clearly be a highly political process, especially if other sections of that society are for any reason opposed to such changes.

Identify the Marginalized People Within a Community

We would also stress the importance within community development of first identifying any categories of people who have traditionally been marginalized or excluded, and who are likely to continue to be within a process of community development unless special steps are taken to

> **Key Strategies to Involve People in Community Development**
>
> - Cultivate desire and commitment to change.
> - Identify the marginalized people within a community.
> - Use the process of empowerment, participation, and building local organizations.
> - Work within the wider context of cultural and political realities.

avoid this. The strategy of strengthening such categories of people by engaging in a category-based approach to community development may well be critical. However, depending on the nature of the prevailing community relations, such efforts may be misunderstood and resented by the wider community unless simultaneous action is taken to improve social integration and social cohesion at that wider level.

Use the Process of Empowerment, Participation, and Building Local Organizations

The core of the community development process stresses empowerment, participation, and building local organizations. The key here is involving people within an approach that is empowering—whatever else is taking place. Participation, however, also means that people are encouraged to take the leading role in identifying their needs, suggesting strategies for meeting these, and participating fully in whatever action follows. This overall process is furthered by local organization building, for it is within these local organizations that local people pool their expertise, develop a better understanding and appreciation of each other, and establish strong bases on which to move ahead. While no community is likely to be completely self-sufficient, or should be, there will be a strong focus within this process on community self-reliance and the utilization of community-based initiatives.

Work Within the Wider Context of Cultural and Political Realities

Finally, we would emphasize that the whole process of community development occurs within, and must be seen to occur within, a wider context. Community development workers need to be highly aware of this, and ready to tailor the specific approach they adopt to the prevailing reality, especially at the cultural and political levels. Moreover, local community members need to become highly aware of their wider context, whether as a resource source, in terms of their potential participation within it, or as a past or present source of oppression, exploitation, or opposition to their advancement.

Conclusion

All of the above programs and strategies will play roles within each of the fields of international social work discussed in the following chapters. Moreover, it is in those chapters that we shall provide field examples showing how the above strategies are incorporated into each of the fields of action covered in this text. The strategies included in this chapter are thus basic strategies of relevance across the breadth of international social work and of basic importance.

Summary

- Empowerment is a key principle and strategy in international social work practice. Although the concept is contentious, it can be effectively employed in work with individuals, families, groups, communities, organizations, and institutions to enable them to gain control over their lives and environment.

- Capacity building is an important strategy that facilitates development or well-being of the whole society. It is closely connected to several related principles and covers varied capacities and targets from individual to organizational levels in social work and development practice.

- Although no community can be self-reliant in the contemporary globalized world, the principle of self-reliance and the use of self-help groups are prominent in social work and development practice. Social workers need to use several strategies to promote and practice self-help and self-reliance as these help to counter overdependence on external factors.

- Societies experiencing frequent tensions and conflicts require proactive strategies to maintain social cohesion and integration. Democratic, sociolegal, and economic strategies, and multicultural values both at micro and macro levels, may facilitate social cohesion.

- Income generation strategies and programs have played a key role in enhancing income and quality of life of specific populations trapped into poverty and other related difficult circumstances. Social workers can contribute to further building these strategies and programs by providing intellectual and training inputs and by facilitating microcredit schemes, microenterprises, and collective action, if needed.

- Community development, though contentious in terms of concept, is a broad and important strategy that incorporates several other strategies and emphasizes a particular process involving change, that addresses the plight of most oppressed and deprived populations by empowering them, and that adopts participatory and local organization approaches within a wider socioeconomic and political context.

Questions and Topics for Discussion

- Using different concepts of empowerment, summarize your understanding of empowerment.
- Despite large macroeconomic development programs, why do you think local-level economic activities and income-generation programs are needed?
- What do you think capacity building should cover at individual, group, community, and organization levels?
- If you were given the task of capacity building, what kind of approach would you follow?
- Why do you think there is so much emphasis on self-help and self-reliance in development practice?
- As an external worker, what precautions would you take to encourage self-help and self-reliance of communities?
- Critically review the strategies for self-reliance.
- Why do heterogeneous societies often experience social tension, conflict, and civil wars?
- Critically review strategies suggested to enhance social cohesion. Do you agree with them?
- Critically review key income-generation programs presented in this chapter. As a social worker, which of the income-generation programs would you prefer to initiate?
- How do you understand community development as a concept and a broad strategy?
- What is the process involved in community development and why is such a process important?
- Discuss community development as a strategy, as a process, and as a goal.

Possible Areas for Research Projects

- In a specific local development context, analyze various strategies employed to facilitate community development, and evaluate the impact of the strategies on individuals and communities.
- Document the application of strategies and programs presented in this chapter in terms of the process and outcome.
- Locate two case studies of community development, one emerging from central initiatives and another involving grassroots-level efforts and participatory approaches, and compare the two by analyzing the processes involved.
- Carry out a comparative analysis of the process of application of these strategies and their likely outcomes in one of the following contexts: a poverty alleviation situation, postconflict reconstruction, recovery from natural disasters, and forced displacements.

Further Reading

Campfens, H. (Ed.). (1997). *Community development around the world: Practice, theory, research, training.* Toronto, Canada: University of Toronto Press.

Freire, P. (1972). *Pedagogy of the oppressed.* London: Sheed and Ward.

Hulme, D., & Montgomery, R. (1995). Co-operatives, credit and the rural poor. In J. Mullen (Ed.), *Rural poverty alleviation* (pp. 99–118). Aldershot, England: Avebury.

Lee, J. A. (2001). *The empowerment approach to social work practice.* New York: Columbia University Press (see Chapter 3).

Mondros, J. B., & Wilson, S. M. (1994). *Organizing for power and empowerment.* New York: Columbia University Press.

Social Development Issues, 25(1/2), 2003.

United Nations. (1995). *World summit for social development report.* New York: Author (pp. 66–81).

5

The Field of Development: Background and Issues

The purpose of this and the following chapter is to present local-level development as a field of international social work. This chapter provides a brief introduction to the overall development field. It is a vast and complex field to which many text and other books, along with a wide range of journals and reports, are devoted. And while it is true that social workers are and should be involved across the whole spectrum of development work, given our focus on developing countries in this text we have elected to concentrate on but one aspect of this broad field, namely local-level development (grassroots level community development), for several reasons. First, the majority of social workers in developing countries working in the development field are focused on local-level development. Second, this is the level at which social work expertise most clearly applies, which is not to deny social work's relevance at other levels. Third, the local level is the one most likely to be neglected both in the key texts on development and by many of those in the field responsible for development work—especially those local levels where poverty is concentrated and marginalized populations are to be found. It

is, therefore, appropriate for all of these reasons that we focus our discussion at the local level.

We have elected to introduce development in this chapter by presenting the various paths to achieving development, dividing these basically into three categories, namely, imposed development, where agents external to the state play the dominant role; state-controlled development, where development is a state-initiated and -directed process, often described as a top-down approach that focuses on macroeconomic and political policy, but with assumed implications at the micro level; and externally assisted development, or the tendency for development in many contexts to be dependent on external aid and investment.

Imposed development, as an ongoing process, is perhaps not all that relevant today, although there remain many who believe that western countries control the development process to their own advantage (e.g., Monbiot, 2003; Hoogvelt, 2001; Korten, 1995). Certainly western countries do wield considerable power, given the nature of trade, investment, and aid patterns and institutional structures. However,

Learning Objectives

The objective of this chapter is to encourage readers to think about the major paths to international development followed over the last 50 years, and to explain the importance of local-level development within the overall development process. Toward this end, the aim is to develop a beginning understanding of

- The legacy of past development trends, especially imposed development in the context of colonization and neocolonization.
- The various state-devised paths to development.
- The role in development of external aid.
- The need for local-level development.

the relevance of imposed development lies also in the legacy of colonial history, as is discussed later. Externally assisted development has constituted a significant aspect of development since the end of World War II and continues to do so. Most states, however, also play a crucial role in their own development, despite their colonial or other heritage and the importance to them of external aid; and many international agencies are involved in assisting states to strengthen their development roles.

Following our brief overview of the nature of, and current issues associated with, these three categories of paths, we discuss local-level development. This is presented partly as an alternative to the above approaches but, more important, as an essential complementary approach that is all too often devalued. The following chapter then presents some of the key programs and strategies through which local-level development is pursued.

Global Development Since 1945: The Various Paths to Development

In his excellent history of the "short twentieth century 1914–1991," Eric Hobsbaum (1995) outlines the extent and range of changes that occurred around the world in the 1914–1991 period. At the end of the Second World War, large numbers of peoples lived under colonial control in largely rural agrarian countries, where the norm was subsistence living in extended family groups having little contact with the world beyond. By the end of the century, all this had changed. The great majority of those subject to colonial rule had secured independence, and the changing fortunes of the greatly increased number of states impacted significantly on the lives of the majority of people. Hobsbaum's "golden years" of 1950 through 1973 (1995, chap. 9), with its massive economic growth and rapidly expanding globalization, while essentially belonging to the developed capitalist countries, was in other ways a worldwide phenomenon affecting in various ways almost the entire global population. Much of the developing world, sometimes gradually and sometimes not so gradually, was becoming more industrialized, more urbanized, more populated by individuals and nuclear families rather than extended families, more consumption- oriented, more engaged in various forms of migration, and more connected to global communication, economic, cultural, technological, and other systems. Its classes of well-educated or middle-class people, whose numbers were, in many countries, growing rapidly, and its large youth populations were certainly increasingly a part of the global village, and the many others who did not feel themselves to be a part of that world, and who were certainly not sharing in its affluence, were nevertheless being drawn into its webs, for good or bad. On the positive side, for example, health and education levels rose, often dramatically, while on the negative side many peoples became increasingly subject to the vagaries of the global marketplace and financial crises, to the growing wave of political instability and conflict, and to poor governance.

Many of the massive and widespread changes that hit the developing countries were due to their colonial past; others were the repercussions of changes occurring in the industrialized developed world; others again, however, were the outcome of a concerted effort to develop on the part of many developing states, and a major drive to facilitate that development by the developed industrialized countries. Beginning with the American Marshall Plan to reconstruct Europe and the U.S. efforts to build a strong Japanese economy, along with the establishment of the international economic agencies of the World Bank (WB) and International Monetary Fund (IMF), the development enterprise grew exponentially in the decades after World War II. Large sums of money were channeled into development through the international economic agencies, the various agencies of the United Nations (UN) such as the United Nations Development Programme (UNDP) and the World Food Programme (WFP), the international aid programs of virtually all western countries, and the rapidly expanding number of nongovernmental organizations (NGOs) engaged in development work. As Todaro (1997, p. 547) puts it: "The money volume of official development assistance (ODA), which includes bilateral grants, loans, and technical assistance as well as multilateral flows, has grown from an annual rate of $4.6 billion in 1960 to $58 billion in 1992."

By 1999, however, the annual rate had fallen slightly to $56 billion; while in terms of developed countries' GNP, the percentage allocated to ODA had declined steadily from 0.51 percent in 1960

to 0.29 percent in 1999 (Todaro and Smith, 2003, p. 648). The Organisation for Economic Co-operation and Development (OECD) reported in 2005 that, in 2003, a total of $69 billion had been provided in ODA, and that only five (all European) countries met the 0.7 percent of gross national product (GNP) target set by the UN. This flow of ODA is in itself a highly controversial topic. (See Goulet, 1995, on the ethics of development.) Concerns are frequently expressed regarding, for example, the proportion provided in loans with debt burden consequences (see George, 1988), the strings attached to much ODA, the use of ODA to influence developing countries' political and economic decisions, including the highly controversial structural adjustment programs of the IMF, the amounts of ODA diverted from their goal by corruption, and the dependency burden that can flow from ODA. ODA also has much to do with resulting inequalities (Seabrook, 1993; Thompson, 2003). Todaro (1997, pp. 551–554) and Todaro and Smith (2003, pp. 648–660) provide a useful discussion on why donor countries provide aid and less developed countries accept it. (On ODA, see also Randel and German, 1997, pp. 247–257.)

Development aid, post–World War II, gave rise to what some refer to as the development industry. The UN, national governments, and others embarked on a massive program of development aid of various kinds; a large literature was produced on the topic; and events gave rise to what Todaro (1997, p. 7) calls development economics. Arguing that development economics is not the same as the economics of either advanced capitalist nations or centralized socialist countries, he writes,

> It [development economics] is nothing more or less than the economics of contemporary poor, underdeveloped, Third World nations with varying ideological orientations, diverse cultural backgrounds, and very complex yet similar economic problems that usually demand new ideas and novel approaches.

Todaro proceeds to analyze the meaning of development, the common characteristics of developing countries, and the nature of development economics, and we commend this analysis to social work students and practitioners. It is helpful at this point to reproduce Todaro's (1997, p. 16) definition of development in full:

> Development must therefore be conceived of as a multidimensional process involving major changes in social structures, popular attitudes, and national institutions, as well as the acceleration of economic growth, the reduction of inequality, and the eradication of poverty. Development, in its essence, must represent the whole gamut of change by which an entire social system, tuned to the diverse basic needs and desires of the individuals and social groups within that system, moves away from a condition of life widely perceived as unsatisfactory toward a situation or condition of life regarded as materially and spiritually better.

We should appreciate that Todaro has arrived at this definition after long involvement in studying and writing about development. Has the world achieved over the last 60 years the development implied in Todaro's definition? His work, and that of many others, shows that there have been a variety of "paths to development" endorsed over the 50-odd years of post–World War II global development efforts. Easterly (2002), for example, identifies and analyzes a number of paths to development within what he considers to be an "elusive quest for growth." His "paths," however, are confined to economic theories of development. Other writers, like So (1990), present their discussion of "paths" in terms of the various schools of development thought.

We have developed our own typology of paths to development. It is not a comprehensive typology but rather one that enables social workers to become aware of certain trends and related issues in this field, and also to enable newcomers to this field to find their way around this complex and large literature and field of endeavor. We shall consider the selected paths because a general knowledge of each is highly advantageous to workers involved in development, and particularly local-level development. We are not implying that the paths discussed are inherently good or bad, right or wrong, but rather that each, apart from imposed development, represents an important approach to development, often depending on whether that specific approach is complemented by other approaches adopted simultaneously or addressed in the past.

Imposed Development

Imposed development occurs where the course of development is controlled, or strongly influenced, by outside players. We shall consider briefly three forms of imposed development: that which occurred during the colonial period, that strongly influenced by neocolonialism— "the continuation of the colonial system in spite of formal recognition of political independence" (Hoogvelt, 2001, p. 30), and development imposed by the IMF's Structural Adjustment Programs. (See Hoogvelt, 2001, for a comprehensive critical analysis of the history of the political economy of development.) However, we should recognize that the term has also been applied to even the provision of humanitarian aid (e.g., Harrell-Bond, 1986, whose work on emergency assistance to refugees is called *Imposing Aid*), implying that it can have relevance at the micro level.

Development Under Colonialism

The colonial period occurred between 1500 and, according to some analysts, 1973, with various phases identified during this period (So, 1990, pp. 208ff.). While colonialism and its impact are often discussed in generalities, as Randall and Theobald (1998, pp. 11ff.) point out, it was in fact an "enormously varied experience." This variation, these authors suggest, was due to three factors: the approach adopted by the colonizing power, the nature of the preexisting society, and the way in which colonial rule ended (p. 12). Smith (1983, pp. 30–32) discusses the differences between the colonizing powers, and this is obviously a very important factor in recent developments in the former colonies, especially in Africa, while the manner in which colonial powers withdrew is frequently discussed as often problematic.

There are several characteristics of colonialism that should be noted (see Potter, 1992). One important point is that the establishment and maintenance of colonies usually involved active aggression toward, and the subjugation of, the inhabitants of the colonies (Hoogvelt, 2001). A second important point is that the boundaries and ethnic composition of many modern states are a direct outcome of the colonial powers engaging in territorial demarcation (Smith, 1983, p. 27). For example, in relation to what occurred in sub-Saharan Africa, Stoetz et al. (1999, pp. 44–45) write,

> The European scramble for Africa was codified into the configuration of nation states that endures today. In 1884, delegates from 14 European nations met in a Conference of Great Powers, and the following year they signed the General Act of the Berlin Conference, formalizing the partitioning of sub-Saharan Africa. The Berlin Treaty chopped Africa up into parcels according to the interests of Europeans, completely disregarding the ecological and social features that had defined the continent for centuries.

A third important point is that the motivation of the colonial powers was largely economic, and they proceeded to exploit their colonies for their own economic purposes. They exploited natural resources in many cases, such as silver and gold; and, after turning many nations into cash crop–growing nations, producing products of value to Europe and North America, they then exploited those cash crops. So (1990, p. 112) gives

the example of India and the production of cotton, while sugar, rubber, and bananas are other examples involving a range of countries. A fourth important point is that colonial administration created administrative structures that "were superimposed upon those of the subordinated populations" (Smith, 1983, p. 29). This process commonly involved the use or creation of an elite, often being a specific ethnic or racial grouping and thus creating a new "ethclass" (an ethnic group with class status), or it could involve the recruitment of an existing "native elite" (So, 1990, p. 114). In particularly the former case, this frequently resulted in significant social divisions that were to come more and more to the fore postindependence (Smith, 1983, p. 59), a tragic example being Rwanda, but for the colonial powers it served as a mechanism for reinforcing their control (Smith, pp. 70–71). On this point in relation to sub-Saharan Africa, Stoesz et al. (1999, p. 45) write,

> Europeans instituted a colonial administration that was ruled by whites, but one in which certain tribes were selected for mediation with the African population. Consequently few Africans were to acquire even a rudimentary knowledge of how to govern a modern nation-state. Compounding matters, colonial preference for certain tribes over others aggravated tribal jealousies.

By contrast, in colonial Malaya it was the colonial preference for certain racial populations, and in Ireland for a certain religion, that had similar consequences (Enloe, 1973). Malaysia's "bumiputra policy" of 1970, that aimed at giving the native-born Malays 30 percent of the overall equity pie by 1990, was an attempt to reverse the trend established under colonialism (see UNDP, 1996a, p. 60).

Finally, we should note that colonialism was also responsible for certain forms of social welfare development (Midgley, 1995a, pp. 51ff.). Midgley notes that "colonialism had long been concerned with the exploitation of the natural and agricultural resources of the colonies" (p. 52), but that "this situation began to change in the early decades of the twentieth century when some colonial administrations introduced development plans designed to foster economic growth."

He goes on to discuss the example of Britain and its Colonial Development and Welfare Acts, which "fostered the idea that the colonies were . . . potentially viable economic entities in their own right." With this new thinking, gradually the idea of linking "the expansion of the social services with the overriding need for economic development was generally accepted" (Midgley, 1995a, p. 53). From an early stage in colonialism, however, an aspect of much colonial policy was its "civilizing mission." Mac-Pherson (1982, p. 45) quotes a British colonial policy statement:

> There can be no room for doubt that it is the mission of Great Britain to work continuously for the training and education of the Africans towards a higher intellectual, moral and economic level than that which they had reached when the crown assumed responsibility for the administration of this territory.

MacPherson goes on to present two case studies, one the health services in Papua New Guinea and the other social services in Tanzania. He concludes that the overall legacy of colonialism was dependency and underdevelopment (p. 72), while specific areas of welfare development had many deficiencies that continued after independence. For example, health policies resulted in "curative bias, extreme maldistribution of services, extreme inequalities in access, and the dominance of Western medicine" (p. 62). As Midgley (1981, p. 52) explains, "Social welfare services, which were established in the colonies before independence, were based on practices in the metropolitan countries." Furthermore, "the social services in developing countries evolved incrementally to deal not with absolute need but to meet the growing demand for health, education and housing, especially in

the urban areas" (p. 53). Hence the colonial legacy in the welfare field was not one that would serve the former colonies well as they moved beyond independence.

Neocolonialism Postindependence

The end of the colonial period did not, for the most part, see the end of imposed development (see Hoogvelt, 2001). The phenomenon of neocolonialism often meant that the extent of external influence continued little changed. As Randall and Theobald (1998, p. 11) point out, "experience of colonial rule in Latin America, where most countries gained their independence by the 1830s, explains less about their subsequent development than does continuing American neoimperialism." Imperialism (and neoimperialism), Hoogvelt writes "exists wherever there is deliberate transnational political interference, including military interference, for the purposes of the mobilization, extraction and external transfer of economic surplus from one political territory to another" (2001, p. 160).

This lack of change can be partly understood on the basis of dependency theory (So, 1990, part II; Randall and Theobald, 1998, chap. 4; Todaro, 1997, pp. 82–84). As Randall and Theobald write,

> It [dependency theory] holds that no society can be understood in isolation from this [international economic] order and in fact the condition of underdevelopment is precisely the result of the incorporation of Third World economies in the world capitalist system which is dominated by the developed North. (1998, p. 120)

In the case of Latin America, that domination was exercised largely by the United States. This neoimperialism, however, also comes about in part because of the behavior of Latin American elites, although similar situations occurred worldwide. As Randall and Theobald (1998, p. 15) put it,

In Latin America and elsewhere, elite groups are more oriented, economically and culturally, towards North America and Europe than towards their own countries. That is where they have their bank accounts, maintain business links, own homes and send their children to school.

In her discussion of "neo-colonial imperialism," Enloe (1973, p. 55) quotes an African-American scholar:

A neo-colony is a colony that is no longer needed as such. In the African situation, this meant that the colonizer had completed his work of industrializing the territory. He had disrupted the indigenous way of life of its inhabitants, replacing traditional values with those of the West. . . . All that remained was to establish the indigenous bourgeoisie, sympathetic to the Western culture which had created it, at the political helm, and the country would then be granted "independence." The colonizers could then withdraw their forces back home. They sit comfortably in their living rooms, reaping economic gains from all over the world.

In practice, many scholars (e.g., Hoogvelt, 2001) seem to agree with this view that the end of colonialism represented a change largely in the forms of western control, aided by the growth in neocolonial linkages with certain classes within the former colonies. Most of the newly independent countries continued to exist under a large measure of western control or in a dependency relationship with the West, often resulting in limited or unbalanced development.

The World Bank's and IMF's Structural Adjustment Programs

Although many states are among the members of the international economic institutions, namely the World Bank, IMF, and WTO, these institutions are dominated to a large extent by western states, and particularly by the United States. It is not, therefore, surprising that many people view these institutions as agents of the West and thus of neocolonialism, imposing conditions on weaker countries even as they may distribute aid to them. Todaro (1997, pp. 526ff.) and Todaro and Smith (2003, pp. 613ff.) outline the history and purposes of the various structural adjustment and stabilization packages or programs developed by the WB and IMF. While in theory of benefit to the countries receiving the packages and to the broader world community, two aspects of these packages concern us here. One is that they are clearly imposed by the two organizations in question, for the price in rejecting them is virtually impossible to live with. The second aspect is that "they have been found to contribute to rising hardships amongst the poorest groups in developing countries" (Todaro, 1997, p. 530). (See also Stoesz et al., 1999, pp. 122–123; Simon, Spengen, Dixon, and Narman, 1995; Bello, Kinley, and Elinson, 1982; George and Sabelli, 1994; Hoogvelt, 2001; Todaro and Smith, 2003, pp. 613–615.) Moreover, they have often funded large projects, such as large dams, that have resulted in ecological degradation and the involuntary displacement of people without needed support. Not only, therefore, are they seen by many to be a crucial aspect of western dominance of the development process, especially during times of crisis, but they are also seen to impose hardship on the vulnerable for the benefit predominantly of outsiders to the country in question. (See Easterly, 2002, chap. 6, for a critical analysis; and for some critical case studies, see Simon et al., 1995, on Africa; and Bello et al., 1982, on the Philippines.)

Imposed development has been presented as largely development imposed, in one sense or another and to varying degrees, by external powers. The three types are summarized in Table 5.1. Of course, there is also a degree of internally imposed development emanating from the most powerful sectors of a national population, but at least in most such cases people will eventually have a voice in their own

Table 5.1 Imposed development

	Colonialism	Neocolonialism	The WB's and IMF's Structural Adjustment Packages
I m p o s e d D e v e l o p m e n t	Cold or active aggression, violence, and subjugation	American neoimperialism	Major agents of neocolonialism
	Territorial demarcation with colonizers' self-interest	Domination by the developed north countries	Countries have little say in the package and cannot escape from it
	Exploitation of colonies' human and natural resources for colonizers' economic prosperity	Colony elites' strong affiliation to colonized countries	Large-scale projects causing ecological damage and peoples' displacement with little concern to their well-being
	Administrative structures reinforced colonizers' control and divisions in colonies	Replacement of colonies' traditional values and practices with those of the West	Lead to hardships among the poorest groups
	Limited urban-centered social services to achieve the above three points	Ensuring economic gains for the West	Western dominance in the development process
	Dependency and underdevelopment	Continuation of western control in different forms	Benefit to outsiders
		Facilitate different degrees of instability in colonies when western control is threatened	Dependency and economic growth without distribution
		Dependency, limited and linear development	

development. Such was not the case during the colonial period, and supporters of one form or another of dependency theory and of neoimperialism would argue that this situation has not essentially changed in modern times.

State-devised Development Policies

To some degree this path to development contradicts the previous path of colonialism and dependency, but in practice not all countries were subjected to excessive external control; while in most other if not all cases, it was always going to be in the end a balance between the initiatives taken by those with responsibility for the development of their state and the influences exerted from outside. Ultimately successful development is dependent on a state accepting and exercising control of its own development, and, while colonialism prevented many states or future states from doing so for a period, it is doubtful that neocolonialism would constitute more than an additional, yet highly significant factor, that any state must take into account in an era of globalization (Hoogvelt, 2001, chap. 10). If we accept this premise of state responsibility for development, this still leaves open the precise path to development to be taken by any state, and the variations over the past 50 years have resulted in considerable debate. We shall consider the policies most commonly adopted under four headings: macroeconomic policies, political policies, human resources development policies, and human development policies, although clearly the areas indicated are ideally complementary, despite the fact that often commentators emphasize one area over the others. The first three policy trends are commonly perceived as state-led and top-down approaches, and hence criticized for these reasons when excessive reliance is placed upon them; while the last one is commonly presented as an alternative, people-centered and bottom-up approach to development.

Macroeconomic Development

While macroeconomic policy in developing countries is very much influenced by global events and often significantly assisted (some would say distorted) by external aid, it is largely the prerogative and responsibility of state governments. The success of macroeconomic development in developing countries has, however, varied greatly, as a perusal of World Bank and UNDP reports at any point in time make clear. This has led to considerable attention being given to why some countries develop faster and further than do others. Much attention has focused on various factors perceived as relevant. Some studies stress a country's location and natural resource endowment; others attribute significance to cultural factors; others again focus on a country's relationship with other economic centers within the global economy; and in recent years much attention has been given to the nature of governance, especially its freedom from corruption and inefficiencies and the qualities of those who lead it. Clearly, each and all of these factors, and no doubt others, can be highly relevant in determining state economic levels achieved. (See Easterly, 2002, for a discussion of most of these factors.)

A second approach to understanding economic development has concentrated on the theoretical level, seeking for models that demonstrate what it is that drives economic development. Todaro (1997, chap. 3, or Todaro and Smith, 2003, chap. 4) provides a useful summary of this literature in his discussion of five

theories of economic development, namely the linear-stages theory, structural-change models, the international-dependency revolution, the neoclassical counterrevolution, and the new growth theory. Let us outline briefly the essence of these theories.

The linear-stages approach builds on work by Rostow and the Harrod-Domar growth model. (See Todaro, 1997 and 2003, for explanations of this work.) The approach envisages five stages through which countries pass in their economic progress, with the key factor being prevailing levels of savings and investment.

The structural-change models accept that capital formation is important but emphasize also the establishment of a modern industrial sector.

The international-dependency revolution argues essentially that the underdevelopment of many countries is due to a highly inequitable and exploitative capitalist system favoring the rich and powerful states.

The neoclassical counterrevolution focuses on the importance to economic development of the neoliberal endorsement of supply-side economic policies, and policies such as the privatization of public corporations, encouragement of free markets and trade, and the minimization of government regulation of economic activities.

The latest theory, new growth theory, explains disparities in economic development by endorsing the neoclassical approach while focusing strongly on human capital formation and the promotion of knowledge-intensive industries.

Todaro's own conclusion is that all five theories have some credence, and that there is no one path to economic development. He also endorses the emphasis on the purposes to which economic growth is put as being more important than the growth itself.

This last conclusion of Todaro's is one on which it is important to dwell. Many writers, while fully acknowledging the importance of economic growth, focus mainly on what follows from that growth or what that growth is used for. An interesting national example here comes from the state of Bhutan where state policy emphasizes not Gross National Product but Gross National Happiness! Back in the 1980s, several prominent writers were stressing the importance of "growth with equity." An excellent summary of such arguments is presented in the UNDP's 1996 *Human Development Report,* which focuses on the relationship between economic growth and human development. It highlights the all too common phenomena of "jobless growth"; "ruthless growth—where the fruits of growth mostly benefit the rich, leaving millions of people struggling in ever-deepening poverty"; "voiceless growth—where growth in the economy has not been accompanied by an extension of democracy or empowerment"; "rootless growth—which causes people's cultural identity to wither"; and "futureless growth—where the present generation squanders resources needed by future generations" (pp. 2–4). The emphasis here is clearly on the reality that economic growth may be, and usually is, an essential aspect of development, but that it is not sufficient unless balanced by, and complementary with, other aspects of development (see Sen, 2001).

When we come to consider local-level development, we shall see that even in those developing countries that enjoy reasonable levels of economic growth, the benefits of that growth are not equitably distributed, and so it often becomes necessary for local-level development to focus on the economic dimension through local job creation and income-generation schemes. At the same time, local-level development will be focusing on how the locality or group in question can gain access to the opportunities available through macroeconomic growth. Simultaneously, one hopes that, from the other end, efforts are being made through capacity building, decentralization, and other policies to extend the outreach of those

goods and services and opportunities that are the product of economic growth.

Political Development

It is difficult in practice to distinguish economic policies from the political contexts within which they emerge; hence to a significant degree economic development mirrors its political context, whether that economic development is being driven by state decisions or is a product of international domination by certain powers. As an example of the role of political development, Stoesz et al. (1999, p. 13) consider three patterns of development that have emerged within the Asian context. The three are "the authoritarian capitalism of the 'four tigers' (Hong Kong, Singapore, South Korea, and Taiwan), the market socialism upon which China has embarked, and the welfare state capitalism being attempted in India." An important point to note here is that, despite the political differences among these three examples, all of the countries referred to have achieved high levels of development; and differences between them may well be due more to the nature and history of each country than to the precise nature of the political regime.

Other writers have explored the links between democracy and development. While some writers have maintained that democracy is an essential prerequisite to economic and social development, others point out that some democracies have failed to develop while some nondemocracies have progressed extremely well. As Diamond, Linz, and Lipset (1989, p. 33) put it, "democracy is not incompatible with a low level of development," and they cite India, Sri Lanka, and Papua New Guinea. However, they go on to write,

This is not to deny the general positive correlation between democracy and development in the larger world. Nor is it to ignore the pressures and props for democracy that derive from a higher level of socioeconomic development, with the expansion it yields in income and education, and thus political participation.

Does democracy then lead to development, or does development lead to democracy? (See Sen, 2001, chap. 6.) The UNDP (2002, p. 3) concludes that "advancing human development requires governance that is democratic in both form and substance—for the people and by the people." Or does development at least sometimes require a stronger political hand to guide its progress than democracy often permits—a popular argument in some countries but one for which the UNDP (2002, p. 4) maintains there is no evidence? The debate raises the question of what constitutes democracy. As Randall and Theobald (1998, p. 38) point out, "political scientists are finally acknowledging the historically and culturally exceptional and contingent nature of democracy in the west," and therefore accepting that democracy can assume various forms. They go on to say,

> From the late 1980s, a vast literature has emerged seeking to explain and evaluate the phenomenon of democratization both in the Third World and more globally. Partly for this very reason no single theory of democratization has gained ascendancy. . . . [The] tendency to identify democracy with its western, liberal, variant echoes the ethnocentricity of the earlier political development literature. (pp. 40, 44)

While the debate continues on the precise relationship between political forms and development, there can be little doubt that the process of government is often as important as the form, and there has, particularly since the 1990s, been much concern with corruption and inefficiencies within many political systems worldwide (e.g., Easterly, 2002, chap. 12; World Bank, 1997). As Randall and Theobald (1998, p. 40) comment,

> By 1989 the World Bank was calling for "good governance," though at this stage, the emphasis was mainly on fighting corruption, promoting accountability and efficient administration.

Increasingly, although never consistently, the content widened to include democratic accountability through multi-party elections.

From this brief look at the political path to development, we would have to conclude that, while the political factor plays an important role in development, it is a factor that varies greatly in its impact on development. Moreover, it is obviously only one factor in achieving development, and the degree of its importance will vary from place to place and from time to time. In addition to the above points, one way of appreciating the place of political development is to envision society as composed of several sectors. The sector of governance is clearly of importance, as also is the economic or for-profit sector discussed earlier. In addition to these two, however, are the civil society sector and the sector which, in our view, constitutes the foundations of any society, namely the sector of individuals-families-communities. The importance of civil society, and of its role in political development as well as in other areas of society, is stressed by many writers. Randall and Theobald (1998, p. 205) express it well:

> The closer we approach the industrial era, the more civil society expresses itself in highly institutionalized formal organizations such as trades unions, professional associations, independent political parties, pressure groups and other voluntary associations. Such bodies obviously played a crucial role in the emergence not only of modern democracy but of welfare state capitalism—a system in which the state in committing itself to underwriting the standard of living of the masses generates a degree of confidence in the public character of the state: that the state exists to serve civil society.

Political development cannot be imposed on a nation by outsiders (highlighted again by international efforts to rebuild political systems postconflict, as in Cambodia, Bosnia-Herzegovina, Kosovo, Afghanistan, and Iraq) or by minority power groups within a nation; ideally it represents the formalization of the aspirations and values of local communities, mediated through the structures of civil society, which in turn holds the political system that emerges accountable to the people.

However, political leadership, formation, and developments at national, regional, and global levels are often far from this ideal situation. Many political leaders receive their training in the West, nurture allegiances with the West, and transfer huge personal financial reserves to the West. On the one hand, they often play with nation-building emotions of communities and the masses and, on the other hand, they accept implicit and explicit interference in the political and economic development of the country, simply to remain in power, irrespective of whether they have democratic, socialist, or communist forms of government. There are some political leaders and developments that resist western hegemony and oppose external interference; and there are others that change their international allegiances depending on circumstances. Political developments, including leadership, have highly significant implications for national development, through the formation of blocs, international sanctions, global isolation, and external interference in national development.

Human Resource Development

The next path to development that we need to consider is human-resource-led development. Behrman (1990), in an ILO (International Labour Organisation) document, poses the key questions:

> To what extent is it possible for developing economies to change their comparative advantages from primary commodity and other low skill labour-intensive products to more skill-intensive goods and services through the deliberate expansion of human resources? To what extent is it desirable to adopt a human resource led strategy that

favours human resource investments through policies beyond what would occur in the normal course of development? (Executive Summary)

Perhaps we should start with a definition of two key terms. Todaro (1997, p. 697) defines human capital and human resources as follows:

> Human capital: Productive investments embodied in human persons. These include skills, abilities, ideals, and health resulting from expenditures on education, on-the-job training programs, and medical care.

> Human resources: The quantity and quality of a nation's labor force.

Both definitions have a strong economic thrust, understandable in a text on economic development. We shall suggest, however, a broader appreciation of human resources.

Human resources development is essentially focused on investing in people. However, this investment is for various purposes, achieved through a variety of programs, and undertaken by a range of development agents. One key purpose is economic development, as is implied in Todaro's definitions above. Todaro argues that "a country's potential for economic growth is greatly influenced by its endowments of physical resources . . . and human resources" (1997, p. 33). He continues,

> In the realm of human resource endowments, not only are sheer numbers of people and their skill levels important, but so also are their cultural outlooks, attitudes towards work, access to information, willingness to innovate, and desire for self-improvement. . . . Thus the nature and character of a country's human resources are important determinants of its economic structure.

In terms of the evidence of a link between human resources and economic development, Behrman (1990, p. 89) writes,

There seems to be some evidence about the association between human resource investments and development, though there are some outliers for which such an association does not appear to hold very well (e.g. Cuba, Sri Lanka, the Philippines, Kerala in India, Brazil, Togo). But there is surprisingly little systematic quantitative evidence for the proposition that human resource investments cause substantial development.

On the basis of the available evidence, Behrman is inclined to the position that, while expenditure on basic education and health is clearly warranted, other prohuman resource developments are probably not. Todaro's point above, that many other factors come into play in determining economic outcomes, is emphasized by other writers such as Landes (1998). Landes focuses on such factors as geography and culture as significantly influencing final outcomes.

A further aspect of the link between human resource development and economic development relates to people as consumers and participants. Economic development is contingent on finding markets for products, either at home or abroad, and markets depend on people's ability and willingness to consume. This ability is influenced largely by people's participation in economic development, while the willingness relates to cultural and value factors. So along with people's direct contribution to economic development as productive assets, which would seem to rest on some human resource development efforts, human resource development is in reality required to render people active participants in the economic process at all levels. As Midgley (1995a, p. 159) puts it, "Investments in human and social capital are urgently needed if people are to have the educational levels and skills to utilize the opportunities created by economic development."

A second purpose of human resource development is to facilitate political development. If people are to be active participants in the political life of their society they need, generally speaking, to be literate and to enjoy reasonable health, and certainly to be free from having to devote all their time and energy to surviving. Hence, human resource development, that at least serves to meet basic needs and to provide basic health and education, would appear to be a prerequisite for political development. However, as Corner (1986, p. 14) points out, political considerations might also induce a government to deliberately neglect human resource development. She writes: "Particularly in respect to education, human resource development strategies tend to promote political change rather than preserve the status quo," leading some governments, preoccupied with maintaining their power, to shy away from it.

A third and very specific purpose of human resource development is poverty reduction. As the World Bank (1990, p. 79) writes regarding investing in people,

There is overwhelming evidence that human capital is one of the keys to reducing poverty. Moreover, improvements in health, education, and nutrition reinforce each other. But the poor generally lack access to basic social services. There is too little investment in their human capital, and this increases the probability that they and their children will remain poor. To break this vicious cycle, governments must make reaching the poor a priority in its own right.

Corner (1986, p. 14) links poverty reduction to the political issue:

The political powerlessness of the poor is both a cause and a consequence of the poverty of their human capital. It must therefore be recognized that a prerequisite of a successful human resource development anti-poverty strategy is a measure of political influence and that one inevitable consequence of success is an increase in political power for the poor, a fact that may not be appreciated by many governments.

A final purpose of human resource development relates to the achievement of quality of life for all people within a society (see Sen, 2001, pp. 144ff.). In this sense, human resource development is people-centered development that has as its ultimate objective the overall quality of life of all people. However, while a high level of social service delivery accessible to all is fundamental to human well-being, such enhancement of quality of life needs to coincide with economic development so that people have available the opportunities which they are now equipped to access. The UNDP (1996, chap. 3) has contrasted Sri Lanka's high level of achievement in the field of social service delivery, but low level of economic development, with India's high level of economic development alongside a low level of social service delivery to many parts of the country, and especially to women. Clearly these two levels of development need to complement each other.

The achievement of human resource development is through programs mainly in the fields of education and labor force development, health and nutrition, and family planning. Considerable work has been devoted to identifying forms of education that will prepare people for productive activity during their years of working age, and through formal and informal education programs and a system of lifetime learning. Investing in health is regarded by the World Bank (1993, p. 17) and others as "a crucial part of well-being" but also "justified on purely economic grounds." The issues that arise relate largely to the scope of such investment, the extent to which the "user-pays principle" (i.e., users pay for services rather than services being subsidized by the state) should be applied, and the core one of efficiencies and effectiveness embodied in the many alternative approaches to service delivery. Such issues are extremely important but also exceedingly complex and situation-specific.

The final aspect of investing in people is who takes the responsibility. A survey of the literature and experience in the field suggests that it is a shared responsibility. At the highest level, the international community has sought to establish the relevant rights, identify appropriate achievement targets, establish basic criteria, suggest relevant agendas for pursuing the various objectives, and offer technical assistance. At the national level, responsibility tends to be shared between the government sector, the for-profit sector, and the nongovernment not-for-profit sector. Within this overall scheme, the World Bank (1991b, p. 69) and others tend to give to government the leading role, while exploring partnerships with the other sectors. Individuals also assume a role, however, as they invest in themselves through education, health, and so on, in the expectation of higher economic and quality of life returns in the future. Moreover, we might note that both neoliberal and neoconservative thinking see the individual agent as of central importance. (See Sen, 2001, chap. 5, for a full discussion of this area.)

Human Development

Very early in the post–World War II development process, various commentators pointed out that development was too often viewed in terms of its benefits for national economies, usually in terms of GDP and growth levels, or for the corporate world, and too infrequently in terms of its impact on people. Certainly by the early 1980s, writers were arguing for an alternative development paradigm. Korten and Klaus (1984) present this as people-centered development, of which the central concerns are "to enhance human growth and well-being, equity and sustainability" (p. 299). Roundtables on human development were organized in the 1980s (e.g., Haq and Kirdar, 1985, 1987), referring to human development as "the neglected dimension" of development. A central theme was that "human development is both an input and an objective of development" (Haq and Kirdar, 1985, p. :xvi). These roundtables criticized the human impact of much economic development and argued for "redirecting policy and planning toward the human dimension" (p. 3). The concept of human development, however, came into its own with the UNDP's annual *Human Development Reports* commencing in 1990. These reports argued that development should be "woven around the people" (UNDP, 1991, p. 1), or "of the people, for the people, by the people" (UNDP, 1993, p. 3), while illustrating how many existing development trends were detrimental to the well-being of people. In particular, the UNDP argued against economic growth that was not beneficial to the people in several crucial ways (UNDP, 1996a, pp. 2–4). In 1992, Friedmann (1992, p. 8) presented an excellent overview of the "politics of alternative development," presenting alternative development as essentially an ideology. A similar approach was adopted by Ekins (1992), although he placed a much greater stress than many did on ecological factors.

Midgley (1995a) highlights similar criticisms of past development trends in his discussion of "distorted development." Midgley writes,

> The phenomenon of persistent poverty in the midst of economic affluence is one of the most problematic issues in development today. In many parts of the world, economic development has not been accompanied by an attendant degree of social progress. The phenomenon is often referred to as distorted development. Distorted development . . . is . . . a failure to harmonize economic and social development objectives, and to ensure that the benefits of economic progress reach the population as a whole. (pp. 3–4)

For some writers, distorted development reveals a strong tendency to favor urban areas and their populations over rural areas, or some parts of the country over others, or some groupings (ethnic, racial, religious, class, caste, etc.) of the population over others, or men over women—the frequently discussed gender bias in development (e.g., UNDP, 1995; Elson, 1995a; O'Connel, 1996). Biased or distorted development is

commonly seen as resulting in major inequalities within nations, and also between nations (e.g., UNDP, 1996a). Correcting distorted development was commonly said to require a much greater emphasis on social development, and the World Summit on Social Development (United Nations, 1995), and much other work strongly affirm this point. For example, Midgley (1995a, p. 8) succinctly defines social development as "a process of promoting people's welfare in conjunction with a dynamic process of economic development." For Midgley and most writers, some basic degree of economic development was an essential prerequisite to human development; and this basic level of economic development has often not been achieved, as the World Bank's *World Development Reports* regularly reveal. Easterly (2002, p. 291) argues that "the problem of making poor countries rich was much more difficult than we thought." There is no panacea for poverty and no single economic strategy for achieving growth. Yet the urgency of the quest remains: "The well-being of the next generation of poor countries depends on whether our quest to make poor countries rich is successful" (Easterly, 2002, p. 15).

Few writers have seen social or human development as an alternative to economic development but rather as complementary; in one sense as rectifying the frequently unfortunate consequences of economic development, and in another sense as addressing other aspects of human well-being or dimensions of development (see UNDP, 1996, chap. 3).

This linking of human or social development with economic development became for many an integrated model of development. Stoesz et al. (1999) present an "integrated model of development" as the final chapter to their text on development. Their model (p. 263) is taken from the UNDP's 1996 *Human Development Report*. However, various UN documents were emphasizing the importance of integration at least as early as 1971, when one report referred to integrated development as "an attempt to achieve a balanced growth in the human and material resources of nations" (United Nations, 1971, p. 8). This particular UN report stresses the importance of community development generally, and of people's participation in particular, for achieving this goal. The notion of an integrated approach to development was a logical and commonsense conclusion to any realistic analysis of the impact of development. Yet many politicians, economists, and others clearly believed that, if the economic house was in order and economic growth was being achieved, other dimensions of development, such as social, cultural, and ecological, would take care of themselves. This manifestly false assumption of a trickle-down effect has been difficult to shift and tends to be reinforced today by the neoliberal or conservative ideology. The need to emphasize the focus on human development therefore remains extremely important.

Externally Assisted Development

While most state-devised development has occurred with some degree of external assistance of various kinds, the focus here is on development that is predominantly funded and driven by external assistance. It is important to focus on this path to development because of its overall significance since 1945, and because in many ways it tends to negate the key principles upon which our approach to development is based, especially the principles of self-reliance, participation, and empowerment. External assistance, in general terms, can be described as foreign aid, which Todaro (1997, p. 546) defines as follows:

The concept of foreign aid that is now widely used and accepted is one that encompasses all official grants and concessional loans, in currency or in kind, that are broadly aimed at transferring resources from developed to less developed nations on development or income distribution grounds.

Foreign or development aid can take various forms. On the basis of the channel through which aid is provided, aid can be divided into multilateral aid (e.g., provided through a body such as the UN), bilateral aid (government to government), and aid channeled through the NGO sector. On the basis of type of aid, it can be divided into aid provided to government budgets generally, project aid (tied to the implementation of a specific project), food aid, and humanitarian aid (aid in crisis situations such as natural disasters and wars).

It is assumed that most developing countries will require aid to some degree and for some period, although some countries have sought to develop without external assistance (e.g., the People's Republic of China). It is further assumed that only the western developed industrialized countries and Japan are rich enough to provide aid to the extent usually required. However, a key question arises: Why should any country provide aid to another? One would like to think that the main reason is what Rieff (2002, p. 43) calls "the humanitarian imperative—that when people are suffering, even if they are strangers, it is our collective obligation as human beings to come to their aid." While Rieff is here referring to humanitarian aid, the same rationale could be applied to development aid provided to eradicate poverty and enhance human well-being. Rieff (p. 57) comments further on this point:

What we now call humanitarianism, our ancestors called charity. The idea that it is a moral obligation of the more fortunate to assist the less fortunate and that those who are in need may legitimately expect help is one that is normative in all the world's major religions. Call it altruism, call it pity, call it solidarity, call it compassion, but the impulse to help is so deeply rooted in human culture, that, whether it is intrinsic or learned, it can rightly be described as one of the basic human emotions.

Without necessarily negating this point of view, especially as it applies to the majority of aid workers, most commentators proceed to voice considerable cynicism regarding the motivation for states providing aid (e.g., Easterly, 2002, chap. 2; Cassen, 1994, p. 136; Hoogvelt, 2001, pp. 191ff.).

Todaro (1997, p. 550) summarizes donor country purposes for providing aid as follows:

> Donor countries give aid primarily because it is in their political, strategic, or economic self-interest to do so. Some development assistance may be motivated by moral and humanitarian desires to assist the less fortunate (e.g., emergency food relief programs), but there is no historical evidence to suggest that over longer periods of time, donor nations assist others without expecting some corresponding benefits (political, economic, military etc.) in return.

Hayter and Watson (1985, pp. 242ff.) elaborate on the self-interest aspect by suggesting that aid is used "to reward friends and penalize enemies," "to open up markets," to finance projects which are "essential for the profitable operation of foreign investors," and to enable private firms and banks "to get rid of otherwise uncompetitive products." Even more sinister, Hoogvelt (2001, p. 191) refers to Mark Duffield's view that

> the new aid agenda reverses earlier developmentalist goals of "incorporation" of peripheral areas into the world system, and instead now serves as a policy of management and containment of politically insecure territories on the edge of the global economy.

These are common themes, although clearly none of them should be used to generalize about the purposes of aid. However, the self-interest motive appears to be validated by the way in which aid is allocated. As Todaro (1997, p. 549) points out, one might expect it to be allocated on the basis of relative needs, whereas "most bilateral aid seems unrelated to development priorities." Eurostep (a network of NGOs from European

countries) and ICVA (the International Council of Voluntary Agencies), in agreeing with this view, spell it out as follows:

> Over 3000 million people live in Low Income Countries with per capita incomes below $675 a year. In 1990, these Low Income Countries received 62% of DAC ODA [aid provided through the Development Assistance Committee of the OECD and the EU]. By 1994, these countries' share of aid slipped to 53%. In 1995, low income countries received barely half (51%) of total ODA. A smaller share of a smaller cake. (Randel and German, 1997, p. 248)

The figures are indicative of the fact that aid is not allocated on the basis of need at all, with disproportionate shares going to those countries of greatest political interest to a donor country (see Todaro, 1997, p. 549). And, as the end of the above quote states, overall amounts of aid have been declining in recent years, partly due to what Krueger, Michalopoulos, and Ruttan (1989, p. 305) refer to as "aid fatigue." (Initially, ODA grew greatly in volume but has, since the early 1990s, decreased both overall and as a percentage of donor countries' GNP, as detailed earlier in the chapter.)

All the indications are that the poorest countries can place minimal reliance on aid to assist their development; and that, even when many poor countries do receive aid, they will have difficulty securing it on terms that are appropriate to their development needs and goals.

Given all the perceived deficiencies in the development aid program, one might wonder why developing countries are willing to receive aid, let alone to become dependent upon it. Todaro (1997, pp. 554ff.) suggests one major and two minor reasons. The major one is economic, due to developing countries accepting uncritically the proposition "that aid is a crucial and essential ingredient in the development process." The two minor reasons are political and moral: political, in that "aid is seen by both donor and recipient as providing greater political leverage to the existing leadership to suppress opposition and maintain itself in power"; and moral in that "many proponents of foreign aid in both developed and developing countries believe that rich nations have an obligation to support the economic and social development of the Third World." Hayter and Watson (1985, pp. 245–246) emphasize Todaro's political reason.

What then can we conclude regarding the overall impact of aid? Cassen (1994) surveyed a large sample of aid activities in seven countries and concluded that the impact of aid is broadly positive, but far from perfect, and that it seldom relieves poverty. Reasons for the inadequacies of aid are seen to relate to donor policies and processes, recipients' weaknesses, and an overall failure to coordinate the many aid projects. In the humanitarian aid context, Rieff (2002) concludes, "We know that aid too often does nothing to alter—and very often reinforces—the fundamental circumstances that produced the needs it temporarily meets" (p. 24); and

independent humanitarianism does many things well and some things badly, but the things it is now called upon to do, such as helping to advance the cause of human rights, contributing to stopping wars, and furthering social justice, are beyond its competence, however much one might wish it were otherwise. (p. 334)

Even at the purely economic level, there is a debate regarding aid that is well expressed by Todaro (1997, p. 556):

On one side are the economic traditionalists, who argue that aid has indeed promoted growth and structural transformation in many LDCs. On the other side are critics who argue that aid does not promote faster growth but may in fact retard it by substituting for, rather than supplementing, domestic savings and investment and by exacerbating LDC balance of payments deficits as a result

of rising debt repayment obligations and the linking of aid to donor-country exports.

Todaro expresses the hope that, in the future, the probably lower volume of aid will be geared more to the real development needs of recipients, and that enlightened self-interest may yet come to include a focus on "eliminating poverty, minimizing inequality, promoting environmentally sustainable development, and raising levels of living for the masses of LDC peoples" (pp. 557–558), but he acknowledges that this point has not been reached. Finally, an IMF review of aid states the overall impact of aid in the following stark terms:

Simply put, over the past 30 years, the vast majority of developing countries—84 out of 108—have either stayed in the lower-income quintile or fallen into that quintile from a relatively higher position. Moreover, there are now fewer middle-income countries, and upward mobility of countries seems to have fallen over time. (Curtis, 1997, p. 13)

While most commentators on aid are critical of many of the realities they identify, this does not mean that they reject the concept of aid as helpful in the development process, or even as essential to the development process (e.g., Cassen, 1994, p. 14). Some criteria seen as necessary to render external aid of real assistance to development are emphasized by those same authors who have misgivings about aid. Curtis (1997, pp. 10–11), for example, reminds us that aid is but one aspect of the complex relationships between donor and recipient states:

Aid is only one part of the relationship between developed and developing countries. International trade, investment, conflict prevention and debt relief are far more important for determining the opportunities for equitable human development in an era of globalisation.

Krueger et al. (1989, p. 308) emphasize the importance of dialogue between donor and recipient states resulting ideally in some convergence of views. They concede, however, that such dialogue is often adversely influenced by strong donor interests:

> When donor interests strongly influence the flow of aid resources, the effectiveness of policy dialogue is reduced. Donors find it extremely difficult to utilize policy dialogue to promote better policy in the recipient country when the representatives of that government are aware that the security or trade interests of constituents in the donor country carry more weight than the policy reform objective. (p. 309)

What these writers are out to achieve is an appropriate economic policy environment in the recipient country, without which any aid is unlikely to make a significant contribution to development. The writers, however, do have clear views as to what constitutes such an environment, namely "an outward-oriented strategy and rapid growth of exports" (p. 307).

Other writers maintain rather that it is the right of developing countries to determine the direction of their economic and social policies, and any pressure on the part of donors, whether states or institutions such as the World Bank, is unacceptable.

A further criterion that may determine the ultimate outcome of aid is the specific purposes to which the aid is put. There has been debate over the efficacy of funding large infrastructure developments, especially if such are either ill-conceived (e.g., some massive dams or international airports), or geared to enhancing the status of an individual leader or government, or to promoting the interests of potential foreign investors in that country. An example of a policy designed to encourage a beneficial approach to aid is the *20:20 Compact* conceived at the 1995 World Summit on Social Development (see UNDP, 1997, p. 113), by which aid is used to enhance the provision of social services. "This compact calls on donors to commit 20% of aid resources and on recipient governments to commit 20% of public expenditures to the provision of basic services" (Curtis, 1997, p. 9).

This could be seen as implying that aid should be made available on the basis of certain conditions being met, in this case a commitment to increasing basic social services as an antipoverty and human resources development strategy. Recently, in 2003, the Australian government announced that it would consider making aid to Pacific countries conditional on countries showing a commitment to eradicating corruption in government. How feasible or ethical is such a policy?

Overall, we might conclude that the provision of aid should always be strongly influenced by the prevailing situations existing in recipient countries—the opposite to the perceived tendency to relate aid largely to situations and agendas existing in the donor countries. Prevailing conditions could include the situations in relation to governance, economic policy, poverty levels, social services provision, political stability, and so on, the intention being to ensure that the aid provided would be beneficial, geared to development needs, and appropriate in type and conditions applied. When aid is provided along such lines, the obvious consensus among commentators is that it is highly likely to make a significant contribution to the development process in the countries concerned and even globally. However, there remains clearly a dilemma as to the extent to which donors can or should exert influence over the ways in which aid is utilized by recipients.

Local-level Development

All of the paths discussed to this point have largely involved the macro level of society, and have been aspects of what is commonly referred to as top-down development undertaken largely by the institutions of the state. By contrast, the essential focus of the local-level path to development is on the individuals-families-communities sector of society, the micro level, and represents bottom-up development. Bottom-up development came to be seen as either complementary to or a correction of the uneven impact of top-down development. It was never envisaged as an alternative path to other forms of development undertaken by state institutions; indeed to the contrary, state institutions were commonly seen as possessing the ability to facilitate local-level development while engaging in development at other important levels. Friedmann (1992, p. 7) writes in relation to this point,

> Although an alternative development must begin locally, it cannot end there. Like it or not, the State continues to be a major player. It may need to be made more accountable to poor people and more responsive to their claims. But without the State's collaboration, the lot of the poor cannot be significantly improved. Local empowering action requires a strong State.

Early discussion of the local-level development path was often in terms of community development. As a United Nations (1971, p. 1) report puts it, "After approximately 20 years as a UN-supported program, community development has gained nearly universal recognition as a force for inducing social and economic change in developing countries." This community development was carried out by workers deployed by either governments or NGOs. Of great interest was the fact that many governments very early on established large-scale community development programs, such as in Korea, Tanzania, India, and Mexico; however, much of this work was seen in hindsight to possess significant shortcomings (Dore and Mars, 1981; Campfens, 1997; see also Chapter 4). Many scholars in the development field regarded this early community development thinking not only as too

top-down but also as too idealistic, in part because it regarded communities as natural units of organization (Esman and Uphoff, 1984, p. 49). In addition, many evaluations of state-run community development schemes were critical of them because no trust was or could be developed between the workers, funded and deployed by the state, and the peoples among whom they worked. These criticisms led in some quarters to a growing emphasis on local institutional development as an alternative to community development. Uphoff, one of the scholars to do this, explains that "local" can be community but can also be group or neighborhood or several communities together (Uphoff, 1986, p. 10). His model (p. 11) identifies three local levels—locality, community, and group. The development approach is then to work with existing local institutions, defined as "complexes of norms and behaviors that persist over time by serving collectively valued purposes" (p. 9), and promoting local institutional development where and as necessary (see also Esman and Uphoff, 1984).

Other writers, from at least the early 1970s, have referred to local-level development in terms of NGO involvement in small-scale projects. Cernea (1989, p. 124) suggests that these small-scale NGO programs were basically of three types:

1. small production-oriented projects (e.g., the establishment of a tree nursery by a women's group and the construction of a small tank irrigation system);

2. production support service projects (e.g., building a village or group storage facility or a road and setting up a village-to-market transportation service); and

3. social service projects (e.g., a health room, a community hall, an ambulance service, a sports terrain, or a house for a teacher).

In all these approaches, the basic principle was "putting people first" (Cernea, 1991; Chambers,

1983; Ekins, 1992), engaging in people's capacity building, and thereby facilitating a bottom-up development process. There was also always a strong focus on participation. David (1993, p. 11) summarizes the overall approach as follows: "The people are the motivating force and a local, people-oriented development strategy is the sine qua non of human development today."

It is stated above that local-level development is in many contexts complementary to, or a correction of the more macro top-down approaches. It is, however, often more than this. If we recall Midgley's (1995a) discussion of distorted development, we shall appreciate that it is very easy and very common for prevailing national (and even international) development trends to favor certain levels, sectors, or geographical areas within a nation. For example, development frequently occurs in the interests of the advancement of the emerging middle-class, urban sector, or in more productive and better located geographical areas. While often well-intentioned, inevitably such trends result in impoverished and undeveloped areas. This situation is aggravated if the advantaged sections represent an ethnic, racial, or religious grouping that is clearly distinguished from the bypassed populations. In such cases, distorted development is not only driven by economic development models that favor urbanization, industrialization, and wealth generation, but also by a desire to advantage a specific ethnic group over others while preserving their power base.

It will be obvious that the above types of scenarios render essential a focus on local-level development, for several reasons. First, there is the reality that macro-level development often does not trickle down to certain populations and areas, or will take so long to do so that generations will languish in poverty. Local-level development may be all the development that these people will see, assuming that it occurs. Second, if local impoverished and marginalized populations are to battle for access to or a share of macro-level development, they may need to be strengthened through people's capacity building, organized through local institutional development, and empowered through participation in the process of local-level development. Third, active local-level development should bring the needs, if not the very existence, of such populations to the attention of those sharing in the benefits of existing development, and especially of those guiding it, so that a change process is initiated within the actual development models and goals of the nation, and not just in the rhetoric.

The need for local-level development is obvious, so obvious that one might be led to ask why it is not a major component of development in developing countries. There are several reasons why the prevailing local-level development situation in many poorer countries has not developed beyond some isolated local projects. First, we should not underestimate the difficulty of workers functioning effectively in many contexts, whether nationals or expatriates but especially if outsiders. Living conditions can be hard, working situations often unsupportive, poverty and various social problems deeply entrenched, local levels of negativity and suspicion high, and the local resource base available on which to build very limited. Second, there exists no ready-made potential pool of already trained workers. Any locals who have been upwardly mobile may be very unwilling to return to work in their impoverished area of origin; many nationals who qualify in social work, development studies, and so on may well prefer the easier and more lucrative work opportunities in the more developed areas; and most expatriates may well see such work as beyond their cultural, social, and even professional competence. The only viable solution may be to recruit, train, and deploy locally. Third, national authorities and ruling classes may essentially not be in favor of liberating disadvantaged populations, or even of diverting national resources to them. While this may in part reflect basic group selfishness, it may also have strong political and group relations overtones. Finally, many of the poorer nations do not receive sufficient aid and investment, are too burdened by external debt, and are too held back by poor governance and internal divisions and conflict to be able or willing to devote resources and energies to local-level development among the poorer sections of their populations. It is for these reasons that the situations in both poorer countries and poorer areas of relatively well-developed countries will depend, for some time to come, on the ability of either the international community or national governmental or international nongovernment organizations to devise appropriate programs of local-level development. International social work should be able to make a significant contribution to this goal, at the international, national, and local levels.

Conclusion

Katherine Kendall, a preeminent leader in the early development of international social work, wrote the following in the preface to one of the few social work texts on international development (Stoesz et al., 1999, p. ix):

> International development is seen as one of the most pressing human welfare issues of the day. Despite the enormous strides that have been made since World War II in life expectancy, reduced infant mortality, nutrition, annual income, and education, the process of development has left untouched millions of people who live in absolute poverty.

Yet the social work authors of this text make virtually no reference to the role of social work in the international development field, and very few schools of social work incorporate many aspects of this field in their curricula. However, schools of social work are starting to teach social development, and to see community development as a key dimension of social development and so crucial to the development process. Yet few of these schools report optimistically on students' responses to this field of practice.

In this background chapter on international development, we have sought to introduce the reader who is new to this field to the various paths that development has taken. Statistical accounts of the development progress of all countries are readily available from the World Bank and UNDP in their annual World Development and Human Development reports, while more detailed national reports are also produced regularly by the World Bank and the regional bodies of UN/ECOSOC. There is indeed a wealth of literature on development generally, but much less on local-level development that also outlines the way in which social workers and others might contribute to that process. We have concluded this chapter by focusing on local-level development as the dimension and level of development to which social work skills are most readily applied. In the following chapter we shall present some of the key approaches and strategies that social workers and others can use in this context. What we wish to stress here, however, is the importance of social work adopting this field as critical to the well-being of millions of people, and as one to which social work can respond and should be responding.

Summary

- Since World War II, many countries have experienced various degrees of development and of social, economic, and political change.

- Many countries have been subjected to imposed development through the processes of colonization and neocolonialism, such as the WB's and IMF's Structural Adjustment Packages.

- Macroeconomic development theories—the linear-stages approach, structural change models, international dependency revolution theories, neoclassical counterrevolution theories, and new growth theory—have influenced the development policies and realities of many countries, often with adverse effects. There is no one path to development. Important lessons can be learned and useful aspects employed from all theories.

- Political developments play crucial roles in the development process. Genuine democratic processes, people's participation, good governance and good leadership irrespective of political form, balance of power issues, and political stability are all important aspects of political development.

- The path of human resource development not only facilitates economic development but also political development, poverty reduction, and improvements in quality of life. Responsibility for this development has to be shared at local, national, and international levels.

- Human development is at least as important as economic development, and should be recognized and practiced.

- To facilitate development, many countries receive external aid that is sometimes geared toward the needs of donor countries. External aid has been reduced in recent years and come under considerable criticism from the perspectives of geopolitical and economic interests. External aid for development is important, but the culture and politics of aid should address the felt needs and prevailing conditions of receiving countries. It also should be directed to those countries that need it most.

- Without local-level development, macro development strategies cannot be fully and effectively realized.

Questions and Topics for Discussion

- What values should underpin the development process?

- Discuss the phenomenon of imposed development. What do you understand by the term?

- How should we understand development, and what roles can and should an "international development enterprise" play in a country's ongoing development?

- Which of the various paths to development would you emphasize for a country's development process, and why?

- What should be the role of external aid in development and what are currently the major issues with it?

- What potential is there in local-level development when actions taken at other levels are ineffective or even counterproductive?

Possible Areas for Research Projects

- Select a country or region with which you have some familiarity and trace its development history, bearing in mind the various paths to development. Consider the paths taken in terms of development outcomes (as measured by the WB or UNDP).

- Study the pros and cons of aid-dependent development, perhaps with a specific country or region in mind, and determine, on the basis of your analysis, what role it should play.

- Examine a country's (or a small region's within a country) development process over a period in terms of adherence to, or departure from, the integrated-perspectives approach (presented in Chapter 2).

- In a selected context, identify the barriers involved in preventing either external aid or macro-level development from permeating through to the local level.

Further Reading

Easterly, W. (2002). *The elusive quest for growth: Economists' adventures and misadventures in the tropics.* Cambridge, MA: MIT Press.

Hoogvelt, A. (2001). *Globalization and the post-colonial world.* Basingstoke, England: Palgrave Macmillan.

Isbister, J. (1991). *Promises not kept: The betrayal of social change in the third world.* West Hartford, CT: Kumarian.

Stoesz, D., Guzzetta, C., & Lusk, M. (1999). *International development.* Boston: Allyn & Bacon.

Todaro, M., & Smith, S. C. (2003). *Economic development* (8th ed.). Harlow, England: Pearson.

UNDP. (1996). *Human development report: Growth for human development.* New York: Oxford University Press.

6

The Field of Development: Programs and Strategies

In the previous chapter we outlined the reasons why local-level development (sometimes referred to as grassroots level community development) should be the development priority of international social work, while accepting that social workers are and should be involved at all other levels and dimensions of the development field. In this chapter, after exploring further the meaning of local-level development, our focus is on the most common programs and strategies found in local-level development within developing countries.

Learning Objectives

- To encourage readers to think about how development can work at the local level, and the roles that social workers or others might play in the process.

- To introduce readers to the key programs and strategies used in the field of local-level development.

  Specifically, this chapter aims to develop an understanding of

- The meaning and significance of local-level development or grassroots-level community development.

- The importance of the integrated-perspectives approach in global, national, and local-level development.

- Personnel issues in local-level development.

- Some specific aspects of local-level development.

- Some broad approaches, strategies, and programs used within local-level development.

- The importance of, and need for employing, integrated comprehensive programs.

Local-level Development

The Meaning and Significance of Local-level Development

Social development is often said to be necessary at all levels, ranging from the international to the local, and here we need to clarify what precisely we mean by the term *local*. Earlier it was pointed out that, in the 1960s, local was commonly seen as synonymous with community, with community development being the term used to encompass local-level development. Then as we saw, writers like Esman and Uphoff (Esman and Uphoff, 1984; Uphoff, 1986) moved toward a more complex appreciation of the term local. For these writers, local could refer to a group, neighborhood, community, or several communities together. Uphoff (1986, p. 11) produced a model of what he called "Levels of Decision Making and Activity." Five levels together could be seen as constituting local, although Uphoff confines his meaning of local to the first three of the following:

locality level (a set of communities having cooperative or commercial relations);

community level (a relatively self-contained socioeconomic-residential unit);

group level (a self-identified set of persons having some common interest; maybe a small residential group like a hamlet or neighborhood, an occupational group, or some ethnic, caste, age, sex, or other grouping);

household level; and

individual level.

We shall retain all five levels because social work as practiced at the local level will inevitably involve all five levels. The skill in local development work often lies in the complex task of understanding the required meaning of local in a specific context, and therefore the level of intervention. As Uphoff (1986, p. 11) says "Many mistakes in development assistance derive from too gross an understanding of this apparently simple term," namely *local*.

Accepting the above understanding of local, we need to consider the significance of the local level in development, especially in light of the fact that it receives hardly a mention in many major texts on development. Let us commence by considering the local level as one of the sectors that constitute a society.

Referring to the local level as individuals-families-communities, we can regard it as one sector of society alongside the other three sectors of society: the marketplace or economic sector, the governance of the state or institutional sector, and the civil society sector. In our model of society (see Figure 6.1), society is depicted as a triangle. The base of the triangle is the individuals-families-communities sector, which functions as the foundation of society. Accepting that the other two sides of the triangle are the economic and governance sectors, the space within the triangle is then civil society. Civil society interacts with all three sides of the triangle. Most of its constituent parts emerge from the individuals-families-communities sector, as local organizations come together to form a wide range of more or less societywide associations, organizations, and movements. Some of its constituent parts, however, emanate from and contribute directly to the economic sector, such as trade unions and employer associations. Other parts emanate from, or at least participate directly within, the governance sector, such as political parties and movements, civil service unions, and the like. We would argue, on the basis of this model, that a well-functioning society is built on firm foundations. Without a strong individuals-families-communities sector, as we shall go on to interpret this, a society will not possess a strong civil society or representative governance or an effective economic sector. Although some forms of the economic and governance sectors can be imposed for a period

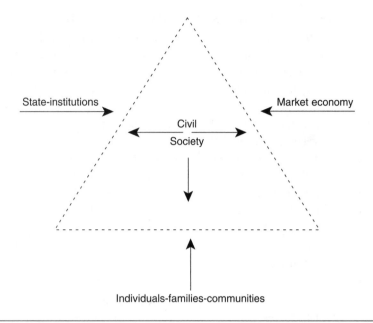

State-institutions

Market economy

Civil
Society

Individuals-families-communities

Figure 6.1   The four sectors of a society

from outside, or created and controlled by an internal elite, all sectors depend ultimately on strong foundations at the local level. So, in development terms, while the development of all sectors is important, the creation of strong foundations is of particular importance, and it is this task that local-level development assumes as its overall goal.

If we wish to be more specific, we can discuss several ways in which important aspects of society depend on the foundations established at the local level. One argument is that ultimately it is people who constitute a society's most important resource, but like all other resources people require development, and this development begins at the local level. A crucial element of this is capacity building at the individual, family, and community levels. A second argument is that important societal qualities, such as social capital and social integration, cannot ultimately be imposed from above but rely on local-level developments (World Bank, 2000/2001, 2001). A third argument is that macroeconomic development is, to a significant degree, dependent on economic

developments at the local level, such as the household economy, the community economy, and the informal economy, while other levels of economic development require that the local level functions effectively as producers and consumers within the economic system.

In addition to its inherent significance, the significance of focusing on local-level development is in part due to the extent to which that level is neglected by the overall development process, as a result, for example, of biased or distorted development (Chapter 5). Local-level neglect also occurs when overall development is stymied by corrupt and inefficient governance and an underdeveloped formal economic sector, resulting in low levels of development and usually high levels of poverty at the local level. To the extent that these blocks to development cannot be rectified quickly, local-level development may be the only level at which practitioners can attempt to move forward the whole process of development for large populations; and doing this has been shown to be feasible, even in the face of development failure, or blockages to development, at the macro level. Moreover, even slight improvements at the local level may flow upward through a somewhat stronger civil society, exerting greater pressure for positive change within the macro political and economic sectors.

Finally, we would argue that, for social workers, the local level is the level where the need for their skills, the relevance of their range of knowledge and skills, and the significance of their value base is greatest. In developing countries particularly, an effective social work education program should see large numbers of graduates being available for local-level development work, which is unfortunately not the case in most developing countries.

The Integrated-perspectives Approach and Local-level Development

The integrated-perspectives approach both highlights the importance of local-level development and guides its implementation. The four perspectives, singularly and together, point to the need for a strong focus on development at the local level. The global reality is that hundreds of millions of people still today continue to eke out an existence or struggle to survive, particularly in impoverished rural areas, the remote parts of many countries, on isolated islands, and as marginalized indigenous or minority populations largely excluded from mainstream development. Each of our four perspectives cries out against this reality. The global perspective reminds us that these peoples are members of the global community, have a unique contribution to make to the world in a variety of ways, and deserve to be given an appropriate place within the global community. The human rights perspective reminds us that all these people possess the right to development, and to enjoy a lifestyle and standard of living consistent with what it means to be human. The ecological perspective shows us how deleterious it is for poor people, their local

environments, and the global ecology if they are kept in poverty and forced to exploit their natural environments in unsustainable and harmful ways in order to survive. Finally, the social development perspective shows us how we can ensure that these people find their rightful place within the human family.

There is simply no way in which we can value, affirm, and seek to implement these four perspectives without placing a strong emphasis on local-level development in those localities requiring such, for it is at the local level that many of the realities that our four perspectives set out to address are most widely manifested and often most deeply entrenched.

Personnel Issues in Local-level Development

While there does not appear to be much detailed discussion of the question of personnel in local-level development, apart from a number of UN reports in the 1970s, the implications in what is said on the topic generally are frequently that local personnel either can facilitate the whole process or are essential as motivators to initiate action. The more impoverished a situation, where people are struggling to survive, and the more disempowered a people, the less likely is local-level development to take off without external intervention. The nature of this external intervention is characterized by the personnel engaged in it being referred to as enablers, facilitators, or motivators. As such they may be local personnel who, as volunteers or paraprofessionals, are recruited and trained for such work; alternatively, they may be people from cultural or ethnic backgrounds similar to those of the local people in question but who are drawn from the ranks of high school or even university graduates, depending on the availability of such people for the levels of pay being offered. (In some countries, unemployment rates among new graduates have made it comparatively easy to recruit such personnel into local-level development for at least short periods while they await employment opportunities: for example, Sri Lanka and Bangladesh in the 1990s.)

However, another theme common in the literature refers to the shortage of personnel for employment in local-level development. The perceived reasons for this vary. Sometimes it relates to the prevailing culture and a difficulty in fitting such personnel as are available into local cultural frameworks; sometimes it relates to the prevailing living and working conditions, especially in the more impoverished areas of a nation, and the unwillingness of personnel "with prospects" to accept such work; and sometimes it seems to be more because few people are being trained for and deployed into such work. There would appear to be a much greater number of relatively untrained local staff, guided or trained by outside professionals, engaged in local project work, whether undertaken by local NGOs or by international organizations. Such work is very different from what is being discussed here. Projects tend to be discrete time-limited programs undertaken at the local level, but usually with limited participation of local people at any level. The effectiveness of such project work in bringing about sustainable change has been often questioned.

So far as professional social work is concerned, the reality in many less developed countries requiring staff in local development work is that there exists either no school or few schools of social work, and any graduates usually prefer to work in urban areas, often in the civil service, and in any case usually in relatively well-paid and comfortable jobs befitting their perceived status. Such circumstances produce few social work graduates available for and willing to enter local-level development work, even if there were the agencies willing to employ them. One example here is Thailand. A recent report (Senanuch, 2005) indicates that at least 40 percent of graduates from the country's two schools of social work are working outside the profession, and that very few of the remainder choose to work with the poor. Few students opt to study community development, while the main curricula devote minimum time to development or poverty issues. This situation is beginning to change in some countries with the introduction of rural schools of social work (e.g., in India), but change is coming extremely slowly and to a very limited degree. If social work, or any other profession for that matter, is to supply the frontline grassroots workers required for local-level development work, it will need to develop education and training models very different from those introduced to date.

The UN has long been aware of the importance of personnel at the local level. In 1979, a UN report called *Social Services in Rural Development* stated,

> Frontline workers constitute the heart of the social service delivery system and their training requires special attention. Limitations of resources dictate that training full-fledged professional workers is neither possible nor desirable if the needs of the majority of the rural poor are to be met reasonably soon. (p. 35)

In 1988, a UN document on social development concluded that

> to overcome the shortage of trained personnel in many countries, comprehensive training programmes should receive high priority. . . . Appropriate training should be provided at all levels. (United Nations, 1988, p. 10)

A few years later, the secretary-general's report on the implementation of these guiding principles commented,

> A technical assistance programme should be devised for training all categories of personnel required to ensure an effective execution of micro-level programmes at the individual, family and community levels. (United Nations, 1991, p. 5)

Also in 1988, an ESCAP plan of action on human resources development pointed to the need for "enablers of human resources development":

Appropriate enablers of human resources development must be identified. . . . Enablers of human resources development include those individuals, groups and organizations whose active intervention can catalyse the human resources development process. (UN/ESCAP, 1988, p. 12)

An ESCAP Social Development Strategy in 1992 stated,

The professional capabilities of the personnel responsible for the implementation of the national programmes of action will need to be strengthened. (UN/ESCAP, 1992, p. 36)

Many reports in the development field over the years have indicated a need for appropriate personnel, especially at the local level, but almost never do they spell out precisely who these personnel should be or how they might be recruited, trained, and deployed. Even the descriptions used of such workers are confusing: for example, social service personnel, social welfare workers, frontline workers, paraprofessional workers, community development personnel, rural development staff, community social workers, and social workers (all found in UN documents of the 1980s and 1990s). The three general terms indicating categories of personnel most commonly found are professionals, usually in specific areas such as health, education, and agricultural development; local development workers, usually seen as paraprofessionals, untrained workers, or volunteers; and social welfare personnel to address specific welfare needs. Seldom are the terms, or the categories they signify, developed in any detail, and one often gains the impression that their utilization reflects considerable wishful thinking. In practice, we are unaware of major training schemes being developed in relation to any of these three areas, which may be why local developments in all three areas—social service delivery, local-level development generally, and local responses to welfare needs—appear to be restricted to the work of a comparative handful of NGOs covering a small fraction of the existing need. Furthermore, the call for large numbers of trained personnel seems to have become less frequent, with any emphasis found being largely on in-service training of NGO personnel. One wonders, however, how much the work of NGOs at the local level is significantly constrained by their inability to employ personnel with appropriate skills.

It appears clear to us, from a review of the literature and from our observations, that there continues to be a major need for frontline workers across the range of social development concerns at the local level, but that this need is today less in the forefront of thinking than it was in the 1970s and 1980s. While development thinking has been increasingly pushing the responsibility for local-level development back onto the people, their communities, and local organizations, few in the field appear to think that the local level in many situations will assume this responsibility without facilitators, both working at this level and with the ability to channel necessary resources of various kinds through to this level. Moreover, many evaluations of work undertaken at the local level indicate significant levels of success from people-centered local development initiatives undertaken at the local level with the assistance of facilitators (see Cernea, 1991; Carroll, 1992; Nee and Healy, 2003; Vohra, 1990; UN/ESCAP, 1996a, 1996b). One must, therefore, conclude that the availability of much larger numbers of appropriately trained facilitators will result in much wider deployment of such staff and far more effective social development at local levels. One key question for us here is, then, whether social work education in developing and developed countries has the capacity, and indeed the responsibility, to take this level of education and training seriously, even if it requires the incorporation within the profession of an undergraduate level such as social work assistants. We shall consider this question in Chapter 14.

Case Examples

Personnel in Family Planning in Bangladesh

A case example showing the need for appropriate personnel comes from an experience with family planning in poverty-stricken villages in Bangladesh. Initially a government family planning office sent out extension workers who were educated middle-class town women speaking upper-class Bengali. As one analysis put it, these workers were separated from the village women by "a gulf of arrogance and indifference." The scheme failed to reach the poor. Then an alternative NGO scheme that was introduced flooded the countryside with cheap birth-control pills, using undertrained field workers who offered little education or supervision in the use of the pills. This approach was seen to do more harm than good.

(Example from Hartman and Boyce, 1982, p. 29.)

Personnel in Child Health in Indonesia

Another case example using volunteers comes from Indonesia, and was assessed by the UN as successful. The program was designed to promote child health at the village level. It recruited 800,000 women health volunteers to provide leadership in child health in 57,000 villages. Working through a village-based "integrated services post," the voluntary workers played many roles themselves (e.g., monitoring children's physical development and running education sessions), while also acting as liaisons between the local mothers and available health staff (e.g., for immunizations and midwifery services). The volunteers received training but attendance was uneven and some of the volunteers were assessed as performing poorly.

(Example from UN/ESCAP, 1994a, p. 29.)

Goals and Strategies Pertaining to Local-Level Development

The question of goals, strategies, and skills required by local-level development is clearly a huge area regarding which we can do little more than provide a synopsis concerning how we see the field in practice terms. It could be argued that the entire area of social work literature and experience related to working with individuals, families, and communities is relevant, provided that it is appropriately modified for the developing country and locally specific context. In addition, there is a large literature (although not in the major texts and often of a general nature) in the development field relating to local-level development in various contexts, particularly rural but also urban. Despite these two bodies of literature, there appears to have been little work done on developing an overview of the goals, strategies, and skills pertaining to local-level development. Once practitioners possess such an overview, they can explore the wider literature for more detailed material on specific aspects of the field that can be applied, directly or indirectly, to whatever specific situation they confront.

The Six Levels of Focus of Local-Level Development

Within local-level development there are various levels on which workers might focus, although ideally a focus on any of the following areas should occur within a broad understanding of the situation pertaining to all of the other areas outlined below. We are suggesting that there are six main levels of focus. These are individuals, families, communities (in a broad sense to cover neighborhoods, localities, communities in the common sense of the term, and sets of communities), population groups, local organizations, and local institutions and governance. Social work is very familiar with the first four, may well regard the fifth as an aspect of community development, and tends to avoid the sixth. We believe that all six are important to local-level development practice, for the following reasons.

A focus on *individuals* is sometimes assumed to be a luxury that cannot be afforded within the situations of mass need that often present in developing countries. There are several reasons why such an assumption is erroneous, including the argument from rights, but let us focus on two other basic ones. One basic reason is that all other units—families, local organizations, and so forth—at the local level consist ultimately of individuals, whose capacities and commitment levels are fundamental to the effective functioning of those units. As individuals are the basic resource on which all development ultimately

depends, it is essentially a matter of the capacity levels, attitudes, values, and so on of individuals that will determine the final outcome. A second reason is that, in any context, but particularly in the developing country context, there will be a number of people who have been damaged by the poverty, abuse, exclusion, or marginalization they have experienced, or who possess disabilities for which they have never been provided with the available strategies to overcome, or have been psychologically and physically damaged by experiences of war, natural disaster, and displacement. This individual welfare aspect of local-level development is critical if development opportunities are to be made available to all people and if all people are to be drawn into the development process, while human rights and social development principles imply that this must be the case.

Practitioners at the local level will work with individuals, even if this is within the context of other work, and must take the needs of various categories of individuals into account as they plan and implement all activities undertaken locally. They will thus ensure that community-based and other responses to need are so designed that they will cater to the needs and rights of a wide range of individuals.

Case Example

Prostheses in Cambodia

A good example of local-level development focused on individuals is in the field of disability. In Cambodia, because of extensive use of antipersonnel mines, many rural adults and children were deprived of any opportunity of participating in development after losing a limb. The provision of artificial limbs was critical to such people's future well-being and even survival in some cases. Local organizations worked with an appropriate Australian university faculty to develop, manufacture, and fit appropriate artificial limbs, and to instruct recipients in their effective utilization.

(Example from personal communication with staff of Faculty of Health Sciences, La Trobe University, Melbourne, Australia.)

Case Example

Public Health in the Philippines

A case example comes from the Philippines. In attempting to raise public health levels at the household level, a health board was prominently displayed at the village center. Each household was indicated by a drawing of a house which was segmented, with segments signifying sanitation, type of flooring, and other facilities. The segment was then colored to show whether the household had made no change, was in the process of changing, or had achieved the desired goal. Thus a degree of public pressure was used to bring about household changes and so raise public health levels in the community as a whole.

(Example from UN/ESCAP, 1996a, p. 61.)

The second main level of focus is *families*. In many aspects of local-level practice the family constitutes a key focus. Many caring services are located in the household; the household economy is of very great importance, especially in areas lacking broader economic development; the provision of health and education frequently relies on the cooperation of all members of a household; human rights are very significant at the household level, especially in relation to females and children; and it is the family unit that is usually most affected when things go wrong. Many local-level development programs focus, therefore, on the family unit, and the wealth of knowledge and understanding applicable to family functioning should be made available to practitioners concerned directly with this level of local practice. All local workers, however, will always need to bear in mind the roles of the family, the pressures on families in a specific context, and the likely implications for families of any activities undertaken locally.

Many local-level development programs focus to a significant extent on individual families. These include programs concerning family planning and household public health measures (e.g., home sanitation), household economic programs, and home improvement programs. However, the delivery of such programs, while essentially concerned with family well-being and sometimes targeting specific categories of families, is often undertaken at the community level. This allows economies of scale through programs providing, for example, mass education, while often also enlisting the general community as a support for achieving set goals.

The third main level of focus, *communities*, has always been a key focus in local-level development, although as noted earlier the concept and viability of community has long been a topic for debate. We are adopting a broad definition of community to embrace the concepts of neighborhoods, localities, and both separate communities and communities existing within a specific area. The community development work that emerged in the developing world from the 1960s on, and the strong focus on local rural development during the same period, both placed a strong emphasis on community. Various national programs sought to deploy community workers at all village levels (e.g., in India and Indonesia), and other government-led programs relied on community leaders (e.g., Thailand), while many NGOs engaged in community development work. For a time following this period, it almost seemed as if communities were being regarded as a focus belonging to the past, with the current focus being on individuals at the local level, civil society functions, and state programs. More recently, with the neoliberal emphasis on a smaller state and smaller state budgets, but also because of a renewed interest in the potential of communities, responsibility for development has been increasingly thrown back onto the local level, but often with little exploration of the real ability of the local level to respond.

The fourth level of focus is *group life*—a concept that is also somewhat difficult to pin down. In one sense, the focus is on identity groups to which individuals belong on the basis of their perceived religion, ethnicity, race, caste, or some other such attribute. In another sense, categories of people might be determined on the basis of class, occupational grouping, or age. Activities might thus, for example, be geared to teenagers, the elderly, working-class people, or those employed in a particular industry such as forestry, fishing, or mining. While groups with which people identify, or within which they feel a sense of belonging, may exist in any local area, such groupings become important as a level of focus for practitioners when they constitute the basis of significant social divisions. Many societies are characterized by deep divisions on any or all of the above bases, and when this is reflected at the local level, which is almost invariably the case to some degree, workers may be compelled to focus initially on specific groups, even if the ultimate goal is to build social cohesion across local diversity.

There are many examples of a group focus, including programs with lower-caste groups in India, with street children in most developing countries, and with women migrant workers in Hong Kong and elsewhere (see Chapter 13).

The focus on *local organizations,* while familiar to community development workers, is not so central to most social work practice. Local organizations in the development context are sometimes referred to as people's organizations, because they are formed by people at the local level to facilitate meeting needs, pursuing interests, or realizing aspirations. Esman and Uphoff

(1984, p. 18) define local organizations as "organizations which act on behalf of and are accountable to their membership and which are involved in development activities." Local organizations constitute the building blocks of civil society. Forming at the local level initially, such organizations often go on to associate with their counterparts in other localities in various ways, eventually in many cases becoming national organizations. This association or cooperation is designed to increase the possibility of people achieving the goals that led initially to the establishment of such organizations, by increasing their power to influence either governance or the economic sector. Workers in their practice at the local level are regularly involved in facilitating networking between people, which networks eventually coalesce in many cases into local organizations. Once these organizations are formed, local workers will frequently continue to work with them to strengthen them and facilitate their achievement of identified goals. (See Cernea, 1991, and Esman and Uphoff, 1984, for a wide range of examples of local organizational development.)

Our sixth and final level concerns *local institutions,* including local government. As mentioned earlier in Uphoff (1986, p. 9), "institutions, whether organizations or not, are complexes of norms and behaviors that persist over time by serving collectively valued purposes." He later comments, "An institution is an organization that is valued by persons over and above the direct and immediate benefits they derive from it." According to Uphoff, the benefits of institutions "tend to be 'public goods'" (p. 14). As examples we might mention governance, law and order, banking, or religion. The reason for including this area here is the perceived importance, in developing countries in particular, of promoting institutional development at the local level, which according to Uphoff can be done through "assistance, facilitation, and promotion" (p. 19). What must be stressed, however, is that the values, norms, and behaviors on which institutions are based must be those of the people concerned, and not those of outsiders desiring to impose a set of foreign institutions on a people. (For some case studies, see Uphoff, 1986.)

Four Basic Emphases in Working at the Local Level

Regardless of which of the above six levels a worker focuses on, there would appear to be four basic emphases in working at the local level. The four are

- working directly with *individual units,* whether families, communities, or whatever;
- working with the *interactions between various units;*
- working with *collectives of units* of whatever kind; and
- working with the *formal structures established by units* at the local level.

Let us consider each of these emphases and their relevance.

Working with individual units is going to be extremely important when the units concerned are unable to function effectively in society, both in fulfilling their own purposes and in linking with other units to fulfill collective goals. Engaging in unit capacity building and improved functioning, raising the level of self-confidence and self-esteem, and so on may be the specific objectives of working with individual units. Clearly this can apply across the range of units, from individuals to local institutions.

Working with the interaction between units at the local level basically revolves around strengthening social capital for purposes such as enhancing social cohesion. Families can be at odds with each other—a condition Banfield (1958) and others have called "amoral familism"; communities may be at odds with each other—a condition we might call "excessive communalism"; groups may be in conflict or engaged in excessive competition with each

other, as exemplified in ethnocentric behavior or religious fundamentalism; and local organizations and institutions may be experiencing difficulty in appreciating each other's roles and cooperating for the general or public good. This emphasis on interaction is extremely important if social capital is to grow and bind people together for their mutual benefit and the promotion of the public good—the essence of social capital being mutual trust and cooperation.

Working with collectives of units of whatever kind is ultimately essential at the local level, in that it is only through cooperation and collaboration between units that progress is finally achieved, whether social, economic, political, cultural, welfare, or ecological in nature. The emphasis within social development on achieving an integrated and comprehensive approach to overall development is for this reason. Local workers will, therefore, often be found encouraging and facilitating ways of units working together in the achievement of their identified goals.

Finally, within most local areas a series of social, economic, political, cultural, legal, and other structures are ultimately formalized, giving rise to a range of local organizations and institutions with designated roles within the local context. In many situations, however, such developments remain for a period in an embryonic and fragile state; and local-level workers may see the strengthening of such structures as the major emphasis in their local involvement. Often the focus will not cover all such structures, but will focus on those such as local governance structures, economic structures, and social service delivery structures.

Two Key Approaches to Local-level Development

Although the following two approaches are essentially complementary, and should therefore be held together by practitioners, their separation has been a reality in much social work practice as it has evolved in the past. The two approaches are the remedial and developmental approaches.

We are taking the *remedial approach* to mean a focus on remedying presenting problems without necessarily addressing the root causes of those needs or modifying structures so that such problems will not arise. It is the obvious approach where the local worker is strongly aware of a range of often serious presenting problems. There are several points that need to be made regarding this approach. In many areas of developing countries, the extent to which basic needs are being met is far from acceptable, and a worker could be forgiven for automatically assuming that the presenting task was to meet these needs however and wherever possible. In some situations, a worker may consider that the people themselves are insufficiently aware of their own needs to be willing to engage in meeting them, and that the key challenge is "awareness-raising" in regard to these problems. Finally, in the development field, many commentators have argued that remedial work can only be based on evaluations of their situation made by the people themselves, and then carried out essentially by the people after they have considered the situation and decided how to approach the problem. This approach implies that situations not considered by local people to be a problem will not be addressed—an outcome that some local workers find difficult to accept. Accepting that the social development principles and values should always apply, the remedial approach is a valid and often necessary approach, as long as it does not utilize available resources to the extent that the second approach, the developmental, becomes impossible. This is because a failure to go back to root causes, and to engage in the developmental approach on the basis of that understanding, is likely to see no end to the emergence of presenting problems—a situation to be avoided if at all possible.

The *developmental approach* implies that the emphasis is, from the beginning, much more on what might and should be than on what is. The danger here is that the vision for the future on which developmental work is based may well represent an outsider's vision rather than one held by the local people. So again the social development perspective is important to ensure that the whole approach is essentially a participatory one. Within the developmental approach, the worker may focus on capacity building, influenced by an understanding of what capacities lie latent, could be developed, and would be beneficial to future development (see Chapter 4). Alternatively, the worker may focus on local organization development as holding the key to realizing the local potential, gearing this frequently to economic development or to another dimension of development. As another alternative, the focus may well be on local income-generation opportunities, in terms of development mainly of the household, community, or informal economy, but sometimes of the formal economy at the local level. While the developmental approach is essentially looking ahead, it cannot be oblivious to presenting local needs, and will seek to ensure that strategies utilized will ensure that these needs are met as progress is made toward achieving designated and agreed-upon goals.

Key Strategies and Programs Appropriate to Local-level Development

While we shall discuss a range of specific types of programs, it is important to emphasize, first, that what follows is by no means an exclusive list and, second, that ideally local-level development will involve many of these programs being run together and integrated with each other. Wherever possible, local-level development should be undertaken through what has been called a *comprehensive integrated approach*. Commonly this will involve an NGO or an appointed team of workers acting as the key

---

Key Strategies and Programs for Local-level Development

- Basic literacy courses

- Primary school education

- Basic health care

- Adult education, basic training, and people's capacity building

- Awareness-raising and empowerment

- Local income-generation programs (includes microenterprise schemes)

- Credit schemes and people's banks

- Community-based welfare programs

- Self-help groups and promotion of self-reliance

- Collective responses to specific situations

- Leadership development

- Local organization and institution promotion and capacity building

- Linking local organizations to government agencies and international structures

- Comprehensive community development programs

---

agency. That agency should initially establish coordinating mechanisms that bring together village or community representatives, existing local NGOs, and any government structures operating within the area. It is crucial that all sections of the population and all local agencies within the designated area understand each other's concerns, roles, and activities, and come together within structures that will both achieve this goal and maximize cooperation and collaboration. A comprehensive integrated approach, concerned with all dimensions of local life and involving all members of the local population, directly or indirectly, reflects the social development, human rights, and ecological perspectives that are today widely accepted (at least in theory) and key elements in our conceptual approach. (See the final section of this chapter for an example of the comprehensive integrated approach.) The alternative to this comprehensive approach is the initiation within an area of a number of small-scale projects, undertaken by

a variety of agencies and implemented with little or no attempt at coordination or meaningful levels of people's participation.

The balance of this section is devoted to strategies and programs deemed to be commonly of central importance to comprehensive community development programs.

Basic Literacy Courses

Basic literacy plays a crucial role in people's ability to participate in and benefit from local-level development. Many such courses are provided on a relatively informal basis, involving little in the way of infrastructure and material inputs. They do, however, require teachers, who may be recruited from the local population and trained and assisted in performing this role, or may be outsiders brought in for the purpose. There is considerable expertise available to assist in devising such courses and selecting the most effective teaching methods.

Case Example

Literacy in Papua New Guinea

An example of a basic literacy program is one conducted in Papua New Guinea. This involved utilizing western experts to devise the literacy program and western workers to train local leaders. These local leaders were then supported in the establishment and running of literacy courses at the village level. The secret to the success of this program lay in the design of the approach to literacy learning, and the training and support of local leaders. That is, the best possible literacy development methods were employed within a program that was fully responsive to local culture, socioeconomic realities, and the people's aspirations.

(Example from personal communication with social worker involved.)

Primary School Education

A key element in overcoming the cycle of poverty and in building a sound basis for further local development is the provision of primary school education. Research shows that the returns from investment in primary school education are indisputable and much higher than for higher levels of education (World Bank, 1991b, p. 64). It is thus a critical aspect in local development.

Ideally education is the responsibility of the state, or of local government if the provision is decentralized. In many developing countries, however, states are not sufficiently well-developed or funded to be able to provide universal primary school education—at least not without some assistance from the local level. It is not uncommon, for example, for local-level development to be involved in providing the physical structures within which a primary school will function, in providing part of the salary of a teacher, in actively supporting the school system in other ways, or even of utilizing local partly trained personnel as a substitute for a qualified teacher. An alternative scenario to the above, especially where the local

area is extremely impoverished, is for an NGO to undertake some or all of the above roles; but even where this is necessary, every effort should be made to maximize community participation from the very beginning.

In developed countries few social workers are concerned with the central aspects of education. In developing countries, however, this cannot be the situation. It is important that social workers appreciate the importance of primary school education, have an appreciation of key curriculum issues such as the extent to which the curriculum should be related to the local situation (e.g., to income-generation opportunities open to these children in the future), understand the various barriers that often stand in the way of children attending and benefiting from school and have some insights into how to address these barriers, and have explored their role in building school-parent-community relationships so that the school becomes an integral part of the local scene. Even if local workers are not involved in developing the primary school system itself, they will invariably be involved in the community's ability to foster, support, and effectively and fully utilize that system.

Case Example

Primary Schools in China

An example from the People's Republic of China is a program established by a government-supported autonomous NGO whose concern was with the effectiveness of primary schools in impoverished rural areas. Under the name of Project Hope, the program aimed at improving the physical conditions in schools or building new ones, enhancing the roles of teachers, and ensuring the ongoing attendance at primary school of children from poor families. Utilizing donor monies, involving local community officials and others, but particularly recruiting members of the China Youth Foundation as outreach workers, the program sought to rectify a situation where only one-third of children graduated from primary school, with four million dropping out each year. By 1996, the program had assisted 860,000 families with school fees, encouraged and assisted many other families to keep their children in school, established 300 new primary schools (using local community involvement to a very high degree), and supported underpaid teachers in various ways. This program has been assessed as highly effective in improving primary school education, involving youth in a very worthwhile program, and educating families and officials on the importance of primary school education.

(Example from UN/ESCAP, 1996a, p. 29.)

Basic Health Care

A glance at the relevant statistics (e.g., UNDP annual reports) will quickly reveal the extent to which the coverage of health services is limited in the majority of developing countries. What is critical to local-level development, however, is the availability of at least basic health care in every locality across every country. Not only is this a commitment agreed on by all governments at the international level, but the precise nature of basic health care has been carefully researched by the World Health Organization (WHO) in terms of what provisions are essential and how these are best delivered in cost-effective terms (see World Bank, 1993). It is this level of basic health care that every local worker should both appreciate and be committed to achieving, with of course the full involvement of the local people.

As with primary schools, the roles of local communities are critical in achieving the set goal. The local community may assist in constructing a basic health center and even in paying staff to some degree, often in nonmonetary ways.

Staff may even need to be recruited locally and provided with basic training, ideally ongoing supervision, and the ability to refer people to professional health services as necessary. It is also important that the local communities be educated regarding key aspects of health provision, such as the importance of basic hygiene and public health and how to achieve this in the local context, the nature and importance of immunization in their situation, and the identification of key symptoms for common local illnesses. Local communities may be able to establish loan schemes to assist local people to reach the nearest doctor or hospital when this is essential. Sometimes a basic health insurance arrangement for this purpose is attached to a local small-scale credit scheme or people's bank.

All social workers engaged in local-level development should receive at least some elementary education in basic health care and public health provision, and should ensure that, whatever their specific activities, they remain fully aware of the health factor and how to maximize beneficial health standards at all levels.

Case Example

Basic Health Care in Sri Lanka

A government-run initiative in an extremely impoverished area of Sri Lanka used health concerns as its entry into local communities, largely because health was critical to enabling the poor to move into income generation and out of poverty. Over a period of approximately two years, the process was one of awareness creation, group organization, and health activities. Local support teams were selected for training by the poor people themselves, and these would then work with the government's village development officers. The focus of the health program was on mothers, with the major concerns being health education and an antimalaria program. Rural women's development societies were formed as a framework for involving women with each other, fostering empowerment and solidarity, and channeling health supports and services. The aims were to overcome ignorance, dependency, and helplessness, and to encourage communities to assume responsibility for their own health. While basic health was the focus, the program aimed also at enhancing literacy, income-generation activities, and community development generally.

(Example from UN/ESCAP, 1996a, p. 106.)

Adult Education, Basic Training, and People's Capacity Building

Invariably throughout the local-level development process, local people become aware of deficiencies in their knowledge and skills levels. Sometimes this may be within a context where many people greatly underestimate their own capacity to learn and grow in knowledge and abilities; at other times, people are highly eager to learn and brimming with self-confidence in this regard. The worker's task in this area is invariably influenced by local circumstances and prevailing cultural attitudes, so that the approach adopted should be one that is suited to the local situation.

As the need to learn emerges, workers are faced with several options. They may themselves be able to provide the knowledge and teach the skills, and may elect to do so; they may decide that it is better to offer the people the opportunity of a visit from an outsider to run an appropriate course; or they may decide to use the identified need to encourage local people to explore how to access the wider society to meet the need, such as contacting a government department office for information or even training related to agriculture, forestry, marketing, and so on. Over a longer period, they may even talk with relevant communities or organizations regarding the possibility of establishing a local adult education center, where relevant materials could be kept and various courses organized from time to time—an important repository of resources in many villages today.

While no social worker will possess all of the knowledge and skills local people might need, all could be expected to appreciate the importance of people's capacity and knowledge building in the broadest sense, to be able to identify possible mechanisms for achieving this locally, and to be ready to facilitate a community's desire to enhance its ability to engage in its own capacity building, or at least developing processes for achieving this goal.

Case Examples

Training in Chile

A well-established NGO in Chile is engaged in a range of development projects. The basic process used is that NGO staff train "local monitors, or community promoters" who are then responsible for implementing the project. The training of these monitors has been evaluated as beneficial to both them and their communities, because of the leadership abilities developed. A specific aspect of this NGO's program is to run courses in such areas as electricity and sewing, contributing both to the range of capacities available locally and to income-generation opportunities for course participants. While clearly beneficial, a criticism of these programs has been that they seldom result in collective action or raise overall economic (income, employment, and production) levels.

(Example from Carroll,1992, chap.13.)

Capacity Building in South Korea

Another example, from South Korea, of what was basically referred to as a capacity-building program, was the establishment of a social welfare center in an urban area by a school of social work. While the center provided a variety of services within an "integrated urban services" approach and had several aims, one key aim was capacity building. Several types of capacities were targeted, including management capacities at the local level; vocational training of the mothers of the children attending the day care program; the capacity of parents to adapt to the urban environment, including sex education, child rearing, and family planning; leadership training for youth; and leadership training for local community leaders. Relating capacity building to a variety of child, health, and other program delivery is quite common.

(Example from Chi, 1987.)

Awareness-raising and Empowerment

While social workers in western countries are at least conscious of the need for self-awareness, seldom does awareness-raising in others receive much attention. By contrast, an emphasis has been placed on awareness-raising in a variety of development contexts in developing countries. While in Latin America there has been a strong emphasis on awareness-raising and empowerment in the context of oppression (see Chapter 4), a second context where the concept is raised is that of extreme poverty, usually in situations where people have come to accept their poverty as in some sense indicative of what they deserve or what they are worth. And a third context is that of culture, where certain circumstances may, for example, be accepted as representing the hand of fate.

The assumption often found in the development literature is that an awareness of reality is an essential prerequisite to people participating fully in their own development process, in that awareness will frequently lead to a determination to initiate changes and efforts to do just that. In some circumstances, however, workers should never encourage or promote self-awareness without standing ready to support people when that awareness results in a desire to take action. Awareness-raising is thus one step within a broader process.

It is suggested that awareness-raising can be achieved through dialogue between people and a worker, often undertaken informally, for example utilizing situations where people typically gather for other purposes in circumstances that involve resting or waiting. A second strategy is social learning—learning that occurs within group contexts and largely as a result of posing problems and seeking their resolution through action. In practice, however, awareness-raising is likely to occur, or be possible, within a wide variety of situations (such as oppression, exclusion, local problems such as drug addiction, and access to existing facilities); and an observant worker, aware of the need for such, will utilize opportunities as they arise. (For a discussion of empowerment, see Chapter 4.)

Case Examples

Organization in India

Awareness-raising and empowerment programs target a range of powerless people. One urban NGO in India targeted mainly pavement dwellers who often found themselves powerless in a vice between politicians and large urban developers. This NGO encouraged the organization of youth and women for social action initiatives, and then provided ongoing support as they undertook these.

(Example from UNDP, 1997, p. 97.)

Collective Action in Kenya

A movement in Kenya has organized 100,000 women to plant more than 20 million trees, clearly in part in response to soil erosion but also with the aim of initiating collective action to fight poverty by making people aware of how they could respond to needs through collective action. This campaign advocates greater political commitment to eradicating poverty, a sense of public responsibility, and people-centered solutions to problems.

(Example from UNDP, 1997, p. 99.)

Empowerment in Cambodia

From Cambodia comes an example of empowering ordinary people to confront local abusive and exploitative leadership. In many villages, people experiencing this type of leadership lacked solidarity and strong relationships. The role of NGO staff in these circumstances was to work patiently with the people, listen to their frustrations, and assure them that it was not normal to live with such violence. As people developed insight into their situation, the social workers acted as mentors, gradually showing that another way could be imagined. Finally, workers organized courses on human rights, which usually resulted in a decision to establish a local human rights association and challenge behavior that was outside the law, including the behavior of local leaders (sometimes referred to as warlords). Almost invariably this led to a drop in the level of violence, but, equally significantly, to an enhanced awareness of rights and a sense of being empowered.

(Example from Nee and Healy, 2003.)

Local Income-generation Programs (See also Chapter 4)

Inadequate development levels are commonly associated with insufficient income-generation opportunities and therefore poverty. Hence a major strategy for any local-level development worker must be to utilize every opportunity to enhance people's capacity to secure a higher income than in the past, and if possible one that is adequate for meeting basic needs such as health services, nutritious foods, children's clothing and books for school, and adequate housing.

Income-generation activities can range from very minor activities such as a better farming method that increases crop yields, to major income-generation programs that train and employ local people, to making credit available that people can use to create income, through to policy measures such as land reform. Such

---

Case Example

Income Generation in the Philippines

One example of many where income-generation initiatives are related to a housing improvement program comes from the Philippines. In this government-initiated program, the first goal was to upgrade slum areas with actions relating to legal tenure, area amenities, and quality of individual homes. At the same time, residents were shown how to establish low-initial-capitalization enterprises based largely on the home. Food processing, simple garment manufacture, and vending were the most common enterprises, sometimes requiring skill development programs and short-term loans. It was found that the improvement in the housing situation was a key to rendering viable a range of income-generation activities. The program was run by a team that included architects, engineers, and economists, but appeared to be weak at the social level with consequences at which we can only guess.

(Example from Habitat, 1989.)

---

activities can be on the individual and family levels but are in practice more likely to be, and are usually more effective, on the small group and community levels.

Essentially all social workers engaged in local development practice should be aware of the economic dimension of development and knowledgeable about successful methods for generating income. Some workers, however, will at times need to place a major emphasis on such programs, studying carefully the strategies and methodologies successfully utilized in various places.

Credit Schemes and People's Banks

Both credit schemes and people's banks have been widely used in a variety of contexts and at various levels. The rationale for such schemes is usually twofold: the inability of people to secure credit from formal institutions such as major banks because they possess no collateral and are regarded as bad risks; and the frequent need for small amounts of capital if people are to improve their lot in life. On the basis of such rationales, a variety of schemes have been successfully implemented. Credit schemes are essentially designed for the poor and, at least in the Asian context, usually target women. They

range from large well-known schemes such as the Grameen Bank in Bangladesh (see Stoesz et al., 1999, chap. 12), with large amounts of capital, administrative structures, and many clientele; to tiny local schemes with small capital, no staff, and a coverage of a few villages. In these credit schemes, there is some initial input of capital for loan purposes, which then grows from the interest rates charged and the high repayment rates almost invariably achieved.

People's banks vary from credit schemes in that there is usually no initial capital grant to get them started. Local people are encouraged to save regularly, usually minute amounts, and to bank their savings; they then have the right to borrow from the accumulated capital in turn and on the basis of submitting acceptable income-generation proposals. A key feature of these banks is the encouragement members receive from each other, the sharing of ideas regarding achieving savings and effectively using small amounts of capital, and the development of basic skills such as very simple bookkeeping and financial calculations. Invariably members also develop considerable skills in the general area of income generation.

Most successful credit schemes and people's banks are essentially self-help groups, or mutual support groups, operating in the field of income generation, although some grow beyond this to become formal organizations. The key to their success is the full participation of members as contributors, recipients, and supporters of each other. The role of the social worker may be simply to feed in the idea, put local people in touch with others running such

schemes, perhaps enable local representatives to attend a workshop on the subject, and generally facilitate the implementation of the scheme. The worker skills involved are basic social work skills; the crucial element is a worker's recognition of the importance and potential of such schemes.

Case Examples

Credit Scheme in Papua New Guinea

While some credit schemes are very large and sophisticated, most are very local, small-scale, and basically self-help schemes. In one scheme in the highlands of Papua New Guinea, the local women were encouraged by a local social worker to investigate the benefits of credit schemes by attending a weekend workshop. Becoming enthusiastic about the possibilities, the women secured a small grant from an Australian aid organization and established a credit scheme. Under the scheme, local women could apply for an interest-bearing set-period loan to initiate an approved income-generation program. Association members visited each project regularly, assisting with any problems encountered and being generally supportive. Loans were almost invariably repaid and the initial fund grew. The higher incomes achieved increased school attendance by enabling parents to equip their children with books and shoes, and raised health levels by making basic medications available (e.g., antimalarial tablets). Most important, the scheme raised local morale and resulted in a wide range of improvements to village life, such as when the men worked voluntarily to improve local drainage and roads, and to construct a shorter road to the nearest market.

(Example from UN/ESCAP, 1996a, p. 51.)

People's Bank in Sri Lanka

An example of a people's bank comes from a poor area in south Sri Lanka. Based on an idea developed by a Sri Lankan academic, the 52 people's banks in this area in 1996 operated as follows. With limited membership in each (usually around 30), the members meet weekly to hear ideas about saving, to bring and bank their weekly savings, no matter how small, and to feel encouraged in their lives by the support of the group. Then members are eligible to request a loan for an income-generation project from the bank's accumulated funds. All projects funded are monitored closely and well supported. Although these banks tend to have only a marginal impact on economic levels in the community, they are important in building confidence, introducing the concept of saving, encouraging people to think of possible entrepreneurial endeavors, and creating strong local support structures. Based entirely on the self-help principle, with no outside experts or paid staff, all that was required was for social workers to introduce the idea and provide initial support or facilitation.

(Example from UN/ESCAP, 1996a, p. 98.)

Credit Scheme in Thailand

It is perhaps helpful here to give, as our final case example, a government-initiated credit scheme for the urban poor of Thailand. In its Seventh National Economic and Social Development Plan (1992–96), Thailand introduced a credit scheme to increase the organizational capacity of urban poor communities and the availability locally of capital. By 2004, some 1,000 communities had joined the scheme, each receiving an initial community grant. These savings and credit associations are operated by their members, consisting usually of 5 to 15 persons. Members meet regularly and pay a set amount into the group fund. They can then apply for an interest-bearing loan. Allocations are either decided by the leader(s) or determined by lottery. While these local credit schemes have been on the whole quite successful, it is reported that many of the urban poor did not join a group because they felt unable to make a regular contribution through regular savings, they had no time to attend meetings, and they did not feel able to trust other members and the group leaders. The scheme seemed to require members to have already a regular, if small, income and an ability to save.

(Example from Senanuch, 2005.)

Community-based Welfare Programs

Workers will frequently find themselves engaged in situations where a specific social problem is widespread, facilities for individual treatment inconceivable in the context, and the potential of the community to develop a community-based response to the problem at least worth exploring. Community-based intervention is intervention where the community is a major player in the instigation of the program, and community members are the major players in its implementation. The rationale for such programs is that local people and organizations are fully aware of the presenting need, adversely affected by it directly or indirectly, and potentially possessed of the motivation and capacity to engage in a planned response to the situation.

Successful community-based welfare programs have been developed in response to a range of social needs, including disability, HIV/AIDS, drug addiction, mental health, isolated elderly, child care and juvenile delinquency, and AIDS orphans (see UN/ESCAP

1989a, 1989b, 1995a, 1999a, 1999b; Moroka, 1998; Kaseke and Gumbo, 2001). Most programs have emerged from the efforts of local social workers or have involved local workers in various ways in their implementation. Some programs have engaged staff to play key ongoing roles in the program while others have operated essentially without paid staff. All must have, however, community participation as the major input component, involving people's time and the development and utilization of their capacities. Moreover, all such schemes usually involve significant community education, designed both to provide knowledge and understanding and, as necessary, to bring about significant changes in prevailing attitudes concerning the specific condition being addressed and the persons who suffer from the condition. This community education element may be one of the major roles for the local worker, requiring significant skills in community education. Workers need also to be skilled in addressing local prejudices, discrimination, and fears, often rooted in strong cultural belief systems.

Case Examples

Community-based Health Care in Indonesia

Among the many examples of community-based welfare programs is a community-based health care program in Indonesia. Under this program, UNICEF provided a nutritional first-aid package for each village. These packages included weighing scales, growth charts, oral rehydration salts for managing diarrhea, vitamin A and iron supplements, and immunization kits. The ministry of health assisted in the establishment of the program in some 2,000 villages, but the local mothers ran the program, achieving an 80 to 98 percent response rate from local mothers, resulting in significant health outcomes. An evaluation concluded that one-half of the improvement in village nutrition levels came from this program.

(Example from UNICEF, 1996, p. 55.)

Drug-abuse Reduction in China

A community-based drug abuse reduction program in southern People's Republic of China aimed at educating the community regarding drug abuse and facilitating community-based responses to the problem. The outcomes included a heightened awareness of the nature and dangers of drug abuse, the eliciting of many community ideas regarding reducing the incidence of drug abuse, and an effective reaching out to and assisting of drug abusers. While well-trained workers were required to initiate the program, once this phase was successfully accomplished, the extent of community awareness and understanding, the emergence of community leadership and volunteers, and the establishment by the community of a variety of programs ensured that the overall program was sustainable without further inputs, and highly effective in achieving its goals.

(Example based on interview with person in charge of program.)

Collective Responses to Specific Situations

Many traditional societies possessed collective responses to tasks that presented themselves at particular times in the year or from time to time (Pawar and Cox, 2004). While modern communities have tended to move away from such schemes, the ability to work together still often emerges in the face of a natural disaster emergency in both developed and developing countries. Within local-level development, one strategy is to capitalize on this traditional or innate ability to cooperate by deliberately fostering collective responses to presenting needs. This will be particularly effective when the reality is that the traditional focus on collective action is still remembered but has been significantly undermined by socioeconomic and sociocultural changes. Sometimes a worker from the outside is best able to rediscover a forgotten traditional response and propose its regeneration, albeit in appropriately modified form, to facilitate the local response to a situation of some concern to many.

Situations that may respond to the collective approach can vary greatly. It may be practical tasks, such as harvesting individuals' crops in turn, working together on constructing or reconstructing after a disaster each other's homes, purchasing in bulk resources that all require, or sharing the need to carry produce a long distance to market. It may, however, be a social need such as the need to settle disputes between community members (perhaps traditionally done by elders), to provide support for individuals in need (such as AIDS orphans in much of Africa; see Kaseke and Gumbo, 2001), or to enhance young people's abilities to benefit from educational opportunities. Finally, it may be a need to organize a defense against some outsiders or some possible eventuality—traditionally a common reason for collective action but also unfortunately a very modern and urgent need in many countries plagued by natural disasters, conflict, and war.

Collective action is in practice a very basic strategy, applicable in much local-level development without necessarily emerging as a formal program in any sense. The process of

Case Examples

Women's Collective and Organized Action in India

One well-known collective response is a trade union of poor women (SEWA) established in India. Drawing its membership from petty vendors, home-based producers, and casual laborers in urban and rural areas, its aim is to enhance women's income-earning opportunities and improve their working environment. It establishes savings and credit cooperatives, producer cooperatives to help women to get better prices for their goods, training courses to improve skill levels, and legal services for those requiring such. It also operates essentially as a welfare collective.

(Example from Ghai, 1994, p. 221, and UN/ESCAP, 1994b, p. 33.)

Farmers' Cooperatives in East Africa

In East Africa, cooperatives were established initially because African cash-crop growers (essentially peasant farmers) were up against monopolistic white farmers and Asian middlemen. While highly effective for a period, partly because their actions benefited other more powerful groups, many withered when, after independence, nobody powerful supported them ideologically or practically. It would seem, from this example, that local cooperatives ideally require well-established and relatively powerful outside support systems or to be part of national federations.

(Example from Curtis, 1991, p. 47.)

operating collectively, wherever the need and possibility for such exists, is what matters, and it is a process that is very consistent with the integrated-perspectives approach we have adopted. Collective action tends to be more ecologically sound and sustainable, recognizes the rights of others, and accords with such social development principles as participation and self-reliance.

Leadership Development

The focus in local-level development, as far as leadership training is concerned, seems to be mainly on two levels. One level is working with existing leaders providing any support or capacity building that they request; while the other level is a "training the trainers" approach. In any community there tend to be a range of leaders, such as traditional leaders including religious leaders, those who play leadership roles within

local organizations, and natural leaders who tend to emerge in any situation requiring such. Such people are frequently concerned regarding various deficiencies in development in the local context, and one role of local workers is to work with such people in pursuing whatever goals or tasks are identified, provided, however, that the decision making and overall approach adopted is participatory and not one dominated by self-elected leaders pursuing personal or elitist goals.

Training of local trainers is also an excellent approach to initiating many aspects of local-level development. As there will almost inevitably not be sufficient appointed personnel available, and because the utilization of local people is consistent with a self-reliant, empowering, and participatory approach, the recruitment of local personnel to be trained as future trainers of others is highly appropriate. Frequently trainees will be brought together from a number of villages or locations, trained in whatever aspect of

Case Examples

Local Approaches to Leader Selection

The work of Uphoff on leadership training reveals that particular types of leaders are required for different purposes, and that every community has a pool of potential leaders who need to be tapped and recruited in specific ways. He gives the example of a program in the northern Philippines where two leaders were always selected: an external leader for linking to government and so on, and an internal leader for day-to-day managerial tasks. He also gives the example of the Saemaul Undong scheme in South Korea, where the selection of leaders for training was left to the community, which almost invariably bypassed village headmen and elected younger and more dynamic leaders—something that others might not have dared to do. In a further example from Sri Lanka, farmer representatives were selected to engage in a discussion on the qualities that local leaders should have if group action was to be effective. Eventually these meetings selected local leaders for training and program leadership by consensus, not by voting.

(Examples from Uphoff, 1986.)

Leadership Training in the Solomon Islands

In the Solomon Islands, a church-run leadership training program recruited village youth for a two-year leadership training course, as long as they were supported in their application by community and family and showed a commitment to the village. The course covers English language, various aspects of agriculture, basic woodwork, and mechanics. The aim is to develop skills useful to the local community and to strengthen attitudes that inspire graduates to commit themselves to the further development of their entire community. Much of the practical training is done on a group basis to encourage a focus on group projects within their own villages. Trainees also self-manage the training center's daily chores (e.g., growing and preparing foods) and engage in financial management to further enhance skill levels that will be of benefit to their communities. Finally, graduates are followed up in their villages at least once a year to offer ongoing guidance and support.

(Example from Bamford, 1986, p. 8.)

development is envisioned, and ideally supported as they carry out their training role on returning home. Sometimes this process of training trainers is an ongoing aspect of the local development process, perhaps attached to a local community-run adult education center. Often the process requires also some material inputs, such as basic equipment that local people can use with benefit.

Local Organization and Institution Promotion and Capacity Building

Depending on the extent of development of organizations or institutions in any given location, the emphasis of a social worker may be on facilitating the establishment of an appropriate organization or institution, or on strengthening existing structures through a process of capacity building. The ideal situation is that the perception of the need to form or strengthen specific structures emerges or evolves as the local people come to understand the nature and importance of these structures, and participate more and more actively in their establishment and development. However, one reason for local reluctance to proceed too far along this path may be a lack of confidence in local ability to establish and maintain a specific

Case Example

Center for Social and Economic Development in Bolivia

The Center for Social and Economic Development (DESEC) in Bolivia is a local development association initiated as a private sector program to assist campesinos. The basic local institution is also called the Center—a voluntary association of resident peasants who solve problems collectively. When there are several centers in an area, each elects representatives to the regional federation. Each also provides representatives for the national-level body. The DESEC provides technical services, home construction, health services, and agricultural services, supported in so doing by the national organization. The centers are open to small farmers and landless laborers, leadership is arranged through local elections, and financial grants are available from the government. This initiative has been evaluated as outstanding.

(Example from Esman and Uphoff, 1984, p. 313.)

structure. In such circumstances, a local worker can do much to facilitate the process. Many international agencies undertake considerable institutional capacity building, in relation to both local NGOs or people's organizations and to local governance structures; however, the work that we are referring to here is done at a much earlier stage in the development process.

Linking Local Organizations to Government Agencies and International Structures

Local organizations can be very isolated and lacking the networks that make possible the dissemination at the local level of externally available knowledge, skills, and other resources. The potential for such networking is frequently there. What is lacking may be knowledge of external resources, certain capacities to make contact with these external resources, or a lack of confidence in initiating the process. What the local social worker can do is overcome any of these deficiencies and facilitate the establishment and smooth operation of appropriate networks that will result in local access to necessary external knowledge and resources.

The Place for Integrated Comprehensive Programs

The above mentioned aspects of practice are all ones that are commonly encountered in the field and in the literature. While they are presented here in very general terms, it should be appreciated that their precise utilization by workers will depend on the realities of local cultural systems, need profiles, sociopolitical structures, and so on. There are no universally or regionally applicable blueprints for the implementation of any of these programs or strategies. Moreover, this list of possibilities is not and never could be complete. The range of approaches to local-level development is virtually unlimited. Hence social workers should view the above approaches, albeit frequently successful, as only a starting point for triggering the professional imagination of the active and committed local-level development practitioner.

It will also be clear, from the examples given, that seldom are programs confined to only one of the above types. It is usual for programs to combine at least several of these possibly discrete approaches. Where circumstances permit, agencies and personnel engaged in local-level development tend to prefer to undertake a truly comprehensive development program although there is some evidence that funding bodies sometimes resist this trend as being too open-ended from a costing and accounting point of view. The comprehensive approach tends to integrate the above discrete strategies, in one form or another, and often others within a program aimed at raising the level of an entire region by focusing on virtually all dimensions of development and engaging virtually all levels at which development can be undertaken. The following case example from the Philippines provides a good example of a highly successful program of this type.

Case Example

Local-level Development Program in the Philippines

The Philippines has been through long periods of colonization, a period of hostile occupation, and a significant period of internal dissent and subversive and terrorist activities. As a society, it developed many feudal features, and has long been dominated by a powerful elite that controls many aspects of social, economic, and political life. Corruption has been a constant problem, undermining most attempts to bring about significant change. Moreover, despite significant amounts of development aid and close ties with the United States, the prevailing feudal characteristics and corruption have resulted in significant distorted development. The existence of such trends tends then to aggravate existing levels of crime and subversion, as well as political instability. Overall, despite its advantages of being, for example, an English-speaking country linked with the United States and located within the fast-developing Southeast Asian region, the Philippines has continued to manifest all the signs of a developing country.

The UNDP's Human Development Index in 1999 (UNDP, 1999) places the Philippines at the 77th ranking within 174 ranked countries, and the statistics presented by the UNDP and World Bank raise many concerns. Even in the area of gender discrimination, an area in which the Philippines has been active at many levels and has proclaimed excellent policies, the country ranks on the UNDP's gender-related development index at 65th place out of 143 countries, and on the gender empowerment measure at 45th place among 102 countries. Development in the Philippines still has a long way to go.

The area of this case study, Negros Occidental, was one where sugarcane plantations (haciendas) had long dominated the economy and most of the productive land area, with the plantations owned by the so-called sugar barons—part of the feudal elite. Many of the local people had provided labor for the plantations in the busy periods, but for the balance of the year survived on marginal land and some employment stemming from the tourist industry. Then in the mid-1980s recession hit the sugar industry and the livelihoods of many local people simply disappeared as many plantation owners stopped cultivating their land and moved into more profitable pursuits. As this occurred in the immediate aftermath of a disastrous economic period for the country and a period of political turmoil culminating in the overthrow of the Marcos regime, the new Aquino government took immediate action. In 1988, the Comprehensive Agrarian Reform Program was introduced to acquire unused land for redistribution; and an Integrated Social Forestry Program made upland areas available for 50-year leases, designed to assist people while also addressing the ecological degradation of upland areas through illegal logging. Other initiatives concerned irrigation and social services. All of these central government initiatives had potential application to Negros Occidental.

It was clear, however, that despite these national initiatives, nothing would change in a place like Negros Occidental unless a process of change was initiated locally. With significant leadership from a new provincial governor, a group of persons established a food-for-work program, which was in essence a large-scale comprehensive regional development program based on local-level development to run for five years with the objective of turning around the province's fortunes and addressing the widespread poverty. The food-for-work element, available through the UN's World Food Programme, was crucial, for the plan was to use this program to pay for the services of the poor who would constitute the labor force required for local developments. The aforementioned acts initiated by the central government would be utilized as fully as possible, while the UNDP agreed to contribute significant resources, but the key resource ultimately would be the local people.

The program was run by a team of 18 young graduates drawn from a range of disciplines. This team approach was of critical importance to providing maximum support to these 18 young people undertaking very demanding roles. The program was implemented at all levels by a network of Local Implementing Agencies (LIAs), which included government agencies, NGOs, and POs (people's organizations). Each LIA was responsible for a series of agreed-on projects which they implemented with the support of the team. This network of LIAs required much work on the part of the team to bring them to the point where they could understand the roles and restrictions of each other so that close collaboration would be possible. Such collaboration was crucial and called for a dedicated and sensitive approach by team members.

The program was designed to achieve comprehensive development in each designated local level. On the ground, this would consist of a team member contacting local people to discuss problems and concerns. This might result in an NGO placing a staff member with the community in a community development role, or in the identification of specific projects in which a government agency (e.g., an agency for health, education, irrigation, agriculture, or forestry) would become directly involved as part of the local LIA's action plan. Where a need or potential for food-for-work initiatives was identified—such as in building a school or clinic, constructing a small dam and irrigation system, or establishing a network of rice paddies—local poor people would be recruited to do the work under guidance and paid through the food-for-work program. This provided useful capacity building, enabled workers to identify and respond to special needs, led to poor people feeling a sense of acceptance, purpose, and a viable future, and at the same time constructed a facility that would benefit the community as a whole.

In many cases, local initiatives brought together people in communities or revitalized existing communities, resulting in the establishment of POs determined to build or strengthen various dimensions of community life. These communities interacted with each other at various levels, thus ultimately strengthening provincewide networks.

By the fourth year of the five-year program there were 63 project sites and a much larger number of specific projects, all designed to contribute to meeting community needs with and through the full involvement of community members. Considerable training and capacity building were occurring, many local income-generation opportunities were being established, the various sectors were collaborating with each other, and levels of motivation and participation were extremely high. The province's infrastructure—of schools, clinics, paved roads, irrigation systems, and so forth—had expanded enormously. Government agencies had moved from being formal bureaucratic structures, providing a service to a small number of situations that they selected, to being people-centered operations operating relatively informally in close cooperation with local community groups to provide services in a much larger number of locations. Many NGOs had been revitalized and learned what participatory local-level social development really meant. Many POs had formed and were demonstrating people's newfound ability to work with government agencies, NGOs, and others in their ongoing development. Both NGOs and POs had also learned much about a range of income-generation activities, including artificial reef building, various agricultural pursuits, and a range of basic trades.

Each project was remarkable and inspiring, but let us briefly describe one project where one of the authors spent time. This project started with the identification by the team of nine households engaged in illegal logging in an uplands area and having virtually no access to social services. In 1991, through the outreach of the program, they were offered uplands land on the basis of a 25-year lease with the right to renew for an additional 25 years. The households accepted the offer and the task of building disparate households into a unified and viable community commenced. The numbers grew quickly to 25 households, and these households began the work of community building. In this they were aided by the deployment of an NGO staff member who worked with the people as a community development worker for well over a year. All parties regarded the role of that person as pivotal, for these households had a limited capacity to envisage the potential of the land and the importance and process of community building.

With the assistance of the catalyst, the households gradually evolved a plan for the establishment of their village that consisted of a series of specific projects. They would construct a dam and a mini-irrigation scheme to bring water to rice paddies. With this irrigation they would develop an area of intensive cultivation, producing rice, vegetables, and flowers that could be sold to the people down on the coastal plain. A further area would be devoted to forestry, partly to yield a longer-term income and partly to restore the area's ecological balance. Much of this work, however, would require skills which the people did not possess, so training and education were important. Finally, the households needed to become a community, served by a school and possessing a range of facilities in the area where housing was being erected.

All in all, it was a mammoth undertaking for these people. Even trusting each other as the basis for engaging in joint community initiatives was difficult, and some friction, distrust, rival leadership, and so on were not uncommon during the first few years. However, the households did gradually learn to work together, to establish their community structures, and to engage in collaborative measures. This was greatly aided by the resident catalyst, the periodic visits of a team member, and especially by the experience of working together on joint projects. These joint projects represented the pooling of labor on community schemes, facilitated by the food-for-work arrangement; the working with the various GAs acting as LIAs on specific projects; and the whole experience of learning together in classroom contexts and in the field.

In three years, a disparate collection of impoverished and marginalized households had become a flourishing community, both socially and economically. Their dam was both beautiful and the heart of a successful irrigation system. Their fields were highly productive, and thousands of small trees dotted the reforested area. Their children attended school, and the village was a happy and comparatively well-serviced place to live. Almost daily a community person would head off with cut flowers to sell, while others pursued other income generating activities, some operating on an individualistic basis, and some on a cooperative basis. To the outside visitor, there was no mistaking the people's pride in their achievements and their ability to function successfully as a social and economic unit.

The entire program was based firmly on the principles of participation, self-reliance and sustainability, culminating in a focus on people in communities. The strategies adopted throughout included:

Use of a team and NGO staff as project catalysts;
A people-centered community-based approach;
A basic strategy of social mobilization, especially of the poor;
A focus on education, training and capacity building; and
An emphasis on income generating outcomes.

This program is an excellent example of poverty alleviation at one level, but more important, of local-level social development. The key to poverty alleviation is ultimately community development. If that development is buttressed by a network of government service agencies committed to sustainable community development, and by a political system geared to providing an enabling environment for development, the potential for community development is greatly enhanced. Sustainable community development itself, however, must ultimately be manifested in effective POs, initially established for development purposes but ultimately finding their place within civil society, which is that level of community development which links the needs and wishes of the people to the macro structures and policies of society. (Further information on this case study is available in UN/ESCAP, 1996 (i) & (ii); & Cox, 1998.)

Conclusion

Local-level social development in general terms calls for the range of approaches that are basic to social work, but many contexts call for a range of additional strategies that we have sought to reflect in our overview, as well as a capacity for flexibility and to be innovative. There is a wealth of material in this area, unfortunately more in the form of case studies and evaluations than of detailed accounts of methods of intervention.

If the social work profession can bring about the deployment of significant numbers of workers able to contribute to frontline local-level operations in places requiring such, it would significantly change the face of development and enhance the well-being ultimately of millions of people. Moreover, if the profession can train reasonable numbers of social workers to engage in devising, promoting, supervising, and otherwise supporting local-level development programs, whoever the frontline personnel might be, that too will represent an essential and valuable contribution to building better societies within which people can secure a better way of life than many millions have experienced in the past.

Summary

- The local level consists of "individuals, families, groups, communities, and locality (a set of communities)," and is one of the four sectors of any society. Although it is very significant as the foundation sector, it has often received less attention than the other sectors, and social workers may be able to change this situation. The integrated-perspectives approach reinforces the need to focus at the local level.

- Lack of adequate numbers of appropriate personnel for local-level development is a real issue that needs to be addressed. Can social work meet this challenge?

- Social workers need to focus their practice on individuals, families, communities, groups, and local organizations and institutions, and on the interaction between these units, using both remedial and developmental approaches as appropriate.

- A combination of relevant strategies and programs needs to be employed, incorporating empowering and participatory values and in a coordinated and comprehensive manner, to achieve local-level development.

- The history of development across the globe suggests that there is gradual recognition of the integrated-perspectives approach, but current and future development planners and practitioners need to adopt and implement such an approach.

Questions and Topics for Discussion

- What do you mean by local-level development, and how important do you consider it to be?
- What do you see as the main personnel issues in local-level development?
- How important is combining the various strategies in local-level development, and what combinations present as crucial in achieving desired outcomes?
- How would you compare the roles of the team members in the Negros Occidental development program with your understanding of community development?
- Review and reflect on
  - the six areas of local-level development;
  - the four basic emphases in working at the local level;

– the two key approaches to local-level development; and
– the key strategies and programs listed for achieving local-level development.
Can these be employed in a coordinated and integrated manner?

- Identify and develop examples of a few key strategies that you have come across in the field.

Possible Areas for Research Projects

- Select an area with which you are familiar and devise an ideal local-level development program.
- Select a local-level development initiative known to you, and analyze the strategies utilized and the perceived benefits of these.
- Consider some case studies of local-level development in terms of the personnel used in the programs, and discuss your findings in terms of social work's roles in local-level development in developing countries.
- Undertake a case study on local-level development with a view to examining areas of focus and the way (integrated or otherwise) key strategies and programs are employed.

Further Reading

Carroll, T. F. (1992). *Intermediary NGOs: The supporting link in grassroots development*. West Hartford, CT: Kumarian.

Ife, J. (2002). *Community development: Community-based alternatives in an age of globalization* (2nd ed.). Sydney, Australia: Longman Pearson.

Korten, D. C., & Klaus, R. (Eds.). (1984). *People-centered development*. West Hartford, CT: Kumarian.

UNDP. (1993). *Human development report*. New York: Oxford University Press.

Uphoff, N. (1986). *Local institutional development: An analytical sourcebook with cases*. West Hartford, CT: Kumarian.

7

The Field of Poverty:
Background and Issues

Poverty has been termed the most significant problem confronting the modern world, and, with one-third of the world's population significantly affected by poverty, the statement is not surprising. Others have referred to poverty as the greatest scandal confronting the modern world, in that globally humanity possesses the wealth and the knowledge to eradicate poverty; what is lacking is the political will to do so. Finally, poverty is widely regarded as the world's most intractable problem, given that, despite a wide range of commitments to its eradication, it continues largely unabated in its overall dimensions, despite significant progress on many other fronts and in many parts of the world.

In the early history of social work, poverty tended to be seen as one of those socioeconomic problems beyond the competence of a profession such as social work to tackle, although this has certainly been changing in recent decades. This chapter does not set out to demonstrate that it is within the competence of social work to eradicate poverty, but it does strongly suggest that it is within its ability to significantly reduce

poverty in certain developing country contexts, and that, in almost every context, social work has the competence, and the responsibility, to seek to alleviate the impact of poverty on the lives of many people.

In the first section of the chapter we consider poverty in the light of our integrated-perspectives approach, which we shall argue provides us with a sense of direction in approaching this serious and complex problem. We shall then briefly review global poverty in terms of its current dimensions, progress in reducing its global incidence in the last fifty years, and trends in the distribution of poverty globally.

The second section introduces the exceedingly complex concept of poverty, focusing on identifying and defining the various facets or types of poverty that exist globally and that social workers encounter. Within this section, we shall consider the nature and causes of each type, as well as the various approaches to the reduction of the various types of poverty that have been attempted in developing countries in recent decades, indicating where possible the

Learning Objectives

- To develop a beginning understanding of the nature, causes, and types of poverty in developing countries.

- To encourage readers to think about the links between poverty and phenomena such as conflict, natural disasters, ecological degradation, and high population growth rates.

- To be able to apply the integrated-perspectives approach to an understanding of the phenomenon of global poverty.

- To understand ways of defining poverty and forms of poverty.

degree of success associated with each approach and considering the possible reasons for success and failure.

In the following chapter we turn to consider the role of social work in relation to poverty and the identification of programs and strategies commonly used, by social workers and others, in poverty alleviation work.

Perspectives on Poverty: The Integrated-perspectives Approach and Poverty

In the following section we shall often refer to the ways in which global factors impact, positively and negatively, on the nature and incidence of poverty wherever it occurs. It follows that any effective program to eradicate or reduce poverty must be global in nature, as has been often affirmed. Even local programs aimed at alleviating poverty will need to take global factors into account, even if there exists no potential to interact directly with or influence these factors. Both the impact of global factors on local situations and the advantages of drawing on the potential benefits of global systems and programs must be prominent in workers' minds if they are to intervene effectively. An obvious example is the negative impact of a multinational corporation (MNC) relocating an operation, with resulting large-scale employment loss, and the possibility of local people, usually through their

government, persuading another MNC to compensate for the loss by establishing a plant locally and drawing on those local resources. A somewhat different example is appreciating the impact of an International Monetary Fund (IMF) Structural Adjustment Program in a local context and working with the IMF and others, including the national government, either to change the arrangements or take steps to offset the impact. The global perspective within the integrated-perspectives approach is thus critical within the poverty alleviation field of international social work practice.

Equally important is the human rights perspective, for on what other basis can one argue against the scourge of poverty? The humanitarian argument, especially if it amounts to a charitable approach, is not what the poor require or deserve. And while arguments based on religion may be effective in some contexts, they will not usually be widely adopted and are thus too precarious. We are thus effectively left with the human rights argument as one that is formally and globally accepted, at least in principle, and one which if implemented will result in campaigns to eradicate existing poverty and protect against future poverty. Poverty eradication requires an in-principle rejection of any form or degree of poverty, along with active campaigns to achieve that goal. Similarly, poverty alleviation at the local level requires an equally firm commitment to work against poverty as basically contrary to all people's rights.

The significance of the ecological factor in the poverty field is frequently discussed. There can be no doubt that ecologically unsustainable practices have been contributing to poverty for some time, while the negative impact of poverty on ecological systems is also apparent. It follows that an effective antipoverty campaign at any level will call for a knowledgeable and deliberate inclusion of the ecological perspective at every step of the process. If the world gets this wrong, no adherence to people's human rights will be worth the paper it is written on. The protection, sustainable utilization, and respect for the inherent importance of the ecological environment are vital to success in raising all people's standard of living to a level above that where poverty begins to have a negative impact on the environment.

Our final perspective, social development, is the one that gives direction to all efforts to combat existing poverty and prevent future poverty. All of the reasons contributing to poverty, all of the dimensions at which the problem of poverty must be tackled, all of the strategies on which poverty reduction and alleviation are based, and all of the values that underpin a commitment to eradicate poverty are encompassed within the social development perspective—that is, the approach to building strong, healthy, and just societies. The social development perspective is not a blueprint for poverty alleviation or for any other goal; rather it indicates the parameters of policy and program development to achieve such goals. This will be demonstrated in the next chapter where we consider effective approaches and strategies for combating poverty.

Global Poverty: Current Dimensions and Trends

The global poverty situation is a complex one, reflecting the complexity of both the phenomenon of poverty and of the world in which it is found in economic, political, cultural, and other terms. However, we are fortunate in having available detailed and authoritative analyses of global poverty prepared by the UNDP and World Bank, on which we shall draw substantially in providing the following overview.

When reflecting on the current incidence of poverty worldwide, it is easy to overlook the fact that substantial progress has been made in recent decades in reducing poverty. As the UNDP (1997, p. 2) expresses it, "In the past 50 years poverty has fallen more than in the previous 500. And it has been reduced in some respects in almost all countries."

The World Bank (2000/2001, p. vi) adds that "in 1990–1998 alone the number of people in extreme poverty fell by 78 million." Progress throughout the twentieth century was, however, not just in the incidence of income poverty but also in what the UNDP calls "poverty from a human development perspective" or "human poverty." Writing of the experiences of developing countries since the 1950s, the UNDP comments,

By the end of the 20th century some 3–4 billion of the world's people will have experienced substantial improvements in their standard of living, and about 4–5 billion will have access to basic education and health care. It is precisely these gains that make eradicating poverty not some distant ideal—but a true possibility.

While we may take some comfort from these observations, the fact remains that the current incidence of global poverty remains extremely high—high enough for the UNDP to refer to the situation as "a scandal" and the World Bank as "shameful" (World Bank, 2000/2001, p. 1). The UNDP (1997, p. 2) writes,

Although poverty has been dramatically reduced in many parts of the world, a quarter of the world's people remain in severe poverty. In a global economy of $25 trillion, this is a scandal—reflecting shameful inequalities and inexcusable failures of national and international policy.

In its latest report on poverty, the World Bank (2000/2001, p. vi) summarizes the current situation as follows:

Of the world's 6 billion people, 2.8 billion live on less than $2 a day, and 1.2 billion on less than $1 a day. Six infants of every 100 do not see their first birthday, and 8 do not survive to their fifth. Of those who do reach school age, 9 boys in 100, and 14 girls, do not go to primary school.

Given that "less than $1 a day" constitutes extreme poverty, and "less than $2" poverty, the proportion of the world's population suffering from poverty remains extremely, and unacceptably, high.

In a paper released by the World Bank in 2000, the bank outlined the global trends in income poverty during the 1990s as follows:

The decline in the number of poor between 1993 and 1998 is due almost exclusively to a reduction in the number of poor people in East Asia, and notably in China. But progress was reversed by the [Asian financial] crisis [in 1997], although only partly as poverty remains well below what it was a decade ago, and appears to have stalled in China.

In South Asia, the share of the population living in poverty declined moderately through the 1990s, but not sufficiently to reduce the absolute number of poor. The actual number of poor people in the region has been rising steadily since 1987.

In Africa the share declined slightly but the numbers of people in poverty increased. The new estimates indicate that Africa is now the region with the largest number of people living below $1 per day.

In Latin America the share of poor people (below both $1 and $2 per day, the latter being more relevant for the region) and the numbers increased.

In the countries of the former Soviet bloc, poverty rose markedly—both the share and the numbers increased.

Chapter 2 of the UNDP's 1997 report on poverty describes in considerable detail the "progress and setbacks" relating to poverty that have occurred in recent times. While the detail provided by the UNDP and World Bank is important in illustrating the complexity of both the poverty phenomenon and the task of reducing its incidence, the critical point for us to note here is the UNDP's final conclusion:

Progress in reducing human and income poverty is marked by discontinuity and unevenness. . . . (p. 48)

Some people lift themselves from poverty. Others stay poor. And still others become newly poor. Poverty is thus constantly being created and re-created. It disappears in some places but reappears elsewhere, at other times. (p. 61)

The UNDP is particularly concerned with gender, rural-urban, ethnic, and regional (within countries) disparities in the distribution of poverty. Regarding the contemporary face of income poverty, the UNDP (1997, p. 48) writes, "Today a poor person is more likely to be African, to be a child, a woman, or an elderly person in an urban area, to be landless, to live in an environmentally fragile area and to be a refugee or a displaced person."

While the face of global poverty has been changing, in terms of the causes of global poverty and its impact on people generally and on specific population categories, five factors, clearly often interacting factors, seem to emerge from the general literature. These factors and their interrelationships are diagrammed in Figure 7.1

The first factor is that of geography. Landes (1998, p. 5) writes, "On a map of the world in terms of product or income per head, the rich countries lie in the temperate zone, particularly

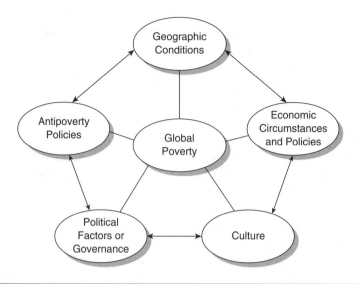

Figure 7.1   Factors affecting global poverty

in the northern hemisphere; the poor countries, in the tropics and semi-tropics." Landes goes on to spell out some of the reasons for this state of affairs. From a different geographical stance, the UN often separates out the small, landlocked, and island states as having greater difficulties in developing than others. In this case it is not geography in global terms, but the geographic features of individual states. Similarly, one can categorize countries in terms of their natural resources, and, while some countries have been able to overcome a low level of natural resources, many others have suffered from this geographic characteristic. Finally, the geographical location of countries in terms of prevailing trade routes, or facility in trading with other nations, has often been a significant factor in their development and therefore poverty levels. Geography is clearly a factor in the global distribution of poverty, but the experience of some countries suggests that it is not an insuperable factor.

A second but more contentious factor is culture. We quote from Landes (1998, p. 516) again: "If we learn anything from the history of economic development, it is that culture makes

all the difference." Landes discusses situations where the prevailing culture was conducive to economic development and others where it was not. Without such a theory, it is difficult to understand why certain parts of continents remain pockets of poverty long after other parts have surged ahead. Culture may be the vital determining factor in encouraging some peoples to commit themselves to regular and sustained work, to exercise appropriate frugality to permit savings, to show initiative and inventiveness in confronting economic and other challenges, and thus to inculcate the types of values required by a modern economy.

A third factor is the economic one. Some nations will, at vital points in their national development, experience global economic circumstances that are highly conducive to high growth rates, which in turn offer the conditions for overcoming poverty. This is often said to have been the case for Hong Kong, Singapore, South Korea, and Taiwan. Alternatively, nations may embark on a specific economic development strategy that proves highly beneficial to national development and poverty reduction. Or, finally, nations may or may not be highly attractive to developed countries or MNCs, for a variety of reasons, resulting in highly varying levels of aid, investment, and trade opportunities.

A fourth factor is the political one. Again for a great variety of reasons, nations may experience situations of good, stable, and effective governance, that both facilitate and initiate development and the redistribution of the profits of development, or the opposite. Clearly the fortunes of many countries have been and are closely associated with the nature of their governance.

The final factor is the set of antipoverty policies and programs that a country initiates. Dixon and Macarov (1998), in the conclusion to their global review of poverty, suggest that few countries initiate antipoverty programs, even fewer do so effectively, and poverty remains a reality despite a variety of policy initiatives. The implication of their analysis and that of others is that the eradication, or even the significant reduction, of poverty requires a high level of political commitment, an understanding public, and a set of effective policies and programs across a range of areas, including development generally (rural and urban, economic and social, political and ecological dimensions), job creation, social services and social security, and community development. For a variety of reasons, some of which Dixon and Macarov explore, the great majority of developed and developing countries fail to initiate and effectively implement an appropriate set of antipoverty strategies.

In the following section we shall seek to elaborate on this complex phenomenon of poverty, before turning our attention finally to the role of international social work in poverty alleviation.

Global Poverty: The Various Types or Facets of Poverty

Several times we have referred to the concept of poverty as complex, and the purpose of this section is to unravel and make sense of that complexity. Our initial concern is with globalization and poverty, or the impact of global factors on the incidence, distribution, and forms of poverty. We then consider a typology of poverty that flows from the development process. Third, we turn to a typology relating essentially to population categories and the ways in which societies respond to these categories. Fourth, we consider what we are calling *consequential poverty*, or poverty that is essentially caused or aggravated by other phenomena such as conflict and natural disasters. Finally, we consider types of poverty in terms essentially of the forms that the actual poverty takes.

Whether poverty is seen as relating closely to global factors, to the development process, to population categories, or to other phenomena (consequential poverty), all types of poverty vary on two important dimensions. First, any type of poverty can be either absolute or relative. Absolute poverty indicates an inability either to survive, or to adequately meet one's basic needs despite surviving. It represents abject living conditions, the lack of basic capabilities to function within society, and a life situation of significant insecurity and vulnerability. By contrast, relative poverty "is a lack of the resources required to participate in activities and to enjoy living standards that are customary or widely accepted in the society in which poverty is being measured" (World Bank, 2000/2001, p. 23). Second, any type of poverty can be chronic or acute. Chronic poverty is often the situation where people are born into poverty and live out their lives in poverty. It may also, however, be poverty that is brought about by an accident or event resulting in a disability or life situation that leaves one unable to earn an income, without access to social welfare provisions or family supports. Both forms of chronic poverty are still all too common. By comparison, acute poverty is short-term poverty resulting from a sudden, but temporary, loss of employment or of income, as the result of illness, an economic downturn, a natural disaster, or other events. While poverty can, in such circumstances, be severe, its impact is often mitigated by the knowledge that it is probably short-term and that those affected can often survive this period by drawing on savings, selling assets, borrowing, or, in some countries, applying for welfare benefits or relief.

Globalization and Poverty

As has been said, poverty is the greatest problem confronting the modern world, yet one might have assumed that 50-odd years of accelerated globalization in such areas as development activity, trade, and investment flows, and knowledge regarding the phenomenon of poverty, alongside the establishment of a range of global economic and political structures, and together with a huge increase in global wealth and scientific ability, would have made poverty a thing of the past. And in fact poverty has fallen dramatically in these 50 years. The World Bank (2000/2001, pp. v–vi) maintains that "the 20th century saw great progress in reducing poverty and improving well-being," but then concludes that "at the start of a new century, poverty remains a global problem of huge proportions." Indeed, one can take a number of specific countries as examples and show how far they have progressed in recent decades in a variety of ways, including in the reduction of poverty.

Yet despite such national-level progress in some countries, situations have remained unchanged in some other countries and deteriorated in yet other countries since the 1980s, so that overall global figures of poverty and inequality have altered little, and if anything increased, since the 1980s. Global figures on poverty are confusing, with specific figures given depending on the definition of poverty being used, on whether reference is to absolute numbers or percentages or trends, and on what is the precise coverage of global. Generally, however, it is agreed that overall absolute poverty figures have changed little in recent decades, while

inequality has increased significantly (see World Bank, 2000/2001, pp. 3–6, 16–17).

The UNDP (1996a, p. 1) points out that, since the 1980s, "economic decline or stagnation has affected 100 countries, reducing the incomes of 1.6 billion people." How can we explain the juxtaposition of significant global progress at all levels of human activity and continuing high levels of even extreme poverty in some parts of the world? Is it the selfishness of certain countries or governments, of the Western world generally, of an emerging global upper or entrepreneurial class, or of a loosely defined racial-religious world grouping that is largely to blame? Or is it, as some maintain, the nature of the newly emerging global systems, that by their very nature result in a dichotomized world—a world of "the haves" on the one hand and "the have-nots" on the other? (See discussion in UNDP, 1999, chap. 1.) Or is it a question of culture, with some cultures and countries being better equipped at converting possibilities into success, in such a way that eradicates poverty, than are others? All three views have their supporters, and no doubt there are also other alternative views possible. If the world is to eradicate poverty, it is critical that we explore the possible reasons for the persistence of poverty and so come to understand the links between globalization and poverty, despite the difficulty inherent in researching such a topic.

It cannot be said that the failure to reduce global poverty reflects an unwillingness to try, at least at the rhetorical level. On a number of occasions, the international community has endorsed a commitment either to eradicate poverty or to reduce its incidence by a certain percentage by a certain year, the latest being the Millennium Development Goals agreed to within the UN by 189 countries in 2000 (see World Bank, 2000/2001, p. 6; UNDP, 2003). Moreover, agencies like the UNDP and World Bank have carefully monitored progress, as have the various UN/ECOSOC regional bodies. Finally, agencies like the World Bank and Asian Development Bank have made loans and grants to states conditional on governments incorporating in proposals a poverty reduction aspect. If rhetoric and donor requirements are anything to go on, we should have started to see a significant reduction in global poverty rates some time ago. The reality, however, is that this has not occurred, and we need to examine possible reasons for the failure of global rhetoric to translate into success on the ground.

One reason commonly advanced is that development initiatives tend to be top-down, aiming at macro or state-level economic and political changes and anticipating that such will flow down through the systems to exert a positive influence also at the micro level. There is ample evidence, however, that this does not occur—for a variety of reasons. Those controlling activities at the top often ensure that the benefits of development go largely to themselves, their extended families, their ethnic group, or their class. Much large-scale development is controlled by MNCs which tend to repatriate profits to the country where they are headquartered, or distribute them among largely western employees and shareholders. Then a significant amount of the potential impetus of most schemes is dissipated through corruption and mismanagement. Finally, the connection between the aspects of development addressed directly and the areas of poverty is often extremely tenuous, to the extent that a flow-on effect would be unlikely even if all else worked according to plan. It is for this reason that the need to target poverty directly is often asserted.

A second possible reason for the failure of global developments to impact on poverty is the nature of the prevailing ideologies underpinning most global activity. It is widely claimed that neoliberalism and neoconservatism (see Chapter 3), and the structural adjustment and other programs to which they have given birth, are inherently biased toward advancing the interests of those individuals or groupings who are already advantaged in society (see Hutton, 2003). Moves to reduce the size of government, remove subsidies from essential goods and

services, and reduce the size of the welfare state and promote a user-pays approach to service delivery will inevitably impact immediately and significantly on the poor, while there is no significant evidence to show that such moves are ultimately beneficial in reducing poverty. Nor do many commentators believe that the push for free trade will benefit the poorer countries of the world; rather it will enable the powerful countries to either exploit or bypass the poorer ones. Moreover, neoconservative politics seem likely to drive wedges between various parts of the world, promoting neoimperialism, undermining the effectiveness of the UN, and promoting negative reactions in the West toward significant sections of the global population. At the moment, such ideologies appear to be much stronger than human rights–based, or humanitarian, or world citizenship-for-all ideologies, and this state of affairs does not augur well for a concerted effort to eradicate poverty.

Finally, it can be argued that the strong belief in many quarters in the need for and potential of continuing economic growth is very difficult for many to accept (see Easterly, 2002). First, it is commonly maintained that any question of the world moving toward the levels of consumption prevailing in western countries is absurd in sustainable development terms, and it is instead often argued that western countries need to de-develop in many ways. Second, it is apparent that much development today is not only ecological vandalism and unsustainable but is contributing significantly to global poverty rates. The destruction of the world's forests, the overfishing of the world's oceans, the impact of climate change on people's well-being in ecologically precarious areas of the globe, and so on, all in the name of economic growth, are more likely to contribute to poverty rates, than the profits generated are likely to be used in the cause of poverty reduction. It can also be argued that a combination of development trends and of prevailing ideologies is creating rifts between peoples globally and nationally, heightening frustration levels, undermining social cohesion nationally and internationally, and resulting in an increase in the worldwide incidence of conflict, which in turn devastates whole societies, results in widespread poverty, and undermines global progress and therefore global ability to respond effectively to poverty.

If we extend our discussion of poverty to include relative poverty, there can be no doubt that globalization, particularly in the communication and knowledge dissemination areas, creates a much greater awareness in a greater proportion of the world's poor of the comparison of their poverty-stricken conditions with the conditions enjoyed by most people in the western world. Such knowledge must contribute to resentment and therefore to radical behavior and terrorism. It must also encourage many people to join the global movements of asylum seekers, illegal immigrants, and migrant workers, often further contributing to their own poverty and sometimes further destabilizing the world.

It is comparatively easy to suggest arguments as to why globalization trends might well be adding to, rather than reducing, global poverty levels, although there is admittedly still a significant degree of speculation in such arguments. On the other hand, we cannot ignore the potential of globalization to contribute to the eradication of poverty. If trade arrangements, grant monies, debt relief, and investment flows can be expanded, controlled, or supervised, in the best interests of the world's poorest nations and peoples, much could be achieved (see UNDP, 2003). However, such developments will need to be handled sensitively and humanely, and in the interests of people as well as in the interests of corporations, governments, and profit margins. It is also highly feasible to see the UN, other global institutions, individual governments, the NGO sector, and the corporate sector working together to raise global development to levels that remove poverty from the face of the globe. It is widely believed that this is possible if all

parties are truly committed to this goal. Finally, it is not inconceivable that global wealth be harnessed toward such a goal, for example, through a global system of taxation and redistribution such as has been successfully applied within many states. After all, developments within the European Union have demonstrated the potential to do this at the regional level. Hence it seems to be not globalization per se that exerts a negative impact on global poverty levels, so much as the manner in which globalization is handled by those who exercise control over it.

We shall examine two facets of poverty that stem directly from this discussion of globalization and poverty.

The Poverty of the United Nations' List of Least Developed Countries

The UN has designated the poorest countries of the world as Least Developed Countries (LDCs), of which in the late 1990s there were some 44 to 55, depending on the classification criteria used (e.g., World Bank, per capita income of $695 in 1993, or a UNDP Human Development Index score of below 0.5). The reality is that, in these countries, high proportions of the population receive virtually no monetary income and live in absolute or extreme poverty in income and often other terms. In terms of social characteristics, these countries have usually a life expectancy of from 44 to 58 years, 60 to 67 percent of people with no access to health services, and illiteracy rates of up to 73 percent. Their population growth rates are generally high, and the great bulk of the population live in rural areas and depend on agriculture. Many LDCs possess the geographical disadvantage of being either a landlocked or small island state, and are not uncommonly subjected to extreme climatic phenomena, such as frequent cyclonic storms and floods and periodic droughts. Finally, many LDCs have, in recent times, experienced civil war or at least political instability, often resulting from ethnically or religiously diverse populations and low levels of social cohesion.

In 1990 it was clear that not only were conditions in the world's LDCs shocking, but some were regressing in comparative and real terms. Accordingly, the UN organized a conference on LDCs that drew up a program of action for revitalizing these countries. A similar program had in fact been drawn up in 1980 but had failed. The 1990 report (United Nations, 1990, p. 4) stated,

> Despite national and international efforts on behalf of these countries, the social and economic situation of the LDCs as a whole worsened during the 1980s . . . the marginalization of the LDC group in the world economy has in fact become more accentuated, [while] in most LDCs there has been a deterioration of productive capacity and physical infrastructure, [while] particularly worrying was the rapid deterioration in the social conditions of the LDCs.

The program of action for the 1990s stressed, in addition to economic reforms, the mobilizing and developing of human capacities, in accordance with the values of people's participation, democracy, gender equality, good governance, strong institutions, a role for NGOs, and strengthening of human capital. In 1995, ESCAP published a midterm review of the implementation of this program in relation to the Asia-Pacific region. The report acknowledged some economic improvements, but in regard to the social and human dimensions of development, the report is basically negative. It states that "the problem of absolute poverty remains pervasive," environmental degradation continues to be a product of poverty and a lack of incentive not to overexploit, policy reforms have "tended to aggravate the problem of unemployment" and there are few suitable safety nets, women remain disadvantaged, "the problem of human resource

development remains acute," and many social indicators such as illiteracy rates remain unacceptably high (UN/ESCAP, 1995b). The program of action also stressed the importance of the LDCs' external environment, and the ESCAP midterm review again found progress on this front scarcely encouraging. Total ODA (Official Development Assistance) had further declined, the severe debt situation remained unabated, and the prices of food imports had increased.

On the global front, the United Nations Conference on Trade and Development (UNCTAD) reported in 1997 that about one-half of the LDCs showed improved economic performance but highlighted many ongoing problems, due in part to "the continued stagnation of aid flows and the persistence of their external debt problem." Many statements in this 1997 report are disturbing. For example,

> Development has proved elusive for a significant number of LDCs during the last ten years. In fact these countries have experienced regress, their economies have declined, social conditions have worsened markedly, and they have become increasingly marginalized from the mainstream of the world economy. Regress is not the result of a temporary cyclical economic downturn but is a chronic process with important structural characteristics, particularly the degradation of state and social institutions.

The secretary-general of UNCTAD concludes his overview:

> The key message of this part of the report is that urgent action by the international community to help LDCs tackle the widespread problems of economic and social regress, state failure and internal conflicts in LDCs should be a priority. The potential human and economic costs of regress are enormous, and not confined to the regressed economies themselves.

Many writers on globalization are convinced that that process results in the marginalization of countries such as the LDCs (e.g., Ghai, 1997; Pieterse, 1997; Frank, 1996; Townsend, 1994). As one UNRISD (1995b, p. 39) report put it, success in the prevailing global economic environment requires a strong state, large reserves of foreign exchange, and adequate foreign aid or credit—all requirements that LDCs lack. Moreover, ODA levels to LDCs have been declining, despite the commitments in 1990 to increase them. Also, by 1997, "with scheduled debt service repayments estimated to be in the order of one-third of the aggregate export earnings of LDCs, external obligations clearly exceed many of these countries' capacity to pay" (UNCTAD, 1997, p. 27). Finally, "the LDCs, with 10 per cent of the world's people, have only 0.2 per cent of world trade—half their share of two decades ago" (UNCTAD, 1997, p. 9).

In 2003, the UNDP (2003, pp. 15–17) concluded that global forces for development are bypassing hundreds of millions of the world's poorest peoples. It states that the reasons why economic development continues to bypass the world's poorest people and places include poor governance, the international trade system, geography, a reliance on primary commodities, rapid population growth, and the heavy burden of disease.

While external solutions are important to LDCs, one cannot be optimistic that change will come from external factors in at least the short term, given recent trends. Moreover, macro-level economic and social development will continue to be frustrated by prevailing political and governance conditions. In these circumstances, is there any potential for bottom-up or local-level social development? To date it has proved difficult to establish social work and social development training programs in the LDCs, and insufficient donor funding has reduced the ability of external agencies to embark on significant people-centered social development in most LDCs. However, we shall return to this question later in the text (Chapter 14).

Globally Induced Poverty

The concept of globally induced poverty arises from some common misunderstandings of the concept of globalization and its impact on poverty levels. Few writers condemn globalization per se, and indeed it would be foolish to do so. However, even highly reputable commentators on globalization warn that it can and does have adverse effects, depending, in the eyes of many, on how it is handled and regulated. A very balanced overview of globalization and its impact on poverty is contained in the UNDP's 1997 report on poverty (see Chapter 4) and 1999 *Human Development Report*. The first report begins the discussion with a clear statement of the overall situation:

Lacking power, poor countries and poor people too often find their interests neglected and undermined.

Globalisation has its winners and its losers. With the expansion of trade and foreign investment, developing countries have seen the gaps among themselves widen. Meanwhile, in many industrial countries unemployment has soared to levels not seen since the 1930s, and income inequality to levels not recorded since the last century.

A rising tide of wealth is supposed to lift all boats. But some are more seaworthy than others. The yachts and ocean liners are indeed rising in response to new opportunities, but the rafts and rowboats are taking on water—and some are sinking fast. (p. 82)

The report proceeds to attribute the adverse impact of globalization on poverty to three causes: poor national macroeconomic policy, unfavorable terms of trade for poor countries, and rules of the game that are biased against poor countries (pp. 84–85). Having considered the reasons why poor countries do not usually benefit from globalization, the report goes on to point out "that even less certain than globalisation's benefits for poor countries are its benefits for poor people within countries. And this impact of globalisation on internal poverty relates to both developing and industrial countries." The UNDP confirms this conclusion in its 2003 report (UNDP, 2003, p. 16).

Other writers are, however, basically unhappy with a form of globalization that effectively removes jurisdiction over the economies within their borders from national governments. As Korten (1995, p. 92) puts it,

> A government must have jurisdiction over the economy within the borders of its territory. It must be able to set the rules for the domestic economy without having to prove to foreign governments and corporations that such rules are not barriers to international trade and investment.

The core of the problem for Korten is that

> when the economy is global and governments are national, global corporations and financial institutions function largely beyond the reach of public accountability, governments become more vulnerable to inappropriate corporate influence, and citizenship is reduced to making consumer choices among the products corporations find it profitable to offer. (p. 92)

For Korten, the global system is inherently flawed in its current state. He writes,

> A globalised economic system has an inherent bias in favor of the large, the global, the competitive, the resource-extractive, and the short-term. Our challenge is to create a global system that is biased towards the small, the local, the cooperative, the resource-conserving, and the long-term—one that empowers people to create a good living in balance with nature. (p. 270)

Korten's major concern is with the philosophical stance of, and the power held by, the world's MNCs—a concern shared by others such as Madeley (1999), whose book is subtitled *The Impact of Transnational Corporations on the World's Poor.*

Hoogvelt (2001), on the basis of her analysis of the relationship between globalization and development, draws a graphic but widely supported conclusion:

> Globalization . . . has rearranged the architecture of world order. Economic, social and power relations have been recast to resemble not a pyramid but a three-tier structure of concentric circles. All three circles cut across national and regional boundaries. In the core circle we find the elites of all continents and nations, albeit in different proportions in relation to their respective geographic hinterlands. We may count in this core some 20 per cent of world population who are "bankable." They are encircled by a larger, fluid, social layer of between 20 and 30 per cent of the world population (workers and their families), who labour in insecure forms of employment. . . .

> The third, and largest, concentric circle comprises those who are already effectively excluded from the global system. Performing neither a productive function, nor presenting a potential consumer market in the present stage of high-tech, information-driven capitalism, there is, for the moment, neither theory, worldview, nor moral injunction, let alone a program of action, to include them in universal progress.

There is little doubt that globalization in its current form is doing little to alleviate much of global poverty, and probably is adding to it in some circumstances. The more difficult question is whether globalization is inherently flawed or whether the problem lies in the way in which it is being controlled globally and nationally. Let us conclude with the views of the WB and UNDP, whose views are both authoritative and, one would hope, highly influential. Even the World Bank (2000/2001, chap. 10) agrees that globalization is a major concern:

> The lives of poor people are also affected by forces originating outside their countries' borders—global trade, capital flows, official development assistance, technological advance, diseases, and conflicts, to name just a few. Actions at the global level are therefore crucial complements to country-level actions. They can accelerate poverty reduction and help narrow the gaps—in income, health and other dimensions—between rich countries and poor. (p. 179)

Its report goes on to discuss four key areas of international action for poverty reduction:

> expanding market access in rich countries for developing countries' goods and services;
>
> reducing the risk of economic crises;
>
> encouraging the production of international public goods that benefit poor people;
>
> ensuring a voice for poor countries and poor people in global forums.
>
>   Also important for poverty reduction is development cooperation—foreign aid and debt relief. . . . Other global forces that affect the poor include international labor migration, commodity price volatility, global warming and environmental degradation, promotion of political and human rights, and the international arms sale and trade in illicit gems that spur on prolonged conflict in countries. (World Bank, 2000/2001)

Finally, the UNDP's (1997, pp. 91–93) report concludes,

> To seize the opportunities of globalization, the poorest developing countries need,
>
>   1. A more supportive macroeconomic policy environment for poverty eradication. . . .

>   2. A fairer institutional environment for global trade. . . .
>   3. A partnership with multinational corporations to promote growth for poverty reduction. . . .
>   4. Action to stop the race to the bottom. . . .
>   5. Selective support for global technology priorities. . . .
>   6. Action on global debt. . . .
>   7. Better access to finance for poor countries. . . .

In many respects the world is sailing through the current era of globalization with neither compass nor map. Too little is known about the links between globalization and poverty, an area that demands much more intensive study. But regardless of the future direction of globalization, we know enough about the basic measures that need to be taken to attack poverty. The speed of globalization makes them all the more urgent.

Poverty and the Development Process

Our first typology of poverty is related to, or stems from, the development process (see Isbister, 1991; Allen and Thomas, 1992; Easterly, 2002). For those familiar with the history of western industrialized nations, we can employ that historical process to help us to understand how various types of poverty emerged there, and then consider the relevance of that process for developing countries. If we go back to the premodern period, we are confronted with a number of traditional societies. These were largely rural societies populated in the main by tenant farmers (in feudal societies) and small landholders, with some nomadic peoples. These economies were largely subsistent, with a degree of barter exchange and perhaps some mutual support schemes. People were basically poor to very poor. Meeting their basic needs was a precarious process, affected by climatic conditions, natural disasters, strength of family and tribal groups, and war between social groupings. Accordingly, life expectancy levels were low to very low, capacity building opportunities were extremely limited, and there was very limited freedom of choice. People's well-being was often ultimately determined by the geographical conditions and by political patronage or feudal systems and what these entailed. While the phenomenon of subsistence poverty was, in general terms, very real, especially in terms of the lack of freedom and choice that it imposed on people, the severity of that poverty varied greatly, dependent largely on climatic conditions. For example, in many parts of the world a cold or hot dry season left people dependent on food supplies accumulated during the good season, and sometimes with inadequate housing, water, and other essentials; while in other parts of the world people experienced what has been called "subsistence affluence," meaning that they experienced good living conditions, in terms at least of food and housing, throughout the year (for example, in parts of the Pacific).

The western world then experienced the agricultural revolution. Land was amalgamated into larger holdings, some technology was introduced, and the phenomenon of the cash crop emerged. Trade was expanding and society began to reflect the newly emerging opportunities. Some people became rich; some survived the changes and remained viable; while others became landless laborers, deprived of opportunities to be subsistent and displaced by technology, apart from short periods when their labor might be in demand. These changes had two effects. On the one hand, many of the rural population became extremely poor and barely survived, even when times were good; when times were bad they starved. On the other hand, the changes resulted in a major exodus from many rural areas, either abroad as in the massive flows of Europeans to the lands of the New World, or to the rapidly emerging urban centers within the

country. In these newly formed urban areas, many of the newly arrived lived in deplorable slums among unhygienic surroundings, and survived on extremely poorly paid work in very poor working conditions within either the emerging industrial sector or the urban informal economy. The industrial revolution had arrived, bringing with it accelerated urbanization, and urban poverty existed on a large scale. Hence, across countries and regions, a varying degree of rural poverty existed side by side with a varying degree of urban poverty, and only very slowly did conditions in both sectors improve.

In time, most western industrialized countries learned to handle these new rural and urban conditions, and the extent and severity of both types of poverty were, over a relatively long period of time, markedly reduced. In a later period, however, these nations became aware that, while the mainstream society and economy were functioning quite well, and often becoming exceedingly middle-class and prosperous, there existed a parallel society and economy that was not doing very well at all. These were basically the socially and economically excluded, or the marginalized. They might represent indigenous populations of aboriginal origins (First Nations peoples); they might include those unable or unwilling to adapt to modern society, if indeed they would be accepted, such as the Roma people of Europe; they might include racial or ethnic minorities whose participation in society was limited by prevailing mainstream attitudes toward them (e.g., attitudes in parts of Europe toward former migrant workers, who won the right to permanent residence, and toward illegal immigrants); or they might include categories such as rural youth, school dropouts, individuals with psychiatric conditions, unmarried mothers, and so on, for whom society appeared to offer few opportunities, and sometimes little acceptance. Europe led the way globally in seeking to devise policies, structures, and programs that were socially and economically inclusive in their operations, so as to overcome the phenomenon of exclusion. However, such goals proved difficult to achieve and a new form of poverty had emerged—the homeless, long-term unemployed, socially marginalized, and so on, who lived frequently in or on the verge of poverty. Beyond Europe, the continuation of pockets of poverty is apparent in many otherwise affluent countries (see Dixon and Macarov, 1998; Kelso, 1994; Hong Kong Council of Social Services, 1996).

Turning to the developing world, all of the above types of poverty can be found, often existing simultaneously, because of the developing world's highly accelerated and uneven progress through the stages outlined above. Subsistent traditional societies are not unknown; rural poverty contains the largest number of people in poverty; urban poverty, with people living in slums, shantytowns, and urban settlement areas, is the fastest growing form of poverty; and pockets of socially and economically excluded reflect the pluralistic nature of many of these societies, with inadequate levels of social cohesion, a continuing inability to accept those who appear different from the norm, and a tendency for many societies to leave behind, in development terms, some pockets of the population. Thus the developing world reflects the western experience, but while in the latter case that experience was spread over some centuries, allowing countries time to adjust and work out socioeconomic and political-policy solutions, in the developing world it was often concertinaed within a rapid development process over a few short decades. Hence in the developing world we see the juxtaposition of various types of development-related poverty, just as we see the juxtaposition of various development stages such as a traditional economy, a rural economy, an informal urban economy, a formal urban economy, and a global economy inserting themselves into many developing countries through, for example, free trade zones. Clearly, therefore, the reasons for and nature of the various types of poverty vary, especially in the developing world, for they reflect different aspects of a nation's development process occurring more or less simultaneously, in part a result of colonial and neocolonial influences. Moreover, however, the rapid pace of change and the juxtaposition of various types of development, each with its consequent poverty, has been extremely difficult for developing countries to respond to, by contrast with the historically much slower pace of change in the western industrialized world.

Subsistence Poverty

Subsistence-level living was common in traditional premonetary societies, and the great majority of people were therefore poor in at least income terms. Most were also poor in terms of basic health and education needs, but whether they were poor in terms of nutrition and shelter was dependent largely on the environment in which they lived, as pointed out previously. Not surprisingly, the most basic definition of poverty is the capacity to survive. As Dixon and Macarov (1998, p. 4) define it, poverty "may mean nothing more than having the resources to purchase or grow sufficient food for oneself and one's dependents." One might add also to gather food and to possess shelter from the elements. Subsistence poverty is often associated with chronic hunger. As Allen and Thomas (1992, p. 28) put it, "Chronic hunger is one aspect, probably the most fundamental, of a wider set of deprivations understood as poverty. Chronic hunger and poverty are closely related." We should note also, however, that a phenomenon easing the impact of overall poverty for the great majority of individuals was the strength, and inclusive and supportive nature, of the family, clan, or tribal group.

Rural Poverty

Until comparatively recently the great bulk of global poverty was rural poverty. Indeed, Mullen (1995, p. 1) reports a "dramatic increase in magnitude of rural poverty worldwide during the 1980s." Even in 1997, the UNDP reported that "about three-quarters of the world's poorest people live in rural areas, dependent on agricultural activities for their livelihood" (pp. 7–8). With increasing rates of urbanization this situation is slowly changing, but still today a majority of the world's poor live in rural areas. In addition to this statistical dominance of rural poverty, it is also commonly said that rural poverty is worse than urban poverty. The World Bank (1990, p. 29) stated this clearly, and the situation does not appear to have changed significantly:

> Poverty as measured by low income tends to be at its worst in rural areas, even allowing for the often substantial differences in cost of living between town and countryside. The problems of malnutrition, lack of education, low life expectancy, and substandard housing are also, as a rule, more severe in rural areas.

However, even in poorer countries rural areas vary greatly in poverty terms. As the World Bank's 1990 report went on to say,

> Many of the poor are located in regions where arable land is scarce, agricultural productivity is low, and drought, floods and environmental degradation are common. In Latin America, for example, the worst poverty occurs predominantly in arid zones or in steep hill-slope areas that are ecologically vulnerable. Such areas are often isolated in every sense. Opportunities for non-farm employment are few, and the demand for labor tends to be highly seasonal. Others among the poor live in regions that have a more promising endowment of natural resources but lack access to social services (education and health) and infrastructure (irrigation, information and technical assistance, transport, and market centers). (p. 30)

Two common characteristics of rural poverty are high illiteracy rates and very low income

levels (UNDP, 1997, p. 42). Illiteracy rates are commonly twice as high in rural areas as in urban areas, which in turn reflects rural-urban disparities in access to social services. Levels of income poverty are also much higher in rural areas, which is understandable given the common lack of paid employment for landless people. Chambers (1983, pp. 103ff.) picks up the point of the disadvantages against which many of the rural poor struggle and presents a model of "five interlocking disadvantages which trap them in deprivation: poverty itself, physical weakness, isolation, vulnerability, and powerlessness" (p. 103). Within his model (see pp. 112–113), Chambers sets out the key roles of each of the five areas of disadvantage that constitute the "deprivation trap," but the core element is poverty itself:

> Poverty is a strong determinant of the others. Poverty contributes to physical weakness through lack of food, small bodies, malnutrition leading to low immune response to infections, and inability to reach or pay for health services; to isolation because of the inability to pay the cost of schooling, to buy a radio or a bicycle, to afford to travel to look for work, or to live near the village centre or a main road; to vulnerability through lack of assets to pay large expenses or to meet contingencies; and to powerlessness because lack of wealth goes with low status: the poor have no voice. (p. 112)

In addition to the causes of rural poverty set out by the World Bank (isolation, etc.) and by Chambers (impact of specific aspects of their poverty situation on the poor as people), other causes of rural poverty include a range of inappropriate government and private sector policies and practices. Among the most common of these receiving coverage in the literature are

inadequate development of the rural sector by governments;

inadequate employment choices in rural areas, which policies like rural industrialization can overcome (e.g., as in the People's Republic of China);

Western control of the prices of both rural products (e.g., through stockpiling and the release of subsidized production onto global markets) and of rural machinery usually imported by developing countries;

insufficient access to capital loans at reasonable interest rates allied to exploitation by moneylenders;

exploitation by rural elite groups of various kinds;

inadequate social services in rural areas, especially compared with urban areas;

inappropriate land ownership systems, such as feudal landlords or very small holdings resulting from inheritance systems;

the exodus from rural areas in many countries of significant numbers of educated and skilled persons, and especially youth; and, according to some,

TNCs' introduction of genetically modified crops that, for example, may force farmers to purchase seed each year rather than saving some from the previous harvest.

If rural poverty is widespread and often extremely severe in its impact on people, it is also the area of poverty to which a large number and wide range of poverty reduction or alleviation programs have been directed. As a result, there exist a set of policies, programs, and strategies that have been found to be effective against rural poverty, in at least some circumstances, and these we shall consider in Chapter 8. (For comprehensive discussions on rural poverty alleviation, see Mullen, 1995; Chambers, 1983, 1993; Nayyar, 1996.)

Urban Poverty

The concept of urban is not straightforward. While the UN suggested that settlements of over 20,000 people be defined as urban, of over 100,000 as cities, and of more than five million as big cities, Drakakis-Smith (1987, pp. 1–2) has pointed out that,

> there is little homogeneity in the nature of urban growth in the Third World, and this is perhaps not surprising in view of the large number and varied nature of the countries involved. Capital cities can range from small agglomerations of less than 20,000 in the Pacific to the massive 16 million of Mexico City [one of many now well over 20 million].

What is clear is that there is no uniformity in what is regarded as urban, in size, lifestyle, or living conditions.

While urban centers have a long history, the modern city is largely the product of recent developments epitomized in the agricultural and industrial revolutions. The speed and size of these developments have meant large influxes of people into urban areas over short periods of time, often giving rise to atrocious living conditions and to employers' ability to exploit the large labor force that became available. Thus Kelso (1994, p. 7) argues that the modern city and its poverty are closely related to the workings of the modern capitalist system. This urban poverty has consisted essentially of poor living conditions, especially in terms of housing and the availability of essential services, and low wages in the formal sector or a precarious financial existence in the informal sector.

Urban poverty has long been apparent in the developed world, but governments showed little interest in it before the 1960s. (See Kelso, 1994, on the United States, and Higgins, 1983, on the United Kingdom.) Despite significant anti-poverty campaigns at that time, urban poverty has increased in recent decades over much of

Europe, North America, and Australasia, and there remains a great deal of pessimism regarding the possibilities of significant reductions in the near future (Dixon and Macarov, 1998, p. 277). Moreover, along with and related to urban poverty levels, there has been the urgent need in western countries for expensive urban renewal in poorer and badly run-down areas.

In the developing countries, "the impact of European expansion from the sixteenth century onwards transformed urban structures" (Gilbert and Gugler, 1992, pp. 16ff.), because third world urbanization was essentially the outcome of European capital penetration, as these scholars see it. Certainly the urban centers that preceded colonialism and the new centers that emerged with it often experienced massive influxes of rural emigrants seeking employment. This migration was due in part to rural-urban disparities, reflecting an unbalanced development process; partly to rural development policies that resulted in large numbers of landless laborers among the rural poor; and partly to the attraction that cities had for at least some rural people. Even improvements in rural living standards, where these occurred, often meant that "population pressures on the available land became severe in many areas" (Gilbert and Gugler, 1992, p. 63). However, the overwhelming evidence is that most of this rural to urban migration was economically motivated; and, furthermore, that most of these migrants considered that they had improved their conditions by migrating (p. 69). Hugo (1987, p. 153) found that "income levels are generally higher in urban than in rural areas," and that urban-bound migrants usually benefited from this, and most research tends to agree with this finding.

One sometimes is led to believe that rural to urban migrants were made up largely of the rural poor, who swelled the numbers of urban poor in the slum and settlement areas and so contributed directly to urban poverty. This thesis cannot be substantiated as a generalization. By and large, rural to urban migrations have contributed significantly to urban economies, because, as Hugo's (1987, p. 155) and other research shows, "rural to urban migrants in developing countries are on average better educated than those who remain behind," and also more likely to be "the more dynamic individuals in the village, those with leadership potential, and those more receptive to innovative ideas." Moreover, most ultimately saw their migration as successful, having secured a higher income and found access to more opportunities than existed at home. Did rural to urban migration then contribute to urban poverty? In a direct sense no, although certainly recently arrived migrants were often found among those in poverty. Poverty in the long term, however, was far more an outcome of the conditions that prevailed in urban areas than it was of the migration origins of many of the poorer urban residents.

One factor driving rural to urban migration has been a degree of urban bias in development policies (Midgley, 1995a, p. 73), which has been falsely promoted under the influence of structural-change models. (See the Lewis theory of development outlined in Chapter 5.) Such an urban bias, however, has not precluded urban poverty, as the World Bank (1990, p. 30) points out:

Although urban incomes are generally higher and urban services and facilities more accessible, poor town-dwellers may suffer more than rural households from certain aspects of poverty. The urban poor, typically housed in slums or squatter settlements, often have to contend with appalling overcrowding, bad sanitation and contaminated water.... The evidence suggests that urban areas do offer more opportunities for higher paid work, and this implies that, on balance, urbanization helps to reduce poverty.

While urban poverty in the West was closely associated with labor-intensive industrialization, most developing countries have fostered capital-intensive industrialization (Gilbert and Gugler, 1992, p. 88), so that the prevailing labor situation in most cities of the developing world is one of surplus at virtually all levels of the labor market. As Gilbert and Gugler (1992, p. 94) put it,

> Unemployment, underemployment and mis-employment, adding up to a massive waste of labour in Third World cities, relate to three dimensions of inequality. The sharply differentiated incomes of the affluent and the masses, allowing the few to pay so little for the services of the many, foster misemployment. The privileged position of the protected labour-force compared with that of the bulk of the urban workers, causes unemployment when it encourages workers to hold out in the hope of joining the protected labour-force; and it leads to underemployment as the mass of urban workers, with little capital equipment, compete for limited markets.

Estimates of the proportion of urban labor forces working in the informal sector go as high as 65 percent, and this sector is often typified by poor or dangerous working conditions, exploitation, child labor, and significant insecurity.

In addition to the labor market situation, the conditions in slum and squatter settlements, the phenomenon of street dwellers, and inadequate access to basic facilities are significant dimensions of urban poverty (see Blair, 1974). At the same time, many urban residents and observers of their conditions have viewed their slums as at least in part "slums of hope" (see Lloyd, 1979)—an attitude that is still very prevalent. Despite conditions being often horrendous, many of the urban poor ultimately improve their situations by obtaining income, renovating their homes slowly, and providing their children with access to schooling. Even those who end up disappointed are encouraged by the possibilities of improvement and the examples of those who do ultimately make it. Hence urban poverty is not infrequently seen as a temporary phenomenon at the personal level, although not overall.

In practice, the actions of many governments, NGOs, and POs have done much in many places

to gradually improve housing conditions, expand other facilities, improve working conditions, facilitate income-generation schemes through the provision of credit and training, and promote community capacity building and development. Despite many such programs, it must still be said that research on urban poverty tends to conclude on a pessimistic note regarding the ongoing overall incidence of urban poverty (UN/ESCAP, 1993; Gilbert and Gugler, 1992; Rao and Linnemann, 1996). On the other hand, because we have many examples of programs that work, it can also be argued that greater dedication to an expansion of such programs could achieve wonders. We shall examine some of the key strategies in the next chapter.

Poverty and Specific Population Categories

It is clear that, within specific cultures, reflecting social structures and often reinforced by development processes, certain population categories will be more affected by poverty than will be other sections of the same population. The basic process is a cultural devaluing of selected population categories, reflected in attitudes toward these categories that result in a degree of negative discrimination. In turn these values and attitudes are reflected in the prevailing social structures (social exclusion), resulting in a degree of structural discrimination against members of the population category in question which in turn results in higher poverty levels. Among the categories that come most readily to mind are the following: women, especially those in conditions that leave them vulnerable to gender bias; children, especially when regarded as the possessions of adults who are at liberty to exploit and abuse them; persons with disabilities who are regarded as less than full human beings; and members of racial and ethnic minority groupings who are regarded and treated as inferior to mainstream social groupings.

In many cases it is a combination of being a member of a specific population category and being in, or being perceived to be in, a particular social situation that results in exclusion, alienation, or discriminatory behavior. For example, women who conceive a child out of wedlock (single mothers), or who dishonor their husbands, are frequently socially ostracized for their behavior and likely to end up in poverty. Similarly, children who, for whatever reason, leave their family of origin and exist on the street or in youth gangs are likely to find few opportunities in most societies. Finally, those who are racially different and members of an indigenous minority regarded as comparatively uncivilized, especially when choosing to live in certain places or with particular lifestyles, are likely to experience extreme hardships.

We shall consider briefly three such categories—women, children and minority groups.

The Feminization of Poverty

It has been common in recent times to refer to the feminization of poverty (UNDP, 1997, p. 64; Pierson, 1998, p. 71), usually meaning that women are more likely than men to be found among poverty-stricken populations. In 1990, the UNDP (1990, p. 22) wrote in its report on poverty,

Poverty has a decided gender bias. A large proportion of poor households are headed by women, especially in rural Africa and the urban slums of Latin America. Female members of a poor household are often worse off than male members because of gender-based differences in the distribution of food and other entitlements within the family.

In the same year the World Bank (1990, pp. 2, 18) commented,

The weight of poverty falls most heavily on certain groups. Women in general are disadvantaged. In poor households they often shoulder more of the workload than men,

are less educated, and have less access to remunerative activities. . . .

The available figures on health, nutrition, education, and labor force participation show women are often severely disadvantaged. Women face all manner of cultural, social, legal, and economic obstacles that men—even poor men—do not.

In their poverty reports a decade later (UNDP, 1997; World Bank, 2000/2001), the indications were that little had changed. The UNDP, drawing on its GDI (Gender-related Development Index) and GEM (Gender Empowerment Measure) measures, concluded, "First, no society treats its women as well as its men. . . . Second, gender inequality is strongly associated with human poverty."

One key element in the situation is that of access for women, especially poor women, to opportunities for capacity building, not just as a matter of practical access but as one of rights. As Elson (1995a, pp. 75–76) notes,

Thus the fundamental issues of women's poverty go beyond lack of access to paid employment outside the family; they stem from the fact that women are poorer in rights than are men, not just in relation to land and capital, but even in relation to their own persons in their own right, in ways that take into account the complexities of integrating getting a living with raising children and taking care of others.

Women tend to be not fully recognized by the state as citizens, as holders of rights on their own account; rather they are construed to a greater or lesser degree as dependents of men.

However, when women cease to be dependents of men, forming female-headed households, their situation usually worsens. For a range of reasons, including male migration, women widowed or deserted during conflict, the displacement of women, and a breakdown in family relationships, the number of women heading households has grown significantly, thus adding to the burdens borne by women while often failing to improve their social status or access to economic resources such as capacity building and employment. Even in two-parent households, it is frequently the women who are on the front line in poverty terms and requiring empowerment if poverty is to be meaningfully tackled, as the UNDP (1997, pp. 6–7) points out:

> Already women are on the front line of household and community efforts to escape poverty and cope with its impact. But too often they do not have a voice in decision-making—in the household, in the community or in national and international arenas.

Gender equality needs to be part of each country's strategy for eradicating poverty, both as an end and as a means to eradicating other forms of human poverty, "and if poverty reduction strategies fail to empower women, they will fail to empower society" (UNDP, 1997, pp. 6–7).

In a useful article, Elson (1995a) analyzes the place of gender issues in the poverty alleviation approaches of the UNDP (1990) and World Bank (1990), and suggests some guidelines for action. (For examples of social work with poor women, see Abrahams and Peredo, 1996, and UN/ESCAP, 1994b.)

Child Poverty

When poverty is endemic in a situation, or increases suddenly for whatever reason, there is no doubt that children are especially vulnerable. As the UNDP (1997, p. 3) expresses it, "Children are especially vulnerable—hit by malnutrition and illness just when their brains and bodies are forming. Some 160 million children are moderately or severely malnourished. Some 110 million are out of school." As this statement points out, it is the reality that childhood is a period that is critical for children's development and hence for their entire future. Adults may be able to sustain periods of even severe poverty and

bounce back afterward, but for children the experience may leave them seriously impaired for the rest of their lives.

In a wide range of all too common situations, children's health, education, and physical and intellectual development are adversely affected by deprivation of the essential requirements for their development during critical points in that process. At the same time, children do not have the status, strength, or capacity generally to acquire a fair share of available resources, let alone receive an additional share because of their developmental needs. Children may be abandoned, orphaned, forced into providing a service to adults that damages them further, or simply neglected.

Because children have long been regarded and treated as the possessions of adults and basically lesser beings, the focus in recent times has been on the rights of children, with a Convention on the Rights of the Child entering international law in September 1990 (see UNICEF, 1997, pp. 9ff.). However, it is clear that the attitudes of many general publics and governments will have to change significantly if the goals of this convention are to become reality. The plight of children resulting from conflict, the HIV/AIDS epidemic, their exploitation as child labor, their abuse as child prostitutes and slaves, and their status as victims of poverty generally remains an enormous challenge, as the regular reports of UNICEF make abundantly clear (see UNICEF, *State of the World's Children* annual reports). Even in the so-called developed countries, the numbers of children living in poverty continues to be a major concern (see Dixon and Macarov, 1998; Bradbury, Jenkins, and Micklewright, 2000).

Minority Group Poverty

As the UNDP (1997, p. 43) points out, "uneven progress in reducing poverty is reflected in disparities among different ethnic groups in a country," whether that country be developed or developing. They go on to say that indigenous peoples will frequently suffer even more than other types of minorities: "In almost all societies where they are to be found, indigenous people are poorer than most other groups." The World Bank's (2000/2001, p. 28) report on global poverty fully agrees:

> Disadvantaged in many developing and developed countries and transition economies, ethnic minorities and racial groups often face higher poverty. The indigenous populations have a much higher incidence of income poverty in a sample of Latin American countries for which data are available. . . .

Evidence for India shows that scheduled castes and scheduled tribes face a higher risk of poverty. These are among the structural poor who not only lack economic resources but whose poverty is strongly linked to social identity, as determined mainly by caste.

A term that is now commonly applied to the situation of minority groups in Europe is *social exclusion* (Commission of the European Communities, 1993, pp. 20–21). The UNDP (1997, p. 17) notes also the significance of this phenomenon in the developing world.

Whatever the term used, the reality is that "worldwide, low status ethnic minorities experience poverty at high rates" (Meerman, 2001). Meerman continues,

> Moreover, poverty reduction is particularly difficult for those minorities that have a history of severe exploitation and discrimination because they inherit social disadvantages which reinforce the general causes of poverty. Many countries have attempted to promote the economic progress of this latter group with differing results.

The causes of this state of affairs may lie largely with majority group attitudes, former slave and outcaste status, newly arrived immigrant status, or other factors; what changes little are the consequences of their status, namely high levels of illiteracy, undereducation and overt or covert discrimination, relatively low incomes, low labor force participation, and high incidences of disability, illness (physical and mental), and crime. Poverty among low-status minorities is not only difficult to overcome but requires a focus on their status in society and strategies to change that state of affairs. (For some discussions of indigenous minority group poverty alleviation and social development generally, see Stoesz et al., 1999, chap. 10, on Native Americans; Pearson, 2000, on Australia's aboriginals; and Singharoy, 2001, on India's indigenous populations.)

Consequential Poverty

What we are here calling consequential poverty is not strictly consequential in a straight cause-and-effect sense. Rather it includes situations where poverty is so closely associated with other phenomena that it is usually impossible to tackle that poverty without at least simultaneously doing something about the other phenomena. For example, modern conflict inevitably leads to large-scale poverty, in the sense that, in most postconflict situations, there is widespread unemployment, many people have exhausted or lost whatever savings they had, housing has been badly damaged and needs repair if it is to afford adequate shelter, and the normal provision of social services has been badly disrupted. The major overall task in such a context is postconflict reconstruction—a situation with which we are all too familiar in modern times, at least through the media. Poverty reduction or alleviation is a part of the reconstruction task and cannot be tackled in isolation, despite the temporary importance of humanitarian aid. Although the conflict may in fact have aggravated existing poverty, as well as caused additional poverty, the close association of the two phenomena is obvious (see Chapter 9).

We shall consider four examples of consequential poverty: poverty associated with, respectively, conflict, natural disasters, ecological degradation, and high population growth rates.

Conflict-related Poverty

In 1997, the UNDP's *Human Development Report* found that 30 countries were experiencing a declining Human Development Index, and that nine of these were "among those with a deadly population-displacing conflict" (p. 65). In stating this fact, the UNDP is highlighting the clear association between conflict and poverty, an association also noted by the World Bank (2000/2001, p. 50). The UNDP (1997, pp. 65–66) describes this association in several ways. First, the poor are exposed to conflict "because modern wars are fought mainly in poorer countries." Second, "wars strike poor households and communities because they strike civilian populations at large." Third, "many of the casualties are women and children." Fourth, "conflicts in poor countries block or handicap poverty eradication efforts." Fifth, "in addition to those affected by warfare, many poor people fall victim to the supposedly peaceful alternative—economic sanctions" (e.g., Haiti and Iraq).

The UNDP's 1996 report spells out some of these points in more detail:

Since the Second World War the number of conflicts in the world has increased more than fivefold, more than 90% of them internal. Bombs, bullets and landmines might be thought the greatest risks in conflict, but many more people die from indirect causes—such as the disruption of food and water supplies or the disruption of health services. In today's conflict zones more than 100 million people are chronically malnourished. In the Horn of Africa in the early 1990s, mortality and disease rates were more than 20 times as high as normal. This takes a terrible toll on children. (1996a, p. 24)

The association between conflict and poverty is both close and extensive, and it continues into the important postconflict reconstruction phase on which we shall focus in Chapter 9. Social workers are far more likely to be involved in the postconflict phase than during conflict, but they still require an understanding of the nature of the association between the two phenomena of conflict and poverty in a range of contexts.

Natural Disaster–related Poverty

The World Bank (2000/2001, p. 170) states that "over the past 10 years the incidence of natural disasters has increased," pointing out that many such disasters are both "human-made" and "natural." The report goes on to point out that "developing countries, especially their more densely populated regions, suffer the brunt of natural disasters," in that "97% of all natural disaster–related deaths were in developing countries." Furthermore,

Poor people and poor communities are frequently the primary victims of natural disasters, in part because they are priced out of the more disaster-proof areas and live in crowded makeshift houses. The incidence of disaster tends to be higher in poor communities, which are more likely to be in areas vulnerable to bad weather or seismic activity. And there is evidence that the low quality of infrastructure in poor communities increases their vulnerability.

So we find that poor people are more frequently affected by natural disasters, and that,

while natural disasters hurt everyone affected by them, poor families are hit particularly hard because injury, disability and loss of life affect their main asset, their labor. (p. 171)

Beyond the direct impact of natural disasters on the poor, the incidence of natural disasters will frequently result in more poverty, at least in the short term, while the high cost of repairs after the advent of a natural disaster reduces the monies available for other purposes, including poverty reduction programs, as the World Bank (p. 172) goes on to note.

The need to replace damaged infrastructure in disaster-stricken countries diverts government resources from longer-term development objectives and consumes a significant share of multinational lending resources.

Poverty and natural disasters tend to create the proverbial vicious circle. A high incidence of poverty, resulting in the poor being forced to live in precarious conditions, increases the vulnerability of the poor to natural disasters. Hence, as the World Bank points out, what is required is action to lessen people's vulnerability to disasters (pp. 172ff.). This may include general preparation for disasters, resettlement of people from disaster-prone areas, neighborhood improvement programs such as improving quality of housing or drainage, and environmental conservation and reforestation. Clearly arrangements for, and training in, postdisaster responses are also very important, including workfare programs: "Workfare programs can usefully be introduced or expanded in disaster areas in conjunction with reconstruction operations, providing a livelihood to people who can no longer support themselves" (World Bank, 2000/2001, p. 176).

Ecological Degradation–related Poverty

The association between poverty and ecological degradation is a close one, as studies over nearly 20 years have shown. One aspect of this association is the vulnerability of the poor to the impact of ecological degradation. As the World Bank (1990, p. 30) expresses it, "Many of the poor are located in regions where arable land is scarce, agricultural productivity is low, and drought, floods and environmental degradation are common."

Another aspect is the impact of poverty on ecological degradation. To quote from Durning (1990, p. 145), "As the global poverty trap tightens and the world's poor become increasingly insecure and dispossessed, the conditions for

ecological degradation spread to more of the earth's fragile lands."

The World Commission on Environment and Development (1987, p. 3) stresses this link:

There has been a growing realization in national governments and multilateral institutions that it is impossible to separate economic development issues from environment issues; many forms of development erode the environmental resources upon which they must be based, and environmental degradation can undermine economic development. Poverty is a major cause and effect of global environmental problems. It is therefore futile to attempt to deal with environmental problems without a broader perspective that encompasses the factors underlying world poverty and international inequality.

Reports such as the above are concerned about the association between poverty and ecological degradation in both rural and urban contexts. In the former, the association arises, for example, from situations where landless people are forced onto marginal or common lands where they often have no alternative but to exploit the environment in a manner that is destructive and unsustainable. In the latter, ecological degradation is closely associated with the sprawling shantytowns. As Durning (1990, pp. 147–148) writes,

The shantytowns of the poor are found in areas eschewed by the better-off: in floodplains, on perilous slopes, around—sometimes in—garbage dumps containing unknown quantities of toxic materials, and near hazardous industrial zones. The fact that Bhopal [a city in India where a major industrial discharge of toxic material took place] victims were overwhelmingly poor was no coincidence: industrial accidents worldwide take the lives of those who cannot afford to live far from the belching stacks.

Of course this is not to imply that agricultural and industrial pursuits, and development policies generally, might not be equally deleterious to the environment. Recent research on global warming is indicating that the world could be facing a highly precarious future unless all countries manage to reduce significantly their levels of gas emissions resulting in the greenhouse effect. The 1997 Kyoto Agreement, which came into effect in February 2005, seeks to gain universal endorsement to achieving this goal, but some major industrialized countries have to date failed to endorse it.

There are several messages arising out of the above points, but two stand out. One clear point is that significant alleviation or reduction of poverty is essential if the environment is to survive. The second is that ecologically sound and sustainable development is essential if future growth in poverty levels, and indeed disaster for all, is to be avoided. The World Commission on Environment and Development (1987, pp. 51–56) identifies several strategic imperatives for sustainable development, which place a strong emphasis on the human, public, and community dimensions.

In recent years, the international focus on "environmental sustainability" and "sustainable development" has grown even stronger, highlighting again the very close links between poverty and the world's environmental problems. These are well summarized by the UNDP (2003, chap. 6) as it reports on the seventh Millennium Development Goal, and outlines the public policies required to ensure environmental sustainability.

High Population Growth–related Poverty

A brief overview of the global demographic situation highlights the core of the problem of the link between poverty and high population growth rates. The world's population grew from 4.4 billion in 1980 to 5.9 billion in 1998, and the United Nations Population Fund estimates that it may reach 8.5 billion by 2025 (UNPF, 1993).

The increase of some 90 million people per year during the 1990s occurred almost entirely within the developing world. In 1998, the low-income countries had 3.5 billion people, the middle-income ones 1.5 billion, and the high-income countries 885.5 million (World Bank, 1999/2000). Population is thus greatly skewed in its distribution toward the poorer parts of the world, and current population growth rates are worsening the situation. In 1998, the average population growth rate was 2.0 percent for low-income countries, 1.5 percent for middle-income countries, and 0.7 percent for high-income countries: however, rates in many of the poorest countries were over 3 percent—as high as 3.9 percent in Niger, 3.8 percent in Angola, and 3.6 percent in the Congo Democratic Republic and Turkmenistan.

However, the relationship between population levels and growth rates and poverty is not a simple one. Poverty certainly contributes to high fertility rates to ensure that a few children will survive to care for their parents in their old age. As economic standards, social services, and levels of security improve, fertility rates almost invariably decline. As the World Bank (2000/2001, p. 49) expresses it, "There is evidence that better education is associated with higher contraceptive use and lower fertility." Whether high population growth rates result in higher levels of poverty depends in part on issues of resource distribution and migration potential, but it is clearly the case that they have a high possibility of doing so: hence the long history of efforts to achieve birth control, although with very uneven outcomes. Experience suggests that it is better to focus on improving social and economic indicators and to leave fertility rates to be handled by the people themselves.

But what, however, is the relationship between demographic changes and economic developments, with a consequent impact on poverty? The World Bank (2000/2001, p. 49) writes,

Malthus's grim prediction on the effects of population growth on economic development failed to materialize—since the turn of the 18th century the world's population has increased more than fivefold, and thanks to improvements in technology of all kinds, the per capita incomes have increased by even greater multiples. The links between demographic change and development are more subtle than this.

For example, the report notes a different impact of declines in fertility on workforce participation rates and economic growth in East Asia and Latin America, while in the developed world the economic consequences of an aging population and high dependency rations are frequently debated.

On the existing evidence, one is led to the conclusion that the high population growth rates in many of the poorest areas of the world are certain to exacerbate existing poverty and result in larger numbers of people living in poverty. External intervention seems to be essential to push up education and health levels, and so bring down population growth rates before most of these countries can embark on significant development and hence significant poverty reduction. However, care will have to be taken to ensure that the forms of development supported are sustainable in each given context.

Definitions and Forms of Poverty

From the above discussion on types of poverty it will already be clear to the reader that poverty is a complex concept to define, and its definition is almost inevitably determined by the perceived major form that poverty takes. In other words, if poverty is perceived mainly in terms of income levels, the human condition generally, basic needs, or capabilities, the phenomenon will be defined accordingly. We shall therefore consider the major forms of poverty identified and the definitions associated with these forms.

Income Poverty

The most commonly perceived form of poverty is income poverty. This is partly because income levels are comparatively easy to identify and measure, partly because it is consistent with the dominant role of economics in the field of development, and partly because it permits a degree of comparability of poverty levels across regional, national, and other boundaries.

The UNDP (1997, p. 16) used the following definition of income poverty: "A person is poor if, and only if, her income level is below the defined poverty line. . . . Often the cut-off poverty line is defined in terms of having enough income for a specified amount of food."

The concept of a basket of food required for survival and the cost of that basket in a specific context, measured against prevailing income levels, is, as the UNDP says, a common strategy. While people clearly require more than food, the focus on food is usually seen as indicating an overall situation regarding the acknowledged many dimensions of poverty.

The World Bank (2000/2001, p. 1) begins its review of global poverty by acknowledging the multidimensional nature of poverty:

Poor people live without fundamental freedoms of action and choice that the better-off take for granted. They often lack adequate food and shelter, education and health, deprivations that keep them from leading the kind of life that everyone values. They also face extreme vulnerability to ill health, economic dislocation, and natural disasters. And they are often exposed to ill treatment by institutions of the state and society and are powerless to influence key decisions affecting their lives. These are all dimensions of poverty.

However, the report goes on to point out that "using monetary income or consumption to identify and measure poverty has a long tradition" (p. 16), and this report proceeds to use

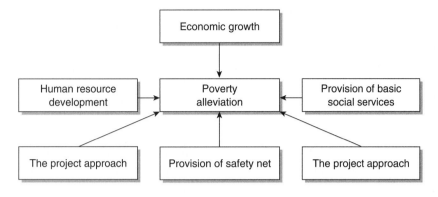

Figure 7.2   Approaches to poverty alleviation as presented by the World Bank

income poverty data extensively, while acknowledging poverty's other dimensions. This multidimensional view of poverty is reflected in the bank's approach to poverty alleviation in 1990 (see Figure 7.2). While the World Bank's presentation of addressing global poverty includes the project approach among others—that is, an approach that is limited in its objectives, timescale, and budget (e.g., a series of water wells, or a basic health clinic or primary school, or the provision of fishing boats), the overall approach advocated is comprehensive. In practice, however, much work in this field in developing countries is, unfortunately, limited to projects (see World Bank, 2000/2001, pp. 130–133).

It is common for many surveys of poverty to use an established poverty line to determine the numbers and characteristics of people in poverty, and a poverty gap (distance of people's income from the poverty line) to determine the severity of poverty. The arbitrary nature of a poverty line and the fact that establishing the line is often a political act are widely acknowledged.

Human Poverty (or Quality of Life Poverty)

It was the UNDP that introduced the concept of human poverty, relating this closely to its concept of human development. As it writes in its 1997 report,

If human development is about enlarging choices, poverty means that opportunities and choices most basic to human development are denied—to lead a long, healthy, creative life and to enjoy a decent standard of living, freedom, dignity, self-respect, and the respect of others. (p. 15)

Consistent with its recognition of human development as multidimensional, the UNDP defines human poverty by drawing on three perspectives of poverty—income, basic needs, and capabilities—to create a Human Poverty Index (HPI). This HPI concentrates on the three essential elements of human life already reflected in its HDI, namely, longevity, knowledge, and a decent living standard. These elements are measured by focusing on specific variables:

percent of people expected to die before age 40;

percent of adults who are illiterate;

percent of people with access to health services and safe water; and

percent of malnourished children under five. (p. 18)

It acknowledges "the inescapable element of judgment" in selecting elements and variables (p. 16) but concludes that its choice has emerged from a participatory democracy process and reflects "the concerns and worries of vulnerable people." The UNDP's 1997 *Human Development Report* ranks countries according to this HPI and compares countries' performance on this index with their performance in terms of an income-based measure of poverty.

While we might be tempted to use even broader sets of quality of life indicators that have been developed (e.g., UN/ESCAP, 1990), the difficulty arises in determining how to measure many quality of life indicators, and then also how to collect the necessary data. The UNDP acknowledges this desire to view poverty broadly but finds itself constrained by practical considerations.

Basic Needs Poverty

Basic needs poverty moves back from quality of life considerations to ask which basic needs are essential to survival, and then to determine whether people have access to what is required by them to meet those basic needs. The UNDP (1997, p. 16) defines the basic needs perspective on poverty as follows: "Poverty is deprivation of material requirements for minimally accepted fulfillment of human needs, including food."

In extreme poverty situations it is essential that the focus be initially on meeting basic needs, but the intention must be that the poverty reduction or alleviation strategies will move beyond a narrow definition of basic needs as quickly as possible. The basic needs approach is much too focused on survival needs and too little on rights.

Capability Poverty

A perception of poverty in terms of capabilities has not been common, but it makes considerable sense when poverty intervention strategies are seen essentially as enabling people to progress on a self-reliant basis. The UNDP (1997, p. 16) describes this perspective on poverty as follows:

Poverty represents the absence of some basic capabilities to function—a person lacking the opportunity to achieve some minimally acceptable levels of these functionings. . . . The capability approach reconciles the notions of absolute and relative poverty, since relative deprivation in incomes and commodities can lead to an absolute deprivation in minimum capacities.

In an earlier work, Allen and Thomas (1992, p. 28) spelled out the basic human capabilities as including "to take part in society, to obtain health care, and to achieve an adequate standard of living." Other writers might focus on basic vocational training as providing people with the ability to be competitive in the job market or to take initiatives in the income-generation field. As the UNDP says, the relative areas of functioning will vary, as will also, therefore, the required capabilities. (For a comprehensive discussion of "poverty as capability deprivation," see Sen, 2001, chap. 4.)

Conclusion

Poverty is the most widespread of global problems, and the most complex because of its interaction with such a wide range of other occurrences. Yet, given the world's wealth and knowledge base, and if a greater measure of stability could be achieved, poverty could be eradicated. That it has not been, and that it does not look like it will be in the near future, is due largely to two reasons. First, many situations lack stability (political, economic, or social), so that reducing poverty in some contexts is invariably balanced by its increase elsewhere. The second reason is that much of the world's wealth is controlled by a relative handful of persons, corporations, and states, and the utilization of that wealth in poverty eradication rests almost entirely on the will to do so of those who control this wealth.

It is encouraging that poverty reduction has proved successful in a number of countries; that the international community is committed to halving extreme poverty by 2015; and that the general public can be motivated to contribute generously to a situation such as the tsunami tragedy of December 26, 2004, that hit many areas bordering the Indian Ocean. However, further significant poverty reduction will take more than general international statements of commitment and public benevolence. Until we find ways to achieve sustainable forms of development, near universal good governance, an end to conflict between communities of people, and the effective redistribution of available resources, poverty will continue to be a major global phenomenon affecting hundreds of millions of people.

As social workers, we should be campaigning for an end to poverty in every way possible, and this requires a comprehensive understanding of the poverty phenomenon, in terms of its nature, causes, and possible solutions. This is why the above introduction to and further study of poverty is so important.

Summary

- The integrated-perspectives approach provides a framework for understanding the complex phenomenon of poverty and pursuing poverty alleviation strategies at all levels.
- Although substantial progress has been made in reducing poverty, the current level of global poverty is extremely high. Geographic, cultural, economic, political, and socioeconomic policy factors appear to play crucial roles in causing poverty, and need to be considered in its alleviation.
- The globalization process needs to be steered more toward poverty reduction globally as internationally agreed.
- Different facets of poverty can be understood through an analysis of the development process.
- Poverty is closely associated with war, conflict and forced displacement, natural disasters, ecological degradation, and high population growth rates.
- Definitions of poverty are often contested. Multiple measures are required to understand this complex phenomenon.

Questions and Topics for Discussion

- Why are current globalization trends seen as problematic in their impact on global poverty rates, and what changes are needed to improve the situation?
- Is the development process inevitably going to be biased in its impact on selected peoples and areas, and if so, what are the implications of this?
- Reflect on the integrated-perspectives approach presented in Chapter 2 and the phenomenon of poverty, and relate the two in terms of the causes of poverty and the desired directions of poverty alleviation strategies.
- Discuss the five broad factors connected to poverty.
- What do you understand by consequential poverty? How can we approach the reduction or alleviation of such poverty?
- How are the various definitions or identified types of poverty likely to influence ensuing policies and programs, and, in the light of this, what definitions of poverty do you prefer?

Possible Areas for Research Projects

- Study a selected country or region in terms of the apparent impact of globalization processes on poverty rates.

- Study the poverty of a specific population in terms of the factors that seem to be responsible for that population's plight, and consider the implications of your analysis for addressing that poverty.

- Using a comparative approach, study the impact of economic growth rates, or political processes, on poverty levels in selected countries.

- In a national or regional context, analyze the phenomenon of poverty by employing the integrated-perspectives approach.

- Review successful and unsuccessful poverty alleviation policies and programs known to you.

Further Reading

Chambers, R. (1993). *Rural development: Putting the last first.* Harlow, Essex, England: Longman. (Original work published 1983)

For overviews and discussions of international poverty, readers are referred to the following works:
UNDP. (1997). *Human development report: Poverty.* New York: Oxford University Press.
UNDP. (2003). *Human development report: Millennium development goals: A compact among nations to end human poverty.* New York: Oxford University Press.
World Bank. (2000/2001). *World development report: Poverty.* New York: Oxford University Press.

8

The Field of Poverty: Programs and Strategies

The focus of this chapter is poverty alleviation at the local level in developing countries, identifying programs and strategies that have been found to be relatively effective. However, it should be appreciated that policies and programs at the macro or national level designed to eradicate or reduce poverty will always have implications for what should, and perhaps can, occur at the local level. In some countries, effective national policies and programs have virtually rendered unnecessary a focus on poverty alleviation at the local level. However, it is also not surprising that some countries that have produced excellent poverty alleviation programs at the local level have continued to possess high levels of poverty nationally, essentially because of a lack of complementary action at the macro level. In the majority of countries, and probably in all developing countries, action at both levels is required; and therefore we commence this chapter with a brief consideration of macro poverty reduction programs adopted in recent years because that level of action is essential to poverty reduction, and it is the extent of its success that will determine the degree of action required at the local poverty alleviation level.

It should also be appreciated that an active and comprehensive approach to development, again at the national as well as the local level, should obviate the need to target poverty specifically, because the overall development process will take into account the extent and nature of prevailing poverty. Indeed, an effective overall development program will always be preferable to a poverty alleviation program, because the latter targets only those in poverty. The common reality, however, is that the development process tends to bypass the poorer sections of a society, making a targeted poverty alleviation program essential. Therefore, the focus on local-level development set out in Chapter 6 is critical in large part because of deficiencies in the overall development process. In terms of the focus of this chapter, it will be appreciated that the programs and strategies set out in Chapter 6 as the key to local-level development are equally applicable to local-level poverty alleviation. Indeed, the two aims cannot be separated.

Learning Objectives

- Within a context of macro poverty eradication and reduction policies and programs, to understand the continuing need for, and potential of, poverty alleviation programs and strategies at the local level.

- To develop a beginning understanding of the ways in which poverty alleviation can be pursued at the local level.

- To understand and apply relevant principles and to follow appropriate poverty alleviation programs.

- To develop interest in and commitment to social work's contribution to poverty alleviation work locally and globally.

However, there are additional programs and strategies to those discussed in Chapter 6 that are especially designed for poverty alleviation, and it is on these that we focus in this chapter, while asking readers to bear in mind the range of programs and strategies presented in Chapter 6 as very relevant to this context.

Finally, we need to remind readers that the basic programs and strategies discussed in Chapter 4 are also very relevant to this chapter, both at the general level and as programs and strategies capable of being adapted to poverty alleviation goals. Readers should therefore keep the contents of that chapter in mind as they read this chapter.

Poverty Alleviation in Context

In order to place the main international social work role in poverty alleviation in context, let us briefly review the key components of antipoverty campaigns in recent decades. These campaigns were intended to eradicate poverty if possible, and the Copenhagen World Summit on Social Development in 1995 stated, "We commit ourselves to the goal of eradicating poverty in the world, through decisive national actions and international cooperation, as an ethical, social, political and economic imperative of humankind."

Alternatively, and more realistically, campaigns were aimed at "reducing by half the proportion of people living in extreme poverty by 2015" (see World Bank, 2000/2001, p. 6; UNDP, 2003).

The most widely adopted strategy for achieving poverty reduction was macroeconomic development. As an Asian Development Bank (1999, p. 20) report on poverty stated, "The critical role of economic growth in providing the employment opportunities and government revenues necessary to tackle poverty was recognized by all countries."

In addition to economic growth per se, economic policies relating to taxation, interest rates, and inflation control are clearly also significant for poverty reduction. However, another important aspect of macroeconomic development in this context is its global focus, including the utilization of export industries and negotiation of trade agreements.

While clearly macroeconomic strategy has achieved considerable success in overall poverty terms in many places, it has done little to benefit poor countries, poor regions within countries, and many categories of poor people (UNDP, 2002, p. 2).

Macro rural development programs have also received a high priority and often been very effective in reducing rural poverty, especially land reform programs (e.g., Taiwan and South

Korea), technical assistance to farmers, price controls on rural products, and rural industrialization (e.g., People's Republic of China). Frequently, however, it has benefited a proportion of rural people while forcing others into either greater poverty or migration.

Microeconomic development has received a high priority in both rural and urban areas. The two most common strategies have been microcredit schemes and microenterprises aimed at income generation, and frequently these two strategies have gone hand in hand. Many of these schemes target the poor, although it is acknowledged that frequently they fail to reach the poorest of the poor (see UNDP, 2002, p. 2).

Social service strategies have constituted another common approach to poverty reduction, directed sometimes at basic needs poverty but more commonly at capacity building. Some countries have managed to improve greatly overall education and health levels, while elsewhere such services have failed to reach poorer regions, communities, and people. Social services have been widely perceived as a necessary element of poverty reduction programs but not a panacea.

Our final category of strategies are community-based ones, a category that has received official prominence only much more recently than the other categories discussed above. The community-based approach is seen ideally as appropriate to situations where the government does not opt out but takes specific action to facilitate communities' engagement in their own poverty reduction or alleviation.

The overall impact of the above poverty reduction strategies is difficult to assess, given the variety in the situations to which they have been applied and in the ways in which they have been implemented. However, it does seem possible to draw certain conclusions from the experience to date, albeit in general terms:

1. The extent, and perhaps nature of, the application of these strategies in developing countries has often failed to achieve significant reduction in overall poverty levels, although with some significant East Asian exceptions, and with some dramatic local successes, such as those in much of urban India.

2. It has become increasingly clear that the application of any of the above types of strategies alone will not reduce poverty, because of the multidimensional nature of the phenomenon. Comprehensive and well-coordinated poverty reduction programs are essential.

3. Poverty reduction strategies generally fail to reach the major pockets of poverty, resulting rather in a creaming effect on the population in poverty; hence the emphasis is increasingly on pro-poor or poverty-targeted strategies.

4. Finally, a major reason for failure to significantly reduce poverty is frequently attributed to the political aspect of poverty reduction, identified as a lack of political commitment to the task. This is presumably because such strategies are expensive and not popular with the influential sections of the electorate, or because the political party in power represents only selected vested interests.

As we consider the roles of international social work in poverty alleviation (and we shall use this term rather than poverty reduction because it more closely reflects what is feasible in this context), it is essential to keep the above conclusions in mind. Their implications include

• that social work, while assisting in any or all of the above strategies, may need to engage in an approach to poverty alleviation at the local level that essentially complements the strategies referred to above;

• that international social work should develop a commitment to the poorest sections of the global population living in poverty, these being the people most likely to be bypassed by other and more macro poverty reduction strategies;

• that frequently international social work will have to operate in this area in spite of political apathy toward what is being done, or even opposition to it (e.g., to empowering the poor); and

• that in many circumstances, international social work should expect to achieve no more than an alleviation of the degree of existing poverty, but should see even that as a highly commendable, worthwhile and necessary short-term goal.

We are not implying that all international social workers working in the poverty field should be involved only in action at the levels here implied. Social work involvement is needed at all of the levels indicated in the various action plans for poverty reduction (e.g., UNDP, 1997, pp. 110ff.; World Bank, 2000/2001, pp. 37ff.). However, it is unlikely that the overall poverty situation will change dramatically or quickly, unless social workers or others can contribute to filling the gaps existing in poverty reduction action to date.

A Model of Poverty Alleviation for International Social Work

In the previous chapter, we considered our integrated-perspectives approach to poverty reduction or alleviation, and that analysis is critical in directing international social work practice in its contribution to global poverty reduction. The importance of each of our four interacting perspectives is abundantly clear. We must approach poverty as a global phenomenon on which globalization trends have a significant impact; we must approach poverty reduction or alleviation not just as essential for addressing people's needs, but as essential for addressing people's rights; appreciating the link between poverty and ecological issues, we must ensure that

poverty reduction or alleviation is ecologically responsible and sustainable; and we need to approach poverty reduction or alleviation within a social development framework as the ideal approach for simultaneously addressing the root causes of poverty, factors influencing poverty, and the consequences of poverty.

In the previous chapter, we also discussed various types and forms of poverty as relatively discrete entities, implying that intervention required identifying the precise form that poverty was taking in a specific context and directing intervention accordingly. While that analysis and its utilization in intervention is important to social work practice, here we want to take a different tack and present a model of poverty alleviation for international social work practice and its significance for intervention (see Figure 8.1).

The model presents poverty as a dynamic process. The beginning point of the poverty process or cycle is some form of social marginalization or exclusion. This is often the root cause of poverty, for example in the form of differentiating between groupings in society based on gender, ethnic, racial, or religious differentiation. A significant outcome of social marginalization or exclusion is active discrimination against groupings negatively perceived. This discrimination spills over from the social into the economic sphere, among others, and an almost inevitable outcome of this occurring is economic marginalization or exclusion, the second point in the model. Economic marginalization or exclusion in turn will reinforce social marginalization or exclusion. Although some excluded groups are able to establish a parallel economy that favors fellow members of the particular social grouping, and so protects against poverty to at least some degree, more frequently it results in poverty as members of the grouping are excluded from many areas of employment or income generation, and often also from vocational education and training that provides access to the various occupations.

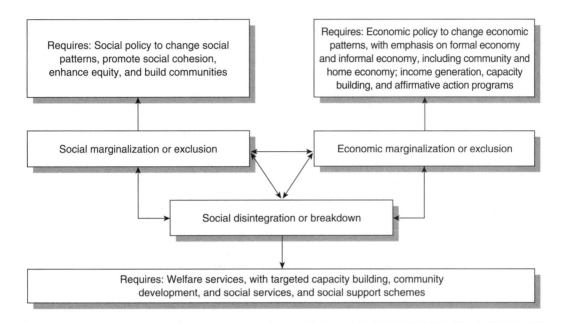

Figure 8.1   A poverty alleviation model

The third point in our basic model is social disintegration or breakdown. The operative process here is that some of those who are socially and economically isolated will be adversely affected by both the fact of exclusion and the ongoing discrimination they experience as a consequence of this, not only in terms of poverty but of self-esteem, self-confidence, ability to form and maintain relationships, and perhaps emotional stability. The proportion of people so affected will depend upon a range of factors, but among these is the extent of solidarity and mutual support systems operating within the group as a whole—for example, ethnic and other groups with stronger networks and internal structures will protect individual members against social disintegration and breakdown more than will those with weaker ones. In other words, the social disintegration or breakdown can affect virtually entire groupings (e.g., some indigenous populations) or entire communities, in which case a high proportion of families and individuals will suffer, or it may affect only a small proportion of comparatively isolated

families and individuals. In sum, social and economic marginalization or exclusion, independently or together, contribute to social disintegration or breakdown. Then the more the social disintegration or breakdown individuals, families, and communities experience, the more likely it is that they will be further socially or economically marginalized or excluded.

The relevance of this dynamic triangular model is that intervention will be largely determined by the extent to which the process has proceeded around the triangle, with intervention adopting both a remedial and a preventative approach. If the situation shows clear signs of social marginalization or exclusion that has not to date exerted a major economic or social disintegration impact (as perhaps with some newly arrived immigrant populations), then intervention will be aimed at addressing this situation. If, however, there are many indications of social disintegration, then that condition must be addressed directly before the social and economic marginalization can be rectified for these people.

The second aspect of the model sets out the various types of intervention that should be considered at each of the three points in the process. The social work profession has, or should have, at its fingertips, policies and programs designed to overcome, or at least significantly improve, the causes and impact of social marginalization or exclusion, economic marginalization or exclusion, and social disintegration or breakdown. Such policies and programs will invariably need to be adapted to each specific socioeconomic-cultural-political context, and professional skill in this area lies in an ability to analyze a situation and design an intervention strategy that draws upon and adapts proven approaches. In all three areas of intervention, programs implemented should ideally have a developmental, preventative, and remedial impact on both the broader situation and the persons affected by that situation.

Local-level Poverty Alleviation and the Role of Social Work

The goal of the model presented here is poverty alleviation. To embark on poverty eradication at the local level is clearly unrealistic, for the local level will always be affected by actions taken at other levels over which it has no control. To some extent this is also true of poverty reduction. Certainly the objective of community-based poverty programs would be to reduce the extent of poverty as far as possible, and it would be highly unlikely to have situations where no one could be moved right out of poverty. The more likely outcome of activities focused exclusively at the local level, however, would be that the severity of the poverty being experienced by a significant number of people would be reduced (i.e., poverty alleviation). Technically many people may remain below an established poverty line, or they may hover around the poverty line being sometimes above and sometimes below, but what we would expect to achieve would be that the overall depth and severity of their poverty would

be reduced and its impact on lives alleviated, not least because people would be given a sense of empowerment and the capabilities to take more control of their own situations and draw on local resources and potential.

We have also deliberately selected this level of operation for our main emphasis because we anticipate that, in the poorest of the developing countries, the majority of social work graduates in an ideal situation (currently seldom the case) will be field operatives, working with local communities and frequently electing to work with the poorest communities in the country. This is not to say that these workers should not be aware of what needs to be and can be achieved at other levels, or that they cannot contribute at those other levels at least indirectly. We envision that the social work profession will possess and act on the overall vision of what poverty reduction requires, ensuring that the experience and suggestions of field operatives are regularly fed into the overall process. Individual workers, however, are likely to spend most of their time on the front line of change within local communities, but ideally not isolated and unsupported in their important roles. Questions of the education levels of these workers are discussed elsewhere (Chapters 1 and 14), and may vary to suit different conditions, but at the very least these workers require a comprehensive understanding of the poverty phenomenon, and of the skills and knowledge necessary to work with individuals, families, and local communities within a community-based approach to poverty alleviation.

The importance of the community-based approach will be obvious. In no developing country are the resources likely to be available for a lot of individually oriented practice, even if such were appropriate, which is often not the case for social and cultural reasons. While individuals make up communities, and so are always in a sense the focus, as far as possible the programs and strategies adopted will need to be community-based, not only to cover as much need as possible but equally importantly because communities possess

- Participation—the strategy is a fully participatory one at every step;

- Self-reliance—the strategy is designed to maximize the utilization of resources available locally, human and material, and to minimize external inputs (see Chapter 4);

- Sustainability—the strategy is designed to be sustainable in its use of resources, thus protecting the well-being of future generations; and

- Empowerment—the strategy is designed to empower all those who participate in it (see Chapter 4).

potential over and above that of the individuals involved. Furthermore, the responses to identified needs will in most cases not be agency-based, as they usually are in most developed countries, but community-based and resulting in time in the formation of people's organizations (POs) or local organizations (LOs). Moreover, increasingly this alternative option is seen as not only driven by necessity, but as possessing potential that is different from, and sometimes preferable to, that likely to be possessed by agencies, whether governmental or nongovernmental.

What then is a community-based approach to poverty alleviation, and how might social workers go about implementing such? There is indeed a wealth of experience on which to draw in answering these questions, and the following outline draws upon that accumulated experience.

The Community-based Nature of the Model

There are two aspects to the poverty alleviation strategy being presented here: namely, the principles on which it is based and the processes that it utilizes. The key programs that it incorporates will be discussed in the next main section.

Principles

The principles on which this poverty alleviation strategy is based are extremely important, and not only to this strategy but to all social

development. Because these principles are discussed elsewhere in this publication, we need only list them here. The four key principles are listed in the box.

Processes

By *processes* we mean the basic processes utilized by the workers in implementing the strategy. From experience in the field, it is clear that these processes are usually as important to success as the programs that are being initiated. They are very much part of the embodiment of the principles on which the strategy is based, yet they are also basic to the programs being introduced. What is interesting and significant is the degree to which these processes are found in the field, not essentially because workers are taught to use them but because it becomes apparent to workers at the community level that they are integral to working with people severely affected by poverty. Let us consider the key processes involved. (See UN/ESCAP, 1996b, for further discussion of the processes.)

Small-cell Formation. The basis for the adoption of this process is that the poor very commonly lack self-esteem and self-confidence, are largely accepting of their fate because they can do nothing else, and tend to maintain a low profile because they have too often been victimized and oppressed. This is particularly true of poverty-stricken women, especially in female-headed households, and of the members of lower-caste and lower-class people. It is, therefore, unrealistic to assume that such people can begin immediately to engage in activities to address their poverty. Many will need a period of months before they begin to believe that change is possible and have the confidence and courage to embark on action.

The small-cell formation process is one in which people in poverty, living in close proximity to each other and with similar characteristics (all female, all mothers, etc.), are encouraged to meet together in small groups of commonly no more than five persons, along with the worker who has already contacted them individually and sought to establish some basic trust. The participants in a cell are encouraged to talk about their situation, their concerns and difficulties, their children and the dreams they had or have for them, and generally the experiences of their everyday life. It is seemingly helpful to be able to verbalize their situations in front of others who either share or understand their plight. It is perhaps the beginning of empowerment and a sense of self-awareness—that is, making conscious an awareness of their plight or what Freire and others have called conscientization.

The group will be encouraged to meet regularly along the above lines until members begin to suggest specific activities, at which point the group moves into the second stage.

An Action Focus. Excessive discussion of one's plight without any hope or plan for change can be discouraging or depressing. The worker will, therefore, be slowly inserting into discussion the question of what actions these persons believe would be helpful, even if the suggested actions are "if only" ones—that is, if only we could change this, find this, do this, and so on. As ideas emerge, the worker will encourage discussion of these and be ready to throw in feasible suggestions for implementing what is being suggested. The rationale is to encourage the group to engage in small actions that are, perhaps with

outside help, within their abilities and such as will help promote hope and confidence. Ideas may be around accommodation facilities, some aspect of child care, literacy classes for themselves or some other area of basic training, or a small savings scheme. At this stage, while the nature of the action may be important, even more important is engaging in action per se.

The Establishment of People's Organizations. While the small-cell process is an extremely important starting process, the numbers of people involved are obviously small and, as such, the groups are not greatly empowering. At the appropriate time the worker will raise with the group the possibility of meeting with other such groups, perhaps to combine forces in some proposed enterprise. Gradually, as cell groups get together, the basis emerges for a PO made up of people of similar backgrounds, facing similar dilemmas, and possessing some key ideas as to the directions for change. These POs present an organizational base from which to pursue their goals. They offer a much stronger basis for action than the small cells, exemplifying the fact that one moves forward more effectively from a strong base. In developing countries, LOs or POs are the basic building blocks of civil society, whatever the specific focus of a PO might be, and they will vary greatly. (For a discussion of this approach being used in the U.S. context, see Piven and Cloward, 1979.)

Adult Learning. A key process throughout the entire poverty alleviation strategy is that of adult learning. The adage that knowledge is power contains considerable truth at all levels in society. Poor people require knowledge, including the knowledge or awareness that they are themselves worthwhile people with rights and potential for development. Adult learning will, therefore, include learning about oneself and one's situation, learning knowledge and skills to which one has never had access before, and social learning or learning from doing things together with others and looking at the outcomes of doing so.

This adult learning may be initially in the small-group context with the worker as the important stimulus to knowledge building, but gradually it will come to include the bringing in of outsiders who have knowledge to impart. Not only is this imparting of knowledge important, but people need to discover the external sources of knowledge that exist and are accessible to them, and develop confidence in approaching them. Finally, a community may elect to establish an adult learning center where learning activities occur on a regular basis, but it is important that the community establish such a center when ready for it, rather than it being an imposition from outside. It is equally important that the community establish a committee to run the center and consult regularly with the entire community.

A Team Approach. Effective poverty alleviation requires effective workers; however, this type of work is often extremely difficult. Frequently the poor eke out an existence in remote regions, or as marginalized people rejected by the wider community, or as an exploited population with others having a vested interest in maintaining their poverty and therefore subservience. Whatever the precise circumstances, poverty alleviation work is difficult and sometimes also risky. The team approach recognizes this fact and is a structure whereby workers are linked to and supported by the other members of the team, and withdrawn from their demanding frontline work on a regular basis for debriefing, socializing, evaluation, planning, knowledge-building, and generally to rediscover or renew their sense of purpose and commitment.

Such teams are not hierarchical, are led by a team leader who is either elected or fully supported by members, are highly supportive of the individual, provide a context in which workers can express their reactions to their work and can work through their emotions, and ensure that

workers are approaching their tasks in the most effective ways. Ideally the team has a headquarters to which all members can travel, from which backup can be secured as necessary, and within which members can from time to time relax and be renewed in strength and purpose.

Poverty Alleviation Programs and Strategies Used in International Social Work

While this poverty alleviation set of strategies is built on principles and utilizes certain processes, its core is the programs that it incorporates or on which it is ultimately based. The following programs and strategies have been selected for several reasons. They are widely used in a wide variety of contexts; when implemented well they have been shown to be highly effective in alleviating various aspects of poverty; they are eminently feasible in most if not all contexts, although local circumstances may well require modifications to the essential form; and together they cover the most fundamental aspects of poverty. It should again be noted that the extent of the poverty alleviation achieved will largely depend on what is happening at national, regional, and global levels. This set of strategies is not a panacea for poverty reduction; however, when implemented successfully at the local level along the lines suggested it will always alleviate poverty to some degree and for some people. But how deeply it will cut into poverty, and how broad will be its coverage, will ultimately depend on a range of factors that are not specifically addressed by this strategy. This is not, of course, to imply that such strategies do not have positive reverberations at other levels, especially when implemented within a significant number of a country's poverty-stricken communities.

The focus on local-level poverty alleviation is not meant to imply either that this level is the key to poverty work, for indeed it is poverty reduction policies and programs at the national level that are ultimately the key to significant poverty reduction. Nor do we imply that social workers have a more important role at the local than at the national level. It is rather the circumstances in the poorer developing countries that render both the local level and a poverty alleviation focus major challenges to which social workers can and should respond, and in many cases are responding. We remind readers again that the local-level development approach discussed in Chapter 6 is also highly relevant to poverty alleviation, as the following discussion and case examples will show, and readers should read this chapter in conjunction with both Chapter 6 and Chapter 4, which together represent the range of major programs and strategies that we have identified as relevant to local-level poverty alleviation work.

The following discussion is divided into three sections, remembering that development-based programs are addressed in Chapter 6: poverty alleviation programs where community-based social services are the key focal point; programs where a social welfare response is the key strategy; and programs that possess a comprehensive approach.

The Development of Community-based Social Services

Ideally social services should be provided by central or regional government agencies, with significant amounts of taxation and other revenues devoted in particular to health and education services. However, many developing countries lack the resources to provide even basic social services at an adequate level across the country. Often they lack the required funding for this purpose, although many countries could give it a higher priority for the funds that are available than they do; but many also find it difficult to provide qualified staff to the more isolated areas and the more impoverished communities, either because the numbers of qualified staff are

inadequate or because staff refuse to serve in such settings.

It is important to remind ourselves that a lack of access to basic social services is a major cause of poverty. It results directly in capability and basic needs poverty, and indirectly impacts significantly on income poverty. Moreover, those without access to basic services will lack the basic well-being required to address their poverty, assuming that the opportunities to do so are there. Their poor health levels and inadequate literacy skills will, in particular, be fundamental limitations in any efforts to take the initiative. Hence it is of fundamental importance that these basic needs are addressed and, if they are not being addressed at the national level, then it is incumbent on local workers to find feasible community-based alternatives at the local level.

A common strategy is to encourage local people to band together and build a health clinic, primary school, child care center where mothers can gather for a variety of inputs, or some other type of community center. Depending on the circumstances, workers may need to help the local people to acquire the necessary building materials or food-for-work support if the poor are to devote time to these purposes under supervision. Not only are these centers potentially important in themselves, the process of erecting them can serve to pull a population together, build confidence, and even develop some basic skills.

Once the base is there, the urgent requirement is for staff. It may be that central governments will provide staff once a community has built the facility; or it may be that government will provide all or part of the salary, provided that the community can secure a worker. In the latter case, the only option may be for the community to select a local person for basic training in the required skills, with the poverty alleviation worker organizing the training, resulting in a paraprofessional approach that is certainly preferable to no service. Where the government provides only part of the worker's salary, the community may have to make up the balance in kind, for example by keeping the staff member provided with food. Alternatively, persons recruited in this way may have to accept that they will have to continue to make some provision for their own and their family's well-being, through farming and so on. Both of these two situations are encountered.

A key element in this approach is that the involvement of the community will itself have positive results. Local people will learn that they do not have to accept a lack of services, that they have the potential to make some contribution themselves, and that they are able to put pressure on governments and others to respond to their needs. Moreover, the whole process should make them more aware of various health and education issues, and that very awareness is conducive to further changes in personal and community behavior.

Of course the ultimate outcome of such a program may be very basic premises, a partly trained and poorly paid worker, a poorly equipped facility, and only relatively minor improvements in levels of community health, education, and so on. What is important, however, is that it is a start. A community may now be much less accepting of the previous lack of services, much more knowledgeable about the nature and importance of the various services, and much more committed to work toward the ongoing improvement of local services. In the meantime, they may also be aware of the extent to which community members can support a basic facility, as parents assisting at school or in some other way, and can extend the impact of a center by engaging in relevant change processes at the home, neighborhood, and community levels.

For the last outcome to occur, the use of adult learning models to raise levels of awareness of public health issues, of home-based learning, and of using community systems to encourage households to strive for sanitation, accommodation, child care, and other standards that they now appreciate is extremely important. So while the construction of a community center might be the practical element in the program, the accompanying process of community education in basic social, health, and education needs and standards is also vital. An aware community can do much to improve local standards, as many communities have demonstrated over the years.

The participatory, self-reliant, and empowering nature of this community-based approach to social services will be obvious (see Chapter 4).

Case Examples

Health Care and Community Building in the Philippines

Our first example comes from the Philippines and is based essentially on the importance to poverty alleviation of primary health care. The communities that were targeted in this program had some major and special health problems, along with no access to formal health services. The whole area was also regarded as one with no strong tradition of community action or collective enterprises.

The NGO that initiated the program, despite its roots in the health field and its aim to improve health standards, decided on a relatively comprehensive approach to poverty alleviation with a key focus on training. This is indeed true of most highly successful programs, the core aim of which is community-based social services. The work was carried out by a team of workers of high caliber and strong commitment. Their basic approach was to immerse themselves in a locality and operate as proactive catalysts. It was found that three months of initial immersion was usually required before a worker gained trust and a program could get off the ground. While the agency appreciated that government departments had extreme difficulty in reaching the communities in question, the work was based on a participatory model that included government agencies, nongovernment agencies, and existing local organizations, at least at the planning and reporting-back levels, but preferably also at an action level.

The key objective of the people-centered outreach was to build communities that were aware, active, and organized for ongoing action. A key element of the program was to recruit and engage community workers in the development process, revolving their roles initially around health concerns, and to enhance community capacity by training these persons and others.

The community health volunteers, as they were called, were health educators and represented the first line of curative health; they engaged in nutritional education and promoted family planning. Each trained health worker was made responsible for 15 households, maintaining contact with them, gathering relevant data on their health situation, and gradually undertaking an educational role. Workers were trained to identify health indicators and to use these effectively in their promotion work.

Within this general health program, a special program was concerned with children's health and reducing infant and child mortality. This special project covered more than 46,000 families, among whom infant mortality was 50.4 per 1,000 live births. Health volunteers were recruited and trained specifically for this project in which local officials were also fully involved.

A strategy employed by the agency's project officers was to keep the people asking *why* until the causative roots of any problem were identified by the people themselves—a process akin to conscientization. This phase would then lead into community planning and the implementation of agreed-on projects.

The program resulted in a 17.3 percent improvement in health status, an increase in use of safe water from 17.5 to 61.3 percent, while immunization rates rose from 30.1 to 57.2 percent. The impact on poverty levels was noted as significant but not measured. Community drug stores were established to ensure the availability of essential medical supplies.

While the program required significant aid monies, the approach adopted was that the program would provide a maximum of 30 percent of required resources, encouraging and assisting the communities to locate the balance, internally or externally. This was designed to strengthen community self-reliance.

There were several important strategies adopted by this outreach program:

1. The program was structured around a careful analysis of the prevailing context, including the nature and depth of the poverty, the realities of political instability, and the level of community inertia.

2. The program was well grounded in a local medical school to ensure the appropriateness and effectiveness of its health focus.

3. Agency staff were carefully selected on the basis of qualifications and motivation, and were deliberately built into a strong supportive team—essential but difficult when workers were placed in remote and highly impoverished areas.

4. The initial phase had to be a proactive one of outreach with a period of immersion to build trust and understanding.

5. Despite the focus on health, the program appreciated the importance of addressing health issues within a broader context of community building, preparation for income generation, a focus on microenterprises, literacy and education programs, and so on. It was thus an integrated approach despite its central focus being on health.

6. The program sought always to work in partnership with other organizations, and to encourage particularly government agencies to think more about how they might increase their effectiveness in these very poor communities.

7. The program was a highly participatory one at the community level, seeking to build self-confidence and self-reliance by utilizing local resources fully and ensuring that all developments flowed from local decision making.

(Example from UN/ESCAP, 1996a, p. 61.)

Social Services and Education in Bangladesh

Our second example of a community-based social services approach to poverty alleviation comes from the work of an NGO in Bangladesh. Initially a charity, this NGO changed its focus to social services for the disadvantaged sections of society, and especially disadvantaged women. Its main programs concerned the promotion of nonformal education for adolescents and adults, including literacy and other skills training. It established an institute to train people in the design and management of nonformal education. Then around this educational core, the agency engaged in providing credit to illiterate women and housing for the victims of natural disasters, which are very common in the region.

The charter of the agency states that its fundamental objective is the promotion of nonformal primary and adult functional education, including continuing education and income-generation activities. In implementing this objective, five types of programs were developed: preprimary education, early primary education for children, literacy programs for adolescents, adult literacy programs, and continuing education programs. An example of programs that emerged from these core ones was one that offered illiterate women a package program including literacy, human development, skills training, and seed capital for income-generation projects.

The preprimary education program offered a six-month course of drawing, singing, moral education, and personal hygiene. It involved more than 12,000 children in the year of evaluation.

In its early primary education program, in addition to reading, writing, and numeracy, the course covered environment, health and sanitation, food and nutrition, and disease prevention. This program covered more than 34,000 children.

The literacy program for adolescents provided basic literacy as well as need-based and work-oriented education, in an 18-month course with follow-up. More than 8,000 participated at 295 centers in the year of study.

The adult literacy program covered functional literacy over a 12-month program, and included family life, domestic budget matters, and civic consciousness. Some 46,000 people participated in the program over a four-year period.

Finally, the continuing education program was essentially a follow-up program provided through village community centers. It encouraged socializing, reading, and cultural activities, as well as the ongoing needs of neoliterates. The program catered to some 42,000 in a given year in 225 centers.

This entire program has been highly successful in achieving its major goal. It involved large numbers and was evaluated as having had very positive direct results. The indirect benefits from the opportunities the programs opened up to participants, especially in terms of poverty alleviation, are difficult to assess but are also thought to be considerable.

Agency staff included people from a range of professions and backgrounds.

(Example from UN/ESCAP, 1996b, p. 5.)

The Social Welfare Response to the Poor

Given that a welfare response is usually focused on individuals and that these poverty alleviation strategies are all community-based, their inclusion at first glance might seem a little strange. They form, however, an important group of strategies within the overall strategy because of the presence within any poverty-stricken population of individuals with specific disabilities requiring a degree of personalized assistance. To deny these people the welfare services they need is to deny them access to the overall poverty alleviation strategy, and that is unacceptable from human rights and humanitarian perspectives. However, it is also unacceptable to see them solely as people with welfare needs. The great majority of people with all forms of disability still possess some potential to participate in society and thereby find an opening for self-reliant approaches to moving out of poverty. Unfortunately, in many developing societies such potential goes unrecognized, with people with a disability being seen as different and unable to participate in normal life.

In this type of poverty alleviation strategy, the provision of welfare services to selected individuals will be in effect the first step in making it possible for them to take their place in society. While the service provided will often need to be personalized to some degree, the best approach is to identify categories of disability for which a general solution can be identified. These categories may include the physically impaired victims of landmines, the victims of some past experience through which they were traumatized, individuals with intellectual disabilities, those with specific forms of psychiatric disorders, and those suffering from chronic health conditions. Current levels of knowledge have provided the helping professions with at least some responses to such people's needs, and the implementation of these responses will enable many such people to participate in poverty alleviation programs, providing of course that appropriate levels of understanding and acceptance exist among those members of the general public with whom they will be participating.

The tasks of workers are to identify those in poverty with specific welfare needs, educate the general community regarding the true nature of those needs, and devise programs that will either prepare such people to participate alongside others in the poverty alleviation programs, or, if necessary, to participate in suitably modified programs. While a degree of individual attention may be necessary and possible, it will be more feasible to arrange group programs for addressing specific needs; and such programs should be highly participatory and inclusive, as far as possible, of a strong self-help and mutual help focus. Let us consider a few examples.

Case Examples

Community Group and Welfare Needs in China

In an urban area in the People's Republic of China, a local community group set out to identify and assist categories of people with particular welfare needs. It found a number of people with mental health and intellectual disabilities who were completely dependent on others and yet who clearly possessed some ability to participate in income generation and be more independent. The group accordingly established a sheltered workshop that afforded income-generation opportunities within the potential of these people. The role of the group was to secure funds to establish the workshop, to work on the marketing side, and to be generally supportive of what was basically a self-help enterprise.

The group also located a small number of wheelchair-bound people living in difficult conditions because no one addressed their access problems. The group located a number of ground floor accommodation arrangements suited to modification for wheelchair access. In this way they provided a small number of disabled persons with reasonable accommodation, and enhanced opportunities for participating locally.

A third initiative of the group arose from locating several elderly persons living alone and unsupported, yet requiring significant assistance. For these people the group established a hostel for the elderly, worked with the residents in developing mutually supportive arrangements, and arranged for a local hospital to provide daily nursing care.

It should be pointed out that these initiatives were carried out by a community group composed of individuals with no relevant training and no resources beyond what they could raise from the local community or government agencies. In the process of establishing these community facilities, the group was conscious of the need to educate the general community regarding the needs of the identified categories of needy individuals. The approach of the group to meeting needs was, however, essentially a welfare one.

(Example from author's field visit.)

Supportive Employment Program in Hong Kong

A second example comes from Hong Kong. Traditionally, responding to the vocational needs of Hong Kong's estimated 269,000 people with disabilities had been based on segregated services such as day activity centers and sheltered workshops. It was found that only 2.9 percent of the workshop population moved into open employment, and the Supportive Employment Program was established to change that situation. The work was pioneered by an NGO providing supportive employment for people with intellectual disabilities.

The program began with a mobile cleaning crew, working with on-the-job supervision in warehouses, schools, and so on. It then organized a group employment approach by arranging for intellectually disabled persons to work as a packaging team in the food industry. As participants became more independent, they were referred out to supported jobs with individual coaches. Once supervision could be minimized, they were discharged to open employment.

The scheme achieved for those involved some five times the income received in a sheltered workshop, enhanced the quality of life of these people, and was an empowering process.

(Example from UN/ESCAP, 1994a.)

HelpAge International

HelpAge International is a global network of not-for-profit organizations that has initiated schemes in a range of developing countries to assist older people to remain active and independent. Here are two examples. In India, through two NGOs, HelpAge India and GRAVIS (Gramin Vikas Vigyan Samiti), HelpAge International financed income-generation projects such as goat-rearing; making envelopes, candles, and *agarbatti* (incense sticks); *durrie* (rope) weaving; and agriculture and food security projects to make older persons self-dependent. In Cambodia, through associations of older people, it supported loan schemes, savings groups, and rice and fertilizer banks to enhance social and economic benefits to the elderly and their families.

(Examples from HelpAge International, 2005a, 2005b.)

Save The Children

Sri Lanka is one country where Save The Children locates children who have lost a limb, arranges for an artificial limb to be made and fitted, and provides the young person with a week's training in how to use the new limb. Through such services, those thousands of people injured by land mines and so on are provided with renewed hope and the opportunity to participate in the development of their country.

(Example from Save The Children, 1992, p. 39.)

Programs That Utilize a Comprehensive Approach

It is not being implied that a successful poverty alleviation strategy will incorporate either all of the above programs or only those programs discussed above. Poverty is a complex phenomenon, and workers will need to evaluate carefully any situation to determine the major forms and causes of poverty. The range of programs adopted will then reflect that evaluation, as well of course as the availability of resources.

However, each of the above programs is very common, largely because they are all concerned with either capacity building or income generation, both of which are integral to effective poverty alleviation and because they are not necessarily resource-intensive. Essentially poverty alleviation is about ensuring that individuals, groups, and communities have the capacity to tackle their own poverty and gain access to opportunities for securing an income essential to overcoming poverty and achieving well-being.

However, the tendency to establish what are seen from the beginning to be comprehensive poverty alleviation programs should be noted. We have provided one example of such at the end of Chapter 6, but it may be helpful to consider two others.

Case Examples

Rural Development in Bangladesh

Our first example is that of a program run by a government agency in Bangladesh engaged in rural development. The agency's aim is to assist the small and marginal farmers and the rural poor who have no assets to improve their socioeconomic conditions, mainly through the establishment of cooperatives but within an integrated rural development program. This program was developed in a country with enormous poverty that faced regular natural disasters and contained a high degree of political instability. While the core focus of the program throughout has been economic, increasingly social development has become a major aspect of the approach. The following project is only one that made up the overall program of this agency, but it is the largest one and one evaluated as highly successful.

There are five basic strategies in this project: mobilization and organization, creation of capital, training, provision of credit, and creation of marketing facilities.

The key strategy was the formation of separate organizations for men and women without assets at village level. This was done through field organizers recruited locally—all graduates, but for whom there were few employment opportunities. Field organizers visited the villages in their allotted area, established contact with the target group, and assumed a proactive role encouraging group formation. As the groups formed and nominated leaders, the organizers became facilitators. Groups were composed of either men or women, but not both, with an overall target of 50 percent women. The groups commenced as informal ones but became eventually registered bodies—essential in the legal context.

The second strategy, the creation of capital, was achieved through members' savings, often extremely small sums, which in effect purchased shares in the society. Inculcating a habit of saving was important, as was learning to handle funds responsibly. The fund created was also a critical step toward self-sufficiency, and gave members a sense of ownership of their society. As the fund accumulated, members were eligible to draw loans from it.

Training was the third strategy. The project had its own training teams employed continuously in the provision of training. In addition, training available from the staff of other government agencies expanded the range of expertise available. Most important, however, was the program of training "bio-technicians" drawn from the ranks of societies' members. These persons were trained to train others and receive a small payment from those trained, with the aim that ultimately they would sell their services. Field organizers also undertook some training. The wide range of training available was an important aspect of the project, being of course often linked to income generation.

The fourth strategy was the provision of credit, and this was closely linked to the training strategy. Making credit available was based on the understanding that income-generation activities required credit, although often only small sums, and that credit was not available to these people through the normal financial markets. The provision of credit was related also to members' savings records. Loans were for 12 months and interest-bearing, with weekly repayments expected, and the loans were "protected" by a five-member solidarity group—a support group of fellow members that acted also as a social pressure to some degree. While the amount of credit available was often less than ideal, the repayment rate ran at 93 percent.

The creation of market facilities was a crucial strategy to income-generation success, but it took different forms in different districts.

This project, at the point of evaluation, had 1,309 societies and around 33,000 members. In addition to its set aims, it was seen as highly successful in awareness-raising, confidence building, and status raising among members, especially women. The societies per se gave members a much-needed power base for pursuing their rightful share of the nation's resources and facilities. Overall, the project was a significant vehicle for social development.

In addition to the key aims of the societies, they were utilized by the agency as avenues for the provision of cell latrines to every family, the promotion of family planning, the establishment of an immunization program, and the fostering of literacy and education generally. Sometimes these were achieved with agency funding and sometimes by linking the societies to other sources of funding and assistance.

Looking at the above project in context, it should be noted that in reality Bangladesh has suffered from a plethora of poverty alleviation programs, the overall impact of which has not always been beneficial. Moreover, programs tend to focus on the easier areas of the country and on those persons potentially more amenable to change. Finally, it is apparent that the richer sections of the Bangladesh population tend to resent these poverty alleviation programs, and are sometimes able to frustrate them in significant ways. All these are among the reasons why the significant investment in poverty alleviation in Bangladesh, while alleviating the poverty of thousands of families, has overall failed to make a significant dent in poverty levels in that country.

(Example from UN/ESCAP, 1996a, p. 10.)

Poverty Alleviation in Sri Lanka

Our second example comes from Sri Lanka and concerns probably the best-known NGO in that country. Based on Buddhist teachings and the teachings of Mahatma Gandhi, the central purpose of the organization was to put forward a vision of a new society order. It set out to organize the poorer sections of both rural and urban society and contribute to building a more just society. To this end, it both draws individuals, particularly youth, into a movement for change and runs a series of special programs. At the point of study, the organization had more than 30,000 village youth actively involved in improving local conditions, and was running five main programs. These programs were in the areas of empowerment and poverty eradication; the development of economic enterprises; early childhood development; rural technical services; and rehabilitation, reconciliation, and reconstruction in areas affected by the long civil war.

The poverty alleviation program targets the poor, directly seeking to facilitate them satisfying their basic needs by their own efforts, and to empower them through capacity building and enhancing their potential. The program is designed to run over a period of six to seven years in any one place, and is in five stages, thus emphasizing that poverty alleviation is a slow process.

Stage one requires the village to request the NGO's involvement, thus indicating motivation and some awareness. In some extreme situations, however, an outreach proactive approach is used, as long as a clear request precedes any further step. The key objective of stage one is the establishment of a local group interested in local development and ready to be a vehicle for achieving it. To achieve this, the organization assumes a proactive role through the provision of a local worker, while assuring that all decisions are made by the people. The worker identifies community leaders and offers training, tending to favor the younger and better-educated community members in the process.

Stage two is essentially the people establishing a development plan. This process is never hurried and may take 12 months, during which more leadership emerges and training takes place. The climax of this stage is the establishment of a society, registered as a legal entity—essential for various purposes such as negotiating with government departments.

During stage three the NGO worker gradually withdraws as the society strengthens and engages in development. The initial focus is usually economic development, and the society has access to the agency's program that specializes in developing economic enterprises. Usually a savings scheme is developed during this stage from which eventually loans to members can be made. The objective is now an effective income-generation program, in preparation for which the society is encouraged to conduct a feasibility survey that analyzes problems and resources and identifies potential income-generation activities.

Stage four, the implementation stage, sees the establishment of an action committee consisting of members carefully trained for guiding economic enterprises. Its role is to facilitate groups' negotiation for resources. The community should now be actively involved in building a stronger and better society, based especially on income generation but not limited to that objective.

By stage five, the community is totally independent, reliant on its own resources and usually employing a rural enterprises manager. It should be engaging in its own ongoing development program with no external assistance beyond the occasional advice of the agency if this was requested.

There are a number of crucial strategies used in this poverty alleviation program. It targets the poor, but at a whole village level. In addition, it tends to target youth and women as the better change agents. The program uses facilitators who are critical in the early stages, with each facilitator covering five villages. Most of the facilitators are youth, recruited and trained by the agency. Third, the staged approach occurs over an extended period, ensuring that the community is able to develop with and through the program, in a process of empowerment. At the village level, the key is to build good leadership, and again the tendency is to target youth for this purpose. Training of these youth and others is the most critical input throughout the program, based on the belief that development demands knowledge and skills.

Because of this agency's origins, there is also a spiritual dimension to the program. At the core of poverty alleviation and ongoing development is a personal awakening—the spiritual, moral, and cultural awakening of individuals. There is also a strong emphasis on the ecological dimension, consistent with Buddhist thinking.

It should be noted too that one of the first developments to occur locally is the establishment of a preschool center, where the key emphasis is on nutrition and primary health concerns. The development of awareness and knowledge in this field is critical in itself, but the center serves also as a focal point for local women and the beginning of organizing the community. The preschool teachers are trained volunteers, ultimately paid in some way by the mothers.

This agency believes passionately in the ability of people to build communities of harmony, prosperity, and mutuality, although often assuming that some external guidance and support is provided in the process, and it is regarded as one of the most successful agencies in doing this throughout the developing world.

(Example from UN/ESCAP, 1996a, p. 91.)

Conclusion

Social work in developing countries has often ignored poverty or become involved in charity-based responses that do nothing to address the causes of poverty. The explanation for this may be that poverty seems to be in reality so widespread and entrenched a phenomenon that no approach seems feasible. At other times, it seems so complex a phenomenon, in terms of its many root causes, that resolving poverty seems to require the resolution of virtually every other major problem—inadequate health and education services, low levels of economic development, conflict, ecological degradation, political corruption, poor governance, and ethnic prejudice.

It is critical to focus, internationally and nationally, on the eradication of poverty while appreciating that the possibility of achieving this goal in any complete sense is minimal. However, the goal of eradicating absolute poverty, through poverty alleviation, might be feasible. On the other hand, every success in addressing any of the causes of poverty is likely to reduce the incidence of poverty, while socioeconomic progress in a wide range of areas will do the same. This is why there have been significant advances in poverty reduction in recent decades. Unfortunately, however, poverty reduction tends to favor certain sections in society over others, and pockets of extreme poverty are likely to remain because of remoteness of location, indigenous minority group status, different ethnic origins from those of the majority population, or a deeply entrenched class, caste, or gender-based system. It is this entrenched poverty to which social work should give priority, along with the poverty reduction and poverty alleviation effects of local-level development (see Chapter 6). This is not to ignore social work's important roles in contributing to addressing root causes of poverty, and in promoting policy, program, and structural changes that are likely to have a positive effect on poverty reduction. Essentially, however, the focus of the social work profession should be primarily on the more neglected aspects of entrenched poverty through various poverty alleviation strategies.

Accordingly, this chapter focuses on the various approaches to poverty alleviation applicable to situations of entrenched poverty. We appreciate the difficulty of such work, and in many situations its inherent unpopularity; and we appreciate also that the social work profession in most developing countries currently does not have either the types or numbers of social workers willing and able to undertake such work. We would argue, however, that these difficulties need not and should not stop the profession from undertaking such work, wherever it may be required. It is imperative for the many millions of people enmeshed in absolute poverty (at least 1.3 billion), as well as for the security and well-being of the globe as a whole, that social work complements the official efforts in poverty reduction at the macro level by engaging in poverty alleviation at the micro level. In many respects, we know how to achieve this goal, as the above case examples and many others show; all that can be lacking is the commitment to expanding the scope of the many successful initiatives to date. This is indeed a major challenge to the social work profession within developing countries and globally.

Summary

- International social work practice can contribute to poverty alleviation work at the local level.

- A comprehensive and integrated model that addresses social and economic exclusion, and inter alia social disintegration, is necessary for effective poverty alleviation.

- Participation, self-reliance, sustainability, and empowerment are the key principles in poverty work.

- Social workers' experience suggests that the formation and sustenance of self-help groups and POs, supported by practical action and adult learning, are important parts of the process.

- The focus of poverty alleviation programs and strategies may be on community-based social services, state or locally provided welfare provisions, or a comprehensive approach that integrates capacity-building and income-generation activities.

- On the whole, case examples suggest that poverty alleviation work has been found to be most effective when utilizing community-based and people-centered approaches, and involving specific principles, processes, and programs.

Questions and Topics for Discussion

- Examine the major global antipoverty strategies and how social workers can contribute to such campaigns at regional, national, and local levels.

- Critically review the poverty alleviation model presented in this chapter.

- Can you see social workers and others in developing countries engaging in the approaches to local-level poverty alleviation outlined in the chapter?

- How crucial to poverty alleviation are the principles of participation, self-reliance, sustainability, and empowerment, and to which of these, or other principles, would you give priority?

- Are community-based approaches likely to be viable in the typical community, or do they require a particular set of circumstances?

- What characteristics and training do personnel engaged in local-level poverty alleviation require to manage the challenges adequately?

- Critically review the key processes employed by workers while working with extremely poor people. Reflect on your personal strengths and possible areas for improvement for undertaking such work.

- Analyze the last two case examples and identify basic strategies and processes employed in their poverty alleviation work. What leads us to classify them as a comprehensive approach?

Possible Areas for Research Projects

- Take the characteristics of a specific poverty-affected context (from the literature if necessary) and develop a poverty alleviation program likely to be effective in that context.

- Consider the literature on significant reductions in poverty levels in specific contexts, and extrapolate the characteristics of the programs and strategies that seem to have been largely responsible for the outcome.

- Undertake a field study of a poverty alleviation program and document key principles, processes, and programs that did and did not work.

- Evaluate material available to you on microcredit schemes, and make an assessment of their significance as a poverty alleviation strategy in their own right (i.e., when not part of a comprehensive program).

Further Reading

Poulton, R., & Harris, M. (1991). *Putting people first: Voluntary organizations and third world organizations.* London: Macmillan. (Original work published 1988)

UN/ESCAP. (1996). *Making an impact: Innovative HRD approaches to poverty alleviation.* Bangkok, Thailand: UN/ESCAP.

UN/ESCAP. (1996). *Showing the way: Methodologies for successful rural poverty alleviation projects.* Bangkok, Thailand: UN/ESCAP.

9

The Field of Conflict and Postconflict Reconstruction: Background and Issues

History is replete with accounts of wars between the members of various types of social groupings, wars usually fought by the warriors or soldiers of the opposing groups, with differing proportions of civilian casualties and varying degrees of destruction of property and environment. In addition, empires such as the Greek and Roman embarked upon the invasion and conquest of territories, seeking bounty and slaves. Then, in recent centuries in Europe and increasingly elsewhere, wars between nation-states became a familiar phenomenon, with increasing numbers of civilian deaths and destruction of property and infrastructure as the weapons used expanded to include airborne and rocket-propelled bombs and so on. Such wars culminated in the two world wars of 1914–18 and 1939–45.

In past decades, wars saw social workers and other humanitarian workers working with the Red Cross, religious organizations, and other NGOs. Other social workers were involved with former soldiers undergoing rehabilitation and reintegration into families and communities within their western homelands. Also, increasingly people of all disciplines engaged in a general campaigning for peace, while some NGOs and social movements engaged in lobbying at the UN and in national parliaments to bring about a more peaceful world.

In more recent decades, there has been a marked shift away from wars between states toward civil wars fought largely within state borders, often targeting civilians and devastating infrastructure (see Brown, 1993; UNHCR, 2000, p. 9; Duffield, 2001, pp. 13–15; Stewart and Fitzgerald, 2001; Debiel and Klein, 2002; Kaldor, 2003, pp. 119–128). These civil wars have commonly spread over long periods of time with no clear declaration of war or signing of final peace treaties. With these changes in warfare, there has been a marked increase in the numbers of social workers and others involved directly and indirectly in conflict zones. Many have been and are working with humanitarian agencies in both conflict and postconflict situations. Increasing

Learning Objectives

- To assist readers to appreciate the extent and nature of modern conflict.
- To encourage readers to consider the nature of postconflict reconstruction in the modern context, and specifically the roles of the helping professions in that work.
- To introduce readers to some key concerns regarding humanitarian aid work.
- To apply the integrated-perspectives approach to an understanding of the nature of and intervention in situations of conflict and postconflict reconstruction.
- To analyze the postconflict situation and the postconflict agenda by employing appropriate models.

numbers are also engaged in reconstruction efforts, rebuilding communities and state structures in the aftermath of often devastating destruction. Many other workers are working with war victims who have been displaced by war or fled the scene, engaging with asylum seekers across a range of countries, working in displaced-persons centers, and assisting the many victims of torture and sufferers from other traumatic war-related experiences, wherever they may be.

Despite this large increase in social work involvement in conflict and postconflict situations in recent years, all indications are that the demand for such work will increase further in the coming years. As it does so, the sophistication in the application of social work knowledge and skills to the many aspects of conflict situations will continue to grow, as we have seen it doing in the last decade or so. Furthermore, the social work profession, along with many others, will become increasingly disturbed by the nature and extent of modern conflict; hence efforts to achieve greater and more lasting peace will increase. As this happens, social work will intensify its efforts to improve its capacities in areas of practice such as reconciliation between previously warring parties, the strengthening of community relations and social cohesion, the rebuilding of communities, and the building of stronger and more harmonious multicultural societies.

The Integrated-perspectives Approach to Conflict and Peace Issues

Modern conflict, although composed largely of internal wars, is global in many ways. First, the widespread prevalence of conflict renders it a global phenomenon that calls for a global response. Second, among the causes of conflict are such factors as the nature of the distribution of global wealth, trends in aid, and trade and investment, and, therefore, the distribution of social and economic opportunities and the extent to which the world is based on equity, social justice, and human rights. In other words, people's frustration with external developments and with their own situation in global terms is frequently an additional aggravating internal factor. Third, the response to modern conflict is and must be global. Activities involved in ending conflict, securing peace, providing humanitarian aid, and engaging in postconflict reconstruction require well-coordinated international efforts. Finally, responding to conflict and the aftermath of conflict at the human level must call upon the combined global resources of the helping professions, including social work. Invariably workers will move in from around the world to work alongside local workers. Moreover, these workers will require international support, not just monetary and material support but the support of a profession involved in promoting knowledge, developing skills, and improving training in this particular field, and in creating international pressure groups and lobbying in this difficult and often dangerous area of operations. Finally, Kaldor (2003) has devoted a whole book to the thesis that global civil society is an important answer to war, and we agree that the further development of global civil society is very important.

The human rights perspective is obviously a key one. Not only is the abuse or neglect of human rights a common causal factor in conflict, but it is also human rights that must guide the resolution of conflict and the postconflict reconstruction effort. This will only occur if, first, the importance of the human rights perspective is constantly promoted to ensure its place within the often all-pervasive political and economic perspectives; and, second, if all workers engaged in this field are trained in human rights and to instinctively seek out solutions to prevailing situations that are human rights based. For social workers, an additional level of operations is working to protect the human rights of those categories of people whose rights are so readily overlooked—demobilized soldiers, child soldiers, rape victims, those persons disabled by land mines, soldiers wielding machetes, the traumatized, and other such disadvantaged and politically unimportant groupings. (See Duffield, 2001, and the *World Reports* from Human Rights Watch on this question.)

The ecological perspective is also of fundamental significance in this area of practice. Modern conflict frequently has a devastating impact on the environment, sometimes deliberately so, and the rectification of this damage is frequently too focused on strategic areas inhabited by important sections of the population. International social work should focus particularly on the less strategic aspects of the ecological impact of conflict, because it is those aspects that will be more closely associated with the poorer and more disadvantaged people. International social workers should also be so familiar with

ecological issues that they can ensure that their efforts, in for example rebuilding communities, will be along ecologically sustainable lines. Indeed, reconstruction may provide opportunities to rectify past tendencies that have been found to be ecologically damaging.

Finally, as in other areas of international social work practice, it is social development that guides the choice and development of intervention strategies in the postconflict reconstruction work. As we shall see, it is today often argued that all such work should be developmental and not relief-driven (see Duffield, 2001, chap. 2). More than this, however, the social development focus on a multilevel, multidimensional comprehensive approach is extremely pertinent in the postconflict context, and the postconflict reconstruction agenda that we shall present in this chapter is firmly based on that premise.

The Extent and Nature of Modern Conflict

In recent decades, conflict has both become more common and changed in nature from the experience of wars such as the Second World War in Europe and the Korean War. Harris (1999, p. 3) writes,

> In each year of the 1980s and 1990s, there have been between thirty and forty "major armed conflicts" in progress. The Stockholm International Peace Research Institute defines a major armed conflict as one involving "prolonged combat between the military forces of two or more governments, or if one government, at least one organized armed group involving the use of weapons and incurring the battle-related deaths of at least 1000 people during the entire conflict."

Until the breakup of the former Soviet Union and Yugoslavia, virtually all major armed conflict occurred in developing countries.

The increase in the number of conflicts globally since 1989 has been mainly due to an increase in civil wars since the end of the Cold War; for it seems that the Cold War, through the actions and influence of both the United States and the former Soviet Union, prevented some potential conflict situations from erupting into violence (see UNRISD, 1995a, p. 6). A UN report in 1993 (UN/Department of Economic and Social Development, 1993, p. 146) reported that

> there has been a great escalation of violent conflict since the end of the cold war. . . . In the period 1989–1990 there were 33 armed conflicts with more than 1,000 casualties. Only one of these conflicts was fought between nation states. The rest were all civil wars—conflicts between ethnic, religious or other groups in one and the same nation.

The situation did not improve in the course of the 1990s, and in 2001 it was reported by the UN that 36 civil wars were in progress.

Causes of Conflict

Conflict almost always has complex causes. Most writers agree that, in former colonial states, an underlying cause is the colonial legacy. (See UNHCR, 2000, chap. 2, "Decolonization in Africa.") Harris and Lewis (1999, p. 8) write,

> Colonial states were typically imposed by force and deceit, with few roots among the indigenous people of colonized regions. In this process, colonial authorities commonly resorted to violence, along with authoritarian legalism, to compel compliance. Today's post-independence states are often little more rooted among the people than the colonial ones, continuing basically to be external structures artificially and forcibly imposed from above. Post-independence states have often inherited and embraced colonial instruments of violence and used them to subjugate and terrorise their populations.

It also seems clear that a major cause is often the reality that ethnically and religiously pluralistic states are increasingly unacceptable to one or more parties, resulting at times in a violent struggle for independence or a degree of autonomy. One thinks, for example, of East Timor, Sri Lanka, Ethiopia, Chechnya, Aceh in Indonesia, and the former Yugoslavia. In other situations, tensions between rival ethnic or other groups have been long-standing and violence frequently erupts as one party seeks to achieve dominance over others, as in parts of Central America, Fiji, Cambodia, Vietnam, and many African states such as Sudan. (See Duffield, 2001, chaps. 8 and 9, for a case study of Sudan's internal war and responses to it.) The interference in a nation's affairs by one or more other states is also not uncommon, as Afghanistan, Iran, and Iraq exemplify, while war between neighboring states, or would-be states, still occurs, as we saw in the Iran-Iraq and Iraq-Kuwait conflicts, and still see in the Israel-Palestine conflict. Nor is conflict over disputed territory so uncommon, as Kashmir exemplifies. Finally, it is clear that the nature of the development process is frequently also a factor. When development is uneven, unable, or unwilling to overcome poverty, or results in poor governance, the stage is set for conflict if a triggering event occurs (Duffield, 2001, pp. 113–117).

Characteristics of Conflict

While the nature and immediate causes of war vary, as important as the number of modern wars is their nature. The most significant characteristics of modern war are

- the focus on civilians as targets, who are often more at danger than those in the armed forces and represent a huge proportion of casualties;
- the use of mercenaries, or draftees who often go unpaid, and the tendency of both groups to plunder and otherwise exploit the situation for personal gain;

- the focus on the destruction of infrastructure, food supplies and sources, and homes, leaving massive numbers of people homeless and in danger of starvation, and requiring a massive rebuilding program postconflict;
- the displacement of very large numbers of people, internally and across borders;
- the use of torture and rape, which may not be new but are often now on a major scale;
- the involvement of child soldiers as a comparatively new element (UNICEF, 1996, chap. 1);
- the widespread use of land mines that continue to cause civilian casualties long after the war (see reports of the Mines Advisory Group, U.K. and Canada); and
- the messy nature of modern wars in terms of the absence of a declaration of war, the periodically negotiated cease-fires that are generally untrustworthy, and the tendency of such wars to drift on for extended periods, creating insecurity among many of the population. (See, for example, Zwi, 1995; Macrae and Zwi, 1994.)

As Shawcross (2000, p. 13) puts it, "the world was now in a period of nonstructured or destructured conflict, sometimes called 'identity-based.'" The UNHCR (2002, p. 23) wrote recently,

Since the end of the cold war, conflicts have become more messy—internal, ethnic or communal in nature—which in turn are often more difficult to resolve than conventional struggles between states. The study concluded that warlords, the military, local and international entrepreneurs and even groups within a refugee community itself have vested interests in prolonged fighting which may continue for decades.

Impact of Conflict

The impact of war has always been horrendous, especially for those caught up in the fighting and for their families. However, the impact of modern wars is, if anything, more horrendous than ever. Since 1945 it has been estimated there have been more than 22 million war casualties, 84 percent of these being civilians. An even larger number of people have been physically or psychologically maimed by war, and such impairments, while always devastating, are far more so for the people of developing countries, and it is they who have composed the majority of the victims of war. Economies have been invariably devastated by war, and the rebuilding of these economies, while always difficult and long-term, is even more so if the country continues to be perceived as unsafe for investment or as unlikely to offer much of a return on investment. Yet it is of course not only the economies. Frequently a country's infrastructure, both physical and institutional, has been substantially destroyed, and a major reconstruction task confronts those involved postconflict. This huge task may be rendered more difficult by the death, flight, or emigration of many of those who would otherwise have provided leadership during this period. Not least in importance is the fact that social infrastructure has also suffered a major blow. Communities have been physically destroyed but also socially divided by the interethnic, religious, or class nature of the conflict. Family life and support structures have been significantly undermined by the numbers of members lost or separated or affected by the psychological scars of the war. Postconflict rebuilding will, therefore, require also a rebuilding of personal and family lives, as well as of communities.

The Role of the United Nations

The role of the UN in relation to war began to change as the circumstances of conflict changed. As Robertson (2000, p. 25) points out, prior to 1993 the UN "declined to act against any state which objected to having its internal repression investigated or condemned." He goes on to say that only after 1993—"after the Cold War was over and as the specter of 'ethnic cleansing' returned to Europe"—was there sufficient superpower resolve to enable the Security Council of the UN to begin to play its rightful role in the many conflicts occurring. While UN action varied, it was often involved in negotiating a peace, supplying a peacekeeping force, and addressing human rights abuses and crimes against humanity, as well as of course providing humanitarian aid and assisting displaced persons. While the UN has been at specific times criticized for its lack of action, as for example in the period before the outbreak of hostilities in Rwanda in 1994 (see Shawcross, 2000, chap. 5), or had inadequate resources provided to it by the member states to do justice to a particular situation, its intervention has nonetheless become more and more important as time goes on. However, the UN's response to conflict is still very much determined by its member states, both as voting members within the Security Council and as contributors of finances and personnel to any agreed-on UN response. We might also note here that, although the UN Security Council dominates in conflict situations, often in conjunction with prevailing superpowers and such bodies as NATO, the role of global civil society is not unimportant (Kaldor, 2003).

The Role of Global Civil Society

Many nongovernment members of the international community play major roles in influencing UN decisions and in their implementation. In addition, many of these nongovernment bodies initiate their own programs in response to conflict and postconflict situations, and their roles are of great importance in achieving a successful outcome. The onset of conflict will see the UN and some governmental bodies becoming involved, as, for example, in East Timor

where the Australian government made a huge response. Among the NGO agencies also responding will be the Red Cross, Medecins Sans Frontieres (MSF) and other medically oriented bodies, and some of the human rights organizations such as Amnesty International (see MSF, 1997, and reports from Human Rights Watch). As time goes on, a wide range of additional NGOs will become involved, especially in working with displaced persons, aiding war victims, and providing humanitarian aid. Ideally, organizations from the various sectors work in close collaboration with each other. However, the postconflict situation often sees a massive expansion in the numbers of agencies involved, both governmental and nongovernmental, and across a range of fields of endeavor, and close collaboration is in practice difficult to achieve.

The Postconflict Response

Our focus here is very much on the postconflict, rather than the conflict, situation because that is where social workers are mostly involved, although in addition to the Red Cross, many humanitarian aid, refugee, and medically oriented NGOs (e.g., MSF) are heavily involved also in conflict situations. The postconflict response is to some extent a continuation of activities commenced during the conflict. These activities will normally include, first, a response to the conflict, involving diplomacy, the provision of armaments, some training of military personnel, and a degree of profiteering from the conflict. The fact that this aspect of the response is very mixed, often political and profit-oriented, does not constitute the best foundation for ongoing international intervention postconflict, because it will be difficult for many to trust the motives of the agencies involved. This is one of the reasons why it is usually preferable for the UN to take control as soon as possible.

Second, a humanitarian response will be launched during the conflict. The plight of refugees, internally displaced persons, prisoners of war, and other war victims will require, and receive where possible, a range of responses from a variety of organizations. Given the desperate situation of many of those so afflicted and their dependence on aid, it is not surprising that a culture of dependency is sometimes created. At the same time, however, it must be acknowledged that external aid usually falls well short of needs, and that many people are drawing on personal strengths and previously underdeveloped coping mechanisms in a desperate effort to survive. Whatever the balance between creating dependency and enhancing coping mechanisms, the legacy of external aid is an important factor in the postconflict situation.

A third type of activity involves human rights. A range of groups will be involved throughout the conflict in monitoring human rights abuses, and seeking to use the findings to increase external pressure on the warring parties. A continuing focus on human rights issues, including on the possible commission of crimes against humanity during the conflict, is an important aspect of the reconstruction and rebuilding process. It bears a close relationship to the task of reconciliation.

In addition to the types of agencies emerging from the conflict years, postconflict there will now arrive a further group of agencies entrusted with imposing the peace agreement. This is essentially an international political process, brokered in the final stages of the conflict by the UN, by regional bodies such as the European Union or African Union, by NATO and other regional bodies, and by various state powers.

Finally, the end of the conflict is likely to bring an influx of organizations seeking to play a role. Most will have humanitarian goals, but some will focus on economic development and some on the provision of specialized services. Along with the altruists are likely to be organizations that are vying for the available aid monies in order to keep their organizations afloat, some who are out to make a profit from exploiting some aspect of the presenting needs, and even a few presenting fraudulently as aid agencies in order to siphon off some of the funds. To provide some idea of numbers, in Bosnia-Herzegovina, after peace was declared late in 1995, some 240 organizations entered the country to play a role in that postconflict situation. Even the very arrival of agencies in such numbers, especially in developing countries, has an impact on the local economy, such as on the prices of food and accommodation, while the relatively luxurious living style these agencies at times adopt can cause widespread resentment, especially when even their own local staff are excluded from certain facilities as is sometimes the case.

The Postconflict Situation and the Postconflict Reconstruction Agenda

Given the nature of modern conflict, and the importance to global stability and the global economy of getting states affected by conflict back on their feet again, tremendous efforts have gone into postconflict reconstruction in recent decades, as indeed occurred in the aftermath of World War II with the Marshall Plan. The recent experience has resulted in a significant literature on the topic (e.g., Harris, 1999; War-Torn Societies Project, UNRISD, 1998; Kumar, 1997a). We have sought to pull together the key elements in the recovery process, from the perspective of a worker in the field, in two models, depicted in Figure 9.1 and Table 9.1.

Figure 9.1 provides a model of the component parts of the postconflict situation, useful for carrying out an analysis of any situation. Table 9.1 presents the postconflict agenda that outlines the major tasks to be undertaken and can be used as a checklist in devising a response at any level. While not all aspects of the situation, or all parts of the agenda presented, lie within the province of social work, it is important that social workers and others employed in these situations are aware of the overall challenge, and of the importance to their work of aspects other than those in which they may be directly involved. Let us comment briefly on the various elements in both models.

The Postconflict Situation: An Analysis

Figure 9.1 presents a model of the postconflict situation. It begins with identifying two significant related factors instrumental in determining the nature, and especially the dimensions, of the international response to the situation. These factors are the location of the conflict and the prevailing international context. Clearly certain areas of the world, such as the Balkans and the

Middle East, are regarded as of more strategic importance than many other areas, such as parts of Africa. If a conflict is located in a politically or economically sensitive area, its resolution will receive far more attention than it might otherwise receive, although it may also be a more politically orientated response than we might otherwise see. Similarly, the prevailing realities of international relations will play a significant role. If, for example, the major powers are otherwise occupied, or if the conflict in question relates to an existing international relations situation, or if involvement in the resolution (or prolongation) of the conflict fits with an existing agenda of a major power, then the nature of the involvement of the various parties will be significantly affected. Hence responses to conflict and postconflict situations are often driven by factors external to the conflict.

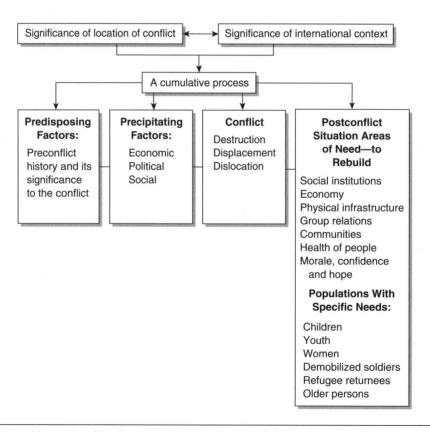

Figure 9.1   The postconflict situation

Table 9.1   The postconflict agenda

A. Peacekeeping for an Interim Period and Provisional Government or Administration

Enforcement of peace agreement

Return of displaced persons and their reintegration

- relationship to host society
- resumption of property rights
- provision of requisites for well-being

Demobilization of soldiers and their reintegration

- relationships with civilians and between opposing forces
- provision of requisites for well-being

Reconciliation

- prosecution for those accused of crimes against humanity
- truth and reconciliation commissions

B. Comprehensive Approach to People's Well-being

Immediate needs of individuals and families generally

- shelter, involving often wider property issues
- food aid, merging into self-reliant provision
- health, education, and social services generally

Immediate needs of populations with specific needs, including children, youth, women, elderly, disabled, demobilized soldiers, and returnees

- specific education and health services
- special accommodation arrangements
- counseling and rehabilitation services

Immediate needs of communities

- sense of community
- mutual support arrangements
- income-generation activities
- rebuilding of community focal points

Immediate needs of society

- law and order, police force and court system
- political life—elections and governance
- physical infrastructure—roads, bridges, etc.
- economic systems—banking, credit, markets, investment, etc.
- social cohesion—identity, values, social relations

C. Root Causes of Conflict at All Levels, Including Predisposing and Precipitating Factors

All activities undertaken in such a way that they contribute to establishing a firm foundation for ongoing development of the society

The second part of the model is concerned with the conflict itself, which is presented as a cumulative process. It is common to assume that any crisis situation is brought about by a combination of predisposing and precipitating factors. The distinction is important because the first group of factors is frequently overlooked in devising the postconflict response, yet their acknowledgement, if not resolution, may be crucial in addressing the root causes of the conflict, and thus rendering unlikely a recurrence of conflict in the future. Predisposing factors are those that well precede the conflict but reflect its origins. While perhaps long quiescent, they constitute collective memories that are readily revived by those political leaders seeking to foment or provoke conflict. These factors may not have been adequately dealt with in the past and so can readily reemerge. Precipitating factors are those that dominate the lead-up to and outbreak of conflict. They can be economic, political, or social in nature, and not uncommonly are a combination of all three types.

Many recent conflicts are widely perceived as ethnic or religious in nature, and there is certainly some truth in these assertions. A UNRISD report (1995a, pp. 6–10) states, "In recent years numerous ethnic, religious and racial conflicts have belied predictions that 'development' would dissipate ethnic loyalties. . . . This upsurge in ethnically-based conflicts has been caused by a number of factors. . . ."

Others point out, however, that political leaders often play the ethnic or religious card because it will generate support for their political agenda, or result in unrest or insecurity that they can exploit. The fact that this is possible means that the ethnic relations situation in question retains elements of uncertainty, or of subconscious resentment or anger. It would also seem that many conflicts coincide with a deteriorating economic situation that is affecting people's well-being and sense of security. Finally, it is often the case that a particular political event, such as an election, strike, or riot, is also contributing to a sense of insecurity. The UNHCR (1997, p. 12) states, "The international community has become increasingly concerned with other sources of instability, including issues such as communal conflict and social violence, poverty and unemployment, organized crime and terrorism, as well as migratory movements and mass population displacements."

This report places a strong emphasis on the various forms of insecurity that occur, or are fostered, in the lead-up to the conflict, and then are greatly intensified by conflict, displacement, and the other ongoing consequences of conflict. A comment by M. Sahnoun (1996) is also worth quoting:

> The challenges to peace and democracy do not necessarily take the shape of sudden explosions of large-scale armed conflicts. These challenges work their own way to the surface through inflation, local tensions, political exploitation of different economic and social situations, increased factionalism, open clashes, outside interference, arms supplies, and, finally, larger and larger confrontation.

Ideally, these aggravating factors are identified and responded to, but when they are not they feed into the conflict situation. In addition to the above factors, it is also important to note the link between development progress and conflict. As Zwi (1995, p. 101) points out, factors promoting conflict include an absolute and relative lack of economic development and environmental resources, and the inadequate or inequitable distribution of national resources. He concludes that "violent conflict is an expression of economic, social, political and environmental stress." Some writers have commented that "scarcity and competition for resources as causes of conflict tend to be neglected" (Vontira and Brown, 1994), and it is apparent that such neglect would be counterproductive in efforts to resolve the postconflict situation (see Minear, 1994, p. 2).

Finally, the conflict itself is highly significant because of the costs it imposes on all involved. As already pointed out, it results in widespread destruction of lives, habitation, sources of livelihood, infrastructure, and institutions. It leads to widespread disintegration—of individuals, families, communities, and societies. It usually results in large-scale displacement, and in significant dislocation of many kinds. The violence, terror, and insecurity that people experience in conflict reinforce past experiences, intensify latent fears, revive old prejudices, and reveal subconscious resentment and anger against identified others. In this way, the realities of conflict become intertwined with the range of predisposing and precipitating factors; and it is this complex mix of experiences, feelings, and attitudes that confronts workers in the postconflict situation.

It is of vital importance to view conflict as a cumulative process because, as the UNHCR (1997, p. 175) points out, "the primary purpose of the reconstruction process must be to avert a "re-creation" of the conditions which produced the conflict in the first place." This means that all factors seen as feeding into the conflict need to be considered carefully and, where desirable and feasible, addressed. Of course this perspective presents the whole reconstruction challenge as one of major proportions. It is already a major task just to respond to the immediate consequences of conflict, and the cost of doing that can be staggering. To address also the range of factors underlying the conflict, from the development process to ethnic relations to political life to redistribution policies and so on, might appear impossible, and often is. The key point, however, is the need to recognize that a patching over of problems is just that. If the basic situation remains unsustainable, it may be only a matter of time before the whole conflict and reconstruction cycle will be repeated. What should be examined, at the very least, is whether the foundations of a viable and sustainable future can be laid in the course of the reconstruction process.

Before we turn to this question, however, we need to address the third dimension of the model, namely the areas of need that the postconflict situation presents. While the primary need is rebuilding, this is not to suggest a reestablishment of the situation that existed prior to conflict: the challenge is to rebuild in a manner that shows awareness of the root causes of the conflict and is consistent with the new context, for conflict invariably changes a situation. A further point invariably emphasized is the need to adopt a holistic approach. A statement by Flora MacDonald is indicative of this view:

> For reconstruction to be successful, it has to be part of an overall strategy that integrated all four elements being considered at this conference: reconstruction, reconciliation, demilitarization, and effective multilateral engagement. It has to embrace the reconstruction of governing institutions at community, local and national levels; expansion of economic opportunities; inclusion of previously disenfranchised groups; restoration of environmental balance; and rebuilding of spiritual and cultural values. (UNHCR, 1996, p. 27)

A World Bank staff member puts the point this way: "Peace consolidation and postconflict rebuilding encompass multiple, interrelated and expensive operations which, to have a lasting impact, also require reinforcing national and local institutions and entities of civil society as well as economic revitalization" (from undated notes distributed by P. Weiss-Fagen).

While it is important to bear in mind the need for a holistic approach, it is also important to identify separately the many dimensions of the whole that need to be addressed within the reconstruction process. The model identifies seven dimensions of rebuilding that will always require attention, although of course the relative importance of each, and therefore the choice of priority areas, will vary. Let us comment briefly on each of these seven dimensions.

Social Institutions

The social institutions of society suffer significantly from conflict. For example, the legal and political systems are invariably among the worst affected. Society is polarized or factionalized, decision making is centralized and often personalized or in the hands of the international community, and systems break down or are abandoned. The key task is, therefore, the building up of the range of national state institutions, and also ideally those of civil society. Among these, the establishment of governance, of an adequate police force and prison facilities, a banking system, and the rebuilding of health and education service provision are often emphasized.

Economy

The economy is clearly also central. In postconflict situations, unemployment rates are extremely high, food production and distribution are often in disarray, dependency levels are high, the willingness and ability to engage in entrepreneurial activities are likely to be low, and the society's economic institutions are probably nonoperational. The urgency of rebuilding the economy cannot be overstated. It is crucial to general well-being, to the return home of displaced persons, to engendering confidence in the future, to encouraging investment, and to creating a conducive environment for development programs.

Physical Infrastructure

The country's physical infrastructure is invariably a casualty of conflict. Roads and bridges are destroyed to curtail military movements, or suffer from neglect and the passage of heavy military equipment, and the distribution of basic utilities—water, electricity, and gas—is usually severely curtailed during conflict because of damaged and neglected infrastructure. It is important to restore this infrastructure as quickly as possible.

Group Relations

Rebuilding intergroup and intragroup relations is of fundamental significance if communities and society are to work together. At the very minimum, peace is an essential precondition for reconstruction; yet peace-building is an extremely difficult and often a very slow process. As Otunnu (1996, p. 6) says, the wounds of internecine wars "have an intensity, a quality of passion and hate, which is very difficult to deal with in the aftermath of war." He suggests the need to focus on "three kinds of wounds: the wounds born of exclusion, the wounds born of alienation, and the wounds born of the conduct of war" (p. 8). (See Norell and Walz, 1994; UNHCR, 1997.)

Communities

Rebuilding of communities is commonly stressed because for most people communities are the focal point of their lives. Healthy communities can also be seen as a significant basis for rebuilding the economy (see Duffield, 2001, chap. 6, on the importance of nonformal economies in this context), civil society, and peace through social cohesion. Even the rebuilding of psychosocial health, morale, and self-esteem will depend in part on the quality of community life achieved. However, rebuilding communities is a slow and painstaking process, often requiring competent community development workers. Sometimes it can be best achieved by focusing a group of people on the rebuilding of homes, communal facilities and infrastructure, income-generation opportunities, and a food supply system, but sometimes a significant focus needs to be on social cohesion. (See, for example, Maynard, 1997.)

Health

The issue of health should be at the heart of rebuilding, especially if it is the people themselves who are seen as the most important rebuilding resource, as they should be. Sometimes, however, rebuilding is regarded largely in material terms and the responsibility of outsiders, and then health issues are marginalized. There are four major areas of health consequences of conflict: physical health, mental health, provision of health services, and public health measures. Physical health concerns include civilian war injuries, disabled soldiers, children's health, communicable diseases, and HIV/AIDS. Mental health concerns "result from loss and grief, social isolation, loss of status, loss of community and, in some settings, acculturation to new environments" (Zwi, 1995, p. 107), while the incidence of trauma-related conditions will also be high. The collapse of health services will affect morbidity and mortality rates, while contributing to suffering, and the collapse of infrastructure will affect health levels generally and leave people exposed to serious epidemics. Health and education services are an important dimension of rebuilding.

Morale, Confidence, and Hope

Finally, rebuilding morale, confidence, and hope is important because it is the people themselves to whom the rebuilding of their society must ultimately be entrusted, and for this they require these attributes in reasonable measure. Personal and group motivation levels are a key to successful reconstruction; and while each success also builds confidence, at times individuals and groups require activities specifically aimed at rebuilding morale, confidence, and hope.

The model emphasizes that certain categories of persons have very specific needs in the postconflict context and will often require specialized services from professional workers. Let us briefly consider these categories.

Children

The vital development phase of childhood is frequently disrupted by conflict. Adults are often preoccupied with survival, schools are closed, and a range of normal experiences are unavailable. As a result, many children are psychologically damaged, orphaned, left behind in their education and intellectual development, traumatized, malnourished, and so on (see Rosenblatt, 1983; UNICEF, 1996; Reichenberg and Friedman, 1996).

Youth

Most youth will have had their education disrupted and will face an uncertain future because of possessing few skills. Some will have served as soldiers, even at a young age, and been forced to kill (see Goodwin-Gill and Cohn, 1994). Many will have experienced or witnessed violence and torture—experiences they will never forget. Some will have been separated from families and survived by acquiring survival skills not ideal for youth or normal life. The wounds of youth will often be significant and require treatment.

Women

Women are often described as the major civilian target in war. As Cranna (1994, p. 163) points out, rape is often organized in a systematic manner (see also UNHCR, 1997, pp. 160–161). Many women are left without support and in very difficult circumstances to care for the very young and the very old. Postconflict, many women find themselves heading a household, often in societies that have not as yet accepted female-headed households, socially or economically. Finally, the burden on women in the reconstruction phase is often as great as the consequences of their experiences during conflict (see Sorensen, 1998; Jacobs, Jacobson, and Marchbank, 2000).

Demobilized Soldiers

Many who fight in modern civil wars are unwilling participants, often young and impressionable, and very likely to have been socialized during their engagement into patterns of behavior inappropriate in the postconflict context. Many have lost contact with their families, and often they have not been paid for their services and are left destitute. The demobilization process for many soldiers is complex and difficult, and usually not assisted by their image and status in communities. A study of demobilization in Haiti concluded that "expecting full reintegration in a few years in some demobilization cases may be asking for the impossible" (Dworken, Moore, and Siegel, 1997, p. 61). Often demobilized soldiers are forced by survival needs into activities in the postconflict period that add to their unpopularity and do not constitute a good basis for a future life, such as mafia-style black market and extortion activities.

Disabled Persons

Disabled victims of war are often marginalized. They seem unable to contribute to reconstruction and constitute a burden on society. Moreover, some societies are traditionally not accepting of those seen as less than persons—such as the disabled. Among those disabled by war are the physically disabled, the victims of land mines and so on; the mentally disabled, with neuroses and psychoses precipitated by war; and the emotionally disabled, the traumatized. While rehabilitation is what these people require, in the realities of postconflict situations such services are often seen as a luxury.

Returnees

Many displaced persons will desire or be obliged to return to their homes, and many factors affect the success of returning. Some will have had negative experiences from displacement and bring the fruits of these home with them; some will be confronted with local hostility, either because they are seen as having

engaged in a cowardly escape and so not as deserving of assistance as those who stayed to defend or fight, or because they are members of the ethnic or religious group regarded as the enemy and not wanted back; and most will return to the realities of destroyed homes, a scarcity of food, and an absence of employment opportunities. Whatever the particular circumstances, the plight of returnees looms large in any postconflict situation (see UNHCR, 1997, chap. 4 and pp. 170–171).

Older Persons

Many older persons will not survive a period of intense conflict, but those who do will often confront significant difficulties. They may have no or little family support; there will usually be no welfare system for them; they will often be seen as, or see themselves as, less entitled to aid than children and workers; appropriate health and caring facilities for the elderly will not be a high priority; psychologically they may feel themselves to be a burden on others; and they will be grieving for a lost past and the victims of the conflict known to them.

There is, of course, much to understand regarding the many areas of specific need outlined in the model, in terms both of the precise nature of the needs and the programs best suited to responding to those needs. All areas will require a degree of targeted intervention, ideally by personnel with expertise in the area. Frequently, however, the workers who happen to be there in the field will find themselves having to respond to the great diversity of presenting needs, trying to acquire as they go some understanding of the presenting needs and experimenting with various intervention strategies. At the very least, such workers need to be able to carry out a needs assessment, while developing some basic understanding of a situation. Using the model provided as the basis for such an analysis, and applying the principles discussed, will provide a starting point.

The Postconflict Agenda

There is widespread support in the literature and the field for a comprehensive approach to the postconflict situation, which is eminently logical (see Harris, 1999, chap. 4). One cannot separate addressing root causes from the more recent causes of the conflict if a successful resolution of the situation is the goal; one cannot separate reconciliation from reintegration of returnees and others, for the latter depends to a significant degree on the former; and, similarly, one cannot separate humanitarian relief from development, for the former will not provide a sustainable base for a people's future. Yet while it is the logical approach, the comprehensive approach is difficult to secure in practice.

In any operation, the scope of activities will reflect the goals. If agencies arrive with the goal of feeding people their focus will naturally be on food relief, and many agencies are goal-specific in their approach. Similarly, if an overwhelming desire of governments is to return refugees or asylum seekers to their country or place of origin, that goal may largely close out a concern for the returnees' long-term viability or even short-term safety. Finally, if the goal of the international community is to achieve peace at any price, they may accept compromises that bring about a tenuous peace but frustrate the achievement of other goals of reconstruction and ongoing development. A comprehensive approach implies the acceptance of a range of goals that together will support and enable the achievement of an acceptable and sustainable level of well-being as quickly as possible, as well as of long-term development. While ideal, such an approach is often not possible in the existing circumstances; however, it should still function as the model for whatever is feasible in any context.

There has been a major debate over the relationship between humanitarian aid and ongoing development (see Duffield, 2001, chap. 4; Rieff, 2002, chap. 2; Gorman, 1993, chap. 1). A common assumption in the 1980s seems to have been that the two approaches were separate and

different, with often the former seen as short-term and the latter as long-term, or the one addressing survival needs and the other developmental needs. This division has since then been challenged for various reasons. First, the aid-development division was based on the assumption of a linear progression from the cessation of conflict to postconflict aid and then development. This assumption was flawed. For example, conflict was often intermittent, with no clear cessation point; and development needs were clearly ongoing, even if at times interrupted by conflict. The division was also based on the assumption that the goals and nature of aid and development were different, but in the field this distinction was difficult to discern. For example, was the rebuilding of shelter aid or development, and was not the speedy provision of income-generation opportunities the best form of aid, as well as of development? Critics of the aid-development division were also concerned that aid could undermine development, for example, by engendering a degree of dependency on aid and of insecurity in regard to self-reliance.

Despite the important debate surrounding humanitarian aid and its relationship to development, to which we shall return later, the prevailing view in the 1990s came increasingly to be that aid, which is usually essential, can and should be provided in ways that promote development, so that both sets of goals were aspects of the comprehensive approach. (UNHCR, 2000, p. 142, provides a good summary of the history of this line of thought.) We shall return to this principle shortly, but first we shall explore the various elements in the comprehensive approach as set out in Table 9.1.

The Comprehensive Postconflict Agenda

The comprehensive postconflict agenda is today widely endorsed in theory. A UNHCR report (1997, p. 174) sets out the components of such an approach in terms of a range of what it calls "peacebuilding tasks":

The peacebuilding process incorporates a dozen different but interlocking tasks: strengthening the capacity of existing institutions; holding free and fair elections; monitoring and promoting human rights; addressing the problem of accountability for previous human rights violations; building a strong civil society; demobilizing combatants; removing landmines and unexploded ordnance; reforming the security services; restoring education and health facilities; assisting war-stricken children; reviving agricultural production; rebuilding the physical infrastructure; and instituting macroeconomic policy reforms. What is more, all of these peacebuilding activities must be carried out simultaneously if displaced populations are to be effectively and sustainably integrated in their own society.

The European Union, in a 1997 document regarding Bosnia-Herzegovina, spoke in terms of consolidated programs with four elements: the rehabilitation of identified dwellings, the rehabilitation of social-physical infrastructure, the development of the local economy, and the development of local institutions. A wide range of writers and reports refer to a great range of activities as needing to play a role within reconstruction programs. Table 9.1 presents the range of tasks that are commonly identified or implied as together constituting the comprehensive approach.

Group A tasks include four tasks that represent large-scale responses to the postconflict situation. The peace agreement has to be enforced; people in temporary situations need to be returned to their homes or settled in a semipermanent situation elsewhere; those armed forces personnel who are now on the loose need to be integrated into civilian life; and the animosity between the warring parties has to be tackled at a preliminary reconciliation level at least. The inability to develop an adequate response to any of these four situations is likely to jeopardize the whole reconstruction process.

Group B tasks represent a comprehensive approach to people's well-being. Individuals will need shelter, food, personalized assistance, and access to health services. Communities also possess needs, and the response to those needs is essential to meeting individual needs in a sustainable manner. The community-based response to presenting needs is, in addition, often the most effective response, given available resources. Finally, there is a range of needs that can best be met at the societal level, and all of those listed are essential aspects of the reconstruction of society.

Group C tasks reflect the longer-term dimension and relate specifically to the root causes of the conflict. If the preconflict political, economic, or social system was significantly flawed to the extent that social cohesion was jeopardized, then the reconstruction of society must ensure that ultimately it takes place along lines that are conducive to the longer-term well-being of all groups in the society, and to harmonious relations between them.

The comprehensive nature of this agenda should not be perceived as a comprehensive set of separate items. The many necessary dimensions of reconstruction must be interlinked. This is in part because they are interdependent, with success in any one area being frequently dependent on success in other areas; but it is so also because many areas of the agenda can be, and perhaps even must be, approached together within the one program or set of programs. Fundamentally, people have to be responded to as complete persons, and not treated in terms of externally determined specific aspects (e.g., various physical, emotional, or mental aspects) as so often happens when outsiders intervene; moreover, communities and societies are entities, and attempts to compartmentalize them will ultimately prove counterproductive; and, third, development is demonstrably an integrated and comprehensive process, and can only be an adequate response to people's needs when it is such.

Any discussion of a comprehensive approach immediately throws up the need for a coordinated approach. It also highlights the need to operate on the basis of goals that are long-term and associated with a people's or a society's ongoing development goals and needs. Finally, it implies a program of major proportions and significant cost. Each of these implications can be seen as militating against a comprehensive approach being easily and effectively implemented. However, the gains of a successful comprehensive approach in terms of the benefits of peace, the value of securing the future well-being of an entire population, and the global significance of bringing about long-term stability to any part of the world should not be underestimated. In these ways, the comprehensive approach will represent money well spent, whereas a patching-up job, which may degenerate again into conflict after a period, may not only represent money poorly spent but also be responsible for perpetuating insecurity and causing further suffering. Even if the comprehensive approach cannot be fully implemented, given specific circumstances, it remains the ideal goal and worth striving for, even at a less than ideal level. Finally, it should be emphasized that the comprehensive approach may be used to guide a national level operation, a local community one, or some level in between.

The Humanitarian Aid Debate

Although humanitarian aid (for definitions see Beigbeder, 1991, pp. 2–3) is required and provided in a variety of contexts, conflict and humanitarian disasters tend to be inseparable. Situations requiring humanitarian aid commonly precede an outbreak of conflict, almost invariably accompany it, and usually continue long after a degree of peace has been achieved. Given the nature of current civil wars, the need for humanitarian aid may exist for up to 80 percent of an entire population, and may well continue for a significant proportion of the population for upwards of a decade. In addition

to the link between conflict and the need for humanitarian aid, virtually every refugee and displaced person situation requires an aid program. The need for humanitarian aid exists among refugees in flight, refugees residing in camps of various kinds, and refugees in the process of being repatriated and facing reintegration in their original homeland. Finally, humanitarian aid is invariably associated with emergencies and ongoing poverty arising from economic crises and natural disasters, at least in developing countries.

In all three types of situations, current thinking focuses on either preventing crises and conflict, or at least reducing people's vulnerability; protecting people who are caught up in crises— protecting them from, for example, danger and exploitation; providing people affected by emergencies of various kinds with whatever aid is required and for as long as it is required, which is often for a prolonged period; and providing aid in such a way that people's chances of returning to some degree of normality in their lives is enhanced. Duffield (2001, pp. 75ff.) discusses the nature of what he calls "the new humanitarianism." He writes,

> The new humanitarianism reinforces earlier policy commitments to linking relief and development, conflict resolution and societal reconstruction. The new humanitarianism reflects a willingness to include the action and presence of aid agencies within an analytical framework of causal and consequential relations. (p. 75)

The new humanitarianism is a genuine, if particular, response to the complexity of the new wars. A concern with consequences and processes has to be part of any reappraisal. What is important in understanding its particularity, however, is not so much the practical veracity of the new development-oriented humanitarianism— whether it will be any more successful than the regime it has replaced—as its implications for liberal governance. A concern with limiting harmful consequences while encouraging beneficial processes demands new forms of surveillance, appraisal, and monitoring if desired outcomes are to be achieved (Duffield, 2001, pp. 80–81).

Many commentators maintain, however, that the major continuous focus is invariably, and understandably, on the third area of activity, namely the provision of emergency humanitarian aid as quickly and as expeditiously as possible, and to as many in need of such as possible. (For an overview of the nature and history of humanitarian aid, see the introduction in Beigbeder, 1991.)

The question that confronts us here is whether social workers have a role in humanitarian aid and the potential to make a significant contribution (see Van Rooy, 1998, on civil society and aid).

Social Workers and Humanitarian Aid

As far as social workers are involved in conflict and postconflict situations, in work with displaced persons and refugees, and in poverty alleviation work resulting from economic crises and natural disasters, they will invariably be involved, directly or indirectly, with humanitarian aid programs. It is, therefore, incumbent on such workers to develop an appreciation of the many complexities surrounding humanitarian aid, and to explore carefully the potential of their making a valuable contribution to this important area of international practice.

Given the nature of such work, it would seem desirable not only that all social workers involved internationally develop a deep appreciation of humanitarian aid, but that some social workers, from whatever part of the world they originate, specialize in this area of activity. Moreover, in those countries most vulnerable to the types of emergencies requiring a humanitarian aid response, it would seem to be highly desirable that the education of social workers

includes content on humanitarian aid. Whether they are involved at the planning, management, or operative level, or even coordinating their own work with humanitarian aid programs, knowledge of this crucial area of activity will be important in a large majority of countries.

Understanding Humanitarian Aid Today

Accepting that all social workers at the international level require a knowledge and understanding of the complexities, limitations, and dangers of humanitarian aid provided in response to what are frequently complex emergencies, let us consider some of the key issues that arise in this area of activity.

The Expansion and Dimensions of Humanitarian Aid in Recent Times

The UNHCR (1997/1998, p. 41) has stated regarding the expansion of humanitarian assistance:

During the past decade, the resources devoted to humanitarian assistance have soared. Among official aid agencies, spending on emergencies has increased five-fold over the last decade. The rise in the share of emergency assistance in the total bilateral aid spending of the industrialized countries is even more dramatic, increasing from 1.5 percent in 1991 to 8.4 percent in 1994.

With more than 30 civil wars raging at any one time, upwards of 40 million displaced persons and refugees, an increase in the number and severity of natural disasters in the 1990s, and economic crises hitting Asia and South America, and ongoing in parts of Africa, it is hardly surprising that all aspects of humanitarian aid have exploded in recent times. There are some unfortunate consequences of this expansion. One is that the amount of funding requested for most emergencies is not forth-coming; and the other may be that many in the Western world have become almost immune to such phenomena.

The Key Agencies Involved in Humanitarian Aid

Several agencies of the UN have emergency response as part of their mandate. Of these, the central one is perhaps the Office for the Coordination of Humanitarian Affairs (origi-nally the Department of Humanitarian Affairs, established in 1992), but others include UNHCR, WFP, UNICEF, UNDP, and WHO. In addition to these UN bodies, many INGOs have key roles to play in humanitarian aid. Among the best known are the International Com-mittee of the Red Cross (ICRC), Medecins Sans Frontiers, Oxfam, World Vision, Care Inter-national, International Rescue Committee (IRC), and Save The Children. As there are some 1,500 NGOs registered with the UN, many of whom work within the humanitarian aid field to at least some degree, the above list contains only a few of the better known ones.

It follows that, in any emergency situation, a wide range of agencies will be found, giving rise to the commonly mentioned problem of coordi-nation. The UNHCR (1993, p. 92) writes,

> A serious crisis is likely to involve dozens of relief agencies, while a protracted and highly visible one may attract literally hundreds of more-or-less independent participants. A monumental effort is required to assure that their actions are complementary, or at least do not work at cross-purposes. No single entity can exert authority over the diverse actors, although cooperation is in the inter-ests of all.

The UN will seek to coordinate its agencies and the private ones that work with them by des-ignating a "lead agency" to take overall charge of

any humanitarian operation; or an individual may be appointed as an emergency coordinator or a special representative (UNHCR, 1993, p. 92). At times the NGOs involved will establish a coordinating body (e.g., in Thailand during the region's response to displaced persons and post-conflict reconstruction), but at other times they operate in flagrant competition with each other for media coverage, areas of involvement, and grant monies.

Complex Nature of Many Humanitarian Disasters

In its 1993 report, and speaking only of refugee emergencies, the UNHCR distinguishes between "traditional refugee emergencies" and the more complex ones which it describes as follows:

> In other, more complex, situations, armed conflict, political instability, drought, ethnic tensions, economic collapse and the deterio-ration of civil society have occurred in daunt-ing combinations. . . . Multiple emergencies within a region . . . interact with each other in unpredictable ways and at several levels. (p. 86)

The report goes on to point out that, in com-plex emergencies, "operations are inevitably con-ducted under somewhat chaotic conditions" and call "for extraordinary logistical and organiza-tional feats." It is virtually impossible to overstate the difficulties confronting organizations and their staff in delivering humanitarian aid to very large populations in desperate circumstances and within complex political, economic, and social contexts. If mistakes are made, and they are (e.g., see Rieff, 2002), this is hardly surprising.

Centrality of Politics

A recurring theme in much of the writing on this topic is that most situations are, first, highly political, and only second humanitarian. It follows that aid agencies cannot operate in an apolitical manner. As Terry (2002, pp. 220–221) puts it,

> As all the cases illustrate, however, by the fact of their participation aid organizations were necessarily implicated in the larger political picture, particularly when in receipt of funds from governments pursuing a political agenda. Whether they acknowledged it or not, unless they intervened equally on both sides of a conflict or ensured that their aid accrued no benefit to a warring party—something impossible—aid organizations were supporting one side by default.

Rieff (2002, p. 26) writes, "Humanitarian aid workers have increasingly accepted the idea that their work has to be political as well, abandoning the notion of humanitarianism-against-politics for the politics of humanitarianism."

Finally, Duffield (1994) argues that complex emergencies generate a particular and radical form of political economy. He writes,

> Prompted by the post–Cold War continuation of internal conflict in many parts of Africa, a new analysis of complex emergencies is emerging. This argues that complex disasters, such as famine in certain parts of Africa, have a distinct political economy structured by relations of power and gender. (p. 52)

Hence Duffield (1994, p. 65) concludes,

> In complex emergencies humanitarian policy can only develop as part of a political process. In the past, aid agencies have often depoliticised policy by reducing it to a technical matter of organization or good practice. This found acute expression in the former Yugoslavia where humanitarian aid has been deployed consciously as an alternative to political engagement.

Duffield (2001, chap. 4) develops these points further. The two related arguments commonly found in the literature are that complex emergencies possess a strong political component in their origins, which the international community must address, and that the humanitarian response to emergencies will invariably possess a political dimension that must be recognized and handled.

The Limitations and Dangers of Humanitarian Aid

A UNHCR (1997/1998) report lists four limitations and dangers of humanitarian aid, all of which appear frequently throughout the literature. The first limitation reflects our previous point:

> First, humanitarian action alone cannot resolve complex political emergencies and situations of forced displacement . . . humanitarian action cannot be a substitute for political action or decisions.
>
> Second . . . it has become all too clear that humanitarian action can play only a very limited role in protecting human rights and safeguarding human security in situations of ongoing conflict.
>
> Third, there is a need both to acknowledge and address some of the unintended consequences of humanitarian action . . . when food and other aid is indiscriminately pumped and dumped into a crisis area, local markets and social security networks are liable to be undermined. At the same time, large-scale relief operations can easily create a harmful dependency—both physical and psychological—amongst the beneficiaries of external assistance.
>
> Fourth, there is perhaps an even more important need to recognize that humanitarian action can easily be drawn into the logic of an armed conflict, thereby prolonging or even intensifying it. (pp. 44–45)

These points listed by the UNHCR are exemplified not only by their own literature but by writers like Duffield (2001), Rieff (2002), and Terry (2002), among others. They show, for example, how the aid provided can be siphoned off to support armed forces; how crises can be manipulated to secure external aid; how the provision of humanitarian aid can legitimize movements and individuals; how the location of aid can bring about population movements, perhaps thereby supporting the ethnic cleansing of an area; how aid can support the strong in any situation and further undermine the weak; how aid can completely undermine the formation of self-reliant responses; how the provision of refugee camps with their aid programs can provide either a recruiting ground for armed forces or a place to which fighters can withdraw for a period of recuperation; and so on. The dangers seem endless and often serious, leading Rieff (2002, p. 24) to conclude, "Giving aid has proved to be a more ambiguous act than aid workers ever imagined."

Humanitarian Aid and Its Associated Principles

Terry (2002, pp. 19ff.) provides an important discussion of the search for principles on which to base humanitarian action. She begins with an examination of the principles of the Red Cross:

> Three of the seven fundamental principles of the Red Cross movement, humanity, impartiality, and neutrality, provide the most broadly based principles to guide humanitarian action and form the basis of the various codes of conduct that have appeared in recent years.

A fourth principle of the Red Cross, that of independence, she sees as "a precondition for genuinely upholding the other principles." She defines the four principles as follows:

> The "humanitarian imperative" declares that there is an obligation to provide humanitarian assistance wherever it is needed, and is predicated on the right to receive, and to offer, humanitarian aid. Impartiality implied that assistance is based solely on need, without any discrimination among recipients because of nationality, race, religion, or other factors. The principle of neutrality denotes a duty to refrain from taking part in hostilities or from undertaking any action that furthers the interests of one party to the conflict or compromises those of the other. Independence is an indispensable condition to ensure that humanitarian action is exclusively concerned with the welfare of humanity and free of all political, religious, or other extraneous influences. (p. 19)

Discussing each of these principles in turn, Terry finds problems with at least the implementation of, if not the assumptions of, all of them. For example, in regard to neutrality she asks if it is either morally acceptable or even possible in situations of total war. Rieff (2002, p. 21) finds it impossible to condone the silence of the ICRC regarding Nazi concentration camps early in World War II and regarding the situation in Biafra (which seceded from Nigeria in 1967 with horrific violence). In both cases, the ICRC "refused to compromise their neutrality and go public" because it would imperil what they were seeking to do. In relation to the principle of impartiality, Terry concludes that this is only possible if an organization is financially and politically independent—and most NGOs are not. For example, most governments will not allow humanitarian aid to get in the way of prosecuting a war or achieving a peace. Finally, the humanitarian imperative is not clear-cut if the very provision of assistance can endanger a people's well-being—and there are many examples of where it has done so, directly or indirectly. The kind of issue that concerns Terry is this:

How can the humanitarian imperative or the requirement that assistance be impartial prevail alongside the need to ensure that certain human rights are upheld before aid is given? (it being a UN requirement that international partners "collectively apply human rights conditionality to the assistance program"). (p. 26)

Terry goes on to discuss "the paradoxes of humanitarian action," namely "the tensions inherent in trying to assist populations without contributing to the forces responsible for their suffering."

It would seem that whatever principles one chooses on which to base humanitarian action, there will at times be the danger that the application of the principle will backfire in some way, resulting in an outcome very different from that intended. Rieff (2002, pp. 249ff.) discusses the stated principles of CARE, related to its work in Afghanistan in 1997, and concludes,

The mission statement, like that of many other relief agencies, was pure rhetoric, designed, it seemed, to make aid workers, their donors, and the general public feel better. In fact, in Afghanistan a serious commitment to humanitarian relief and a serious commitment to human rights, as long as the Taliban remained in power, were irreconcilable, and every relief worker knew it.

Rieff goes on to show that for the UN, the United States, most NGOs, and indeed most parties, the importance of humanitarian aid "was largely instrumental." We saw the beginnings of a rights-based humanitarianism in the UN—"a move from the philanthropic perspective of needs to the political principle of rights" arising out of the conviction that "there were no humanitarian solutions to humanitarian problems." "To be effective, aid must always be political, and . . . the destruction of the Milosevic regime in Serbia or of the Taliban–Al Qaeda

nexus in Afghanistan [or of the Saddam Hussein regime in Iraq] were examples of what was needed" (pp. 253–254). Is humanitarian aid doomed to serve the objectives of whatever political forces are dominating a particular humanitarian crisis; or perhaps even worse, to be caught in between the competing views of the many parties involved in most conflicts? Is humanitarian aid in the end largely a matter of self-interest? As Rieff (2002, p. 85) puts it,

This question of the degree to which, in crisis after crisis, humanitarian groups have proved unable to distinguish, even in private, between [their own institutional interests] and the interests of those they are pledged to serve is one of the great issues in contemporary humanitarianism.

The Temptation and Dangers of Turning Humanitarian Aid Into a Technical Enterprise

While the core objective of humanitarian aid would seem logically to be the alleviation of suffering, it is clear that historically and in contemporary terms it is frequently intertwined with many other objectives, such as colonial ambitions, missionary zeal, human rights commitments, gaining power and influence, and appeasing consciences at whatever level. At the operative level, the delivery of aid is surrounded by numerous dilemmas, for both the organizations involved and their staff. It is not surprising, therefore, that there has developed a tendency to treat the whole field as a technical enterprise.

It has become important to "sell" the need for aid to governments and publics in acceptable ways. Part of this process is a manipulation of the media, selecting for the media situations and images that constitute good public relations (Duffield, 2001, pp. 76ff.). It is clearly important to find the best technological approaches to virtually all aspects of aid, in the interests of efficiency and accountability if not of ensuring the maximum good. It is important to hire the latest forms of security at the operative level, to avoid the pilfering of aid, the distorting by force of distribution arrangements, and the endangering of personnel (see Duffield, 2001, pp. 65–68). As Terry (2002, p. 236) puts it,

> The expansion of humanitarian activity at the end of the Cold War and the proliferation of NGOs has created a veritable "aid industry." Larger global budgets for humanitarian aid—$6 billion in 1995—and the readiness of aid organizations to expand the notion of "humanitarian" activity beyond the provision of life-saving relief into areas of postconflict peace-building and reconstruction have opened up new markets for Western commercial interest, and aid is becoming an enterprise. . . . Most organizations have embraced the expanded role, and the technocratic approach seems likely to flourish in the future.

Terry writes of the tendency for aid agencies to employ private security firms:

> The ethical and practical issues raised by the hiring of private security are too numerous to be dealt with in this book: suffice it to suggest that if humanitarian action has been reduced to a logistical exercise, better to contract a supermarket chain to deliver aid with the protection of DSL (Defence Systems Limited), and at least avoid the humanitarian pretense. (pp. 234–235)

Rieff (2002, pp. 86–88) concludes that "humanitarianism is an impossible enterprise"; that the confusion of roles within humanitarian aid "has become unsustainable"; and that "the future of humanitarianism is up for grabs."

While there may be no easy answers in regard to humanitarian aid, what is clear is that the suffering of victims is real, the need for assistance is usually urgent, and that,

call it altruism, call it pity, call it solidarity, call it compassion, the impulse to help is so deeply rooted in human culture that whether it is intrinsic or learned, it can rightly be described as one of the basic human emotions. (Rieff, 2002, p. 57)

What is also clear is that humanitarian aid must never be allowed to be reduced "to its technical components for the sake of 'proving' efficiency to donors, thereby demeaning the ideas on which humanitarian action is based" (Terry, 2002, pp. 52–53). For this reason alone, the social work and other helping professions should not turn their backs on the aid enterprise, leaving the bulk of such activities to commercial operators. To do so would be to deny the very foundations of humanitarianism as mutual aid.

Institutional Constraints to Learning in the Humanitarian Aid Context

It is significant that Terry (2002) has titled her book *Condemned to Repeat?*—raising the question of whether humanitarianism is doomed to repeat its errors. In her final chapter she includes a section on "institutional constraints to learning" which contains some important messages. She writes first of team members' interpretation of their experience, recognizing that staff work in highly stressful situations which "are compounded when insecurity and concerns about the misuse of aid generate questions about the viability and side effects of the aid program" (p. 225). She considers four coping strategies commonly adopted by staff. These are

- overworking—together with a focus on the immediate and micro-level dimensions of the problem;
- detachment—becoming detached from the people they are trying to assist in an effort to ease feelings of guilt and frustration;
- transference—rationalizing behavior by transferring guilt away from themselves

toward other factors, like politics, donors, the host government, and even the victims; and

- reality distortion—creating illusions of success to enable them to feel a sense of self-worth and accomplishment in the midst of institutional inadequacy or failure.

As Terry (2002) concludes, these psychological coping strategies impact upon the way that experience is interpreted, particularly in generating a defensiveness toward criticism that impedes the ability of individuals to admit to, and learn from, mistakes (p. 228).

Terry goes on to discuss "the culture of justification," pointing out that in humanitarian action it is the satisfaction of the donor that ensures financial viability. She writes,

> Thus aid agencies have a strong institutional incentive to portray humanitarian action as an indispensable remedy for human suffering. For the most part, accountability to donors takes precedence over ensuring that target populations receive timely and appropriate humanitarian assistance, and the negative consequences of humanitarian action are downplayed. (p. 229)

She goes on to discuss aid organizations' "perceived need to amplify the gravity of a situation or selectively report the worst aspects of it in order to arouse sufficient awareness and action to raise a response," referring to the use of "disaster pornography" and the "CNN factor" (p. 230). The overall effect of these trends is "that it discourages open discussion among the organizations about the failures or negative consequences of humanitarian action" (p. 231).

Terry's (2002) next section is on "the logic of institutional preservation" (pp. 232ff.). There are three main aspects of this logic that are important to note:

> First, underpinning the logic of institutional preservation is the aid community's ingrained

belief that humanitarian action is indispensable to the survival of refugees and other victims of disasters.

> The second aspect of the logic of institutional preservation is ... [that] the humanitarian enterprise will prevail owing to the nature of democratic governance in the West—the "politics of pity."

> The third aspect of the logic is the way in which aid agencies have used the western focus on humanitarian action, "although it is known that humanitarian action is not the answer to crises generated by conflict," to turn aid into an enterprise and adopt a technocratic approach. This too is a way of protecting aid organizations from the dilemmas they confront in the field.

For whatever reasons, and there are clearly many, one often hears in the field the comment that international work seldom appears to learn from past mistakes and come up with better strategies. Sometimes this is due to the rate of turnover of staff in particular areas of activity and to the tendency not to record experiences; sometimes it is the utilization by staff of a variety of defense mechanisms or coping strategies, as suggested above; and sometimes it is due to the aid organizations ensuring that nothing that they say or do will undermine their operations and ongoing viability, as Terry explains above. Whatever the reasons, the literature is replete with criticisms of the overall humanitarian aid situation and of specific situations; and the need is, as Rieff and others argue, to rethink and revamp this whole humanitarian response to global crises and the needs they generate.

The Importance in Humanitarian Aid of Looking Ahead to After the Emergency

The final issue that we wish to raise here is another that runs throughout the literature on humanitarian aid in several different forms. The issue is partly a concern with the possible negative consequences of aid. For example, aid is frequently seen as creating dependency and reducing the possibilities of a healthy level of self-reliance emerging. Gorman (1993, p. 8) expresses this very vividly:

> Among refugee experts, the Palestinian case serves as a prime example of how not to cope with a refugee problem. Indeed, the term "Palestinization" has taken on the connotation of a disease to be prevented. To avoid the Palestinization of refugees, refugee experts argue that it is necessary to encourage self-reliance among refugees from the earliest phases of a refugee situation.

A second possible negative consequence is where aid inappropriately assumes the responsibilities of states. As Duffield (1994, p. 58) expresses it, "In crude terms, the process has been characterized by NGOs replacing the state in the provision of basic welfare services."

Adopting the more positive approach, it is commonly argued that those providing humanitarian aid must always do so in ways that maximize the possibility of a satisfactory long-term outcome of the crisis and postcrisis situations. For example, Gorman's (1993) entire book is concerned with the links between refugee aid and development. As he writes in his preface, his book's key theme is that

> the world continues to face a crisis of economic underdevelopment and of refugee movements. This book addresses these twin predicaments, arguing that they are in a very real sense linked and that neither can be fully resolved without taking into account the other. (p. 1)

To take another example, Duffield, Macrae, and Zwi (1994, p. 231), in the conclusion to the book edited by Macrae and Zwi (1994), write, "Development of sustainable peace is therefore deeply related to developing new mechanisms of international accountability and to promoting new strategies for disbursing international relief and development assistance."

They then set out six bases for change. These include, in summary, "acknowledging the structural conditions that promote violence"; "developing a framework of international law that promotes the rights of victims of violence and underdevelopment"; avoiding intervention "becoming a selective political tool of a unipolar world order"; establishing "an independent, international monitoring system" developing "tools to monitor and evaluate the impact of relief assistance on the evolution of conflict"; and giving conflict-affected communities "a voice in determining the course of international action to prevent, mitigate and resolve structural and political violence."

As a final example, writers focusing on the postconflict situation, where humanitarian aid is usually critical, frequently point out that the ultimate objective of aid is to get a country back on its feet again. They argue that the manner in which aid is provided can either contribute to long-term recovery or set back the whole process to a significant degree. In this context, the process of providing aid must be linked to a country's long-term recovery.

In all these situations, aid is not an end in itself, vital though its provision is for the survival or well-being of people. Yet aid is likely to become an end in itself when the motivation for its provision relates either to the donors who make it possible or to the organizations who are dependent on its provision. Humanitarian aid must be given only for humanitarian reasons, and, as every social worker knows, a people-centered approach encompasses both short-term and long-term objectives. The basic reason for any aid is the ultimate well-being of the recipients. If aid contributes to people's short-term survival but leaves them ultimately in an invidious or impossible situation, it has failed its main objective. And that, so many writers say or imply, is what the current approach to humanitarian aid is frequently doing.

Personnel in Humanitarian Aid Responses to Crises

Who are the aid workers? Who is it that sends out reports on the need for humanitarian aid, negotiates with the powers that be to allow aid into a situation, drives the aid trucks across hostile lands to deliver the aid, distributes the aid in chaotic situations while controlling a desperate crowd, organizes the masses of people seeking aid and ensures that the aid is distributed equitably, and responds to the many personal needs among the victims of disaster as they desperately seek aid? While there are many excellent discussions of the contexts of humanitarian aid, its successes and failures, and the many paradoxes, issues, and controversies that surround these operations, the many thousands of aid workers are usually reduced to a silent, impersonal, and anonymous category of "the aid workers," apart from the common use of interviews with individual aid workers in media reports. Writers tend to be mainly concerned about the macro issues, as in Macrae and Zwi's (1994) excellent book *War and Hunger: Rethinking International Responses to Complex Emergencies*; but who are the aid workers?

Hugo Slim, of Oxford's Brookes University, presented a paper in 1994 on "the continuing metamorphosis of the humanitarian professional." In his paper he suggests that the majority of contemporary humanitarian emergencies require relief workers to have rather different skills than were required in the eighties. This is because the nature of emergencies has changed—"the overriding feature of complex emergencies is their thorough politicalness and their domination by conflict." The paper goes on to discuss the following areas requiring specific skills:

negotiation;

conflict analysis and management;

propaganda and humanitarian broadcasting;

working in urban terrains, in that urban settings have become far more common in the nineties;

human rights monitoring, because of "a significant merging of humanitarian and human rights agendas";

armed guards and protection;

working with the UN military—another aspect of "the militarisation of the international relief system";

the longevity of emergencies and the need for a developmental paradigm;

the importance of being a country specialist;

peace-building and rehabilitation; and

personal security and emotional health, because "many relief agencies and their staff experience periods of powerlessness" and "are often robbed, attacked and even killed."

Slim's central point is that the majority of workers, engaged with complex emergencies as they were presenting in the early 1990s, were facing situations that commonly called upon all of the above traits. If workers did not possess the necessary skills in advance, and were unable to undertake short training courses, then they had to discover them as they went—a situation to be avoided if at all possible for the sake of the workers and their effectiveness as workers, and thus of the recipients of aid (see Stearns, 1993).

Conclusion

Conflict, with all its human consequences, and postconflict reconstruction, especially of communities, are critical aspects of international work to which social workers are being drawn in increasing numbers. However, it is a difficult and often dangerous field that workers need to enter with an understanding of the nature of modern conflict and the challenges of postconflict work. We have presented this field largely in terms of an agenda, in order to show clearly what is involved in such work and the importance of integrating all aspects. We have included also a discussion of humanitarian aid in this chapter because, while by no means confined to this field of work, it is invariably a critical component of responding to conflict. In the following chapter we shall present some of the programs and strategies that are particularly relevant to this area of international social work.

Summary

- Conflict and achieving peace and postconflict reconstruction require the integrated-perspectives approach for effective work.

- Modern conflict has increased and changed from earlier times due to a range of factors. Often civilians bear the brunt of these conflicts. Despite their limitations and criticisms of them, the UN, governmental organizations, and global civil society agencies play significant roles in restoring peace and order.

- International social work practitioners interested in postconflict reconstruction need to understand thoroughly the postconflict situation and agenda, although these vary to some degree with location. Many factors lie behind, precipitate, and aggravate modern conflict.

- The postconflict agenda includes at least seven dimensions of need and six population groups with specific needs.

- The postconflict agenda essentially involves peace-building tasks with provisional administrative arrangements to enforce peace, achieve reconciliation, meet immediate needs at all levels, restore law and order, and address the root causes of the conflict.

- While humanitarian aid is essential, often controversial, and debatable, it is critical that it be provided in accordance with social development principles.

Questions and Topics for Discussion

- In what ways do the characteristics of modern conflict render external intervention a difficult and often dangerous process?

- Are there potential roles for the helping professions while conflict is ongoing, and, if so, what roles might they play?

- Given the complexity and extent of the consequences of conflict, is comprehensive postconflict reconstruction a feasible goal?

- Given the differences between the basic relief and developmental approaches, how critical to the future and how feasible is adopting the developmental approach?

- What are the critical issues in delivering humanitarian aid, and what roles can the helping professions usefully perform in this field?

- Discuss the usefulness of the integrated-perspectives approach in understanding peace and postconflict reconstruction and intervening in such situations.

- Discuss the postconflict agenda in terms of your thoughts on priorities.

Possible Areas for Research Projects

- Consider conflict in a country of interest to you and analyze its extent, causes, and impact, as well as international responses to it.

- In selected conflict/postconflict situations, analyze the roles of the major external players involved, and draw your own conclusions regarding appropriate external intervention in such situations.

- Using secondary sources, identify the roles in postconflict reconstruction played by social workers and others from the helping professions, and suggest additional roles that they might play.

- If possible, reflectively document your own or another social worker's experience of a postconflict situation.

- Analyze a selected conflict/war situation known to you, on the basis of the integrated-perspectives approach.

- Undertake an analysis of a postconflict situation in terms of its impact, available resources locally and externally, and various levels of responses with a view to developing appropriate programs and services.

Further Reading

Cranna, M. (Ed.). (1994). *The true cost of conflict.* London: Earthscan.

Macrae, J., & Zwi, A. (Eds.). (1994). *War and hunger: Rethinking international responses to complex emergencies.* London: Zed Books.

Rieff, D. (2002). *A bed for the night: Humanitarianism in crisis.* London: Vintage.

Shawcross, W. (2000). *Deliver us from evil: Warlords and peacekeepers in a world of endless conflict.* London: Bloomsbury.

UNHCR. (2000). *The state of the world's refugees: 50 years of humanitarian action.* New York: Oxford University Press.

10

The Field of Conflict and Postconflict Reconstruction: Programs and Strategies

In the previous chapter we presented a postconflict reconstruction agenda, including a discussion of humanitarian aid, emphasizing the importance of this agenda being implemented in a comprehensive and coordinated manner. Reconstructing or rebuilding a country after conflict, especially given the nature of modern civil wars, is a complex, massive, and highly expensive undertaking. Yet it is an undertaking that the international community is being called upon to carry out with growing frequency. We begin this chapter by considering the roles of international social work in the reconstruction enterprise. While social workers may be, and probably are at times, engaged in all aspects of reconstruction, there are some aspects of the process that appear to be more closely related to the traditional areas of social work expertise. These are particularly the delivery of psychosocial programs among those suffering from traumatic war experiences, which draws on the clinical expertise of social work; and rebuilding communities, which is a specific application of community development. A further specific dimension

of postconflict reconstruction is the need to promote reconciliation, more harmonious community relations, and a sustainable peace. While social work has not traditionally worked in this postconflict area, the challenges of community relations and of reconciliation or conflict resolution in the industrial and multicultural western contexts have traditionally formed part of social work. We shall consider the question of applying that expertise in the postconflict reconstruction field. The field of refugee work, also highly relevant in the postconflict context, we shall leave until Chapter 12, but that chapter should be read in conjunction with this one, because of the overlapping of work with displaced persons and work in the conflict and postconflict contexts. Similarly, because of the nexus between responding to the impact of conflict and laying the foundations for ongoing development, as spelled out in Chapter 9, the programs and strategies pertaining to local-level development outlined in Chapter 6 are also of some relevance in this context. Finally, the material covered in Chapter 4 is also applicable in this context.

Learning Objectives

- To introduce some of the key strategies in postconflict reconstruction from a helping professions perspective.

- To encourage readers to consider the importance of rebuilding people, families, and communities postconflict, in addition to rebuilding economies, infrastructure, and institutions, and how these two fields should be related.

- To help readers to understand the basic strategies needed to work with people and agencies in postconflict situations, and the importance of following the integrated-perspectives approach in such situations.

- To encourage readers to consider the roles of international social work in implementing the postconflict reconstruction agenda.

Implementing the Comprehensive Postconflict Agenda

Given that postconflict reconstruction represents the early stages of a social development initiative designed to get a society back on its feet and able to move ahead, it is not surprising that the principles that should underpin it are the principles that underpin social development in any context.

Principles Behind the Comprehensive Approach

The major principles of the comprehensive approach are that it is people-centered, participatory, based on human rights and fundamental freedoms, empowering, and sustainable. What is different from many other social development situations is that the postconflict circumstances, in the minds of many observers and participants, tend to militate against operating on the basis of these principles. For example, it may be assumed by some players that the local population has been rendered destitute and subjugated by violence and terror to the extent that a patronizing or paternalistic approach is appropriate, as well as this often

being the approach seemingly necessitated by the requirements of donor agencies or the perceived urgency of situations. It may be argued, for example, that short-term humanitarian aid is of paramount importance, even if it is neither sustainable nor empowering. Finally, the urgent needs are often not perceived in a people-centered manner; instead, institution building, infrastructure reconstruction, and establishment of economic systems are seen as essential tasks to be carried out by experts and corporations, regardless of the population to be served by them and who will ultimately staff them. The reality is, however, that in such circumstances the need to focus on all of these principles is more important than in many other contexts, and a significant tendency to overlook them can jeopardize the entire postconflict operation's longer-term success.

Strategies Relevant to the Comprehensive Approach

In discussing some general strategies, we are not implying that there exists a blueprint that can be applied to all postconflict situations. As the UNHCR (1997/1998, p. 175) puts it,

There is no blueprint for peace. Looking at war-torn societies, such as Afghanistan, Bosnia,

Guatemala, Rwanda and Mozambique, it is quite apparent that the circumstances that lead to, sustain and eventually bring an end to civil wars and communal conflicts are extremely diverse. Peacebuilding strategies must reflect this diversity, and be carefully tailored to the situation at hand. They must also be based on a rigorous analysis of the circumstances which have led to violence.

There are, however, strategies that should be considered carefully as relevant to any postconflict situation. A number of strategies were considered by a UNHCR workshop in 1997 (UNHCR, 1997), and there have been many other discussions on this subject.

Utilizing a Developmental Rather Than a Humanitarian Relief Approach

The fundamental approach that characterizes all of the following strategies is the integrated-perspectives approach, for the reasons presented in the previous chapter. First, let us focus on the differences between a narrowly conceived relief effort and an approach that leads appropriately into the redevelopment phase, referred to commonly as the developmental approach. The following main differences between the developmental and relief approaches have been adapted from an unpublished 1996 Brookes University, Oxford, paper (Slim, 1996).

The Relief Approach	The Integrated-perspectives (Developmental) Approach
Piecemeal	Comprehensive and integrated
Address the issues at hand	Focus on issues with global and local considerations
Relief-oriented actions	Act in due regard to human rights and ecology
Remedial	Developmental
Donor-led	Client-led
Act quickly	Act slowly
Spend quickly	Spend over time
Don't admit failure	Failures accepted
Symptom focus	Causes focus
Return to normality	Instigate change
Short-term	Long-term
Material	Nonmaterial and material
Reactive	Proactive
Does not challenge power	Challenges power
Nonparticipatory	Participatory
Project focused	Program focused
Specified and technical	Nonspecified and attitudinal

The implication of the above list of differences is that the overriding strategies should be to ensure that relief is provided, as it usually must be, as far as possible in a manner that is consistent with developmental requirements. Such strategies will also be consistent with the principles listed above. There are many examples in the field of the developmental approach. For example, some programs merge food supply with food production; some programs engage in the provision of health or education services, in conjunction with community self-help programs, revolving around building the structures required and helping to staff them; some aid programs operate on a food-for-work basis; and any programs that involve the people as the major participants, in both the decision-making and implementation phases, are developmental in nature. Such developmental activities should be guided by the integrated-perspectives approach outlined in Chapter 2.

Strategies for the Postconflict Situation

Let us consider some specific types of developmental strategies relevant in the postconflict context, and especially those consistent with traditional social work skills.

Strategies That Strengthen People's Capacities

- Establishing health facilities and services
- Establishing various education and child/youth care facilities
- Establishing community support centers
- Provision of posttrauma and other rehabilitation services
- Establishing nurturing and self-help groups
- Providing leadership and paraprofessional training

Strategies That Rebuild Communities and Civil Society

- Facilitating community development generally
- Enhancing reconciliation and community relations generally
- Enabling families to rebuild their homes or construct alternative accommodation
- Engaging community members in the rebuilding and operation of facilities
- Facilitating local institutional building
- Strengthening local community and civil society organizations

Strategies That Facilitate Income-generation Initiatives

- Enabling those with land to become productive again
- Facilitating community-based market and credit systems
- Establishing food-for-work reconstruction enterprises at the local level
- Employing local people in as much of the reconstruction work as possible
- Providing training consistent with short-term employment opportunities

The question that arises is whether these strategies, when implemented in the postconflict situation, are essentially different from their application to social development situations generally or within poverty alleviation programs. Their implementation will clearly be affected by the extent of devastation caused by the conflict, the degree to which people have been demoralized and traumatized, the continuation and degree of bitterness and antagonism that characterize the society in conflict, and the extent and nature of the available resources, including external aid, which varies greatly in quantity and in when it becomes available. Hence we cannot generalize across postconflict situations because circumstances vary widely. Moreover, at the local level where many social workers will be deployed, these issues are relevant only in determining the starting points or the immediate priorities, and the extent to which workers must rely on local resources.

For example, if the impact of conflict on the local people has been devastating, an initial strong focus on nurturing, healing, and strengthening will be called for, using group approaches as far as possible, before much community-based capacity building is possible. Similarly, if the bitterness, hatred, or mistrust between rival sections of the community is intense, the tasks of reconciliation and gradually rebuilding trust must be among those taking priority. In relation to resources, both overall situations and the circumstances of the various agencies will differ in terms of the amount of external resources available for various aspects of local-level rebuilding. This variation will in turn affect the extent to which local workers will need to rely on local resources, both human and otherwise; and this will affect the degree of difficulty confronting workers and people in achieving set goals, rather than the strategies employed. Finally, the local resource pool will vary greatly between situations, depending on whether the conflict occurred within a relatively developed country, such as the former Yugoslavia or even Sri Lanka with its comparatively high levels of human resource development, or a relatively underdeveloped country, such as Afghanistan, Laos, or one of many countries in Africa.

In every situation, however, workers' starting point must be an analysis of the situation, in terms of the impact of conflict on a particular area and population, the extent of local resources available, the potential availability of external assistance, and developments at the national and regional levels. Only after such an analysis has been undertaken can agencies determine the overall nature of the programs they should or can provide. While this is clearly the logical approach to situations, the reality can result in a very different outcome. We have been told by workers in the field that they arrived in the local situation already running flat out in attempting to respond to presenting demands. The moment their doors were open, so to speak, they were inundated, and several years later would say that they had never had the luxury of time to assess the situation and develop a plan. This, however, is not an acceptable excuse. While postconflict situations represent high levels of very demanding needs and often chaotic conditions, to respond to needs effectively will always require the establishment of a considered program likely to achieve maximum effectiveness as quickly as possible.

Part of the problem in responding to postconflict situations is that this area of activity is, in any organized sense and in relation to modern civil wars, relatively new. Moreover, the reality has been that most approaches have not been well designed, for the above reasons, and workers have tended to operate in crisis mode for relatively short periods of time before withdrawing, mainly for their own health and protection. While commendable in itself, a consequence of the overall strategy adopted has been that few workers, or even agencies, accumulate a pool of evaluated expertise and strategies, and then make this knowledge available to newcomers to the field. While this has been beginning to change in recent times, we have still a long way to go before we can assure ourselves that we know how best to respond to postconflict situations, and are passing on that knowledge to the majority of workers entering such situations. In the meantime, while drawing on all available knowledge, we need to take the lessons learned from social development in a wide variety of contexts and apply those lessons to the realities of any postconflict situation. And indeed, it is already clearly established by experience in the field that there is considerable overlap between typical social development situations in developing countries and typical postconflict situations, despite the existence also of important differences.

A final part of the problem in this context is the propensity of the international community to launch a major response to a situation as soon as a degree of peace has been secured, driven by a sense of compassion aroused by the conflict alongside a degree of international concern about the consequences of continuing conflict. The extent of this response, however, does seem to be determined by the role of the media in generating public compassion, which varies greatly; the assessment of donor governments of the strategic importance of the country in question; and to some degree preexisting public attitudes in the donor countries. Once the initial goals have been achieved, there is a tendency on the part of nations, donors, and at least part of the nongovernment sector to pull out. This is because the memory of the conflict begins to recede and the high cost of intervention begins to weaken state resolve and public compassion, while the chances are that another conflict or crisis situation will have emerged to dominate international concern. While it is perhaps understandable and acceptable that certain sections of the international community will pull out after only a comparatively short period of involvement, it is also arguable that such situations should continue to be regarded as urgent

development situations, with the development agencies within the UN, government, and nongovernment sectors ensuring that ongoing development needs are adequately responded to long-term. This is most likely to occur if, right from the first days of the international community's involvement in a situation, the focus is developmental and the overall strategy one of capacity building, based on self-reliance and participation principles, at all levels of society.

Some Key Areas of International Social Work in the Postconflict Situation

From our analysis of the literature and field experience, we suggest that there are several core areas of activity where social workers, along with other members of the helping professions, should be focusing. This is not meant to imply that social workers are not and should not be involved in other aspects of postconflict work. We would argue, however, that the profession should give serious consideration to developing knowledge and skills in relation to those areas of need most closely related to social work's traditional areas of expertise. The areas we shall discuss here are delivering psychosocial programs, rebuilding communities, and engaging in peacebuilding and reconciliation work.

Delivering Psychosocial Programs

The ruinous effect of war, as Maynard (1997, p. 204) terms it, has been a continuous theme running through human history. We are more conscious of it today perhaps because there are more wars, because more people and especially civilians are affected, and because the media and people's mobility make most of us more aware of such situations. There are many accounts of the psychological and social impact of war, so let us summarize how the situation is often seen. Maynard discusses four clusters of traumatic war experiences to which soldiers and civilians alike are frequently exposed.

Four Clusters of Traumatic War Experiences

Exposure to Fighting and Torture

While professional soldiers may become hardened to killing people and the possibility of being killed, many of those who are involved in civil wars are engaged in such fighting for the first time. Moreover, some are compelled to fight, some may be mere children when recruited to bear arms and kill, and many are involved in wars in which former neighbors may be pitted against each other. The use of torture and mutilation adds to the horror, as does the fact that fighting is often on the streets, in homes, and in places associated with normal life and pleasure—the marketplace (e.g., Sarajevo), coffee shops (e.g., Israel), or pubs (e.g., Northern Ireland) being often the targets of brutal attacks.

Such experiences cannot fail to have an impact on the majority of people—an impact that may stay with them for decades or even the rest of their lives. Of course the degree of fighting and brutality varies, as does the period over which it is experienced. While some children born into civil war know nothing but war conditions for all or much of their impressionable years (e.g., in Palestine, Cambodia, parts of Sri Lanka, South Sudan, Somalia, and elsewhere in sub-Saharan Africa), for others it is a brutal interruption to their childhood years. Finally, we should note that it has been found that the difference in the impact between those engaged in the fighting and being subject to torture, and those who witness such events, is minimal. Lewis (1999, p. 99) comments, "In fact, many studies have revealed that those who have witnessed atrocities are often more adversely affected than those who have been maimed and tortured."

Exposure to Abusive Violence

Abusive violence perpetrated against soldiers, prisoners of war, and civilians is a feature of modern warfare. The violence comes in many forms: attacks on defenseless people, using such weapons as machetes; the rape of women, often publicly or in front of their children; the maiming of civilians, such as the cutting off of a hand or foot (Republic of Congo and Liberia); the wanton destruction of property, especially homes; the use of booby traps, for example in a child's toy (e.g., in Bosnia); the widespread use of land mines against civilians (e.g., Cambodia); the use of torture to secure information (e.g., Iraq); and the use of a wide range of tactics to engender as much fear in a population as possible. We might also include kidnapping of civilians, as was occurring in Iraq in 2004–05. Experiencing and witnessing such atrocities can be highly traumatizing.

Deprivation

Deprivation is both used as a weapon against a population and an inevitable consequence of war. People are commonly deprived of food, shelter, and health care. The last can be extremely serious when infectious diseases hit a population exposed to unhealthy living conditions and without nutritious foods. In the midst of severely traumatizing experiences, many are deprived of even their normal psychological supports. Some will feel abandoned. Some people are effectively deprived of their sense of identity, no longer treated by anyone around them as a person with a history and personality. Many are deprived of their belongings and of any sense of security. Some even are deprived of their faith and of hope. Severe and prolonged deprivation has a major impact on most people.

Loss of Meaning and Control

In the midst of war-torn societies, people feel that life, relationships, values, beliefs, and so on no longer have any meaning for them. Their world has been turned upside down. They feel bewildered and disoriented. Moreover, they feel caught up in, and carried along by, events completely beyond their ability to influence or control.

In addition to the psychological impact of war, there is also a social impact. Lewis (1999, p. 99) writes, "In most war-torn countries, the impact of prolonged violent conflict on social systems has been devastating, weakening societal, communal, and family level structures and their decision-making systems." Adding another dimension, Maynard (1997, p. 207) writes, "In war-torn societies, healthy social patterns between dissimilar groups are replaced by distrust, apprehension, and outrage, impairing community cohesion, interdependence, and mutual protection."

The social impact of war, which will of course take some considerable time to recover from even after conflict is at an end, makes it far more difficult for individuals to handle the psychological impact of conflict. Maynard goes on to express this very well:

> The psychological and social damages of war are inexorably intertwined. Poor individual psychological health erodes community stability through the exhibition of paranoia and blatant mistrust, irrational behavior, and the need for constant care. At the same time, ruined social institutions and inter-group relations further the impression of chaos, exacerbating mental vulnerability. As a result, internal warfare can have extreme deleterious effects on the psychosocial health of communities subjected to violence. (1997, p. 207)

The psychological impact of the experiences of enduring "multiple traumas including physical privation, injury, torture, mutilation, rape, incarceration, witnessing torture or a massacre, as well as the death of family members" results in a relatively limited repertoire of responses, according to Lewis (1999, p. 98). These are "sleep disturbance, lability of mood (including sadness and irritability), undue fatigue, poor concentration, and diminished memory." Parker (1996, p. 80), quoting some Dutch work, writes of the "survivor syndrome" and its symptoms:

> There is widespread agreement that a clear-cut "survivor syndrome" can be identified ... composed of the following symptoms and signs: anxiety, chronic depression states, some disturbances of cognition and memory, a tendency to isolation and withdrawal, many psychosomatic complaints and, in some cases, an appearance that suggests a similarity to the "living corpse" stage of concentration camp prisoners—who have regressed to such apathy and hopelessness that death was imminent.

Parker goes on to say that this syndrome is similar to the widely recognized post-traumatic stress disorder (PTSD). Maynard (1997, p. 206) lists the symptoms of PTSD as the following:

> The wide-ranging symptoms include anxiety, depression, substance abuse, social withdrawal, hostility, estrangement, despair, isolation, meaninglessness, anticipation of betrayal, hyper-vigilance, and destroyed capacity for social trust. In PTSD specifically, the subject over-responds to stimulation of memories and often relives the original trauma.

However, both Parker and Maynard go on to discuss the strong possibility that responses to traumatic experiences are culturally determined, pointing out that most of the research on PTSD has been carried out in a western context. Workers should, therefore, be aware that the presenting symptoms, in nature, severity, or expression, may well vary from culture to culture. Moreover, very little work has been done with perpetrators to help us understand why they act as they do and what the longer-term consequences are for them.

Responses to the Victims of Trauma

Let us turn to the question of ways of responding to the victims of trauma, or, in other words, to the range of psychosocial programs found to be helpful. Before we turn to some specific suggestions, however, there are two important points to be noted. One is that experience and research to date on this topic, in a postconflict setting, remains relatively limited, and writers on the topic acknowledge that there is little guidance available when it comes to drawing up a program. The second very important point is that we must be very cautious in applying western practice to the majority of postconflict situations that lie in the developing world. With these two caveats, let us look at what programs are suggested.

Therapy

We leave it to the local worker to judge what relevance therapeutic methods will have, but our second caveat certainly applies here. Parker (1996, p. 83) writes in regard to the therapies:

One thing is clear. The so-called "talking cure" or "talk therapies" (such as psychotherapy and psychoanalysis) probably have little to offer in the non-Western world. The "use of talk therapy" . . . is firmly rooted in the conception of the person as a distinct and independent individual, capable of self-transformation in relative isolation from particular social contexts.

In Africa and many other parts of the non-Western world, most therapy directly involves other family members and sometimes the wider community. It is probably not very helpful to individualize the suffering of a person whose recovery is bound up with the recovery of the wider community. In other words, effective healing in the aftermath of war is greatly influenced by the local context.

Some workers make reference to group therapy, in which a group of fellow sufferers share their experiences and insights with each other. This seems to signify, for individual sufferers, that they are not alone, and enables them to consider how others are handling a similar situation. It may also be therapeutic, as many suggest, simply to talk about the traumatic experiences, instead of bottling them up, feeling ashamed that one was in some sense responsible for what happened, feeling embarrassed to talk about certain symptoms being experienced, or withdrawing into oneself and shunning social contact.

Involvement in the Reconstruction Process

It is common for writers and workers to refer to the benefits for the traumatized from being engaged alongside others in reconstruction tasks. While the benefits are indirect, they seem to include the social experience of working alongside others, the therapy of hard work enabling one to at least momentarily forget the immediate past, and the nurturing of hope by focusing on rebuilding for the future of self, family, community, and nation. Lewis (1999, p. 106) writes,

In Mozambique, the actual physical work of reconstruction—such as the building of homes and the planting of fields—was considered to be particularly crucial to the post-war healing of individuals and communities. . . . Through the processes involved in simply living and working, the people themselves were "the living proof that people were living their lives in a good way once more." The very work of reconstructing the local infrastructure . . . had profound personal significance to the participants as an indicator of recovery.

Reconciliation and Conflict Resolution Initiatives

While reconciliation is discussed in a later section, we should note here its relevance to the healing process. Many writers argue that it is a critical step in the healing process, involving a conscious forgiveness of the perpetrators of violence and abuse that enables one to rise above negative emotions of anger and so on and begin to move forward. There is also, however, a communal aspect. Maynard (1997, p. 209) writes that "restoring a trustworthy community has the most healing effect on PTSD sufferers," and others share this view.

Community-based Approaches

The importance of a community-based approach is often stressed in this context. Lewis (1999, pp. 101–102) states,

> Goodwin-Gill and Cohn (1994) advocate that treatment for war-related mental trauma should be deinstitutionalised, emphasizing community-based strategies that take advantage of existing human and material resources. They explain that the aim of this strategy should be to reduce the stigma attached to psychological therapy. . . . Similarly, approaches which focus largely on the psychosocial healing of the individual should not replace a concern for broader social, political and economic reconstruction. . . . Summerfeld, too, recommends that war-related traumatisation should not be viewed as an injury sustained by an individual, but rather a process or processes impinging on social and cultural organization at various levels: family, community and society.

There are many ways in which a community-based process can be interpreted in practice. The work of reconciliation and the involvement of traumatized people in reconstruction and in group therapy all fall into this category, as does community rebuilding.

The Involvement of Traditional Healers, Religious Organizations, and Cultural Strategies

The dangers of imposing assessment and response processes from outside a situation have already been stressed. Under this heading, writers are emphasizing the importance of identifying indigenous responses to trauma and stress, and seeking to mobilize these in support of the postwar healing process. Lewis (1999, pp. 102ff.) writes extensively of the significance of adopting this approach because, as she says, "The ways in which people embody and give meaning to their distress are significantly influenced by their particular cultural context" (p. 102). She writes, "In Mozambique, for instance, local social institutions and healers already provide both meaningful interpretations of people's suffering, and particular mechanisms for managing it."

She says that, in that country, "traditional healers specializing in war trauma have played a key role in reconstructing shattered lives" (p. 104), and that "in Mozambique the churches are recognized for their role in promoting reconciliation, offering forgiveness, and helping both adults and children reaffirm the process of reconstruction" (pp. 105–106).

It is not always easy for outside professionals to place their trust in traditional healers and local religious groups, but the important question is, who do the people involved trust, rather than who do the external workers trust.

The Five Stages of Psychosocial Recovery

Many writers emphasize that psychosocial recovery is a process, but Maynard (1997, pp. 209ff.) is more specific and suggests five phases within the process. Phase 1 is "establishing safety"—"critical to any healing is removing the danger and replacing it with the foundations of security." Phase 2 is "communalization and bereavement"—"communalization, the act of sharing traumatic experiences, perceptions, resulting emotions, and responses with other people in a safe environment, in conjunction with a period of mourning over the losses, is a major part of the healing process." Phase 3 is "rebuilding trust and the capacity to trust"—"the critical next step to a healthy psyche and interpersonal relationships is reconstructing the confidence and commitment between adversaries." Phase 4 is "reestablishing personal and social morality"—"healing psychosocial wounds requires reconstructing the concept of themes (what is right) and reestablishing guidelines for individual behaviour" and social ethics. The fifth and final phase is "reintegrating and restoring democratic discourse"—"a healthy society is one that accepts an amalgamation of the diverse elements of society."

The reader may not accept these five as the five vital or only phases. What is important, however, is to follow Lewis's logic and consider the existence of phases within a programmed response to psychosocial healing in the postconflict context. (On trauma and responses to it, see also Welsh, 1996, and Straker, 1993.)

Case Examples

Both of our case examples come from Bosnia and Herzegovina. Unfortunately, this is partly because professional psychosocial programs were much more common in this Balkan state, more developed and better recorded, than in most postconflict situations.

Family Rehabilitation in Sarajevo

Our first example is concerned with family psychosocial rehabilitation, and was established by an INGO with religious affiliations. The project was carried out in Sarajevo, using professionally qualified staff, and involved 300 families containing 1,574 individuals. The program rested on the assumption that the majority of Sarajevans had been daily exposed to fear and stress throughout the four years of war. It was based also on the belief that, despite war scars, many families and individuals had demonstrated considerable strength.

While the program set out to provide assistance, it did so in a way that might demonstrate which psychotherapeutic methods would produce the best results. It also sought to establish when normal reactions to traumatic events became abnormal. The agency appreciated that existing research showed that people varied considerably in their reactions to traumatic events and in the time required for recovery. Although the core of the program involved 300 families, 2,305 families were visited and assessed in the implementation of the project, it being found that only a minority required intensive care. Other families required assistance with child development issues, refugee returnee status, alcoholism, conflict situations, care of the elderly, and information regarding rights and meeting needs. Most families required some material assistance, including hygiene kits.

Psychosocial work that was undertaken had to encompass a number of individuals in each patient's immediate circle, and involved significant time to establish friendly relations between therapists and patients—said to be generally the most difficult aspect of the task and requiring considerable patience.

The project revealed a major need for a range of services, including the education of professionals in utilizing preschools and schools in a beneficial therapeutic manner; counseling centers for premarital, marital, and family relations work; specialized services for juvenile delinquents; establishment of a family trauma center; a program for child victims of war; a program for families with missing members; an SOS line for children and adults; and an emergency supported home for the homeless.

(Example from Catholic Relief Services, 1996, p. 1.)

Program for Health Workers in Sarajevo

The second example is a program designed for women who continued to provide health services in Sarajevo throughout the four years of war. These women had to work with a variety of injuries, and did so usually in facilities without water, electricity, gas, food, and medications. The strain involved in doing this constantly was enormous. After the war, the social work services unit at the local university combined with a German NGO to assist the rehabilitation and social integration of these female health care workers.

The program revolved around arranged 21-day breaks away from Sarajevo in groups of 26 women. The objectives were to facilitate overcoming burnout and the experiences of personal trauma (including loss of family members and of homes, and various physical and psychological consequences of the war years). The women participated in group and individual sessions, with two group sessions and two individual sessions for each woman each week. Staff had been especially trained for this type of work as well as for psychiatric, psychological, or social work.

The program also utilized work therapy, conducted through the active participation of the women in all aspects of their break away. There were also programs of "active relaxation," involving a wide range of activities.

The program covered 286 women in a five-month period, with follow-up arranged to continue for as long as was needed.

(Example from Catholic Relief Services, 1996, p. 29.)

Rebuilding Communities

Three points would seem to be indisputable in relation to rebuilding communities. One is that communities play a critical role in the functioning of society from the perspective of human development and human well-being, so that it is logical to argue that rebuilding communities will play a fundamental role in the postconflict reconstruction agenda. The second point is that rebuilding communities falls well within the ambit of the social work profession, given its focus from the earliest days on community development. Third, it is widely agreed that those traumatized by conflict benefit from engaging in the rebuilding process, and for most people this has to be at the local community level. Yet the prevailing reality would seem to demonstrate a lack of acceptance of these points.

Kumar (1997b), in the initial chapter of the book he edited, discusses an extensive list of activities pertaining to rebuilding war-torn societies, yet he makes no mention of community rebuilding. The one chapter in the book that ostensibly covers this area, that of Maynard (1997) which is titled "Rebuilding Community,"

in practice focuses on the subject matter of its subheading—"psychological healing, reintegration and reconciliation at the grassroots level." There are direct and indirect references throughout the book to the importance of community, but the process of rebuilding communities is not addressed directly. Is it assumed that it will occur without intervention, or result from other aspects of reconstruction? This seems to us to be symptomatic of an unwillingness to focus resources directly on community rebuilding in the postconflict situation. Is it because to do so would require a large number of professionals to be deployed across the large number of communities, or because such work is seen as far less important to the key agencies involved than are state-level institution building, economic development, and infrastructure reconstruction? Furthermore, we have found no focus on this area of activity by social work, although the adaptation of its community development practice to cover this area could well have been, and in our view should have been, undertaken in recent decades.

The chapter by Spence (1999) in another text on recovery from armed conflict (Harris) is appropriately titled "The Centrality of

Community-Led Recovery." Yet she quotes from UNRISD research to argue that, in postconflict situations to date, the major agencies involved have largely ignored local communities and grassroots organizations. Spence, having listed the elements of recovery as "economic reconstruction, political reconstruction, social reconstruction, repatriation and demobilization" (p. 210), writes,

> Social reconstruction after war is surely the most vital factor in any recovery process. Addressing the effects of conflict involves addressing the needs of those communities which experienced it and the healing of both those that perpetrated the war and those who suffered because of it. . . . Given that the human resource of any country is its most powerful factor, as it is people who provide the energies which enable political, economic and infrastructural reconstruction to take place, it is vital that recovery policies take heed of the effects of war on the civilian population.

Spence refers to several situations where it seems clear that community participation was a key to overall success in reconstruction, and that that participation was dependent on being sensitive to community needs and strengthening community structures.

Spence also makes the important point that wartime communities are neither merely the victims of conflict nor inactive during conflict. Many become empowered to become active participants in their own survival and recovery process, thus beginning the process of reconstruction and recovery before the fighting is finished (pp. 208–209). She later writes,

> The reality of post-conflict situations dictates that while governments and international agencies are still devising recovery and reconstruction policies, communities will already be experimenting with their own recovery processes. It is unrealistic to expect civilians

to await directions from above as to how reconstruction will operate. . . . It is vital that other actors in the recovery process recognize the importance of these self-generated schemes and cooperate with them rather than imposing what they consider to be more beneficial.

She further writes of communities that have been through a war,

> They may have discovered new ways of coping; the role of women in the community may have been strengthened as men are conscripted; they will be capable of adjusting to harsh conditions; and they will all share a common desire to return to normalcy as soon as possible. It is these abilities which will guide communities in their transition to recovery. (p. 218)

Whether Spence is implying that the typical community will require no outside support in the rebuilding or recovery process, but only recognition by the other agents of the importance of its role in the overall process, is not completely clear. She does argue that the reconstruction policies of governments and others need to be sensitive to community needs, flexible, and locally based; while the extent of empowerment and organizational development at the community level needs to be significant. While we fully agree with Spence that "the basis for recovery from disaster is community competence and an acknowledgement by other actors in the recovery process that involving communities will lead to stronger economic and social systems" (p. 220), we would argue that in many situations this community competence does not and will not occur spontaneously. (See, for example, Nee and Healy, 2003, regarding the postconflict situation in Cambodia.)

During conflict, communities are affected adversely in a range of ways. Members flee or are killed or conscripted, family and other systems are dislocated, individuals are traumatized and some give up hope, and community resources are damaged. While it is obviously also true that many individuals develop new coping skills and discover inner reserves, and that peoples are sometimes bound together in strong mutual dependence responses to difficult presenting situations, there is still a long struggle involved in overcoming adversities and rebuilding strong and healthy communities. And when this process does not start early, those who are able to do so will leave for the cities where recovery is faster and opportunities greater, or will even migrate abroad if it is possible to do so, thus further depriving the community of important human resources. Given the danger that many communities will languish in a recovery backwater for months or years, the challenge is to initiate community development programs that are feasible in the context and will bring communities quickly to the point where they can expect to be active participants in the wider reconstruction process. The questions then are, of what elements are such community development programs composed, and what staff do they require?

We agree fully with the following finding from the UNRISD War-torn Societies Project (1998, p. 16): "The main resources that allow a society to rebuild after a war lie undoubtedly in the people themselves, their resilience, creativity, pragmatism and capacity to adapt."

Local solutions and responses to rebuilding challenges are often more effective, cheaper, and more sustainable than nonlocal responses. In addition, they contribute to restoring dignity, confidence, and faith in local capacities to cope.

The question is, how do we ensure that this state of affairs becomes the prevailing reality? We suggest the following strategies as critical wherever feasible.

Some Specific Strategies for Community Rebuilding

The following strategies are derived in part from the literature but arise also from observations and experience in a range of contexts. The strategies listed below may be implemented by international and national intergovernmental and governmental agencies involved in the reconstruction process, NGOs, or individual workers; moreover, they all are capable of interpretation as strategies for implementation or as principles underpinning all action. The strategies are as follows:

- take steps to ensure that communities are active participants in as many of the reconstruction programs as possible;
- develop a community-based component within as many reconstruction programs as possible;
- ensure that all steps possible are taken to facilitate the healing of people and communities;
- be aware of what active communities are doing, acknowledge their actions, and incorporate them within wider plans wherever possible;
- be aware of which communities are inactive, assess why they are so, and encourage NGOs to implement appropriate programs to redress such situations;
- direct some basic resources to communities in need of rebuilding, and facilitate their involvement in their own rebuilding; and
- encourage the organization of training workshops for local leaders on community rebuilding, including, as appropriate, credit schemes, income-generation opportunities, and the formation of local organizations.

Case Example

A Local NGO in Postconflict Cambodia

Cambodia, basically a rural country, was devastated by a long period of war and oppression. The following comments regarding the process of rebuilding communities in the aftermath of conflict comes from the director of a local NGO that operated with international NGO support. The NGO worked through the initial period of survival (relief) and into the period of social change (development), recognizing that the seeds of change must be discovered in the villages, not imposed by the agency. Outsiders could only facilitate the process. The reconstruction of rural life after the violent conflict was depicted as a period of many challenges but also new opportunities.

Workers in the process of rebuilding communities had to bear in mind two facts about the country: that the kinship network was the essential support system available; and that this was a society with a very weak justice system where the power of local leaders was paramount. Survival for most families depended on finding a patron able to offer physical protection, economic assistance, and even moral support. This relationship imposed on the client obligations of loyalty to the patron in all circumstances, and labor assistance when requested. This system of patronage further entrenched the position of the powerful, but was seen by most people, especially the poor, as indispensable.

However, the traditional network of relationships had been sorely tested by conflict and, in the aftermath of the conflict, was further tested by the growth of the cash economy, the threat of HIV/AIDS, and external material assistance. Moreover, the experience of conflict and oppression had entrenched attitudes of uncertainty and hopelessness, resulting in people waiting for others to provide the answers to their needs rather than seeking them themselves. Indeed, all aspects of community culture had been disrupted by war. Corruption had become a survival strategy for many, and an unknown number of people were suffering from traumatic experiences; levels of trust were extremely low; and a "system of lies" was a common method of handling situations, especially by authorities, thus further damaging relationships.

During the 1990s, international aid was greatly needed, and both the aid received and the hope of it coming resulted in high levels of dependency and so an undermining of development potential. Most aid agencies had little understanding of community realities. INGOs even began to be seen by locals as potential patrons, although they were unaware of this happening. Gradually, however, INGOs rightly identified the rebuilding of civil society as a priority, and they facilitated the emergence of an estimated 800 local NGOs by 2003. It was expected that these local NGOs would promote grassroots empowerment and maximize bottom-up development. In practice, these new indigenous organizations proved to be very fragile and too dependent on entering into contracts with overseas organizations. From the point of view of their staff, these NGOs were little more than a source of resources to provide for families. Inevitably distrust built between these NGOs and both their international partners and local government.

The NGO director making these comments and his agency sought an alternative path to change: one that began with people's desire for a better life. This meant facilitating a gradual change in attitudes, perceptions, and beliefs, and promoting an acceptance of the dignity and worth of all individuals. Rather than doing this in a direct manner, it was seen that it could be done by the way that skills and strategies were taught to local people—that is, demonstrated by the workers. It was also seen as particularly important to promote human rights because of the tradition that respect for status was much more important than respect for rights; however, the way in which this was done was also critical—it had to reflect people's experience and culture. It was best done where actions were initiated that were educative, such as involvement in conflict resolution locally.

The key to moving forward, however, was seen to be the restoring of trust, starting with small networks of trust that were gradually expanded. The second foundation for development was seen to be education. Both would need to be slow processes. The process began by building trust through encouraging the establishment of cooperatives around responding to needs, while building education into every step. A crucial part of this process was enabling local people to analyze and critique the prevailing system and possible solutions in order to identify the best way forward. A strategy developed for achieving this was one of moving from story to critical reflection. A concern is named within a group, the group encouraged to present it through story, and the presentation to be followed by reflection before any action is undertaken.

Village or community reconstruction will occur only when a critical mass become convinced that change is needed and possible, and can together choose the best way to act. The essential process is to locate and support purposeful networks, encouraging the growth of local initiatives. The role of the development practitioner in this is "learning, relating, listening, mentoring, and making new knowledge and experience available in a timely way." Sharing stories together may be a good starting point, including painful stories shared in community, this being also of therapeutic value. Encouraging a differentiation between past and present, encouraging visualizing the future, and sharing where training and other resources might be available were all important roles.

The logical starting point for networking is a web of interlinked grassroots associations, many of which in fact did exist. Existing associations deserve to be respected as independent organizations with goals, and not superceded by outsiders forming new organizations to suit their projects. Existing groups and new networks of such can be assisted and nurtured, promoting trust and solidarity, and promoting also the inclusion of vulnerable and isolated persons. These grassroots organizations can be enabled to network with government departments, to link with the institutions of society, and ultimately to influence developments at this level, for example by challenging serious corruption.

As the networks of local associations strengthen, they will be able to ensure food security, shelter, protection under the law, and access to national health and education systems. They will have developed the ability to negotiate effectively. However, this will occur only gradually and with the strengthening of local community bonds and structures. This whole process begins with a social worker "mentoring key individuals within the community."

There are, according to this report, no easy answers. "The move beyond violent solutions begins with the insight and reflection of women and men capable of imagining that life could be different, and capable of acting together to make a difference to their immediate world."

(Example from Nee and Healy, 2003.)

Securing and Maintaining Peace and Promoting Reconciliation

The pursuit of peace has not been a common theme in national or international social work. One social work educator who spoke and wrote of it frequently in the 1980s was Sanders (1985, 1988), while Healy (2001, p. 247) makes a brief reference to "peace and conflict studies" within social work. However, in this context the topic is of central importance, while the pursuit of peace here is not basically beyond social work's role in conflict resolution in other contexts. Certainly it is not sufficient for international social work to be involved in responding to the consequences of conflict; it should also be actively involved in promoting peace. While it is peace in a positive sense that needs ultimately to be achieved in postconflict situations, the immediate goal is commonly referred to as reconciliation. We shall therefore consider initially social work's involvement in the reconciliation process in postconflict situations. However, peace must also be sought, both to prevent future conflict and to build harmonious and cohesive societies within which strong and inclusive social development can occur, and that too is a challenge with which international social work can and should assist. Let us consider first the question of postconflict reconciliation.

Promoting Reconciliation in Postconflict Situations

Although they were writing in 1994, the words of social workers Norell and Walz (1994, p. 99) still seem to summarize the current state of affairs regarding reconciliation work at the local level:

> For the peacemaker, a major obstacle in moving toward a nonviolent resolution of civil conflict has been the inability of ethnic groups to forgive and reconcile previous incidents of violence. While efforts at international mediation have had some limited success in gaining cease fires, efforts to promote forgiveness and reconciliation, which would reduce future conflict, are less common. Currently, little is known about the process of reconciliation as an intervention to be used with ethnic groups in conflict.

Herrick and Meinert (1994, p. 130) in the same year lamented that neither the education nor traditional practice of social work were "designed to promote social harmony, prevent ethnic conflict, intervene in ethnic conflict, and deal with its consequences," including reconciliation work. Yet the importance of reconciliation cannot be overstated. Galtung wrote in 1995, in an article published in a UNRISD newsletter,

> If resolution and reconstruction are carried out without reconciliation, then all the traumas, hatred and damage done to the social structure and the culture of society will hit back, sooner or later. A society left deeply divided after war is a pathological society,

and this pathology will ultimately run its course.

We might start by clarifying the terminology related to this activity. Norell and Walz (1994, p. 100) suggest that "reconciliation is not only a matter of healing memories and receiving forgiveness," but also "a matter of changing structures in society that provoke, promote, and sustain violence." They define reconciliation as follows: "Reconciliation is the process one goes through to remove a particular type of conflict from one's life through forgiveness and altering the conditions that occasioned the conflict (e.g. structural changes)."

The first step in the process is mediation that is designed to halt the violence. This is followed by forgiveness—"a stage of reconciliation in which the victim lets go of the feelings of hate and anger toward the perpetrator for past acts of violence." It is hoped that victims who can forgive will trigger the impulse to repent in the perpetrator, and some form of repentance is almost always necessary for reconciliation to be achieved. Norell and Walz (1994, p. 102) write of this stage,

> Repentance, however, can occur only in the face of objective evidence of wrong-doing and the actual admission of guilt. Both sides must acknowledge the violence of aggression and the violence of retaliation. Some blurring of who is victim and who is aggressor often results from this process.

A further stage that often accompanies repentance is restitution. As the authors write, "Each culture tends to develop its own particular forms of restitution"; but restitution, whatever its form, "offers a way of restructuring the relationship between victim and perpetrator." The final stage in the reconciliation process is presented as follows:

> The final stage in reconciliation is the normalization of the relationship between previously warring parties. Each must get to the

place where societal business can be carried out without bearing baggage from the past. The history of past traumas may be recalled but is defused. Past traumas can no longer serve to build an ethnic group's identity or contribute to its solidarity. (Norell and Walz, 1994, p. 103)

A central outcome of the overall process is, in Maynard's (1997, p. 215) words, "rebuilding trust and the capacity to trust." Her words are well worth noting:

Betrayal during the course of combat, particularly in today's interpersonal warfare, undermines faith and confidence in others. Further, the process of dehumanizing the opposition diminishes its power and thus respect. Restoring the adversary's humanness and honor is an essential step in recovering from psychological trauma; it also plays a critical role in reestablishing interpersonal relationships and thus community-wide interaction. Renewed trust in a war-torn society includes general belief in the good intentions of other community members, reliance on them for common services, willingness to assume a responsible role in society, and commitment to the joint future of the community.

Reconciliation in conflict situations is undertaken at many levels. The peace process undertaken by the UN or others is an essential step toward reconciliation. The establishment of procedures through which war crimes and crimes against humanity can be prosecuted is also an important step. In the aftermath of the apartheid regime in South Africa, a Truth and Reconciliation Commission (TRC) was established "to promote nation building, national unity and reconciliation among all South African citizens" (Mamphiswana and Netshiswinzhe, 1999, p. 66). They continue: "The crux of the TRC . . . is that of healing the wounded and traumatized nation through disclosing the crimes

committed during the late apartheid days" (p. 67). Similar bodies were established in El Salvador, Rwanda, and East Timor, and one is at last in the process of being established in Cambodia—long after the cessation of conflict. Our concern here, however, is with the reconciliation process at the local level, where all evidence suggests that whether it takes place or not is due almost entirely to the insights and abilities of both social workers at this level and members of the communities previously embroiled in conflict. While few workers have been trained in the area to date, many do possess the insights and basic skills to implement a program.

The UNHCR has advocated for some years the importance of providing workers and community leaders with training in this area. In 1995, the UNHCR Executive Committee stated that the committee

recognises the role refugee community education can play in national reconciliation and encourages UNHCR, in cooperation with other organizations, to strengthen its efforts in assisting host country governments to ensure the access of refugees to education, including the introduction into such programmes of elements of education for peace and human rights. (UNHCR, 1997)

A workshop convened by the UNHCR in 1997 focused both on training for a general role in the field of peace and reconciliation, and for specialized training of workers who might become part of mobile peace troupes. Training is clearly a high priority in this area, but let us turn our attention to the strategies frequently suggested for workers in the field.

Reconciliation Through Engaging in Common Tasks

A strategy frequently suggested is encouraging members of the previously warring groups to work together in the reconstruction process. Maynard (1997, p. 214) writes that "relief and development projects may have trust-building attributes." She later comments that "direct physical engagement in rehabilitation activities serves as a relatively safe step toward committing to the future of the community" (p. 220). Herrick and Meinert (1994, p. 130) write that "it is important to engage in activities whereby both parties to the conflict develop some mutual responsibility for what is taking place." Finally, Harris (1999, p. 48) quotes Johan Galtung as saying, in 1995, that "the tasks of conflict resolution, post-war reconstruction, and national reconciliation should ideally be approached together, with the conflicting parties reconciled by working together on resolution and reconstruction."

Strategies to Encourage Forgiveness

Norell and Walz (1994, p. 101) write,

The capacity to forgive can be developed in several ways. It can be facilitated through increasing the victim's understanding and insight into the aggressor's situation and conditions; it can be achieved through the victim's honest desire to end the conflagration by stepping forward to break the cycle of violence; and it can also come through the victim's faith or spiritual beliefs.

However it comes, what is important is that community members develop an ability to forgive those who they believe to have been the perpetrators of violence. This is neither an easy nor a quick process, but social workers can engage in encouraging and enabling the first steps to be taken.

Conflict Resolution Strategies

The importance of conflict resolution is obvious, and the helping professions have considerable experience generally in this area. In order to promote conflict resolution, writers

suggest the training of community leaders in the process, and the organizing of the community for this purpose. It is particularly important to establish situations where intergroup dialogue can occur.

Educational Strategies

The UNHCR's 1997 discussion paper places a strong emphasis on "education for peace, conflict resolution and human rights." It suggests that peace and human rights components can be inserted into a wide variety of education contexts, and gives as an example an education-for-peace case study from Tanzania (pp. 32ff.). In relation to human rights education, this paper emphasizes the need to focus on the values underpinning human rights and to encourage thinking in terms of responsibilities as well as rights. Maynard (1997) also advocated workshops on human rights.

Strategies for Practitioners in Their Day-to-Day Work

Norell and Walz (1994, pp. 108ff.) suggest a number of specific strategies for practitioners in the field, including the following:

Listening to individuals:

"It is important that victims of violence be allowed to tell their stories again and again. This deintensifies the trauma of their experience." This can also be encouraged on a group basis by establishing situations where victims can tell their stories to each other, thus creating a situation of "peer counseling."

Maintaining ethnicity:

"Individuals and ethnic groups need to feel secure in their ability to maintain their ethnicity before they can compromise with other ethnic groups. Political and religious leaders ignore, and even at times denigrate ethnicity. But ethnicity is important to most participants."

Encouraging compassion and attention:

These authors point out that quick action is often not sustainable. "Compassionate practitioners need to feel or suffer with those with whom they work," while avoiding overidentification with the victim.

Seeking traditional models of reconciliation:

"Within cultures, there are time-honored ways to promote the resolution of conflict and reconciliation between parties. To seek, honor and lift up these processes will strengthen reconciliation within the culture."

While reconciliation work has certainly not received the attention it needs and requires more research, workers in the field have been successfully using a range of strategies of which the international worker in the current climate needs to be aware. (Readers are referred to the social integration and cohesion section in Chapter 4 for material on strategies that may also be relevant in the reconciliation process.)

Building Cohesive and Harmonious Societies

Within the field of peace and war or conflict, the emphasis should clearly be on the utilization of strategies that will contribute to building harmonious relations, maintaining peace, and so preventing conflict. It is both a preventative and a developmental approach, with indeed the focus on the latter as societies seek to develop (an ongoing process) in ways that will promote social cohesion.

The key goal in achieving social cohesion (or social integration or social harmony) is to ensure that a society is fully inclusive in all its dimensions and at all levels. As the World Summit for Social Development (United Nations, 1995, p. 68) put it,

The aim of social integration is to create "a society for all," in which every individual, each with rights and responsibilities, has an active role to play. Such an inclusive society must be based on respect for all human rights and fundamental freedoms, cultural and religious diversity, social justice and the special needs of vulnerable and disadvantaged groups, democratic participation and the rule of law. The pluralistic nature of most societies has at times resulted in problems for the different groups to achieve and maintain harmony and cooperation, and to have equal access to all resources in society. Full recognition of each individual's rights in the context of the rule of law has not always been fully guaranteed. Since the founding of the United Nations, this quest for humane, stable, tolerant and just societies has shown a mixed record at best.

In a paper prepared at UNRISD for this summit, Bangura (1994) discusses the complex interaction between "identity, solidarity and modernization." He suggests that "to capture the benefits of modernization, societies are expected to break out of the boundaries of ethnicity, embrace a secular nation state identity, develop a rational-scientific view of development and treat individuals as autonomous entities."

However, as he goes on to say, the process of modernization affects different groups in a society differently, and "when benefits and costs seem to correspond to ethnic, racial or religious affinities, people may come to see development in terms of those cleavages. Economic recession and programmes of stabilization and restructuring may, in turn, deepen such cleavages" (p. 2).

Bangura explores the roles of ethnic, religious, and political identity in relation to social integration and concludes,

Ethnicity and religious behaviour are forms of consciousness that often represent appropriate responses to the chaotic conditions of modern life. They provide richness to the human condition which the impersonal forms of modernity cannot handle. But it is evident also that most present-day conflicts and wars tend to be fuelled by particularistic values and identities.

There is indeed a long history of intrastate instability and conflict, and many writers over the years have addressed this topic (e.g., Enloe, 1973; Smith, 1983). Most of this discussion has been concerned with the developing world. In developed countries, the focus historically has been on either community relations across racial and ethnic social divisions inherited from the past, or on the challenges of building cohesive, harmonious, and successful multicultural societies in the face of highly diverse populations created by immigration programs or, more recently, influxes of illegal immigrants and asylum seekers. Whatever the nature or analysis of situations giving rise to concerns about social cohesion or integration, the emphasis invariably comes down to what intervention strategies are feasible and likely to be successful in such contexts. How do social workers and others go about the task of building successful societies in the face of significant pluralism? Let us look at some responses to this question.

The World Summit on Social Development (United Nations, 1995) suggested a number of key areas of action:

governments should promote and protect all human rights and fundamental freedoms, including the right to development (p. 69);

governments should encourage the fullest possible participation in society (p. 70);

governments should act to eliminate discrimination and promote tolerance and mutual respect (p. 71);

governments should "promote equality and social justice" (p. 72); and

governments should respond to the special needs of the vulnerable and disadvantaged groups (p. 73).

Bangura (1994, pp. 32ff.) places the emphasis on, first, socioeconomic development—for example, "Policies of economic development need to be sensitive to problems of marginalization, social inequalities and political disequilibrium for development itself to be sustainable." In this context, Bangura examines the common redistribution policies:

The major redistributive policies attempted in most plural societies have been based on proportionality and affirmative action. The first type seeks to ensure that jobs, political appointments, educational opportunities and public investment programmes are distributed in ways that reflect population ratios. This involves the use of quotas, subsidies and special funds for disadvantaged groups. The second type, though similar to the first, seeks primarily to redress imbalances created by discriminatory practices, often of a historical nature. In this case, quotas, subsidies, special funds and other forms of redistributive mechanisms may be used to reach the disadvantaged population, but the aim is not to create ethnic balance. (p. 33)

Bangura's second emphasis is on institutional changes: "The second broad area relates to institutional changes and policies to ensure that groups do not feel alienated from vital political processes that shape their lives" (p. 35). In this context, Bangura focuses particularly on representation and participation. His final conclusion is worth noting:

This discussion demonstrates that no single policy is sufficient to address the problems of social order, political stability and participation in ethnically plural societies. At the same time, no ethnically plural society is likely to avoid using the policies of devolution and power sharing in the long run if it is to enjoy political stability and an acceptable level of social cohesion. However, such policies may have to reflect the historical experiences and social structures of individual societies and have to be based on solid foundations of civic and common citizenship rights. A policy that is based exclusively on ethnic group rights is likely to freeze relations between groups, promote ethnic chauvinism, entrench group privileges, punish individuals who seek to straddle or transcend group politics, and frustrate social interactions based on individual interests. (p. 39)

An Australian scholar, McAllister (1990, summary page 1), reviewed the literature on community relations in terms of Australia's multicultural policies, and drew the following conclusions. He identified four broad approaches to intervention:

Encouraging contact between individuals, through voluntary and informal activities, for example, or through education and housing policies;

Group representation, involving ethnic pressure and interest groups acting on behalf of particular communities, individual representation and the promotion of role models;

Promoting inter-group co-operation, encompassing community education, the dissemination of positive information through the media, and the spreading of superordinate goals such as national unity or citizenship; and finally,

The promulgation of *justiciable rights,* such as equal opportunity, affirmative action

and contract compliance legislation, and anti-propaganda legislation.

He then went on to conclude that three particular intervention strategies had the best chance of success (1990, summary page 2):

Altering the size, distribution and resources available to ethnic pressure and interest groups, as well as increasing individual representation, together form a *representational strategy;*

Combining role models and superordinate goals together form the basic components of a *mass media campaign* to improve community relations; and

Community education provides the basis for an intervention strategy based on *local communities,* targeted for their potential for intergroup conflict.

Many practitioners and scholars have concluded that a bottom-up approach of strengthening minority groups is also of great importance, on the premise that a strong and cohesive ethnic/racial/religious or whatever group will be much better able to participate in the broader society, whether as consumers of goods and services, including employment opportunities, or as contributors to a society's development.

While these last suggested strategies have been developed in, for example, western societies built on large-scale immigration, the need is to assess the applicability of these to the pluralistic, postconflict developing society.

Case Examples

Education for Peace Among Refugees in Tanzania

The first of these case examples concerns a program run by the UNHCR designed to promote peace between opposing groups of refugees occupying the same refugee camps in Tanzania. There were several aspects to the program.

First, regular meetings were convened of community representatives. The aim was to build dialogue between groups and help the community to work together for a common good.

Second, community centers were constructed in each camp as a practical demonstration that groups had to work together, initially in deciding how to build and utilize these centers.

Third, a network was established to promote cross-group dialogue. While initially somewhat artificial, in time this became a true forum for dialogue and a vehicle for reconciliation.

Fourth, a cross-camp "Drawing for Peace" competition was introduced for schoolchildren. The drawings were displayed in each camp and viewers invited to cast a vote. These excited a lot of discussion.

Some women from the camps proposed a peace initiative of their own, in the form of groups discussing the impact of war on their children and their own reactions to this.

The program also prompted a regional conference for religious leaders as a peace initiative.

In reporting on the above developments, the UNHCR points out that "there were many in the camps who saw any peace initiative as threatening or even 'collaborating with the enemy.' These people intimidated the 'peace activists,' threatening their well-being, security, and, in some cases, their lives."

(Example from UNHCR, 1997, p. 45.)

Education for Peace in Sri Lanka

In this program, the government, assisted by UNICEF, established an "Education for Conflict Resolution" program. A core group of people were trained in some of the different forms of conflict resolution used in various countries, and eventually produced ten different training manuals aimed at principals, teacher trainees, teachers, and pupils. These were written in a form that was in harmony with Sri Lankan culture, especially Buddhist culture and the cooperative principles common to village life. They drew also on meditation designed to create a sense of inner peace.

In 1992–94, the project trained 3,500 principals, 500 master teachers, 3,000 teachers, and 7,500 student leaders. These in turn have reached approximately 420,000 of Sri Lanka's 4.5 million schoolchildren. In 1995 the program moved also into a media campaign to reach parents and the community as a whole.

(Example from UNICEF, 1996, p. 32.)

Peace Education in Somalia

Within a local region with no formal judicial structures, communities have utilized traditional forms of justice to resolve many of the issues arising from the war, such as damage to livestock and repatriation of family members. Peace conferences have been organized by communities and officiated over by tribal elders. An INGO has assisted the process by providing transport to these peace talks as required. The scheme, while small-scale and local, has apparently been quite successful. Minimal external action was needed to initiate and facilitate the process, and what eventuated was essentially consistent with local cultural tradition.

(Example from UNHCR, 1998.)

Conclusion

The involvement of members of the social work profession in conflict and postconflict situations on a relatively significant scale is comparatively new, resulting to a very large degree from the changes to conflict that have occurred since the late 1980s and which are discussed in the previous chapter. Nonetheless, that involvement by the profession is still far less than it should be and than it is likely to be in the near future.

Even without considering the direct involvement of social workers in theaters of conflict and postconflict reconstruction, it would seem essential that all members of the profession should possess some understanding of modern conflict; its causes, extent, and nature; but particularly of its impact on people's well-being across the globe. The impact of modern warfare has been enormous and extensive. The breadth of the impact covers the soldiers affected by conflict who eventually return home, and their family members; civilians caught up in conflict and obliged to live for many decades with its horrific consequences; the impact on the numbers of persons displaced by conflict, who can be found scattered across the globe as refugees and asylum seekers; the economic and political impact of conflict on the majority of countries; and even the impact that constant and vivid monitoring of conflict situations by the media has on many viewers. Social workers need an understanding of this disturbing phenomenon, whether or not they might ever find themselves working in this field.

The three key areas in which increasing numbers of social workers will hopefully be involved are

building peace, at the preventative and remedial levels, through for example reconciliation projects and programs to enhance social cohesion;

healing the wounds of conflict, wherever the many victims of conflict are to be found and whatever the nature and causes of their suffering; and

rebuilding the lives of families and communities, but especially of communities given the dimensions and centrality of that need.

While it has become increasingly clear as to what should be done in this field, there is still much to learn regarding how best to approach the presenting needs. Although the extent of social work experience in the field has been increasing steadily, very little of that experience has been documented and even less utilized in framing appropriate intervention strategies. What is now required is

pulling together extant experience systematically;

carrying out more research in this field; and

devoting more resources to teaching and training in this area.

Following on Chapter 9's overview of the conflict and postconflict situations, this chapter has considered the past and possible future roles of social work, but we are well aware that the available written materials on which to base the chapter, especially material emerging from social work theory or practice, have been relatively limited, despite the now considerable field experience.

We trust that this chapter will inspire more social workers to consider this whole field carefully from a social work perspective, and that some graduates will be led to seek employment in this extremely needy field.

Summary

- International social work in postconflict reconstruction may be guided by the integrated-perspectives approach, following certain principles and incorporating selected strategies. Central to it are psychosocial programs and community rebuilding.

- The delivery of psychosocial programs involves a good understanding of traumatic war experiences in cultural contexts, and accordingly developing needs-based responses to effectively work with the victims of trauma so as to facilitate their psychosocial recovery.

- Although often given less importance, community rebuilding is a fundamental activity in the postconflict situation, and such an activity should be undertaken by valuing and involving local people, resources, and solutions.

- Security and maintaining peace involves the process of reconciliation, conflict resolution, and building harmonious relations at all levels.

Questions and Topics for Discussion

- Discuss the suggested strategies for responding to postconflict situations.

- In light of the discussion of psychosocial programs and community rebuilding, what do you consider to be the critical issues in their implementation in the postconflict situation?

- Why do you think there seems to be minimal emphasis on community rebuilding, and how might this be rectified?

- In your view, what are the three most important strategies in community rebuilding?

- What are the importance and the potential of reconciliation work in the aftermath of recent conflicts of which you have some awareness?

Possible Areas for Research Projects

- Carry out a critical analysis of the current understanding of community development and its potential application to community rebuilding in the postconflict context.

- Consider the literature on the helping professions' roles in conflict resolution and reconciliation work generally, and determine their application to the postconflict context.

- Consider Western understanding of and responses to post-traumatic stress disorder, and their relevance to postconflict reconstruction work in non-Western contexts.

- Examine the possible reasons for the perceived low emphasis on community rebuilding, and devise strategies to respond.

- If possible, document the experiences of some humanitarian aid workers with a view to learning lessons for guiding future work.

- Systematically document the process of reconciliation and securing peace in postconflict situations.

Further Reading

Danieli, Y., Rodley, N. S., & Welsæth, L. (Eds.). (1996). *International responses to traumatic stress: Humanitarianism, human rights, justice, peace and development.* New York: Baywood.

Kumar, K. (Ed.). (1997). *Rebuilding societies after civil war: Critical roles for international assistance.* Boulder, CO: Lynne Rienner.

UNRISD. (1998). *Report on war-torn societies project.* Geneva: Author.

11

The Field of Displacement and Forced Migration: Background and Issues

One consequence of many situations confronting the modern world, such as conflict, natural disasters, and ecological degradation, is the displacement of millions of people from their homes, social support structures, means of livelihood, and often country. These peoples have been referred to as the world's *displaced persons, the uprooted,* or *forced migrants.* Whatever term is used, the needs presented by these people are frequently massive, complex, and exceedingly difficult to resolve. The field of forced migration has attracted many social workers, since at least World War II, who have participated in the international community's response, as well as in local responses, to these forced migrants. However, as most countries today possess at least some of these people, usually as either displaced persons or asylum seekers, this is also an international concern that has reached into social workers' day-to-day workplace in almost every country. As a result of considerable intervention among displaced persons, both internationally and locally, a huge amount of practice experience has been acquired, and one purpose of this and the following chapter

is to give newcomers to this field a sense of what working in this field of international social work involves.

The chapter is divided into two main parts. The first part presents the forced migration situation as it confronts us today, but with some reflection on developments in this field since World War II. In the second part of the chapter we engage in a critical analysis of the field, focusing on causal factors and factors influencing the nature of global and local responses and their consequences. This leads us to the importance of possessing an appropriate conceptual framework for analyzing situations and intervening in this field, and we turn to our integrated-perspectives approach as providing that framework.

Forced Migration: The Presenting Situation and Its Background

The field of practice covered in this chapter is diverse and therefore difficult to conceptualize in

Learning Objectives

- To understand the concept, nature, types, and extent of forced migration.

- To understand the plight of the displaced and other forced migrants, and of common international, government, and public reactions to that plight.

- To develop a beginning appreciation of the situations in which forced migrants are often placed, the implications of these, and feasible positive responses to them.

- To analyze forced migration situations by applying the integrated-perspectives approach so as to understand the broad causes of displacement and migration and to develop suitable responses.

- To understand various forced migration situations from the point of view of social work intervention.

an overall sense. Yet all the various situations covered by the term "forced migrants" have elements in common, such as similar causes, characteristics, and consequences; and call for a range of relatively similar responses from social workers and other members of the helping professions. The field of forced migration is an extremely complex one in the modern world, presenting major legal, administrative, and humanitarian dilemmas, and affecting the lives of tens of millions of people every year. (On the refugee crisis generally, see Zolberg, Suhrke, and Aguayo, 1989, and Kushner and Knox, 1999.) Moreover, it has in recent times proved to be a situation where the international community and individual governments have extreme difficulty in determining and implementing an adequate, in humanitarian terms, yet politically acceptable response.

The Nature of Forced Migration in the Contemporary World

We are using the term "forced migration" to describe a wide range of situations. The difficulty in doing so, however, is that the concept of *force* becomes both broad and vague. The force behind population movements may be economic, social,

ecological, or political in nature, sometimes referred to in the migration field as *push factors*, as distinct from *pull factors*. Such migration will vary considerably in the degree of force, and therefore in terms of its importance as a push factor; and the situations to which forced migration can give rise vary. The term *forced migration* is not, therefore, an ideal one. What we are seeking to do is to distinguish this broad population of so-called forced migrants from the populations of voluntary, official, and relatively permanent migrants, who set out to change their country of residence, and short-term travelers such as tourists. A World Council of Churches publication (WCC, 1996, p. 10) identifies the common characteristics of those uprooted by force as follows:

People leave their communities for many reasons and are called different names—refugees, internally displaced, asylum seekers, economic migrants. As churches, we lift up those who are compelled by severe political, economic and social conditions to leave their land and their culture—regardless of the labels they are given by others. Uprooted people are those forced to leave their communities: those who flee because of persecution and war, those who are forcibly displaced because of environmental devastation and those who are compelled to seek sustenance in a city or abroad because they cannot survive at home.

Another publication on forced displacement (DeMartino and Buchwald, 1996, pp. 195–96) summarizes the impact on people of being forcibly displaced:

> Forced displacement is one of the most stressful human experiences. The chief causes of displacement—conflict, persecution, violence, or social and political collapse—very often result in multiple and prolonged exposure to extreme stress. While fearing for their lives, refugees also feel a deep sense of humiliation and extreme helplessness. They long not only for a safe haven, food, shelter, and medical first aid, but also for social justice, legal protection, and encouragement to restore their sense of community, their shattered human dignity, and their personal identity.

Our own definition of forced migration is the following:

> By forced migration we mean migration situations where a significant force—political, economic, or social in nature—is exerted on people to leave their habitual place of residence, in circumstances often of extreme stress, resulting in departure for a comparatively unknown destination and under conditions of travel and entry that frequently offer little if any security to those migrating.

There are four critical elements in this definition, each of which is of major significance when it comes to responding to the needs of forced migrants. The first element is the existence of a degree of force. People seldom engage in migration lightly, for the majority of people have a strong attachment to a home. The fact that migration is forced will also breed frustration and resentment against the prevailing forces, and make it more difficult to adapt

to a new situation because one is there, in a sense, under duress. The second element is that forced migration is always associated with a degree of stress, and often extreme stress, which often is the outcome of a period of highly traumatic experiences. The effects of stress and trauma are, therefore, often found among forced migrants. The third element is the fact that the destination is either completely unknown or vague. At one end of the spectrum, people leave under pressure with no sense of where they will end up; at the other end of the spectrum, people know that they are seeking freedom, security, a better future, and so on, and know vaguely that there are places or countries that offer these conditions, one of which they decide to seek out, but their whole plan is full of assumptions—about the destination, their reception, and their long-term future. The final element is the lack of security. Some forced migrants expect to be welcomed with open arms, but have no evidence that this will occur; while others anticipate hostility, resentment, and generally negative responses from receiving populations and governments, but still continue on in hope or aim to avoid discovery. The reality, however, is that the great majority of forced migrants exist, for often prolonged periods, in situations of significant insecurity. All four elements leave forced migrants far more vulnerable than other categories of migrants, and therefore in need of sensitive and sympathetic reception, which is in practice the opposite of what many receive from officialdom. It is, therefore, incumbent on the helping professions to try to remedy, or at least ameliorate, this unfortunate situation, difficult though this will often be.

The specific categories of "forced migrants" covered in this chapter are described by the following terminology: *displaced persons, asylum seekers, refugees, illegal immigrants,* and *migrant workers.* Let us consider the definition of each category and its size and nature in the contemporary situation.

Displaced Persons

The term *displaced persons* has come into regular usage in recent years. It is a term that covers several distinct categories of people, as set out in the diagram in Figure 11.1. Basically, however, it covers people whose movement away from their normal place of residence has not been of their free choice, being due to factors beyond their control. People are regularly displaced by war, conflict, invasion, and the like: basically they are fleeing imminent danger. Others are displaced by persecution or the fear of such, and such displacement occurs commonly under regimes where the human rights of some sections of the population are regularly abused. Displacement may also be caused by natural occurrences, whether sudden such as an earthquake, tsunami, volcanic eruption, or violent storm, or over a long period of natural change, such as desertification or salinity problems. It simply becomes impossible, either suddenly or gradually, for some people to survive in their previous place of abode, and many are thus compelled to move. Finally, some people are forcibly relocated as a result of development projects, such as major dam constructions (see Cernea and McDowell, 2000), or because of a government-imposed transmigration program (e.g., Indonesia).

Displacement may mean displacement to another part of one's country of residence, the so-called *internally* displaced persons, or across borders into a foreign country—the *externally* displaced. The subcategory of internally displaced persons has become one of growing concern in the last decade or so. In its 1997/1998 report, the UNHCR (1997/1998, p. 99) suggested the following definition of internal displacement:

In this discussion, the term "internally displaced people" will be used to denote those persons who, as a result of persecution, armed conflict or violence, have been forced to abandon their homes and leave their usual place of residence, and who remain within the borders of their own country.

By 1995, the UNHCR was reporting that the numbers of the internally displaced exceeded the numbers of refugees, who, under the UN's 1951 definition, are externally displaced. However, of the more than 15 million internally displaced persons, the UNHCR was then accepting responsibility for only 6 million. In 1999, the UNHCR reported that there were an estimated 20 to 25 million internally displaced persons around the globe, stating, "Millions of displaced persons get only passing attention from the international community" (Wilkinson, 1999, p. 5). Many of these people are invisible, while others are out of reach of the international community for political reasons. However, the overriding reason for ignoring the plight of most of these people is that the international community is not able, or willing, to amass the resources required to take action. The UNHCR has in fact adopted a 30-point set of principles entitled *Guiding Principles on Internal Displacement* to guide the behavior of nations (principles that to date have been largely ignored), together with a set of criteria that limits the UN's own involvement in such situations (UNHCR, 1999, p. 11). The number of internally displaced persons of concern to the UNHCR had fallen to 5.3 million at the end of 2003, out of a total population of concern of 17.1 million (UNHCR, 2004, p. 6). (For case studies of the internally displaced, see Cohen and Deng, 1998.)

Asylum Seekers

Some of those who are displaced across borders apply to the government of the country in which they find themselves, or to the UN, for asylum or refugee status. They are asking that their reasons for leaving their country of origin and entering that other country be recognized as

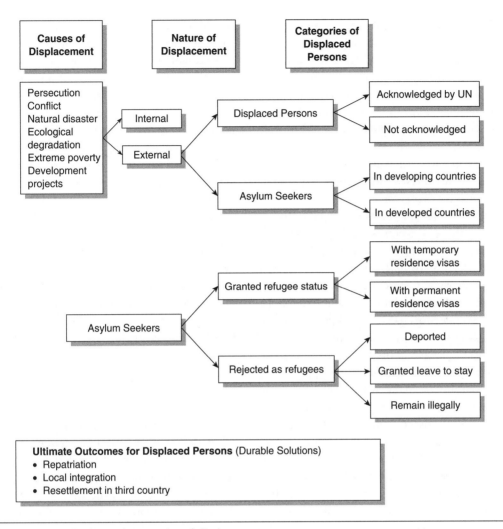

Figure 11.1   Causes and categories of displacement

valid reasons for seeking asylum, and that they be granted refugee status under the 1951 UN Convention and Protocol Relating to the Status of Refugees (this Convention defines refugees and provides a comprehensive codification of their rights internationally) and temporary residence under the protection of the Convention. Whether asylum is granted or not will clearly have major significance for such people. However, as the UNHCR pointed out in 1993,

There is a gap between the individual's right to seek asylum (Universal Declaration of

Human Rights, Article 14 [1]) and the state's discretion in providing it. In this legal no-man's land, each state makes its own decisions as to whom it will admit and why. (p. 32)

Asylum seekers have been defined within the European Union as follows: "Asylum seekers are persons who consider themselves as refugees and who seek, therefore, asylum as well as recognition of their refugee status in the territory of another state (Kumin, 1998, p. 7).

However, a distinction is being made, in reality, between those who claim asylum in a developing country and those who reach a western country before making application for asylum. The western world tends to regard the former population as genuine asylum seekers, presumably because they claim asylum in the first possible country after fleeing, and the latter population as bogus in the sense that what really drives them is not a need for asylum but a desire to settle in a western country. The logic applied is this: Why otherwise would they not request asylum at the first possible opportunity?

A major reason for western governments making this distinction is the huge increase in asylum-seeker numbers from the 1970s to the early 2000s. (Since 2003, the numbers of asylum seekers arriving in western countries have begun to fall.) Estimated asylum applications in Europe went from approximately 13,000 per year at the beginning of the 1970s to approximately 200,000 per year at the end of the 1980s. In 2003, France had the largest number, with 59,800 applications, followed by Germany with 50,600, and the United Kingdom with 49,400. Canada and the United States also experienced a steady rise in the number of claimants in this period. Overall claims in Canada rose from 5,000 in 1983 to 40,000 in 1988 and were 31,900 in 2003. In the United States, the increase was from some 20,000 in 1983 to some 100,000 in 1989. However, by 2003 numbers had fallen to 43,300. The Australian experience was similar but on a much smaller scale. While applications for asylum processed were in the hundreds during most of the 1980s, they rose to over 10,000 in 1990–91 and stood at 9,500 in 1999. "Since 1982, the major western receiving countries have received 8.7 million applications, peaking in 1992 at 858,000 submissions. During the entire period almost two million people were officially accepted as refugees and granted asylum, in the form either of permanent residence status or a temporary residence visa" (UNHCR, 2002, p. 13).

The whole area is highly controversial. Many western countries are inclined to treat these asylum seekers as illegal immigrants. While their applications are usually processed, as indeed they should be under international law, in many countries the applicants are held under inhumane conditions, in what is known as mandatory detention, while awaiting the outcome of their applications, with many suffering considerably from the overall experience. (See Mares, 2001, on the situation in Australia.) Many are held in prison-like reception centers, not permitted to work, and provided with only the most basic of health and education services. While those who are rejected may be deported or leave voluntarily, some become part of an underground population living in fear and deprivation. Even those granted asylum in the form of a temporary residence visa (often a three-year visa) are frequently made to live in virtual poverty by governments, their situations rendered humane in some situations by caring communities or NGOs. (On asylum in the industrialized world, see UNHCR, 2000, chap. 7.)

Refugees

The term *refugee* is technically confined to those asylum seekers who are granted refugee status under the terms of the 1951 UN refugee convention. Refugee status brings these people under the protection of the UN, or specifically the United Nations High Commissioner for Refugees (UNHCR); there have also been other populations not granted refugee status but designated "people of concern to the UNHCR," which designation brings with it a comparable level of protection and assistance. People granted refugee status may or may not receive asylum in a specific country; that is something that the UNHCR may have to seek for them, it being ultimately dependent on the goodwill of individual governments.

Under the 1951 UN Convention and Protocol Relating to the Status of Refugees, a refugee is defined as follows:

The term refugee shall apply to any person who . . . , owing to a well-founded fear of being persecuted for reasons of race, religion, nationality, membership of a particular social group or political opinion, is outside the country of his nationality and is unable or, owing to such fear, is unwilling to avail himself of the protection of that country; or who, not having a nationality and being outside the country of his former habitual residence as a result of such events, is unable or, owing to such fear, is unwilling to return to it.

The perceived problems with this definition, as they have emerged with time, are its exclusion of the internally displaced; its focus on persecution, which is not defined here or in other UN conventions, and which may not include, for example, victims of war; and its gender bias, in that it tends in most situations to be males who are, or are seen to be, the direct focus of persecution, despite the fact that women and children inevitably suffer extensively. The consensus of opinion today, however, is that if a new definition was sought from the international community, any agreed definition would be more restrictive than the existing one, such is the concern in many countries of being inundated by refugees.

Illegal Immigrants

Illegal immigrants are those who have entered into a jurisdiction that is neither their own by birth or citizenship nor one to which they have a right of entry without obtaining permission in the form of a valid entry visa. The difficulty arises from the diversity of this population. For example, asylum seekers in particular circumstances may be said to have no inherent right to cross the border illegally and request asylum, being instead declared to be illegal immigrants and therefore subject to whatever consequences exist for those entering illegally. A second category of illegal immigrants is composed of those who enter a country illegally for work purposes as migrant workers, but in situations where the government, because of its desire to attract workers, is not strict about

enforcing entry requirements. While generally permitting such entry for labor force purposes, those entering are, strictly speaking, illegal immigrants, possessing no rights and subject to periodic crackdowns (usually for political reasons) on illegal immigrants and forced deportation. A third category of illegal immigrants is composed of those who enter a country, bypassing entry requirements, with the intention of exploiting what that country has to offer or in order to commit criminal acts in that country. The final category consists of legal entrants who remain in the country after their temporary visa has expired—"the overstayers." These four categories of illegal immigrants are not always treated the same by the states that they have entered, or remained in, illegally.

While flows of illegal immigrants have a long history, a comparatively new and alarming development has been the huge increase in trafficking of human beings that involves illegal migration. In 2000, the UNHCR reported (Kumin, 2000, p. 19),

To be sure trafficking is hardly a new phenomenon, but experts believe it has ballooned into a $7 billion annual global business with links to the worldwide arms trade, drugs, prostitution and child abuse. The poor, the vulnerable, refugees and asylum seekers are all targeted, both by hardline traffickers who often recruit and move victims across national boundaries and then coerce them into activities which amount to little more than modern day slavery, or by somewhat more benign "smugglers" who promise to transport desperate "clients" into another country for a simple cash payment.

The government of the United States has estimated that "50,000 women and children are trafficked into that country each year to work as prostitutes" (Kumin, 2000, p. 19), and a similar situation prevails in Europe and, to a lesser degree, Australia. It is also a common phenomenon in the more developed parts of Asia. This is an area of major concern to many organizations and individuals. (Le Breton's 2003 book, *Trapped,* vividly documents human trafficking in the Brazilian context.)

Migrant Workers

Technically migrant workers are those who enter a country with legal work permits but no entitlement to permanent residence rights. They are accepted as migrant workers because of the country's need to expand its labor force, perhaps temporarily, but without an intention or desire to increase (and thus diversify) its population through a formal immigration program. Migrant worker visas are usually time-specific and may have a number of other requirements attached, such as inability to change employment without permission, bring immediate family members with them, or access certain facilities and social services available to others in that country. There is the constant danger of migrant workers being exploited and denied basic rights, and so becoming second-class residents, often barely tolerated by the general public. Our concern here is only with those people who are forced into going abroad to work for the very survival of themselves and their families, and who have minimal ability, without assistance, to avoid the exploitative nature of many local recruitment agencies and arrangements.

While the boundaries between the above five categories of forced migrants are at times difficult to delineate, for the reasons indicated, they are all extremely significant populations in the contemporary world, with each giving rise to situations of unacceptable erosion of rights and undermining of well-being that frequently require intervention. It is because social workers have been very much involved in these interventions that this field of activity is included here as a highly important aspect of international social work practice.

Forced Migration Movements and Numbers in Recent Times

Some formal arrangements for refugee protection and assistance were established between World Wars I and II; however, our focus here is on the post–World War II period. Since international arrangements for the protection of refugees were established after World War II, the scope and dimensions of situations coming broadly under the umbrella of displaced persons, or refugees and those in refugee-like situations, have increased enormously. As the UNHCR (2000, p. 275) puts it, "The dynamics of displacement have changed greatly over the half-century of UNHCR's existence. So too, have international responses to the problem of forced displacement." (Chapter 11 of this report is well worth reading on this topic.)

The three major changes that have occurred are that the concept of *refugee* has become far more complex, giving rise to the plurality of terms discussed above; that the numbers of so-called refugees have grown exponentially; and that the location of displacement today is predominantly within developing countries. Each of these three changes has altered the dynamics of international intervention and reduced the willingness and ability of particularly western nations to respond in the manner in which they were disposed to respond immediately after World War II. Let us consider each of these changes in more detail.

Refugees were initially seen as mainly European persons displaced during World War II or fleeing from communism. As such they were welcome for resettlement in western democratic countries. Then, as the causes of displacement diversified, so too did the perceptions of displaced persons. Some were seen as political refugees; others as economic refugees, who were simply desirous of reaching a country with a higher standard of living and better prospects for themselves and their children; while others again were seen as neither political nor economic refugees—for example, ecological refugees, as changes in local ecology resulted in displacement. The population was further divided between the internally and externally displaced. Hence it became difficult to view this diverse population as made up of individuals or categories possessing equal status, requiring a similar response, and being within the mandate of the same conventions or set of organizations. Furthermore, it was widely considered that authorities had to respond with care so as not to create a pull or incentive factor that would increase the numbers moving out of situations and requesting acceptance. Indeed, national governments and others spoke frequently of, and often acted on the basis of, the importance of deterrence in this context.

The second change was a massive increase in numbers of refugees and those in refugee-like situations. For example, when the UNHCR was formed in 1951, it was estimated that some 1.25 million people in various parts of the world came within its terms of reference; but by 1998, the UNHCR was caring for some 22 million people, and there were at least as many displaced persons who did not come under its mandate. As the UNHCR (1997/1998, p. 2) reported, "In total, some 50 million people around the world might legitimately be described as victims of forced displacement." And just as the numbers are huge, so too is the cost of caring for them— a cost which is seldom met in full by the governments asked to contribute to the UNHCR budget, thus leaving a proportion of refugees bereft. In 2001, the UNHCR reported that it was caring for some 23 million people, but by 2002 the number had fallen to 19.8 million "which included 12 million refugees, 6.3 million persons internally displaced within their own countries (IDPs) and other 'groups of concern,' 940,800 asylum seekers and 462,700 returnees" (UNHCR, 2002, p. 13). At the end of 2003, the total population of concern to the UNHCR stood at 17.1 million (UNHCR, 2004, p. 6).

The third significant change since World War II has been the change of location from predominantly Europe to the developing countries. In 2002, the UNHCR (2002, p. 13) reported, "Developing countries produced 86 percent of the world's refugees in the last decade, but also provided asylum for seven out of ten of those fleeing."

The occurrence of unstable regimes, blatant disregard of human rights, and civil wars have, in recent years, been mainly in developing countries, where the low levels of development and discontent with the economic and political situations have exacerbated adverse living conditions and contributed to the motivation to flee. There are several consequences of this change in location. First, refugees and displaced persons in developing countries are commonly found in situations where the logistics of bringing in and distributing humanitarian aid, and of providing protection, are such that many displaced persons are neither assisted nor protected, with casualty rates among such people increasing greatly in recent times. Even the workers in these contexts are in greater danger than was previously the case, and there are frequent casualties among their ranks. A second consequence is that those fleeing will, if possible, bypass neighboring developing countries and attempt to reach a western country—these are the so-called *jet age refugees.* This frustrates western nations and leads them to question the bona fides of the people involved, in the sense that if what they sought was refuge, why did they not request it in the nearest country? It is seen in the West as better for all concerned, but especially for westerners, if refugees travel only to a neighboring developing country and there seek asylum. A third consequence is that the general public in the Western world is not nearly as understanding and accepting of, or sympathetic toward, such people as they were of those fleeing communism; and these attitudes militate against western governments appearing to be too accepting of such refugees or asylum seekers. Moreover, in some western countries many members of the general public clearly feel threatened, economically and socially, by the well-publicized influx of displaced persons. And even if the public does not lack sympathy for such people in general terms, they seemingly become tired of the endless demands on their pockets and patience, resulting in what is termed "compassion fatigue."

The precise causes of contemporary movements are sometimes difficult to identify, and we are largely left to assume that they reflect the realities of the modern world. These realities are those of modern civil wars, human rights abuses, unstable governance, increasing severity of natural and ecological disasters, growing patterns of socioeconomic inequality, and highly uneven levels of development. How far each of these factors contributes to the forms of mobility being discussed is impossible to say; but it is logical to argue that each factor will contribute to decisions to leave in at least some situations or countries, with the destinations being mainly the more advanced, more secure, and more prosperous countries. Other factors, such as global crime and terrorism, will have minimal effects in numerical terms but can have a disastrous impact in other ways, as recent events have demonstrated. DeMartino and Buchwald (1996, p. 195) argue that "most of today's forced displacements are caused by armed conflict," and that "threats and persecution are other main causes of refugee movements."

We need also to be aware, in general terms, of the likely consequences of such movements, in which basically four specific categories of actors are involved. Two sets of actors are countries, namely the countries from which people are moving and the countries to which they move; and the consequences in both cases would seem to be mixed. First, the countries of origin may lose some of their more enterprising citizens with the abilities and initiative to make a significant contribution to those countries; on the other hand, those who successfully locate elsewhere may send large amounts of remittances to relatives and communities back home, thus contributing significantly to the local economy and to levels of well-being. The receiving countries, for their part, have the high initial costs of resettling refugees, processing asylum seekers, or seeking out illegal arrivals, but those who remain tend to integrate and become at least eventually net contributors to the economy, sometimes even displaying above-average entrepreneurial flare and even an inventive capacity. Since the early 1990s, the overall numbers of asylum seekers, the numbers permitted to work,

and the numbers finally permitted to stay are all highly relevant factors in the cost-benefit equation. So how the costs and benefits balance out, for both categories of countries overall and for individual countries, will vary greatly no doubt, but there is a widespread sense in the research literature that both sets of countries tend on the whole to experience net gain, at least most of the time. On the other hand, the prevailing sentiment among the general public in most receiving countries today is that they are being manipulated and exploited, subjected to huge financial costs, and exposed to the threat of diseases, such as tuberculosis, and to crime or terrorism; and these prevailing sentiments do not augur well for future social cohesion nationally and peaceful relations internationally. (See, for example, Huntington, 2002, pp. 198–206.)

The third and fourth categories of actors involved are the people, namely the family and fellow community members who are left behind, and those who move away. How do these categories of persons fare on the whole? Once again there seem invariably to be pluses and minuses. It is difficult for those who remain behind to accept with equanimity the departure of their relatives and friends, although in these days "the tyranny of distance" is not nearly as great as it used to be. On the other hand, possessing contacts in other parts of the world can be advantageous. These relatives and friends may, for example, periodically remit home a part of their earnings or even sponsor others to join them abroad. It is, however, the experiences of the fourth and final category of actors that is the most significant and of greatest concern in this text—those engaged in such mobility. Here too many writers present a cost-benefit analysis, but to the workers involved with these people it is apparent that the costs, for at least a significant proportion of people, are high indeed. First, it is seldom easy to leave one's home and kin. Second, the travel experience for these people is anything but straightforward. They often live in constant fear of detection, arrest, imprisonment, deportation, and so on. They may exist for long periods in very difficult circumstances, such as those that many refugee camps and asylum-seeker holding centers represent. Third, if these people are in a community illegally, they live in fear of being apprehended; may face discrimination, exploitation, and even forms of blackmail; and are afraid that if they use hospital and other essential facilities they will be detected and deported. If and when they are granted some form of legal status, the early years of struggling to save some money from a low income, to be divided between those back home and set aside to secure their own future, are extremely difficult ones, often involving great sacrifices and periods of ill health, depression, and despair. If they do ultimately succeed, the years leading up to that point may have taken a toll that no successes will ever fully compensate for, and they will commonly find themselves projecting the real rewards of migration onto their children, desperately hoping that they will not let them down by making them feel that all their sacrifices have been for nothing.

Recent Forced Migration in Africa

The situation in Africa has been selected for highlighting because it most clearly typifies what is happening in the field of forced migration, albeit at the extreme end of a continuum. The following is based largely on the presentation of "Africa at a Crossroads" by the UNHCR (Wilkinson, 2003), although there is a considerable literature and media coverage on many aspects of recent civil war and forced migration developments in Africa. (See also Duffield, 2001, chap. 8; Cranna, 1994, chaps. 4–6; Shawcross, 2000, chap. 10; and Rieff, 2002, chap. 5.)

Two recurring themes in presentations of the situations in Africa are the political and the humanitarian. The political theme is characterized by references to ethnically and politically divided states, unstable and corrupt governments and political systems, and dictatorships, which together in turn generate a lack of civility, increased lawlessness, interethnic conflict, and low levels of economic investment and consequent poverty.

The humanitarian theme revolves around, on the one hand, the massive levels of need and the excessively inhumane treatment of people, and, on the other hand, the huge amounts of aid monies required that seem to sink into a bottomless pit, giving rise to compassion fatigue and refugee fatigue. The Western world seems alternatively compelled to respond to the excessive suffering and inclined to turn away because of a seeming inability to bring about change. This ambivalence characterizes both western governments and potential individual donors.

The dimensions of the overall problem in Africa are truly enormous. The UNHCR (Wilkinson, 2003) reports the total number of uprooted people "at a staggering 15 million," people fleeing in the face of events that "seem almost incomprehensible." Added to the figures of those who flee are the figures of those who do not make it—the casualties of war, conflict, violence, torture, and inhumanity.

A few figures from some specific situations, given in the box on page 278, reveal the dimensions of the problem.

Nor did the situation improve greatly in 2004. A major news item in that year was the situation in the western region of southern Sudan, where thousands of civilians died and an estimated 1.2 million people fled their homes. By year's end, however, government and rebel forces in Sudan had signed a peace agreement to end the 22-year-old rebellion in the south—a conflict that has resulted in more than 2 million deaths. While one review of 2004 in Africa (Carroll, 2004–2005) saw some faint glimmers of hope for the continent, these existed within an overall situation of considerable gloom.

Let us briefly consider Africa in terms of our integrated-perspectives approach.

The Global Perspective. In global terms, many people and not a few governments (e.g., the United States for a period in the 1990s) are inclined to regard Africa and its problems as a

In Rwanda, the "world's largest genocide in recent times" saw one million people die and untold thousands flee into neighboring countries—"almost a million people crossed into Tanzania over four horrible weeks," and "there were some two million people squatting in appalling conditions just outside Rwanda" (Shawcross, 2000, p. 120). Some three million people have perished in the Republic of Congo (described as "Africa's first World War") and 2.5 million were forced to flee. The Sudan has been immersed in civil conflict virtually since its independence in 1956, and two million have died while four million "roam the desert wastes" (see Duffield, 2001; Cranna, 1994). The entire West Africa region has been "destabilized after war erupted once more in Liberia in 1989, with 2.4 million Liberians displaced and 500,000 killed"; and "Burundi is one of the world's poorest and smallest countries, but a decade-long conflict there killed more than 200,000 people and produced nearly one million uprooted persons, or nearly 14 percent of the total population."

Ten countries in Africa in 2003 were home to major displaced populations, ranging in numbers from 109,000 in the Republic of Congo to 690,000 in Tanzania; the UNHCR, in 2003, was assisting over 3.5 million refugees and other displaced persons across the face of Africa.

In many parts of Africa, the forced migration caused largely by conflict has been aggravated by other events, including the HIV/AIDS epidemic that in 2001 claimed more than two million lives and left large numbers of bereft orphans; malaria, measles, tuberculosis, and diarrheic diseases that have killed some eight million people; and starvation, due to a combination of conflict and drought, that has taken a huge toll—in 2003 "an estimated 40 million Africans in Ethiopia, Eritrea, the Sahel and West Africa face starvation according to the World Food Program." (All quotations and figures from UNHCR, 2003. See also UN reports on Africa, and Shawcross, 2000.)

long way away, perhaps a lost cause, and perhaps not of any great significance in global terms. This could not be further from the truth. (One significant development may be that, in 2005, the U.K. government is giving Africa priority in its aid and development activities and encouraging the European Union to do so also.) Africa is a vital part of the globe. For example, what is happening to the people of Africa is resulting in a large migration movement northward, with many Africans slipping into Europe by whatever routes available; what is happening to the ecology of Africa is having global consequences; the political instability of Africa provides hotbeds for terrorism and global crime; and the huge dimensions of suffering in Africa are having, and must have, a major impact on the average world citizen's sense of guilt, shame, and moral indignation.

The Human Rights Perspective. In human rights terms, Africa is probably the least known continent, and there is a tendency to regard its peoples as still not fully a part of the modern world, and therefore perhaps as not possessing human rights to the same degree as others. However, the very concept and nature of human rights cries out against such an attitude. The peoples of Africa possess the same rights as others, and those rights have been systematically abused for far too long. If human rights are permitted to die in Africa, they may not long survive elsewhere, for the very concept will have been seriously undermined.

The Ecological Perspective. High population growth rates, unsustainable development trends, conflict, and natural disasters have for a long time been playing havoc with Africa's fragile natural environment. To place at risk such a major part of the world's resources is not only unacceptable in moral terms but sheer lunacy in every sense; however, to arrest the decline requires large-scale and urgent efforts to combat all of the problems faced by Africa today.

The Social Development Perspective. As many African writers have long been saying, the answer to Africa's problems lies in a comprehensive, integrated, multidimensional, multilevel, and strongly value-based approach to that continent's development. Without social development there will be no peace, no sustainable environment, unsustainable levels of population growth, and no eradication of the various diseases plaguing the continent.

A Critical Analysis of the Forced Migration Situation

The first part of this chapter has described the forced migration situation that has been escalating since World War II and has today reached frightening proportions. As was pointed out in the above case example on Africa, the tendency in recent years has been to respond to this alarming situation on two levels—the political and the humanitarian. The political level has increasingly become the predominant response of western governments, concerned that forced migration is already impacting too heavily on western peace and prosperity, with an inevitable political backlash at the ballot box. Western governments have been experimenting with a range of policies that might be effective in containing forced migration to the developing countries. These policies include building "walls" around western countries (e.g., the "fortress Europe" mentality, or Australia's patrolling of the surrounding seas, or interdiction measures off the U.S. coast); paying or bribing or otherwise encouraging selected countries to keep potential asylum seekers within their borders (e.g., Poland, Mexico, or Indonesia

at various times); treating illegal arrivals harshly as a deterrent to others making the trip (e.g., mandatory detention in poor conditions, as in Australia); removing arrivals to offshore sites and treating them as persons on foreign soils (Australia's "Pacific solution" to boat arrivals); and convincing international airlines that they should act as the western world's migration officers by refusing to transport persons without a valid visa or paying all associated costs when they do so.

For much of the international community, however, the response is humanitarian aid. Rieff (2002, pp. 20–21) writes,

> The humanitarians . . . came from Western Europe, Canada, and the United States and seemed, whether willingly or unwillingly, to have become the rich world's designated consciences in all these landscapes of disaster. . . . Their specific mandates vary, but their basic remit is to bring aid . . . to suffering populations.

Rieff goes on to quote the words of an earlier UN High Commissioner for Refugees, Sadako Ogata: "There are no humanitarian solutions to humanitarian problems." While a natural and laudable response, the humanitarian response will never be a fully adequate one—never finally resolving any situation. (See Chapter 9 on humanitarian aid.)

The critical analysis of the world's forced migration situation that we present is based on the application of the integrated-perspectives approach to both the causes of the situations and the prevailing and necessary responses to them. While we shall consider the four perspectives involved separately, it will be clear that the four overlap, interconnect, and in every sense represent an integrated whole.

The Global Perspective

While the complex of factors that precipitate forced migration is usually predominantly local, such as poverty, inequality, biased development, depressed economies, political suppression, and human rights abuse, it is almost always obvious that these local factors reflect global factors, in reality and in perception. It may be unfair trade arrangements and pricing mechanisms, outside support for a corrupt and oppressive government, the refusal of outsiders to provide assistance, the perception of negative attitudes toward a racial or religious population, or the very existence of countries where the quality of life is vastly superior. Whatever the actual or perceived global factors, they will frequently influence the decision to flee and perhaps the ultimate choice of destination. Moreover, the decision of outside authorities (the UN or particular governments) to respond or not will further contribute to the size and urgency of the exodus; while the dimensions of the longer-term humanitarian response will also have an impact.

The responses to forced migration must be global in nature, as recognized and demonstrated through the support for UN initiatives and the constant reference to global burden-sharing in relation to forced migration. However, in the long run, the forced migration situation will become manageable only when that global response is not just remedial but preventative in nature. When people worldwide experience the security of knowing that they will be protected from abuse of all kinds by a concerned and active global community, then they will flee only in dire circumstances. In any event, world economic, political, social, and ecological systems based on human rights, social justice, sustainability, and equity principles will go far to avoid the development at the local level of conditions that might lead to a need or decision to flee.

The Human Rights Perspective

The abuse of human rights of all types lies at the heart of most forced migration. People denied their political, economic, social, and cultural rights; people denied the right to develop their potentials and achieve a reasonable standard of living; and people whose rights are regularly abused are inevitably going to consider leaving that situation as one of their options. The fact that only a very small proportion of people in such situations can and do leave is irrelevant; it takes only a small proportion to depart to have dire consequences for those individuals, the countries to which they flee, and the persons and countries they leave behind.

Hence it will only be when the world community takes human rights seriously, in the sense of developing a commitment and an ability to protect all peoples' rights to a significant degree, that the pressures that contribute to forced migration will be considerably diminished. The adequate protection of peoples' rights is a highly important preventative measure in this context. Beyond this, however, the range of responses that have been and will be made to the phenomenon of forced migration must be based fairly and squarely on human rights. At present, many of the political responses to forced migration flout human rights conventions, as the UN Human Rights Commission and others have frequently said. Moreover, some aspects of the humanitarian responses to forced migrants fail to take human rights adequately into account, becoming preoccupied with the delivery of aid, sometimes without regard for the consequences of aid of this nature.

The Ecological Perspective

At this stage, only a small proportion of the total volume of forced migration is a direct result of ecological degradation, as people's livelihoods are threatened, or made impossible, either by changing natural conditions (often aggravated by aspects of development such as encroaching deserts, increasing salinity, the drying up of inland seas, and reduction in fish and wildlife stocks) or by specific development processes (such as the large-scale destruction of forests or wetlands). In many other situations, ecological degradation is a result of either widespread poverty or warfare that deliberately destroys food supplies and natural areas, and one outcome of these situations is forced migration. Finally, forced migration may be the result of generally poor development practices, basically either unsustainable development or development that favors some vested interests at the expense of many others. The introduction of large-scale cash crops, the construction of large dams, and the widespread introduction of mechanization can all result in significant levels of forced migration. This may be because the nature and requirements of the natural environment, and its ability to support the population that was there, are ignored; or because development renders superfluous, in employment terms, a significant proportion of a population.

If the ecological factor is a significant causal factor, it is equally one that needs to be taken into account as responses to forced migration are developed. For example, forced migrants are often gathered, or gather themselves, in areas where food, shelter, and medical care are made available. The impact of these large gatherings of people on the local environment can be devastating (e.g., through gathering fuel for cooking), resulting inter alia in the further impoverishment of the local population and even more forced migration (a common occurrence in parts of Africa).

The Social Development Perspective

It will be obvious to the reader by now that the social development perspective is vital in both appreciating the causal factors behind forced migration and understanding how best to respond to forced migration situations. Underdevelopment or neglected development, as well as biased or distorted development, is often associated with the many other factors that lead to forced migration. A country enmeshed in civil war, or governed by a corrupt and inefficient government, is not one that will be able or

willing to support efficient and sustainable development. Equally, a government that favors the development of one area of a country or one section of a population over others will jeopardize peaceful and harmonious community relations, leading readily to conflict with all its consequences, including forced migration.

Equally important, however, is the now common assertion that responses to forced migration situations must be guided as much by sustainable social development considerations as by humanitarian relief or other considerations (Gorman, 1993; Duffield, 2001). The ultimate aim is to provide people with adequate foundations for ongoing social development. This applies to the responses to individuals in refugee camps and displaced-persons contexts, to repatriation arrangements, and to the post-conflict reconstruction process that is providing for both the local people and forced migration returnees. The social development perspective underpins and determines the basic directions of both preventative and remedial responses to forced migration.

Specific Aspects of International Social Work's Involvement in Forced Migration Situations

It is appropriate that social work can and should be involved in all aspects of the forced migration field. Social workers may engage in policy development, general administration, program development and management, training and supervision of personnel, community education, humanitarian aid, and so on. However, an examination of the field and of experience to date suggests that they are more likely to be involved in some aspects of forced migration situations than others, and that the knowledge and skills underpinning social work practice lend themselves more to some contexts than others.

While there are many situations in which forced migrants often find themselves, and which challenge the helping professions to identify appropriate forms of intervention, we have selected and shall describe seven such situations, leaving to the next chapter the discussion of some intervention strategies appropriate, to varying degrees, in all seven contexts and no doubt others.

Camps and Holding Centers for Refugees, Displaced Persons, and Asylum Seekers

Many refugees, displaced persons, and asylum seekers find themselves in centers that provide temporary accommodation, a degree of humanitarian aid, processing arrangements, and a highly varying degree of security. Beyond these characteristics, the centers vary greatly. Some are virtually prisons with residents having no freedom to leave, while in others, individuals are free to come and go. Some provide a range of "normal" facilities, while others are stark and offer only the barest of necessities, or sometimes not even those. Some centers are well staffed by caring people, while others are run by military, government, or other personnel, some of whom are as likely to take advantage of the refugees as to assist them, and who certainly do not see themselves as there predominantly to provide services in response to presenting needs. Often the perceived role of these center personnel is to control such situations, and perhaps also to distribute aid as best they can. There is, in practice, a wide range of prevailing agendas. Finally, some centers are "home" to those staying there for a matter of weeks only, while in other cases the stay can be in excess of a decade. After surveying a number of "protracted situations that can last for decades," the UNHCR (2002, p. 26) comments,

Any civilian forced to abandon home, country, and often even close family, undergoes major traumatic stress. This may be alleviated

if displaced populations return home quickly, but for people faced with years of uncertain exile, the psychological and physical burdens are crushing.

When displaced persons are kept for a long period in some form of holding center, the impact on them depends in part on the nature of, and conditions within, such centers, and these vary greatly as has been said. Despite such variations, we need to be, in general terms, aware of the ways in which this period of waiting in limbo impacts on people regardless of the prevailing conditions. First, such centers represent high levels of deprivation—deprivation of freedom, basic comforts, privacy, dignity, individuality, independence, a sense of identity, security, support, basic services, and sometimes hope. Second, the long period of waiting induces boredom, encourages endless and often unhealthy contemplation of what happened in the past and might happen in the future, creates a sense of helplessness, results often in feelings of guilt and anxiety, and can give rise to psychological conditions that make suicide or a lapse into a psychiatric condition a real risk. The impact of a period in such conditions is, however, understandably different for different categories of people. For example, women face a particular risk of being raped or sexually exploited, but can also at times find strength and purpose in the care of children, the elderly, and others. Overall, workers and researchers tend to suggest that men are more at risk, being deprived of all their former roles that affirmed their maleness and sense of identity (see Hitchcox, 1990, pp. 218–219). Buchwald (1991, p. 3) sums up the situation:

Refugees, as beneficiaries of assistance programmes, are often "overinstitutionalised." They begin to find it difficult to solve their own problems and lose some of their coping mechanisms. Traumatized by the circumstances of fleeing their homes, stressed by the artificial living conditions in refugee camps, suffering a loss of identity and being deprived of meaningful activities to fill their day-time hours, they will become more and more dependent on whatever agency personnel can offer them. In the emergency phase, they may already present anxiety, loss of self-confidence, disorientation, hopelessness, psychosomatic complaints and post-traumatic stress disorder. . . . As the initial emergency stage moves into one of continuing relief, cases of depression and neurosis, apathy, aggression and an attitude of "learned help-lessness" may evolve.

Writers lament that various authorities have shown a strong tendency to label refugees. Zetter (1991) has written at length on the tendency to label refugees and, in so doing, to emphasize the nonparticipatory and powerless nature of their situation. A UNRISD (1993, pp. 2ff.) report refers to "the tyranny of labels," pointing out that inappropriate and excessive use of labels often results in inappropriate treatment of refugees. Therefore, Ingram (1989), Wilson (1992), and others stress the importance of giving refugees some control over such conditions as their food acquisition, and over what they do with food provided by donors (e.g., sell or exchange it), arguing that it is erroneous, unnecessary, and unhelpful to assume that refugees have to be dependent and passive recipients of humanitarian aid. In some camps, for example, the residents may be able to engage in food production and should be encouraged to do so (see Kreitzer, 2002). The whole question of refugee dependency is indeed much discussed. Most field workers regard this state of dependency as, to some degree at least, a myth, pointing out the many situations where refugees must and do take major responsibility for their own well-being. On the other hand, many bureaucratic approaches to refugee care treat refugees as if they are completely dependent. Many workers echo the words of a UNRISD (1993, p. 6) document that states that, while not detracting from the value of

external assistance, it is critically important "to emphasize that the knowledge, capacities and coping strategies of the people themselves are their chief means of survival and hope for the future."

In relation to therapeutic intervention, while it is widely accepted that trauma affects refugee populations on a large scale (e.g., Danieli, Rodley, and Weisæth, 1996), it is also recognized that refugees sometimes resist being diagnosed as in need of therapeutic intervention, fearing that it may have negative consequences for their future by, for example, excluding them from available resettlement opportunities (see Knudsen, 1991). Therapeutic intervention, while necessary, must, therefore, be approached with care and seen in the context of the refugees' wider agenda. Mollica (1990) wrote, in regard to the well-documented mental health crisis in the Thai-Kampuchean border camps, of the exclusive emphasis of relief agencies on "safety, shelter and material relief," and of a culpable failure to introduce an appropriate mental health program; and he proceeds to spell out a feasible program for such a context.

These are but a small sample of the many articles highlighting the complexities and needs of refugee camps and comparable situations, the dangers associated with them, and the need to introduce radical changes to them. (See issues of the journals listed at the end of this chapter for further articles on this issue.) Unfortunately, in the decade since most of the articles referred to above were written, little has changed, except that the emphasis is more on large, temporary, and semistructured holding camps in Africa, while the holding centers in which asylum seekers are often detained in the West represent some further erosion of humane conditions as the emphasis is placed increasingly on deterrence as the key policy toward asylum seekers. (See, for example, McMaster, 2001, on Australia's detention policies.)

The varying array of centers represents one important context where social workers and others are required to assist those in refugee and refugee-like situations. Their roles will include trying to humanize conditions, developing as far as possible a sense of community, facilitating a range of social and recreational activities, introducing health and education services, and providing psychosocial programs, as well as assisting in the running of such centers in ways that are not deleterious to well-being while consistent with the other accepted objectives of the centers. All their efforts, however, will depend on workers possessing a comprehensive understanding of the impact on people of refugee status, and of life lived in limbo at all stages in that process.

The Repatriation Process

Of the three "durable solutions" for refugees put forward by the UN (repatriation, local integration, and resettlement in a third country), by far the most common today is repatriation. Ideally repatriation occurs in a context where peace has been restored in the refugees' homeland and where conditions are such that those returning can quickly begin to live a normal life. Unfortunately, this ideal is increasingly not the reality. As the UNHCR (2000, p. 152) reports,

> During the 1990s, it became increasingly clear that in post-conflict situations, refugees often go back to situations of fragile peace where tensions remain high, where there is still chronic political instability and where the infrastructure is devastated. Such countries are often precariously perched between the prospect of continued peace and a return to war.

As the UNHCR points out, repatriation during the 1990s was of three kinds. The ideal is *voluntary organized repatriation*. This involves the refugees waiting until conditions for return are at least satisfactory, the international community (usually the UNHCR) being willing to organize the return, and the resources being available to provide transport and some short-term assistance after arrival home. Some have estimated

that such returns represent only some 10 percent of all returns (UNHCR, 1997/1998, p. 49). The second form of repatriation has been termed *spontaneous repatriation*. The great majority of refugees who return to their home countries do so on their own initiative and at the time of their choosing (as far as they have choice regarding anything), rather than under a formal repatriation plan. This poses a dilemma for those organizations involved in protecting refugees because, as the UNHCR (1997/1998, p. 148) explains,

> Recent experience has demonstrated that refugees frequently go back to countries which are not fully at peace. As one expert on this issue has written, "most repatriations occur during conflict, without a decisive political event such as elections or a peace agreement and without a major change in the regime or the conditions that originally caused flight."

In many cases, refugees return to situations of conflict and instability because they are repatriating under duress or because they feel that it is in their best interests to repatriate, even if conditions are not completely safe at home.

The third and last form of repatriation is *repatriation under duress,* sometimes called *forced repatriation* or *repatriation emergencies* (see Bayefsky and Doyle, 1999). The UNHCR's 1993 report explains,

> A special category of repatriation concerns movements caused by people fleeing from danger in their countries of asylum. . . . Repatriation under emergency conditions is at the extreme end of the spectrum of unplanned and unorganized movements. (p. 111)

As the UNHCR points out in its 1997/1998 report (p. 147), sometimes returning under duress is due to the actions of "host governments, host communities and other actors, with the specific intention of forcing refugees to go back to their homeland." This means, in effect, that "the principle of non-refoulement [that refugees will not be forced to return home] ... has been flouted on a regular basis during the past few years." At other times, return is due to a general deterioration of conditions in the country of asylum—a common situation in Africa in the past decade.

There are many other problems associated with repatriation. First, there are many obstacles to repatriation. Continuing violence and persecution is obviously one, but others include an unwillingness on the part of the government or sections of the community at home to receive the returnees (e.g., Bosnia and Herzegovina), the existence of land mines in the returnees' homelands (e.g., Cambodia), disputes over the ownership of houses and land, and an absence of essential humanitarian aid, basic services, and income-generation opportunities. Sometimes the return is as difficult, or even more difficult, than the exile itself (UNHCR, 1997/1998, p. 153). This UNHCR report summarizes the problems of return under the following headings: physical insecurity, social and psychological insecurity, legal insecurity, and material insecurity (pp. 154–159).

Finally, repatriation has reintegration as its objective, and until this is achieved repatriation is incomplete. Yet often preventing reintegration are continuing conflict, the ongoing repercussions of conflict, and low levels of development. As the UNHCR (1993, p. 112) expresses it,

Unless return is accompanied by development programmes that address people's immediate needs as well as longer-term goals, it may undermine rather than reinforce the prospects for reconciliation and recovery. ... There is a growing realization that extreme deprivation and competition for resources can re-ignite conflict and undermine the achievements of a fragile peace.

With repatriation being the eventual outcome for most refugees and displaced persons, we need to consider what interventions are open to the social work profession to assist in this process.

The Process of Local Integration

The second durable solution for refugees, and the second most common outcome of forced migration, is integration within the country to which the person has fled and sought or found asylum. Little is written about this outcome for refugees, but it is a situation with which the UNHCR is involved. It reported (2004, p. 5) that "by the end of 2003, 73 per cent of the 6.5 million refugees hosted by developing countries had access to assistance provided by or through the UNHCR."

Sometimes it happens by default, in that, if nothing else happens and displaced persons remain in their place of exile, the situation of local integration eventually comes to be accepted as the long-term reality. This can happen with displaced persons, illegal immigrants who may eventually be granted an amnesty permitting them to stay, and asylum seekers who on rejection go underground and remain in the country indefinitely.

Local integration for displaced persons is most common when there are strong similarities and even bonds between those in exile and the local host community (for example, the situation of many Afghans in Pakistan and of many Central Americans in southern Mexico; see Stein, 1997). Not only are such displaced persons accepted by the community, but governments are more inclined to ultimately accept them as permanent residents. The integration process of these people is not essentially different from that of many formal immigrants, despite the differences in the starting point and early experiences. On the other hand, those early experiences of possible persecution or conflict in the homeland, of fleeing, and of being in exile in another country may take their toll and render the integration process more difficult than for other migrants. Social work appears to have had minimal involvement in such situations to date.

Resettlement in a Third Country

The final solution, open mainly to those found to be refugees in the formal sense of the 1951 convention, is acceptance for resettlement by a third country—usually a western country. In recent times, less than 1 percent of all refugees have been offered resettlement, with the proportion probably closer to 0.5 percent during most of the 1990s. Apart from any impact from the refugee's background, which is of course often considerable, the resettlement of refugees is little different in essence from the integration of all immigrants; however, at times it is more difficult because complicated by past experiences (see Cox, 1989; Balgopal, 2000). Social workers have long had an involvement in refugee resettlement in all the major countries of resettlement.

Displaced Persons Not in Any Form of Organized Center

In many circumstances, those displaced are scattered across a wide area and to some degree lost among the local permanent inhabitants. The areas over which they are scattered may, on the one hand, be forest, bushland, or mountain slopes, being areas that commonly offer little shelter from either the elements or marauding forces, and little sustenance. Alternatively, the area may be a heavily populated one where the displaced are easily "lost" and where they may or may not be welcomed. Clearly it is much more difficult to locate these dispersed populations of displaced persons and make provision for their well-being, yet they may well be in a more vulnerable position than those in centers. Strategies used have included establishing centers within a region of dispersal, making humanitarian aid and medical services available, and hoping that those displaced will hear of these centers on the grapevine and reach them. Sometimes air drops of food are used where displaced persons are dispersed in isolated or difficult terrain, and occasionally workers set out in four-wheel-drive vehicles in an attempt to locate, rescue by

guiding them to centers, or assist those fleeing. The local community may offer aid or may be quite antagonistic toward those moving through and perhaps exploiting their countryside for firewood, food, and so on.

Illegal Immigrants Existing Within the General Community

Illegal immigrants will invariably maintain a low profile, avoiding authorities and facilities that ask for identification papers, such as schools and hospitals. This deliberate avoidance of facilities places them at considerable risk and leaves them deprived of essential services. In relation to work, they will tend to seek out forms of mass low-paid and nonunionized employment, where employers are willing to turn a blind eye to their illegal status knowing that they are the more easily exploited. Most western countries have such areas of employment, often rural in nature but also home-based and sweat-shop industries; but many developing countries also have such areas of employment and attract illegal workers. Unfortunately the authorities are usually well aware of these situations and, when raids on illegal immigrants are politically desirable, will sweep such situations and deport those apprehended. While it is often not difficult for the helping professions to establish contact with illegal immigrants, it does call for a special kind of operation to establish trust and involves the risk of offending authorities.

Development Displacement

Development displacement has been a significant phenomenon in many countries. The displacement and relocation of populations has been due to various reasons, including a desire to change population density disparities (e.g., Indonesia), ethnic distribution policies (e.g., the former USSR), construction of large dams (e.g., India and China), a desire to gain access to natural resources (e.g., through mining and forestry in Asia, Latin America, and elsewhere), and land and agricultural reforms in many developing countries. There has been some limited social work involvement in the relocation and local integration of some of these displaced populations, but social work internationally has been more concerned with lobbying for the protection of the rights of such displaced populations, especially where traditional lifestyles appear likely to be irreparably destroyed.

Migrant Workers in Foreign Countries

There is a great range of migrant worker situations, from top executive personnel in multinational firms to illiterate rural individuals. Here we are concerned with situations where migrant worker opportunities are forced on people because of their precarious circumstances, and where the nature of the migrant work undertaken carries a high risk of deleterious effects on the workers and their families. Intervention in such situations is usually required at various levels: the policy-program level, seeking to humanize such schemes and ensure the protection of those involved; the sending-community level, educating and preparing intending workers,

assisting the reintegration of those returning, and ensuring the support of the family members left behind; and the receiving level, seeking to establish protective devices and supporting structures for those working in any context. Female migrant workers have been found to be particularly vulnerable, but males can also be exposed to unacceptable conditions. (See Cox, 1997; chap. 13, and ILO publications on migrant workers.)

Conclusion

The challenge to the social work profession and others is to devise programs that will reach out in some or all of the above situations, and to evolve strategies that will prove successful in each of the contexts presented. This is no mean challenge. We are talking about millions of people in total, distributed across a very large number of countries, and existing often in circumstances that make even access difficult, let alone the successful devising and implementation of appropriate programs. In the next chapter we shall consider the range of programs that potentially have application to all the above situations.

Summary

- Forced migration is a broad concept that encompasses a range of situations that force people to leave their homelands and head for unknown and uncertain destinations—a situation full of insecurity. Although forced migration has dramatically increased in recent times, responses to the needs of forced migrants remain far from adequate.

- The root causes of displacement and migration lie in global and local political contexts, the denial of human rights, ecological degradation, and overall lack of or distorted development. Prevention of and remedies for forced migration call for addressing global, human rights, ecological, and social development factors, as suggested by the integrated-perspectives approach.

- Forced migrants can be found in eight difficult situations (refugee camps and centers, repatriation, local integration, resettlement in a third country, scattered displaced persons, illegal immigrants, development-displaced persons, and migrant workers) where social workers can play significant roles.

Questions and Topics for Discussion

- What do you understand to be the key elements of forced migration, in terms of major causes, issues arising, and responses?
- By employing the integrated-perspectives approach, analyze the causes of displacement and migration.
- What do you consider to be the relevance today of "compassion fatigue" and a fear of asylum seekers or illegal entrants as invading foreigners?
- What are the main potential roles of social workers and others of the helping professions in the most commonly found forced migration situations?

Possible Areas for Research Projects

- Select a specific situation of forced migration and analyze its causes, nature, and outcomes with a view to developing conclusions regarding possible intervention strategies.
- Survey a population's response to a perceived or hypothetical forced migration situation, such as an influx of asylum seekers.
- Select a specific situation of forced migration and develop an intervention strategy focusing on human needs and responses to them.
- Drawing on secondary sources, analyze forced migration trends in selected countries, exploring the links between these and the integrated-perspectives approach.
- Undertake an analysis of various countries' current policies and responses to forced migration, examining them particularly from a human rights perspective.

Further Reading

For general texts on forced migration we recommend the following:

Le Breton, B. (2003). *Trapped: Modern day slavery in the Brazilian Amazon.* Bloomfield, CT: Kumarian Press.

Loescher, G. (1993). *Beyond charity: International cooperation and the global refugee crisis.* New York: Oxford University Press.

UNHCR. (1997/1998). *The state of the world's refugees.* New York: Oxford University Press.

UNHCR. (2000). *The state of the world's refugees.* New York: Oxford University Press.

Zolberg, A. R., Suhrke, A., & Aguayo, S. (1989). *Escape from violence: Conflict and the refugee crisis in the developing world.* New York: Oxford University Press.

For recent analyses of the global situation of displaced persons, the best source is the UNHCR's regular publication, *The State of the World's Refugees.*

Readers are referred also to the following journals for a range of useful articles on forced migration and intervention in these contexts:

Journal of Refugee Studies
Canada's periodical on refugees: *Refuge*
International Journal of Refugee Law
UNHCR journal, *Refugees*

12

The Field of Displacement and Forced Migration: Programs and Strategies

The field of displacement and forced migration has been a major one for social workers, particularly since the end of World War II. Many social workers were working in Europe with refugees displaced by that war, and social work with immigrants gradually emerged as a specific and significant field as many western countries (e.g., Australia, Canada, and the United States) embarked upon formal immigration programs—programs that initially included large numbers of refugees from mainly Eastern Europe. At the same time, a body of literature began to emerge as mental health, health, and helping profession personnel generally wrote about experiences and research in refugee camps and among uprooted populations. As the centers of refugee work moved from Europe to the developing world, there was something of a hiatus in social work involvement in this field, apart from the handful of personnel who worked for various religious refugee agencies, the UNHCR, and the IOM (International Organization for Migration). However, as more and more other agencies focused on the refugee field, whether exclusively or alongside humanitarian, development, or postconflict activities, the numbers of social work and other helping profession personnel in the field began to increase quite rapidly. Unfortunately, it took much longer for a solid body of literature to emerge, a process greatly assisted by the refugee studies centers at Oxford University and York University, Canada—both of which continue to be active in this field and to disseminate literature helpful to practitioners.

The refugee field has, in addition to welfare concerns, fostered a strong legal dimension, allied in part to human rights law but with significant independent existence. While that body of literature is of great interest to those who specialize in this field of international social work, we shall not enter that territory. Equally important is the work of the UNHCR and other agencies in the areas of refugee protection and aid. This body of literature is perhaps even more critical to specialists in this field than the legal work, but we shall also not enter that area. (The

Learning Objectives

- To familiarize readers with a range of useful programs addressing the prevailing conditions, past experiences, and specific needs of forced migrants.

- To encourage readers to consider suitable programs and strategies for the various forced migration situations.

International Journal of Refugee Law is an excellent source for readers interested in this area.) The focus of this chapter is essentially on the types of programs pertaining to forced migration that social workers and others can be expected to provide across the various forced migration situations outlined at the end of the previous chapter.

A General Overview of Social Work Programs in Forced Migration Situations

In this chapter we discuss a number of programs that are generally important in the forced migration context, and in which social workers and members of the other helping professions have major roles to play. Given the diversity of forced migration situations outlined in Chapter 11, it is not being suggested that all programs are equally applicable to all contexts or always able to be implemented in an identical manner. However, it is probable that all should be seriously considered as of possible importance in any forced migration situation, and then decisions taken as to which programs should take priority and precisely how those selected should be implemented. We first list the programs, grouping like with like, and then indicate briefly their nature. We shall later consider a number of the more key programs in some detail, discussing the strategies and skills each requires and illustrating these with case studies.

Most of the programs listed in Table 12.1 will be self-explanatory, but a brief rationale for each in the forced migration context may be in order.

Advocacy programs are important because the motivation of forced migrants is frequently misunderstood; their presence or very existence is seen as constituting a threat; and the cultures that they represent are sometimes seen as alien and unwelcome. Advocacy programs are important to ensure that relevant general publics and officials fully understand a situation and its origins, and hopefully develop positive attitudes toward the situation and the people involved.

Outreach programs are often called for because many forced migrants are either not easily located or deliberately remain hidden, fearing some form of retribution. It is important to reach out to these people in ways that will both locate them and allow them the security of making contact in their own time and in a nonthreatening context.

Humanitarian aid programs are often essential because forced migrants will usually have traveled light and lack ready access to necessary provisions. While social workers may at times actually provide humanitarian aid, they will more often be involved in putting forced migrants into touch with such programs and ensuring that they do receive access to them.

Health programs are more important within a forced migrant situation than is commonly the case because the very act of and conditions surrounding fleeing leave people suffering from, and vulnerable to, a range of conditions that will require treatment. Moreover, the crowded conditions of many gatherings of displaced people and the lack of sanitary measures render people vulnerable to the outbreak of various diseases, making public health measures very important.

Table 12.1   Social work programs in forced migration situations

General Programs	*Specific-area Programs*
Pertaining to prevailing conditions	***Pertaining to families and family members***
Advocacy programs	Children's education and psychosocial programs
Outreach programs	Services for refugee women
Humanitarian aid programs	Family services programs
Health programs	Family reunion programs
Programs designed to humanize existing conditions	Intercountry casework programs
Pertaining to people's past experiences	***Pertaining to specific needs***
Trauma counseling programs	Repatriation and reintegration programs
Rehabilitation programs	Integration programs
Support programs	Human rights programs
Social and recreational programs	Legal-oriented programs
Pertaining to group situations	
Self-help programs	
Community building programs	
Community relations programs	
Pertaining to future needs	
Education programs	
Skills development and capacity-building programs	
Income-generation programs	

Programs humanizing existing conditions are necessary in many contexts. Refugee camps and asylum seeker centers, for example, will often have been established in a hurry, contain few resources, and be managed by staff with few ideas of how to normalize or humanize conditions to the extent possible. Even when resources are scarce, there will always be scope for programs that can improve conditions. These programs are especially critical when migrants are to remain long-term in the conditions in question, to offset the often negative effects of long stays in such centers.

Trauma counseling programs represent a response to the traumatic experiences through which many forced migrants have passed. These may be experiences of extreme violence, torture, sudden separations from loved ones, the loss of loved ones through violence, or traumatic escape experiences. There is now considerable experience in responding effectively to posttrauma conditions, and such programs are critical.

Rehabilitation programs will cater to the specific needs of individuals whose past experience has left them wounded, maimed, or disabled in some way.

Support programs are designed for the general population in forced migration contexts, appreciating that a majority of people are in situations where they both need support and have been deprived of their traditional support structures.

Social and recreational programs may sound like a luxury, but they are far from being so. Social and recreational programs fill many needs. They occupy people in an enjoyable way and break the monotony and boredom confronting many forced migrants left in limbo while their status and futures are being resolved. Such programs can also be therapeutic, and ideally they should be planned by competent leaders to achieve such ends. Programs may be specifically planned for traumatized children, rape victims, elderly people, and others, with programs designed to address specific areas of need. Finally, such programs will help to break down the isolation that can be a real danger in such contexts.

Self-help programs are designed to bring people in similar circumstances together to enable them to support each other and, given appropriate self-help programs, lead each other through their particular difficulties, and enhance capacities to respond to future events as much as is possible in the circumstances.

Community building programs can assist by linking people within communities that offer a stronger base from which to face the future. The degree of community life possible will vary greatly, but any strengthening of potential community bonds will be beneficial for many people in forced migration circumstances.

Community relations programs are needed to respond to those situations where a group of forced migrants is experiencing difficult intergroup relationships with either a host population or some other group of forced migrants. In either set of circumstances, it is important to avoid prolonged insecurity and potential conflict by building better community relations.

Education programs, while obviously important for future well-being, are often not practical in a formal sense in the prevailing circumstances. Where they are practical, however, or where informal programs can be developed, it is important to seize every possible opportunity to further the development of children and young people, while also providing appropriate adult education programs.

Skills development and capacity-building programs cover a range of skills areas, the focus usually being on those skills identified as important to a people's future. Language skills, occupational skills, and life skills may be the focus. Not only should these skills facilitate future adjustment to new circumstances, but the pursuit of new skills is in itself beneficial in terms of morale, self-esteem, confidence building, and simply passing the time constructively.

Income-generation programs have more scope than is often realized. They can apply within refugee camps, among a dispersed population, and in many other situations. They should be carefully planned to ensure their feasibility in the circumstances, and may well need to be guided by workers able to facilitate the process (e.g., by providing training and ensuring access to external resources).

Children's education and psychosocial programs are an attempt, first, to compensate for the extent to which normal developmental experiences are missing from the lives of most children caught up in forced migration. The focus may be on formal education, but is more likely in the circumstances to be on informal education. Second, such programs set out to address the negative impact on children of past experiences of conflict, flight, separation, and so on—that is to say, psychosocial programs are incorporated within education programs. It is often possible and beneficial to involve parents in these programs in some way.

Services for refugee women are important because such women compose a high proportion of displaced populations, bear a significant burden during periods of conflict and escape from conflict, and are frequently very much at risk in the situations in which they find themselves after flight. The incidence of violence and rape among refugee women is very high; the need for specific protection arrangements is very real; and the provision of a range of services targeting women is a high priority. The UNHCR (1991) has published *Guidelines on the Protection of Refugee Women,* while various other publications also focus on refugee women (e.g., International NGO Working Group on Refugee Women, 1989).

Family services programs are important because family life and relationships suffer greatly from many of the circumstances leading to forced migration. Married couples may have experienced lengthy periods of separation; one or both parents may have had experiences which they find they cannot share with their partner; parents may have been preoccupied with events and become emotionally distant from their children; grandparents may be perceived as, or perceive themselves to be, a burden, thus straining these relationships; and family members may not have shared equally in the decision to leave, resulting in ongoing tensions and the attribution of blame if things do not work out well.

Family reunion programs are designed to assist in the reunion of families separated during conflict or flight; often family members are not even aware whether other members of the family survived. Family members can be so preoccupied by these fears that reunion, or at least knowledge about significant others in advance of physical reunion, is essential if they are to move ahead. These services are the objectives of so-called tracing services, such as that provided by the International Red Cross.

Intercountry casework programs can assist where families are separated from each other, being often in different countries, and facing situations that require a joint decision, the obtaining of information or documentation from the other party, or the ability to work through situations of disagreement or conflict. International Social Service, headquartered in Geneva, is one international organization specializing in this field (see Cox, 1986).

Repatriation and reintegration programs will not be applicable to all forced migrants, but in reality a very high proportion of displaced persons, refugees, and asylum seekers end up returning home. That process is often far from easy at every step, and ideally the process should be prepared for, expedited to make it as smooth as possible, and followed up to ensure that a satisfactory degree of reintegration occurs.

Integration programs are required by those forced migrants who do not return home but are permitted to settle in the country to which they fled or in another country. Integration is seldom a straightforward process, and will usually be assisted by appropriate integration programs run by qualified workers.

Human rights programs highlight the need for forced migrants to be protected from abuse of various kinds. Their status is usually such that they are readily abused, exploited, discriminated against, and in other ways rejected as unwanted aliens. It is critical that programs ensure the availability of human rights workers able to negotiate, and monitor, a human rights regime that will protect these people.

Legal programs recognize that the legal needs of forced migrants will often go beyond the area of human rights. They may require legal advice or representation while their status is being determined, or when prosecuted for entering a country illegally, or when subjected to persecution by members of the host population. The legal status of such people is such that legal support schemes are often an essential service, yet normally beyond their means and sometimes frowned on or even refused by authorities.

Having presented briefly each of the program areas listed, we shall now consider some of the key ones in more detail, particularly in terms of the specific strategies that can with benefit be adopted in each case. While some of these strategies are useful in a range of fields of international and local social work, they are considered here because of their specific relevance to the forced migration field.

Strategies:

- Ensure that those with special needs or additional difficulties are reached.
- Focus on the most disadvantaged.

Some Specific Programs and Strategies for Responding to Various Forced Migration Situations

In many forced migration situations, the provision of humanitarian aid is crucial to people's very survival. Usually people have fled virtually empty-handed, and are obliged to exist in a relatively inhospitable situation and in large numbers. Securing sustenance without external aid is often virtually impossible. Fortunately, there are various international agencies that focus on the provision of humanitarian aid of various kinds, and have considerable experience in the logistics of responding to crisis situations. Yet frequently things go wrong. Sufficient material aid is not made available; it is virtually impossible to reach a situation with the aid; distribution can be only at some fixed points which forced migrants are obliged to reach but find it difficult to do so; and the type of aid provided may be inadequate for meeting certain needs. There is little that social workers and other workers can do about such difficulties. It is necessary for the UN and others to convince donor and recipient governments to cooperate quickly and fully to prevent the loss of lives.

Humanitarian Aid and Its Distribution

The role of social workers is more likely to be to assist in the distribution of aid in such a way as to ensure that those with special needs or added difficulties are reached. Sometimes the reality is that food distribution is so organized that it goes only to the young and fit who are able to fight for a share, while the sick, mothers with young children, and the elderly miss out. Sometimes the distribution is effectively politicized, with only some groupings in a conflict situation obtaining access to the aid. If local workers are aware of the risk of this, or of it actually happening, they may be able to devise distribution strategies, or negotiate arrangements with people's leaders, in an effort to avoid what may be tragic inequities. What strategies workers adopt will depend on the prevailing conditions; one important element, however, is to focus on the most disadvantaged. (See Chapter 9 for a more detailed discussion of humanitarian aid in general.)

Case Example

Difficulties in Providing Aid to Refugees in Croatia

Some examples of the difficulties in providing aid to refugees come from Croatia. Here authorities admitted that the cost of transporting donated food was three times the value of the food delivered, while acceptable food could have been purchased locally. Second, they felt unable to sell donated food that came in too small quantities to distribute equitably, for fear of being accused of corruption.

Third, they had problems with agencies insisting on distributing food in ways that ensured maximum publicity and, in some situations, caused riots. Finally, the practice in this context of providing refugees with cooked food, while of great benefit to contractors, often resulted in unpalatable food. It was also noted that those in control of the overall refugee situation failed to appreciate "how fundamental food preparation and the social rituals of commensality (eating together) are to the restoration of communal life."

(Example from Harrell-Bond, 1996, p. 26.)

Programs Humanizing Existing Conditions

The conditions in which refugees, displaced persons, asylum seekers, and other forced migrants find themselves are frequently less than ideal. This is often because such facilities must be established rapidly, in situations where resources to do so are inadequate, or in circumstances where political parties and others are determined to maintain harsh conditions for essentially political reasons, including punishment and deterrence. However, it also happens to a degree because those responsible for the logistics of establishing such facilities possess little awareness of the needs of those who will be occupying them, or of the possible impact of certain conditions. Furthermore, they may, on the basis of past training, be led to establish the facilities on a military or institutional basis, not appreciating how deleterious this might be. Finally, those operating such facilities may run them in ways that are counterproductive to the needs of certain categories of people living there. They may, for example, fail to provide adequate protection for the vulnerable and support for family groupings, and may not see the importance of enabling natural support structures to form. They may equally be unaware of the advantages likely to flow from involving the people living in the facility in its running.

The task of humanizing centers of various kinds where forced migrants are being detained or accommodated is extremely important, given our understanding from research and experience of the negative impact that such facilities can have on those who live within them. One thinks of the problems associated with institutionalization and dependency, of the consequences on emotional health of monotony and boredom, of the frequently devastating effect of a loss of most roles in life, of the heightened anxiety levels resulting from waiting for a long period in limbo for the results of an application for refugee status or resettlement in a third country, and of the fear and sense of insecurity that some residents face every hour of every day—fear, for example, of violence and rape.

The challenge to social workers and others in any such context is to consider existing needs and potential dangers, devise conditions and programs that will assist those in the situation, and convince those in authority of the importance of introducing such changes. Ideally, such work should be carried out in close consultation with the forced migrant population. They are likely to have ideas of helpful programs, to offer assistance with the implementation of changes decided on, and to benefit personally from such involvement. What specific programs are initiated will, of course, be determined by the prevailing circumstances.

In presenting guidelines for the care of refugee children in camps, the UNHCR (1994, pp. 46–47) writes,

> Camp Environment: Where camps are unavoidable, measures which enable families and refugee communities to live as normally as possible in economic, social and cultural terms will benefit refugee children. Models of previous community life may be replicated through

> *As far as possible, the social worker's approach should be*
>
> - empowering,
>
> - engaged in capacity building, and
>
> - indirectly therapeutic in acknowledging the trauma, stress, anxiety, and other conditions that prevail.

economic activities of adults, home gardening and workshops for training and production. Opportunity for at least primary education must be ensured. Access to the wider world by allowing freedom of movement outside of camps can be extremely valuable to children.

Examples of other specific steps to humanize camp conditions include the provision of a recreation center or meeting place, organization of sporting events, facilitating the organization of religious festivals, encouraging the celebration of family milestones, permitting people to cook and assume control of as many aspects of the camp as possible, and addressing the refugees by name.

On the other hand, humanizing refugees' conditions may be seen as an ethical dilemma (see Case Example).

Trauma Counseling Programs

Petevi (1996, p. 166) presents a good introduction to this topic in the following comments:

Trauma, affecting refugee populations on a large scale, is being progressively recognized by UNHCR and the international community. This acknowledgement is increasingly reflected in humanitarian relief assistance. Preventive and remedial responses to trauma are starting to be introduced at the first stages of refugee influxes, depending on the situation. The need for rapid, preventive, population-based interventions is also being recognized as a means to respond to the psychological needs of the highest possible number of refugees; and, with a longer-term view, to preserve their psychological, intellectual,

---

Case Example

Concerns With Humanizing Camps in Hong Kong

An NGO working in Hong Kong's closed camps for Southeast Asian refugees wanted to create an environment beneficial to the refugees' physical and mental health. In doing so, however, they saw the danger of their programs contributing to the perpetuation of a situation that the refugees did not want and that was also not in their best interests. At the same time, the NGO's aims to build self-reliance and self-respect ran counter to the administration's idea of an orderly and tightly controlled camp. The agency continued to work to make the prisonlike conditions more humane, but lost several staff over the ethical issue and found themselves at times in confrontation with administration and some of the refugees.

(Example from Community and Family Services International, 1991.)

---

and social functioning, as well as their future human and socioeconomic development. Empowerment of refugees, through family reunification, autonomy in structuring daily activities, schooling, gathering in groups, undertaking professional and income-generating activities, reconstructing personal and group networks, etc., becomes a further step in this direction and contributes to mobilizing coping skills and resources in the refugee community. Through early intervention in this domain, an important contribution can be made to national reconciliation and peace by allowing the refugees to express, analyze, ventilate and exchange their experiences on an individual and community basis, and thus eventually catalyze problems.

There are many sources or causes of trauma for refugees and displaced persons, and De Martino and Buchwald (1996) provide a useful summary of the general situation regarding forced displacement, which they regard as "one of the most stressful human experiences." Many displaced persons have experienced torture and "other forms of violence which may have been as severe as torture" (WHO/UNHCR, 1996, p. 110), and such experiences frequently give rise to a set of debilitating but clearly recognizable symptoms.

This WHO/UNHCR (1996, p. 111) report lists the most common reactions to severe violence, commenting,

Someone who has suffered severe violence or torture may have most of these reactions. Every person is different and some people can tolerate suffering better than others, but any person who complains about several of these reactions will probably need extra support.

Petevi (1996, p. 180) rightly warns that "special" behavior is observed in every refugee and displaced population, but emphasizes that the behavior "should not, however, be considered as pathological, but should be dealt with as normal responses to abnormal situations." Among the more specific reactions to traumatic experience, Petevi (p. 181) lists

flashbacks to the traumatic situation with intense anxiety, nightmares, panic attacks, and sleep disturbance;

avoidance behavior to escape these intense feelings of anxiety and helplessness; social retreat, emotional and somatic anesthesia;

hyperarousal with startled responses and psychosomatic corollaries (i.e., phobic reactions), aggressiveness, clinging, self-medication with alcohol or drugs; and

sadness and depression related to the loss of home, health, community, and culture and to the death of family members and friends. Refugees and displaced persons are especially affected by the violent death and maiming of children.

While it is important to understand the common symptoms among those who have experienced torture, violence, and situations of extreme stress, and to understand the causes for these symptoms, it is especially important that workers know how to respond to such conditions. As important perhaps as the specific programs found to be helpful is a set of principles guiding such work. Let us consider a few of these. First, it should be recognized that programs can operate at different levels, and the choice of level in any context is very important. The levels are those of the individual, group, family, and community. Some believe, for obvious reasons, that individual psychotherapy and other such programs have very limited scope in such situations as the aftermath of armed conflict.

Second, whatever approach is adopted must be culturally appropriate. As De Martino and Buchwald (1996, p. 202) warn, "Some NGOs have warned against therapists transplanting their own methods to different cultures without careful reflection on their appropriateness."

Five principles:

- Choose appropriate level for intervention.
- Be culturally appropriate.
- Draw volunteers and staff from among the forced migrants.
- Introduce psychosocial support programs into existing services.
- Restore dignity and mobilize capacities.

A third principle is that staff and volunteers for this work should as far as possible be drawn from among the refugees themselves. As De Martino and Buchwald (1996, p. 200) point out, "They had suffered the same trauma and could therefore show a deep understanding for the problems shared with them and help revive traditional approaches to healing." Such people will often, of course, require careful, albeit basic, training and ongoing support.

Fourth, wherever possible it is considered best that psychosocial support programs be introduced into existing services for assistance and protection, thus avoiding any possible stigmatizing effect.

Finally, the ultimate goal of all such work is to restore dignity and mobilize capacities. As De Martino and Buchwald (1996, p. 201) comment,

> The psychosocial worker has to restore the dignity and mobilize capacities which have been blocked in order to help people to develop new strength for adjustment and become actively involved in day-to-day responsibilities. Through this healing process, psychosomatic symptoms like sleeplessness, nightmares, and pains should gradually disappear.

In addition to following such guiding principles arising out of past experience, there are also a number of specific programs that might be considered, using either a group or a community-based approach. Petevi (1996, pp. 183ff.) discusses

mobilizing coping skills and resources within the wider community;

helping individuals to understand their own behavior, and not, for example, see it as a sign that they are losing their sanity;

developing natural support networks within the extended family or the community;

establishing self-help groups for those who have been through similar experiences;

providing people with employment opportunities to foster autonomy and self-esteem;

making sporting and leisure activities available; and

providing debriefing opportunities:

> Debriefing is a specific intervention which helps refugees discuss and work through traumatizing events and integrate them into their memory in a healthy way. It contributes, among other things, to preventing the creation of socially isolating secrets and myths at their inception, curtails intentions of hatred, revenge etc. It is especially useful to groups that have lived through the same experience. (p. 184)

The specific methods suggested by De Martino and Buchwald (1996, pp. 201–202) are the following:

Guided communications, in which the problems are discussed and solutions are elaborated, can be conducted at the group and individual level.

Nonverbal therapy can also turn into a powerful tool, such as meditation exercises in an appropriate cultural or religious context.

Creative methods such as games, theater, or painting in which the trauma is reflected can create a strong impact by removing the trauma and rebuilding self-confidence both for the artists and the spectators.

Special visual aids such as picture books or videos have proved particularly helpful.

Physical exercises, and breathing and relaxation techniques, can have beneficial effects in the long term.

Specific populations may require specially devised programs. Refugee children, demobilized soldiers, victims of torture, rape victims, and so on may well have to be assessed and their needs responded to separately, although care must always be taken not to separate any group from the wider community of which they are or should be naturally a part, and so, for example, stigmatize them.

While a major responsibility for such work can be laid upon communities, and individuals recruited from communities and trained, the roles of professional workers in locating and assessing needs, devising programs, recruiting and training local staff and providing them with ongoing support, and ensuring that such work is integrated into wider programs of reintegration, reconciliation, reconstruction, and social development are all of major importance.

Case Examples

Therapeutic Testimony in Chile

In a program for political refugees in Chile, the use of testimony as a therapeutic tool was developed. Testimonies were drawn up by therapists and ex-prisoners together, partly for accumulating evidence against the regime but, equally important, as a therapeutic process. The process was cathartic and assisted people to reconnect with reality.

(Example from Agger and Jensen, 1990, pp. 118–119).

Therapeutic Effect of Narratives

Elsewhere in the refugee field, testimonies are often referred to as narratives, either biographical or presenting a situation of suffering and exile in general terms. In the Balkans, refugees were often asked to write their personal narratives, one of which we share here:

My life story:

I was born on April 19, 1982 in Vukovar.

I lived in Prilyevo [a suburb] in December 8, 1944 street.

Now I live in Vukovar Avenue [in Zagreb] at No. xx, 6th floor.

My feelings are sad, because of Dad and my uncle.

My Dad has been listed as missing for 2 years and 3 months now.

My uncle died in a camp (Sremska Mitrovica) which was found out in March 1992.

While there was shooting in Vukovar I lived in the cellar.

I was hungry, and what little we had had been eaten.

People died quickly, killed by mortars and bullets.

I remember when the army took people out of the cellar; we went out.

Not far from me was my house which was hit by 3 mortars.

The house across the street was destroyed to its foundations, a "sow" mortar fell on it.

While we were going along the street we looked at all those horrors.

A body with the upper part missing was lying in a ditch.

I felt sad and lonely as if I was in a foreign land.

I would like to go back to Vukovar, but it's not easy.

When we saw the Bulgarian Cemetery on the TV we started to cry for my mother's sadness, there were more than 1,000 graves in it.

(Example from Prica and Povrzanovic, 1996, p. 91.)

Therapeutic Theater in Croatia

In a refugee camp in Croatia for children from Vukovar, children in a theater workshop reconstructed symbolically their own house and, ultimately, the town—"a fairy site of their lost childhoods and untroubled happiness." Other children worked with a skillful creator of puppets to develop their stories, the rehearsals of which "presented occasions for therapeutic work, while the performances were to some extent a chance to relive suppressed emotions, confront them, accept them, search for possible solutions, and survive."

(Example from D. Cox's field notes taken in Bosnia-Herzegovina in 1997.)

Support Programs

Social workers have long been aware of the value of support programs in many different contexts, despite the fact that such services appear vague to outsiders. We are all aware of what it means to be supported in any context, and the more difficult is the situation being faced the more important support becomes. The term *support* suggests that, to a significant degree, there is little concrete that persons providing support can do. They will not change the situation being faced, provide any specific resources, or engage in any specific type of service. They will simply be there, to provide a helping hand as and when necessary, to offer comfort and encouragement, and to convey to people the sense that they are not alone or deserted. Support services are a recognition of the fact that many people in situations like forced migration do have specific

Support services include

- providing the opportunity to talk things through;
- providing some information or advice;
- acting as a linkage through to various specific services;
- sharing tasks with people in tangible ways, thereby encouraging them to believe that they can and should continue to engage in those tasks; and
- providing appropriate backup when the going gets too tough.

needs, but are at the same time just trying to survive in an extremely difficult situation—physically, socially, economically, and emotionally.

Support services can be an effective preventative strategy, minimizing the possibility of crises occurring with individuals, families, or groups. As such, they can avoid unnecessary suffering and unnecessary costs on the part of agencies already stretched to the limit. Moreover, these need not be expensive services to maintain. While what is said above may be seen as applying to workers external to a situation, this is not necessarily the case. Among most populations are individuals with a natural propensity to identify the need for support and provide it appropriately. With some training and backup, these individuals can operate as effective support personnel in any situation. They have the advantage of a common language, of identifying with the general population, and of being already within the situation, as well perhaps of doing such work on a voluntary basis. These individuals may be members of the displaced population itself, and it is these who will be sought out in the context of a refugee camp, for example, but they may also be members of a host population who can provide support to, for example, a population of returnees. The role of the external worker is, then, to recruit and train, and if possible support, a team of support workers. This strategy has been used effectively both in refugee camps and in a postconflict situation such as that in Bosnia-Herzegovina.

Social and Recreational Programs

This is a further program area that is too readily undervalued. Faced with humanitarian needs, protection needs, and so on, social and recreation needs may appear as a luxury undeserving of program space or the deployment of scarce resources. Yet, as with support services, the key goal should be people's survival, and the question is then what roles do social and recreational programs play in achieving that goal. The key points that need to be made are, first, that humans are social beings who find it very difficult to survive for any length of time emotionally isolated from others; and, second, that recreational activities can be therapeutic and so reduce the onset of reactions to stress that are debilitating.

Social programs will focus mainly on enabling appropriate group formation and facilitate the welding together of such groups. Groups enable people to share experiences, to find support in numbers and mutual sharing, to exercise more power or control over a situation, to provide mutual support opportunities, and to permit a degree of relaxation in the midst of a familiar group reality. All of these objectives are important in the forced migration context, and workers aware of this fact will be doing all possible to facilitate group formation. This may be through putting people with similarities together or in contact with each other (a self-help group approach); it may be through establishing focal

> *Three key points:*
>
> - The importance of social and recreational programs should never be overlooked by workers in the field;
> - however, such programs should eventually be run by the people themselves;
> - so the challenge to workers is to initiate the process by engaging potential leaders or establishing a process that can quickly be handed over to the members.

points and facilities where a group can get together; it may be through suggesting activities that the group could with benefit undertake; or it may be by providing on a temporary basis some leadership for the group formation process.

Recreational programs are programs organized by workers to provide opportunities for a particular group of people to relax for periods and push their anxieties to the back of their mind. One sees refugees in camps engaged in sport, children in many contexts playing games, groups of people putting some effort into organizing for a forthcoming cultural festivity, or small groups celebrating some occasion. These programs are in a sense insignificant in the overall scale of things, yet important well beyond the time and resources required to initiate them. They are a part of humanizing situations that are in danger of dehumanizing those involved, or of normalizing abnormal situations.

Much can, therefore, be done with very few demands on workers' time and energies.

Children's Education and Psychosocial Programs

The definition of a *refugee child* in this context is a person who is under the age of 18 years and has been displaced from his or her usual environment by war or other events. Many children become separated from their parents in such contexts and are commonly referred to as *unaccompanied children* or *minors*. Other children remain in the company of family members but possess particular needs to which a response is required. As the UNHCR's "Policy on Refugee Children" (UNHCR, 1994, p. 166) puts it, "Three interrelated factors contribute to the special needs of refugee children: their dependence, their vulnerability and their developmental needs (i.e. their requirements for healthy growth and development at different ages)."

The numbers of refugee children are huge. It is commonly accepted that approximately half of the world's displaced or uprooted are children. This means that, in 2000, there were 25 million children in an uprooted state, of whom the UNHCR was caring for 10 million (UNHCR, 2001, p. 7). In the African context, the numbers of displaced children are even higher, in that reports are concerned with "children separated from their families in emergency situations of war, natural disaster and famine"—the unaccompanied children that represent a major concern to social workers and others across Africa. (See the issue of *Journal of Social Development in Africa*, 1993, that focuses on unaccompanied displaced persons.)

Research carried out by Boothby (1992) and others (see Athey and Ahearn, 1991) vividly document the impact on children of the experience of violence and war in their home country, of loss as they flee and assume refugee status, of deprivation and exposure to traumatic situations as they live in refugee camps and asylum seeker detention centers, and of surviving on the streets and elsewhere. Millions of children have been exposed to horrific situations in recent decades, and the impact of such exposure will depend on the extent of exposure and the developmental age and situation of the child.

The types of experience which many refugee children experience and which place a child at particular risk include trauma, loss, and severe deprivation. The coping behaviors that children employ when confronted with such stressors vary by developmental stage and by their ability to draw on various resources (Athey and Ahearn, 1991, p. 4).

These children can be found among the many streams of displaced persons, in refugee camps, abandoned on the streets of foreign cities where they join the local street children and survive as best they can, in detention centers established for asylum seekers, and among the flows of returnees going home, where they merge with the many other children seeking to get over their war and loss experiences and move ahead. In all such situations, there is a major need to develop programs that target various categories of uprooted children and respond to their needs. Experience and the literature identify various types of responses, including the following ones.

An important long-term need is to reunite children if possible with their parents or other family members. Boothby (1992, p. 15) gives an example from the Mozambique situation:

> The tracing and reunification effort would begin with an active search to identify all children in need of assistance in locating lost family members. Procedures were devised to identify and document unaccompanied children in orphanages and other child care institutions, hospitals and feeding centers, living on the streets in urban areas, and with substitute families in *deslocado* centers or refugee camps in neighbouring countries.

This is often a very complex process, presenting difficulties in identifying the children and the parents, in locating parents or relatives, and in achieving a satisfactory reunion after all that all parties have been through.

A second area of intervention is to make immediate provision for the ongoing development and education needs of the children, which cannot of course be separated from the children's psychosocial needs. The more stable a situation is the easier will be the establishment of such programs, but even in relatively stable situations, like refugee camps and detention centers, it can prove very difficult to persuade the authorities to approve such programs and then to obtain the necessary resources. If the stay in camps is an extended one, the need for such programs becomes even more urgent, as a UNHCR (1994, p. 46) report spells out:

> The emotional development of children may be adversely affected by remaining for years in the artificial environment of a refugee center or camp where normal life activities are impossible. In such circumstances, refugee children are restricted in their freedom of movement, grow up dependent on care and maintenance support, and often live in poor conditions with little to keep them occupied. . . . Children suffer from the negative effects of extended stays [in camps] on the well-being of adult family members and the destructive effects on the family unit. . . . Refugee children sometimes face serious adaptation problems when they finally leave the camps.

This report goes on to suggest a range of activities through which "developmental, emotional or psychological problems can be identified."

Education is very important for refugee children to ensure that they do not fall too far behind in their development at all levels. If they do fall behind to a significant degree, as so often does happen, the chances are that they will never catch up once they are repatriated or resettled elsewhere. Their entire future is thus jeopardized if basic education services are not forthcoming. However, the reality is that the area of psychosocial rehabilitation is often even more critical for refugee children. In its publication on mental health of refugees, the WHO/UNHCR (1996) has a section on the mental health of refugee children. The publication by Ahearn and Athey (1991) is also very helpful in this context, focusing largely on the research literature. There are in fact quite a few reports of psychosocial programs undertaken with refugee children. The following, for example, was undertaken with Bosnian refugee children in Macedonia in 1993–96 (Catholic Relief Services, 1996, pp. 55–61). The program involved some 300 children aged 7 to 15 years, and had four phases.

> The Introductory Phase—The first phase was the phase of meeting, establishing contacts, introducing the rules of group work, reestablishing confidence and support. . . .

> The Opening Phase—The second phase was oriented towards seeking new methods (ways) of communication through using various working modalities (very often non-verbal ones—lines, drawings, movements, sounds, voices) as the field, the tools for symbolic processing of the contents, with active participation in selection by the children. For instance, we worked very concretely on the following aspects: *deblocation of creativity* . . . ; *stimulation of initiative; child's identity* (numerous games involving names); *intensive emotions; fears* (acting out through process of removing fear); *feelings of aggression* . . . ; the decrease of *anxiety* within the group.

> The Phase of Searching for Personal Meanings—This is the third phase, marked by *the story-telling method*. . . .

> The last phase is The Phase of Integration— Here the main activity work is on *My Book on War*. The work on this book represents the first attempt at direct work on children's war-caused traumatic experiences, and the first chronology of their personal experiences (both the painful and the nice ones), through a story that the child himself needs to put down. . . . The aim of the work in this phase is to connect the most sensitive, often suppressed

contents of the child's experience and to include them into the whole of his life space. (Unkovska, 1996, pp. 60–61)

In the same publication (Catholic Relief Services, 1996, pp. 115ff.), there is a report on a psychosocial program conducted in six kindergartens in Sarajevo in 1996, reflecting a program (Head Start) being implemented in 19 eastern and central European countries under the Soros Foundation. There is a strong emphasis on creating the right atmosphere in the room (sense of security, of feeling loved, of being accepted as competent, of being encouraged to be independent, etc.), while engaging in activities "to heal the war consequences caused by traumas and stress." The program strives to avoid constantly questioning the children about traumas, marking them as different or disabled, or isolating them from their current environment, which continues to be stressful.

In addition to programs conducted with the children themselves, ideally involving family members and others, workers with refugee children place a strong emphasis on working with the children's immediate environment. As Boothby (1992, p. 115) puts it,

> For children who live in displaced communities and refugee camps which lack safety and other basic necessities of life, a PTSD [post–traumatic stress syndrome] approach is not sufficient. Instead, the intervention goal is to create a more positive social reality for the child through broader assistance efforts that help to support or re-establish the child's primary relationships to parents, families, communities and, in some cases, larger ethnic groups.

This approach is essential in part because "the longer they [refugee children] live in the midst of danger and adversity, the more likely it is that their personalities, behaviour, and moral sensibilities will become altered in the process" (Boothby, 1992, p. 120). Athey and Ahearn (1991) also stress this point. They conclude

---

Three important strategies:

- Reuniting children with families if possible.
- Making immediate provision for the developmental and educational needs of children.
- Working with the children's immediate environment.

Case Example

Education Programs for Refugee Children in Africa

In many parts of Africa, the UNHCR has long run a range of education programs for refugee children. With various governments offering places in their schools, the UNHCR meets the costs of study, including travel costs, a personal allowance, and so on. UNHCR social counselors monitor the program and provide the support often needed when the refugee children are separated from their community, are worried about their families who are either missing or still in refugee camps, and experience a range of frustrations. In evaluating the scheme, the UNHCR emphasizes the importance of a strong counseling service, of careful selection of students, and of a series of specialized holiday and remedial programs.

(Example from Guebre-Christos, 1989, pp. 143–145.)

---

their overview of the mental health of refugee children as follows:

> This overview suggests that policy and program development should be designed explicitly to strengthen communities and assist refugees in rebuilding their own communities within the larger society. Ways to support families should also be developed since the family is so critical to the child's adjustment. (p. 16)

Building community may be much more difficult in some contexts than others, but it will always be possible to strengthen communal bonds among refugees and to facilitate strong bonds and mutual support.

Services for Refugee Women

The particular needs of refugee women have long been recognized. "The International NGO Working Group on Refugee Women was created in 1986 to maintain the focus on women refugees by sharing information among NGOs on refugee women and by monitoring and advocating for refugee women's issues with UNHCR" (International NGO Working Group on Refugee Women, 1989, p. 9). It produced *Working With Refugee Women: A Practical Guide* in 1989. In 1991, the UNHCR brought out its *Guidelines on the Protection of Refugee Women* (UNHCR, 1991) and it has placed a strong emphasis on the needs of refugee women in all its programs.

While all refugees are vulnerable, it is commonly accepted that women are among the most vulnerable. Lobo and Mayadas (1997, p. 422) write,

> In recent conflicts women have had to flee with children and the elderly across national, cultural and language barriers without the traditional male support. This has exposed women to moral and physical danger and

other forms of exploitation. Special programs have been designed to address the victims of exploitation, particularly those who have been sexually abused.

The problem goes back in part to the reality that women are often targeted in modern civil wars, with rape used as a weapon against a defenseless civilian population. As Cranna (1994, p. 163) writes about one civil war,

> The war in Bosnia-Herzegovina has been characterized by extensive incidences of rape organized in a systematic manner and often condoned by local officials. Muslim women have suffered most from this crime and the most reliable estimate puts the number of Muslim women raped at 20,000. . . . For many the psychological trauma that accompanies rape will stay with them for a life time.

Women are also targets while fleeing, while it has not been uncommon in refugee camps for those in authority to demand sexual favors in exchange for the women's rightful access to humanitarian aid and other services.

It is also commonly said that women carry the burden of displacement, given that they greatly outnumber male refugees, usually carry responsibility throughout for children and elderly, and are often left as heads of households in cultures where such a status is not widely recognized or provided for. This overall situation exists throughout the period in exile and becomes particularly pertinent within the repatriation-reintegration process.

Given the vulnerability of women to exploitation of various kinds, it is not surprising that the program focus has been on protection. The UNHCR (1991, p. 7) writes,

Women share the protection problems shared by all refugees. Along with all other refugees, women need protection against forced return to their countries of origin; security against armed attacks and other forms of violence; protection from unjustified and unduly prolonged detention; a legal status that accords adequate social and economic rights; and access to such basic items as food, shelter, clothing and medical care.

In addition to these basic needs shared by all refugees, refugee women and girls have special protection needs that reflect their gender: they need, for example, protection against manipulation, sexual and physical abuse and exploitation, and sexual discrimination in the delivery of goods and services.

In the light of this analysis of protection needs, this UNHCR document outlines guidelines that should be adhered to by all governmental and nongovernmental organizations, and suggests a range of programs that can be implemented. It is particularly concerned with camp design and layout; access to food, water, firewood, and other distributed items; access to appropriate health care; education and skills training; and economic activities. These areas, and some others, are also canvassed in the practical guide to working with refugee women published by the International Working Group on Refugee Women in 1989. Many recommendations are set out and detailed in both these documents, together with many case studies of different types of programs with refugee women in the NGO Working Group publication. The area is too broad to even summarize in this publication, but interested workers will have no difficulty in locating material covering this field of work.

A key strategy:

- Develop and employ appropriate measures to protect women.

Case Examples

Women's Organization in Guatemala

Mama Maquin is an organization created by Guatemalan refugee women in Mexico. Among other activities they raise the consciousness of refugee women about their rights as women and take action on these rights, participate in the creation and implementation of necessary services, are involved in the peace and repatriation talks, and ensure that Mama Maquin organizations within Guatemala are present to receive and assist refugee women and their families on return.

(Example taken from WCC, 1996, p. 66.)

Program for Chilean Women in Argentina

In a program for refugee women from Chile exiled in Argentina, an NGO focused on integrating the women within Argentina, while not losing sight of their eventual return to Chile. The NGO implemented labor scholarships that trained women through on-the-job experiences as apprentices in a trade, or through technical training in workshops or businesses. It also supported and encouraged the creation of support groups. Within these groups, the women were quick to organize a range of activities for themselves.

Program for Women in Palestinian Refugee Camps

In Jordan, an NGO developed a program within the largest of the Palestinian refugee camps. In a cultural context where women were not permitted to work outside the camp, yet required work opportunities, the NGO established a center for training and employment with the focus on making clothing for specialized niche markets, such as hospital uniforms.

Employment Programs for Refugee Women in Somalia

In Somalia, the ILO combined with a local NGO to develop programs within four adjacent refugee camps. The aims were income-generation, marketable skills development, and the strengthening of refugee associations, especially women's associations. Many employment opportunities were found with the aid agencies servicing the camps, both within their aid programs and in the income-generation activities they initiated within the camps. This initial work spawned at least another 12 Somali NGOs and a significant integrated camp development project that engaged in setting up a variety of agricultural and microenterprise schemes that created even more employment. Some expatriate workers assisted in these developments while the refugees themselves played significant roles.

(Examples from International NGO Working Group on Refugee Women, 1989, pp. 163, 130, and 126.)

Family Reunion Programs

The likelihood of family members being separated from each other in periods of conflict and population displacement is high indeed. Families may make a decision to separate, to the advantage of some or all family members—for example, sending away a child as many Southeast Asians did—or separation may be an accidental consequence of the ensuing chaos. Whatever the origins of the separation, refugees and displaced persons frequently arrive at an interim destination with no knowledge of whether other family members survived, and if they did, of where they now are. In such circumstances, it is very difficult for most people to settle down and focus on their own needs. Fortunately,

Two key strategies:

- Link forced migrants to available databases.
- In regard to family reunion, monitor refugees' reactions to news received and try to ensure that they are supported when the news is bad.

family reunion needs in such circumstances have long been recognized, and some agencies have developed considerable expertise in setting up a central database for family reunion purposes, gathering data on people's whereabouts, and making that information available to those seeking to locate relatives and friends. The International Red Cross stands out in this regard as having much experience and an ability and readiness to establish this service in most refugee situations. The task of the local social workers is thus simplified. Usually they need only to make sure that the people with whom they are in touch are linked into the database, although they may also be able to assist the Red Cross in expediting the whole process. When refugees are massed in camps and camplike situations, the family reunion process tends to work quite well; however, refugees can be scattered and thus not even aware of such a service. Hence, it is incumbent on workers in all contexts to be aware of this need, of the programs available, and of how to connect individuals to those programs as required.

The second important aspect of the worker's role in relation to family reunion is to monitor refugees' reactions to news received, or try to ensure that they are supported when the news is bad. On receiving news, refugees may be inclined to rush off to find and join a loved one, may be devastated by grief, may misinterpret what they have been told, or may, in general terms, respond to the news in ways that are inappropriate or detrimental to their own well-being. While the reality of the news will always be there, a worker qualified to facilitate decision-making processes and to assist people to handle grief, anxiety, or other emotions will often have an important role to play in this context.

Repatriation Programs

Repatriation of the various categories of forced migrants has become very common in recent years. (See Chapter 11 for a general discussion.) It is a process that varies greatly, however, with both the category of forced migrants involved and the particular circumstances surrounding the repatriation. These variations have great significance for intervention. One important variable is the degree of free choice involved. Some situations constitute in reality forced repatriation with virtually no choice involved, while other situations permit complete freedom of choice. Choice will, however, depend significantly not just on the attitudes of relevant authorities but on the availability of alternative courses of action. A second variable is the degree of involvement of formal agencies in the repatriation. In some situations, spontaneous repatriation occurs and people return with no agencies involved. In other situations, the UNHCR or a government agency may negotiate the return but do little to expedite its occurrence. In other situations again, not only is repatriation negotiated but transport is arranged, an aid package provided to aid reintegration, and workers may even accompany the returnees and stay to assist during the initial postarrival phase. A third important variable is the degree of confusion, chaos, and uncertainty surrounding the repatriation. Situations can vary from relatively peaceful and organized returns to reasonably secure situations to exactly the reverse. Workers need to assess each situation in terms of such variables and plan their roles accordingly.

Some might wonder why refugees and others return of their own accord to situations that are less than ideal. It is important to appreciate that, in probably the great majority of situations, there exist strong forces drawing people back home. One set of forces relates to the importance for most people of home. The identification with a house, land, countryside, a social network, a culture or way of life, and a nation is often very strong; and, despite the knowledge of, for example, war devastation, the death of many people, continuing insecurity, and an uncertain future, many people simply want to go home. A second set of factors relates to the conditions endured during exile. Prolonged periods in refugee camps, asylum seeker holding centers, or alien countryside encampments provide no incentive for staying longer than necessary—sometimes this is one reason why those in power maintain basic conditions. Nor is it just the physical conditions. A period spent in limbo in situations where minimal activity is possible, and where one has a great deal of time to reflect on one's situation and grow anxious, is extremely difficult to handle long-term for most forced migrants. A third and final set of forces relates to the availability of alternatives. Unless forced migrants can at least imagine a viable and satisfactory alternative to returning home, they will choose repatriation; and today satisfactory alternatives are seldom available.

The repatriation of refugees or displaced persons is a field of work within which there is significant experience. By contrast, the repatriation of illegal immigrants generally and asylum seekers from western countries, while occurring quite frequently, is seldom attended to with the same concern for the people involved. This is partly because the repatriation process is more one of deportation, with a strong emphasis on the speedy implementation of court or administrative orders by officials, and with no significant role possible for the helping professions, or even friends. However, in some circumstances, both asylum seekers and illegal immigrants can decide to return home voluntarily, in which case there is scope for worker facilitation of the process. We shall focus this discussion on the repatriation of refugees and displaced persons, but the reader should be aware of the possible application of what is suggested to other situations.

There are basically four steps within the repatriation process where appropriate intervention is often possible and may well make a significant difference to the outcome. These steps are preparation for the future return, the actual transition, reintegration postreturn, and the community-relations situation postreturn.

Preparation for Future Return

Ideally refugees and others should be prepared for whatever it is that lies ahead of them, especially when the future is likely to hold significant difficulties and dangers. The better prepared people are, the more likely it is that the next stage of their lives will be successful. Given, however, that the majority of displaced persons returns home, and that their successful reintegration is the key objective of return, all programs should be geared toward this objective from the earliest stages of a refugee operation. There are three key strategies involved here.

Capacity Building

It will be obvious that returnees are likely to benefit from the possession of specific capabilities. The focus in this context will be on the choice of capabilities covered, the mode of training, and the possibility of using a "training the trainers" approach, so that some of the refugees are provided with the necessary skills to assist others, both in this stage and later. In most cases there is a strong emphasis placed on vocational skills suited to the economy in the country to which refugees are returning. Such capacity building was common in the refugee camps along the Thai-Cambodia border and in the Palestinian camps.

Psychological Preparation

Many displaced persons will face returning with significant levels of apprehension, anxiety, and even fear, and it is beneficial if these emotional reactions can be dealt with, usually through a group work approach. Within this group approach, the emphases will include

the provision of accurate information and the opportunity to discuss it;

allowing participants to voice their concerns and fears and work these through within the group, benefiting from becoming aware that others share the same fears and that discussing them gives them a different reality; and, in some circumstances,

acting out some scenarios involving situations that may arise on return (role plays), thus assisting people to think through what they might do if such scenarios eventuate. (An example here is being confronted with

hostile neighbors who are members of a perceived enemy group.)

Material Support Packages

It is not uncommon for the UNHCR or a particular government agency to provide returnees with some basic resources to assist with reintegration. The package often includes some money, some basic food, some tools, and perhaps some seed. Workers can advocate for the provision of an appropriate package and ensure that recipients think through how best to utilize what is provided. Unfortunately, these packages are often provided more as a bribe to encourage return than to expedite return, and workers need to be aware of this motivation and ensure that, despite this agenda, the package is used beneficially.

Case Examples

Prereturn Training for Cambodians

Cambodian refugees in camps around Southeast Asia were on the whole fortunate to have had access to western-based NGOs' programs in education and employment skills. Many received technical training or training as health service providers, teachers, social workers, community organizers, translators, and administrators. Most hoped to gain employment in their fields on returning to Cambodia, although few believed that that process would be easy.

Preparation for return was seen as needing to include sessions on health conditions in Cambodia (quite different from those in the camps); and sessions for the especially vulnerable individuals—those with disabilities, the elderly, orphans, and so forth—on what to expect on their return and where they might look for any support required.

(Example from UNHCR, 1993, p. 104.)

Lack of Preparation for Refugees From Sierra Leone

By contrast, the preparation of refugees for return to Sierra Leone from surrounding countries was impossible. The UNHCR had no precise details of who would be returning or of their final destinations. In some cases, it was difficult to gain access to the refugees concerned, for various reasons including danger to workers. Hence planning the return and preparation of people was impossible.

(Example from UNHCR, 1997.)

Predeparture Plan for Refugees Returning to Mozambique

The predeparture plan for the repatriation of refugees to Mozambique included registration of everyone, vaccination and health screening programs, and the provision of information about the situation in specific areas of Mozambique. There was a major focus on the danger of the estimated 2 million land mines scattered around the country.

(Example from UNHCR, 1993, p. 108.)

Assistance Plan for Refugees Returning to Mali

An example of a repatriation assistance package is that provided to Tuareg refugees returning to Mali. This package included tents, mosquito nets, and food. On arriving in their home area, they also became eligible for a settlement grant.

(Example taken from UNHCR, 1997/1998, p. 151.)

The Actual Transition

The actual transition takes many different forms. It may be undertaken on foot, by truck or van, by bus, or by air. It may occur in small groups or involve massive numbers moving together. The concern is that those planning the repatriation may be focused on the logistics of the operation and have little time to consider, or have any insight into, the people dimension. The stress associated with the movement, and hence the impact on the sick and disabled, children, the elderly, and mothers caring for several children, should be carefully considered, and everything possible done to ensure that all involved have a reasonable chance of handling the ordeal. This should mean that members of the helping professions are involved in the planning process as fully as possible. The focus should be on the mode of transit, facilities available during transit, necessary supplies carried with or by the people, and the arrangement of who travels with them to maximize support. It is especially important to ensure that the needs of the most vulnerable are met during the transition, and that the separation of such people from family or support groups is prevented. Ideally workers will carry out such planning in close consultation with those being repatriated—at least through their leaders.

Whether there is any possibility of workers accompanying the returnees will depend on many factors, but every effort should be made to ensure that vulnerable returnees, especially when returning to comparatively unknown, devastated, or insecure situations, are accompanied, met at the other end, or at least well prepared for all eventualities. If workers are not available for this purpose, members of the group can be selected, or asked to volunteer, for training to act as support personnel for the journey and initial reintegration period. It would not be difficult to inculcate certain basic skills in selected individuals that would enable them to provide relevant support services, as a preventative measure, and to recognize and respond appropriately to certain danger signs if these occur, and the UNHCR has often adopted this approach. However, workers need to be aware that all returnees will possess a degree of anxiety and be faced with many tasks on arrival, often leaving them too preoccupied with their own situations to be concerned about others.

Integration Postreturn

Returnees can face many problems postreturn. Some may find themselves displaced again, within their own country, because their property has been taken over by others, their land has been mined or in other ways rendered unusable, or their economic situation in their original place of residence is not viable. Returnees may move from rural to urban areas in search of relief or employment, to other rural areas, or to live with relatives or friends. The precise situation postreturn will clearly affect reintegration.

One key element postreturn is the community relations situation prevailing between returnees and other groupings in their place of residence. Sometimes returnees are confronted with neighbors, community members, and local authorities who have no sensitivity to their rights or needs, sometimes because they regard their flight as desertion. This is discussed in the following subsection.

A vital first task is securing adequate shelter. This may mean temporary accommodation or urgent temporary repairs to the returnees' own homes. Longer-term, it may mean assistance with rebuilding or relocation, or legal and administrative assistance to acquire access to their rightful property. The property issue is often a complex and sensitive one, with rival legal and moral claims to rightful possession being not uncommon. In Bosnia-Herzegovina a property commission was established to handle what was there a large and complex problem.

A vital second task is securing a source of sustenance. As immediate employment is unlikely to be available to most returnees, they must often seek to access humanitarian aid programs. Some, however, will become dependent on relatives and friends who had not left, or who are still in exile but in countries that permit employment. It is imperative that some short-term source of sustenance is achieved, and many returnees require assistance in achieving this, but beyond that point long-term income generation becomes a major challenge. In at least some situations, workers may be able to consult with returnees and others in devising locally feasible income-generation schemes.

Finally, the integration needs of specific family members need often to be addressed. Children, youth, women, men, the elderly, and the disabled can all be confronted with category-related as well as personal needs. Meeting those needs will call for a range of local initiatives, including psychosocial programs, self-help programs, community development programs, and social service programs, including health and education services provision.

Case Example

Assistance in Communities of Tuareg People Returning to Mali

The UNHCR facilitated the integration of Tuareg refugees returning to Mali by constructing new and rehabilitating existing water supply sources; distributing seeds, tools, and other agricultural inputs; providing training in irrigation techniques; establishing microcredit and income-generation projects; and repairing and constructing schools and furnishing them. An important aspect of this and many other such integration projects is that no real distinction is made between former refugees, returning internally displaced persons, and the resident population. This is in the interests of equity and harmonious community relations.

(Example from UNHCR, 1997/1998, p. 151.)

The Community Relations Situation

Two situations that involve community relations are quite common. One is where returnees are unpopular among their own people who did not flee. The act of fleeing may be perceived as cowardice, betrayal, or simply taking the easy way out, while those who remained might see themselves as the heroes who stayed to defend property, communities, or country. In such circumstances, those who remained might see themselves as rightfully possessing first claim to property, including that which they occupied during the conflict, and also to humanitarian aid, employment opportunities, and capacity-building programs. This places the returnees in a very difficult situation. It is a particularly invidious situation when local authorities support the claims of those who stayed on against those of the returnees.

The second situation is where a divided community, one in which competing groups fought against each other during the period of conflict, continues to be bitterly divided; or even worse, where one party won significant rights in the peace negotiations and now controls the local situation, while the returnees belong to the rival party. In these situations, returnees will not be welcome. They may be met with violence as they attempt to rebuild their homes and so on; or they may be ostracized and have few opportunities open to them. Their return might even be perceived as an attempt by outsiders to change the demographic balance and so influence future elections or other events.

Such situations confronting returnees at the local level are of course part of the nationwide need for reconciliation programs (see Chapter 9), almost invariably required after the types of situations that result in large-scale displacement of people. While these programs need to be instituted at various levels, they will frequently be needed also at the local level; hence, they become an integral element within the overall repatriation and integration plan. However, the field of reconciliation relating to a conflict and post-conflict situation is still very new. At the national level, interesting experiments have occurred with truth commissions, as in South Africa, and the prosecution of war criminals, as in the former Yugoslavia and Rwanda. Both approaches can be helpful in publicly acknowledging what occurred during the conflict. What impact they have on longer-term community relations is difficult to say, as we are still too close to such situations.

Reconciliation at the local level will be more akin to traditional community relations experience, which has been typically with racially divided communities, particularly in the United States, and with countries experiencing large-scale immigration, such as Australia, Canada, and the United Kingdom. Whether the strategies for intergroup relations developed in such contexts are directly applicable to the post-conflict situation cannot as yet be determined; however, it seems logical to suggest that they have a place, even if requiring adaptation, as would probably be necessary anyway given that most postconflict situations are located in developing countries. Let us consider some of the traditional strategies in terms of their relevance to postconflict situations.

Education Strategies. These strategies focus on ensuring that people have access to the facts pertaining to the groupings in question, to their coexistence in communities, and to what has occurred in the past. Such education can be attempted in many different ways (e.g., printed word, television shows, and street theater), depending on the context, but there will always be a strong emotional component involved in people's responses, often distorting the cognitive level. In other words, people have strong feelings and attitudes that "the truth" may do nothing to change.

Participation Strategies. It has long been believed that, in many situations, people's negative feelings will be dissipated once they have the opportunity to meet, and preferably get to know, members of the opposing group. Strategies may include bringing people together to work on common tasks, such as rebuilding, or in social contexts, or even to discuss the situation and engage in some planning for the future. Clearly relationships have to be at a certain level before people from rival groups can be brought together with positive outcomes.

Discussion Group Strategies or What Was Originally Called "Revelation." In the postconflict and refugee returnees situations, it may be particularly important that community members are brought together to discuss their views of what occurred during the period of conflict. Such groups can give people an opportunity to vent their anger and make accusations, and for members of the other party to respond and present the situation from their viewpoint. Whether this will result ultimately in a fairer or more accurate assessment of what has occurred among at least some parties, whether it will lead to expressions of sorrow and even apologies, or whether it will result in a degree of forgiveness, will depend largely on the circumstances and partly on the local leadership available. However, the skill of group leaders could also be a major factor, which raises the question of whether reconciliation work can and should be taught to workers likely to encounter such situations. There may be a strong element of negotiation involved in such group work, and certainly conflict mediation skills will be important.

Equalizing Opportunities. These have been traditionally seen as very important strategies. They assume that part of the community relations problem lies in structural issues, such as lack of equal access to particular facilities or opportunities. While the postconflict situation is essentially different, for example, from race relations in the USA, it is not unlikely that one or more parties have emerged from the conflict with greater access to power and resources than other parties, resulting in significant frustration, anger, and other emotions which will aggravate emotions already there from the past. It may, therefore, be important to explore this aspect of a situation and see what can be done to change arrangements or structures. This may, of course, be difficult to achieve at the wider level, but some progress may be possible at the local level.

Training of Various Authorities and Leaders. Rather than intervene directly, it may be preferable to work through community leaders or public officials. If such people can be convinced by skilled workers of the importance of reconciliation and positive community relations for the future of all concerned, they may be able in turn to guide their constituencies toward such.

Integration Programs

While reference has been made above to the integration, or reintegration, of returning refugees or displaced persons, there are other contexts where integration is important. One so-called durable solution for displaced persons is to remain in their place of first asylum and be integrated there. This solution has been quite common in some parts of the world. Furthermore, the third durable solution of resettlement involves integration within the country of resettlement, and, while less common today, this form of integration has been the reality of hundreds of thousands of refugees since the end of World War II.

Integration is a complex process about which much has been written in developed countries over the years. (See, for example, Cox, 1987, 1989, for discussion of the literature to that time and a focus on Australia.) It is commonly seen as a multistage process involving several parties and affected by a range of important variables. It is seldom without its difficulties for the newcomer, even when the differences between the newcomer and the host population are relatively

Table 12.2   Summary of four steps in the repatriation process

Steps	Strategies/Process
Preparation for future return	– Capacity building – Psychological preparation – Material support packages
The actual transition	– Stress associated with the movement – Mode of transit, facilities available during transit, supplies, and accompanying person – Needs of the most vulnerable – Separation of family members
Integration postreturn	– Adequate shelter – Source of sustenance – Integration needs of specific family members
Community relations postreturn	– Education strategies – Participation strategies – Discussion group strategies – Equalizing opportunities – Training of various authorities and leaders

few. When a different race, culture, and set of past experiences are involved, it can be a very difficult process indeed. Where forced migrants are involved, significant differences between the immigrants and the host population are often the reality. Moreover, forced migrants are by definition people who did not choose, in the full sense of the word, to be in that situation. They were obliged to flee and may well find themselves grieving both for a home and lifestyle now gone, as well as for many relatives and friends who did not make it in trying to escape.

There are many integration programs that have been tried and tested, particularly in western countries. Some of these will be relevant in the context being discussed, but we should be aware that, particularly in impoverished developing country environments, there may be additional factors at work. Among the integration programs commonly discussed are

- preparation for the period of adjustment;
- development of capabilities, such as language, that will aid integration;
- education of the host community;
- a focus on community relations, as described under repatriation programs;
- the provision of opportunities, such as employment, to newcomers without disadvantaging members of the host population;
- facilitation of ethnic group development and community development to provide newcomers with a support base and some sense of power in the context;
- access to necessary health, education, and other services and facilities, on as equal a basis as possible as pertains to the host population; and
- category-specific services to meet the needs of specific sections of the newcomer population.

> *A key strategy:*
>
> • Raise awareness among the displaced of both the prevailing situation and of human rights issues.

Case Example

UNTAC and Human Rights in Postwar Cambodia

UNTAC (the UN Transitional Authority in Cambodia) that administered Cambodia after the war possessed a human rights component. The organization managed to free some political prisoners, to ban certain forms of treatment in prisons, and to foster indigenous human rights groups. These groups were extremely successful, with memberships eventually totaling several hundreds of thousands.

(Example from Shawcross, 2000, p. 57.)

Human Rights Programs

Forced migration situations are permeated with human rights abuses. They are frequently a cause of flight, a factor in the process of escaping, and characteristic of many situations in which forced migrants often find themselves. Many refugees are not safe in refugee camps; many asylum seekers exist in conditions that, in some people's opinions, epitomize breaches of their human rights; and many returnees return to situations where they possess no or few rights and have no one to advocate for them. The situations vary greatly but the constant is that those human rights that have been guaranteed by various conventions are not enforced.

In these situations, the roles of social workers include advocacy, protection, and awareness-raising campaigns specifically in relation to human rights. Advocacy represents an attempt to change the situation by making sure that the facts are known to those with power to intervene, that those engaged in the abuse are identified to the public and authorities, and that alternative arrangements likely to be beneficial are well publicized. Protection signifies a recognition that the abuse situation may not change dramatically or

quickly, and that it is incumbent on social workers to identify ways in which vulnerable groups can be given some protection and then strive to have the alternative arrangements implemented. Finally, the forced migrants often have no awareness of the regime of rights, and of the illegality or unacceptability of what is happening to them. It can be helpful for social workers to raise the level of awareness, among the displaced, of both the prevailing situation and of the people's rights under various conventions. What actions forced migrants can take for themselves will vary, and are ultimately up to them, but they should at least have the option to speak out on their own behalf by being in possession of the pertinent facts.

Legal Programs

In addition to the human rights issue discussed above, many forced migrants ideally can benefit from legal advice or representation. Frequently they are obliged to make applications regarding their current and desired status, to provide information to authorities regarding their past experiences and reasons for fleeing, to resist attempts to deport or repatriate them, or to argue for certain rights for themselves or their families. When lacking experience in handling such situations, and especially when poorly educated and perhaps even illiterate, their ability to present themselves and their situation adequately may be very limited. If, in addition, they are fearful about the possible consequences of divulging certain facts or accepting certain proposals, their ability to be effective in their own defense will be even more limited. Hence the need for legal advice or representation is often considerable. Frequently such assistance is available to asylum seekers in developed countries, but it is seldom available in many other contexts; and the goal of providing formal legal services to all forced migrants is clearly an impossible one. While field-workers in such contexts may not be a very adequate substitute for legally qualified personnel, there may be no option but that they fulfill this role.

It is, in any case, possible and desirable that those moving into the international field receive a basic education in the legal aspects of commonly prevailing situations. This training should cover the major aspects of human rights law and the specific rights pertaining to refugees, asylum seekers, and others. It should also cover the potential role of the social worker in assisting forced migrants at the legal level in several commonly identified situations. Realistically, it may not be possible for the

typical worker to play this role on a one-to-one basis; and alternative strategies include

- group information and discussion sessions,
- the training of some members of the group in the basics of relevant situations, and
- lobbying hard for legal personnel to be made available.

Forced migrants are extremely defenseless in many situations in which they find themselves, and the way in which governments fall back on legal approaches to resolving situations of forced migrants makes it essential that workers in the field take this aspect of their work very seriously.

Community Development Programs

It is unusual in the literature to find reference to community development programs in forced migration situations, but some such situations are so stable and long-term that there seems to be no reason why a community development approach should not be adapted to such a context. However, as the following case example from Hong Kong's closed camps for Southeast Asian refugees in the 1980s reveals, doing so may not be without some ethical dilemmas and significant opposition from various parties.

Case Example

A Case Study of a Community Development Program in a Refugee Camp in Hong Kong

The NGO that implemented this program identifies empowerment as the key goal of any community development strategy, with participation of the target population in service delivery as the key to empowerment. The agency recognized, however, that describing community development as planned social change within a community or group of communities had limited application in an institutionalized community, especially one that possessed no clear civic rights and significant uncertainty regarding the future of the people involved.

The community development process in this situation began with a stock-taking of existing power relationships, including past critical experiences of the group, the existence of traditional power structures within the group, identifying influential persons, and relationships with camp management. This was achieved through purposive interaction with community members, which also involved achieving reasonable rapport between the group and workers. The next step was to identify the interest groups in the community (e.g., Women's Association, Buddhist Association, youth groups, foster care providers, and senior citizens groups), and the presence of issues that were important avenues for community organization (e.g., handicapped persons, emotionally disturbed people, unaccompanied minors, security and violence issues, and camp hygiene issues).

The most important aspect of the community development strategy was to identify the needs of the community, and to try to mobilize the resources of the community and external resources around these needs. The list of needs included the following types: social, health, hygiene, security, cultural, economic, and those of special groups. This identification of needs was seen as an ongoing process.

The NGO also ensured that it became involved in all orientation sessions for newly screened-in refugees, and it produced an information booklet for this purpose.

The following difficulties were encountered:

Some difficulties were experienced with camp managers, who were essentially trained for managing criminals.

Ethnic structures of the camp were a critical factor in the strategy, with ethnic rivalries constantly marring the peace of the camp.

The high level of apathy among refugees, engendered by long-term incarceration in camps and the institutionalized environment, made high levels of participation difficult to achieve.

On a cultural level, most Vietnamese refugees had no concept of liberal democratic politics, and found it difficult to accept a right of individuals to participate in decision making affecting their lives.

The role of the community development worker as facilitator and catalyst, and the rapport each established, were the most crucial tools. The community development paraprofessional workers were important role models and links between agency and community. All invitations, for example, had to be personalized by these workers. In addition, the following were found to be essential:

The community structures that emerged required some economic freedom.

Community leaders needed space within which to gather and work.

Information gathering had always to be undertaken in a culturally appropriate manner.

Elected community leaders needed to receive some token payment.

The creation of a program advisory committee representing all parties was important.

The NGO saw this overall strategy as responding to the microscopic reality of the totality of "refugee reality." The ability of the process to articulate community needs at high levels was widely accepted as most important, although the NGO staff, when acting as power brokers, often felt powerless.

The NGO concluded that it would be naïve to think that such a community development strategy could result in dramatic changes in the empowering process of refugee inhabitants of such a closed refugee camp, but that even limited progress was very important to strive for. (This study is taken from Community and Family Services International, 1991.)

Conclusion

In this chapter we have sought to convey something of the enormity, complexity, and urgency of working with the various forced migrant populations around the world. There is a lot of experience in this field, and a lot of literature documenting that experience (although much of it is not readily accessible except through specialized libraries such as that of the Refugee Studies Programme at Oxford University), and we have sought to identify and convey some of the key conclusions of that literature. We are aware, however, that much of the literature referred to reflects a period when attitudes toward displaced persons, asylum seekers, and refugees were far more sympathetic than they are at the time of writing, and the whole field far less politicized than it is today. Instead of social workers in this field working harmoniously alongside a range of authorities, they will today often find themselves in conflict with some authorities, while working with other authorities and agencies that are not as well supported as they need to be. In other words, this field of work has become increasingly difficult, even as the need for it has grown significantly. It is, therefore, all the more important that the social work profession commit itself to expanding its understanding of, and ability to contribute to, this important field.

The social services division of the UNHCR and others have done considerable work on exploring how best to contribute to the plight of the various categories of displaced persons, and their work should be disseminated and incorporated into the curricula of schools of social work. No doubt we shall learn much more over the next few decades on how best to assist displaced persons in a range of situations in which they are commonly found, especially if we undertake the necessary research in this field. More difficult, however, will be the task of identifying feasible "durable solutions" (a UN term) for those populations of asylum seekers, displaced persons, and others toward whom at present there often exist such negative attitudes, and whose situations and treatment are so frequently completely unacceptable from a humanitarian and human rights perspective. Identifying acceptable outcomes for these forced migrants will be extremely difficult, and will require the ingenuity, commitment, and compassion of the social work profession along with a range of other professions and individuals.

Summary

- Social workers can contribute to most types of programs, applying a range of effective strategies.
- Social workers should focus on the most disadvantaged forced migrants. They need to intervene at levels that are culturally appropriate, and which creatively and constructively engage the forced migrants.
- Priority should be given to strategies that meet the educational and psychological needs of children and that protect women.
- To facilitate family reunion, social workers should link forced migrants with existing databases and monitor their responses to news of family members.
- Repatriation and reintegration require systematic planning, with the steps including preparation, the actual transition, reintegration, and fostering harmonious community relations.

- Appropriate education, employment, and welfare programs need to be developed for forced migrants involved in third-country resettlement.

- Social workers should raise awareness of human rights among forced migrants and lobby for appropriate legal services.

- The growing phenomenon of forced migration is becoming more complex and difficult. By strengthening their commitment to this field, social workers can contribute significantly to the well-being of forced migrants.

Questions and Topics for Discussion

- Review the general and specific programs outlined as relevant to forced migration situations.

- In relation to the specific programs referred to in the text, what do you consider to be possible strategies, and what might be the roles therein of social work and the helping professions generally?

- If you were a social worker in the forced migration field, which program would you prefer to work with, and what knowledge and skills would you need to have?

- What difficulties and dilemmas are social workers and others likely to face when working in forced migration situations?

- How idealistic are the programs and strategies presented in terms of the nature of the majority of forced migration situations to which they might potentially apply?

- Which human rights apply to forced migrants, how do they tend to be observed, and what implications do they have for future action?

- Assuming that you are asked to work with a group of forced migrants, identify your existing strengths and possible areas of improvement for engaging confidently in such work.

- Analyze the case study presented near the end of this chapter and identify key programs, strategies, and issues in it.

Possible Areas for Research Projects

- Undertake an evaluation of a known, or documented, social work program undertaken within a forced migration context.

- Document a repatriation program for forced migrants and identify factors facilitating effective repatriation.

- For a selected country, analyze the impact of recent (anti)migration policies, regarding asylum seekers or others, and identify relevant programs that have been or could be developed to assist the people involved.

Further Reading

Lobo, M., & Mayadas, N. S. (1997). International social work practice: A refugee perspective. In N. S. Mayadas, T. D. Watts, & D. Elliott (Eds.), *International handbook on social work theory and practice* (pp. 411–428). Westport, CT: Greenwood.

WHO/UNHCR. (1996). *Mental health of refugees.* Geneva: WHO.

For recent analyses of the global situation of displaced persons, the best source is the UNHCR's regular publication, *The State of the World's Refugees.*

Readers are referred also to the following journals for a range of useful articles on forced migration and intervention in these contexts:

Journal of Refugee Studies
Canada's periodical on refugees: *Refuge*
International Journal of Refugee Law

13

International Social Work With Specific Populations

In the previous chapters we have focused on four fields of international social work, each field concerning a well-recognized area of activity occupying the international community and generating significant bodies of literature. Other fields that could have been discussed include natural disasters, the health and education fields, and disability. While fields such as these represent one way in which international social work is organized, many agencies and individual workers elect rather to focus on a specific population. The situations of all such populations are closely associated with one or more of the well-known fields; however, they represent discrete populations with specific characteristics that call for a highly targeted response to presenting needs. There are many such populations, but we have selected four on which to focus here largely as examples, although each of these populations has become of concern to social workers and others in developing countries.

One common characteristic of most such populations, and certainly of the following four, is their vulnerability. The UNDP (1997, p. 12) has defined vulnerability as follows: "Vulnerability has two faces: external exposure to shocks, stress and risk; and internal defencelessness, a lack of means to cope without suffering damaging loss."

While many people in the world face vulnerability of one kind or another (see UNDP, 1999, p. 90; Friedmann, 1992), the vulnerability faced by specific populations arises from the characteristics of these populations and their situations, and as such calls for particular understanding.

A second common characteristic of most such populations is marginalization, meaning that the population in question is marginalized by the local mainstream population. The marginalization might be social (facing a degree of social exclusion); economic (facing a degree of discrimination in employment markets, etc.); or political (possessing no power in society and no access to political participation). Marginalization is a major factor in creating vulnerability, but not all vulnerable people are marginalized.

In practice, most vulnerable marginalized populations have been certain types of racial-ethnic minority groups, certain types of immigrant groups, certain child and youth populations, and

Learning Objectives

A study of this chapter should enable readers to

- Understand the nature and significance of four specific populations—street children, child laborers, migrant workers, and AIDS orphans—as vulnerable marginalized groups.
- Reflectively apply the integrated-perspectives approach (Chapter 2) to an analysis of and work with such marginalized vulnerable groups.
- Understand key strategies and programs employed to work with each of the four specific groups.
- Understand common aspects of responding to marginalized vulnerable groups and applying key strategies.

certain categories of men and women. All such populations are prone to poverty, low levels of health and education, high levels of personal suffering, low levels of self-esteem, very restricted social networks, and an endangered sense of identity. Often the innate ability of the individuals involved to establish strong group formations with fellow victims in self-help type arrangements is also fairly limited, largely because of their situations.

The populations which we shall consider here are street children, child laborers, migrant workers, and AIDS orphans.

Street Children

The United Nations Convention on the Rights of the Child (1989) is a widely endorsed convention that obliges state signatories to introduce policies and programs to protect and uphold the rights of children. (For a discussion on this Convention, see Save The Children, 1999.) In the Convention on the Rights of the Child and in other areas of international usage, "a child means every human being below the age of eighteen years unless, under the law applicable to the child, majority is attained earlier." However, in some states, a child is defined as a person under the age of 21, or occasionally some other given age beyond eighteen.

Definitions and Numbers

The definition of a street child is somewhat more difficult. A common form of definition is the following:

Street children are those who spend most of their time on the streets whether working or not; have only tenuous ties, or no ties at all, with their families; and have developed specific survival strategies.

The definition is deliberately vague as to what the child is actually doing on the streets and the relationship that the child has with his or her family. It therefore encapsulates the view that street children in fact constitute a very varied population, rendering generalizations unhelpful. Moreover, the detailed circumstances prevailing among children on the street will vary considerably from place to place and time to time, again making general conclusions dangerous.

The numbers of street children are understandably largely unknown. They exist in many towns and cities across many countries and are impossible to number. One estimate in the early nineties put the number at 100 million, while about the same time UNICEF estimated the number to be about 30 million. The reality is that we

Table 13.1   Examples of categories of street children

Focused on reasons for being on the street (SSWAP, 1988)

Helping parents to earn a living
Maltreated by their parents
From broken homes
Parents unable to provide for them
Just playing on the streets
Having no home whatever

Focused on children's relationship to the street and family (NASWE, 1992)

Children on the street—work on the street but do not live there
Children of the street—both work and live on the street, having left their families
Completely abandoned children

Focused specifically on family relationships

Children who see their families virtually daily
Children who see their families intermittently (e.g., on visits to the rural home)
Children who never see their families but know where they are
Children who have no contact with and no knowledge of their families of origin

Focused specifically on intervention strategies (UNDP, 1996b)

Street-based with no family ties
Street children with families
Sole breadwinners
Educated street children with or without family ties

---

do not know; however, it is widely believed that the number is very large and probably growing in recent decades. Indeed, some would go so far as to see it as an inevitable aspect of urban development in developing countries.

Categories of Street Children

Many different categorizations of street children have been suggested, the only common denominator being the belief that the population is very varied. Categorizations are developed for different reasons, reflecting the diversity. Some categorizations focus on reasons for children being on the street; some on the nature of the relationship street children have with their families of origin; and some on intervention strategies by suggesting that different

categories require different approaches. Let us look at a few examples.

In each of the examples in Table 13.1, each category identified is seen as having quite specific characteristics that identify the children, represent important determining factors in understanding their situations, and will influence the manner in which a worker will determine the intervention strategy to be used. Categories reflect both root causes, such as extreme poverty or family breakdown, and specific elements of the prevailing situation, and both are important considerations for the worker seeking to develop helpful intervention programs.

We shall discuss in the next section the various intervention strategies that have been found useful. We should recognize, however, that there are other parties with different agendas. There are those involved in crime, prostitution, and so on who are eager to recruit street children and exploit their situations for their own ends. Then there are those in authority positions who regard street children as a nuisance to others on the streets, or as shaming their city and nation. Authorities have been reported in parts of South America as engaging in killing children on the streets, while elsewhere the goal is to push them out of certain areas, drive them further underground, or simply harass them to discourage their lifestyle and activities. Finally, the general public may adopt a stance toward street children of a particular kind, such as establishing vigilante gangs to drive them away from areas, providing handouts and offering charity, or acting toward the children so as to demonstrate rejection or worse. Workers in the field must appreciate that they cannot always expect the cooperation of relevant others for whatever they are seeking to achieve. As far as the children are concerned, while their right to elect to be on the street should be respected, their right to have other options open to them should also not be neglected.

Intervention Strategies and Skills in Working With Street Children

Let us begin the discussion by looking at four aspects of work with street children where possible options exist, which a worker might need to consider in any particular context, and then we shall consider which strategies appear to have been the more successful.

Work With the Street Children, Their Families, or Their Communities

This is a common set of options that arises in a range of situations, namely with the individual children, their families, or their communities. When one opts to work with street children directly, this may be simply because they are too alienated or separated from their families and communities. When there is a family with which the street child has fairly regular contact, an alternative is to work with the family, and obviously with the street child to some degree, in an attempt to improve family functioning, raise socioeconomic status, and reintegrate the street child within a family where he or she will have a higher level of well-being than on the street. If the street children are drawn from a number of families living within a common community, the third option may be to work to improve the lot of the community, with benefits hopefully flowing through to both the families and the street children. The decision may be based in part on the urgency of the situation existing on the street, and the need for remedial action to be taken in that context. In some situations, work at all three levels may be necessary and possible, perhaps involving a team of collaborating workers.

Work at the Preventative or Remedial Level

This is again a common choice confronting workers. It is often clear that remedial work, while essential for a number of individuals, will in effect be a patching-up job for the individuals concerned, while doing nothing to prevent others from joining the street children's ranks each week. Preventative work, which in this case might focus on the root causes such as underdevelopment and poverty, may seem like abandoning the current street children population in the vague hope that the achievement of better conditions generally will reduce the numbers coming onto the streets in the future. It is a difficult choice, and most of us would opt for attempting to do both, which is obviously the ideal answer. However, the two options call for different strategies, according in part to prevailing levels of development, and each requires different kinds of workers.

Develop Responses at the Institutional, Community, Center, or Street Level

Again these options have their equivalents in many contexts. In this context, the institutional approach, sometimes called the correctional approach, tends to see the street children as delinquents who need to be removed from the streets, incarcerated for a period, and hopefully rehabilitated. Most field-workers would oppose both this definition of street children and this approach to the problem. Criminalizing victims can have very adverse effects on the individuals involved and on community perceptions of the problem. There seems also to be little evidence that it commonly has a positive outcome.

The community approach here has limited meaning, unless by it we mean the communities from which the street children originally came and with which they may still have links. The issue here really is whether the inevitably long-term nature of community work is going to achieve positive results within a time frame that will benefit the current population of street children. It may represent long-term preventative work.

The center-based approach assumes that it is possible and desirable to remove the street children from their street environment for at least short periods. Clearly individuals' use of these centers must be on a purely voluntary basis, so much will depend on whether the centers and their staff are regarded as trustworthy and an answer to perceived needs. The centers may address basic health and education needs, provide further education or vocational training, or offer opportunities for the street children to express their needs and fears and receive helpful support and advice. These centers can have much to offer street children, as many programs have demonstrated, but require very skilled and dedicated staff operating a program that is acceptable to the young people themselves. It is possible, however, that the centers cater only to street children possessing a degree of understanding, maturity, and initiative. They may not be accessible to other children who may require, in effect, an outreach program through which to establish an initial level of trust. Only then might some of these children be attracted to centers.

Street-based Approaches

The street-based approach is essentially an outreach approach designed to make contact with those street children who are difficult to reach. Because it is designed for the most difficult or troubled young people in the most difficult situations, it is, generally speaking, extremely difficult work. It may be designed to link some street children back to centers, but in other situations it may have to function as a street-based alternative to the center. The worker is then faced with the challenge of how to provide health services, education, job training, and other tangible assistance, as well as support, counseling, and a link with the wider society for those wishing to make use of it. There are those who are skeptical whether street-based programs have any impact at all. One difficulty is that any impact that they do have is often intangible and even unobservable. It is certainly clear that workers in such programs come under great pressure and may even confront a degree of danger—from street children themselves, criminals, police, and even members of the general public. A writer in Latin America presents a common point of view (Raffaelli, 1997, p. 98):

> The outreach approach is more viable in its ability to reach large numbers of children where they actually live, but the ultimate success of street-based programs is questionable, given the dangers of living on the street and the difficulty of moving from street life into mainstream society. In the words of one experienced youth work educator, "There is no rehabilitation on the streets . . . salvage work means setting limits, and the street knows no limits." Most street youth advocates believe that homeless youth need a safe living situation off the street, where they can participate in creating an alternative to the families they have lost. The role of social workers and other service providers in promoting positive youth development in those alternative settings is critical.

> *Four broad areas of options in working with street children:*
>
> - Work with the street children, their families, or their communities.
> - Work at the preventative or remedial level.
> - Choice of street-based approaches.
> - Choice of responding at institutional, community, family, center, or street level.

Let us now turn to some specific strategies that are regarded as beneficial in the street children situation across a range of specific contexts.

Some Strategies in Working With Street Children

The following strategies emerge time and time again in the literature and in conference papers. Each strategy has been tried in a range of countries and found feasible and beneficial. We shall examine each strategy separately, but it should be clear to the reader that some agencies and workers will be in a position to have a multitiered approach. The following example of such an approach comes from Colombia (Carrizosa and Poertner, 1992, p. 409). It is described as a rehabilitation model and has the following elements:

> The programme's four levels move from engaging the child in the street . . . to moving to a half-way house. . . . If the child demonstrates a commitment to the programme through behaviour changes, the next level is the . . . residential school and the final level is . . . a self-governing community . . . with the ultimate goal being integration into the larger society.

We shall examine each strategy as if undertaken independently.

The Street Educator/Facilitator Strategy

As a report from the Philippines describes this strategy, "The street-based approach reaches out to children in their street or places of work. Street educators conduct informal dialogues with the children to get to know them, understand their situation, offer assistance, and impart desirable values" (NASWE, 1992, p. 7).

A Latin American article suggests that "this approach assumes that the best way to fight the problem is to educate and empower the children" (Carrizosa and Poertner, 1992, p. 409). Frequently such programs work with the street children in the identification of problems, and then use those problems to explore possible solutions. The process allows for a degree of informal education to occur. It encourages the children to question the society that has created their situation, but also to consider what options are available to each of them as individuals. When the children themselves explore possible options, this may permit the worker to facilitate those children making contact with the services and opportunities available to them, of which previously they had been unaware. The worker will then provide support and encouragement to those who seek to change their situations. In Latin America in particular, "the outreach approach draws on the model proposed by Paulo Freire (1973), who argued that the educational process must involve the learner as an active agent, not as a passive subject" (Raffaelli, 1997, p. 97). Other writers emphasize that the major roles of the street worker are to make street children aware of the facilities available to them, create an awareness within them of their own life and situation, and facilitate their access to the services they need for their personal growth and development and future well-being (e.g., Rane, 1994, p. 99). This of course assumes that there are such services open to street children, and unfortunately this is not always the case. When they are not already available, an important role of the worker will be to promote their development.

One aspect of such work that is sometimes raised is the importance of encouraging self-help or mutual support structures among the street children. Research shows that street children frequently form groups within which the older and stronger children support others, or the more experienced children advise and guide newcomers to the streets. While this natural occurrence is to be applauded, it is sometimes possible for a worker to deliberately stimulate the strengthening or extension of these bonds. For example, if a child cannot be removed from the streets and is clearly vulnerable, the worker may well be able to persuade other street children to offer that child a type of family or group environment. While we appreciate that such support is sometimes—but certainly not always—provided with ulterior, and usually exploitative, motives, it may still be better than nothing.

Street work among street children is both a viable and often a necessary approach. It must be appreciated, however, that it is potentially very demanding on the worker. The worker operates essentially without on-the-spot supports, faces many demanding situations, is often obliged to work unusual hours, and will usually find such work to be exceedingly draining. Because such work is often undertaken by paraprofessional workers, we would stress the importance of them receiving appropriate training. We would also strongly recommend that such workers operate from within teams, whereby each worker receives the supports that are essential for the worker's well-being.

The Street School Strategy

While the street educator focuses, in education terms, on informal education pertaining to the street children's current realities, the street school strategy is concerned also with preparing the children for entry to the formal school system. In most situations, a combination of informal and formal education will be called for. The street school, however, specifically recognizes that many street children, while currently outside the formal education system, are both capable of entering it at some point and often desirous of doing so if given the opportunity. They may need to remain on the streets for the time being, for reasons beyond their control such as the need to support their families, but may in time be able to enter school and move on to vocational training.

Street schools are established almost literally on the streets to cater to street children's education needs at times and in ways that are consistent with the children's realities. The venue may be a mobile van, a tent, or some other structure. The school focuses on those hours that represent a lull in the street children's normal activities. There may be classes of a kind, or children may come when they wish and pursue, under guidance, their personal study program. Schools cater to a wide age range and a wide range of educational levels. The goal is to assist children to reach the level necessary to enter the formal system at the level appropriate for their age. A wide range of teaching and learning methods is required to cater to this diversity, and the staff needs to be focused on individuals' needs.

Invariably the street children who come to the street schools will bring other needs with them, and the school staff should be prepared to respond appropriately to a wide range of situations, while not losing the central focus on education.

Family-based Strategies

While not all street children have families in the same urban center, many do. An alternative strategy in such situations is to work with the family as a whole, with one of the basic goals being to provide the children with other options to working on the streets. Assisting the parents may enable them to encourage their children to attend school and finance such. Improving intrafamilial relationships may remove another pressure that is resulting in children opting out of family life. Or providing the family as a whole with an improved material situation may be what is called for. Even health and family planning assistance may be the required response, preventing the birth of further children for whom there is no alternative to the street. Finally, educational sponsorship, adoption, foster care, and day foster care have been used to provide individual children with the chance to adopt an alternative path, but these possibilities need to be explored through and with the family.

Such work is, of course, no different from normal family- and community-based strategies. The only difference is that the point of entry is the street children themselves, so that the strategy is in part an attempt to take children off the streets if at all possible.

Center Strategies

As Raffaelli (1997, p. 98) says, "Most street youth advocates believe that homeless youngsters need a safe living situation off the street." Hence there has tended to be a strong focus on the provision of different types of centers open to street children. These range from centers designed to ameliorate some of the worse features of life on the street to specially designed residential centers to which children are forcibly removed. Let us consider the main options.

The *drop-in center* is designed to render life on the streets more bearable, while at the same time bringing street youth into contact with workers who may be able to open up for these children some options away from the street. As one Indian report (Rane, 1994, p. 20) expresses it,

> The drop-in center, established as a support system, provides health, recreational, training, counseling, and washing facilities and supplementary food for street children. . . .

The purpose is to motivate and encourage street children to drop-in at the center at certain hours of the day, and to utilize this time for doing something educational, useful and productive rather than wander around aimlessly on the streets and become targets for exploitation and abuse. . . .

The strategy is to take advantage of the time that street children are in the center, by gaining their trust and confidence, understanding the circumstances of their problems, providing an opportunity for basic services, and providing alternative activities that would keep them off the streets.

Some centers are specifically designed to provide a hot supper and a bed for the night. These are sometimes referred to as night shelters. As the above Indian report observes, "Children themselves have prioritized their prime needs as night shelter and food" (Rane, 1994, p. 101). (See also NASWE, 1992, p. 7.)

The *transitional* or *temporary center* is designed around more lasting goals. It aims to give street children an opportunity to leave the street and be assisted into an alternative lifestyle. In the Philippines, the Lingap Centers are so designed. The NASWE (1992, p. 7) report describes these as follows:

> Lingap Centers offer longer and lasting services. Among these are medical and social treatment for physical injuries and emotional trauma suffered, the restoration and rehabilitation of impaired social functioning, sending the children to school, developing their skills, and preparing them for gainful occupation. Some centers also offer foster care and adoption services.

In 1988, the SSWAP recorded that five Lingap Centers had been set up in the Philippines. It comments,

> The Lingap Center is a transitional home for children. Each center can serve from 60 to 100

children every three months, the estimated length of stay of each child. During this period the social worker of the center tries to work out the return of the child to his parents or transfer to a foster home or child caring agency for a longer period or for adoption. The centers provide services for the physical, social, economic, spiritual, moral, medical, nutritional, and educational needs of street children. (SSWAP, 1988, p. 37)

The *group home* mirrors a common strategy today for children lacking a family home. The idea is to bring a small group of children together with houseparents in a home context, seeking to approximate family life as far as this is possible. Such houses provide a secure environment from which children can go out and participate in schooling, vocational training, or the workforce. The children are free to leave if they wish; however, through the support of not only the house-parents but also social workers and others servicing a number of such group homes, it is hoped that they will be motivated to work toward whatever goals they establish for themselves. Several group home programs for street children have been established in India and elsewhere.

The *correctional center* represents the forced removal of street children to a residential center designed to provide "treatment" in a reform school environment. In this approach the children are regarded as delinquents in need of reform. While such an approach may at times be necessary, it is in marked contrast to the voluntary centers that seek to offer street children the opportunity to move off the streets and on to other things.

Strategies Designed to Meet a Specific Need

There may be several examples available of strategies developed exclusively to cater to one specific need among street children, but the one selected here is one that has featured prominently in the literature and in discussions in recent years. It is the problem of HIV/AIDS and other sexually transmitted diseases (STDs) as they affect street children. Programs addressing these issues are largely preventative and educational in nature.

Reports on street children make frequent reference to the sexual activities of the children. Many are sexually involved with each other, both in sexual experimentation and in seeking comfort from each other; many are sexually exploited while on the streets; and many are involved in prostitution, both heterosexual and homosexual, as a survival strategy. They are thus highly vulnerable to STDs and AIDS. (See Dube, 1997, on the situation in Zimbabwe.) In these circumstances, the call is to develop "street-based STD and AIDS education" (Connolly, 1994, p. 199). In addition to sex education, the provision of condoms is emphasized, along with programs to promote self-esteem and empower street children. Among the educational strategies adopted have been street theater, films, videos, and games, as well as appropriate written material.

In Zimbabwe it was found that traditional AIDS education programs were having little impact among street children, and an innovative "street children peer education strategy" was developed. Mupedziswa, Matimba, and Kanyowa (1996, p. 75) present this strategy as follows:

In brief, the envisaged model involves identifying a number of "key" street children, who are then singled out for special training as peer educators. A peer is a person similar to oneself in such variables as age, background and interest. The strategy targets influential street children who may be interested in receiving such training. The hope is that those trained would then go around the town or city, educating their peers on HIV/AIDS . . . [through] a range of educational activities, including conversations and even organized group sessions.

The arguments for the model are that street children are often difficult to locate, hard to communicate with, and less likely to be influenced by outsiders. Peer educators may not have such problems. The article sets out a number of

Strategies for work with street children:

- The street educator/facilitator
- The street school
- Provision of different types of centers
- Addressing specific issues such as HIV/AIDS
- Work with stakeholders

guiding principles for the success of the model, and sets out the steps required for the effective implementation of the strategy.

Dube (1997, p. 72) rightly points out that

the threat of AIDS and other sexually transmitted diseases, increased drug addiction etc., cannot be separated from lack of choice and opportunity. Our work in the long term should be towards improving the general health and self-image of the children. Giving children the knowledge and the facilities to improve this will increase their self-respect as well as reduce risks to HIV/AIDS infection. . . . Behavioural change on the part of the children can only come from promoting self-worth and creating an environment where children can make informed choices.

Work With Stakeholders

We should not underestimate the importance of educating the general public in regard to street children. It is not uncommon for the general public to perceive them as antisocial elements, delinquents, suppliers of drugs to others, and so on. If any level of work with street children is to be fully successful, it will be important to work with prevailing public attitudes and bring about a better understanding of the whole phenomenon. The general public is one important body of stakeholders.

The second group of stakeholders is composed of specific groups of workers. These include the police and security personnel, transport workers, public health providers, street vendors, and shopkeepers. Such stakeholders regularly interact with, and are often daily affected by, the behavior of street children; hence their attitudes toward them as well as their ability to influence them positively cannot be underestimated. It is important to inculcate in such groups well-based positive attitudes toward the situation and, ideally, an understanding of useful strategies appropriate to each situation.

Case Examples

Drop-in Center in Afghanistan

In Afghanistan, two decades of conflict have led to large numbers of street children, who are often at risk of abuse. Most have been forced onto the street through poverty. It is known, however, that street life can have long-term physical and psychological effects on the child and can perpetuate their poverty. A local agency drew up a plan, with the support of the local community, to establish an emergency drop-in center. The center is managed by a medical practitioner and the staff is made up of social workers. Street children visit the center regularly and have access to basic education, health services, health and hygiene education, food, sport, and recreation. Once a child establishes a pattern of regular attendance, vocational training is also provided, with a choice among a number of trades. The social workers develop friendships with the children, regularly visit their parents if appropriate, and provide follow-up support for the children. In the first year of operation, more than 450 children were admitted to the center and many participated regularly. Some have been successfully reintegrated into schools to continue their education, while most continue their education at the center.

(Example from UN/ESCAP, 1994a, p. 11.)

Outreach Program in Mumbai

Street children are also a widespread and growing urban phenomenon in India, with the number in Mumbai alone estimated at 100,000. Most of these children are deprived of basic needs and face hunger and disease, especially skin diseases. Most are illiterate and effectively denied their right to education. In Mumbai, there are 22 NGOs working for the welfare of street children. One of these conducts an outreach program successful in reaching many street children at railway stations, temples, and so on. The overall program encompasses health service delivery, nutrition, education, vocational training, recreation, and counseling. It also engages in advocacy on behalf of street children generally, and in training others in work with street children. In one year, the agency's outreach program assisted 45 children to reintegrate into schooling, encouraged 25 children to open savings accounts, took 30 children away on a three-day camp for leadership training, engaged 20 children in vocational training, and assisted in various ways a large number of others.

(Example from UN/ESCAP, 1994a, p. 17.)

Street-based Program for Girls in the Philippines

Our third case example is of street-based intervention among girls in the Philippines. Features of the program include street organization among peer groups; the training of selected girls as "street caretakers"; making girls aware of their various life options; building structures among the girls for protecting each other against sexual harassment and the like; assisting the girls to plan responses to their perceived needs; and training girls to provide adequate emergency care and various forms of preventive health services to their peers. If the girls express a desire to rejoin their families, the agency facilitates this by seeking to improve the parenting roles of the girls' parents.

An essential feature of this program is advocacy, particularly among law enforcers, while the girls need also to regain trust in policemen to counteract the negative experiences they had with them. At the community level, the challenge was even greater. The entire community needed to be mobilized to redefine and resolve basic issues pertaining to the survival and development of their children. These issues concerned children's rights, women's conditions, access to services, and distribution of power.

It was observed that the street girls of Manila "continue to struggle with the violence wrought by structural injustices, mass poverty, empty relationships and warped values," resulting in "destruction of body and spirit."

(Example from ChildHope, 1989.)

Child Laborers

One large-scale problem involving children is child labor. This is a complex situation regarding which it is difficult to generalize. While technically child labor might be defined as the employment of children under the legal age for work, even that description covers a range of situations. First, there are the divergent conditions under which children work. As a UNICEF (1997, p. 24) report expresses it,

> In reality children do a variety of work in widely divergent conditions. This work takes place along a continuum. At one end of the continuum, the work is beneficial, promoting or enhancing a child's physical, mental, spiritual, moral or social development without interfering with schooling, recreation and rest.
>
> At the other end, it is palpably destructive or exploitative. There are vast areas of activity between these two poles, including work that need not impact negatively on the child's development.

In relation to minimum age for work, while the ILO establishes a general minimum age of 15 years, the age limits in various countries vary from 12 to 18 (UNICEF, 1997, p. 25). It is also important to appreciate that many children around the world work in the family context, particularly in agricultural activities, and very often in conditions that are not harmful. In addition, many children do after-school work to earn some pocket money or assist their families, and often this is regarded as beneficial. The key issue, therefore, is not so much child labor per se as exploitative child labor, and labor likely to have a negative impact upon a child's development.

Child labor is a common phenomenon. It exists in all parts of the world and in rich as well as poor countries. UNICEF (1997, p. 26) sums up the global situation as follows:

> Worldwide, the big picture looks something like this: the vast majority of all child labourers live in Asia, Africa and Latin America. Half of them can be found in Asia alone, although their proportion may be declining in South-East Asia. . . . Africa has an average of one in three children working. In Latin America, one child in five works.

However, the report goes on to say that the majority of children work for their families, in homes, in the fields, and on the streets, and that the numbers of children working in deleterious conditions is unknown. Certainly child labor includes work in manufacturing, in agriculture, in mining, on the streets, and in the domestic context.

In a more recent report, UNICEF (2005) states,

> Today, more than 350 million children, aged from 5 to 17, are at work. They can be differentiated on the basis of their age, on the effect that working has on their basic rights and, in particular, on the extent to which their work causes them harm. More than 140 million of the total are old enough to be working under international standards. Nevertheless, getting on for half of these—60 million—suffer harm because they are involved in the abuse of the "worst forms" of child labour, from which they should be protected. The remaining 80 million have reasonable jobs, either in industrialised or developing countries.
>
> Out of approximately 211 million working children under 15, more than half (over 120 million) are involved in the "worst forms." So, together with older adolescents, almost 180 million young people below 18 are involved in the "worst forms," approximately 1 in every 12 children in the world today. The vast majority of these, more than 170 million, are engaged in work that is hazardous, posing a health risk and, in some cases, even threatening their lives.

The central issue is not thus children working but the exploitation of children in conditions that are hazardous to their health and well-being. The Convention on the Rights of the Child, in article 32, obligates governments to protect children "from economic exploitation and from performing any work that is likely to be hazardous or to interfere with the child's education, or to be harmful to the child's health or physical, mental, spiritual, moral or social development." When is child labor exploitative?

UNICEF (1997, p. 24) determined that child labor is exploitative if it involves

- full-time work at too early an age;
- too many hours spent working;
- work that exerts undue physical, social, or psychological stress;
- work and life on the streets in bad conditions;
- inadequate pay;
- too much responsibility;
- work that hampers access to education;
- work that undermines children's dignity and self-esteem, such as slavery or bonded labor and sexual exploitation; or
- work that is detrimental to social and psychological development.

Some observers may also wish to raise the question of freedom of choice. Although the free choice of children is a controversial matter, when children are forced into labor, are kept in it as virtual prisoners, and have no choice regarding leaving such work, then the absence of free choice is surely an important additional factor.

Strategies for Addressing Deleterious Child Labor

There are several general or indirect strategies that are commonly put forward as relevant to this problem.

Indirect Strategies

One strategy is *education.* Education is the logical alternative to child labor; hence every step possible should be taken to ensure that children attend school (UNDP, 1996b, p. 91). To this end, Ike and Twumasi-Ankrah (1999, p. 115) suggest a policy of compulsory primary education: "To eradicate the widespread forms of child labor would require a strong government measure involving a compulsory, free primary education for all children," along with vocational training. The Convention on the Rights of the Child insists that primary education must be universal and compulsory, and UNICEF is convinced that if governments enforced this "the extent of exploitative child labor would be significantly reduced" (UNICEF, 1997, p. 48). However, they point out that quality of education is a further factor:

> Education and child labor interact profoundly. As we have seen, work can keep children away from school. At the same time, poor quality education often causes children to drop out of school and start working at an early age. Good quality education, on the other hand, can keep children away from work. The longer and better the education, the lesser the likelihood that a child will be forced into damaging work.

A second strategy is *legislation.* The passage of child labor laws is critical in providing authorities with the necessary weapons for outlawing certain practices. "All countries should establish a coherent set of child labour laws both as a statement of intent and as a springboard for their wider efforts" (UNICEF, 1997, p. 58). While legislation has proved highly effective in many countries, in other countries it has been shown that legislation is a necessary but not a sufficient condition. In India, for example, it is clear that legislation is ineffectual without an independent and incorruptible inspectorate.

Advocacy is a third strategy commonly referred to. Ideally, child advocacy centers carry out research, provide training, develop programs, and seek to influence governments and the corporate world, all designed to reduce the incidence of exploitative child labor. Hopefully advocacy will result in mobilizing society. As UNICEF (1997, p. 63) puts it, "The best guarantee that a government will take its responsibilities seriously is when all sectors of society become involved in a genuine national movement." The

NGO sector, the media, trade unions, employer bodies, and the children themselves all have major roles to play in achieving this outcome.

Finally, *reducing poverty and improving the powerlessness of the poor* is a strategy addressing root causes. It is frequently poverty that impels children into hazardous work. Hence "enabling poor families to lift themselves out of the pit of powerlessness is a fundamental factor needed to bring about long-term change" (UNICEF, 1997, p. 61). The strategies discussed under local-level development and poverty alleviation (see Chapters 6 and 8) are all relevant in this context. Sometimes it is changes in the social structure that are required to achieve this goal, as well as strategies that can be implemented at a local level by those in poverty.

Direct Strategies

While the above strategies are essentially preventative in nature, reducing the numbers of children engaging in exploitative child labor in the future, are there strategies that might be effective in meeting the presenting needs of the current population of child laborers? It is often said that many children engaged in child labor are difficult to access. They are virtually held incognito and captive by those exploiting them, and considerable ingenuity would be required just to make contact with these children, let alone

assist them. An alternative strategy may then be to seek to make contact with and influence the practices of those employing the children. While this may be more feasible in principle, in practice it may be considered unlikely that those willfully exploiting children, presumably to accumulate significant profits, will readily acknowledge and discuss the situation, let alone agree to change it. If this is the case, workers must then look to see whether there are those in positions of authority who can be motivated to take action against exploitative employers.

Given the widespread nature of the practice in some places, and the corrupt nature of many administrative systems, this too may seem like an unfruitful avenue to pursue. However, one should still try. What is more important in this context than lobbying simply to remove the practice is to have thought through, and be ready to present, a set of policies and practices that would be in the best interests of the child while also potentially acceptable to employers and authorities (e.g., a viable work-education combination or government-assisted improved working conditions). Finally, if workers are effective in remedying an employment situation, they must be ready to assist the children involved and their families to find alternative sources of income. Lobbying for an end to any practice, without foreseeing what the outcome will be and making plans to respond accordingly, is irresponsible practice.

Strategies for Addressing Deleterious Child Labor Situations

Indirect strategies:

- Education
- Legislation
- Advocacy
- Reducing poverty and the powerlessness of the poor

Direct strategies:

- Influence the practices of those employing children.

- Persuade relevant authorities to take action against exploitative employers.

- Present a set of policies and practices that cover the interests of the children and are acceptable to employers and authorities.

- Assist the children involved and their families to find alternative sources of income.

- Develop networks for lobbying purposes.

Case Examples

The following comments and case examples come from UNICEF's (1997) experience in this field.

Education for Domestic Workers in Kenya

In Kenya, many poor rural families are glad to be relieved of the responsibility of feeding a child, especially if it is a relative in the town who offers to assume this responsibility in exchange for the child's labor. Usually there is also a promise to educate the child, but there is no one to check that this promise is fulfilled, and often the child receives no education but is subject to long hours of drudgery, discrimination, and isolation. In response to this situation, an NGO in Nairobi's industrial area established a center offering basic education and training, including cooking classes, as well as comfort to young domestic workers. The center is funded by the ILO's International Program on the Elimination of Child Labor. Nearly 100 girls are enrolled in the six-month course that covers basic literacy, cooking, and introduction to skills such as tailoring and typing. The timing of classes is negotiated with employers, who usually agree because the times are fine and no cost to them is involved. The girls can be as young as seven years, and very often are pregnant at fourteen or fifteen, when employers tend to put them out on the street. The agency has found that there is a need for continuing services, as well as for a range of other services for which they do not have the funds. This is the only center in Kenya offering skills training and basic literacy to girls who are domestic workers.

(Example from UNICEF, 1997, p. 34.)

Education Programs

UNICEF has looked carefully at the problem of getting working children back to school, and provides the following comments and examples.

In India's West Bengal state, an NGO has assisted 370 children to quit work and continue their education by providing them with school supplies, health services, and a midday meal. Another 19 children aged over 14 have obtained skilled work based on vocational training received. This is but one of the scores of organizations established in many countries to meet the needs of child laborers. "Education, essential to ensuring better opportunities for child workers, is a common thread throughout these programs. The challenge is to make education economically viable, attractive and relevant for working children and their families" (UNICEF, 1997, p. 50).

Quite commonly, nonformal education is used to get children back into the regular school system. Many programs aim for community-based, sustainable alternatives that have elements of both informal education and survival skills. In Nepal, a two-year program for children released from the carpet factories offers free food, lodging, and a mixture of formal and nonformal education, leading to enrollment in school or placement in employment using newly acquired vocational skills. In India's Uttar Pradesh state, an NGO has opened 60 schools for former bonded laborers that compress five years of basic education into three.

(Examples from UNICEF, 1997, p. 50.)

Income-replacement Programs

"A common problem in dealing with working children is how to keep the poorest, whose income is most critical to their own and their families' survival, in school. Relevant curricula, flexible class schedules and quality education are essential." Ways of covering the direct costs of schooling have to be provided, as well as cash stipends to compensate families for lost income. UNICEF gives some case examples from Latin America.

In Honduras, more than 2,000 young street workers have benefited from formal and nonformal education provided by an NGO that also provides health care, counseling, school supplies, uniforms, and, where needed, partial scholarships and nutritional supplements. Another NGO in Ecuador pays weekly stipends that approximate the earnings of a shoeshine boy, while teaching handicraft production. Participating children must resume regular schooling.

An innovative program, implemented by the government in Brazil, pays an education grant, equal to the minimum wage, to poor families whose children do not miss more than two days of school per month. This program, which includes a savings and credit plan, has dramatically lowered the dropout rate among poor students.

(Examples from UNICEF, 1997, p. 51.)

Migrant Workers and Their Families

The migrant worker phenomenon is highly varied if the term is used to cover the full range of workers from the highly mobile top executives of the Multinational Corporations (MNCs) through to unskilled persons who slip illegally across the border for work purposes. While it is difficult to define a clear dividing line, the focus here is on the highly vulnerable lesser-skilled sections of the movement. Moreover, migrant worker movements are composed of women and men, but at the levels to which we are referring the great majority today are women, and they are generally far more vulnerable as migrant workers than their male counterparts. While much of the following discussion is couched in gender-neutral terms, it should be noted that we are referring, in program terms, to a population composed largely and increasingly of women.

History and Dimensions of the Migrant Worker Phenomenon

Migrant worker movements have a long history, but we can date the modern phase back to the eighteenth century. Migrant worker movements occur where there is a surplus of labor in some areas and a shortage in others. People then migrate, through whatever channels available, in an effort to survive or achieve their life goals.

The specific characteristics of such migration vary greatly. It may take the form of largely unfettered movement, as occurred out of Europe into the new worlds of the Americas and Australasia. It may occur within countries as surplus rural labor moves to fast developing urban areas in search of employment. It may occur within continents, as has happened on a large scale within Africa, Asia, Europe, and Latin America. This intracontinental migration may be formal or informal, legal or illegal, and temporary or inclining toward permanent. Finally, migrant worker movements may be largely male, largely female, male and female adults, or family groups. Most of this migration reflects the uneven nature of development. As some countries progress, their need for labor increases and they may find that labor most readily available from beyond their borders. The sending countries are then those countries where development processes are not providing sufficient employment opportunities, either for a growing pool of skilled people or for a surplus of unskilled workers in rural areas. That the phenomenon is both an ongoing and a highly varied one can be seen by a program in early 2005 to recruit migrant workers for Iraq from West Africa (e.g., Sierra Leone).

In recent decades, the extent of labor migration within Africa, Asia, and Latin America has caused grave concern. While the numbers are small in terms of percentages of national populations, they are large in terms of the numbers of people affected, both positively and negatively, by the whole migration experience. In terms of Asia, for example, a 1996 estimate was that there were "about 3 million Asian migrants employed outside Asia, and 3 million Asian migrants employed in Asia" (Martin, Mason, and Nagayama, 1996, p. 165). Of the three million workers employed within Asia, some 50 percent were not legally recognized foreign workers. This same study added: "Most indicators point to more rather than less migration in the 21st century."

Migrant worker movements are complex in terms of their impact on both sending and receiving countries and on the migrant workers and the families they leave behind. The overall situation is well summarized by the above authors:

> The key to most labor migrations lies inside labor-importing or receiving countries, but the solution to reducing emigration pressures lies in sending countries. Labor-importing countries set migration streams in motion by authorizing or tolerating the entry of foreign workers, and these foreign workers soon make a place for themselves in host country firms and labor markets, slowing down adjustments that would occur if migrants were not available. In the emigration country, families, villages and regions can become dependent on the international labor market, and labor brokers and other middlemen develop a strong incentive to keep migration going. Dynamic processes—what some have called cumulative causation—are then set in motion to perpetuate migration for employment. The presence of migrants makes it unnecessary to restructure certain jobs, or to adjust wages, so that "migrant labor markets" can become isolated from the mainstream economy. Remittances and returns raise expectations, but they rarely spark an economic renaissance themselves, so that some villages can become "nurseries and nursing homes" for workers who support their families by working abroad. (Martin et al., 1996, pp. 165–166)

Benefits and Dangers Associated With Migrant Worker Movements

Potentially there are many benefits flowing from migrant worker movements. The sending countries are able to avoid a variety of costs by exporting surplus labor, and their economies benefit from the remittances sent home and the acquired skills and savings with which workers often return home. The receiving country has some labor shortages met in a way that appears to be cost-effective in the short term, avoiding training costs and local-level wages. However, as the above quotation indicates, there may often be a downside to these benefits, especially in the longer term. Finally, the migrant workers would seem often to benefit by securing an income and using that income to improve their home situation and perhaps even finance a business venture at home. Middlemen can also benefit through engaging in the often lucrative trade in human labor. It is easy to see why these schemes appear tempting to all parties, and there is no doubt that many people and countries have benefited—at least in the short term.

Here it is important that we focus on the dangers associated with migrant worker movements, examining these specifically from the point of view of the workers and their families, although recognizing that the impact at the state level is also very important for the citizens of these states, both workers and their families and others. Social workers need to appreciate these dangers, be able to assess their impact in any situation, and be equipped with the strategies required for addressing such situations.

The Nature of Migrant Worker Movements

The very nature of many migrant worker movements leaves the workers highly vulnerable. If, for example, the workers are part of an unauthorized or illegal movement, they will lack the entitlement to many facilities and benefits that local workers are entitled to, will be open to sudden deportation at times when governments decide—often for political reasons—to move against illegal workers, will be vulnerable to exploitation from unscrupulous employers and others, and generally will live with a sense of insecurity and even fear. If the workers are part of a migrant worker movement where the desire all round is for them to remain permanently

in their work, but where governments are apprehensive about changing the nature of the movement to one of permanent residence, workers remain in a situation of limbo. Often they remain unable to sponsor family members, at least until various parties lobby effectively for the workers to have the rights of permanent migrants, as occurred in parts of Europe in the 1960s and 1970s. The need here is to remove ambiguities from migrant workers' situations while recognizing their need for a normal life.

The Exploitation of Migrant Workers

While migrant worker movements can be exploitative in their very nature, the reality is that migrant workers are often deliberately exploited. Exploitation is common among migration middlemen, who make untrue promises to would-be workers, charge exorbitant fees, provide false visas and other documents, and sometimes disappear when would-be migrants have made an up-front payment. Such exploitation can have a devastating effect on people living close to the poverty line. Exploitation also occurs on the part of employers in the receiving countries, with practices like withholding wages against travel costs, holding passports to prevent workers from leaving, taking advantage sexually and in other ways of vulnerable workers, and imposing work hours and conditions that are entirely unacceptable but from which workers are unprotected. Sometimes even officials in the sending or receiving country exploit workers by imposing charges that are not authorized, or demanding money simply to do their duty. The lower the workers' level of education and the less experience they have, the more they are vulnerable to these forms of exploitation.

Two types of development have occurred over the years to protect migrant workers against exploitative practices. First, there have been many developments within international law to protect this category of people: "International law protects their status as foreigners.

Labor laws guarantee aspects of their working conditions. Human rights are proclaimed for them as for every other person" ("Editor's Introduction," APMJ, 1993).

The International Labour Organisation (ILO) in 1986 issued *The Rights of Migrant Workers: A Guide to ILO Standards for the Use of Migrant Workers and Their Organisations,* and the ILO has worked strenuously for the rights of migrant workers. As a result of its work, a UN Convention on the Rights of Migrant Workers was adopted in 1992. However, as many are quick to point out, migrant workers' rights are seldom supported by the general public, the media, or governments, leaving the UN, the ILO, and a small number of NGOs the lone voices on their behalf.

The second type of development has been the introduction of programs designed to raise the knowledge and awareness levels of would-be and actual migrant workers, to enhance their capacities, and generally to provide support. Some programs have been developed by sending governments, and the Philippines' government has done much in this regard. Some are developed by NGOs and operate at the recruitment level in rural areas, in conjunction with formal preparation programs, and, as far as this is feasible, in receiving countries such as Hong Kong and Singapore. In the receiving countries, NGOs often endeavor to establish meeting points where migrant workers can gather, share experiences, voice complaints, support each other, and develop a degree of self-help capacity. While these programs have provided an excellent service, their coverage is unfortunately not nearly as widespread as one would like to see.

The Family Members Left Behind

The final major problem area to which we shall refer here is the situation of family members left behind. There are several specific difficulties commonly encountered. Because a large proportion of migrant workers today are married women, they leave behind a husband, often with limited domestic experience, and children who may or may not be well supported. Fathers and children have been known to suffer in such circumstances. When fathers go abroad, the women are frequently dependent on the remittances sent back by the men for their livelihood, and sometimes on other male relatives for their protection. When both parents work abroad, children may be left, often in the care of grandparents or other relatives, with minimal guidance and perhaps with more pocket money than they have ever known. Such children can be vulnerable to experimenting with drugs and engaging in other forms of dangerous behavior. In some countries, government and NGO agencies have set up support groups for the family members left behind, while many teachers and religious leaders have also established programs.

The Roles of Social Workers and the Strategies They Employ

There are many roles and strategies that social workers and others can bring to bear in the situations confronting migrant workers. Let us divide the roles into categories relating to steps in the process.

The Recruitment Stage

In regions where people are tempted or forced to seek out migrant worker opportunities abroad, and where recruitment agents are active, it is incumbent on social workers and others to ensure that a public education program is established, that information points are set up where individuals can direct their inquiries, that group counseling/information/discussion sessions are offered, and that local government officials and recruitment agents know that there is someone monitoring their activities. The strategies relevant to such activities will be obvious.

The Preparation Stage

The governments of sending countries should be encouraged to ensure that all departing migrant workers have access to a preparation program. Such a program should include, as necessary, sessions on the legal and administrative aspects of going abroad to work; capacity building courses covering skills involved in going abroad, both for personal protection and for work purposes (e.g., introducing domestic workers to modern methods of housework unfamiliar to them); assertiveness training to enable workers to stand up for their rights more effectively; basic language training for the receiving country; and information regarding services available to them in the receiving country at their embassy, in NGOs, and elsewhere. Sometimes local NGOs will join forces with government by offering some areas of preparation within the government courses or as complementary to them. The Philippines is a good example of a country where several such initiatives are under way.

The Situation Overseas

While overseas, workers can be exceedingly vulnerable. They need agencies that will keep contact with them as closely as possible, monitor their experiences, provide support and assistance as required, and generally ensure that the experience overseas is a positive one. These agencies may be located within embassies and be provided by governments, may be local NGOs, may be expatriate NGOs established for this purpose, or may be international bodies such as the INGOs and divisions of the UN such as UNIFEM (United Nations Development Fund for Women) and the ILO. In some receiving countries such work is extremely difficult, and in practice will not occur without international pressure being brought to bear on the governments of such countries. Social workers in various contexts can do much to plan and lobby for such developments, administer them, and deliver whatever direct services are required and possible.

The Situation of Family Members Left Behind

The challenge to the government and NGO agencies in the sending countries is to ensure that the families of migrant workers survive the experience intact, and are able to make good use of both local facilities and the remittances sent to them by the person abroad. Without such services, families may fall apart, remittances be squandered, children's education and health needs be neglected, and people become too dependent on the person abroad, and, in a few situations, the family may suffer from the stigma of a married woman going abroad to work. Workers at the local level may collaborate with school and health clinic staff to provide support groups, counseling, and information services, and practical income-generation and other opportunities, so that families can utilize remittances well and expeditiously.

The Situation of Returnees

Finally, returning migrant workers can be confronted with a range of needs. The overseas experience might have been traumatic in some ways, making debriefing at the very least necessary; there may be unresolved matters such as missing wages or problems with funds remitted through banks; they may wish to discuss a further term abroad; and they may have concerns about their family or future plans that they desperately need to discuss with a knowledgeable and objective counselor. All returnees should have access to an agency where such needs can be met, and workers there should be experienced in the overall migrant worker process, as well as knowledgeable of specific situations, so that they can handle all presenting matters.

Key Strategies for Work With Migrant Workers

The recruitment stage:

- Establish public education programs.
- Offer group counseling/information/discussion sessions.
- Monitor activities of government officials and recruitment agents.

The preparation stage:

- Offer preparation programs for departing migrant workers.
- Inform departing workers about legal and administrative aspects of work abroad.
- Help migrant workers to develop personal protection and work skills.
- Provide assertive training around assertion of rights.
- Provide necessary language training.
- Advise regarding further assistance and services.

The situation overseas:

- Establish an agency to monitor migrant workers' experiences.
- Provide support and assistance as required.
- Plan and lobby for such developments.

The situation of family members left behind:

- Collaborate with school and health clinic staff to provide support groups.
- Provide counseling and information services.
- Initiate practical income-generation and other opportunities.

The situation of returnees:

- Create debriefing facilities.
- Assist with attending to unresolved matters.
- Explore concerns about family situations and future plans.
- Provide access to appropriate services.

Case Example

Counseling for Workers Returning to Sri Lanka

In Sri Lanka, a counseling service was established for women migrant workers returning suddenly from Kuwait as a result of the Gulf War in 1990. NGO staff, over a 12-month period, interviewed some

84,000 returning women regarding their experience of moving and working abroad and of returning home. The objective was to provide these women with counseling where needed (one-half of all those interviewed were seen as requiring counseling), while also establishing what the major problems were and what ongoing programs could alleviate them. Most of the women going abroad were married women from very poor families who had borrowed heavily to raise the necessary fees. Many experienced significant family problems while abroad; many had traumatic experiences themselves while abroad; and most experienced a range of difficulties, including difficulties of an economic nature, postreturn. Among the 41,572 women seen by counselors, 4,430 severe trauma cases were encountered and referred for specialist assistance. In addition, physical and sexual abuse had been experienced by some two percent of all returnees interviewed.

The program highlighted the vulnerability of women migrant workers in at least the Middle East, and indicated the need for a range of programs. This range included programs for educating the community generally regarding working abroad, with a focus on more impoverished populations; predeparture programs for those intent on moving abroad, designed as orientation or preparation programs with an emphasis on rights and self-protection; family-related programs to address the needs of families where the mother had gone abroad; and postreturn programs to assist with reintegration within the family and local community. It was realized that such programs needed to involve both government and non-government agencies, and that the programs would require access to appropriately qualified personnel. Moreover, most of the local social workers would need to be women.

(Example from Cox, Owen, and Picton, 1994.)

AIDS Orphans in Africa

The HIV/AIDS epidemic is a truly global phenomenon with many consequences. Because of the inadequate understanding of the condition, victims of HIV/AIDS are commonly feared, shunned, and effectively marginalized. We have chosen to focus here largely on children, but this is certainly not because children are the only victims. Nor is the required social work outreach to AIDS victims limited to children (see Sachdev, 1998; Sewpaul and Rollins, 1999). In the case of AIDS orphans, it is the combination of the AIDS phenomenon and the situation of orphans generally that becomes the key concern.

The Nature and Significance of the HIV/AIDS Epidemic

HIV/AIDS is a modern global epidemic, affecting large numbers of persons in virtually all countries. The first cases of HIV were diagnosed in the very early 1980s, and since then the disease has grown to epidemic proportions. It is impossible to know how many have died to date, but the UN puts the total number affected in 2001 at 42 million. Of these, 29.4 million were in sub-Saharan Africa, although numbers in Asia have now started to increase rapidly and are at their highest in India, where the current estimate is close to 4 million persons with the number infected virtually doubling every year. The current HIV/AIDS situation is summarized by UNAIDS, UNICEF, and USAID (2004, p. 3) as follows:

AIDS is the leading cause of death worldwide for people aged 15 to 49. In 2003, 2.9 million people died of AIDS and 4.8 million people were infected. In relation to the numbers orphaned by AIDS, that number grew globally from 11.5 million in 2001 to 15 million in 2003.

Initially the disease was seen as affecting men who engaged in homosexual relationships and those who were intravenous drug users. Gradually, however, the numbers of sufferers with a heterosexual orientation, and the numbers of women, came to equal or surpass those in the former two categories. What is particularly alarming is the number of children being born with the infection or succumbing to it in early childhood. UNICEF has stated that 60 percent of all child deaths are now caused by the AIDS virus, and that it resulted in the deaths of 610,000 children in 2001. It is, therefore, affecting virtually all categories of the population, but with the impact being greatest in the developing world and often in the poorest countries.

The impact of the disease has been enormous. It has devastated family life in many countries, leaving households without a male breadwinner and very many children without parents. In sub-Saharan Africa, there were, in 2003, 12.3 million children orphaned by AIDS—a figure predicted to rise significantly in the future (UNAIDS et al., 2004, p. 10). That these numbers existed within a total orphan population in the region of 143 million is highly significant. The situation is particularly alarming in countries with no developed welfare system to provide adequate care for these children. It has devastated the workforce, undermining companies' profitability and affecting the overall economy. For example, in South Africa one in four adults of working age now has the virus. In many of the world's poorest countries in Africa, it has devastated the food supply, as large numbers of rural people succumb to the disease and become unable to engage in their normal productive work. Some reports go so far as to say that AIDS is fueling the food crisis in Africa. The direct impact of the disease has reached enormous proportions. That impact, however, is significantly aggravated by official and public attitudes toward HIV/AIDS. To some extent, the disease is seen as an affliction of those who flaunt accepted standards of behavior, with the result that those afflicted are most unfairly ostracized. It is also seen, erroneously, as a viral infection that is easily transmitted and to be

greatly feared. Therefore, there is a strong tendency to avoid all who are afflicted, and to seek to ensure that one's children in particular do not mix with even the family members of those who are afflicted.

In terms of medical treatment, while there is no cure as yet for HIV/AIDS, there are medications available that will halt or slow the progress of the disease. Unfortunately, however, the availability of these medications has become a highly controversial issue. The pharmaceutical companies have been determined, for the most part, to retail the medications at what they say are for them reasonable prices, while knowing that those prices simply make them unavailable to the great majority of HIV/AIDS sufferers. In sub-Saharan Africa, for example, only some 300,000 of the 29.4 million who are living with HIV are in receipt of lifesaving drugs, and this situation appears unlikely to change. The whole issue has become beset by politics, both politics over the pricing of AIDS medications and even politics (e.g., in South Africa) regarding whether AIDS is even caused by the HIV virus.

There is no doubt that HIV/AIDS is one of the most serious of the modern epidemics, and one that calls for a global response from the UN and its agencies, the international NGOs, governments, the medical profession, and the many other helping professions, including social work. It is a complex situation, involving community education and awareness-raising, medical care, respite and hospice care, care of orphans and family groups, work on community and official attitudes toward those with the disease, and self-help initiatives among those afflicted. Fortunately much is being done at all of these levels, but every report indicates that much more needs to be done if this scourge is to be brought under control.

There are many points of intervention in the HIV/AIDS situation where social workers can and should be and in practice often are involved. However, we shall restrict our discussion here to the situation of AIDS orphans, a situation currently found largely in Africa.

Programs for AIDS Orphans

As stated earlier, the numbers of AIDS orphans requiring appropriate programs has risen enormously in recent years in many countries, and in March 2004, the UNAIDS Committee endorsed a "Framework for the Protection, Care and Support of Orphans and Vulnerable Children Living in a World With HIV and AIDS" (UNAIDS et al., 2004, p. 21). This framework endorses several important principles (pp. 38–39):

Focus on the most vulnerable children and communities, not only children orphaned by AIDS.

Define community-specific problems and vulnerabilities at the outset and pursue locally determined intervention strategies.

Involve children and young people as active participants in the response.

Give particular attention to the roles of children, men, and women, and address gender discrimination.

Strengthen partnerships and mobilize collaborative action.

Link HIV/AIDS prevention activities and care and support activities for people living with HIV/AIDS with support for vulnerable children.

Use external support to strengthen community initiative and motivation.

Generally speaking, AIDS orphans require the same range of services that other orphans require, namely, extended family care, adoption, foster care, and institutional placement. The two difficulties that commonly emerge, however, are first that most AIDS orphans are in the poorest countries of the world that tend to lack the range of welfare services that might be found elsewhere; and, second, that attitudes toward HIV/AIDS are such that even AIDS orphans are likely to find themselves ostracized and marginalized, being left to fend for themselves as best they can during what is likely to be a short life

expectancy. In relation to Zimbabwe and the matter of social work intervention, Kaseke and Gumbo (2001, p. 57) comment,

The community-based care programme remains the only pragmatic and appropriate response to the problem of orphan care, particularly in circumstances where the extended family system is unable to assist. However, the community-based orphan care programme needs to be replicated at a national scale if it is to make a national impact. For this to happen, and given the general state of poverty in most communities, efforts should be directed at strengthening the capacity of communities to provide care to orphans.

As with many other social needs, in developing countries a community-based response is among the most realistic responses but needs to be facilitated by skilled workers.

While AIDS orphans require the provision of direct services, social workers can also make an indirect contribution by raising the levels of community understanding of HIV/AIDS and its victims, including orphans. For reasons already canvassed, there remains a high level of ignorance and misinformation regarding HIV/AIDS, resulting often in prejudice and fear; hence most writers and speakers at conferences highlight the importance of workers engaging in programs that will raise the level of awareness of the disease and encourage an active response to it. Such programs often need to be directed at various publics, including public officials with the relevant health and welfare responsibilities, members of the various professions, potential employers of people with the disease, and the general public. Moreover, such programs may be general in nature while others will relate to specific individuals who are in need of an advocate. As Miah and Ray (1994, p. 80) write,

Because people with AIDS are largely discriminated against, they often need help gaining access to various services and benefits. [The social worker] must be an advocate against discrimination in jobs, schools, social services, housing, child care, legal assistance and health care.

However, the more important need is still for a widespread education campaign designed to bring about a positive response to this disease at every level of society and internationally. Fortunately, there has been a very strong international campaign that has achieved much success, but much more needs to be done at many local levels.

In addition, social workers can help to reduce the numbers of AIDS orphans. One way is to tackle the problem of the sexual exploitation of girls occurring in situations where the girls have no choice but to be exposed to HIV. There is still widespread "kidnapping" of girls (removal of girls from their families under false pretences) for purposes of prostitution that today exposes these girls to HIV/AIDS and an early death, sometimes leaving orphaned children behind them. A second way is for social workers to lobby governments to contract with pharmaceutical companies for the provision of appropriate HIV/AIDS medications at prices that sufferers can afford. This issue has been highly controversial in recent years, but it is essential that it be pursued and that ways be found to ensure that access to medication exists on a basis of equity. If we can reduce the numbers of people dying from AIDS we shall, of course, reduce the numbers of AIDS orphans. A third indirect approach is through the education of social workers and members of the other helping professions.

It is critical that all those members of the helping professions who are in a position to staff services for HIV/AIDS sufferers, including orphans, and to lobby for an effective response to this epidemic, are fully knowledgeable of the subject and without the fears and prejudices that influence many people's reactions to this disease and those who suffer from it. Ankrah (1992, p. 59) is one of many who have argued for formal courses on this topic within the social work education curriculum. In a study of Arab social work professionals' knowledge of and attitudes toward AIDS, Azaiza and Ben-Ari (1997) found that the majority of their respondents did not have adequate knowledge of and open attitudes toward AIDS, had not received training, and thought AIDS to be predominantly a medical matter. Soliman and Miah (1998), in a study of social work students' attitudes toward HIV/AIDS that covered the United States and Egypt, found that most social work educators in the United States "unambiguously acknowledged the importance of incorporating AIDS/HIV content into the curriculum" while "Egyptian schools of social work have not considered or dealt with the AIDS/HIV issue at all in terms of curriculum development." They concluded that the

> social work curriculum should be attuned and oriented toward enabling students to gain the necessary knowledge, insights and skills to effectively serve the AIDS/HIV infected clients, family members, and the community. . . . Social workers should learn how to influence policies that will commit more funding for public health education and safety. (p. 51)

Key strategies for working with AIDS orphans:

- Emphasize community-based responses.
- Educate and raise awareness among the general public.
- Advocate against discrimination and lobby for needed services.
- Initiate preventative measures.
- Include the topic in social work education programs.

The following case examples come from sub-Saharan Africa, where 80 percent of the world's 15 million AIDS orphans are to be found. Four of the ten worst affected countries are Botswana, Malawi, Zambia, and Zimbabwe (AVERT, 2005), and the following brief summaries of action are provided by AVERT, an international AIDS charity, on its Web site (www.avert.org/aidsorphans.htm).

Case Examples

Botswana's National Orphan Program

In 1999, Botswana developed a National Orphan Program to review and develop policies, build and strengthen institutional capacity, provide social welfare services, support community-based initiatives and monitor and evaluate activities. The program is implemented by both GOs and NGOs. While encouraging community care, institutional care is provided only as a last resort. UNAIDS have estimated that 120,000 children had lost their parent(s) to AIDS by the end of 2003. A trust consisting of community volunteers and local extension staff provide food, clothing, blankets, counseling, toys, bus fares to and from school, school uniforms and other educational needs to needy orphans. An orphan drop-in centre model is used to relieve overburdened relatives and provide opportunities for children to play, do arts projects and practice traditional dance. Many complex issues need to be resolved in implementing community and institutional care programs for AIDS orphans.

(Example from http://www.avert.org/aidsorphans.htm.)

Malawi's AIDS Orphans

According to the UNAIDS estimation, Malawi has 500,000 children orphaned by AIDS at the end of 2003. Although the government of Malawi established a National Orphan Care Task Force in the early 1990s, extreme poverty, lack of administrative capacity and inadequate resources have resulted in very weak support for orphans. Village orphan committees and Anti-AIDS clubs have been educating communities about AIDS epidemic and providing help to needy orphans. As internal resources appeared to have been stretched to the maximum, more money, programs and services are needed for the care of AIDS orphans.

(Example from http://www.avert.org/aidsorphans.htm.)

Project to Support AIDS Orphans in Zambia

In Zambia AIDS orphans are estimated to rise to nearly one million by the year 2014. With no or little support from extended families, some orphaned children are looked after by neighbours, some by orphanages and some are forced to live on streets. Schooling of these children is a major problem as free education is not available. While some lobby local schools to not claim fees from children, others raise money for orphans' school fees. By mobilizing volunteer teachers and space, community schools without fees are also opened. In 2002 INGOs supported a project that offered life-sustaining care and support for over 137,000 orphans and other vulnerable children. The project tries to keep siblings together within extended families and communities. Another project offers educational, spiritual, financial and social support to more than 4,000 orphans.

(Example from http://www.avert.org/aidsorphans.htm.)

Government Policy for AIDS Orphans in Zimbabwe

It is estimated that Zimbabwe has 980,000 AIDS orphans. The government policy emphasizes community based care for orphaned children. First extended family, second substitute family, third formation groups of orphans to live together under the supervision of a caregiver, fourth, an adolescent child-headed household with siblings remaining together with some local supervision and support. Fifth is, if these four are not possible, a temporary arrangement in an orphanage. Not only AIDS affected people, but also carers face the stigma associated with the disease.

(Example from http://www.avert.org/aidsorphans.htm.)

HIV/AIDS and Other Epidemics

The HIV/AIDS epidemic has assumed major proportions and requires a concerted and coordinated effort from all the professions, including social work. However, the reality is that, where the need is greatest, the presence of social workers tends to be minimal. This situation highlights again the need for the profession to stimulate and support the development of social work, at the appropriate levels and with appropriate personnel numbers, in the countries most affected. Even then the profession must explore fully the potential of community-based responses, given the large numbers of people affected by the virus. In addition, however, the universal nature of HIV/AIDS, together with the ambivalence, ignorance, and negative attitudes toward its victims, necessitates the inclusion of content on this epidemic in the curricula of all schools of social work.

While we have focused on HIV/AIDS as an area involving vulnerable marginalized people, it will be obvious to many readers that this is but one of a number of epidemics wreaking havoc on the lives of millions of people. Malaria, various forms of tuberculosis, river blindness, and other diseases have proved difficult to combat and have a devastating impact. While the importance of a medical response to these diseases is clear, related public health issues, community education, and community-based responses to those in need of assistance are all areas where social work has a great capacity to contribute and should be doing so to a much greater extent than is currently the case. This would involve, for example, public health content in social work curricula in many countries.

Conclusion

In this chapter we have presented four examples of populations with very specific problems that call for targeted intervention programs. The needs faced by such populations may be closely related to the larger fields of intervention, such as development and poverty, but are, at the same time, so specific and so urgent that they must be treated as fields of practice in their own right. Whether the curricula of schools of social work should introduce courses on any of these fields will depend on the dimensions and urgency of the problem in their national context. At least equally important to such action is the need to carry out research among such specific populations in need, and to generate a practice literature that can be used in ongoing education and special workshops.

The list of these specific populations is reasonably long. In addition to the four covered here, the needs of victims of trafficking, child prostitutes, child soldiers, homeless youth, indigenous populations in many contexts, people with specific types of physical and intellectual disabilities, and the isolated elderly quickly come to mind. While our overall focus is inevitably on the major social phenomena, such as poverty, these many situations confronting particular populations should never be overlooked and often call for specific attention, not least in developing countries. For many social workers, such populations will be their focus rather than the broader fields, and they will need to be equipped for such roles.

Summary

- Marginalized and vulnerable groups are an important field of international social work practice as such groups exist in all countries. It is important to work with these groups.
- Although the extent of the problem of street children is difficult to determine, social workers and others have developed an understanding of the problem and evolved some effective strategies for addressing this situation.
- Child labor is an important global issue that links all countries through production-consumption processes. Direct and indirect strategies are required to address this phenomenon.
- The large numbers of migrant workers relate to uneven development processes. Although there are benefits and dangers associated with labor migration, migrant workers frequently face significant dangers and endure significant abuse and exploitation. There are some good strategies for addressing this situation.
- The growing problem of AIDS orphans, especially in Africa, requires both local and global responses. Social workers need to develop and use appropriate strategies to encourage community responses, educate the public, advocate on behalf of orphans, and seek to reduce the overall incidence of HIV/AIDS.
- Most vulnerable individuals and groups experience significant degrees of exclusion and deprivation, and critical barriers to advancement. Social workers need to work at all levels to address these situations, employing outreach, participatory, and environmental change approaches, and working to help implement global declarations and programs.

Questions and Topics for Discussion

- What do you understand by vulnerability and marginalization?
- Employing the integrated-perspectives approach (Chapter 2), discuss the causes of vulnerability and marginalization.
- In addition to the four population groups discussed in this chapter, what other population groups are especially vulnerable and marginalized and how can you identify them? Also examine strategies, if known, employed to work with them or suggest appropriate strategies.
- Discuss the significant categories of street children and the bases of these categories.
- Discuss direct and indirect strategies for addressing the phenomenon of child labor.
- Discuss benefits and dangers associated with migrant workers and their families.
- What can social workers do to empower migrant workers and their families and protect them from abuse and exploitation?
- Discuss the plight of AIDS orphans and strategies identified for addressing their plight.
- Discuss the three common aspects and key intervention strategies for international social work practice with marginalized vulnerable population groups.

Possible Areas for Research Projects

- Undertake a cross-country analysis of policies and programs dealing with child labor.
- Develop case studies to document innovative and replicable strategies for responding to marginalized vulnerable population groups of interest to you.
- Undertake a literature survey of the needs of and issues affecting migrant workers.
- Study the effectiveness of key intervention strategies across a range of marginalized vulnerable populations.

Further Reading

Thompson, N. (2003). *Promoting equality: Challenging discrimination and oppression* (2nd ed.). London: Palgrave Macmillan.

UNAIDS, UNICEF, and USAID. (2004). *Children on the brink 2004: A joint report of new orphan estimates and a framework for action.* New York: UNICEF.

UNESCO. (1995). *Working with street children: Selected case-studies from Africa, Asia and Latin America.* Paris: UNESCO Publishing/International Catholic Child Bureau.

UNICEF. (1997). Children at risk: Ending hazardous and exploitative child labour. In *The state of the world's children 1997* (chap. 2, pp. 15–76). New York: Oxford University Press.

UNICEF. (2005). *End child exploitation: Child labour today.* London: UNICEF.

For migrant workers, please see relevant ILO publications (Geneva, Switzerland), and issues of the *Asian and Pacific Migration Journal*, especially Volume 2, Number 2 (1993); Volume 5, Number 1 (1996); and Volume 6, Number 1 (1997).

14

Challenges for International Social Work for the Twenty-first Century

Our definition of international social work, set out in Chapter 1, highlights the role for social work intervention, in education and practice terms, to respond "to the various global challenges that are having a significant impact on the well-being of large sections of the world's population." The definition goes on to argue for the application of the integrated-perspectives approach to the analysis of international situations and responses to them: in other words, our understanding of social work, and its place in the world internationally, needs to synthesize the global, human rights, ecological, and social development perspectives (Chapter 2). However, as the text proceeds it is made clear that social work locally could also, with benefit, be understood through this integrated-perspectives approach. Each of the four dimensions of that approach in effect represents a challenge to the ways in which social work is organized and practiced. Social work practice that fails to take cognizance of the global context, to focus on the human rights of all people, to encompass a

strong ecological sensitivity, and to incorporate a social development approach as that is defined, represents practice that has failed to keep pace with the modern world.

In Chapter 3 we analyze four dimensions of the global context within which social work functions, and each of these dimensions presents challenges to modern social work. The ideological context is of particular importance to social work because recent changes in that context have been exerting a major impact on all aspects of practice. This is particularly true of the dominant neoliberal and neoconservative ideologies, resulting in widespread weakening or dismantling of the welfare state, reductions in government services, more negative attitudes toward the world's disadvantaged and excluded, growing inequality and levels of poverty, and indeed increasingly ambivalent attitudes in some countries toward the roles of the helping professions, including social work. At the organizational level, social work's roles in national government agencies, the NGO sector, and all facets of the international community have been changing dramatically, as indeed those organizational sectors themselves undergo significant changes. The policy dimension is always an important aspect of the context within which social work is practiced, but the emergence of global social policy has profound implications for the roles of social work at all levels, and particularly for its engagement in the policy formulation process. Finally, at no level is social work immune from the key global social problems as delineated by the UN and others. The significance of such issues as global poverty levels, global terrorism, heightened suspicion between global "civilizations" (as used by Huntington and others to denote global ideological groupings; see Chapter 3), significant changes in and deterioration of the global ecology, and widespread movements of peoples around the globe affect every state, the residents of every country, and the professions that express a concern for people locally, nationally, and internationally. Social work practice is profoundly affected by this and the other three dimensions of the global context within which it operates.

How is the profession of social work per se to respond to the challenges of the contemporary world? That question is far too complex and vast to address comprehensively in this concluding chapter, yet it is important that we stimulate social work readers to contemplate this topic.

The Way Ahead for International Social Work: Where Should International Social Work Be Heading in the Twenty-first Century?

In the context of our examination of international social work in this text, and in the light of the various statements on social work ethics and the objectives of the social work profession, we shall in this section draw together the directions that we believe international social work should be taking in this new century. In addition to discussing directions, we shall look also at possible strategies for implementing such changes.

Becoming a Truly Global Profession

It is not acceptable that social work should be strongest in the most developed and richest countries, struggling in many developing countries, and nonexistent in virtually all of the least developed countries (LDCs) of the world, except perhaps for a handful of expatriates working in these countries in aid and development agencies. A social work profession true to its ethics and vision would be seeking to contribute to the development of not only these LDCs but to the less developed areas within many other countries, whether classified as developed or developing.

There are various strategies that the profession could use to further this goal of universality. One strategy would be for the profession to sponsor the establishment of schools of social work in LDCs, and in the rural and remote areas of many countries. This might be done by the international or national professional associations, or by individual schools in more affluent countries, as indeed a few schools in Canada and the United States have already done. A second strategy is for schools in a neighboring country or region to engage in training students from the less developed country or region in need of such, as has been occurring to a limited degree in recent decades (e.g., in India in relation to Bhutan and Nepal, and in Europe in relation to Eastern Europe). A third strategy would be for the profession to encourage the UN (perhaps the UNDP) to undertake the task of establishing social work where the need exists, and for the profession to work closely with the UN in the process of implementation of social work roles related to human development goals.

Reflecting a Truly Global Response to International Needs

The major social needs confronting the world have been frequently identified (see Chapter 3). They include poverty and inequality issues; development issues, both rural and urban; war and peace issues, including civil wars and post-conflict reconstruction; the phenomenon of refugee movements, asylum seeker flows, and displaced populations in their many manifestations; issues of ecological degradation and the impact of natural disasters; global trafficking of people for labor generally and the sex trade specifically; the scourge of HIV/AIDS and other diseases; and abuse of human rights in many areas. It can be readily demonstrated that the knowledge and skills that compose social work, its code of ethics, and its stated objectives all indicate that the social work profession should be playing significant roles in all such fields of work. The reality, however, is that its involvement, while undoubtedly growing, remains comparatively limited.

What strategies could be used to expand social work's contribution to the key areas of global need? First, if all the schools of social work were to teach international social work, encompassing intervention in such fields as those listed, more graduates from developed and developing countries might consider entering such work. A second strategy would be for the international social work associations to run, or join in running, summer schools or other intensive courses on social work in these fields. As a third strategy, it may then be necessary to market to international agencies the potential contribution of social work to these fields. A further strategy, which would complement all of the above, would be to encourage social workers already in these fields to write up these experiences for sharing with other social workers.

Incorporating a Social Development Perspective Within Social Work Education Curricula

We have already seen that the matter of a social development perspective within social work receives considerable coverage in the literature. Reviewing social work internationally in 1997, Elliott (1997, p. 448) wrote,

> The social development model has the potential to be taken beyond a theoretical and ideological framework to an operational model for social work practice which will enhance professional and intercultural exchange at individual, local, regional, national, and international levels.

A number of schools of social work have already moved in the direction of incorporating a social development perspective in the curriculum, and others are contemplating doing so. There is no doubt that a social development perspective moves well beyond the traditional community development focus of the past, and necessitates quite radical changes to the traditional curriculum and the typical school of social work. One change relates to student numbers, for the implementation of social development models in developing countries currently being discussed requires many personnel who could best come from social work, provided that social work addresses the matter of education and professional levels discussed later. Moreover, the typical curriculum will need to focus more on global issues, cross-cultural social work, and selected fields of international practice. Social work needs to move in this direction to be true to itself and to have significance as a profession within the developing world.

How might this goal be achieved? One strategy is to provide schools of social work with appropriate curriculum models that incorporate the social development perspective, so that the curriculum development task is not left to individual schools. This will be the objective of a later section of this text, but it needs to be done at a variety of levels. A second strategy is to establish new schools of social work that focus predominantly on the social development area, allowing such schools to become models for future developments within existing schools. A third strategy might be for the international associations (IASSW and IFSW) or some other body to offer a consultancy service to schools of social work willing to consider such a change.

Introducing a Three-level Model of Social Work Education and Practice

We referred in Chapter 1 to the importance of developing a three-level model of social work practice, reflected in the recruitment practices and education models of schools of social work. The three levels would be those of the social work assistant, trained to work effectively at the grassroots level within specific fields, the social work graduate representing the level that currently dominates, and the senior social worker able to provide leadership across the profession—today's postgraduate student body. If these three levels were graduated in the numbers required by the field, locally and perhaps also abroad, social work could make a significant contribution to national and international responses to global needs.

We appreciate that there has always been a degree of opposition within social work to the profession incorporating a paraprofessional level, but we believe that any adverse effects of doing this would be well and truly offset by the ability of social work to make a more effective and highly visible response to global needs that frequently dominate the international agenda, and thus be seen as relevant to international developments—an essential step in improving the image, as well as the potential, of social work in many contexts. We also believe that, while the numbers and backgrounds of social work graduates remain as limited as they are in many developing countries, the importance of social work must be regarded as equally limited. Social work has no capacity to respond effectively to major areas of global need unless it can establish a level of operation able to contribute effectively to frontline realities. If social work does not accept this challenge, there may ultimately be no choice but to establish a new profession for the purpose of responding effectively to presenting needs. Courses in development studies are already numerous, but to date have tended to be largely economic in orientation and geared to the provision of leadership in this field largely within a project approach; however, this might change with the introduction of additional levels and centers of training. If this happens, social work will be further marginalized, or even disappear as a valid profession in some developing contexts.

The strategy open to social work is to introduce a preliminary or basic social work course from which students could emerge as social work assistants (whatever the terminology used), perhaps specialized in one or two specific areas (e.g., poverty alleviation and local-level development) and with the necessary basic social work skills. Such assistants, following completion of a specified number of years of practice, could go on to apply to study to become graduate social workers, which, to facilitate, would require a more flexible set of admission criteria than currently exist, and some upgrading of facilities, but there is ample evidence that such is feasible. The postgraduate level already exists, but may require some further developments to reflect the requirements of international social work as presented. In many countries, it may be preferable to introduce a new social work undergraduate school, probably outside university circles but planned and run in close consultation with university schools of social work, the professional association, and others. In the international social work context, it would be preferable for such a course to include plenty of exposure to the relevant fields of practice, either through field placements or even by including a degree of in-service training for those already working in the field.

Changes Required to Social Work Education

Various surveys indicate the extent to which social work education has been changing in recent decades. Commenting on Stickney and Resnich's *World Guide to Social Work Education,* published in 1974 but still relevant today, Kendall (1986) discusses how, on the African continent, social work education is increasingly moving towards indigenous models with some social development content. By contrast, in Latin America the emerging alternative foci have been on social change (social reform) and revolutionary change, with both trends adopting a strong liberation theme. The more pervasive Asian theme, however, links social work with social development: "Many schools of social

work in Asia have now adopted social development or developmental social welfare as key objectives" (p. 21). More recent surveys, by Hokenstad et al. (1992) and Watts, Elliott, and Mayadas (1995), further expand on the changes that have been taking place. Our interest here, however, is on the place within the curriculum of international social work, and Healy (1995a) provides a good overview of this issue in the volume by Watts et al.

In examining this question of the place of international social work in the social work curriculum, Healy first considers definitional issues. She concludes that the issue of the definition of international social work remains unresolved. However, she notes that there is some consensus on the key elements that should be included: "Three concepts were held to be essential by more than 50 percent of the respondents: cross-cultural understanding (58.9 percent), comparative social policy (56.9 percent), and concern with global social problems (54.5 percent)" (p. 423). Healy noted some significant differences in views when the various continents were compared. She also observes that the complete range of international content referred to can become a problem:

> A reality which becomes both a positive and a negative for international content is that the field of potential curriculum material is vast. Within this vast array of possibilities, international content in social work programs has tended to focus on only a few areas, leaving other significant areas relatively untouched. (p. 430)

Finally, Healy notes the tendency of some schools to offer a separate course on international social work while others infuse international elements throughout the curriculum.

Despite the above difficulties, the global survey of 1990, to which Healy is referring, found that "of the 214 schools which responded . . . , 155, or 72.4 percent, reported that international content is included in their social work curriculum" (p. 429). North America had the highest proportion of schools with such courses, these being mainly elective courses, while Latin America had the lowest proportion of schools offering such courses. While the overall results are encouraging in many ways, Healy is still led to draw the following important conclusion:

An examination of the current state of international curriculum content in schools of social work reveals a curriculum area in disarray . . . there is little or no evidence of well-planned, comprehensive international curriculum development. International aspects of the curriculum most often appear peripheral to mainstream curriculum; course objectives are poorly developed and not logically linked to broader educational priorities or regional needs; few schools have incorporated internationally related objectives into their overall educational plan; and the profession, as it exists in individual countries and as a worldwide movement, has not thought through the nature of its international contribution. (pp. 431–432)

These are damning words indeed, coming from a social work educator who has devoted more time to international social work than most.

Healy goes on to discuss the perceived specific obstacles to progress in instituting international content, such as limited financial resources, scarcity of teaching resources, lack of faculty competence, and limited time within the curriculum. However, she dismisses these obstacles as relatively minor, while identifying three major obstacles:

Three overarching obstacles in the way the social work profession approaches international social work block major reform in international curriculum. These three interrelated obstacles are: (1) that social work has not

come to terms with the costs of international ignorance; (2) that international aspects of social work are treated as peripheral, not mainstream; and (3) that the profession has not defined its roles in the international context. (pp. 432–433).

Finally, Healy draws her own conclusion:

Social work curriculum can respond through clearly establishing new purposes related to cross-cultural communication and knowledge, global social problems, and capacity for utilization of the worldwide profession and its networks. (p. 436)

We have drawn from Healy's overview at some length because it is the most recent and a very competent analysis of the prevailing situation regarding international social work in the curriculum. We might note, however, that another recent survey of schools of social work in the United States and Canada (Caragata and Sanchez, 2002) found that the schools frequently possessed international links and quite often placed a few students abroad, but did very little to integrate international learning into their curriculum. (See also Johnson, 2004.) We consider that the same can be said of Australia and New Zealand. On the basis of the available evidence, we can say that social work has been stumbling into the international arena for some time now, but still lacks clarity as to where it is headed and why.

However, recently approved educational policy and accreditation standards (EPAS) by the Council on Social Work Education (CSWE, 2001) give rise to hope that many social work programs in the United States may include or integrate international social work into their curriculum content and offer better clarity and vision for international social work practice. For example, the CSWE EPAS document in its preamble states: "Guided by a person-in-environment perspective and respect for human diversity, the profession works to effect social and economic justice worldwide."

Under the education policy, a statement relating to purposes of the social work profession (Section 1.0) includes a global dimension:

Professional social workers are leaders in a variety of organizational settings and service delivery systems within a global context.

Section 4.2 of the foundation curriculum content requires social work programs to

integrate social and economic justice content grounded in an understanding of distributive justice, human and civil rights, and the global interconnections of oppression.

Further, section 4.4 expects the

course content to provide students with knowledge and skills to . . . analyze organizational, local, state, national, and international issues in social welfare policy and social service delivery.

It is also heartening to note that to globalize social work education, the CSWE established the Katherine A. Kendall Institute for International Social Work Education in 2004. One of this institute's primary aims is to foster the mainstream development of international content in social work education (CSWE, 2005).

In the following section we present in more detail our views on the directions that the social work profession should be taking in strengthening social work's role in the international field.

A Model for Introducing International Social Work Into the Curriculum

In discussing the manner in which international social work should be incorporated into the social work curriculum, we have in mind the four key conclusions set out in the above section on where social work should be heading in the twenty-first century. Our discussion is based on the premises that social work should become a truly global profession that makes a truly global response to the major social problems confronting the contemporary world, and that, to become such, it should incorporate a social development perspective within an education model that contains three levels: the paraprofessional, professional, and senior professional levels.

A Three-level Education Model

If social work is to carry out its international roles and national responsibilities in the great majority of developing countries, it requires a three-level education model (see Table 14.1). First, it is imperative that social work schools prepare the appropriate numbers of specifically trained personnel to contribute to the human resources required for the social development field as a whole, including in particular poverty alleviation, local-level development, and enhancing social cohesion, and including specific areas of need, such as displaced persons and postconflict reconstruction where required. While these are among the major needs, there is in practice a wide range of global needs requiring a skilled response. Such fields of work together require very large numbers of personnel equipped with, ideally in our view, some 12 to 18 months of training that concentrates on those fields of practice within which they are most likely to be deployed in the particular context at the particular time. In addition to these key areas of training, these paraprofessionals need also to acquire a range of basic professional skills, some key bodies of knowledge, and an understanding of professional ethics.

To become a fully qualified social worker would require a further two years or so of education, both broadening and deepening training received to this point, which might be made up of a mixture of in-service training, short intensive courses, and a period of full-time

Table 14.1   A three-level model for social work education, and practice in the global context

Level A

Education:	pregraduate social work education and training in some specific areas of practice along with selected basic skills and knowledge
Duration:	total of 12–18 months, including in-service training periods
Title:	assistant social worker
Level:	paraprofessional
Work level:	local (frontline) worker
Major roles:	e.g., local-level social development, frontline operations in refugee and postconflict work, child care work, youth work, community development, family welfare

Level B

Education:	graduate level in social work
Duration:	3–4 years
Title:	graduate social worker
Level:	professional
Work level:	intermediate (usually at agency or regional level)
Major roles:	facilitating development at the local level generally, training and supporting Level A workers, establishing and managing local programs, basic research and social policy work, and available to assist with more complex situations

Level C

Education:	postgraduate level
Duration:	1–2 years
Title:	senior social worker
Level:	senior professional
Work level:	central (leadership in central government and nongovernment structures)
Major roles:	senior management, program planning, senior research officer, senior policy personnel, involvement in graduate and postgraduate education

studies, with the balance between these depending on the prevailing circumstances. Taken as a whole, this further education and training should complement what was contained in an individual's initial basic training, while ensuring that these graduates reach the level of a fully trained social worker. It is desirable for graduates of this level to have reached university education standards, alongside the various other professions.

The senior professional level would be achieved by a further 18 to 24 months of education, coming after a period of practice experience. This educational level would focus on management and leadership qualities in general,

along with specific content in those key fields where these graduates are likely to be exercising leadership.

It is important that the entrance requirements for each level be consistent with local realities, and designed to recruit those individuals most likely to make a significant contribution at the respective level in the priority fields of work. A number of workers would remain at each level, while others would eventually want to progress within the profession, and articulation between levels should make this possible, with additional upgrading opportunities provided as necessary. It may be, for example, that persons with a minimum of four years of secondary school would be recruited into level one; and these persons would require additional opportunities to make it possible for them eventually to reach university graduate status level, if this was their wish and they possessed the ability to do so.

In terms of numbers, a typical developing country may need to prepare social workers each year in the following proportions: over a thousand level one assistant social workers, over 300 graduate social workers, and perhaps 40 or 50 senior social workers. Precise numbers, of course, would depend entirely on the profile of prevailing social needs to which social work could be responding, and the extent of the development of the social work profession within that country. In developed countries, there may be minimal need perceived for level one assistant social workers, although the range of welfare officer, youth worker, community development, child care, and other training courses, as well as the existence of specific pockets of unmet social need, suggest that the significance of this level of social worker may have long been neglected by the profession. On the other hand, it may for some time be incumbent on schools of social work in developed countries, and in a range of developing countries, to prepare professional and senior professional social workers who are able to move immediately into the international fields of practice in any country, as in fact has been occurring in recent times.

A Social Development Focus Throughout the Three Education Levels

At various points in this text, the nature of and need for a social development focus within social work education have been discussed. What we wish to do here is outline some ways in which this objective can be achieved. In doing so, we are drawing extensively on the work carried out by a group of social work educators from across Asia at a workshop at La Trobe University in 1997 (Cox, Pawar, and Picton, 1997a), while also bearing in mind the quite extensive literature on this topic (see Cox, Pawar, and Picton, 1997b; Chui, Wong, and Chan, 1996).

The Social Development Perspective

The model being presented is guided by the following understanding of what the social development perspective signifies. Looking at this understanding, it will be appreciated that the comprehensive nature of the social development perspective, as it is commonly understood and presented here, is virtually equivalent to the integrated-perspectives approach introduced in Chapter 2 and used throughout this text. We have maintained the term *social development* here because it is consistent with the literature; however, readers should feel free to substitute the term *integrated-perspectives approach* as equally applicable.

A social development perspective

Goals:

- Promotion of people's well-being or quality of life
- Enabling people to experience freedom to satisfy their aspirations and realize their potential

Values:

- Respect for people and belief in their capacity to grow and develop
- A holistic understanding of human existence—physical to spiritual

---

(Continued)

- Acceptance of social and cultural pluralism, and incorporation of the centrality of people's cultures and values
- Acknowledgment of the importance of ecological issues and people's links with nature and their environment
- Acknowledgment that social relations are based on the right and obligation to participate, equality of opportunity, and the right of all to social justice

Process:

- A participatory process
- An empowering process

Strategies at the local, national, and international levels:

- Capacity building of individuals, groups, and communities
- Local institution building and support for people's organizations
- Fostering self-reliance
- Creating an enabling environment within which all people can develop
- Participating in the development and functioning of social institutions
- Promoting the provision of adequate resources and services accessible to all
- Promoting a proactive role for the state in supporting participatory planning
- Engaging in the development and implementation of policies to enhance social development
- Coordinating development initiatives at all levels
- Strengthening civil society in all its various aspects

Responding to the broader and specific context:

- Understanding the positive and negative roles of economic, political, social, and cultural development trends within a global and national context, particularly in terms of their impact on people and their well-being
- Understanding people's needs in context
- Acknowledging people's aspirations and the barriers to their realization
- Understanding people's culture and values
- Understanding the range and nature of existing social institutions

*The Parameters of
the Social Development
Perspective Within the Curriculum*

The parameters of the social development perspective within the curriculum context can be divided into the generic and the specific. The generic level includes inculcating an understanding of all aspects of the social development perspective as outlined above. In addition to looking at the goals, values, and strategies common to social development, the generic aspects span the full range of social needs, at all levels from the individual to the international, while embracing the remedial, preventative, and developmental approaches to responding to social needs. In addition to exploring social development, the generic level should include also a skills component. Among the key generic skills pertinent to social development are

- skills relating to intervention in the field and problem solving,
- skills relating to project and program activities,
- skills relating to interaction with wider publics,
- skills relating to enhancing social integration,
- skills relating to generic social development initiatives,
- research skills,
- political skills,
- economics-related skills, and
- policy development skills.

The level at which these skills will be taught will depend on the social work education level.

From the practice perspective, however, in the end these generic aspects of social development need to be made specific to a particular context. The context will imply specific goals of social development, specific presenting social needs, a specific economic-political-cultural context, and specific bodies of knowledge pertinent to any or all of the above. The following list of specialized fields within social development, in which education and training often need to be provided, is not exclusive but does contain fields of widespread importance:

- Poverty alleviation
- Employment and income generation
- Social integration and cohesion
- Rural and remote area development
- Atoll and island development
- Urban slum and settlement development
- Work with children in especially difficult circumstances
- Work with people with disabilities
- Work with families, children, youth, and elderly
- Work with women in the development context
- Work with tribal and indigenous minority groups
- Public health, sanitation, and family planning services
- Shelter and self-help housing
- Formal, informal, and community education at all levels
- Disaster management
- Substance abuse and addictions
- HIV/AIDS, and responses to epidemics generally
- Individual and collective public safety
- Ecological management and sustainable development

All of the above areas can be taught at all education levels, with the content made appropriate to each particular level. The teaching of each field should embrace knowledge, strategies, and skills components.

The Learning Objectives in Introducing Social Development Into the Curriculum

The following are among the key learning objectives behind a social development–oriented curriculum.

Students, on graduating, would have the capability

- to express a commitment to the goals of social development;
- to apply the values that underpin social development and observe their ethical implications;
- to appreciate the contexts of people's lives and well-being at all levels from the individual to the societal;
- to use the strategies fundamental to social development;
- to engage in the two main processes of social development, namely a participatory and empowering approach; and
- to engage in lifelong learning as reflective practitioners.

The Inclusion in the Curriculum of International Social Work Content

It has become increasingly important for the social work curriculum to contain a strong element of international social work content for reasons canvassed at several points in this text. Many schools of social work are doing so, although often, as Healy (2001) points out, the manner of doing so could be greatly improved. Having reflected on this matter, we would like to make the following suggestions as to how international content can best be incorporated into the typical social work curriculum.

The two modes of inclusion commonly discussed are the diffused and specific alternatives. When this topic is diffused throughout the curriculum, the expectation is that all members of the teaching staff will incorporate an international dimension to their subject matter. By contrast, in the specific approach, distinct courses on international social work are included in the curriculum. These two modes of inclusion are not of course necessarily alternatives, and, as with many aspects of the curriculum, it is ideal that a subject is introduced in its own right but then reinforced by being referred to, and expanded on, at various other points in the curriculum. The weakness of the diffused approach as the exclusive approach is that it depends on a high level of central oversight and control of the curriculum. As for the international content itself, some staff will not see it as important, some will feel inadequate to introduce such content, and the introduction may be so diffuse in practice that it makes no real impact on students.

We strongly suggest that every social work course contain some specific international content. If this content is picked up and built on by other staff within other parts of the curriculum, this is ideal; but without specific content it is unlikely that students will develop an appreciation of the international dimension of their profession. We would further suggest that this content not be available exclusively at the elective level. It may be that some key topics should

be included within the core curriculum and others left to an elective, but if such content is taught entirely at the elective level only a small proportion of graduates will come to appreciate this important aspect of social work.

There are several obvious components of the common curriculum where some international content is logical and should be strongly encouraged. Let us list some such components:

- Social policy courses will benefit from both a comparative social policy element and content on global policy.
- Cross-cultural social work courses should strongly reflect the global context.
- The history of social work should cover all areas of the globe.
- Ethics courses should consider social work ethics from an international perspective.
- Law and social work courses should consider international and human rights law.
- Poverty courses should consider poverty around the globe.
- Community development courses should look at community development in various national contexts and its application to many aspects of international practice.

There are, however, some aspects of international social work that are less likely to be reflected elsewhere in the curriculum and, in any case, will benefit greatly from specific content. Among such aspects are

- global social problems and the roles of social work;
- the international community and the contribution therein of social work; and
- the development and organization of social work as an international profession.

In addition to course content, it is important wherever possible that social work students receive some international experience during their preparation for professional life. There are several ways in which this can be achieved:

- Overseas field placements are now not uncommon, although they still involve only a tiny proportion of social work students, and such should be facilitated by schools whenever possible, as the value of them is now well recognized.
- Students can exchange with students from overseas, or do one semester of their course in another country, or at least be encouraged to visit overseas schools when possible.
- Some schools may be able to establish a multicampus curriculum where the various campuses are in different countries, as has occurred in Europe, permitting students a cross-cultural experience dimension to their studies.
- Staff exchanges or visits to overseas campuses can be arranged, giving students direct exposure to teaching staff who normally teach and practice in a very different context.

We are suggesting, then, that the typical social work curriculum should contain international material at various points within the existing curriculum, specific international content in courses devoted to international social work, and opportunities where possible for students to interact with the international field in as direct a manner as possible.

If a specific course on international social work is provided, we suggest that it include, at a minimum, the following topics:

- understanding the global context of practice and globalization processes;
- social work internationally, its reach, codes of ethics, foci of practice, and organization;
- a social development perspective in social work;
- a cross-cultural approach to working internationally; and
- major fields of international work and the roles of social work.

Changes Required to Social Work Practice

When we think of the qualities required by social work practitioners working in international fields, it seems clear that certain qualities will need to be emphasized. It may be that currently some social workers do not possess many of these qualities, while others who do possess them will need to hone them further if they are to cope with the demands and challenges of the international field. Of course the qualities identified will vary to some degree across the various fields of international practice as well as with the nature of practitioners' involvement in the international area. In regard to the latter point, we might distinguish between

Western social workers working within their own country but with a global orientation,

Western and non-Western social workers working in the international field outside their country of origin and most commonly in developing countries, and

local workers in developing countries able and willing to move beyond traditional social work roles and engage with the major fields of international social work practice.

In regard to the first group, their general needs which may require changes will be to develop a global orientation and an understanding of the dominant presenting needs that are global in nature. Westerners among the second group will need to acquire many additional qualities to those that local social work practice usually requires, and many of these are set out below. Non-Western workers in the second group, however, should be better able to work outside their normal context. Finally, local workers in developing countries with social work training and engaged in international concerns are currently very few in number. What is called for, therefore, are basic schemes to recruit and train such people. In many cases this may require social work education programs that differ markedly from those with which we are already familiar. In addition to receiving appropriate basic training, these workers may also require specific training in some of the areas referred to below.

Some General Qualities Required by Social Work Practitioners

International social work practice requires an enhanced ability to think globally both at the situation analysis level and in the devising of intervention programs. Furthermore, international social workers must be able to analyze situations and devise programs without feeling daunted by the scope and complexity of the global context.

Such practice also requires the ability to operate in a wide range of organizational contexts. In many situations, workers will find themselves engaging at different levels and in various ways with community organizations, the national and international NGO sector, both local and overseas governments, and the UN system. Practice may regularly require collaborating with any or all of these types of organizations, working in different structures at different times, or being part of teams drawn from the various sectors. A good understanding of the many sectors that compose the international community is essential.

Along with the ability to span the range of structures engaged internationally is the ability to adopt cross-disciplinary approaches. This involves the need to be familiar with the main orientations and modus operandi of the various disciplines, so that one can work together with other professionals with an understanding of their various roles and potential contributions in specific practice contexts.

International social work practice calls for a heightened level of ability in working across cultural differences. Many social workers in the international fields are working with both

colleagues and clients from cultural backgrounds that differ from their own, while many situations with which they engage will possess significant cultural factors that must be taken into account at every stage in the engagement.

International practice requires, in general terms, a high degree of commitment to the social justice and human rights dimensions of practice, which in turn requires a good level of understanding of the nature and application of these concepts.

Finally, in many situations, practice in the main international fields requires an ability to confront intense suffering, extreme deprivation, high levels of emotional and physical damage, and the devastation of overwhelming loss, and still have the strength and objectivity to function appropriately and effectively in such contexts. High levels of empathy need to coincide with an ability to put to one side personal reactions as one embarks on constructive engagement with the situation.

Some Qualities Required at the Macro Level of Engagement

A key quality required by international social work practitioners is the ability to keep in mind at all times the macro, meso, and micro levels of the presenting situation. While this may be, in a sense, true of all social work, at least ideally, it is essential in much of the international area of operation. This ability is enhanced by training in significant fields, such as poverty alleviation or the displacement field, that covers all three levels.

The macro level of engagement requires a strong emphasis on cross-structural relationships, and the need to formulate and negotiate agreements regarding policies and processes, resource issues, questions of access, and so on. The skills required at this level include political sensitivity, significant organization-based knowledge, negotiation and advocacy skills, and so on.

Some Qualities Required at the Micro Level

Practice at the micro or local level frequently calls for the following qualities:

an ability to be innovative and demonstrate initiative, regarding social work's traditional methodologies as only the starting point for thinking through possible responses;

an enhanced ability to adopt participatory, empowering, and self-reliant approaches to practice, whatever the context or level;

an ability to function for periods without colleagues being present or nearby and providing daily support, requiring significant levels of self-confidence and self-knowledge; and

an ability to be aware of potential dangers, to take steps to ensure one's personal security, and to utilize basic self-defense techniques.

Changes Required in the Nature of Social Work Practice

Undoubtedly, the major change in social work practice called for, when responding to the challenges of international social work, is a significant broadening of the scope of social work and expansion of its range of intervention modalities. Historically, the evolution of social work has been conditioned largely by Western countries' realities and the priorities of their governments. In recent times, however, Western social work has expanded enormously, largely in response to newly emerging needs. A social work focus on drug abuse, domestic violence, women's rights, children's rights, the homeless, unemployment, palliative care, and HIV/AIDS is very obvious today but was virtually nonexistent only a few decades ago. Social work practice has thus already demonstrated a willingness and ability to expand its range of fields and practice modalities.

International social work practice calls for even more radical changes to the social work

profile if it is to reflect global concerns, the great range of global cultures, and the presenting realities in the less and least developed countries. The shift from personal to community-based intervention, while not initiated in the main by the social work profession, is one obvious example. Others include the "barefoot social worker" in parts of rural India, the lone social worker deployed to work in local-level development in remote villages in the Philippines, and the social activist working for people's rights in Latin America. However, it seems likely that considerably more innovation will be required if social work globally is to respond to the range of needs, situations, and cultures.

The question that then arises is, how does one build a profession that is highly flexible in its choice of intervention strategies? Certainly workers need to be highly flexible, but so too does the profession in its perception of what constitutes social work. If the core of social work consists of a clear set of principles and ethics, a clear vision of the essential qualities of the life we seek for all human beings, a set of basic skills such as the ability to form relationships with people or groups, and clear bodies of knowledge pertaining to a range of disciplines, can the profession give these qualities priority over possible methodologies? Methodologies with far-reaching application should, of course, be endorsed and taught to students, but the range of potentially feasible, acceptable, and appropriate methodologies should surely be kept open, and even the utilization of taught methodologies, such as counseling and community development, kept flexible.

We would not wish to recommend specific changes to social work practice because to do so is to contradict the essential need for flexibility in the face of diversity. Rather, we suggest that social workers be trained in the essential ability to analyze situations and develop appropriate intervention responses, while adopting as open and as broad an approach as the individual worker or group of workers will permit. Only then will we see social work practice respond appropriately and effectively to the very broad canvas that international social work practice constitutes.

Careers in International Social Work: Social Work Graduates' Response to International Social Work

We have been assuming that there is scope for social workers to be employed in international social work; however, we need to examine whether this is a valid assumption. When Western writers address this question, they are usually considering the employment prospects for Western graduates to work with international agencies in developing countries, so let us start with this issue. From survey work that he undertook in the United States, Rosenthal (1990) concluded that there were few social work graduates working abroad, despite the fact that they were clearly well qualified for the many work opportunities available. Reviewing the literature on this matter, Healy (1987) found

> that the (international) agencies have not sought social workers and that the agencies have misconceptions about the nature of social work training and expertise, underestimating the breadth of the profession. Nonetheless, the concluding impression . . . was that agencies are seeking skills and attributes possessed by many professional social workers. (p. 406)

So while she concurred that the numbers of U.S. social workers being employed abroad was probably minimal, she noted that

> opportunities for expanding social work's role in planning, directing, and delivering services internationally exist. (Healy, 1987, p. 408)

As Healy (2001, p. 4) implies in her recent book, the participation of social workers from the United States in international social work may reflect the fact that

more than 90% of American professors surveyed expressed no need to read books or journals published outside their own country in order to keep up in their fields—a quite astounding finding of disinterest in their professions beyond national borders, and possibly indicative of ethnocentrism.

Specht's (1990) comments on the focus on clinical social work in the United States referred to in Chapter 1 may be a further reason why comparatively few social workers from that country venture abroad.

Do European social workers reflect a similar lack of interest in working abroad? All indications suggest that the colonial experience, and the interest of countries like the Netherlands and Scandinavian countries in international work generally, have led to much higher numbers of European social workers working abroad than of Americans, although we are not aware of any statistics on the matter. Certainly one encounters more European than American social workers when moving around the field in developing countries.

Apart from social workers from Western countries working abroad, we should also examine whether the graduates of Latin America, Hong Kong, Japan, the Philippines, Singapore, India, South Africa, and so on become involved in international social work to any significant degree. Certainly there are graduates from all of these and other countries who are highly regarded internationally, but it is unclear whether these graduates accept employment beyond their borders to any great extent, despite the work of some noted individuals. What is clear is that undoubtedly such graduates will have much to offer if appropriately educated.

Prospects for Social Workers in International Social Work Careers

What does appear to be widely accepted is that social work education and experience do provide social workers with those skills and attributes required in the international field, and that they are also eminently suited to such work because of the common focus on the importance of cross-cultural factors within many practice situations. It is also very clear that the numbers of personnel being appointed today to work in fields such as those of displaced persons, humanitarian aid, postconflict situations, human rights, and development work of various kinds are larger than ever before. How far employers or recruiting agencies consider social workers for such employment, and how much social workers make themselves available for such employment, are questions to which there appear to be at present no accurate answers. Our impressions are that social workers are readily considered when they do apply and are highly regarded when they are employed, and that more social workers are applying for such work, but we are unable to support these impressions with figures.

In conclusion, we believe that the scope of international work open to social work graduates is expanding rapidly, and that more and more social workers are being drawn into the international field, either as a career or for short periods that inform and complement their international approach to their work at the national and local levels. We also believe that opportunities will rapidly increase further if, first, social workers in developed and developing countries are trained in international social work, and second, more social workers are graduated in developing countries with the skills and motivation to work within the major social development challenges confronting these and other countries at the local, intermediate, and central levels as outlined above.

Local Social Work Staff in International Social Work in Developing Countries

We have focused to this point on nonlocal social workers moving into international social work, but of course the majority of workers employed by many international agencies are local staff, recruited and deployed locally to work either in frontline situations or in program management roles. The question that then arises is, to what extent are these local workers local social work graduates? While again we know of no statistics, we believe their numbers to be extremely small, for several reasons. First, in some countries there are either no schools of social work or a very small number of schools graduating very small numbers of practitioners. While some local people will have studied social work abroad, we believe that number to be also very small. Add to the numbers problem the fact that public service positions are highly attractive to the majority of graduates in many developing countries, and one further reduces the pool available to international agencies. In many situations, we have observed that local staff in international positions are often without qualifications, and yet not well supervised in terms of their work with people and not offered opportunities for in-service training in the more human aspects of their work.

It would seem, therefore, that there is considerable scope for the expansion of social work career opportunities in international work, for both graduates joining international agencies as international staff and for those joining as national or local staff. Hence we need to see schools of social work around the world preparing workers at these two levels, international and national-local, which will require graduating social workers at the assistant social worker, graduate social worker, and senior social worker levels outlined above, and in greater numbers than we have seen to date. In addition to providing more training and more places for social workers interested in moving into international social work, the social work schools and profession will need to embark on research into the major fields of international social work practice, in order to broaden their knowledge base, identify key strategies, and improve the skills of graduates and professionals. If the profession responds appropriately, we believe that far greater numbers of social workers than we have seen to date will move into the career opportunities that are clearly there.

The Global Organization of Social Work

For most of its history, the profession of social work at the international level has relied upon the services of a dedicated band of volunteers, serving as officeholders, committee members, conference organizers, and members of various working parties. It has proved to be financially difficult to maintain staff at a central headquarters and, whenever that has been possible, such staff has been thinly spread over a great range of activities and members, member countries, or member associations. While it seems unlikely that this situation will change in the foreseeable future, we believe that social work's global organizations have vital roles to play if social work is to assume its rightful place in the activities of the international community. Accordingly, different strategies will need to be explored to accomplish the ends we have in mind.

Let us consider, first, the roles that the international social work organizations will need to play if the field of international social work is to develop as we consider it should. The key roles for the international organizations would include those listed in the box below.

We anticipate that, if the international organizations are seen to be taking these roles seriously, financial and other assistance will be forthcoming from governments, the UN, MNCs, and the NGO sector. The international organizations will carry the roles of initiating, coordinating, and promulgating programs and outcomes.

However, as these tasks would currently be beyond the resources of the international organizations, we believe that specific roles will need to be delegated to particular areas of the profession. We anticipate that some national social work associations, some schools of social work, some NGOs, and some research centers would be willing to undertake specific areas of activity under the overall auspice of the international organizations. We anticipate that this is the case because some national associations, schools, and so on have already clearly demonstrated their willingness and ability to be so involved. However, these activities would often carry more weight and gain more support if they had the endorsement of the international organizations, and if it were clear that the specific programs were integrated within a much broader plan and vision.

Each of the five areas listed above as key roles for social work's international organizations

---

1. The sponsorship of education and training in international social work in both developed and developing countries

2. The promotion of social work education generally in developing countries, especially those countries currently without schools

3. The promotion of the roles of social work in the international field across the breadth of the international community

4. The promotion of research into the core fields of international social work practice, with a focus on identifying appropriate programs, strategies, and related skills

5. The dissemination of educational and promotional literature on international social work practice to the profession globally

might have a working group, perhaps jointly responsible to the IFSW and IASSW. These working groups would then enlist the support of various social work entities to find and carry out specific tasks, such as

the general promotion of international social work education and training;

the establishment of workshops on specific subjects, in conjunction perhaps with a global conference;

the establishment of social work education in specific countries, specifically countries with no school of social work, a clear need for such, and local parties keen to play a role in such a development;

the involvement of the social work profession in international efforts in, for example, curtailing global trafficking in women or children for purposes of exploitation;

the initiation of a research project into, for example, how social work might best contribute to community rebuilding in a post-conflict situation; or

the printing and distribution of centrally developed or approved literature pertinent to international social work practice.

The involvement of the international organizations in international social work will probably work best when as many states as possible have national "international social work committees," as we know has been the case in Australia and the United States for some time. If such committees were affiliated with the global structures in an appropriate way, and their collective activities disseminated through an international newsletter,

this would help to promote the cause of international social work at all levels, while providing the various levels with ideas for action.

Conclusion

In this chapter we have sought to identify some key changes to social work education and practice required if the profession of social work is to make a more significant contribution to what we have defined in Chapter 1 as international social work. Because a reasonable amount of change has already been achieved in this regard, we do not believe that what we are suggesting is either unreasonable or impractical. The most difficult challenge may be the establishment of the social work profession in those countries where currently it does not exist, especially in the world's LDCs. This will require a significant commitment from the global profession and the assistance of other organizations, such as the UN. Other areas of change suggested would not seem to be particularly difficult.

The social work profession has the capacity to undertake more research into the various fields of international social work practice, to develop more curriculum content related to international social work, to support those workers who choose to work in this field, and to encourage all social work practitioners to endorse and implement a global perspective in whatever their chosen field of practice. No longer can the social work profession afford to neglect or treat as peripheral this extremely important aspect of practice; and if this text assists in the change process required, the authors will be more than satisfied.

Summary

- Twenty-first-century international social work must ensure that quality social work education and practice is accessible in all parts of the world based on prevailing needs. Toward this end, changes in both educational content and training levels are needed to effectively respond to international issues and needs.

- Social work as a global profession needs to focus on existing and emerging critical issues at both local and global levels, develop innovative responses, reach out to needy populations and areas, employ the integrated-perspectives approach, and adapt to different contexts, while maintaining global minimal standards.

- Although there are encouraging initiatives, the social work profession and social work schools globally need to take systematic steps to introduce international social work curricula into their programs.

- The three levels of training and the integrated-perspectives approach, particularly the perspective of social development, should be introduced as appropriate.

- Social workers should be aware of, and develop the qualities needed to engage effectively in, the field of international social work. Flexibility, openness, innovativeness, and appropriate intervention responses are needed in their practice.

- There appears to be considerable scope for the expansion of social work career opportunities in international social work.

- Global organizations of social work can play key roles in developing the field of international social work and in realizing its vision.

Questions and Topics for Discussion

- Where do you think social work should be heading in the twenty-first century?

- What are the changes needed in social work education to meet global contemporary realities?

- Discuss the three-level education model and the social development perspective as presented.

- Examine your social work curriculum to locate the content of international social work.

- What personal qualities are needed to effectively engage in international social work?

- Locate an advertisement for an international social work or development position, examine suggested selection criteria, and compare your qualities and qualification to see your suitability for the position.

- Make a list of agencies and organizations known to you that work internationally and employ social workers.

- How do you think global social work organizations can contribute to the field of international social work practice?

- What makes social work a global profession and what further needs to be done to achieve the goal of becoming a global profession?

Possible Areas for Research Projects

- Conduct a feasibility study for setting up a social work program where one is not available.

- Undertake a study to outline major fields of international social work practice.

- Conduct a study of social workers engaged in international social work to identify and develop key professional and personal qualities for international social work practice.

- Undertake case studies of global social work organizations and analyze their contributions to building international social work, and based on that analysis suggest strategies for future action.

- Drawing on both primary and secondary sources of information, develop a vision for international social work in the future.

Appendix A

International Federation of
Social Workers (IFSW) International
Association of Schools of Social Work (IASSW)

Ethics in Social Work, Statement of Principles

1. Preface

Ethical awareness is a fundamental part of the professional practice of social workers. Their ability and commitment to act ethically is an essential aspect of the quality of the service offered to those who use social work services.

The purpose of IASSW and IFSW's work on ethics is to promote ethical debate and reflection in the member organisations, among the providers of social work in member countries, as well as in the schools of social work and among social work students. Some ethical challenges and problems facing social workers are specific to particular countries; others are common. By staying at the level of general principles, the joint IASSW and IFSW statement aims to encourage social workers across the world to reflect on the challenges and dilemmas that face them and make ethically informed decisions about how to act in each particular case. Some of these problem areas include:

- The fact that the loyalty of social workers is often in the middle of conflicting interests
- The fact that social workers function as both helpers and controllers
- The conflicts between the duty of social workers to protect the interests of the people with whom they work and societal demands for efficiency and utility
- The fact that resources in society are limited

This document takes as its starting point the definition of social work adopted separately by the IFSW and IASSW at their respective General Meeting in Montreal, Canada in July 2000 and then agreed as a joint one in Copenhagen in May 2001 (section 2). This definition stresses principles of human rights and social justice. The next section (3) makes reference to the various declarations and conventions on human rights that are relevant to social work, followed by a statement of general ethical principles under the two broad headings of human rights and dignity and social justice (section 4). The final section introduces some basic guidance on ethical conduct in social work, which it is expected will be elaborated by the ethical guidance and in various codes and guidelines of the member organisations of IFSW and IASSW.

2. Definition of Social Work

The social work profession promotes social change, problem solving in human relationships and the empowerment and liberation of people to enhance well-being. Utilising theories of human behaviour and social systems, social work intervenes at the points where people interact with their environments. Principles of human rights and social justice are fundamental to social work.

3. International Conventions

International human rights declarations and conventions form common standards of achievement, and recognise rights that are accepted by the global community. Documents particularly relevant to social work practice and action are:

- Universal Declaration of Human Rights
- The International Covenant on Civil and Political Rights
- The International Covenant on Economic Social and Cultural Rights
- The Convention on the Elimination of all Forms of Racial Discrimination
- The Convention on the Elimination of All Forms of Discrimination against Women
- The Convention on the Rights of the Child
- Indigenous and Tribal Peoples Convention (ILO convention 169)

4. Principles

4.1 Human Rights and Human Dignity

Social work is based on respect for the inherent worth and dignity of all people, and the rights that follow from this. Social workers should uphold and defend each person's physical, psychological, emotional and spiritual integrity and well-being. This means:

1. Respecting the right to self-determination—Social workers should respect and promote people's right to make their own choices and decisions, irrespective of their values and life choices, provided this does not threaten the rights and legitimate interests of others.

2. Promoting the right to participation—Social workers should promote the full involvement and participation of people using their services in ways that enable them to be empowered in all aspects of decisions and actions affecting their lives.

3. Treating each person as a whole—Social workers should be concerned with the whole person, within the family, community and societal and natural environments, and should seek to recognise all aspects of a person's life.

4. Identifying and developing strengths—Social workers should focus on the strengths of all individuals, groups and communities and thus promote their empowerment.

4.2 Social Justice

Social workers have a responsibility to promote social justice, in relation to society generally, and in relation to the people with whom they work. This means:

1. Challenging negative discrimination[1]—Social workers have a responsibility to challenge negative discrimination on the basis of characteristics such as ability, age, culture, gender or sex, marital status, socio-economic status, political opinions, skin colour, racial or other physical characteristics, sexual orientation, or spiritual beliefs.

2. Recognising diversity—Social workers should recognise and respect the ethnic and cultural diversity of societies in which they practice, taking account of individual, family, group and community differences.

3. Distributing resources equitably—Social workers should ensure that resources at their disposal are distributed fairly, according to need.

4. Challenging unjust policies and practices—Social workers have a duty to bring to the attention of their employers, policy makers, politicians and the general public situations where resources are inadequate or where distribution of resources, policies and practices are oppressive, unfair or harmful.

5. Working in solidarity—Social workers have an obligation to challenge social conditions that contribute to social exclusion, stigmatisation or subjugation, and to work towards an inclusive society.

5. Professional Conduct

It is the responsibility of the national organisations in membership of IFSW and IASSW to develop and regularly update their own codes of ethics or ethical guidelines, to be consistent with the IFSW/IASSW statement. It is also the national organisation's responsibility to inform social workers and schools of social work about these codes or guidelines.

Social workers should act in accordance with the ethical code or guidelines current in their country. These will generally include more detailed guidance in ethical practice specific to the national context. The following general guidelines on professional conduct apply:

1. Social workers are expected to develop and maintain the required skills and competence to do their job.

2. Social workers should not allow their skills to be used for inhumane purposes, such as torture or terrorism.

3. Social workers should act with integrity. This includes not abusing the relationship of trust with the people using their services, recognising the boundaries between personal and professional life, and not abusing their position for personal benefit or gain.

4. Social workers should act in relation to the people using their services with compassion, empathy and care.

5. Social workers should not subordinate the needs or interests of people who use their services to their own needs or interests.

6. Social workers have a duty to take necessary steps to care for themselves professionally and personally in the workplace and in society, in order to ensure that they are able to provide appropriate services.

7. Social workers should maintain confidentiality regarding information about people who use their services. Exceptions to this may only be justified on the basis of a greater ethical requirement (such as the preservation of life).

8. Social workers need to acknowledge that they are accountable for their actions to the users of their services, the people they work with, their colleagues, their employers, the professional association and to the law, and that these accountabilities may conflict.

9. Social workers should be willing to collaborate with the schools of social work in order to support social work students to get practical training of good quality and up to date practical knowledge.

10. Social workers should foster and engage in ethical debate with their colleagues and employers and take responsibility for making ethically informed decisions.

11. Social workers should be prepared to state the reasons for their decisions based on ethical considerations, and be accountable for their choices and actions.

12. Social workers should work to create conditions in employing agencies and in their countries where the principles of this statement and those of their own national code (if applicable) are discussed, evaluated and upheld.

The document *Ethics in Social Work, Statement of Principles* was approved at the General Meetings of the International Federation of Social Workers and the International Association of Schools of Social Work in Adelaide, Australia, October 2004.

Note

1. In some countries the term "discrimination" would be used instead of "negative discrimination." The word negative is used here because in some countries the term "positive discrimination" is also used. Positive discrimination is also known as "affirmative action." Positive discrimination or affirmative action means positive steps taken to redress the effects of historical discrimination against the groups named in clause 4.2.1 above.

Appendix B

Acronyms

APEC - Asia Pacific Economic Cooperation

APMJ - Asia Pacific Migration Journal

ASEAN - Association of Southeast Asian Nations

AU - African Union (formerly OAU, Organization of African Unity)

CD - community development

COSW - Commonwealth Organization for Social Work

CSWE - Council on Social Work Education

DP - displaced person

ECOSOC - UN's Economic and Social Commission

ESCAP - UN's Economic and Social Commission for Asia and the Pacific

EU - European Union

GATT - General Agreement on Tariffs and Trade (now WTO)

GDP - gross domestic product

HABITAT - UN Centre for Human Settlements

HDI - Human Development Index of the UNDP

HIV/AIDS - human immunodeficiency virus/acquired immunodeficiency syndrome

HPI - Human Poverty Index of UNDP

IASSW - International Association of Schools of Social Work

ICRC - International Committee of the Red Cross

ICSD - International Consortium for Social Development

ICSW - International Council on Social Welfare

ICVA - International Council of Voluntary Agencies

IDP - internally displaced person

IFSW - International Federation of Social Workers

ILO - International Labour Organisation

IMF - International Monetary Fund

INGO - international nongovernmental organization

IOM - International Organisation for Migration

LDC - least developed country

LO - local organization

MNC - multinational corporation

MSF - Medecins Sans Frontieres (Doctors Without Borders)

NASW- National Association of Social Workers

NATO - North Atlantic Treaty Organization

NGO - nongovernmental organization

ODA - official development assistance

OECD - Organisation for Economic Co-operation and Development

PO - people's organization

PTSD - post-traumatic stress disorder

SAP - Structural Adjustment Program of IMF and World Bank

TNC - transnational corporation

UN - United Nations

UNCHR - United Nations Centre for Human Rights

UNCTAD - United Nations Conference on Trade and Development

UNDP - United Nations Development Programme

UNHCR - United Nations High Commissioner for Refugees

UNICEF - United Nations Children's Fund

UNRISD - United Nations Research Institute for Social Development

WB - World Bank

WFP - World Food Programme

WHO - World Health Organization

WTO - World Trade Organization

References

Abo-El-Nasr, M. (1997). Egypt. In N. Mayadas, T. Watts, & D. Elliott (Eds.), *International handbook on social work theory and practice* (pp. 205–222). Westport, CT: Greenwood.

Abrahams, C., & Peredo, A. M. (1996). Social work with poor women and their children in Peru. *The Journal of Applied Social Sciences, 21*(1), 53–60.

Adams, R. (2003). *Social work and empowerment* (3rd ed.). Basingstoke, England: Palgrave Macmillan.

Agger, I., & Jensen, S. B. (1990). Testimony as ritual and evidence in psychotherapy for political refugees. *Journal of Traumatic Stress, 3*(1), 115–129.

Ahearn, F. L., & Athey, J. L. (Eds.). (1991). *Refugee children: Theory, research, and services.* Baltimore: Johns Hopkins University Press.

Alexander, C. (1982). The international code of ethics for professional social work. In D. S. Sanders, O. Kurren, & J. Fischer (Eds.), *Fundamentals of social work* (pp. 45–50). Belmont, CA: Wadsworth.

Allen, T., & Thomas, A. (Eds.). (1992). *Poverty and development in the 1990s.* England: Oxford University Press.

Anderson, S., Wilson, M., Mwansa, L., and Osei-Hwedie, K. (1994). Empowerment and social work education and practice in Africa. *Journal of Social Development in Africa, 9*(2), 71–86.

Ankrah, E. M. (1992). Aids in Uganda: Initial social work responses. *Journal of Social Development in Africa, 7*(2), 53–62.

Asamoah, Y. (1997). Africa. In N. Mayadas, T. Watts, & D. Elliott (Eds.), *International handbook on social work theory and practice* (pp. 303–319). Westport, CT: Greenwood.

Asian Development Bank. (1999). *Reducing poverty: Major findings and implications.* Tokyo: Asian Development Bank.

Athey, J., & Ahearn, F. (1991). The mental health of refugee children: An overview. In F. L. Ahearn & J. I. Athey (Eds.), *Refugee children: Theory, research and services* (pp. 3–19). Baltimore: Johns Hopkins University Press.

AVERT. (2005). Aids orphans and affected children. Retrieved May 4, 2005, from http://www.avert.org/aidsorphans.htm

Azaiza, F., & Ben-Ari, A. (1997). Knowledge of and attitudes to AIDS among Arab professionals in Israel. *International Social Work, 40*(3), 341–357.

Aziz, N. (1995). The human rights debate in an era of globalization: Hegemony of discourse. *Bulletin of Concerned Asian Scholars, 27*(4), 9–23.

Balgopal, P. R. (Ed.). (2000). *Social work practice with immigrants and refugees.* New York: Columbia University Press.

Bamford, G. N. (1986). *Training the majority: Guidelines for the rural Pacific.* Suva, Fiji: University of the South Pacific.

Banfield, E. C. (1958). *The moral basis of a backward society.* New York: Free Press.

Bangura, Y. (1994). *The search for identity: Ethnicity, religion and political violence.* Geneva: UNRISD.

Barker, R. L. (1999). *The social work dictionary* (4th ed.). Washington, DC: NASW Press.

Battistela, G. (1993). Human rights of migrant workers [Special issue]. *Asian and Pacific Migration Journal, 2*(2).

Bayefsky, A., & Doyle, M. (1999). *Emergency return: Principles and guidelines.* Princeton, NJ: Princeton University Center of International Studies.

Behrman, J. R. (1990). *Human resource led development? Review of issues and evidence.* Geneva: ILO-ARTEP.

Beigbeder, Y. (1991). *The role and status of international humanitarian volunteers and organisations.* Dordrecht, The Netherlands: Martinus Nijhoff.

Bello, W., Kinley, D., & Elinson, E. (1982). *Development debacle: The world bank in the Philippines.* Birmingham, England: Third World Publications.

Billups, J. (1994). Conceptualizing a partnership model between social work and social development. *Social Development Issues, 16*(3), 91–99.

Black, J. K. (1991). *Development in theory and practice: Bridging the gap.* Boulder, CO: Westview.

Blair, T. L. (1974). *The international urban crisis.* Saint Albans, England: Paladin.

Boothby, N. (1992). Displaced children: Psychological theory and practice from the field. *Journal of Refugee Studies, 5*(2), 106–122.

Bose, A. (1992). Social work in India. In M. Hokenstadt, S. Khinduka, & J. Midgley (Eds.), *Profiles in international social work* (pp. 71–83). Washington, DC: NASW Press.

Bradbury, B., Jenkins, S., & Micklewright, J. (2000). *Child poverty dynamics in seven nations.* Sydney, Australia: Social Policy Research Centre, University of New South Wales.

Bronfenbrenner, V. (1979). *The ecology of human development.* Cambridge, MA: Harvard University Press.

Brown, L., Durning, A., Flavin, C., French, H., Jacobsen, J., Lenssen, N., et al. (Eds.). (1991). *State of the world 1991, A Worldwatch Institute report.* New York: W. W. Norton.

Brown, M. E. (Ed.). (1993). *Ethnic conflict and international security.* Princeton, NJ: Princeton University Press.

Bruyn, S. T. (2005). *A civil republic: Beyond capitalism and nationalism.* Bloomfield, CT: Kumarian.

Buchwald, U. von. (1991). *The refugee dependency syndrome: Origins and consequences.* Geneva: League of Red Cross and Red Crescent Societies.

Campfens, H. (Ed.). (1997). *Community development around the world: Practice, theory, research, training.* Toronto, Canada: University of Toronto Press.

Caragata, L., & Sanchez, M. (2002). Globalization and global need: New imperatives for expanding international social work education in North America. *International Social Work, 45*(2), 217–238.

Carrizosa, S., & Poertner, J. (1992). Latin American street children: Problems, programmes and critique. *International Social Work, 35*(4), 405–414.

Carroll, R. (2004, December 24–2005, January 6). Bad, but it could have been worse: Year in Africa. *Guardian Weekly,* p. 37.

Carroll, T. F. (1992). *Intermediary NGOs: The supporting link in grassroots development.* Hartford, CT: Kumarian.

Cassen, R. (1994). *Does aid work?* (2nd ed.). Oxford, England: Clarendon.

Catholic Relief Services. (1996). *Psychosocial rehabilitation perspectives: Conference proceedings.* Sarajevo, Bosnia and Herzegovina: CRS.

Cernea, M. M. (1989). Non-governmental organizations and local development. *Regional Development Dialogue, 10*(2), 117–142.

Cernea, M. M. (1991). *Putting people first: Sociological variables in rural development projects* (2nd ed.). New York: Oxford University Press.

Cernea, M. M., & McDowell, C. (Eds.). (2000). *Risks and reconstruction: Experiences of resettlers and refugees.* Washington, DC: World Bank.

Chambers, R. (1983). *Rural development: Putting the last first.* Harlow, England: Longman.

Chambers, R. (1993). *Challenging the professions: Frontiers for rural development.* London: Intermediate Technology.

Chi, Y.-C. (1987). Social development and capacity building: A case example of a social welfare centre in Korea. *International Social Work, 30*(2), 139–149.

ChildHope. (1989). *The street girls of metro Manila.* Manila, The Philippines: Author.

Chow, N. (1997). China. In N. Mayadas, T. Watts, & D. Elliott (Eds.), *International handbook on social work theory and practice* (pp. 282–300). Westport, CT: Greenwood.

Chua, A. (2003). *World on fire: How exporting free market democracy breeds ethnic hatred and global instability.* London: W. Heinemann.

Chui, W., Wong, Y., & Chan, C. (1996). Social work education for social development. *The Journal of Applied Social Sciences, 21*(1), 15–25.

Clark, J. (1993). *The state and the voluntary sector.* Washington, DC: World Bank.

Cohen, R., & Deng, F. M. (Eds.). (1998). *The forsaken people: Case studies of the internally displaced.* Washington, DC: Brookings Institution Press.

Colletta, N. J., Lim, T. G., & Kelles-Vitanen, A. (Eds.). (2001). *Social cohesion and conflict prevention in Asia.* Washington, DC: World Bank.

Commission of the European Communities. (1993). *Green paper: European social policy.* Luxembourg, Belgium: Author.

Commission on Global Governance. (1995). *Our global neighbourhood: The report of the commission on global governance.* England: Oxford University Press.

Community and Family Services International. (1991). *Community development strategies among Vietnamese refugees and asylum seekers in Hong Kong.* Hong Kong: Author.

Compton, B. R., & Galaway, B. (1999). *Social work processes.* Pacific Grove, CA: Brooks/Cole.

Connolly, M. (1994). Experiences of UNICEF initiated projects for street children in Latin America. In A. Rane (Ed.), *Street children: A challenge to the social work profession* (pp. 196–204). Bombay, India: Tata Institute of Social Sciences.

Constable, R., & Mehta, V. (Eds.). (1994). *Education for social work in Eastern Europe: Changing horizons.* Chicago: Lyceum.

Corner, L. (1986). Human resources development for developing countries: A survey of the major theoretical issues. In UN/ESCAP, *Human resources development in Asia and the Pacific* (pp. 1–28). Bangkok, Thailand: UN/ESCAP.

Cox, D. R. (1986). Intercountry casework. *International Social Work, 29*(3), 247–256.

Cox, D. R. (1987). *Migration and welfare: An Australian perspective.* Sydney, Australia: Prentice Hall.

Cox, D. R. (1989). *Welfare practice in a multicultural society.* Sydney, Australia: Prentice Hall.

Cox, D. R. (1997). The vulnerability of women migrant workers to a lack of protection and to violence. *Asian and Pacific Migration Journal, 6*(1), 59–76.

Cox, D. R. (1998). Community rebuilding in the Philippines. In M. D. Hoff (Ed.), *Sustainable community development: Studies in economic, environmental and cultural revitalization* (pp. 45–62). Boca Raton, FL: Lewis.

Cox, D., Owen, L., & Picton, C. (1994). *Asian women migrant workers: Maximizing the benefits of their experiences.* Melbourne, Australia: La Trobe University.

Cox, D., Pawar, M., & Picton, C. (1997a). *Social development content in social work education: Report of a survey of schools of social work in the Asia-Pacific region.* Bundoora, Australia: La Trobe University School of Social Work & Social Policy.

Cox, D., Pawar, M., & Picton, C. (1997b). *Introducing a social development perspective into social work curricula at all levels: Report of a regional workshop.* Bundoora, Australia: La Trobe University School of Social Work & Social Policy.

Cranna, M. (Ed.). (1994). *The true cost of conflict.* London: Earthscan.

CSWE (Council on Social Work Education). (2001). *Educational policy and accreditation standards.* Retrieved March 28, 2005, from http://www.cswe.org/accreditation/EPAS/EPAS_start.htm

CSWE. (2005). *Katherine A. Kendall Institute for International Social Work Education.* Retrieved March 28, 2005, from http://www.cswe.org/

Curtis, D. (1991). *Beyond government: Organizations for common benefit.* London: Macmillan.

Curtis, M. (1997). Development cooperation in a changing world. In R. Randel & T. German (Eds.), *The reality of aid: An independent review of development cooperation: 1997–1998* (pp. 4–18). London: Earthscan.

Danieli, Y., Rodley, N. S., & Weisæth, L. (Eds.). (1996). *International responses to traumatic stress: Humanitarian, human rights, justice, peace and development.* New York: Baywood.

David, G. (1993). Strategies for grassroots human development. *Social Development Issues, 15*(2), 1–13.

Deacon, B. (1997). *Global social policy: International organizations and the future of welfare.* London: Sage.

Debiel, T., & Klein, A. (Eds.). (2002). *Fragile peace: State failure, violence and development in crisis regions.* London: Zed Books.

DeMartino, R., & Buchwald, U. von. (1996). Forced displacement: Non-government efforts in the psychosocial care of traumatized peoples. In Y. Danieli, N. S. Rodley, & L. Welsæth (Eds.), *International responses to traumatic stress* (pp. 193–217). New York: Baywood.

Diamond, L., Linz, J., & Lipset, S. (Eds.). (1989). *Democracy in developing countries* (Vol. 3: Asia). Boulder, CO: Lynne Rienner.

Dixon, J., & Macarov, D. (Eds.). (1998). *Poverty: A persistent global reality.* London: Routledge.

Donnelly, J. (1993). *International human rights.* Boulder, CO: Westview.

Dore, R., & Mars, Z. (1981). *Community development: Comparative case studies in India, the Republic of Korea, Mexico and Tanzania.* London: Croom Helm.

Dorfman, R. A. (Ed.). (1988). *Paradigms of clinical social work.* New York: Brunner and Mazel.

Drakakis-Smith, D. (1987). *The third world city.* London: Methuen.

Dube, L. (1997). AIDS-risk patterns and knowledge of the disease among street children in Harare, Zimbabwe. *Journal of Social Development in Africa, 12*(2), 61–74.

Duffield, M. (1994). The political economy of internal war: Asset transfer, complex emergencies and international aid. In J. Macrae & A. Zwi, *War & hunger* (pp. 50–69). London: Zed Books.

Duffield, M. (2001). *Global governance and the new wars.* London: Zed Books.

Duffield, M., Macrae, J., & Zwi, A. (1994). Conclusion. In J. Macrae & A. Zwi, *War & hunger* (pp. 222–232). London: Zed Books.

Durning, A. (1990). Ending poverty. In L. Brown, A. Durning, C. Flavin, H. French, J. Jacobsen, M. Lowe, et al. (Eds.), *State of the world 1990* (pp. 135–153). Sydney, Australia: Allen & Unwin.

Dworken, J., Moore, J., & Siegel, A. (1997). *Haiti demobilization and reintegration program.* Alexandria, VA: Institute for Public Research.

Eade, D. (1997). *Capacity building: An approach to people-centred development.* Oxford, England: Oxfam.

Easterly, W. (2002). *The elusive quest for growth: Economists' adventures in the tropics.* Cambridge, MA: MIT Press.

Eban, A. (1983). *The new diplomacy: International affairs in the modern age.* New York: Random House.

Edwards, M., & Hulme, D. (1992). *Making a difference: NGOs and development in a changing world.* London: Earthscan.

Ekins, P. (1992). *A new world order: Grassroots movements for global change.* London: Routledge.

Ekins, P., & Newby, L. (1998). Sustainable wealth creation at the local level in an age of globalization. *Regional Studies, 32*(9), 863–872.

Elisabeth, R. (2003). *Social work and human rights: A foundation for policy and practice.* New York: Columbia University Press.

Elliott, D. (1993). Social work and social development: Towards an integrative model for social work practice. *International Social Work, 36*(1), 20–36.

Elliott, D. (1997). Conclusion. In N. S. Mayadas, T. D. Watts, & D. Elliott (Eds.). *International handbook on social work theory and practice* (pp. 441–450). Westport, CT: Greenwood.

Elliott, D., & Mayadas, N. (1996). Social development and clinical practice in social work. *The Journal of Allied Social Sciences, 21*(1), 61–68.

Elliott, J. A. (1994). *An introduction to sustainable development.* London: Routledge.

Elson, D. (1995a). Public action, poverty and development in a gender aware analysis. In J. Mullen, *Rural poverty alleviation* (pp. 59–81). Aldershot, England: Avebury.

Elson, D. (Ed.). (1995b). *Male bias in the development process* (2nd ed.). Manchester, England: Manchester University Press.

Enloe, C. H. (1973). *Ethnic conflict and political development.* Boston: Little, Brown.

Esman, M. J., & Uphoff, N. T. (1984). *Local organizations: Intermediaries in rural development.* Ithaca, NY: Cornell University Press.

Eurostep/ICVA (International Council of Voluntary Agencies). (1997). *The reality of aid 1997/8: An independent review of development cooperation.* London: Earthscan.

Falk, R. (1993). The making of global citizenship. In J. Bretcher, J. B. Childs, & J. Cutler (Eds.), *Global visions: Beyond the new world order* (pp. 39–50). Boston: Southend Press.

Falk, R. (1997). Resisting "globalization-from-above" through "globalization-from-below." *New Political Economy, 2,* 17–24.

Featherstone, M. (Ed.). (1990). *Global culture: Nationalism, globalization and modernity.* London: Sage.

Fook, J. (1993). *Radical casework: A theory of practice.* Sydney, Australia: Allen & Unwin.

Fowler, A. (1991). The role of NGOs in changing state-society relations: Perspectives from eastern and southern Africa. *Development Policy Review, 9,* 53–84.

Frank, A. G. (1996). The underdevelopment of development. In S. C. Chew & R. A. Denemark (Eds.), *The underdevelopment of development* (pp. 48–66). London: Sage.

Freire, P. (1972). *Pedagogy of the oppressed.* Harmondsworth, England: Penguin.

Friedmann, J. (1992). *Empowerment: The politics of alternative development.* Cambridge, MA: Blackwell.

Fuchs, A., Jones, G., & Pernia, E. (Eds.). (1987). *Urbanization and urban policies in Pacific Asia.* Boulder, CO: Westview.

Galtung, J. (1995). *Global governance for and by global democracy.* London: Klewer Law International.

George, S. (1988). *A fate worse than debt.* London: Penguin.

George, S. (1990). *Ill fares the land.* London: Penguin.

George, S., & Sabelli, F. (1994). *Faith and credit: The World Bank's secular empire.* London: Penguin.

Germain, C. B., & Gitterman, A. (1980). *The life model of social work practice.* New York: Columbia University Press.

Germain, C. B., & Gitterman, A. (1996). *The life model of social work practice: Advances in theory and practice.* New York: Columbia University Press.

Ghai, D. (1994). Participatory development. In K. Griffin & J. Knight (Eds.), *Human development and the international development strategies for the 1990s* (pp. 215–246). London: Macmillan.

Ghai, D. (1997). Economic globalization, institutional change and human security. In S. Lindberg & A. Sverrisson (Eds.), *Social movements in development* (pp. 26–42). London: Macmillan.

Gilbert, A., & Gugler, J. (1992). *Cities, poverty and development: Urbanization in the third world* (2nd ed.). England: Oxford University Press.

Gilpin, R. (1987). *The political economy of international relations.* Princeton, NJ: Princeton University Press.

Goodwin-Gill, G., & Cohn, I. (1994). *Child soldiers: The role of children in armed conflicts.* Oxford, England: Clarendon Press.

Gordon, W. (1994). *The United Nations at the crossroads of reform.* New York: M. E. Sharpe.

Gore, M. (1988). Levels of social work provision in relation to needs in a developing society. *Indian Journal of Social Work, 49*(1), 1–9.

Gorman, R. F. (Ed.). (1993). *Refugee aid and development: Theory and practice.* Westport, CT: Greenwood.

Goulet, D. (1995). *Development ethics.* London: Zed Books.

Gray, M. (1997a). A pragmatic approach to social development, Part 1. *Social Work/Maatskaplike Werk, 33*(3), 210–222.

Gray, M. (1997b). A pragmatic approach to social development, Part 2. *Social Work/Maatskaplike Werk, 33*(4), 360–373.

Guebre-Christos, G. (1989). Education of refugee girls: Case study/Namibian students in West Africa. In International NGO Working Group on Refugee Women, *Working with refugee women: A practical guide* (pp. 143–145). Geneva: UNHCR.

Habitat. (1989). *Improving income and housing: Employment generation in low income settlements.* Nairobi, Kenya: Habitat.

Hall, N. (1993). Issue on unaccompanied displaced persons [Special issue]. *Journal of Social Development in Africa, 8*(2).

Hamilton, C. (2003). *Growth fetish.* Sydney, Australia: Allen & Unwin.

Haq, K., & Kirdar, U. (Eds.). (1985). *Human development: The neglected dimension.* Islamabad, Pakistan: North-South Roundtable.

Haq, K., & Kirdar, U. (Eds.). (1987). *Managing human development.* Islamabad, Pakistan: North-South Roundtable.

Harrell-Bond, B. E. (1986). *Imposing aid: Emergency assistance to refugees.* England: Oxford University Press.

Harrell-Bond, B. E. (1996). Refugees and the challenge of reconstructing communities through aid. In R. J. Kirin and M. Povrzanovic, *War, exile, everyday life* (pp. 23–30). Zagreb, Croatia: Institute of Ethnology and Folklore Research.

Harris, G. (Ed.). (1999). *Recovery from armed conflict in developing countries.* London: Routledge.

Harris, G., & Lewis, N. (1999). Armed conflict in developing countries: Extent, nature and causes. In G. Harris (Ed.), *Recovery from armed conflict in developing countries* (pp. 3–11). London: Routledge.

Harris, R. (1990). Beyond rhetoric: A challenge for international social work. *International Social Work, 33*(3), 203–212.

Hartman, A. (1994). Social work practice. In F. G. Reamer (Ed.), *The foundations of social work knowledge* (pp. 13–50). New York: Columbia University Press.

Hartman, B., & Boyce, J. (1982). *Needless hunger: Voices from a Bangladesh village.* San Francisco: Institute for Food and Development Policy.

Hayter, T., & Watson, C. (1985). *Aid: Rhetoric and reality.* London: Pluto.

Healy, L. (1987). International agencies as social work settings: Opportunity, capability, and commitment. *Social Work, 32*(5), 405–409.

Healy, L. (1995a). Comparative and international overview. In J. D. Watts, D. Elliott, & N. S. Mayadas (Eds.), *International handbook on social work education* (pp. 421–439). Westport, CT: Greenwood.

Healy, L. (1995b). International social welfare: Organization and activities. In *Encyclopedia of social work* (pp. 1499–1510). Washington, DC: NASW Press.

Healy, L. (2001). *International social work: Professional action in an interdependent world.* New York: Oxford University Press.

HelpAge International. (2005a). *Global network: Asia: Cambodia.* Retrieved April 26, 2005, from http://www.helpage.org/global/AScambodia/AScambodia.html

HelpAge International. (2005b). *Global network: Asia: India*. Retrieved April 26, 2005, from http://www.helpage.org/global/ASindia/ASindia.html

Herrick, J., & Meinert, R. (1994). Ethnic conflict, social development and the role of the helping professions. *Social Development Issues, 16*(3), 122–132.

Heyzer, N., Riker, J., & Quizon, A. (Eds.). (1995). *Government-NGO relations in Asia: Prospects and challenges for people-centred development*. London: Macmillan.

Higgins, J., Deakin, N., Edwards, J., & Wicks, M. (1983). *Government and urban poverty*. Oxford, England: Basil Blackwell.

Hitchcox, L. (1990). *Vietnamese refugees in Southeast Asian camps*. London: Macmillan.

Hobsbaum, E. (1995). *Age of extremes: The short twentieth century 1914–1991*. London: Abacus.

Hoff, M. D. (Ed.). (1998). *Sustainable community development: Studies in economic, environmental, and cultural revitalization*. Boca Raton, FL: Lewis.

Hokenstad, M. C., Khinduka, S. K., & Midgley, J. (Eds.). (1992). *Profiles in international social work*. Washington, DC: NASW Press.

Holloway, R. (Ed.). (1989). *Doing development: Governments, NGOs and the rural poor in Asia*. London: Earthscan.

Holton, R. J. (1998). *Globalization and the nation-state*. London: Macmillan.

Hong Kong Council of Social Services. (1996). *Concern for vulnerable groups*. Hong Kong: Author.

Hoogvelt, A. (2001). *Globalization and the postcolonial world: The new political economy of development* (2nd ed.). Basingstoke, England: Palgrave Macmillan.

Hugo, G. (1987). *International migration of contract labour in Asia: Proceedings of IDRC workshop*. Thailand: Changmai University.

Hulme, D., & Montgomery, R. (1995). Co-operatives, credit and the rural poor. In J. Mullen (Ed.), *Rural poverty alleviation* (pp. 99–118). Aldershot, England: Avebury.

Human Rights Watch. (annual). *World Reports*. New Haven, CT: Yale University Press.

Huntington, S. P. (2002). *The clash of civilizations and the remaking of the world order*. Reading, England: Free Press.

Hutton, W. (2003). *The world we're in*. London: Abacus.

IASSW & IFSW (International Association of Schools of Social Work & International Federation of Social Workers). (2004). *Global standards for social work education and training*. Retrieved June 3, 2004, from http://www.iassw.soton.ac.uk

IFAD (International Fund for Agricultural Development). (1985). *The role of rural credit projects in reaching the poor*. Oxford, England: Tycooly.

Ife, J. (1995). *Community development: Creating community alternatives—Vision, analysis and practice*. Melbourne, Australia: Longman.

Ife, J. (1997). Australia. In N. S. Mayadas, T. D. Watts, & D. Elliott (Eds.), *International handbook on social work theory and practice* (pp. 383–407). Westport, CT: Greenwood.

Ife, J. (2001). *Human rights and social work: Towards rights-based practice*. Cambridge, England: Cambridge University Press.

Ife, J. (2002). *Community development: Community-based alternatives in an age of globalization* (2nd ed.). Sydney, Australia: Pearson Education.

IFSW and IASSW. (2004). *Ethics in social work, statement of principles*. Bern, Switzerland: IFSW.

Ike, C., & Twumasi-Ankrah, K. (1999). Child abuse and child labour across culture. *Journal of Social Development in Africa, 14*(2), 109–118.

ILO (International Labour Organisation). (1986). *The rights of migrant workers: A guide to ILO standards for the use of migrant workers and their organizations*. Geneva: ILO.

Ingram, J. (1989). Sustaining refugees' human dignity: International responsibility and practical reality. *Journal of Refugee Studies, 2*(3), 329–339.

Independent Commission on International Humanitarian Issues. (1986). *Refugees: The dynamics of displacement*. London: Zed Books.

International NGO Working Group on Refugee Women. (1989). *Working with refugee women: A practical guide.* Geneva: Author.

Isbister, J. (1991). *Promises not kept: The betrayal of social change in the third world.* West Hartford, CT: Kumarian.

Jacobs, S., Jacobson, R., & Marchbank, J. (Eds.). (2000). *States of conflict: Gender, violence and resistance.* London: Zed Books.

James, R. (Ed.). (2001). *Power and partnership? Experiences of NGO capacity-building.* Oxford, England: INTRAC.

James, V. U. (Ed.). (1998). *Capacity building in developing countries: Human and environmental dimensions.* Westport, CT: Praeger.

Johnson, A. K. (2004). Increasing internationalization in social work programs: Healy's continuum as a strategic planning guide. *International Social Work, 47*(1), 7–23.

Kaldor, M. (2003). *Global civil society: An answer to war.* Cambridge, England: Polity Press.

Kaseke, E. (1990). A response to social problems in developing countries. *Social Policy and Administration, 24*(1), 13–20.

Kaseke, E., & Gumbo, P. (2001). The AIDS crisis and orphan care in Zimbabwe. *Social Work/Maatskaplike Werk, 37*(1), 53–58.

Kelso, W. A. (1994). *Poverty and the underclass: Changing perceptions of the poor in America.* New York: New York University Press.

Kendall, K. A. (1986). Social work education in the 1980s: Accent on change. *International Social Work, 29*(1), 15–27.

Kendall, K. A. (2000). *Social work education: Its origins in Europe.* Washington, DC: Council on Social Work Education.

Kirin, R. J., & Povrzanovic, M. (Eds.). (1996). *War, exile, everyday life.* Zagreb, Croatia: Institute of Ethnology and Folklore Research.

Knudsen, J. (1991). Therapeutic strategies and strategies for refugee coping. *Journal of Refugee Studies, 4*(1), 21–38.

Korten, D. C. (1984). People-centered development: Toward a framework. In D. C. Korten & R. Klaus (Eds.), *People-centered development* (pp. 299–309). West Hartford, CT: Kumarian.

Korten, D. C. (1990). *Getting to the 21st century: Voluntary action and the global agenda.* West Hartford, CT: Kumarian.

Korten, D. C. (1995). *When corporations rule the world.* London: Earthscan.

Korten, D. C., & Klaus, R. (Eds.). (1984). *People-centered development.* West Hartford, CT: Kumarian.

Kreitzer, L. (2002). Liberian refugee women: A qualitative study of their participation in planning camp programmes. *International Social Work, 45*(1), 45–58.

Krueger, A., Michalopoulos, C., & Ruttan, V. (1989). *Aid and development.* Baltimore: Johns Hopkins University Press.

Kumar, K. (Ed.). (1997a). *Rebuilding societies after civil war: Critical roles for international assistance.* Boulder, CO: Lynne Rienner.

Kumar, K. (1997b). The nature and focus of international assistance for rebuilding war-torn societies. In K. Kumar (Ed.), *Rebuilding societies after civil war* (pp. 1–38). Boulder, CO: Lynne Rienner.

Kumin, J. (1998). An uncertain direction. *Refugees, 2*(113), 5–9.

Kumin, J. (2000). A multi-billion dollar trade in humans. *Refugees, 2*(119), 18–19.

Kushner, T., & Knox, K. (1999). *Refugees in an age of genocide.* London: Frank Cass.

Landes, D. (1998). *The wealth and poverty of nations: Why some are so rich and some so poor.* London: Abacus.

Laqueur, W., & Rubin, B. (Eds.). (1990). *The human rights reader* (Rev. ed.). New York: Meridian Books.

Le Breton, B. (2003). *Trapped: Modern day slavery in the Brazilian Amazon.* Bloomfield, CT: Kumarian.

Lee, J. A. (2001). *The empowerment approach to social work practice.* New York: Columbia University Press.

Leighninger, L., & Midgley, J. (1997). United States of America. In N. S. Mayadas, T. D. Watts, & D. Elliott (Eds.), *International handbook on social work theory and practice* (pp. 9–28). Westport, CT: Greenwood.

Lewis, J. P. (Ed.). (1988). *Strengthening the poor: What have we learned?* New Brunswick, NJ: Transaction Books.

Lewis, N. (1999). Social recovery from armed conflict. In G. Harris (Ed.), *Recovery from armed conflict in developing countries* (pp. 95–110). London: Routledge.

Livermore, M. (1996). Social work, social development and microenterprises. *The Journal of Applied Social Sciences, 21*(1), 37–44.

Lloyd, P. (1979). *Slums of hope: Shanty towns of the third world.* Harmondsworth, England: Penguin.

Lobo, M., & Mayadas, N. S. (1997). International social work practice: A refugee perspective. In N. S. Mayadas, T. D. Watts, & D. Elliott, *International handbook on social work theory and practice* (pp. 411–428). Westport, CT: Greenwood.

Loescher, G. (1993). *Beyond charity: International cooperation and the global refugee crisis.* New York: Oxford University Press.

MacPherson, S. (1982). *Social policy in the third world: The social dilemma of underdevelopment.* Brighton, England: Harvester.

MacPherson, S., & Midgley, J. (1987). *Comparative social policy and the third world.* Brighton, England: Wheatsheaf Books.

Macrae, J., & Zwi, A. (Eds.). (1994). *War and hunger: Rethinking international responses to complex emergencies.* London: Zed Books.

Madeley, J. (1999). *Big business, poor peoples: The impact of transnational corporations on the world's poor.* London: Zed Books.

Mamphiswana, D., & Netshiswinzhe, B. (1999). Promoting social development and change through truth and reconciliation: A case for South Africa. *Social Development Issues, 21*(3), 66–74.

Mares, P. (2001). *Borderline.* Sydney, Australia: University of New South Wales Press.

Martin, P., Mason, A., & Nagayama, T. (Eds.). (1996). The dynamics of labour migration in Asia [Special issue]. *Asian and Pacific Migration Journal, 5*(2/3).

Mayadas, N. S., Watts, T. D., & Elliott, D. (Eds.). (1997). *International handbook on social work theory and practice.* Westport, CT: Greenwood.

Maynard, K. (1997). Rebuilding community: Psychosocial healing, reintegration, and reconciliation at the grassroots level. In K. Kumar, *Rebuilding societies after civil war* (pp. 203–226). Boulder, CO: Lynne Rienner.

McAllister, I. (1990). *Intervention strategies in community relations: A review and critical evaluation.* Canberra, Australia: Office of Multicultural Affairs.

McMaster, D. (2001). *Asylum seekers: Australia's response to refugees.* Australia: Melbourne University Press.

Medecins Sans Frontieres. (1997). *World in crisis: The politics of survival at the end of the twentieth century.* London: Routledge.

Meerman, J. (2001). Slow roads to equality: Enduring poverty among four low-status minorities. In N. J. Colletta, T. G. Lim, and A. Kelles-Viitanen (Eds.), *Social cohesion and conflict prevention in Asia: Managing diversity through development* (pp. 99–153). Washington, DC: World Bank.

Meinert, R., & Kohn, E. (1987). Towards an operationalization of social development concepts. *Social Development Issues, 10*(3), 4–18.

Miah, M., & Ray, J. (1994). Critical issues in social work practice with AIDS patients. *International Social Work, 37*(1), 75–82.

Midgley, J. (1981). *Professional imperialism: Social work in the third world.* London: Heinemann.

Midgley, J. (1995a). *Social development: The developmental perspective in social welfare.* London: Sage.

Midgley, J. (1995b). International and comparative social welfare. In *Encyclopedia of social work* (19th ed., pp. 1490–1499). Washington, DC: NASW Press.

Midgley, J. (2001). Issues in international social work: Resolving critical debates in the profession. *Journal of Social Work, 1*(1), 21–35.

Midgley, J. (1996a). Social work and social development: Challenging the profession. *The Journal of Applied Social Sciences, (21)*1, 7–14.

Midgley, J., Hall, A., Hardiman, M., & Narine, D. (1996b). *Community participation, social development and the state.* London: Methuen.

Minear, L. (1994). *Development without conflict.* Providence, RI: Brown University.

Mines Advisory Group. (Occasional). *Country reports.* Cumbria, England, and Vancouver, BC, Canada: Author.

Mohan, G., & Stokke, K. (2000). Participatory development and empowerment: The dangers of localism. *Third World Quarterly, 21*(2), 247–268.

Mollica, R. F. (1990). Communities of confinement: International plan for relieving the mental health crisis in the Thai-Khmer border camps. *Southeast Asian Journal of Social Science, 18*(1), 132–152.

Monbiot, G. (2003). *The age of consent: A manifesto of a new world order.* London: Flamingo.

Mondros, J. B., & Wilson, S. M. (1994). *Organizing for power and empowerment.* New York: Columbia University Press.

Moroka, T. (1998). Community-based mental health care: A justification for social work involvement in Botswana. *Social Work/Maatskaplike Werk, 34*(4), 344–360.

Muetzelfeldt, M., & Smith, G. (2002). Civil society and global governance: The possibilities for global citizenship. *Citizenship Studies, 6*(1), 55–75.

Mullaly, R. P. (1993). *Structural social work: Ideology, theory and practice.* Toronto, Canada: McClelland and Stewart.

Mullen, J. (Ed.). (1995). *Rural poverty alleviation.* Aldershot, England: Avebury.

Mupedziswa, R. (1992). Africa at the crossroads: Major challenges for social work education and practice towards the year 2000. *Journal of Social Development in Africa, 7*(2), 19–38.

Mupedziswa, R., Matimba, V., & Kanyowa, L. (1996). Reaching out to the unreached: Peer education as a strategy for the promotion of HIV/AIDS awareness among street children. *Journal of Social Development in Africa, 11*(2), 73–88.

Nader, R., Greider, W., Atwood, M., Shiva, V., Ritchie, M., Berry, W., et al. (1993). *The case against free trade.* Berkeley, CA: North Atlantic Books.

Nasr, S. H. (1990). *Man and nature: The spiritual crisis of modern man.* London: Unwin.

NASWE (National Association for Social Work Education). (1992). *Helping street children in especially difficult circumstances: A guidebook for social work practitioners.* Manila, The Philippines: Author.

Nayyar, R. (1996). New initiatives for rural poverty alleviation in rural India. In C. H. Rao & H. Linnemann (Eds.), *Economic reforms and poverty alleviation in India* (pp. 171–198). New Delhi, India: Sage.

Nee, M., & Healy, J. (2003). *Towards understanding: Cambodian villages beyond war.* Sydney, Australia: Sisters of St. Joseph.

Norell, D., & Walz, T. (1994). Reflections from the field: Toward a theory of practice of reconciliation in ethnic conflict resolution. *Social Development Issues, 16*(2), 99–111.

O'Connel, H. (1996). *Equality postponed: Gender rights and development.* Oxford, England: Worldview.

Osei-Hwedie, K. (1990). Social work and the question of social development in Africa. *Journal of Social Development in Africa, 5*(2), 87–99.

Osei-Hwedie, K. (1993). The challenge of social work in Africa: Starting the indigenization process. *Journal of Social Development in Africa, 8*(1), 19–30.

O'Shaughnessy, T. (1999). *Capacity building: A new approach? Principles and practice.* Melbourne, Australia: World Vision.

Otto, D. (1996). Nongovernmental organisations in the United Nations system: The emerging role of international civil society. *Human Rights Quarterly, 18,* 107–141.

Otunnu, O. (1996). Healing the wounds: What nature of wounds? In UNHCR, *Healing the wounds: Refugees, reconstruction and reconciliation* (pp. 6–8). Geneva: UNHCR.

Pandey, R. (1996). Ghandian perspectives on personal empowerment and social development. *Social Development Issues, 18*(2), 66–84.

Parker, M. (1996). The mental health of war-damage populations. *Institute of Development Studies Bulletin, 27*(3), 77–85.

Pasha, M. K. (1996). Globalisation and poverty in South Asia. *Millennium: Journal of International Studies, 25*(3), 635–656.

Pawar, M. (1999). Professional social work in India: Some issues and strategies. *Indian Journal of Social Work, 60*(4), 566–586.

Pawar, M., & Cox, D. R. (2004). *Communities' informal care and welfare systems: A training manual.* Wagga Wagga, Australia: Charles Sturt University Centre for Rural and Social Research.

Payne, M. (1997). *Modern social work theory.* London, Macmillan.

Pearson, N. (2000). *Our right to take responsibility.* Cairns, Australia: Noel Pearson.

Petevi, M. (1996). Forced displacement: Refugee trauma, protection and assistance. In Y. Danieli, N. S. Rodley, & L. Weisæth (Eds.), *International responses to traumatic stress* (pp. 161–192). New York: Baywood.

Pierson, C. (1998). *Beyond the welfare state* (2nd ed.). Cambridge, England: Polity Press.

Pieterse, J. N. (1997). Going global: Futures of capitalism. *Development and Change, 28*(2), 367–382.

Pincus, A., & Minahan, A. (1973). *Social work practice: Model and method.* Itasca, IL: Peacock.

Piven, F., & Cloward, R. A. (1979). *Poor people's movements: How they succeed and how they fail.* New York: Vintage Books.

Polidano, C., & Hulme, D. (1997). No magic wands: Accountability and governance in developing countries. *Regional Development Dialogue, 18*(2), 1–16.

Potter, D. (1992). Colonial rule. In T. Allen & A. Thomas (Eds.), *Poverty and development in the 1990s* (pp. 204–220). England: Oxford University Press.

Poulton, R., & Harris, M. (1988). *Putting people first: Voluntary organisations and third world organisations.* London: Macmillan.

Prica, I., & Povrzanovic, M. (1996). Narratives of refugee children as the ethnography of maturing. In R. J. Kirin & M. Povrzanovic, *War, exile, everyday life* (pp. 83–113). Zagreb, Croatia: Institute of Ethnology and Folklore Research.

Queiro-Tajalli, I. (1997). Latin America. In N. S. Mayadas, T. D. Watts, & D. Elliott (Eds.), *International handbook on social work theory and practice* (pp. 76–92). Westport, CT: Greenwood.

Raffaelli, M. (1997). The family situation of street youth in Latin America: A cross-national review. *International Social Work, 40*(1), 89–100.

Ramanathan, C. S., & Link, R. J. (Eds.). (1999). *All our futures: Principles and resources for social work practice in a global era.* Boston: Brooks/Cole.

Randall, V., & Theobald, R. (1998). *Political change and underdevelopment: A critical introduction to third world politics* (2nd ed.). London: Macmillan.

Randel, R., & German, T. (1997). *The reality of aid: An independent review of development cooperation: 1997–1998.* London: Earthscan.

Rane, A. (Ed.). (1994). *Street children: A challenge to the social work profession.* Bombay, India: Tata Institute of Social Sciences.

Rao, C. H., & Linnemann, H. (Eds.). (1996). *Economic reforms and poverty alleviation in India.* New Delhi, India: Sage.

Reichenberg, D., & Friedman, S. (1996). Traumatized children: Healing the invisible wounds of children in war: A rights approach. In Y. Danieli, N. S. Rodley, & L. Welsæth (Eds.), *International responses to traumatic stress* (pp. 307–326). New York: Bayview.

Rieff, D. (2002). *A bed for the night: Humanitarianism in crisis.* London: Vintage.

Robertson, G. (2000). *Crimes against humanity: The struggle for global justice.* London: Penguin.

Robertson, R. (1990). Mapping the global condition: Globalization as the central concept. In M. Featherstone (Ed.), *Global culture: Nationalism, globalization and modernity* (pp. 15–30). London: Sage.

Robertson, R. (1992). Globalization: Time-space and homogeneity-heterogeneity. In M. Featherstone, S. Lash, & R. Robertson (Eds.), *Global modernities* (pp. 25–44). London: Sage.

Robinson, W. I. (1996). Globalisation: Nine theses in our epoch. *Race and Class, 38*(2), 13–31.

Rosenau, J. (1995). Changing capacities of citizens. In Commission on Global Governance, *Issues of global governance: Papers written for the Commission on Global Governance* (pp. 371–403). London: Klewer Law International.

Rosenblatt, R. (1983). *Children of war.* London: New English Library.

Rosenthal, B. (1990). US social workers' interest in working in the developing world. *International Social Work, 33*(3), 225–232.

Rowlings, C. (1997). Europe. In N. S. Mayadas, T. Watts, & D. Elliott (Eds.), *International handbook on social work theory and practice* (pp. 113–121). Westport, CT: Greenwood.

Sachdev, P. (1998). HIV/AIDS and social work students in Delhi, India: An exploratory study of knowledge, beliefs, attitudes and behaviours. *International Social Work, 41*(3), 292–310.

Sachs, J. (2002). *The dignity of difference: How to avoid the clash of civilizations.* London: Continuum.

Sahnoun, M. (1996). Managing conflict after the Cold War. *Journal of the Institute of Life and Peace, 1*(2), 15–18.

Sanders, D. S. (1982, August–September). *New developments in international refugee work: A challenge to social work education.* Paper presented at the IASSW International Conference, Brighton, England.

Sanders, D. S. (1985). Peace and social development in the Pacific: A challenge to the social work profession. *International Social Work, 28*(4), 21–30.

Sanders, D. S. (1988). Social work concerns related to peace and people oriented development in the international context. *Journal of Sociology & Social Welfare, 15*(2), 57–72.

Save The Children. (1992). *Children at crisis point: Stories from Asia.* London: Andre Deutsch.

Save The Children. (1999). *Children's rights: Reality or rhetoric?* London: International Save The Children Alliance.

Seabrook, J. (1993). *Victims of development: Resistance and alternatives.* London: Verso.

Sen, A. (2001). *Development as freedom.* England: Oxford University Press.

Senanuch, P. (2005). *An investigation into the policy for urban poverty alleviation in Thailand.* Australia: University of Sydney.

Sewpaul, V., & Rollins, N. (1999). Operationalising developmental social work: The implementation of an HIV/AIDS project. *Social Work/Maatskaplike Werk, 35*(3), 250–263.

Shaw, M. (1994). Civil society and global politics: Beyond a social movements approach. *Millennium: Journal of International Studies, 23*(3), 647–667.

Shawcross, W. (2000). *Deliver us from evil: Warlords & peacekeepers in a world of endless conflict.* London: Bloomsbury.

Sherraden, M. (1991). *Assets and the poor: A new American welfare policy.* Armonk, NY: M. E. Sharpe.

Simon, D., Spengen, W. V., Dixon, C., & Narman, A. (Eds.). (1995). *Structurally adjusted Africa: Poverty, debt and basic needs.* London: Pluto Press.

Singharoy, D. K. (Ed.). (2001). *Social development and the empowerment of marginalised groups: Perspectives and strategies.* New Delhi, India: Sage.

Slim, H. (1994, September). *The continuing metamorphosis of the humanitarian professional: Some new colours for an endangered chameleon.* Paper presented at the Development Studies Association Conference, Lancaster, England.

Slim, H. (1996). Beyond working in conflict [Workshop paper]. Unpublished.

Smith, A. D. (1983). *State and nation in the third world: The western state and African nationalism.* Brighton, England: Wheatsheaf Books.

So, A. Y. (1990). *Social change and development.* Newbury Park, CA: Sage.

Soliman, H., & Miah, M. (1998). A cross-cultural study of social work students' attitudes towards AIDS policy: Implications for social work education. *International Social Work, 41*(1), 39–52.

Solomon, B. B. (1976). *Black empowerment: Social work in oppressed communities.* New York: Columbia University Press.

Sorensen, B. (1998). *Women and post-conflict reconstruction: Issues and sources.* (Occasional Paper No. 3, War-torn Societies Project.) Geneva: UNRISD.

Specht, H. (1990). Social work and the popular psychotherapies. *Social Service Review, 64*(3), 345–357.

Spence, R. (1999). The centrality of community-led recovery. In G. Harris (Ed.), *Recovery from armed conflict in developing countries* (pp. 204–222). London: Routledge.

SSWAP (Schools of Social Work Association of the Philippines). (1988). *Direct social work practice in helping street children: Workshop proceedings.* Manila, The Philippines: Author.

Stearns, S. (1993). Psychological distress and relief work: Who helps the helpers? *Refugee Participation Network, 15,* 3–8. Oxford, England: Refugee Studies Programme.

Stein, B. (1997). Reintegrating returning refugees in Central America. In K. Kumar (Ed.), *Rebuilding societies after civil war* (pp. 155–180). Boulder, CO: Lynne Rienner.

Stern-Petersson, M. (1993). Global civilisation: Challenges for sovereignty, democracy and security. *Futures, 25*(2), 123–138.

Stewart, F., & Fitzgerald, V. (Eds.). (2001). *War and underdevelopment* (Vol. 1). England: Oxford University Press.

Stickney, P. J., & Resnich, R. P. (Eds.). (1974). *World guide to social work education.* New York: IASSW.

Stiefel, M., & Wolfe, M. (1994). *A voice for the excluded: Popular participation in development: Utopia or necessity?* London: Zed Books.

Stoesz, D., Guzzetta, C., & Lusk, M. (1999). *International development.* Boston: Allyn & Bacon.

Straker, G. (1993). Exploring the effects of interacting with survivors of trauma. *Journal of Social Development in Africa, 8*(2), 33–47.

Suter, K. (1995). *Global agenda: Economics, the environment and the nation-state.* Sutherland, Australia: Albatross.

Tacey, D. (2000). *Reenchantment: The new Australian spirituality.* Sydney, Australia: Harper Collins.

Terry, F. (2002). *Condemned to repeat? The paradox of humanitarian action.* Ithaca, NY: Cornell University Press.

Thomas, M., and Pierson, J. (1995). *Dictionary of social work.* London: Collins Educational.

Thompson, N. (2003). *Promoting equality: Challenging discrimination and oppression* (2nd ed.). London: Palgrave Macmillan.

Todaro, M. P. (1997). *Economic development* (6th ed.). London: Longman.

Todaro, M. P., & Smith, S. C. (2003). *Economic development* (8th ed.). Harlow, England: Pearson.

Townsend, P. (1994). Possible solutions for poverty alleviation. In Netherlands Ministry of Foreign Affairs, *Poverty and development: Analysis and policy* (pp. 83–95). The Hague, The Netherlands: Ministry of Foreign Affairs.

Townsend, P., and Donkor, K. (1995). *Global restructuring and social policy: An alternative strategy: Establishing an international welfare state*. Bristol, England: The Policy Press.

Turner, F. J. (1986). *Social work treatment: Interlocking theoretical approaches* (3rd Ed.). New York: Free Press.

Ul Haq, M. (1995). *Reflections on human development*. New York: Oxford University Press.

UNAIDS, UNICEF, and USAID (Joint United Nations Programme on HIV/AIDS, United Nations Children's Fund, United States Agency for International Development). (2004). *Children on the brink 2004: A joint report of new orphan estimates and a framework for action*. New York: UNICEF.

UNCHR (United Nations Centre for Human Rights). (1992). *Teaching and learning about human rights: A manual for schools of social work and the social work profession*. Geneva: Author.

UNCTAD. (1997). *The least developed countries 1997 report*. Geneva: Author.

UN/Department of Economic and Social Development. (1993). *Report on the world social situation 1993*. New York: Author.

UN/Department of International Economic and Social Affairs. (1982). *Poverty and self-reliance: A social welfare perspective*. New York: Author.

UNDP. (1990). *Human development report*. New York: Oxford University Press.

UNDP. (1991). *Human development report*. New York: Oxford University Press.

UNDP. (1992). *Human development report*. New York: Oxford University Press.

UNDP. (1993). *Human development report*. New York: Oxford University Press.

UNDP. (1995). *Human development report: The revolution for gender equality*. New York: Oxford University Press.

UNDP. (1996a). *Human development report: Growth for human development*. New York: Oxford University Press.

UNDP. (1996b). *Social development assistance to the poorest of the urban poor and street children* (Project of the Government of Indonesia—Project Document). New York: Author.

UNDP. (1997). *Human development report: Human development to eradicate poverty*. New York: Oxford University Press.

UNDP. (1999). *Human development report: Globalization with a human face*. New York: Oxford University Press.

UNDP. (2000). *Human development report: Human rights and human development—for freedom and solidarity*. New York: Oxford University Press.

UNDP. (2002). *Human development report: Deepening democracy in a fragmented world*. New York: Oxford University Press.

UNDP. (2003). *Human development report: Millennium development goals: A compact among nations to end human poverty*. New York: Oxford University Press.

UN/ESCAP. (1988). *Jakarta plan of action on human resource development in the ESCAP region*. Bangkok, Thailand: Author.

UN/ESCAP. (1989a). *Community-based disability prevention and rehabilitation: Guidelines for planning and management*. New York: Author.

UN/ESCAP. (1989b). *Equalization of opportunities and community-based rehabilitation*. New York: Author.

UN/ESCAP. (1990). *Guidelines on methodological approaches to the conduct of a regional survey of the quality of life as an aspect of human resources development*. New York: Author.

UN/ESCAP. (1991). Government-NGO cooperation in social development. *Proceedings of a seminar on cooperation between GAs and NGOs*. New York: Author.

UN/ESCAP. (1992). *Social development strategy for the ESCAP region towards the year 2000 and beyond*. New York: Author.

UN/ESCAP. (1993). *State of urbanization in Asia and the Pacific 1993*. New York: Author.

UN/ESCAP. (1994a). *Asia and Pacific success stories in social development*. New York: Author.

UN/ESCAP. (1994b). *Working with women in poverty: Nine innovative approaches*. Bangkok, Thailand: Author.

UN/ESCAP. (1995a). *Community-based drug demand reduction and HIV/AIDS prevention*. New York: Author.

UN/ESCAP. (1995b). *Mid-term review of the implementation of the programme of action for the least developed countries for the 1990s: The Asia and Pacific Region*. New York: Author.

UN/ESCAP. (1996a). *Making an impact: Innovative HRD approaches to poverty alleviation*. Bangkok, Thailand: Author.

UN/ESCAP. (1996b). *Showing the way: Methodologies for successful rural poverty alleviation projects*. Bangkok, Thailand: Author.

UN/ESCAP. (1999a). *Strategies for community-based drug demand reduction*. New York: Author.

UN/ESCAP. (1999b). *Manual on community-based responses to critical social issues: Poverty, drug abuse, and HIV/AIDS*. New York: Author.

UNESCO. (1995). *Working with street children: Selected case-studies from Africa, Asia and Latin America*. Paris: UNESCO Publishing/International Catholic Child Bureau.

UNHCR. (1991). *Guidelines on the protection of refugee women*. Geneva: Author.

UNHCR. (1992). *Coping with stress in crisis situations* (Internal training document). Geneva: Author.

UNHCR. (1993). *The state of the world's refugees*. New York: Oxford University Press.

UNHCR. (1994). *Refugee children: Guidelines on protection and care*. Geneva: Author.

UNHCR. (1996). *Healing the wounds: Refugees, reconstruction and reconciliation*. Geneva: Author.

UNHCR. (1997). *Education for peace, conflict resolution and human rights* (PTSS Discussion Paper No. 14). Geneva: Author.

UNHCR. (1997/1998). *The state of the world's refugees*. New York: Oxford University Press.

UNHCR. (1998). *Report on a peace education initiative in Somalia*. Geneva: Author.

UNHCR. (1999). Guiding principles on internal displacement. *Refugees, 4*(117), 11.

UNHCR. (2000). *The state of the world's refugees: 50 years of humanitarian action*. New York: Oxford University Press.

UNHCR. (2001). The world of children at a glance. *Refugees, 1*(122), 7.

UNHCR. (2002). The refugee world at a glance. *Refugees, 4*(129), 13.

UNHCR. (2004). *Global refugee trends*. Geneva: Author.

UNHCR. (Occasional). *The state of the world's refugees*. New York: Oxford University Press.

UNICEF. (1996). Chapter 1, Children in war. In *The state of the world's children* (pp. 12–41). New York: Oxford University Press.

UNICEF. (1997). Chapter 2, Ending hazardous and exploitative child labour. In *The state of the world's children* (pp. 15–73). New York: Oxford University Press.

UNICEF. (2005). *End child exploitation: Child labour today*. London: Author.

UNICEF. (Annual). *The state of the world's children*. New York: Oxford University Press.

United Nations. (1968). *Convention and protocol relating to the status of refugees*. Geneva: Author.

United Nations. (1971). *Popular participation in development: Emerging trends in community development*. New York: Author.

United Nations. (1979). *Social services in rural development*. New York: Author.

United Nations. (1988). *Guiding principles for developmental social welfare*. New York: Author.

United Nations. (1990). *Report on the second United Nations conference on the least developed countries*. New York: Author.

United Nations. (1991). *Fourth Asian & Pacific ministerial conference on social welfare and social development*. New York: Author.

United Nations. (1995). *World summit for social development report*. New York: Author.

United Nations. (Occasional). *World social situation*. New York: Oxford University Press.

Unkovska, L. (1996). Psychosocial program for children from Bosnia in Macedonia. In Catholic Relief Services, *Psychosocial rehabilitation perspectives* (pp. 55–62). Sarajevo, Bosnia and Herzegovina: CRS.

UNPF (United Nations Population Fund). (1993). *The state of world population*. New York: Author.

UNRISD. (1993). *Refugees returning home*. Geneva: Author.

UNRISD. (1995a). *Ethnic violence, conflict resolution and cultural pluralism*. Geneva: Author.

UNRISD. (1995b). *States of disarray: The social effects of globalization* (UNRISD Report for the World Summit for Social Development). Geneva: Author.

UNRISD. (1998). *Report on war-torn societies project: Rebuilding after war*. Geneva: Author.

Uphoff, N. (1986). *Local institutional development: An analytical sourcebook with cases*. West Hartford, CT: Kumarian.

Uvin, P. (2004). *Human rights and development*. Bloomfield, CT: Kumarian.

Van Rooy, A. (1998). *Civil society and the aid industry*. London: Earthscan.

Verhagen, K. (1987). *Self-help promotion: A challenge to the NGO community*. Amsterdam, The Netherlands: Cebemo/Royal Tropical Institute.

Vohra, G. (1990). *Altering structures: Innovative experiments at the grassroots*. Bombay, India: Tata Institute of Social Sciences.

Vontira, E., & Brown, S. (1994). *Conflict resolution: A review of some NGO practices*. England: Oxford University Refugee Studies Program.

Watts, T. D., Elliott, D., & Mayadas, N. S. (Eds.). (1995). *International handbook on social work education*. Westport, CT: Greenwood.

WCC (World Council of Churches). (1996). *A moment to choose: Risking to be with uprooted people*. Geneva: Author.

Weiss, T. G., & Gordenker, L. (1996). *NGOs, the UN, and global governance*. Boulder, CO: Lynne Rienner.

Weissberg, R. (1999). *The politics of empowerment*. Westport, CT: Praeger.

Welsh, J. (1996). Violations of human rights: Traumatic stress and the role of NGOs. In Y. Danieli, N. S. Rodley, & L. Welsæth (Eds.), *International responses to traumatic stress* (pp. 131–159). New York: Bayview.

WHO/UNHCR (World Health Organisation/UNHCR). (1996). *Mental health of refugees*. Geneva: WHO.

Wilkinson, R. (Ed.). (1999). Who's looking after these people? [Special issue]. *Refugees, 2*(117).

Wilkinson, R. (Ed.). (2003). Africa at the crossroads [Special issue]. *Refugees, 2*(131).

Willetts, P. (Ed.). (1996). *The conscience of the world: The influence of non-governmental organisations in the UN system*. Washington, DC: Brookings Institution Press.

Wilson, K. B. (1992). Enhancing refugees' own food acquisition strategies. *Journal of Refugee Studies, 5*(3/4), 226–238.

World Bank. (1990). *World development reports: Poverty*. New York: Oxford University Press.

World Bank. (1991a). *Africa capacity building initiative*. Washington, DC: World Bank.

World Bank. (1991b). *World development reports: The challenge of development*. New York: Oxford University Press.

World Bank. (1992). *World development reports: Development and the environment*. New York: Oxford University Press.

World Bank. (1993). *World development reports: Investing in health*. New York: Oxford University Press.

World Bank. (1997). *World development reports: The state in a changing world.* New York: Oxford University Press.

World Bank. (1999/2000). *World development reports: Entering the 21st century.* New York: Oxford University Press.

World Bank. (2000). *Can Africa claim the 21st century?* Washington, DC: Author.

World Bank. (2000/2001). *World development reports: Attacking poverty.* New York: Oxford University Press.

World Bank. (2001). *Understanding and measuring social capital.* Washington, DC: Author.

World Bank. (2003). *World development reports: Sustainable development in a dynamic world.* New York: Oxford University Press.

World Commission on Environment and Development. (1987). *Our common future.* England: Oxford University Press.

Worsley, P. (1984). *The three worlds: Culture and world development.* London: Weidenfeld & Nicolson.

Wuthnow, R. (1994). *Sharing the journey: Support groups and America's new quest for community.* New York: Free Press.

Zetter, R. (1991). Labeling refugees: Forming and transforming a bureaucratic identity. *Journal of Refugee Studies, 4*(1), 39–62.

Zolberg, A. R., Suhrke, A., & Aguayo, S. (1989). *Escape from violence: Conflict and the refugee crisis in the developing world.* New York: Oxford University Press.

Zwi, A. B. (1995). Numbering the dead: Counting the casualties of war. In H. Bradley (Ed.), *Defining violence* (pp. 100–113). Aldershot, England: Avebury.

Index

About the Authors

Dr. David Cox received his initial university education in arts and social work at the University of Melbourne, and his Ph.D. at La Trobe University in the field of the sociology of migration. He worked in the refugee, migration, and international social work areas for 20 years full-time, before beginning to teach in these fields in schools of social work in Melbourne, becoming Professor of Social Work at La Trobe University in 1988. During his teaching career, he carried out extensive fieldwork, largely with UN/ESCAP and various NGOs. He has published two books in social work with immigrants, and more than 60 monographs, research reports, book chapters, and journal articles in his selected areas. Dr. Cox is married with two children, both currently working in the international field. While formally retired, he is an adjunct professor in social work at La Trobe University. Dr. Cox was made a Member of the Order of Australia in 1984 for his service to the refugee and migration field.

Dr. Manohar Pawar received his M.S.W and Ph.D. at leading schools of social work in India, where he also engaged in considerable fieldwork. He is currently a senior lecturer in social work, School of Humanities and Social Sciences, and a key researcher and an associate director of the Centre for Rural Social Research, Charles Sturt University, Wagga Wagga, Australia. He has more than 20 years of experience in social work education, research, and practice in Australia and India. Earlier he taught at La Trobe University, Melbourne, and at the Tata Institute of Social Sciences (TISS), Mumbai, India.

Dr. Pawar received a Quality of Life Award in 2001 from the Association of Commonwealth Universities, and a Research Excellence Award, also in 2001, from the Faculty of Arts, Charles Sturt University. He has completed a number of funded national and international research projects involving Asia-Pacific countries, and has organized international practica for social work students. Dr. Pawar has published several books and refereed journal articles. Some of his own and coauthored published titles are *Data Collecting Methods and Experiences* (2004, New Dawn Press), *Community Informal Care and Welfare Systems* (2002, Vista), *Job Network and Employment Services in Wagga Wagga* (2001, Bobby Graham), *Towards Poverty Alleviation in Rural Australia* (2000, CRSR), *Social Development Content in Social Work Education* (1997, RSDC), and *Justice Processing Sans Justice* (1993, TISS). Dr. Pawar's current areas of interest include international social development, social work and social policy, social work education, NGOs, and community development.